ELEMENTS OF

Writing

REVISED EDITION

Second Course

James L. Kinneavy

John E. Warriner

HOLT, RINEHART AND WINSTON

Harcourt Brace & Company

Austin • New York • Orlando • Atlanta • San Francisco
Boston • Dallas • Toronto • London

Critical Readers

The following critical readers reviewed pre-publication materials for this book:

John Algeo
University of Georgia
Athens, Georgia

Alice Bartley
Byrd Middle School
Henrico County, Virginia

Wilma Bell
Fairfield Middle School
Highland Springs, Virginia

Anthony Buckley
East Texas State University
Commerce, Texas

Norbert Elliot
New Jersey Institute
of Technology
Newark, New Jersey

Elaine A. Espindle
Peabody Veterans
Memorial High School
Peabody, Massachusetts

Maxine M. Long
Genesee Community
College
Batavia, New York

James Lynch
Van Buren Junior High
School
Tampa, Florida

Jeri McInturff
Chattanooga School
for the Liberal Arts
Chattanooga, Tennessee

Judy Olliff
Dallas School District 2
Dallas, Oregon

Cecilia Owen
Flagstaff Junior High School
Flagstaff, Arizona

Staff Credits

Associate Director: Mescal K. Evler
Executive Editors: Kristine E. Marshall, Robert R. Hoyt
Editorial Staff: Managing Editor, Steve Welch; *Editors,* Cheryl Christian,
A. Maria Hong, Constance D. Israel, Kathryn Rogers Johnson, Karen Kolar,
Christy McBride, Laura Cottam Sajbel, Patricia Saunders, Michael L. Smith,
Amy Strong, Suzanne Thompson, Katie Vignery; *Copyeditors,* Michael Neibergall,
Katherine E. Hoyt, Carrie Laing Pickett, Joseph S. Schofield IV, Barbara Sutherland;
Editorial Coordinators, Amanda F. Beard, Rebecca Bennett, Susan G. Alexander,
Wendy Langabeer, Marie H. Price; *Support,* Ruth A. Hooker, Christina Barnes,
Kelly Keeley, Margaret Sanchez, Raquel Sosa, Pat Stover
Permissions: Catherine J. Paré, Janet Harrington
Production: Pre-press, Beth Prevelige, Simira Davis; *Manufacturing,* Michael Roche
Design: Richard Metzger, *Art Director;* Lori Male, *Designer*
Photo Research: Peggy Cooper, *Photo Research Manager;* Tim Taylor, Sherrie Cass,
Victoria Smith, *Photo Research Team*

ISBN 0-03-050863-0

5 6 7 040 00 99

Authors

James L. Kinneavy, the Jane and Roland Blumberg Centennial Professor of English at The University of Texas at Austin, directed the development and writing of the composition strand in the program. He is the author of *A Theory of Discourse* and coauthor of *Writing in the Liberal Arts Tradition*. Professor Kinneavy is a leader in the field of rhetoric and composition and a respected educator whose teaching experience spans all levels—elementary, secondary, and college. He has continually been concerned with teaching writing to high school students.

John E. Warriner developed the organizational structure for the Handbook of Grammar, Usage, and Mechanics in the book. He coauthored the *English Workshop* series, was general editor of the *Composition: Models and Exercises* series, and editor of *Short Stories: Characters in Conflict*. He taught English for thirty-two years in junior and senior high school and college.

Writers and Editors

Ellen Ashdown has a Ph.D. in English from the University of Florida. She has taught composition and literature at the college level. She is a professional writer of educational materials and has published articles and reviews on education and art.

Jan Freeman has an M.A. in English from New York University. She has taught college composition classes. A published poet, she is a contributing editor to *The American Poetry Review* and the editor of Paris Press.

Madeline Travers-Hovland has a Master of Arts in Teaching from Harvard University. She has taught English in elementary and secondary school and has been an elementary school librarian. She is a professional writer of educational materials in literature and composition.

Elizabeth McCurnin majored in English at Valparaiso University. A professional writer and editor, she has over twenty-five years' experience in educational publishing.

John Roberts has an M.A. in Education from the University of Kentucky. He has taught English in secondary school. He is an editor and a writer of educational materials in literature, grammar, and composition.

Alice M. Sohn has a Ph.D. in English Education from Florida State University. She has taught English in middle school, secondary school, and college. She has been a writer and editor of educational materials in language arts for seventeen years.

Acknowledgments

We wish to thank the following teachers who participated in field testing of pre-publication materials for this series:

Susan Almand-Myers
Meadow Park Intermediate School
Beaverton, Oregon

Theresa L. Bagwell
Naylor Middle School
Tucson, Arizona

Ruth Bird
Freeport High School
Sarver, Pennsylvania

Joan M. Brooks
Central Junior High School
Guymon, Oklahoma

Candice C. Bush
J. D. Smith Junior High School
N. Las Vegas, Nevada

Mary Jane Childs
Moore West Junior High School
Oklahoma City, Oklahoma

Brian Christensen
Valley High School
West Des Moines, Iowa

Lenise Christopher
Western High School
Las Vegas, Nevada

Mary Ann Crawford
Ruskin Senior High School
Kansas City, Missouri

Linda Dancy
Greenwood Lakes Middle School
Lake Mary, Florida

Elaine A. Espindle
Peabody Veterans Memorial High School
Peabody, Massachusetts

Joan Justice
North Middle School
O'Fallon, Missouri

Beverly Kahwaty
Pueblo High School
Tucson, Arizona

Lamont Leon
Van Buren Junior High School
Tampa, Florida

Susan Lusch
Fort Zumwalt South High School
St. Peters, Missouri

Michele K. Lyall
Rhodes Junior High School
Mesa, Arizona

Belinda Manard
McKinley Senior High School
Canton, Ohio

Nathan Masterson
Peabody Veterans Memorial High School
Peabody, Massachusetts

Marianne Mayer
Swope Middle School
Reno, Nevada

Penne Parker
Greenwood Lakes Middle School
Lake Mary, Florida

Amy Ribble
Gretna Junior-Senior High School
Gretna, Nebraska

Kathleen R. St. Clair
Western High School
Las Vegas, Nevada

Carla Sankovich
Billinghurst Middle School
Reno, Nevada

Sheila Shaffer
Cholla Middle School
Phoenix, Arizona

Joann Smith
Lehman Junior High School
Canton, Ohio

Margie Stevens
Raytown Middle School
Raytown, Missouri

Mary Webster
Central Junior High School
Guymon, Oklahoma

Susan M. Yentz
Oviedo High School
Oviedo, Florida

We wish to thank the following teachers, who contributed student papers for the Revised Edition of *Elements of Writing, Second Course.*

Dana Humphrey
North Middle School
O'Fallon, Missouri

Annie Kornegay
Rochelle Middle School
Kinston, North Carolina

Judi Thorn
Jenks East Middle School
Tulsa, Oklahoma

Contents in Brief

Table of Contents

▶ CHAPTER 2 **LEARNING ABOUT PARAGRAPHS** 56

It is beautiful to see the people got to love Papa through all his sickness. While we were carrying Papa's remains to Washington we came past Princeton. The whole college was down at the depot and had strewn flowers all along the tracks,

PART TWO **HANDBOOK**

► CHAPTER *13* **THE SENTENCE** 404

Subject and Predicate, Kinds of Sentences

Roger de la Fresnaye, detail of *Emblems* (c. 1913). © The Phillips Collection, Washington, D.C.

▶ CHAPTER *16* **COMPLEMENTS**   487

Direct and Indirect Objects, Subject Complements

▶ CHAPTER 17 THE PHRASE   504

CHAPTER 18 **THE CLAUSE** 532

Independent and Subordinate Clauses

CHAPTER 19 **SENTENCE STRUCTURE** 555

The Four Basic Sentence Structures

►CHAPTER 20 AGREEMENT 572

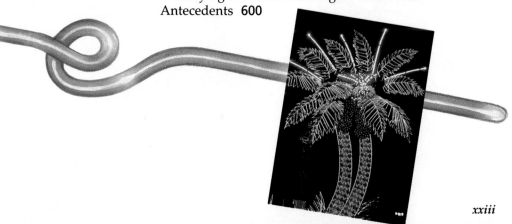

▶ CHAPTER 24 **A GLOSSARY OF USAGE**　　680

Common Usage Problems

▶ CHAPTER 25 **CAPITAL LETTERS**　　707

Rules for Capitalization

CHAPTER 26 PUNCTUATION 736

End Marks, Commas, Semicolons, Colons

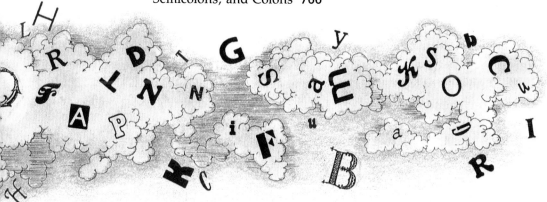

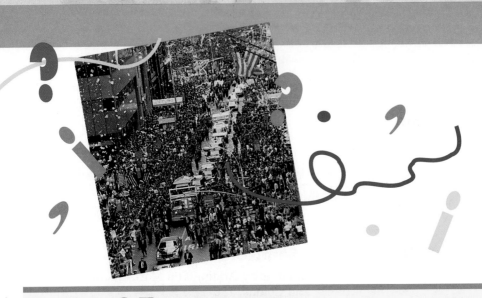

Models

PART ONE

WRITING

INTRODUCTION TO WRITING
What's the Secret?

WRITING HANDBOOK

AIMS FOR WRITING

LANGUAGE AND STYLE

1

WHAT'S THE SECRET?

James L. Kinneavy

Your everyday life isn't mysterious, is it? You get up, get dressed, eat breakfast, and go through your day. There's no mystery to it.

But wait!

Why did you pick that pair of jeans to wear? Why do all your friends want the same kind of jeans? And why did you choose that brand of cereal to eat for breakfast? **What's the secret?**

It's pouring down rain in the morning, but the weather forecasters say it will be sunny later on. How do they know? What's their secret?

Yesterday, your best friend won the election for student council president. You're glad she won, but how did she do it?

It's just another ordinary day, but things are happening all around you. And all these things—and more—share one great secret.

What is it? What's the secret?

©Jay Maisel

The Secret Is . . .

The secret is a power that's so strong it affects almost everything you do. It's the power of communication!

It's the magazine ad that convinces you that those jeans are "right" for you. It's the clever TV commercial that encourages you to choose that brand of cereal and not some other. It's the scientific knowledge that results in an accurate weather report. It's the posters and the speech that convince students to vote for your friend as student council president.

Who has this power? The planners and the talkers and the doers have it. They may be artists, businesspeople, teachers, composers, writers, or scientists. They write the manuals that explain how to repair a bike or program a VCR. They write the scripts that make you laugh or cry or scream during a movie. They design your computer games and write everything you read, even the messages on cereal boxes. They're all the people who communicate ideas to you.

And you're one of them. Every time you talk to someone, jot down a telephone message, scribble a note to a friend, or write an essay in class, you're using the power of communication.

The Key to the Mystery

All these *writers* who influence your life share the same secret. They know how to communicate. They have something to say (a *subject*), someone to say it to (an *audience*), and a way to say it (a *language*).

Think of these elements as a triangle. Language—both written and spoken—is at the center.

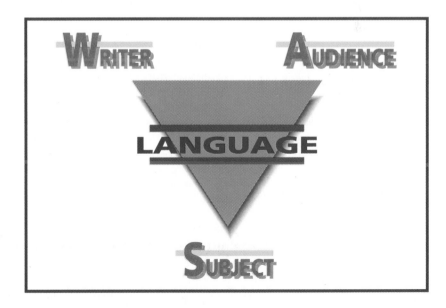

How Writers Write

The Writing Process

Effective communication doesn't just happen. A great deal of thinking and planning goes into it—deciding what ideas to convey and how to get them across to an audience.

Most writers say that their powers of communication work best when they follow a *writing process.* Writers may vary in the way they work through the process, but they all use the following basic steps.

Prewriting	Thinking and planning—choosing a subject, a purpose, and an audience; thinking up ideas; planning how to present the ideas
Writing	Writing a first draft—putting ideas into sentences and paragraphs; following the plan for presenting ideas
Evaluating and Revising	Looking over the draft—deciding what's good and what needs to be changed; making changes to improve the writing
Proofreading and Publishing	Finding and fixing errors; making a final copy; sharing the writing with an audience

Why Writers Write

The Aims of Writing

What reason do you have for writing? Writers always have some purpose, or aim, in mind. All writing has at least one of these four basic aims: to inform, to persuade, to express oneself, to be creative.

To Inform	Writers often aim to give facts and other kinds of information or to explain something.
To Persuade	Writers may want to convince people of something—to buy a product or to vote for someone—or to take some action.
To Express Themselves	Writers may simply want to express their thoughts and feelings.
To Be Creative	Writers sometimes create stories, poems, songs, and plays.

On the following pages are four models. They are all about the same topic—a ballplayer named Casey—but each one has a different aim. As you read, notice how the writing changes as the aim changes.

INFORMATIVE WRITING

Casey strikes out

Five thousand Mudville fans were in attendance yesterday at Sandtown Field when the Mighty Casey took three straight strikes to lose the game for Mudville.

Mudville was down 4–2, with two out, in the ninth inning when Flynn hit a single and landed safely on first base. He was followed by Jimmy Blake, who blasted out a double, driving Flynn to third base.

With the tying runs on second and third, Casey was next in the lineup. The first pitch was straight across the plate, but Casey didn't swing. Strike one. Casey signaled the pitcher, who threw the second pitch. Again, Casey didn't swing, and the umpire called the second strike.

Casey swung hard at the third pitch. He missed. The Mighty Casey had struck out. Sandtown won, 4–2.

READER'S RESPONSE

1. Suppose the Mudville players were your school baseball team. What else would you want to know about the game?
2. Informative writing gives facts and other kinds of information. What are some important facts that you learn about the Mudville game from this article?

PERSUASIVE WRITING

Dear Editor:

I've been a fan of the Mighty Casey for many years. After his poor showing last week, it's time for him to hang up his bat. He acts tough, but his performance in recent games has been disappointing, and last week was the final straw.

Casey let two perfectly good pitches go by. His eyesight must be gone. He can still swing a bat, but what good is that if he can't connect? He's stubborn, and he uses bad judgment. Those things cost us the game.

Mudville has depended on Casey for too long. We need some new, young players who perform well all the time. We need to give old Casey a rest. He's been a great player, but he's long past his prime.

Casey needs to retire. If enough fans speak out, he'll have no choice. Let him know how you feel. Let's get Mudville back in the playoffs again!

Sincerely,

Lyndsey Denis

Lyndsey Denis

READER'S RESPONSE

1. If you were one of Casey's fans, would this letter convince you that Casey should retire? Explain why or why not.
2. What reasons does the writer give for needing to get rid of Casey?

EXPRESSIVE WRITING

Today, I took the longest walk of my life—back to the dugout. It wasn't the first time I've struck out, but it was the worst. I don't know if the fans'll ever trust me again.

Maybe it's time to hang it up. I don't feel good a lot of the time, and I know my running ain't what it used to be. My eyes ain't either. I was showing off some when I let the first one go, but I never should've missed that third pitch! I've always taken chances, and the fans've loved it, but I found out today they don't like me taking chances and failing. I'm too old to change my ways, I guess. But not connecting with a perfect pitch. That's as bad as it gets.

I overheard some people saying I should retire. Maybe I ought to see about managing a team. Baseball's all I know. It scares me to think about quitting.

READER'S RESPONSE

1. Think about a time you didn't perform well, perhaps on a test or in a contest. How did you feel?
2. The article on page 8 gives you facts about Casey. What do you learn about him from this letter to an old teammate?

CASEY AT THE BAT

by Ernest Lawrence Thayer

The outlook wasn't brilliant for the Mudville nine that day;
The score stood four to two, with but one inning more to play;
And so, when Cooney died at first, and Burrows did the same,
A sickly silence fell upon the patrons of the game.

A straggling few got up to go in deep despair. The rest
Clung to the hope which springs eternal in the human breast;
They thought, if only Casey could but get a whack, at that,
They'd put up even money now, with Casey at the bat.

But Flynn preceded Casey, as did also Jimmy Blake,
And the former was a pudding, and the latter was a fake;
So upon that stricken multitude grim melancholy sat,
For there seemed but little chance of Casey's getting to the bat.

But Flynn let drive a single, to the wonderment of all,
And Blake, the much-despised, tore the cover off the ball;
And when the dust had lifted, and they saw what had occurred,
There was Jimmy safe on second, and Flynn a-hugging third.

Then from the gladdened multitude went up a joyous yell;
It bounded from the mountaintop, and rattled in the dell;
It struck upon the hillside, and recoiled upon the flat;
For Casey, mighty Casey, was advancing to the bat.

There was ease in Casey's manner as he stepped into his place;
There was pride in Casey's bearing, and a smile on Casey's face;
And when, responding to the cheers, he lightly doffed his hat,
No stranger in the crowd could doubt 'twas Casey at the bat.

Ten thousand eyes were on him as he rubbed his hands with dirt;
Five thousand tongues applauded when he wiped them on his shirt;
Then while the writhing pitcher ground the ball into his hip,
Defiance gleamed in Casey's eye, a sneer curled Casey's lip.

And now the leather-covered sphere came hurtling through the air,
And Casey stood a-watching it in haughty grandeur there;
Close by the sturdy batsman the ball unheeded sped.
"That ain't my style," said Casey. "Strike one," the umpire said.

From the benches, black with people, there went up a muffled roar,
Like the beating of the storm waves on a stern and distant shore;
"Kill him! Kill the umpire!" shouted someone on the stand;
And it's likely they'd have killed him had not Casey raised his hand.

With a smile of Christian charity great Casey's visage shone;
He stilled the rising tumult; he bade the game go on;
He signaled to the pitcher, and once more the spheroid flew;
But Casey still ignored it, and the umpire said, "Strike two."

"Fraud!" cried the maddened thousands, and the echo answered, "Fraud!"
But a scornful look from Casey, and the audience was awed;
They saw his face grow stern and cold, they saw his muscles strain,
And they knew that Casey wouldn't let that ball go by again.

The sneer is gone from Casey's lips, his teeth are clenched in hate,
He pounds with cruel violence his bat upon the plate;
And now the pitcher holds the ball, and now he lets it go,
And now the air is shattered by the force of Casey's blow.

Oh! somewhere in this favored land the sun is shining bright;
The band is playing somewhere, and somewhere hearts are light;
And somewhere men are laughing, and somewhere children shout,
But there is no joy in Mudville—mighty Casey has struck out!

READER'S RESPONSE

1. This is a famous poem about baseball. Why do you think
   it's a popular poem? What do you like about it?
2. Words like *a joyous yell* and *a muffled roar* help you "hear"
   the crowd when Casey is at bat. What are some words that
   help you "see" Casey at bat?

Writing and Thinking Activities

1. Get together with two or three other students. Look over the four models you've just read about the baseball game and then discuss the following questions.
   a. Which model tries to convince readers to do something?
   b. Which one makes you feel that you're actually there?
   c. Which one mostly states facts about a baseball player striking out?
   d. Which model mostly describes the writer's own thoughts and feelings?
2. Do you know how you communicate? Pick a day to find out. For two hours, keep a record of each time you read, speak, write, and listen. Try to decide what your aim is each time you communicate. Is it to inform, to persuade, to express yourself, or to be creative? Can you see a pattern? Do you have some aims more often than others? Then, get together with a few classmates, and exchange notes. Is their pattern of communication like yours? Or is it different?

3. What aim do you find most in what you read? Bring a magazine or newspaper to class. Meet with two or three classmates to find examples of the four aims of writing— informative, self-expressive, creative, and persuasive. What aim seems to be used most?

4. Creative writing is usually thought of as novels, short stories, poems, and plays. Do you think other kinds of writing are also creative? What about scientific papers and book reports, for example? How might they be creative?

"The bat flashes, there is a new, louder sound, and suddenly we see the ball streaking wild through the air..."

Roger Angell

1 WRITING AND THINKING

Looking at the Process

People aren't born knowing how to play a guitar or a piano. First, they go through a **process** of learning how. Then they have to practice. This is true of writing, too. Becoming a better writer starts with learning and practicing the writing process.

Writing and You.   Do you like to write? Is writing easy for you, or do you have to struggle with every word? Believe it or not, even professional writers run into trouble. They can't think of a new idea, they get stuck looking for the right word, or they know something is wrong but they're not sure how to fix it. What part of writing causes you the most trouble?

As You Read.   As you read the following interview with novelist Ann Petry, notice what she says about where she gets her ideas.

FROM *INTERVIEWS WITH BLACK WRITERS*

AN INTERVIEW WITH

ANN PETRY

INTERVIEWER: Have you ever been unable to write a story which you would have liked to write?

PETRY: I've never abandoned a story or a novel once I started working on it. I've abandoned many ideas before I ever put a pen to paper. I once planned or thought about writing a book for young people about Daniel Drayton and Edward Syres, two ships' captains imprisoned for attempting to help slaves escape from the District of Columbia on the schooner *Pearl.* I didn't write that particular book because I became interested in—actually fascinated by—a slave, Tituba, who was one of three women charged with witchcraft at the beginning of the trials for witchcraft in Salem, Massachusetts. . . .

INTERVIEWER: Is there a part of a novel which is more difficult for you to write than any other?

PETRY: Sometimes. I had great difficulty writing the chapter (*The Narrows*) in which Link is murdered.

INTERVIEWER: Is there some point in the novel where you feel that you have everything in hand and the rest will fall into place?

PETRY: I never have a novel "in hand" until it is completed.

INTERVIEWER: Do you ever experience any conflict between meaning and form, or between what you might like to do in a novel and what you think your reader will be able to understand? Or does the form of a novel develop on its own?

PETRY: The form finds itself.

INTERVIEWER: Do you remember how old you were when you first started to write?

PETRY: Fourteen.

INTERVIEWER: Were you anxious to show your work to people?

PETRY: I rarely ever told anyone that I was writing. And I still don't talk about what I write if I can avoid it.

INTERVIEWER: Do you think of your fiction as autobiographical?

"**...everything I write is filtered through my mind, consciously or unconsciously. The end product contains everything**

I know,

have experienced,

thought about,

dreamed about,

talked about,

lived for."

PETRY: I could say that none of my work is autobiographical, or that all of it is—everything I write is filtered through my mind, consciously or unconsciously. The end product contains everything I know, have experienced, thought about, dreamed about, talked about, lived for. And so in that sense I am any of the characters that I create, all of them, some of them, or none of them.

INTERVIEWER: Could you say something about your writing habits? When do you work? How much revising do you do? Are you subject to moods during the time you are working on a novel?

PETRY: When I'm writing I work in the morning from 8:00 A.M. to about noon. If I'm going to do any revising I do it in the afternoon. The first draft is in longhand. The planning and the writing go hand in hand for the most part. I revise endlessly. And yet the first chapter of *The Street* was written in one sitting and that first draft was the final one—no changes. And there were no changes in a story entitled "Like a Winding Sheet" or in "Sole on the Drums." I do not work at night if I can avoid it. I am not subject to moods. I doubt if my family or anyone else can tell when I'm thinking about writing.

READER'S RESPONSE

1. Do you, like Ann Petry, sometimes abandon ideas before you ever start to write about them? What are your reasons for dropping those ideas in favor of some others?
2. Ann Petry says she started to write when she was fourteen, but she has never liked to talk about her writing with anyone else. How do you feel about your own writing? Do you like to share it, or do you want to keep it to yourself?
3. What do you think Ann Petry means when she says "I could say that none of my work is autobiographical, or that all of it is . . ."?
4. Ann Petry says she writes in the mornings and revises in the afternoons. When do you write best? Do you think your writing is better when you come back later and revise it?

LOOKING AHEAD

In this chapter, you'll learn some techniques that you can work into your own writing process. You'll practice these techniques through all the stages of the writing process—from choosing a topic to publishing. As you work through the chapter, remember that

- writing and thinking work together in the process
- the writing process can be bent or shaped to fit your own style

Aim—The "Why" of Writing

People have a number of different reasons for writing. They talk for the same reasons that they write—because they have something to say, they have some purpose for saying it, and they have somebody they want to say it to.

But these are general reasons for why people communicate. What are the specific purposes that people have when they write? There aren't as many of these purposes as you might think. Look at the following chart.

WHY PEOPLE WRITE	
To express themselves	To get to know themselves, to find meaning in their own lives
To share information	To give other people information that they need or want; to share some special knowledge
To persuade	To convince other people to do something or believe something
To create literature	To be creative, to say something in a unique way

Process—The "How" of Writing

Good writing doesn't just happen. For most writers, it comes from following stages in a process. And the stages are all linked to thinking. In the first stage, prewriting, you'll probably do more thinking than writing. Later, when you're writing your first draft, you may do more writing than thinking.

The following diagram shows the stages that writers usually follow. However, the process differs for every writer. You may spend more time thinking up ideas than your classmates, or you may write down your ideas faster.

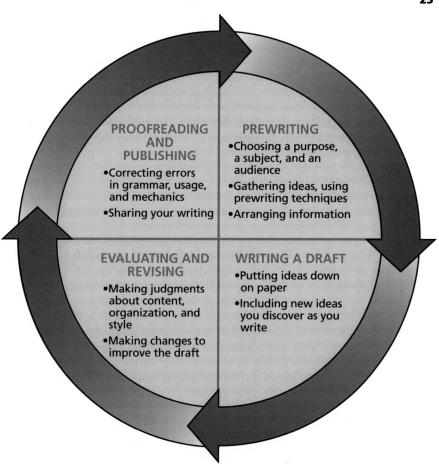

As the diagram shows, at any stage you can return to an earlier one (even to the beginning) if you need to. For example, your ecology club plans to start a recycling project at school. You agree to write a letter to the recycling center to ask for recycling bins. Then you realize you don't know how many bins the school will need. So you go back to the prewriting stage to find ideas and take notes about the information you need.

Topic, *purpose*, and *audience* are also important in the writing process. Sometimes they come together naturally. The topic (recycling), purpose (requesting bins), and audience (adults) determine what goes into your letter. In school, your teacher may assign topics, purposes, and audiences to give you practice for the important writing you do for your own reasons.

 *Prewriting*

Finding Ideas for Writing

Writing begins with looking for something to write about. How do writers find ideas? Often, an everyday experience or a personal interest sparks an idea. But many writers also have special ways, or techniques, they use to find and explore ideas. The following chart shows the ways for finding ideas you'll read about in this section.

PREWRITING TECHNIQUES		
Writer's Journal	Recording experiences and ideas	Page 25
Freewriting	Writing for several minutes about whatever comes to mind	Page 25
Brainstorming	Listing ideas quickly, without judging them	Page 27
Clustering	Brainstorming ideas and connecting the ideas with circles and lines	Page 28
Asking Questions	Asking the *5W–How?* questions	Page 29
Reading and Listening with a Focus	Reading and listening to find specific information	Pages 30–31
Imagining	Using your imagination to think of details	Page 31

For most of your writing assignments, you'll use more than one way to find ideas. For example, you get the idea to write a character sketch of your grandfather from a note in your writer's journal. Then you might use freewriting to recall specific details about him. Feel free to experiment with different ways to find ideas.

Writer's Journal

Many writers keep a ***writer's journal*** in a notebook or computer file to record their experiences, feelings, and ideas. When keeping a journal, try to follow these guidelines:

- Write daily, keeping your journal handy.
- Let your imagination run free. Write down dreams, songs, poems, story ideas. Include drawings.
- Forget about grammar and punctuation. Only your thoughts matter.

 **EXERCISE 1** Keeping a Writer's Journal

If you haven't already started a journal, why not do it now? What's on your mind today? Write a journal entry about whatever it is.

 COMPUTER NOTE: If you keep your journal on a computer or a floppy disk, you may be able to keep it private by using a password. A password lets you protect a document, so that only people who know your password can read it.

Freewriting

Freewriting means writing whatever pops into your head. You don't judge ideas or worry about wording or punctuation. Freewriting can loosen you up for later writing or can give you ideas for topics. When you freewrite, follow these guidelines:

- Set a time limit of three to five minutes, and keep writing until the time is up.
- Start with a subject that's important to you.
- If you get stuck, just write anything. The important thing is to keep your pen moving.

Another form of freewriting is called *focused freewriting* or *looping*. Here, you choose a word or phrase from your freewriting to use as a starting point. Then you freewrite all over again, using that word or phrase as your subject. This practice helps you to focus your ideas for writing.

Here's an example of freewriting notes about pioneers.

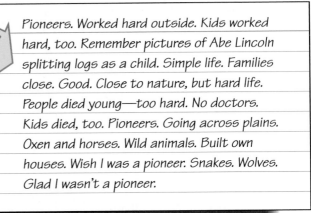

HERE'S HOW

Pioneers. Worked hard outside. Kids worked
hard, too. Remember pictures of Abe Lincoln
splitting logs as a child. Simple life. Families
close. Good. Close to nature, but hard life.
People died young—too hard. No doctors.
Kids died, too. Pioneers. Going across plains.
Oxen and horses. Wild animals. Built own
houses. Wish I was a pioneer. Snakes. Wolves.
Glad I wasn't a pioneer.

EXERCISE 2 ▶ Using Freewriting

Think of a specific time and place that's important to you—perhaps your kitchen on Thanksgiving morning or the school parking lot at 3:00 P.M. Write it on your paper. Now, freewrite for three or four minutes about the place. Just put down whatever comes to mind.

Brainstorming

In *brainstorming,* say what comes to mind in response to a word without stopping to judge what's said. You can brainstorm alone, but group or partner brainstorming is more fun because hearing other people's ideas helps you think of even more ideas. When you brainstorm:

- Write down a subject at the top of a piece of paper. (In a group, use the chalkboard.)
- List every idea about the subject that comes to mind. (In a group, have one person list the ideas.)
- Keep going until you run out of ideas.

Here are some brainstorming notes about teen culture.

HERE'S HOW

clothes—how different	relations with parents
groups dress	friends—and enemies
hairstyles	vacation
music	favorite movies
concerts and stars	bad movies
favorite TV shows	Arnold Schwarzenegger
favorite magazines	dating
hangouts—skating rink	peer pressure

EXERCISE 3 ▶ **Using Brainstorming**

Get together with a partner and have a brainstorming session. Use one of the topics listed below or make up your own. Make a list of your ideas.

1. fads
2. true adventures
3. bicycling
4. summer camps
5. space exploration
6. scary movies

Clustering

In *clustering,* sometimes called *webbing,* you brainstorm ideas and connect them with circles and lines that show how the ideas are related. To make a cluster diagram, follow these guidelines:

- Write your subject on your paper and circle it.
- Around the subject, write whatever ideas about it occur to you. Circle these ideas. Draw lines connecting them with the subject.
- When your ideas make you think of related ideas, connect them with circles and lines.

Here's a cluster diagram on the lives of Plains Indians in the eighteenth and nineteenth centuries. The two main ideas are *where they lived* and *how they lived.*

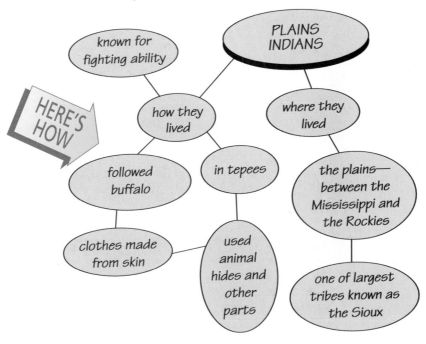

| EXERCISE 4 | Using Clustering |

Turn your brainstorming notes from Exercise 3 into a cluster diagram. Or pick another topic important to you. You can model your cluster diagram after the one above.

Asking Questions

Reporters often get information for news stories by asking the **5W-How? questions:** *Who? What? Where? When? Why?* and *How?* Not every question word applies to every subject. And sometimes you'll think of more than one question for a particular question word. If you were writing a report for your local environmental club, you could ask these questions. The notes in parentheses tell how you might look for the answers.

TOPIC:	<u>How Gorillas Might Be Saved from Extinction</u>
WHO?	Who is working on the effort to save gorillas from extinction? (Check at the library for names and addresses of groups.)
WHAT?	What is needed to save the gorillas? (Read books and articles; interview a zoo director.)
WHAT?	What is done with money given to save gorillas? (Contact groups working to save gorillas.)
WHERE?	Where do gorillas live? (Check in an encyclopedia.)
WHY?	Why are gorillas in danger? (Read books and articles; interview a zoo director.)
HOW?	How can we save gorillas? (Check in a book, or call the education department at a zoo.)

EXERCISE 5 ▶ **Asking the *5W-How?* Questions**

You're a reporter for your town newspaper, and you're writing a feature article about the local skating rink. Write down some *5W-How?* questions that would help you gather the information you need. Your purpose is to inform parents that the skating rink is a safe place for teens to be.

Reading and Listening

Sometimes you'll write about things outside your own experience. So how do you get the information you need? You can read and listen.

Reading. Reading sources include books, magazines, newspapers, and brochures. It saves time to look for your topic by checking the tables of contents and indexes to find the exact pages you need to read. You don't need to read everything. You can skim the pages until you find something about your topic. Then slow down and take notes on the main ideas and important details.

EXERCISE 6　**Reading with a Focus**

Which of the following American Indian peoples interests you most: Mohawk, Seminole, Navajo, Cherokee, or Nez Perce? Look in an encyclopedia or another book to find the answers to the following questions.

1. Where did the tribe originally live?
2. What did they build to live in?
3. What foods did they eat?
4. What kinds of clothes did they wear?
5. Are they known for some kind of art, such as beadwork, pottery, jewelry, or basket making?

Listening. By listening, you can get a lot of information from speeches, radio and TV programs, interviews, audiotapes, or videotapes. To prepare, make a list of questions about your topic. Then, while you listen, take notes on the main ideas and important details.

EXERCISE 7 ▶ **Listening with a Focus**

Listen to a radio broadcast of the top songs of the week (pop, rock, country, or gospel), then answer the following questions. Compare lists with your classmates if you listen to different countdowns.

1. Of the songs you heard, which three do you like best?
2. Who recorded each of these three songs? What number in the countdown is each?
3. What radio station was the countdown on?
4. Who is the host of the show?

Imagining

Can you imagine that you're someone else or somewhere else? Imagining gives you creative ideas for your writing. Trigger your imagination with *"What if?" questions.* "What if?" questions can be silly or serious. Here are examples.

1. What if I became a grown-up overnight?
2. What if something in my life—like TV—didn't exist?
3. What if people could fly like birds?
4. What if everyone looked exactly alike?

EXERCISE 8 ▶ **Using Imagining**

You're developing the plot of a mystery story for a class magazine. The story is about two eighth-graders on a camping trip with their families. Use your imagination and write five "What if?" questions that will help you work out a plot.

EXAMPLES   *What if one of the campers disappears?*
What if strange tracks are found by the river?

CRITICAL THINKING

Analyzing "What if?" Answers

When you ask "What if?" questions for creative writing, you might use any answer, no matter how unusual. But you can also use "What if?" questions to help you explore possibilities for other types of writing—such as reports. These answers need to be more practical, however. For instance, possible answers to *What if stores no longer bag items people buy?* could include these:

1. People could bring their own bags to stores to carry out items purchased.
2. People could make or buy cloth bags to be used over and over.
3. People could hand-carry all the items that they buy in the store.
4. People could fasten helium balloons to items and float them home.

Thinking about these answers, you might decide that answers 1 and 2 would be practical and could help you develop a report on recycling. Answer 3 would work only if people purchased just one or two items. Answer 4 is creative but not practical.

 CRITICAL THINKING EXERCISE:
Analyzing Useful Answers

Now it's your turn. Think about all the items you buy that are enclosed in plastic—in department stores, drugstores, grocery stores, and fast-food restaurants. Use the question *What if no plastic could be used for packaging?* Or make up another "What if?" question. On your own or with a partner or small group, give some answers to the question. Then look over your answers and make a list of the ones that could be used for a report.

Prewriting

Thinking About Purpose and Audience

Most people want to know why they're doing something. *Why* can't I watch this TV program? *Why* do I have to go to bed so early? In the same way, ask yourself, *Why am I writing?* This chart shows the basic purposes you might have for writing and the forms of writing you might use for these different purposes.

MAIN PURPOSE	FORMS OF WRITING
To express your feelings	Journal entry, letter, personal essay
To be creative	Short story, poem, play
To explain or inform	Science or history writing, news story, biography, autobiography, travel essay, office memo
To persuade	Persuasive essay, letter to the editor, advertisement, political speech

Before you write, also ask yourself, *Who will read my writing?* Consider your audience—the readers.

CRITICAL THINKING

Analyzing Audience

Why do you need to think about your audience? Because you're writing to tell them something. You want them to understand what you're saying. You don't want to tell them what they already know—that's boring, like seeing a movie you've already seen.

For example, your hobby is trains. Here's an example of how you might analyze two different purposes and audiences for writing about your hobby.

AUDIENCE:	eighth-graders
PURPOSE:	to inform
WHAT THEY NEED TO KNOW:	different trains I've ridden why I like steam trains best where they still run how steam engines work the difference between steam and diesel engines the oldest steam train I've seen
AUDIENCE:	fifth-graders
PURPOSE:	to describe

WHAT THEY NEED TO KNOW:	how I became interested in trains
	what I like about trains
	my trip to the Green Bay Railroad
	    Museum
	my most exciting steam-train ride
	nearby train trips the students
	    could take

Before you write, ask yourself these questions about your audience—your readers.

- Why is my audience reading my writing? Do they expect to be entertained, informed, or persuaded?
- What does my audience already know about my topic? (You don't want to bore your readers by telling them things they already know.)
- What does my audience want or need to know about my topic? What vocabulary and type of language should I use?

CRITICAL THINKING EXERCISE:
Analyzing Audience

The following paragraph is from a chapter in a travel guide about Zion National Park in Utah. The author's purpose is to tell about his experiences as a park guest and to inform readers about the park's challenges and beauty.

> It took me a little more than half a day to cover the five-mile round-trip hike from the trailhead on Zion Canyon Road to Angels Landing; parts of it were fairly tough going. It's almost 1,500 feet uphill, and the final stretch involves holding on to handrails along a steep, narrow path, but the time and energy were more than worth it. Every step of the way opened a new vista of the "Land of Rainbow Canyons" in southern Utah. I traced the vertical walls of red sandstone as they gradually merged upward into white, while beneath them shales of purple, pink, orange, and yellow revealed what surely must be some of the most brilliantly colored rock in the world.
>
> Michael Frome, *National Park Guide*

You want to persuade a parent, the leader of your scout troop, or another adult sponsor to take you to Zion National Park. The adult you want to persuade knows very little about the park and may be reluctant to even consider the trip. In a small group, discuss ways to change this paragraph for your purpose and audience. Then, rewrite the paragraph in the form of a letter to the adult.

Arranging Ideas

Once you have gathered ideas to write about, the next step in the writing process is arranging them. You always need to arrange your ideas so that readers can follow them.

Types of Order

The following chart shows four common ways of arranging ideas. The right-hand column gives examples of types of writing that arrange ideas in each way.

ARRANGING IDEAS		
TYPE OF ORDER	DEFINITION	EXAMPLES
Chronological	Narration: order that presents events as they happen in time	Story, narrative poem, explanation of a process, history, biography, drama
Spatial	Description: order that describes objects according to location	Descriptions (near to far; left to right; top to bottom)
Importance	Evaluation: order that gives details from least to most important or the reverse	Persuasive writing; description; explanation (main idea and supporting details); evaluative writing
Logical	Classification: order that relates items and groups	Definitions; classifications; comparisons and contrasts

 REFERENCE NOTE: For more information on arranging ideas, see page 98.

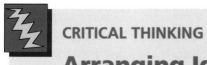

CRITICAL THINKING

Arranging Ideas

How do you know how to arrange your ideas when you write? Sometimes the order you use depends on the kind of information you want to present. For example, your class schedule is printed in the order in which your classes are held (*chronological order*) because class times are most important. Your teacher's list of students is in alphabetical order because it's easier to locate names that way. Sometimes it makes sense to describe items close to you, then those a little further away, and end with items in the distance (*spatial order*). Or you might choose to list your reasons for an opinion with the most important one last because you think this arrangement focuses the reader's attention on your final, best argument (*order of importance*). When you write, your topic, purpose, and audience help you decide which order is best.

 CRITICAL THINKING EXERCISE:
Analyzing the Order of Ideas

Use your new skills to assess how the ideas in the following paragraphs are organized. With two or three classmates, figure out the type of order used in each paragraph. Then, discuss how you identified the order.

1.   Some people really want to be rich. Money is nice, and I want to have enough. But being happy seems more important to me. I know some rich, miserable people, so money must not always make people happy. Okay, so I want to be happy. Next, I want to have time to do things I like to do, like read and be with my friends. I don't like to be rushed all of the time. Then, I guess getting along better with my family would be great.

2. Getting a trampoline really changed the way our yard looked. My little brother's swing set had to be moved from the middle of the yard to the southeast corner. The birdbath was moved to the front yard. The two planters filled with petunias were moved from beside the swing set to near the west fence. The trampoline takes up the whole center of the yard now. Everything else kind of lurks around the edges.

Using Visuals to Organize Ideas

It's hard to understand anything unless it's put in some kind of order—as you know if you've ever tried to find a pair of socks under your bed. The same is true with writing. Visuals—such as charts, diagrams, or other graphic layouts—can help you bring order to your writing.

Charts. To create a chart, think about the different types of information you have. For example, if you gather ideas for a report on gorillas in the wild, you might organize it by making a chart like the following one. You might plan to discuss how many of each kind of gorilla remain in the wild.

Kind	Location	Number in the Wild
Western lowland gorilla	Western Africa	35,000–45,000
Eastern lowland gorilla	Eastern Zaire	3,000–5,000
Mountain gorilla	Rwanda, Zaire, Uganda	3,000–5,000

Tree Diagrams. A tree diagram is another way of organizing main ideas and details. Here is a tree diagram for a report on Matthew Henson, an explorer with Admiral Peary on the first expedition to reach the North Pole.

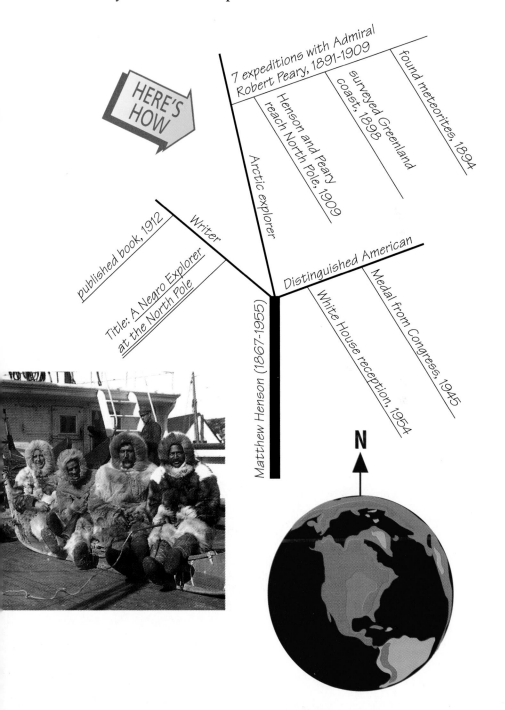

EXERCISE 9 ▶ Making a Chart

With a little practice, charts become easy to create. Try your hand at it. Make a chart to organize the following notes about the advantages and disadvantages of having school year-round.

Students don't forget skills over long summer vacation.
Students can't take long vacations in the summer.
Students can learn more.
Students can't earn money at summer jobs.
Kids can't go to summer camps.
School schedules could more nearly match parents' work
    schedules.
Schools are used year-round.

EXERCISE 10 ▶ Making a Tree Diagram

Tree diagrams help you "see" the structure of ideas. Make a tree diagram using the following notes on the sources of income for eighth-graders. You'll have three sources—parents, outdoor jobs, and indoor jobs.

pet care	kitchen help	running errands
yardwork	gifts of money	posting signs or
allowance	baby-sitting	notices
delivering papers	pay for extra	washing cars
or fliers	jobs at home	

Writing a First Draft

You've done your prewriting by identifying a topic, purpose, and audience, and by organizing your information. Now it's time to start writing.

There's no one right way to write a paper. Some people write their first drafts quickly, just trying to get their ideas on paper. Others go slowly, carefully shaping each sentence and paragraph. These tips may help you.

- Use your prewriting plans as a guide.
- Write freely. Focus on expressing your ideas clearly.
- As you write, you may discover new ideas. Include these ideas in your draft.
- Don't worry about spelling and grammar errors. You can correct them later.

Here's a first draft of a personal essay. You'll find that there are mistakes in it. First drafts always need some corrections. Notice that the writer makes a note to check on something. The writer will replace the note with the proper information and will correct mistakes in a later stage of the writing process.

Last year, my family went to the Yucatán Peninsula of Mexico. We stayed in Mérida, which is an ancient city that has many neat buildings. There are big arches and sculptures and parks. The best part of our trip, though, was going to the Chichén Itzá ruins to see the pyramids. I used to think that pyramids were only in Egypt. [Note: look up name] is the biggest pyramid in Chichén Itzá. It has nine levels, and has a temple on top. It was built a thousand years ago over a smaller, older pyramid. Inside the smaller pyramid is a big cat carved out of limestone. After we came home, we all wanted to go back. The cat statue has green jade eyes. I've never seen such interesting things before. We didn't have enough time to see everything.

WRITING NOTE   When your friends call you on the telephone, you almost always recognize their voices. That's because each friend speaks in a different way—loudly or softly, with a different accent. And each friend has certain words that he or she uses. That makes your friend's voice almost like a fingerprint—no two are exactly alike. And when you write, you have a voice, too. It's made up of the words and kinds of sentences that you use. In your writing, work very hard to have a natural voice—one that sounds like you. Don't use big words or long sentences just because they sound "important." Even when your writing is formal—like a research report—let your natural voice come through.

E X E R C I S E 11   **Writing a First Draft**

If you could change one thing about yourself, what would it be? Do you daydream about being a better athlete, a talented piano player, or a computer wizard? Think about what you'd like to change. Then write a first draft of a paragraph telling what you'd like to change and why.

Evaluating and Revising

Evaluating and revising are two different steps in improving your writing, but you usually do them at the same time.

> Evaluating—deciding on the strengths and weaknesses of your paper
>
> Revising—making the necessary changes to improve your paper

Evaluating

You evaluate writing all the time, whether you think about it or not. You like some books and hate others. You find some written directions easy to follow and others hard. You enjoy certain comic strips but not others.

Self-Evaluation. Because you're so close to your own writing, evaluating it is harder than judging someone else's work. These tips may help make the process easier.

Tips for Self-Evaluation

1. **Reading Carefully.** Read your paper more than once. First, read for *content* (what you say). Next, read for *organization* (how you order ideas). Finally, read for *style* (how you use words and sentences).

2. **Listening Carefully.** Read your paper aloud to yourself. *Listen* to what you've said. You may notice that the ideas don't flow smoothly or that some sentences sound awkward.

3. **Taking Time.** Set your draft aside. Come back to it later and read through it. You'll find it's easier to be objective about it after a little time away.

Peer Evaluation. Most writers, even people who make a living by writing, have someone else read and evaluate their work. You can get advice from others by sharing your writing with your classmates in a peer-evaluation group. In the group, you'll sometimes be the writer whose work is evaluated. Other times you'll be the evaluator.

EVALUATION GUIDELINES

Guidelines for the Writer
1. Make a list of questions for the peer evaluator. Which parts of your paper worry you?
2. Keep an open mind. Don't take your evaluators' suggestions as personal criticism.

Guidelines for the Peer Evaluator
1. Tell the writer what's good about the paper. Give the writer some encouragement.
2. Focus on content and organization. The writer will catch spelling and grammar errors when proofreading.
3. Be sensitive to the writer's feelings. State your suggestions as questions, such as "What does this mean?" and "Can you give an example?"

After your classmates evaluate your paper, think about the comments. Which comments are most helpful? Remember that the final decisions about changes are yours.

CRITICAL THINKING

Evaluating Writing

When you *evaluate* writing, you judge it against a set of standards. You decide whether or not the writing meets each standard. Here are some standards you might use to evaluate your writing. (More detailed standards for evaluating writing appear on page 48.)

1. The writing has a clear main idea.
2. The main idea is supported with details.
3. The order of the ideas makes sense.
4. The ideas flow smoothly.
5. The writing is interesting.

CRITICAL THINKING EXERCISE:
Evaluating a Paragraph

Do you like true-life adventure stories? Read the following paragraph. Then evaluate it, using the standards listed above. Write two comments on what's good about the paragraph. Write two comments on what needs to be improved.

Neg
Ideas not in order,
No naturaly written

os.
Interesting
details

Can you imagine being lost? That's what happened to Steven Callahan, and he wrote about it in the book *Adrift*. He was finally rescued by some fishermen. Callahan's boat sank in the Atlantic Ocean, and he survived in an inflatable raft. He was lost at sea for 76 days. He survived storms, shark sightings, and a diet of raw fish. And, oh, yes, there's something I need to tell you. He spotted ships, but they passed him by. No one else ever survived so long at sea in an inflatable raft. His story is a great one.

Revising

Many writers consider revising the most important stage in writing. They have their first ideas down on paper, and now they can add finishing touches. They may revise their work five or more times before they're satisfied with it.

When you revise, you make handwritten corrections on your paper. You then write or type a new copy. If you have a word processor, you'll find revising easier. You can make changes directly on the draft file and print out a new copy. Use the following techniques to revise.

REVISING	
TECHNIQUE	EXAMPLE
1. **Add.** Add new information. Add words, sentences, and whole paragraphs.	Many of the Amish still live much as they did *when they came to the United States more than 250 years ago.*
2. **Cut.** Take out repeated or unnecessary information and unrelated ideas.	~~They haven't changed much.~~ The women wear long dresses and bonnets; the men wear dark suits and wide-brimmed hats.
3. **Replace.** Take out weak or awkward wording. Replace with precise words or details.	Many Amish use no ~~new things~~ *(modern conveniences,)* ~~like~~ *not even* electricity or telephones.
4. **Reorder.** Move information, sentences, and paragraphs for logical order.	They *using* use mostly horse-drawn *(machinery and make their living by farming.)*

Here's the personal essay from page 41. It has been revised, using the four revision techniques. To understand the changes, see the chart of proofreading and revision symbols on page 54. Notice how the writer has answered the note in the rough draft.

Last year, my family went to the Yucatán Peninsula of Mexico. We stayed in Mérida, which is an ancient city that has many ~~neat~~ *beautiful* buildings. There are big arches and sculptures and parks. *(in the city)* The best part of our trip, though, was going to the Chichén Itzá ruins to see the pyramids. ~~I used to think that pyramids were only in Egypt.~~ [Note: ~~look up name~~] *El Castillo* is the biggest pyramid in Chichén Itzá. It has nine levels, and has a temple on top. It was built a thousand years ago over a smaller, older pyramid. Inside the smaller pyramid is a ~~big cat~~ *jaguar* carved out of limestone. After we came home, we all wanted to go back. The cat statue has green jade eyes. I've never seen such interesting things before. We didn't have enough time to see everything.

You'll learn more about evaluating and revising different kinds of writing in later chapters. But the following general guidelines apply to all kinds of writing.

GUIDELINES FOR EVALUATING AND REVISING

EVALUATION GUIDE	REVISION TECHNIQUE
CONTENT	
1 Is the writing interesting?	**Add** examples, an anecdote (brief story), dialogue, and details. **Cut** repeated or boring details.
2 Does the writing achieve its purpose?	**Add** explanations, examples, or details to achieve the purpose.
3 Are there enough details?	**Add** details, facts, or examples to support the main idea.
4 Are there unrelated ideas that distract the reader?	**Cut** the unrelated ideas.
ORGANIZATION	
5 Are ideas and details arranged in an effective order?	**Reorder** ideas and details to make the meaning clear.
6 Are the connections between ideas and sentences clear? (See pages 71–73.)	**Add** transitional words to link ideas: *because, for example,* and so on.
STYLE	
7 Is the meaning clear?	**Replace** unclear wording. Use precise, easy-to-understand words.
8 Does the language fit the audience and purpose?	**Replace** slang and contractions to create a formal tone. **Replace** formal words with less formal ones to create an informal tone.
9 Do sentences read smoothly?	**Reorder** words to vary sentence beginnings. **Reword** to vary sentence structure.

EXERCISE 12 ▶ Evaluating and Revising a Paragraph

Now it's your turn to evaluate and revise. The following paragraph is the first draft of a paper written to describe a frightening experience. It's aimed at an audience of eighth-graders. With a partner, evaluate and then revise the paragraph. Use the Guidelines for Evaluating and Revising on page 48.

Ever since The Wonderful Wizard of Oz was read to me when I was little, I've wanted to see a tornado. I also liked books about dinosaurs. Maybe I thought that a tornado would take me to some magical place. Tornados are violent circular windstorms that have winds that whirl around and around. When I was eleven, I visited my aunt and uncle in Texas. They live in Texas. We saw black clouds swirling in the sky. It ripped up some big trees. A tornado dropped down out of the clouds and started coming toward the house. It really scared all of us. We were very lucky. It went back up into the clouds before it damaged any buildings. I've seen a tornado. I never want to see another one! No one was hurt, either.

Proofreading and Publishing

After you've revised your paper, most of your work is done. You can relax—now you're in the home stretch of the writing process.

Proofreading

When you proofread, you carefully reread your paper. You correct mistakes in grammar, spelling, capitalization, and punctuation. Again, it's helpful to put your paper aside for awhile. Then focus on one line at a time and read slowly, one word at a time. If you're not sure what's correct, look it up. Afterward, exchange papers with a classmate and proofread each other's paper to try to find errors that need to be corrected.

The following guidelines will remind you what to look for as you review your writing one last time.

GUIDELINES FOR PROOFREADING

1. Is every sentence a complete sentence, not a fragment? (See pages 360–362.)
2. Does every sentence begin with a capital letter and end with the correct punctuation mark? (See pages 708–710 and pages 737–740.)
3. Do plural verbs have plural subjects? Do singular verbs have singular subjects? (See pages 575–588.)
4. Are verbs in the right form? Are verbs in the right tense? (See pages 604–623.)
5. Are adjective and adverb forms used correctly in making comparisons? (See pages 657–664.)
6. Are the forms of personal pronouns used correctly? (See page 437.)
7. Does every pronoun agree with its antecedent (the word it refers to) in number and in gender? Are pronoun references clear? (See pages 594–595.)
8. Are all words spelled correctly? Are the plural forms of nouns correct? (See pages 798–827.)

EXERCISE 13 ▶ **Proofreading a Paragraph**

See how sharp your proofreading eyes are. The following paragraph has five mistakes. See if you can find and correct the errors. Refer to the **Handbook** on pages 402–827 and to a dictionary to correct the errors.

> For the past two weeks, we've had repeated ice storms. On all the sidewalks and on the ground, the ice is now over six inches thick. The main roads are clear, but the side roads are still ice-covered. The main hazard, though, is walking. No one can clear the ice, so the outside is one huge ice-skating rink. schools are closed because the bus drivers don't dare to go off the main roads. School officials are also concerned about students falling and seriously hurting themselves on school property. Most people is simply staying indoors completely.
> *are*

Publishing

After you proofread, you're ready to publish, or share your writing. You've worked hard, and you can be proud of your writing. Here are some ways of publishing your work.

- Read what you've written to the class or to a group of friends.
- Illustrate or decorate a copy of your creative writing, and give it to a friend or relative.

- Post book and movie reviews on a bulletin board.
- Keep a folder of your writing.
- Enter a writing contest. Some award prizes.
- Send your writing to a newspaper or magazine.
  Find out which magazines publish student writing.

CRITICAL THINKING

Reflecting on Your Writing

After you've explored some ways to communicate with an audience, take some time to look at yourself, the writer. One way to do this is by creating a portfolio.

A **portfolio** is a collection that represents different types of your writing and shows your growth as a writer. As you complete writing assignments, choose the pieces that you think say something interesting about you as a writer, and put them in your portfolio. Remember to date each piece so that you and your teacher can trace the development of your writing over time.

By the end of the school year, your portfolio will contain a range of writing types—short stories, reports, and poems, for example—that fulfill a variety of purposes. You will use a variety of thinking skills and writing strategies to create these different types of writing. Therefore, you may sometimes choose pieces for your portfolio that don't completely satisfy you but that do show your progress with different techniques. When considering whether or not to include a piece in your portfolio, be honest but don't be too hard on yourself. One of the challenges of writing is figuring out how to evaluate your work without being overly critical, so that you grow as a writer.

As you reflect on your writing, think about how you used the writing process to create your pieces. By thinking about your writing process, you can identify your strengths and set goals for areas that need work.

CRITICAL THINKING EXERCISE:
Reflecting on Your Writing

Think about the writing you have done recently for different classes. If you still have some of your papers, take them out and reread them. Then, reflect on your writing process by answering the following questions. Date your answers and save them in your portfolio.

1. Which part of the writing process generally goes most smoothly for you? Which part do you find the most challenging? Why?
2. Which part of each paper are you most pleased with and why? Which part would you handle differently the next time you write that type of paper? Do you notice any patterns in your writing? What types of writing do you most enjoy doing?
3. What have you discovered about your writing process? What have you discovered about yourself by reflecting on your writing?

You've worked hard on your writing and should give yourself a pat on the back. Before you share your writing with others, however, follow these guidelines to make sure your paper looks as good as it can.

GUIDELINES FOR MANUSCRIPT FORM

1. Use only one side of a sheet of paper.
2. Write in blue or black ink, type, or use a word processor.
3. Leave margins of about one inch at the top, sides, and bottom of each page.
4. Follow your teacher's instructions for putting your name, the date, your class, and the title on your paper.
5. If you write, do not skip lines. If you type, double-space the lines.
6. Indent the first line of each paragraph.

EXERCISE 14 **Publishing Your Writing**

Can you think of other ways to publish your writing? Get together with two or three classmates to find information about publishers who print student writing. Two reference books to check are the *Market Guide for Young Writers* and *Writer's Market*. Ask the librarian for other sources of information. Then, compile a class booklet of possible publishers.

SYMBOLS FOR REVISING AND PROOFREADING

SYMBOL	EXAMPLE	MEANING OF SYMBOL
≡	at Waukeshaw lake	Capitalize a lowercase letter.
/	a gift for my Uncle	Lowercase a capital letter.
∧	cost ₍fifty₎ cents	Insert a missing word, letter, or punctuation mark.
⌐	by ₍our₎ their house	Replace something.
ℒ	What day is is it?	Leave out a word, letter, or punctuation mark.
∩	rec ie ved	Change the order of letters.
¶	¶ The last step is	Begin a new paragraph.
⊙	Please be patient⊙	Add a period.
∧	Yes, that's right.	Add a comma.

MAKING CONNECTIONS

Writing with a Computer

Pens and pencils will always be required tools for writers, even those who type their finished work. You can carry a pen or pencil anywhere, and whenever a new idea strikes you, you can jot it down while it's still fresh in your mind—even if the only thing you can find to write on is a table napkin or the back of an envelope.

Even though pens and pencils are great for scribbling notes, there are several reasons to switch to a computer when you actually start *drafting*. Computers let you type words and sentences as you think of them, without worrying about putting them in order. If you write in pen and need to rearrange many parts of your draft, you'll have to do a lot of rewriting or retyping. With a computer, you can use your word-processing program's Cut and Paste commands to reorder just the parts you want to move—without doing any retyping at all.

Most computers also let you use special formatting options such as bold, italic, underline, strike through, and different-colored type. You need to follow standard rules when you use these options in your final paper, but when you're drafting, you can use them any way you want.

Computers make it easy to create and change line spacing, paragraph indents, margins, and tabs, too. When you need to make a change, you just change your format settings and print out another copy.

Type and format your next writing assignment on a computer. Attach to the assignment a short note explaining how the computer helped you during drafting. If you don't have a computer at home or in your classroom, check to see if your school library or computer lab has computers you can use, and find out what software is installed on them. Report your findings to the class.

2 LEARNING ABOUT PARAGRAPHS

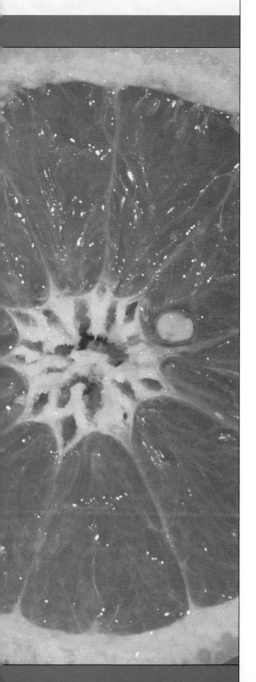

Looking at the Parts

When directors cast a movie, they decide who will play each part. Some actors will have big parts. Others will have only one word to say. Yet, each **part** is important if the movie is to come out right. Paragraphs are like this. Some are big, some are small, but they are all important.

Writing and You. Paragraphs can stand alone, and many do. But most are like links in a chain. They work together to create a longer piece of writing—a magazine article, a short story, a novel, or a letter. Paragraphs separate ideas and yet, at the same time, join them in some way. Why do you think paragraphs come in different sizes?

As You Read. On the pages that follow, you'll find selected paragraphs from a magazine article. As you read, notice how the paragraphs work together to discuss unusual living creatures called slime molds.

from

BEAUTIES
from a
BEAST:

WOODLAND JEKYLL AND HYDES

by Sylvia Duran Sharnoff

During the final stage of their life cycle, slime molds can look like beautiful, minute coral.

It had been a wet spring. Now, in the summer of 1973, panic was spreading in the Dallas suburbs, on Long Island, around Boston. Pulsating yellow blobs were crawling across people's lawns and even up onto their porches. The blobs broke apart when they were blasted with water, but the pieces continued to crawl and grow—reinforcing fears that they were indestructible aliens from outer space or, at the very least, menacing mutant bacteria.

In due time, scientists assured the public that the "unidentified growing objects" were merely a stage in the bizarre life cycle of remarkable but terrestrial creatures called slime molds. Alarming as they can be to those who come across them unexpectedly, slime molds in the crawling stage are so entertaining that some people keep them as pets. In their spore-bearing stage, many slime molds are astonishingly beautiful, overlooked natural treasures.

Early botanists first noticed slime molds in the spore-bearing stage and mistakenly believed they were puffballs, those spherical fungi that sometimes release smoky clouds of spores. Hence, slime molds have traditionally been the province of mycologists, people who study mushrooms and other fungi. The experts who identified the mysterious invaders in 1973 were mycologists. While slime molds are studied by mycologists, and while they may resemble fungi during a part of their life, they take on the appearance of other living things during other portions of their life cycle. They sometimes appear as slimy blobs capable of moving as fast as slugs; in an earlier stage, they take the form of microscopic protozoans. Because of this Jekyll-and-Hyde development, slime molds have been a difficult group to pigeonhole.

> **"Pulsating yellow blobs** were crawling across people's lawns and even up onto their porches."

Plasmodia, the "blobs from outer space" that so alarmed those homeowners, are typically fan-shaped with a delicate, open network of veins and a ruffled leading edge. In some species, they stay microscopic and colorless. Others are large and colorful: violet, pink or red, but most come in shades of yellow. A few species occasionally grow very large, more than three feet across. One mentioned in the scientific literature covered an entire decaying log that was a yard in diameter and ten yards long.

Plasmodia creep about, eating bacteria, fungi, protozoans, and algae, and sometimes cannibalizing sibling slime molds.

Plasmodia transform themselves into dry fruiting bodies called sporophores that can be seen with a magnifying glass.

They generally live under leaf litter on the forest floor or inside rotting logs, where they can squeeze through narrow spaces in search of food.

Aside from the occasional, frightening encounter with large plasmodia, most people have little knowing contact with slime molds: the exceptions are the scientists who study them and the aficionados who keep them as pets. In the early 1900s, an eccentric Japanese folklorist and biological collector named Kumagusu Minakata kept slime molds in his garden. At first he reportedly had to get up every two hours during the night to protect his pets from garden slugs, but then he trained a succession of cats to drive away the vermin.

Forty years ago, a woman named Ruth Nauss kept a "garden" of slime molds in jars and dishes in the living room of her home. She fed them ground oatmeal flakes, their usual diet in laboratories. When she went on vacation, she took the most delicate along with her, tucking them in with a "warm water bottle" on cold nights. She withheld moisture from the hardier ones for several weeks before a vacation to induce them to harden into sclerotia, so she could leave them unattended. At the time she wrote about them, her oldest plasmodium had been crawling around in its dish for more than nine years.

A scientist who studied slime molds wrote in 1892: "Personally, it is not a matter of prime importance whether it be eventually shown that I have been a botanist or a zoologist." A hundred years later, their place in the great chain of life is still imperfectly resolved.

READER'S RESPONSE

1. Do you think slime molds are more like plants or animals? Why?
2. What were your reactions to the people who have kept slime molds as pets? Would you want to keep them as pets?
3. Did reading the selection make you want to find some slime molds to look at? Why or why not?

WRITER'S CRAFT

4. What main idea is the writer trying to convey in these paragraphs?
5. Which paragraphs describe something? Which ones tell a story?

LOOKING
AHEAD

In this chapter, you'll study the form and structure of paragraphs. Even though most paragraphs are part of a larger piece of writing, keep in mind that

- most paragraphs have a central, or main, idea
- sensory details, facts, and examples can be used to support the main idea
- description, narration, classification, and evaluation are ways of developing paragraphs

What Makes a Paragraph

The Main Idea

Have you ever met some of your friends for a game of baseball? You don't always have enough players, but you always have a pitcher and a catcher. You don't have a baseball game without a pitcher and a catcher.

Paragraphs are like that, too. They may not have a topic sentence and a summary sentence, but they have to have a main idea. You don't have a paragraph without a main idea.

The *main idea* is the big idea around which the entire paragraph is organized. Look back at the second paragraph (page 58) in the opening selection. What is the main idea? It is that slime molds are remarkable creatures. The other sentences in the paragraph give specific details about the characteristics that make slime molds unusual and interesting.

Peanuts reprinted by permission of United Feature Syndicate, Inc.

The Topic Sentence

The *topic sentence* states the main idea of the paragraph. It can occur anywhere in the paragraph, but it's usually either the first or second sentence. (Sometimes the topic sentence is made up of two sentences.) Look again at the second paragraph of the opening selection (page 58). The topic sentence occurs first. Can you see how it helps the reader understand the paragraph's main idea?

Sometimes a topic sentence comes later in the paragraph, or even at the end. In these paragraphs the topic sentence pulls the ideas together and helps the reader see how they are related. Sometimes it summarizes, as in the following paragraph.

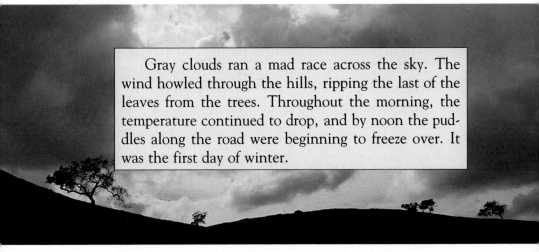

Gray clouds ran a mad race across the sky. The wind howled through the hills, ripping the last of the leaves from the trees. Throughout the morning, the temperature continued to drop, and by noon the puddles along the road were beginning to freeze over. It was the first day of winter.

Many paragraphs have no topic sentence. This is especially true of narrative paragraphs that tell about a series of events. The reader has to add the details together to figure out what the main idea is. Look at the following paragraph. What's the main idea?

When the coyote had finished drinking it trotted a few paces, to above the stepping-stones, and began to eat something. All at once it looked up, directly at me. For a moment it stood still. Then it had turned and almost instantly vanished, back into the shadows

that underlay the trees. From behind the trees, a big black hawklike bird with a red head flapped out and away. Up in the lake, the herons took wing. They, too, circled away from me, angled upriver.

Colin Fletcher, *The Secret Worlds of Colin Fletcher*

Each sentence in this paragraph describes a separate action. But if you put them all together, they suggest the main idea: Colin Fletcher disturbed the animals and they fled.

EXERCISE 1 ▶ **Identifying Main Ideas and Topic Sentences**

All your life you'll be asked to read something and figure out what the main idea is. Sharpen your skills by identifying the main idea in the following paragraphs. If the paragraph has a topic sentence, tell what it is. If there isn't a topic sentence, summarize the main idea in your own words.

1.   There were always dogs about my grandmother's house. Some of them were nameless and lived a life of their own. They belonged there in a sense that the word "ownership" does not include. The old people paid them scarcely any attention, but they should have been sad, I think, to see them go.

N. Scott Momaday, *The Way to Rainy Mountain*

2.   In March of 1996, the Justice Department and the state of California announced a plan to improve emergency telephone service for Californians who are deaf or hard of hearing. Under the agreement, the state will install text telephones known as TTYs or TDDs in 475 emergency telephone centers. A text telephone has a small screen and a keyboard that allow callers to type and receive text messages over telephone lines. Before the agreement, people who were deaf or hard of hearing had to call special 911 centers to get emergency help, and they often had to wait to be transferred to those centers. The Justice Department decided that this two-step procedure was no longer acceptable. Under the Americans with Disabilities Act of 1990, cities must provide telephone emergency services to everyone, including people with disabilities.

3.   I arrived in San Francisco, leaner than usual, fairly unkempt, and with no luggage. Mother took one look and said, "Is the rationing that bad at your father's? You'd better have some food to stick to all those bones." She, as she called it, turned to, and soon I sat at a clothed table with bowls of food, expressly cooked for me.

Maya Angelou, *I Know Why the Caged Bird Sings*

Supporting Sentences

In addition to a main idea and a topic sentence, paragraphs may also have *supporting sentences.* **Supporting sentences** give specific details that explain or prove the main idea. These sentences may use sensory details, facts, or examples.

Sensory Details. When you use words that appeal to one of your five senses—sight, hearing, touch, taste, and smell—you are using *sensory details.* Vivid sensory details help your reader clearly imagine what you're writing about.

Notice the sensory details in this paragraph from *A Wind in the Door.* In the first two sentences, for example, you can "see" Meg move along the wall, you can "smell" the apples, and you can "feel" the cold wind. What other sensory details can you find?

> She moved slowly along the orchard wall. The cidery smell of fallen apples was cut by the wind which had completely changed course and was now streaming across the garden from the northwest, sharp and glittery with frost. She saw a shadow move on the wall and jumped back: Louise the Larger, it must be Louise, and Meg could not climb that wall or cross the orchard to the north pasture until she was sure that neither Louise nor the not-quite-seen shape was lurking there waiting to pounce on her. Her legs felt watery, so she sat on a large, squat pumpkin to wait. The cold wind brushed her cheek; corn tassels hished like ocean waves. She looked warily about. She was seeing, she realized, through lenses streaked and spattered by raindrops blowing from sunflowers and corn, so she took off her spectacles, felt under the poncho for her kilt, and wiped them. Better, though the world was still a little wavery, as though seen under water.
>
> Madeleine L'Engle, *A Wind in the Door*

Facts. Supporting sentences may also contain *facts*. A *fact* is a statement that can be proved true by direct observation or by checking a reliable reference source. For example, if you say that Washington, D.C., is the capital of the United States, that's a fact. It can be proved. But if you say that it's the best city in the world, that's an opinion. Opinions can't be proved. (For more information on facts and opinions, see pages 261–262.)

Look at how the facts in the following paragraph support the main idea that a volcano was erupting. Many of the facts are statistics, or numbers. In the first sentence, for example, facts include the date and time of the boom, as well as the height of the peak. Can you find other facts?

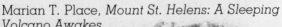

Those who camped overnight on March 28 atop 3,926-foot-high Mitchell Peak were wakened about 2:00 A.M. by a loud boom and whistling sounds. In the brilliant moonlight they watched a great plume of steam rise from the crater. Another eruption at 3:45 A.M. blew ash three miles into the sky and was followed by three quakes registering 4.0 on the Richter intensity scale. Later observers learned the volcano had blown out a second crater. Three small mudflows, not lava, dribbled a thousand feet down the slope. The east and south slopes turned gray from the ash projected by gases roiling from the magma far below the surface.

Marian T. Place, *Mount St. Helens: A Sleeping Volcano Awakes*

Examples. *Examples* are a third kind of supporting detail. They are specific instances or illustrations of a general idea. Soccer and football are examples of team sports played with a ball. Getting grounded is an example of what might happen if you disobey your parents.

In the following paragraph the author gives examples of how animals behave when they're angry.

When animals are angry, they use a different kind of body language. If one animal invades another's territory, the first animal threatens it. Animals may threaten by displaying their teeth or claws. Some try to make their bodies look bigger. Birds fluff up their feathers. Fish stick their back fins straight up and open their gill covers outward. Angry cats arch their backs and make their hair stand on end. These messages say, "I'm a BIG angry animal. Don't come any closer!"

"Animal Body Talk,"
National Geographic World

EXERCISE 2 ▶ **Collecting Supporting Details**

Have you ever collected baseball cards, sea shells, or stamps? You search and choose only the ones you think are best. Now you're going to collect supporting details for topic sentences. Think up at least two details to support each of the following main ideas. With each idea, a type of support—sensory details, facts, or examples—is suggested.

1. Staying alive and healthy is at least partly under your control. (facts and statistics—for example, diet, smoking, or exercise)
2. When I walk around my neighborhood (or city), there's always something going on. (sensory details)
3. No one in my class is just like me. (examples)

Unity and Coherence

A paragraph may have a main idea, topic sentence, and supporting sentences. But the reader may still not understand it fully. What may be missing is unity or coherence.

Unity

When a paragraph has *unity,* all the sentences relate to the main idea. For example, in a paragraph explaining the origin of baseball, every sentence should give some information about baseball's beginnings. Including a sentence about this year's best team will ruin the paragraph's unity. That sentence isn't about the paragraph's main idea—how baseball began.

As you read the following paragraph, notice how each sentence is directly connected to the main idea: how sailors once believed in mermaids.

> Another monster that was equally dreaded by sailors was the beautiful mermaid. Like the sirens, mermaids were thought to be half woman and half fish. Such creatures were said to carry a mirror in one hand and a comb in the other, and from time to time they would run the comb through their long seagreen hair. Most sailors were convinced that it was very bad luck to see a mermaid. At best, it meant that someone aboard their ship would die soon afterward. At worst, it meant that a terrific storm would arise, the ship would sink, and many of the crew would drown.
>
> William Wise, "Strange and Terrible Monsters of the Deep"

EXERCISE 3 ▶ **Identifying Sentences That Destroy Unity**

In each of the following paragraphs, one sentence should make you say, "What's *that* doing there?" Find the sentence that destroys the unity of each paragraph. [Remember: In a unified paragraph, all details are directly related to the main idea or the sequence of actions.]

1. The disappearance of Amelia Earhart remains a mystery. Earhart, who was the first woman pilot to fly across the Atlantic Ocean, crashed in the Pacific while attempting to fly around the world. She was born in Atchison, Kansas, in 1897. Some searchers believe that she survived the crash into the Pacific, because radio distress calls were received. An intensive search for the source of the signals was made. Searchers were not able to find her, however. Finally, the distress signals ceased. In spite of continued searches by airplane and ship, no clue to what became of Amelia Earhart has yet been found.

2.   One reason the mountain bike is popular is because it's built to help the rider keep control even when riding it off paved roads. The extra-wide handlebars improve the rider's balance. Jeremy has a mountain bike, but he only rides on city streets. With its wide tires the mountain bike will roll right over small obstacles that would trip up the skinny tires of a racer. And because the tires are knobby, riders can keep going even if the ground is muddy or sandy. That helps riders keep their balance. Because of these features, mountain bike riders can go almost anywhere.

Coherence

In addition to having unity, a paragraph needs to be coherent. When a paragraph has *coherence,* the reader can easily see how ideas are related. One way to create coherence is to use *transitional words and phrases.* These are words or phrases that show that ideas are connected and how they are connected. The following chart lists some common transitions. Notice that the transitions you use depend, in part, on the kind of paragraph you're writing.

TRANSITIONAL WORDS AND PHRASES

Comparing Ideas/Classification and Definition

also	another	similarly
and	moreover	too

Contrasting Ideas/Classification and Definition

although	in spite of	on the other hand
but	instead	still
however	nevertheless	yet

Showing Cause and Effect/Narration

as a result	for	so that
because	since	therefore
consequently	so	

Showing Time/Narration

after	eventually	next
at last	finally	then
at once	first	thereafter
before	meanwhile	when

Showing Place/Description

above	beyond	into
across	down	next to
around	here	over
before	in	there
behind	inside	under

Showing Importance/Evaluation

first	mainly	then
last	more important	to begin with

Notice how the underlined transitions help show how ideas are related.

Doesn't the earth sometimes seem like one big mess? That's <u>because</u> it is. Think about how much trash you make in one day. Where does it go? The garbageman picks it up <u>and</u> it's gone. <u>But</u> where?

Sometimes trash is burned, releasing harmful pollutants into the air—not a smart idea. Other times it goes to a dump or a landfill, where it's buried with dirt. Not a great idea either, but it doesn't matter anymore, because we're fast running out of space for landfills—so where to next?

"Earth SOS," *Seventeen*

E X E R C I S E 4 ▶   **Identifying Transitional Words and Phrases**

Can you find the words and phrases that connect the writer's ideas? Make a list of all the transitional words and phrases you can find in this paragraph about a family adrift on the ocean in a rubber raft and dinghy.

   The rain continued all night long, and as we bailed the warm sea water out of the raft we were glad not to be spending this night in the dinghy at least. I went over to the dinghy twice in the night to bail out, for the rain was filling her quite quickly, and I shivered at the low temperature of the rain water. The raft canopy offered grateful warmth when I returned, and the puddles of salt water in the bottom of the raft seemed less hostile after the chill of the dinghy. We all huddled together on top of the flotation chambers, our legs and bottoms in the water, and although we did not sleep, we rested, for the work of blowing and bailing now went on around the clock, the bailer passing back and forth between the two compartments.

Dougal Robertson, "Survive the Savage Sea"

Ways of Developing Paragraphs

You've learned about the parts of a paragraph and some ways to give a paragraph unity and coherence. Now think about how you plan to develop your main ideas. Here is a list showing four different strategies for developing your main idea. They're really four different ways of looking at a subject or topic, and they also help create coherence.

WAYS OF DEVELOPING PARAGRAPHS	
Description	Describing parts of a person, place, or thing
Narration	Telling how a person or situation changes over time
Classification	Showing relationships between items
Evaluation	Deciding on the value of an item or making a judgment about its importance

WRITING NOTE Often, you'll use more than one strategy in a paragraph. You may, for example, describe a person and also narrate a story about the person. This blend of strategies will give your writing variety and interest.

Description

What's the sound a rock makes when it is dropped into a bucket of water? What does the Vietnam Veterans Memorial look like? How can you recognize a rattlesnake?

You use *description* to tell what something is like or what it looks like. You use mostly sensory details to tell about what you can see, hear, smell, taste, or touch.

Descriptions are usually organized by *spatial order*—how they are arranged in space. In the following paragraph, the writer uses spatial order to describe part of his family's restaurant.

In a glass case near the cash register, cardboard boxes overflow with bags of fortune cookies and almond candies that my father gives away free to children. The first dollar bill my parents ever made hangs framed on the wall above the register. Next to that dollar, a picture of my parents taken twenty years ago recalls a time when they were raising four children at once, paying mortgages and putting in the bank every cent that didn't go toward bills.

David Low, *Winterblossom Garden*

E X E R C I S E 5 ▶ Using Description as a Strategy

How would you describe your favorite movie star, your sneakers, or the inside of your locker? Choose one of these subjects or one of the five in the following list. List or cluster the details you would use to describe it. Try to appeal to the senses by listing things you can see, hear, smell, taste, or touch. Observe the subject if you can or brainstorm some details. (See page 66.)

1. an amusement park or city park
2. the moment just after a touchdown at a football game
3. a garbage truck or garbage dump
4. your favorite place in the whole world
5. a monster in a late-night, grade-B TV movie

Narration

What happened after Old Yeller died? How do you repair a flat on a bicycle? What caused the Civil War?

To answer any of these questions, you *narrate.* In other words, you tell how a person or how a situation changes over a period of time. You can narrate to tell a story, explain a process, or explain causes and effects.

Paragraphs that use narration are often organized in *chronological order.* That is, events are told in the order in which they occur.

Many narrative paragraphs do not have a topic sentence. Because they are about a series of events, they begin with an action. The other sentences tell about additional actions.

Telling a Story.   You're probably very familiar with one kind of narrating—telling a story. When you tell a story, you tell what happened. The story may be about either imaginary or real events.

Here is a narrative paragraph that tells what happens during a ride in a theme park. You are about to meet a very angry gorilla.

Transporting his passengers on the Roosevelt Island tramway, the operator suddenly announces that King Kong has escaped and is wreaking havoc on Manhattan. Suddenly a wall of water breaks from mains and floods the streets below. Fires rage. Then Kong appears in all his terror, hanging from the Queensboro Bridge. He swats at a police helicopter and sends it crashing to the ground. Then the six-ton, four-story-tall gorilla turns his attention to you, grabbing the tram as if it were a Tonka toy. Twisting and turning the vehicle, he picks it up, blasts you with his banana-scented breath, and hurls you to the ground. Falling at 12 feet per second with 1.75 g's of acceleration, the tram is saved from certain disaster by a single cable.

A.J.S. Rayl, "Making Fun"

Explaining a Process.   Whenever you tell someone how something works or how to do something, you're explaining a process. To help readers follow the steps in the process, you once again use chronological order.

In this paragraph, the writer explains how to pan for gold. Once the gold pan is filled with rock and sand, the panning begins.

> Swirl your pan around and around just below the surface of the water. The water will cause the light sand and gravel to rise to the top. Pour off the sand, pick out the pebbles and repeat the process. When the top dirt is stripped off, you will see black streaks in the bottom of your pan. These are tiny grains of iron magnetite. This is the "pay dirt." Be careful not to wash it away. Magnetite is heavy, but gold is heavier. Your gold, if it is there, will be under the black sand.
>
> Jean Bartenbach, *Rockhound Trails*

Explaining Cause and Effect.   Narrating is also used to explain how one event causes another event. To make the cause-and-effect connections clear, events are often narrated in the order in which they happened.

In the following paragraph, the cause is an October storm. The effects of the storm are what happens to the people, the trees, the animals, and the buildings.

> **Cause**   A storm came this year, against which all other storms were to be measured, on a Saturday in October, a balmy afternoon.... It built as it came up the valley as did every fall storm, but the steel-gray thunderheads, the first sign of it anyone saw, were higher, much higher, too high. In the stillness before it hit, men looked at each other as though a fast and wiry man had pulled a knife in a bar. They felt the trees falling
> **Effect**   before they heard the wind, and they

Effect

dropped tools and scrambled to get out. The wind came up suddenly and like a scythe, like piranha after them, like seawater through a breach in a dike. The first blow bent trees half to the ground, the second caught them and snapped them like kindling, sending limbs raining down and twenty-foot splinters hurtling through the air like mortar shells to stick quivering in

Effect

the ground. Bawling cattle running the fences, a loose lawnmower bumping across a lawn, a stray dog lunging for a child racing by. The big trees went down screaming,

Effect

ripping open holes in the wind that were filled with the broken-china explosion of a house and the yawing screech of a pickup rubbed across asphalt, the rivet popping and twang of phone and electric wires.

Barry Holstun Lopez, *River Notes*

E X E R C I S E **6** ▶ **Using Narration as a Strategy**

When you tell a joke—or any kind of story—you start at the beginning and tell what happens next until you get to the punch line, or ending. Read the directions and then use narration to develop each of the following items.

1. Choose one of the following subjects and list at least three actions that took place.
   A. the funniest thing that ever happened to me (Make up a story, if you like.)
   B. what happened at the Boston Tea Party (Check an encyclopedia or history book.)
2. Choose one of the following subjects and list at least four steps in the process.
   C. how to apply for a job
   D. how to ask someone for a date

3. Choose one of the following subjects and list at least three causes or effects. You may need to do some research on your selected subject.
   E. getting a part-time job after school (the effects)
   F. water pollution (the causes)

Classification

What's country music? What are the differences between a piano and an electronic keyboard?

In answering either of these questions, you would be *classifying.* That is, you'd tell how the specific subject relates to other subjects that belong to the same group. Country music, for example, belongs to the group *music,* which includes rock, jazz, blues, rap, folk, gospel, classical, opera, and other types of music. When you classify, you define (*country music*) or compare and contrast (*piano and electronic keyboard*).

When you write a paragraph to classify, you usually arrange your ideas in *logical order.* Something is called logical because it makes sense; its meaning is clear. When you classify, it makes sense to group or arrange related ideas together.

Defining. When you tell about a subject that's new to your reader, you may have to give a definition. Usually, a *definition* has two parts. First, it identifies the large group, or general class, that the subject belongs to. Second, it tells how the subject is different from all other members that belong to this general class.

Here is a one-sentence definition of tae kwon do. The general class that the subject, tae kwon do, belongs in is italicized. Notice how the other details in the sentence tell how tae kwon do is different from other martial arts.

EXAMPLE   Tae kwon do is an ancient form of *martial art* from Korea that uses kicks and punches in a hard style.

Now here's a paragraph that defines tae kwon do. As you read, think about how the paragraph goes beyond the one-sentence definition.

Tae kwon do is a martial art more than 2,000 years old. An assortment of kicks and punches that focus power with deadly effectiveness, it's a so-called hard style. Hard style? I ask Master Son. "Punch, side kick, roundhouse," Son replies. "One kick, fight finished."

Bob Berger, "Road Warrior"

Comparing and Contrasting. When writing about two or more subjects, you may want to compare and contrast them. *Compare* them by explaining how they're alike. *Contrast* them by telling how they're different. In a single paragraph, you'll probably do one or the other, not both.

Read this paragraph and decide which creature in the drawing below is a moth and which is a butterfly. See if you can find the major differences as you read.

There are three main differences between butterflies and moths. Butterflies are out by day while moths usually fly at night, but this is not an infallible guide since some moths fly by day. Second, moths spread their wings sideways at rest whereas butterflies hold them together over their backs, though again there are exceptions. Third, the butterfly's antennae are long and slender with clubbed ends, whereas a moth's are shorter and feathery.

Gerald Durrell with Lee Durrell,
The Amateur Naturalist

EXERCISE 7 ▶ **Using Classification as a Strategy**

What is it? What makes it different? How is it like or different from something else? All of these questions involve the strategy of classification. Follow the directions below to develop each main idea.

Main Idea	Classification Strategy
1. Japanese schools are very different from American schools.	Compare and contrast the two subjects: Japanese schools and American schools. List some details about each kind of school to support the main idea. (You may need to do some reading about Japanese schools.)
2. Even if you don't know much about dogs, you can't possibly mistake a Saint Bernard for a Siamese cat.	Define the subject. Tell its general class. Then, list all the characteristics that distinguish it from other breeds. (If you need some information about the animal, use an encyclopedia or talk to an owner.)

COMPUTER NOTE: Create charts or tables within your word-processing program, and use them to organize details about a topic. These charts may be particularly helpful when you're comparing and contrasting different subjects.

Evaluation

Did you like the last movie you saw? What didn't you like? Would you recommend the movie to a friend?

In writing a paragraph to answer these questions, you'd be *evaluating.* This is the process of deciding whether something is good or bad—how valuable it is. Remember, though, it's not enough just to give your opinion. You also have to give reasons, or support, for your opinion.

When you write an evaluation, you'll often give the reasons for your opinion in the *order of importance.* That is, you'll tell the most important reason first, the next most important reason next, and so on. Or you may decide to reverse the process and tell the least important reason first. Here is the opening paragraph of an article about the legendary composer and musician Duke Ellington. Notice the reasons the writer gives to support his evaluation.

Duke Ellington considered himself "the world's greatest listener." In music, hearing is all. Given the two or three thousand pieces of music Ellington wrote, he could probably hear a flea scratching itself and put that rhythm into one of his compositions. **Reason** For him the sounds of the world were the ingredients he mixed into appetizers, main courses, and desserts for the appetite **Reason** of his worldwide audience. He wasn't averse to going out in a boat to catch the **Reason** fish himself. He would raise the fowl and the livestock and slaughter them all himself **Evaluation** if there was no one else to do it. But when that musical meal appeared before you none of the drudgery showed. It seemed perfectly natural, as if it had all appeared from behind an invisible door in the air.

Stanley Crouch, "The Duke's Blues"

E X E R C I S E 8 **Using Evaluation as a Strategy**

What's your evaluation—good, bad, or somewhere in between? What are your reasons for your evaluation? Pick two of the following topics and write a sentence expressing your evaluation. Then give two or three reasons to support your opinion.

EXAMPLE *Evaluation: This pizza is delicious.*
Reasons: (1) It has lots of cheese.
(2) It has a crisp, crunchy crust.
(3) The toppings are fresh and plentiful.

1. a recent recording you've listened to or a concert you've attended
2. last week's episode of your favorite TV series
3. a sporting event you attended or watched on TV
4. a new fad or fashion for teenagers

E X E R C I S E 9 **Speaking and Listening: Evaluating a Movie**

Of all the movies you've seen lately, which one is the best? Why? Think of at least three reasons to support your choice of best movie. Jot down your evaluation and your reasons. Then meet with a small group and give your evaluation and your reasons. Listen carefully as others present their evaluations. See if your group can agree on some criteria, or standards, for good movies. How important, for example, is suspense? believable characters and plot? good actors? You may find that the criteria have to be different for different types of films—for example, science fiction, action, drama, and mysteries.

MAKING CONNECTIONS

WRITING PARAGRAPHS FOR DIFFERENT PURPOSES

In this chapter, you've studied the form and structure of paragraphs. Now you can try applying what you've learned as you write paragraphs. Remember that all writing has one or more of the following purposes: self-expression, information, persuasion, and creativity.

Writing a Paragraph to Express Yourself

What makes you feel angry or happy or frightened? What do you think about everyday things that happen to you or that you observe? Personal writing, or *expressive writing,* can help you get in touch with your thoughts and feelings. You may keep these written thoughts to yourself, but perhaps you share them with others.

Write a paragraph expressing how you think or what you feel about a specific subject. Here are some ideas.

- You've just learned that your family will be moving to a distant state next month.
- You just saw something that's made you furious.
- You're at a school dance. Someone you like but have never talked to before asks you to dance.
- You're thinking about a person who's made a big difference in your life. You want to tell that person how he or she has changed your life.

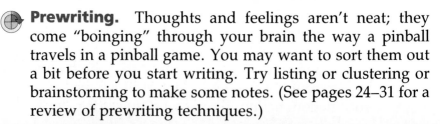 **Prewriting.** Thoughts and feelings aren't neat; they come "boinging" through your brain the way a pinball travels in a pinball game. You may want to sort them out a bit before you start writing. Try listing or clustering or brainstorming to make some notes. (See pages 24–31 for a review of prewriting techniques.)

If you don't like any of the ideas listed above, look through your journal or diary. Try to recall an event or idea that you felt strongly about.

  Writing, Evaluating, and Revising. Write one paragraph explaining what you think and feel. If you're writing only for yourself, just leave your first draft the way you wrote it. But if you want to share your paragraph— and read what others have written—look over your draft carefully. Will your reader be able to follow your ideas?

Proofreading and Publishing. If you plan to share your paragraph, correct all mistakes in usage, spelling, and punctuation. (See the **Guidelines for Proofreading** on page 50.)

Writing a Paragraph to Inform

You take in a great deal of information every day from people, TV, radio, newspapers, and books. But you also give information to your friends and family. You may give directions for playing racquetball, advice on how to care for a pet, or information about the latest styles in clothes.

Write a paragraph using the information in the following chart. It gives statistics (facts stated in numbers) about how junior high students in the United States and in Japan spend their time. The numbers in the chart are hours per week.

Don't try to use all of the chart's information in one paragraph. Focus on what you think is most interesting or important. You can use the topic sentence suggested below or make up one of your own. In your paragraph, focus on differences (as in the topic sentence below) or on similarities. Think of your audience as readers of your school newspaper.

> Topic sentence: If you were a junior high student in Japan, you'd be spending the 168 hours in every week differently than a junior high student in the United States.

TIME SPENT PER WEEK BY JUNIOR HIGH STUDENTS		
Activities	**United States**	**Japan**
Household work	4.6	3.3
School work	31.9	62.8
In school	28.7	46.6
Studying	3.2	16.2
Reading	1.2	2.6
Television	17.5	15.4
Playing games and sports	8.3	3.4
Sleep	59.6	56.6
Other	44.9	13.9

Institute for Social Research, University of Michigan, 1990

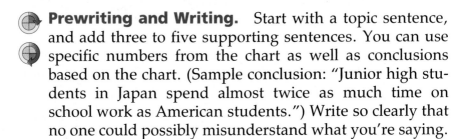

Prewriting and Writing. Start with a topic sentence, and add three to five supporting sentences. You can use specific numbers from the chart as well as conclusions based on the chart. (Sample conclusion: "Junior high students in Japan spend almost twice as much time on school work as American students.") Write so clearly that no one could possibly misunderstand what you're saying.

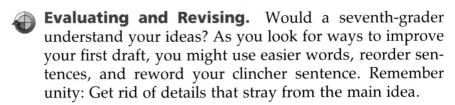

Evaluating and Revising. Would a seventh-grader understand your ideas? As you look for ways to improve your first draft, you might use easier words, reorder sentences, and reword your clincher sentence. Remember unity: Get rid of details that stray from the main idea.

Proofreading and Publishing. Give your paragraph a final polish by correcting mistakes in usage, punctuation, and spelling. Consult your classmates and choose one or two paragraphs to submit to your school paper.

Writing a Paragraph to Persuade

Both in speaking and in writing, persuasion aims to convince someone to take a specific action or to think in a certain way. How persuasive are you? Can you convince people to volunteer to clean up a local park? Can you try to persuade local restaurants to stop using polystyrene cups and plates?

When seen from outer space, the planet Earth looks very beautiful. However, when you look closely, you can see that Earth has many problems.

You've just been appointed Earth Educator in your school. Use some of the facts in the chart below to write one paragraph persuading middle school students to take some action. In your topic sentence, identify the action you want them to take. Don't try to use all of the information in the chart. Just make sure you support your topic sentence with convincing facts and reasons. Here's a suggestion for a topic sentence that you might use.

Topic sentence: Unless we take action now, our beautiful Earth may not be beautiful much longer.

PROBLEM: Too much garbage

THINGS YOU CAN DO:
   Recycle glass, aluminum, plastic, newspaper.
   Don't buy products with a lot of packaging.
   Don't buy polystyrene at all.

FACTS: 1. Americans average four pounds of garbage per day per person. 2. Landfills (where garbage is deposited) are filling up. 3. A third of all our garbage is packaging waste. 4. Almost one tenth of every dollar spent on food goes for packaging that is thrown out. 5. Littered aluminum cans will still be there in five hundred years. Glass bottles last twice as long. 6. Polystyrene doesn't biodegrade at all. It kills turtles and other sea animals. 7. It takes nine times as much energy to make an aluminum can from raw materials as it takes to make an aluminum can from recycled aluminum. 8. Recycling glass and aluminum greatly lessens air pollution and water pollution from glass and aluminum factories.

Prewriting. Use the chart to gather two or three convincing facts and reasons. If you want to write about a different Earth problem, do some research or ask your social studies or science teacher for ideas.

Writing, Evaluating, and Revising. After you've written your first draft, get a classmate's reactions. How convincing is your paragraph? Is there enough supporting information? Have you convinced your classmate?

Proofreading and Publishing. Correct any errors in usage and mechanics. Brainstorm ways of sharing your paragraphs with people in your school and community. You might compile a booklet that you can distribute to adults in your community.

Writing a Paragraph That Is Creative

In 1899, an American artist named Winslow Homer created the painting on page 89 and called it *The Gulf Stream.* Homer knew what the sea and sky looked like because he'd sailed across the Gulf Stream ten times. But how did he imagine the man, the boat, and the sharks?

Your assignment is to imagine a story based on Homer's painting. As in most stories, the main character is involved in some kind of *conflict,* or struggle. Think of a beginning, middle, and end for the story of the man in the boat. Then, write the opening paragraph that describes the story's *setting,* the time and place where the events occur. To develop your paragraph, you'll use description (pages 74–75).

Prewriting. Think through the story first.
- Who is the man in the boat? How did he get there?
- What is he thinking? What will happen to him?
- What part do the sharks and the sailboat on the horizon play in the story?

Jot down some sensory details. If you were on the boat, how would you describe the sky and sea? What would you smell and feel? What sounds would you hear?

Winslow Homer, *The Gulf Stream* (1899). The Metropolitan Museum of Art, Catherine Lorillard Wolfe Collection, Wolfe Fund, 1906. (06.1234) Photograph © 1995 The Metropolitan Museum of Art.

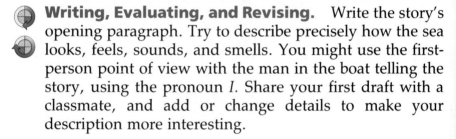

Writing, Evaluating, and Revising. Write the story's opening paragraph. Try to describe precisely how the sea looks, feels, sounds, and smells. You might use the first-person point of view with the man in the boat telling the story, using the pronoun *I.* Share your first draft with a classmate, and add or change details to make your description more interesting.

Proofreading and Publishing. Correct any errors in usage and mechanics. In a small group, read your paragraph aloud. Discuss how others imagine the beginning of the man's story and its end. If you want to, work alone or with a partner to write the rest of your story.

 Reflecting on Your Writing

If you plan to include one or more of these paragraphs in your **portfolio,** date each one and use the following questions to include a brief reflection:

- Which type of paragraph writing did you find easier, the persuasive paragraph or the creative one? Why?
- Explain how you organized your ideas in each paragraph. Did you plan how to organize your ideas before you began writing?
- Did writing only one paragraph on each subject seem just right, or did you want to write more?

3 LEARNING ABOUT COMPOSITIONS

Looking at the Whole

Who's the most important player on a softball team? The pitcher who strikes out the side? Or the batter who gets a hit every time? They're both important because they help make up a whole team. Words, sentences, and paragraphs are also team players. Together, they make up a **whole composition.**

Writing and You. A *TV Guide* article says that one day you'll be able to talk back to your TV set. A science magazine reports that a fossil of a whale has been found deep in the desert. In the newspaper, you read a review of a new movie. These are all compositions. They all explore one idea about a single topic. Where else might you read a composition?

As You Read. In the following article, Nedra Newkirk Lamar uses basic composition form to have fun with the English language.

DOES A FINGER FING?

by Nedra Newkirk Lamar

Everybody knows that a tongue-twister is something that twists the tongue, and a skyscraper is something that scrapes the sky, but is an eavesdropper someone who drops eaves? A thinker is someone who thinks but is a tinker someone who tinks? Is a clabber something that goes around clabbing?

Somewhere along the way we all must have had an English teacher who gave us the fascinating information that words that end in ER mean something or somebody who *does* something, like trapper, designer, or stopper.

" . . . a skyscraper is something that scrapes the sky, but is an eavesdropper someone who drops eaves? "

A stinger is something that stings, but is a finger something that fings? Fing fang fung. Today I fing. Yesterday I fang. Day before yesterday I had already fung.

You'd expect eyes, then, to be called seers and ears to be hearers. We'd wear our shoes on our walkers and our sleeves on our reachers. But we don't. The only parts of the body that sound as if they might indicate what they're supposed to do are our fingers, which we've already counted out, our livers, and our shoulders. And they don't do what they sound as if they might. At least, I've never seen anyone use his shoulders for shoulding. You shoulder your way through a crowd, but you don't should your way. It's only in slang that we follow the pattern, when we smell with our smellers and kiss with our kissers.

The animal pattern seems to have more of a feeling for this formation than people do, because insects actually do feel with their feelers. But do cats use their whiskers for whisking?

I've seen people mend socks and knit socks, but I've never seen anyone dolage a sock. Yet there must be people who do, else how could we have sock-dolagers?

Is a humdinger one who dings hums? And what is a hum anyway, and how would one go about dinging it? Maybe Winnie the Pooh could have told us. He was always humming hums, but A. A. Milne never tells us whether he also was fond of dinging them. He sang them but do you suppose he ever dang them?

Sometimes occupational names do reveal what the worker does, though. Manufacturers manufacture, miners mine, adjusters adjust—or at least try to. But does a grocer groce? Does a fruiterer fruiter? Does a butler buttle?

No, you just can't trust the English language. You can love it because it's your mother tongue. You can take pride in it because it's the language Shakespeare was dramatic in. You can thrill to it because it's the language Browning and Tennyson were poetic in. You can have fun with it because it's the language Dickens and Mark Twain and Lewis Carroll were funny in. You can revere it because it's the language Milton was majestic in. You can be grateful to it because it's the language the Magna Carta and the Declaration of Independence were expressed in.

But you just can't trust it!

"These are but wild and whirling words..."

—Shakespeare
Hamlet, Act 1, Scene 5

READER'S RESPONSE

1. The writer's point is that the English language is tricky. You can't trust it. What do you think? What tricks has English played on you?
2. If English is your second language, think about your first language for a minute. Is it tricky? What are some examples of rules that are irregular or hard to follow?

WRITER'S CRAFT

3. In this article, the writer includes several paragraphs with examples to support her main idea. What is the main idea?
4. The last two paragraphs bring the article to an end. What has the writer done to let you, the reader, know that it's the end?

LOOKING AHEAD

As you work through this chapter, you'll learn about the parts of a composition. You'll learn that most compositions

- have one main idea
- have three main parts: an introduction, a body, and a conclusion
- have unity and coherence so that readers can clearly follow ideas

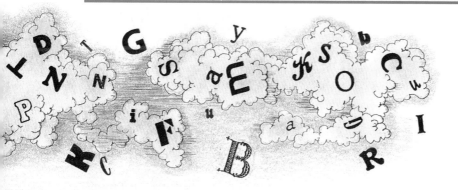

What Makes a Composition

You probably remember a time in elementary school when you stood before a class, knees quaking, to read a composition like "My Dog Spot" or "How I Spent My Summer Vacation." You may not have realized it then, but you were practicing skills that you will use for the rest of your life.

Someday an employer may ask you to write a short composition, or essay, on your goals and interests in life. This composition may help decide whether you get the job. And you'll use these same composition skills throughout school. On a history test, you might write a composition to explain the causes of the American Revolution. In science, you might compose a short composition to explain how a tadpole becomes a frog.

In this chapter, you'll learn the basic parts of the composition form. In later chapters, you'll use that form to explain a process, to write a persuasive essay, to write about literature, and to write a research report.

" 'What I Did This Summer.' This summer, I went to camp. I hated it. I hated every minute of it. I hated my counsellor. I hated the food. I hated the woods. I hated the nature walks and the nature talks. I hated the outings. I hated the campfires. I hated the overnights. I hated . . ."

Drawing by H. Martin; © 1985 The New Yorker Magazine, Inc.

The Composition Plan

Imagine planning spring vacation and looking at an empty suitcase. What will you pack? Well, you might say, that depends on several things. *Where am I going? How long will I be gone? Where will I stay?* You ask these questions so you can plan.

Without planning, you might end up at the beach with your favorite jeans but no bathing suit. Writing compositions takes planning, too. And the more planning you do, the easier your job will be.

The Main Idea Statement

Just like every article you read, every composition has a *main idea.* And that's where you begin your planning. For example, after some thought, you've chosen "movies" as the topic of your composition. What point will you make about movies? This point, or idea, is what your composition will be about. Every detail and each paragraph you write will tie into this main idea. After brainstorming, you might decide to limit the topic of movies to "what makes a good movie." This would become the main idea of your composition.

Early Plans

An early plan, also called an *informal outline,* is one way of sorting your ideas to make your job of writing easier. You put items into groups and then arrange your groups in order.

Grouping.   First, list all the details you can think of on your topic. Look them over, and ask yourself: *Which items are the most alike? What do they have in common? Which items don't fit at all?* (You can cross these out.) Then, arrange all the items into groups. Finally, write a heading for each group that shows how the items in it are related. Here's how one writer grouped and labeled items for a composition with the main idea "what makes a good movie."

—STRONG PLOT— *interesting beginning, high interest level*
—STRONG CHARACTERS— *real and interesting people, sympathetic to viewers*
—SPECIAL FEATURES— *special effects, unusual settings, different time periods, music*

Ordering.   You also have to think about how to order, or arrange, your ideas so that they will make sense. What should you tell your readers about first? second? last?

Sometimes, your ideas will fall right into place. If you're explaining to readers how to program a VCR, a step-by-step process, you would use *chronological* (time) *order.* For the composition on what makes a good movie, on pages 101–103, it made sense to the writer to use *order of importance* (from most important to least important characteristic: plot, characters, special features. Of course, you could also do it in reverse order if it suited your purpose.) If you were describing an old haunted house, however, you would probably want to use *spatial* (space or location) *order.*

You can use any order that makes sense. Sometimes the topic itself suggests the order. Other times, you simply begin at the beginning with important background information and then cover the material in an order that makes sense. With whatever order you use, ask yourself: *Will my readers be able to follow my thoughts easily? Does each group of details make sense from what comes before?*

REFERENCE NOTE: See page 36 for more information about ordering ideas.

Formal Outlines

Another way to plan your composition is to make a *formal outline.* It's similar to the early plan, except it's more structured. It uses letters and numbers to show the relationships of ideas. You won't need to make a formal outline for every composition, but in most cases, a formal outline can help you plan.

There are two kinds of formal outlines. A *topic outline* states ideas in words or brief phrases. A *sentence outline* states ideas in complete sentences.

Here is the topic outline that the writer prepared when planning the composition on what makes a good movie.

Title: Good Movies: Two Thumbs Up

Main Idea: Good movies share certain qualities that make them winners.

I. Plot
   A. Strong beginning
   B. Interesting plot developments
II. Characters
   A. Real and interesting
   B. Sympathetic in some way
III. Special features
   A. Special effects
   B. Interesting or unusual settings
   C. Historical time periods
   D. Music

 REFERENCE NOTE: To learn more about formal outlines, see pages 342–343.

 COMPUTER NOTE: If your word-processing program has a built-in outlining function, you can use it to help create an outline. An outlining function allows you to move whole sections of the outline at once, as you decide how you want to arrange your ideas.

EXERCISE 1 ▶ **Writing the Main Idea**

You've been magically transported back in time to the first Olympic Games. After you have watched the original version of the Olympic competition, you're transported to the 2002 Olympic Games in Salt Lake City, Utah. You jot down the following facts that you learned from your journeys. Ask yourself what point or idea is suggested by these facts, and write a sentence that states the main idea.

- Modern athletes compete for gold, silver, or bronze medals and can make money from endorsements.
- First Olympic games took place in Olympia, Greece, in 776 B.C.
- Modern athletes train for years before competing.
- Now both men and women compete in more than twenty-five different sports.
- Ancient athletes received wreaths of laurel leaves as prizes for Olympic victories.
- Millions watch the modern games in person and through TV.
- Winter sports events were not a part of the ancient Greek games.
- In the Greek games, only men could compete.
- Ancient athletes trained under professional coaches for ten months before the games.
- Today's competitors receive great recognition and lots of attention.
- Tens of thousands of spectators gathered at the ancient games.

EXERCISE 2 ▶ **Creating an Early Plan**

You're still working on your composition about your experiences at the 776 B.C. and the 2002 Olympic Games. With the main idea written, it's time to create an early plan. First, read over the details in Exercise 1 again. Then, group common details under two headings. Finally, arrange the details in each group into an order that you think would make sense to your readers. [Hint: You might want to use chronological order.]

A WRITER'S MODEL

Here's a composition on what makes a good movie. After you read it, look to see how it follows both the early plan and the formal outline. Also, notice how each paragraph topic supports the main idea throughout the composition.

Good Movies: Two Thumbs Up

INTRODUCTION

You are slumped in your seat, jumbo-sized popcorn in your hand. The lights dim, and you're ready for another escape into the world of movies. Maybe you'll find adventure, comedy, romance, or suspense. But maybe you won't. In fact, you may

Main idea

enjoy your popcorn more than the movie. What makes the difference? What makes a good movie?

BODY

Main topic:
Plot

First of all, a good movie draws you into the action quickly. The excitement begins early in Apollo 13, for example, as it dramatizes the thirteenth Apollo space mission. When an oxygen tank in the spacecraft explodes on the way to the moon, the astronauts on board must turn the ship around to try to get back to Earth alive. Who could resist such a suspenseful plot?

A good movie also fulfills the promise of early thrills. Apollo 13 does this by showing the obstacles the astronauts have to overcome on their way back to Earth. With their oxygen running out, the astronauts must direct the spacecraft to reenter the Earth's atmosphere at precisely the right angle, or it will either be incinerated or bounced off into space forever. This plot keeps you riveted, because you want the astronauts to make it home safely.

Main topic: Characters

A good movie also has characters who catch your interest or your sympathy. Jo March, one of the main characters in <u>Little Women</u>, does both. Jo is one of four daughters in the March family, who live in Concord, Massachusetts, during the Civil War. Jo captures your interest because she is so lively and assertive—a tomboy who wants to be a writer, she stages family plays in which everyone, including the cat, has to play a role. But you also feel sympathy for Jo and her sisters as they try to fulfill their dreams in a world that doesn't encourage girls to act like independent individuals. When Jo moves to New York to pursue a writing career, she shows her excitement about her new adventure, even as she struggles with questions about work and love.

Main topic: Special features

Finally, a really good movie has special features. It has something extra that sets it apart from other movies. One of these extras might be

great special effects. For example, <u>Toy Story</u> uses computer technology to create realistic animation that seems three-dimensional. Another special feature might be the setting. <u>The Secret of Roan Inish</u>, for example, draws you into the magical world of a seal-populated island on the western coast of Ireland. A beautiful, unusual setting makes a good story even better.

A historical setting, especially one based on actual events, can also make a good movie. <u>Glory</u> tells the true account of the first African American company to fight for the Union army. This gives the plot a special edge. You just can't help thinking that this is about real soldiers facing real bullets.

Finally, music is another special feature that can improve a movie. Think of <u>The Sound of Music</u>. Without its songs, it wouldn't be nearly as interesting.

CONCLUSION

By the time the lights come up in the theater, you know which was better—the popcorn or the movie. If you're lucky, the movie won out. But if you're not, there are always new movies to see. Maybe the next one will get it right—both the popcorn and the movie will be two thumbs up!

The Parts of the Composition

You have a topic, a main idea, and an early plan or outline. Now you need to think about the three parts of a composition: the introduction, the body, and the conclusion.

The Introduction

Think about a time when you met someone who made a great first impression. Didn't you instantly like him or her and want to get to know that person better? Compositions also make first impressions with their introductions. A lively introduction hooks its readers and makes them eager to read more. A dull introduction runs the risk of boring its readers, who might stop reading.

Capturing the Reader's Interest.   In the composition on good movies, the writer could have written the following introduction.

> Some movies are fun to watch. Some aren't. But good movies do have things in common.

Does this introduction make a good impression? You'd probably agree that it doesn't. It does do one thing—it tells what the composition is about. But it's so boring that most people might not read any further.

Now, take another look at the introduction in the model on page 101. The writer begins by describing a scene familiar to most moviegoers. The writer then encourages the reader to think: What *does* make a good movie?

Presenting the Main Idea.   You'll usually want to include your main idea statement in your introduction. This keeps both you and your readers on track. It's your way of saying, "This is what I'm going to talk about." Do you see how the writer stated the main idea in the last sentence of the introduction on page 101? Even though it's a question, there's no doubt what this composition is about.

Ways to Write Introductions

Writers use a variety of techniques to grab their readers' attention with interesting introductions. Here are three.

1. **Ask a question.** The writer of the composition on good movies ends the introduction by asking a question: *What makes a good movie?* By starting this way, the writer does a couple of things: quickly gets the reader's attention and involves the reader in the paper. Most people would want to read more.

2. **Tell an anecdote.** An anecdote is a short, interesting story. Since most people like a good story, an anecdote is a good way to begin your composition. Notice how the author Joyce Carol Thomas uses an anecdote to introduce an autobiographical sketch.

I was reluctant to leave Ponca City, Oklahoma, where I was born. As we boarded the train to California in 1948, I celebrated my tenth birthday, enjoying the traveling adventure but longing to be back in the place I knew. When I look at my books, I suddenly realize that I have never really left Oklahoma. *Marked by Fire* is set in Ponca City, and so are *Bright Shadow* and *The Golden Pasture*. Going to a new place held its own excitement, too, and the California landscape became the setting of *Water Girl* and *Journey*.

Joyce Carol Thomas, *Speaking for Ourselves*

3. **State an intriguing or startling fact.** A surprising or unusual fact can get your readers' attention right away. The fact can be an eye-opening statement, or it can refer to a surprising statistic. Either way, readers are curious. They can't wait to read on.

> The surfaces of Venus and Mars have been mapped more thoroughly than the oceans that cover 70 percent of Earth's surface.
>
> Tony Reichhardt, "Water World"

E X E R C I S E 3 ▶ **Identifying Types of Introductions**

You've learned about three types of introductions. Can you recognize them? Working with two or three classmates, read the following introductions. Identify the technique used for each. (To make things interesting, one technique is used more than once.) If you disagree on the technique, discuss your reasons with your classmates.

1.   The other day I spotted a T-shirt for sale on the side of the road that read, "I survived Hurricane Hugo, but the aftermath is killing me." I laughed when I saw it, but now it saddens me. Around my neighborhood trees are uprooted, homes destroyed—the debris is everywhere. The hurricane left sixty-five thousand people in South Carolina homeless and eighteen people dead. The hurricane also left millions of changed lives behind it, mine included.

> Jennifer Cohen, "Disaster Hits Home"

2.   Sometimes you feel as though you are full of energy. Other times you are so tired you say, "I don't feel like playing; I don't have the energy." What is this mysterious thing we call energy?

> Laurel Sherman, "Energy: Powering a Nation"

3.   If you are between 7 and 16 years old, you may stand on the surface of planet Mars by the time you are 40.

Scott Stuckey, "A Home on the Martian Range"

4.   Billy Mills enjoyed running across the countryside on the Pine Ridge Sioux Indian Reservation in South Dakota. His legs would fly like the wind as he leaped over logs and chased scurrying rabbits. Running was good training for the boxing matches Billy had with his father, who was an amateur boxer. Little did he know that running, and not boxing, would one day earn him an Olympic medal.

Della A. Yannuzzi, "Billy Mills"

The Body

Think of the parts of the composition as a team. The introduction's job is to grab the reader's attention and announce the main idea. Then the body develops that idea with paragraphs. Each paragraph supports or proves a main point by developing it with supporting ideas.

☞ REFERENCE NOTE: See pages 74–83 for information on strategies of paragraph development.

The body's job is very important, and teamwork is crucial. Maybe you've read compositions that lack teamwork. They might go off on tangents, ramble on and on, or seem disjointed. What's missing is unity and coherence.

WRITING NOTE

Like any long form of writing, compositions are made up of paragraphs. And each paragraph can be made up of several sentences or even just one sentence. What's most important is how each paragraph, no matter how long or how short, helps the writer to support the main idea of the whole composition.

Unity.   You know you have *unity* in your composition when all your body paragraphs develop a point about the *main idea* that you wrote in your introduction. Look at the model on pages 101–103. Do you see how each paragraph has its own main idea (topic)? In every case, the paragraph topic relates to or supports the main idea.

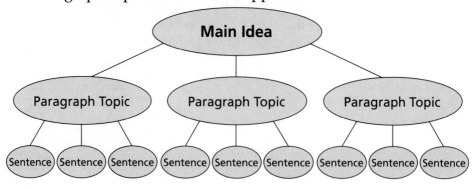

Coherence.   Remember connect-the-dots pictures? By following numbered dots in order with your pencil, you created a picture. The ideas in your paragraphs should be as easy to follow as numbered dots. When they are, your paragraphs have *coherence.* Every sentence leads easily to another. Every paragraph leads to the next.

How can you work on coherence? First, arrange your ideas in an order the reader will understand. Then, make it easy for the reader to see how your ideas are connected.

You can make it easy for readers by using *transitional words and phrases,* such as *next, first, however, in addition to,* and *finally.* They are like the numbered dots. They help readers connect the ideas in your composition. Then readers can see the big picture you've developed.

 REFERENCE NOTE: See pages 71–73 for more information and examples of transitional words and phrases.

EXERCISE 4▶   **Using Transitions**

It's time to connect the ideas! The following list of transitional words or phrases are your dots. Read the four pairs of sentences that show the end of one paragraph and the beginning of the next. Then choose the transitional word or phrase that best ties together the two paragraphs. Some pairs might have more than one right answer. (You won't use all the choices.)

Next	Furthermore
Otherwise	At the last minute
Afterward	First of all
However	Later

1. Of all the annoying people on Earth, my little brother leads the list.
   ____, he uses his age to get his own way.
2. Chen didn't listen to the music. He concentrated on counting the nails in the floor backstage.
   ____, he knew he'd get so nervous that he'd never be able to play his recital piece.

3. When you ask your parents if you can stay out past curfew, explain your reasons carefully. ____, be prepared to answer any objections they might have.

4. I was convinced that all Mexican food was too spicy for me to enjoy. ____, I discovered that real Mexican food is delicious and fun to eat after eating at Luisa's house.

The Conclusion

After you've worked so hard to keep your readers interested, you certainly don't want to leave them hanging in the end. When a composition ends suddenly, readers can feel dissatisfied, let down. Your goal when writing the conclusion is to let your readers know that your composition has come to an end. Here are some of the ways you can do this.

Ways to Write Conclusions

1. **Refer to your introduction.** A favorite technique used by writers is to refer to something in their introduction. This is what the writer of "Good Movies: Two Thumbs Up" (page 101) did. The introduction describes a scene at the movie theater. The conclusion comes back to that scene. The last line also ties the title, introduction, and conclusion together.

> "Maybe the next one will get it right—both the popcorn and the movie will be two thumbs up!"

This statement has a finality to it. It lets the reader know that the paper has come to an end.

2. **Restate the main idea.** One of the most direct ways to end a composition is to restate your main idea *in different words*. In the following example, the writer uses different words to describe the importance of one artist's drawings.

However, Käthe Kollwitz did what few other artists have done—and especially artists who portray children. She would not let us forget the children of the poor and miserable, or the very old, or the overworked mothers struggling for their children. *Their* lives are important, too, she told us in her pictures.

Elsa Marston, "Pictures of the Poor"

3. **Close with a final idea.** Leaving the reader with one last thought can pull your composition together. Here, the teenage writer explaining some of the devastating effects of Hurricane Hugo points to some hope in the crisis.

Yesterday I saw another T-shirt. This one read: HUGO 1, CHARLESTON 0. I thought to myself how wrong that was. The people here have all worked together to rise above defeat. Right now it's HUGO 1, CHARLESTON 1. And gaining.

Jennifer Cohen, "Disaster Hits Home"

E X E R C I S E 5 ▶ **Writing Conclusions**

Remember your trips to the 776 B.C. and the 2002 Olympic
Games? Here's a possible conclusion for a composition
about the two events. As you can see, it's weak. Rewrite
the conclusion to make it more memorable. If you wish,
start over completely. (You may also want to refer to the
notes on page 100.)

> I learned many things about how the Olympic
> games have changed since the first ones in 776 B.C.
> I also realized that some things haven't changed that
> much.

MAKING CONNECTIONS

WRITING AN INFORMATIVE COMPOSITION

As you know, you write for different reasons. You might write to express your feelings, to be creative, to persuade, or to provide information. And you can use the composition form you've been studying in this chapter for any of these purposes.

Now it's time for you to put what you've learned into action. Following are notes on the subject of African American cowboys who helped shape the Old West during the frontier days. (Some of these notes were gathered from an article titled "Black Cowboys" by Suzanne Sobell.) Review the following information. Then, write a short composition to inform your classmates about these African American adventurers.

Main idea: African American cowboys played an important role in the Wild West.

1. Diaries, newspapers, and government reports of the day recorded the accomplishments of several cowboys who were black.
2. Bill Pickett, an African American cowboy, invented the cowboy sport of bulldogging.
3. After the Civil War, about 8,000 former slaves went West and became cowboys.
4. Pickett once survived a five-minute ride on a bucking bull in a Mexico City arena.
5. At least one quarter of all cowboys from the 1860s to the 1890s were black.
6. The legendary African American cowboy Henry Harris became foreman of a cattle ranch in Nevada.
7. Some African American cowboys were broncobusters, cowhands, and wranglers.

8. Pickett was elected to the Cowboy Hall of Fame in 1971, years after his death.

9. A Nevada railroad stop, Henry, is named after Harris.

10. Other black cowboys were popular singers, musicians, and songwriters.

11. One of the most famous of all African American cowboys was Nat Love, who recounted his interesting life in an autobiography.

12. Some African American cowboys were cooks, foremen, and trail bosses.

Prewriting. Look over all the information you've been given. Keeping the main idea in mind, divide and arrange the notes into groups that make sense. Then create an early plan for your paper as shown on pages 97–98. You may not want to use all the ideas.

Writing, Evaluating, and Revising. Begin by putting yourself in your audience's place. How can you capture their attention? What can you say that will get them interested and make them want to read further? As a help, you may want to use one of the ways to write introductions on pages 105–106. Remember to include your main idea in the introductory paragraph.

Next, write your body paragraphs. Make sure that each body paragraph makes a point that ties into your main idea. Use transitions to move easily from one idea to the next.

Finally, write a conclusion that brings your composition to a satisfying, obvious end. You may want to use one of the ways to write conclusions on pages 110–111.

After you've finished writing your first draft, look it over to see how you can improve it. Consider exchanging papers with another student for peer review. Ask the peer-evaluator questions on page 44.

 Proofreading and Publishing. At this point, you may want to take a break from your paper. Come back to it when you're fresh. Then look over your paper one more time. Check for and correct any misspelled words and mistakes in grammar and mechanics. Write or print out a clean copy.

Once you have a clean, corrected copy, think about how you can share it with others. You and your classmates might simply post your compositions on the bulletin board for others to read. Or you may want to use them as the beginning of a booklet on other pioneers of the Old West.

 Reflecting on Your Writing

To add your paper to your **portfolio,** date it and include a brief reflection by answering the following questions:

- How did you decide which ideas to include in your paper?
- How helpful was it to you to make an early plan?
- Which technique did you use to create an interesting introduction? Why did you choose this technique over others?

---

4 EXPRESSIVE WRITING: NARRATION

Discovering Yourself

To excel, athletes reach deep inside themselves for strength and commitment. In the same way, every now and then we need to take a good look inside ourselves. This is how we **discover** who we really are, and how we feel about things.

Writing and You.   Writing about your thoughts and experiences helps you pry loose your deepest feelings. If you want to keep your feelings private, you can write about them in a diary or journal. If you want to share them with others, you might write a personal narrative. Either way, you'll be discovering who you are and how you feel. How well do you think you know yourself?

As You Read.   In the following selection from *The Diary of a Young Girl*, Anne Frank writes in her diary about wanting to become a journalist. As you read, notice how honest Anne is about herself and her feelings.

Olympic Hurdler, Bart Forbes © 1993.

Becoming a —————————

Journalist

by Anne Frank

For a long time I haven't had any idea of what I was working for any more; the end of the war is so terribly far away, so unreal, like a fairy tale. If the war isn't over by September I shan't go to school any more, because I don't want to be two years behind. Peter filled my days—nothing but Peter, dreams and thoughts until Saturday, when I felt so utterly miserable; oh, it was terrible. I was holding back my tears all the while I was with Peter, then laughed with Van Daan over lemon punch, was cheerful and excited, but the moment I was alone I knew that I would have to cry my heart out. So, clad in my nightdress, I let myself go and slipped down onto the floor. First I said my long prayer very earnestly, then I cried with my head on my arms, my knees bent up, on the bare floor, completely folded up. One large sob brought me back to earth again, and I quelled my tears because I didn't want them to hear anything in the next room. Then I

began trying to talk some courage into myself. I could only say: "I must, I must, I must . . ." Completely stiff from the unnatural position, I fell against the side of the bed and fought on, until I climbed into bed again just before half past ten. It was over!

And now it's all over. I must work, so as not to be a fool, to get on, to become a journalist, because that's what I want! I know that I can write, a couple of my stories are good, my descriptions of the "Secret Annexe" are humorous, there's a lot in my diary that speaks, but— whether I have real talent remains to be seen.

"Eva's Dream" is my best fairy tale, and the queer thing about it is that I don't know where it comes from. Quite a lot of "Cady's Life" is good too, but, on the whole, it's nothing.

I am the best and sharpest critic of my own work. I know myself what is and what is not well written. Anyone who doesn't write doesn't know how wonderful it is; I used to bemoan the fact that I couldn't draw at all, but now I am more than happy that I can at least write. And if I haven't any talent for writing books or newspaper articles, well, then I can always write for myself.

I want to get on; I can't imagine that I would have to lead the same

"*A*nyone who doesn't write doesn't know how wonderful it is...."

sort of life as Mummy and Mrs. Van Daan and all the women who do their work and are then forgotten. I must have something besides a husband and children, something that I can devote myself to!

I want to go on living even after my death! And therefore I am grateful to God for giving me this gift, this possibility of developing myself and of writing, of expressing all that is in me.

I can shake off everything if I write; my sorrows disappear, my courage is reborn. But, and that is the great question, will I ever be able to write anything great, will I ever become a journalist or a writer? I hope so, oh, I hope so very much, for I can recapture everything when I write, my thoughts, my ideals and my fantasies.

I haven't done anything more to "Cady's Life" for ages; in my mind I know exactly how to go on, but somehow it doesn't flow from my pen. Perhaps I never shall finish it, it may land up in the wastepaper basket, or the fire . . . that's a horrible idea, but then I think to myself, "At the age of fourteen and with so little experience, how can you write about philosophy?"

So I go on again with fresh courage; I think I shall succeed, because I want to write!

READER'S RESPONSE

1. What did you learn about Anne Frank from reading this selection? Do you have anything in common with her?
2. Would you be interested in reading "Eva's Dream" or "Cady's Life"? How do you feel about Anne Frank's criticism of her own works?
3. Do you agree with Anne that fourteen-year-olds are too young to write about philosophy?

WRITER'S CRAFT

4. What evidence is there in the diary entry that Anne Frank would have been a successful writer if she had lived?
5. Anne Frank addressed her diary entries to an imaginary friend called Kitty. Why might she have included so many details about her life in these diary entries?
6. What reasons does Anne Frank give for wanting to write?

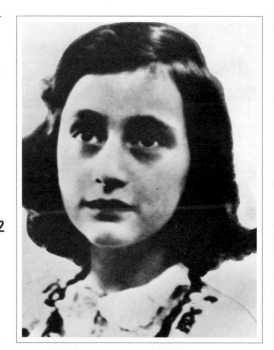

Dit is een foto, zoals
ik me zou wensen,
altijd zo te zijn.
Dan had ik nog wel
een kans om naar
Holywood te komen.
Anne Frank.
10 Oct. 1942

(translation)
"This is a photo as I would wish myself to look all the time. Then I would maybe have a chance to come to Hollywood."

Anne Frank, 10 Oct. 1942

Ways to Express Yourself

Personal expression can occur in different forms and different places: letters to friends, magazine articles, or newspaper columns. A piece of writing is a personal expression when it emphasizes what the writer experiences, feels, and thinks. There are several ways that you can develop an expressive message. Here are some examples.

- in a letter to a friend, writing about an event that was especially important to you
- in your journal, writing your autobiography
- in an article for the school newspaper, defining the word *strong* and explaining what it means to you
- in an essay for social studies class, describing your reactions to past fashions and hairstyles
- in your journal, writing about a visit to the workplace of an adult you know
- in a personal narrative, telling about a job such as baby-sitting or delivering newspapers
- in a letter to a friend, describing the summer camp you're going to
- in an essay for science class, writing about your fascination with a certain type of insect

LOOKING AHEAD

In this chapter, you'll use narration to develop a personal experience narrative. As you work through the writing assignments, keep in mind that an effective personal narrative

- tells about events in the order that they occurred
- uses details about the experience, including sensory details
- shows what meaning the experience had for the writer

Writing a Personal Narrative

 *Prewriting*

Choosing an Experience to Write About

Like Anne Frank, you have had personal experiences worth sharing—personal experiences worth writing about. What was your happiest day? your most exciting moment? your biggest disappointment?

Tap into your personal store of memories. Perhaps you won a big race or took an interesting trip. You can probably recall a number of experiences that had special value for you. Chances are you learned something about yourself on these occasions.

A personal narrative is a good way to explore an important event in your life. As you think about a topic for such a narrative, keep these three questions in mind:

1. **How important was the experience to you? What did you learn about yourself from it?** Don't get the idea that only an earthshaking adventure will do. The smallest incident—important only to *you*—may have taught you a valuable lesson about life.
2. **Do you remember the experience clearly?** You don't have to recall every detail, but you should have a vivid memory of the event.
3. **Are you willing to share the experience with others?** A personal narrative is just that: personal. But it isn't private. Avoid choosing a topic you'd rather keep secret.

"Writing is an exploration. You start from nothing and learn as you go."
E.L. Doctorow

PART 1:
Exploring Possible Topics

It's often helpful to talk over possible topics with others. Think of two topics you might like to explore—for example, "when I forgot Mom's birthday," or "how I won a photo contest." Get together with two or three classmates and share your ideas. What do they think of your possible topics? What do you think of theirs?

WRITING ASSIGNMENT

PART 2:
Choosing a Topic

In Writing Assignment, Part 1 (above), you discussed two possible topics with your classmates. Review those topics here, and make a final decision about the topic for your personal narrative. Use these questions to help you decide.

1. Which experience was more important in your life? A good personal narrative has meaning for *you*.
2. Which experience do you remember more clearly? The more details you can include, the more interesting your narrative will be.
3. Which experience do you feel more comfortable about sharing? Don't write about anything you'd prefer not to share.

Prewriting

Planning Your Narrative

Even though you're writing about yourself, you need to plan your personal narrative. Since other people will read it, you need to make sure it's clear and interesting.

Thinking About Purpose and Audience

When you write, you do so for a reason, a *purpose*. You also expect someone to read what you have written. That someone is your *audience*.

Think about your purpose for writing. Your first thought might be, *It's to get a high grade in English*. That's a worthy goal, but it isn't your true *writing* purpose. When you write a personal narrative, your purpose is to express yourself on paper—and to discover something about yourself in the process. You examine your thoughts and feelings about an event. Then you share your experience with others so that they will understand what you thought and felt.

Who is the audience for a personal narrative? You can always be sure of one reader—yourself. In addition, your teacher will probably read your narrative, and so may your classmates, or a friend, or an adult you trust with your personal feelings. Keep the audience in mind when you write. Include enough background facts and information to make the events in your narrative clear.

Recalling Details

When you write your personal narrative, you'll try to show readers exactly what happened. If you saw a deer, for example, describe the deer in writing so that your readers will *see* it. The way to do this is by including details.

Details are the small, specific parts of an experience. In a personal narrative, they come from your memory. You remember, for example, that the deer you saw was a buck with large antlers and a white tail. When you came near it, the buck stood still for a moment in a clearing in the woods. It stared at you with wide, curious eyes and then bounded away. You heard nothing but the rustling of brush as it fled. You remember the clean smell of the pine trees.

Those are details. They add information about the deer and your experience with it. In this case, they're *sensory details,* because they're based on one or more of the senses—sight, hearing, smell, taste, touch. Details can come from any area of your experience: from events, people, places, or thoughts and feelings.

Events.   Details about events are just what you'd expect them to be. They're the small actions that occurred. Suppose you rode on a float in the last Martin Luther King Day parade. Your details of that event might include (1) breaking both shoestrings in your haste to get ready, (2) helping your younger sister climb onto the float, and (3) waving at people along the street until your arms just ached.

People.   Although you're the center of your own personal narrative, there may be other people in it, too. You observed them at the time. You heard them. When you write, you'll draw on your memories of them to add life to your narrative. Details about people can be anything from the color of their hair (*sight*) to the tone of their voice (*sound*) to the texture of their skin (*touch*).

Places.   Your experience happened in a certain place. It may have been in your house or your neighborhood or your city. The location itself may not have been very exciting. That doesn't matter. Your aim is to make the place, wherever it was, seem real to readers. Once again, sensory details are the key. Remember your sighting of the deer? How did the woods feel? Do you remember "the clean smell of the pines"? What noise did the deer make? Do you remember hearing "nothing but the rustling of brush" as the deer fled?

Thoughts and Feelings.   Finally, look back at your thoughts and feelings about the experience. Were you happy? scared? surprised? There are two ways to share your thoughts and feelings. One way is by stating them directly: "I was scared." Another way is to show your thoughts and feelings through action and dialogue: "I crept forward cautiously. My friend clutched my arm. 'There's something strange floating out there,' she said."

Using a chart like the one on the next page can help you recall and record details of your experience.

Topic: My experience in trying to win a crafts contest			
	What happened	Sensory details	Thoughts and feelings
Background	eight years old; playground coach announced a crafts contest; I told everyone I'd win	blazing sun; playground felt like a hot stove	excited by the contest; sweaty
Beginning	drew picture of a jet airplane; made a clay bowl; strung macaroni into a necklace	kids shouting as they worked; cool, soft feel of clay	confident about winning
Middle	saw other crafts; some were nice; realized materials could be combined	beauty of Luz's cactus-flower drawing; smooth surface of Adela's vase	worried; not bragging
End	did frantic last-minute project—clay bookends; finished third; stayed for picnic	pleased voice of coach announcing winners; smell of picnic for contestants	proud of being third; enjoyed tostadas and lemonade

Reminder

If you need help remembering specific details about your experience

- brainstorm, cluster, or freewrite for ideas (see pages 25–28 of Chapter 1, Writing and Thinking)
- look through your journal for details
- talk to other people who were also part of the experience
- to spur your memory, put the details you can remember in a chart

Arranging the Details of Your Narrative

Most personal narratives begin with important background information. Then writers put events in *chronological order*. This means that you write the first thing that happened, then the second, then the third, and so on. To help your reader follow this time order, you may use transitional words and phrases such as *first, second, then, at last,* and *finally.*

 REFERENCE NOTE: For more help with chronological order and transitions, see pages 75–78 and 71–73.

EXERCISE 1 ▶ **Speaking and Listening: Noting Details About Events**

How good are you at noting details about events? Think of *five* details to show what *one* of the following events might be like. Prepare a short talk to give in class or to a small group about the event based on the five details. Tell your classmates to listen for the details and take notes on them. Do your classmates feel that they are sharing in the event because of your details?

1. going to an auto race
2. shopping on a major sale day at the mall
3. attending a football game
4. entering a pet in a pet show
5. taking a final exam

WRITING ASSIGNMENT

PART 3:
Recalling and Arranging Details

For the personal narrative you plan to write, make a chart like the one on page 128. Under *What happened,* list the events or actions that made up your experience. Under *Sensory details,* list some of the things you saw, heard, smelled, tasted, or touched. Under *Thoughts and feelings,* list how you thought and felt about what happened.

Writing Your First Draft

Understanding the Basic Parts of a Personal Narrative

You already know that a personal narrative

- tells about an important experience that happened to you
- describes important events, people, and places that are part of the experience
- explains the importance of the experience to you

There is no one best way to put together a personal narrative. One writer may begin by describing the story's setting and then tell about events. Another may begin with background and hint at what he or she learned from the experience. Then the writer may go on to tell about events. Two good ways to grab the reader's interest at the outset are with a startling statement or a quotation.

The middle of most personal narratives tells about the experience itself—the details of the event. The conclusion, or ending, usually explains the importance of the experience to the writer. As you read "Cut" by Bob Greene, notice how he has used the basic elements of the personal narrative.

A MAGAZINE COLUMN

Cut
by Bob Greene

INTRODUCTION

Background information

EVENT 1

I remember vividly the last time I cried. I was twelve years old, in the seventh grade, and I had tried out for the junior high school basketball team. I walked into the gymnasium; there was a piece of paper tacked to the bulletin board.

It was a cut list. The seventh-grade coach had put it up on the board. The boys whose names were on the list were still on the team; they were welcome to keep coming to practices. The boys whose names were not on the list had been cut; their presence was no longer desired. My name was not on the list.

I had not known the cut was coming that day. I stood and I stared at the list. The coach had not composed it with a great deal of subtlety; the names of the very best athletes were at the top of the sheet of paper, and the other members of the squad were listed in what appeared to be a descending order of talent. I kept looking at the bottom of the list, hoping against hope that my name would miraculously appear there if I looked hard enough.

I held myself together as I walked out of the gym and out of the school, but when I got home I began to sob. I couldn't stop. For the first time in my life, I had been told officially that I wasn't good enough. Athletics meant everything to boys that age; if you were on the team, even as a substitute, it put you in the desirable group. If you weren't on the team, you might as well not be alive.

I had tried desperately in practice, but the coach never seemed to notice. It didn't matter how hard I was willing to work; he didn't want me there. I knew that when I went to school the next morning I would have to face the boys who had not been cut—the boys whose names were on the list, who were still on the team, who had been judged worthy while I had been judged unworthy.

All these years later, I remember it as if I

EVENT 4

CONCLUSION
Meaning
of experience

were still standing right there in the gym. And a curious thing has happened: in traveling around the country, I have found that an inordinately large proportion of successful men share that same memory—the memory of being cut from a sports team as a boy.

I don't know how the mind works in matters like this; I don't know what went on in my head following that day when I was cut. But I know that my ambition has been enormous ever since then; I know that for all of my life since that day, I have done more work than I had to be doing, taken more assignments than I had to be taking, put in more hours than I had to be spending. I don't know if all of that came from a determination never to allow myself to be cut again—never to allow someone to tell me that I'm not good enough again—but I know it's there.

EXERCISE 2 ▶ **Analyzing the Organization of a Personal Narrative**

After reading Bob Greene's narrative, get together with some classmates and discuss the following questions.

1. Have you ever had a disappointment like Greene's? Are you willing to share it? If so, tell about it.
2. How does the author grab your attention at the beginning? How does he make his personal experience seem real to you?
3. What order does Greene use to organize most of the events of his narrative?
4. What thoughts and feelings does Greene have about being cut? Give examples of his thoughts and feelings in this selection.
5. Personal narratives often reveal the writer's sense of how the experience affected his or her life. How does Greene think the cut affected his life?

WRITING NOTE For some types of writing, such as research reports, you leave out your thoughts and feelings. Instead, you develop the paper with outside sources such as facts and expert opinions. With a personal narrative, however, you *are* the center of attention. You speak directly to your readers, using the words *I, me, we,* and *us.* Your reader sees the experience through your eyes and gets a glimpse inside the personal you. Notice how Bob Greene addresses you—his readers—directly and how the writer of the following narrative does also.

Following a Basic Framework for a Personal Narrative

Bob Greene is a professional writer. His personal narrative deals with an experience that he looks back on as an adult. Still, he includes background information, thoughts and feelings, and sensory details to make the experience real to his readers. In learning to write a personal narrative, you may find it helpful to follow a simpler model, like the personal narrative that follows.

A WRITER'S MODEL

Catch of the Day

INTRODUCTION

Background information

Thoughts and feelings

One Saturday last spring, my friend Kazutaka said, "Let's go fishing." His plan called for a trip to Catherine Creek, which is a great trout stream. People come from far away to catch rainbow trout in the rippling waters of Catherine Creek. Kaz and I are lucky. We live just a short bicycle ride away.

EVENT 1

Sensory details

A light rain stung our faces as we pedaled along the narrow country road toward our favorite spot. By the time we got there the rain had stopped, but the sky was still gray. We walked our bikes to the edge of the creek. We were all alone. The only sound we heard besides the running water was the distant cawing of a crow.

Thoughts and feelings

Sensory details

EVENT 2

What we saw upset us. Three or four people had had a picnic at our fishing spot. They had thrown their trash on the ground and left it there—cans, bottles, napkins, orange peels. What a mess! We put down our fishing poles and began to pick up. We stuffed everything into the plastic bag Kaz had brought for trout. It was a big bag. Kaz is an optimist.

Sensory details

No sooner had we picked up the very last crumpled napkin than Kaz pointed downstream.

EVENT 3

Beneath a large willow tree there was more trash. We walked over and picked that up, too. Then I spotted a plastic ice chest across the creek. Someone had thrown it away. We waded over to it. "It'll make a good garbage can," Kaz said. "I can strap it on the back of my bike."

EVENT 4

EVENT 5

And so it went. We spent more than six hours picking up trash along the creek, all the way to Montour Falls. By afternoon the sun was shining. As we left, loaded down with trash, we saw a tall man with gray hair standing near a car with out-of-state license plates. We waved to him. He shouted, "Beautiful creek you've got here!" That remark alone made us feel that our day's work was worthwhile.

Sensory details
EVENT 6

CONCLUSION
Meaning of experience

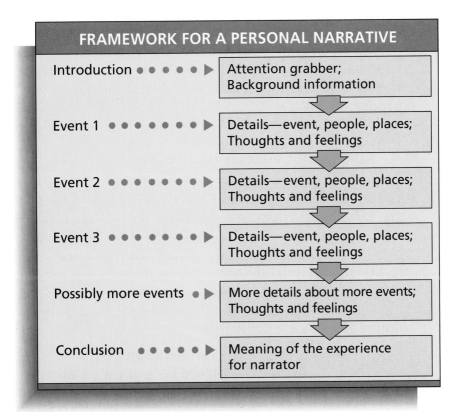

FRAMEWORK FOR A PERSONAL NARRATIVE

Introduction ● ● ● ● ● ▶ | Attention grabber; Background information

Event 1 ● ● ● ● ● ● ● ▶ | Details—event, people, places; Thoughts and feelings

Event 2 ● ● ● ● ● ● ● ▶ | Details—event, people, places; Thoughts and feelings

Event 3 ● ● ● ● ● ● ● ▶ | Details—event, people, places; Thoughts and feelings

Possibly more events ● ▶ | More details about more events; Thoughts and feelings

Conclusion ● ● ● ● ● ▶ | Meaning of the experience for narrator

CRITICAL THINKING

Analyzing Causes and Effects

When you analyze causes, you ask yourself *Why did that happen?* When you analyze effects, you ask yourself *What happened as a result?*

When you write a narrative, recognizing causes and effects plays an important part. You need to think about how one thing is related to something else.

In the Writer's Model on pages 134–135, two friends set out for a fishing trip, but they end up cleaning up the creekside. The friends themselves may have caused this to happen. If one of them had said, "Oh, leave the mess! We came here to fish!" the trash wouldn't have been picked up. The place itself also affected the boys' behavior. The mess at the creek caused them to change their plans from fishing to cleaning up the environment.

As you write your narrative, think about the causes and effects of people, places, and actions. These are the important details that you should include in your narrative.

 CRITICAL THINKING EXERCISE:
Analyzing Causes and Effects

What details are important enough to include in a personal narrative? Which have a cause-and-effect relationship? Get together with several classmates and decide which of the following sets of details have a cause-and-effect relationship by determining whether or not detail *a* caused detail *b*. Then, discuss which sets of details are important enough to include in a narrative about how an argument with a friend started.

1. **a.** My friend wanted to play a joke on me.
   b. She told me the hair on the back of my head looked green today.

2. **a.** We were standing outside by the water fountain.
   b. As usual, the fountain wasn't working.
3. **a.** The bell rang for class.
   b. We had plenty of time to get to class.
4. **a.** I asked another friend if it was true and he said no and laughed.
   b. I was angry with my friend and told her so.

Kudzu by Doug Marlette. By permission of Doug Marlette and Creators Syndicate.

| WRITING ASSIGNMENT | PART 4: **Writing a First Draft** |

Are you ready to write? If not, you may want to spend some time quietly jotting down notes or making a simple outline. Then, begin your first draft. Keep the framework on page 135 in mind as you write. Remember to use the chart you made in Writing Assignment, Part 3 (page 129).

COMPUTER NOTE: When writing your first draft, you can use boldface, italic, or underline styling to mark words, sentences, and sections that you might want to replace or revise later.

Evaluating and Revising

For many students, revising is a chore that won't go away. For professional writers, revising is a natural part of writing. If you dread revising, don't feel alone. Even great writers face tough revising problems, as cartoonist Gary Larson, creator of "The Far Side," shows in the following cartoon.

Edgar Allan Poe in a moment of writer's block.

If possible, let your writing "cool off" for a while before you begin to evaluate and revise. Then use the chart on the following page to improve your narrative. Ask yourself each question in the left-hand column. If you find a weakness, revise your paper, using the technique suggested in the right-hand column.

EVALUATING AND REVISING PERSONAL NARRATIVES

EVALUATION GUIDE	REVISION TECHNIQUE
1 Does the beginning of the narrative grab the reader's attention?	Rethink the beginning; **add** a startling statement or a quotation.
2 Does the narrative include enough background information?	**Add** information or facts that the reader needs to understand events.
3 Are the events arranged in chronological order?	**Reorder** events, putting them in the order in which they happened.
4 Does the narrative include details that make the people, places, and events seem real?	**Add** details based on the five senses: sight, hearing, smell, taste, and touch.
5 Are the writer's thoughts and feelings included in the narrative?	**Add** specific details about thoughts and feelings.

As you evaluate and revise your personal narrative

- use transitions like *first, next, then,* and *later* to make the order of events clear
- use vivid and specific words to help people, places, and events come alive for your readers

| EXERCISE 3 ▶ | **Analyzing a Writer's Revisions** |

Prepare for evaluating and revising your own paper. Analyze the writer's revisions of the first paragraph of the personal narrative on pages 134–135. Then answer the questions that follow.

One Saturday last spring, *(my friend)* Kazutaka   add

said, "Let's go fishing." ~~You'd never guess~~   cut

~~what we "caught"!~~ His plan called for a

trip to Catherine Creek, which is a ~~famous~~ *great*   replace

trout stream. *(are lucky/o We)* Kaz and I/live just a short   reorder/add

bicycle ride away. People come from far

away to catch /fish *(rainbow trout)* in the rippling waters   replace

of Catherine Creek. ∧

1. Why did the writer add *my friend* in the first sentence?
2. How did the second sentence—cut in the revised version—damage chronological order?
3. Why did the writer replace *fish* with *rainbow trout* in the last sentence?
4. Why did the writer move the next-to-last sentence to the end?

| **WRITING ASSIGNMENT** ✏ | PART 5: **Evaluating and Revising Your Personal Narrative** |

Now it's time to evaluate and improve your own personal narrative. Exchange personal narratives with another student. Then, evaluate each other's writing, using the chart on page 139. When you evaluate your partner's writing, give specific suggestions for improvement, and ask for these in return. When you get your paper back, read it carefully. Which suggestions seem good? Which seem off the mark? Finally, revise your paper to correct any weaknesses you and your partner have discovered.

Proofreading and Publishing

Proofreading. Perhaps more than any other form of writing, your personal narrative reflects you. So make it as error-free as you can. Proofread carefully by checking spelling, capitalization, punctuation, and usage.

GRAMMAR HINT

Varying the Position of Adjectives

In narratives you often use adjectives to describe people, places, and events. For interest, learn to vary their position in your sentences. Adjectives often appear before the words they describe.

EXAMPLE The *only* sound we heard besides the *running* water was the *distant* cawing of a crow.

Sometimes, however, adjectives can appear after the word they describe.

EXAMPLES The sneakers, old and smelly, were sitting on the doorstep.

As in the sentence above, when adjectives follow the noun they modify, they need to be set off with commas.

☞ REFERENCE NOTE: For more information on placing adjectives in sentences, see page 447.

Publishing. When you wrote your personal narrative, you had an audience in mind—your classmates, the school community, or a friend or family member. Now is the time to reach out to that audience and share your experience. Here are two ways to do it:

- Give a copy of your personal narrative to a friend or trusted adult who is aware of your experience.
- Present your personal narrative as a dramatic monologue to your class. Use appropriate tone and gestures to add zest to your monologue.

WRITING ASSIGNMENT

PART 6:
Proofreading and Publishing Your Personal Narrative

Proofread your personal narrative carefully, and correct any errors. Then, use one of the suggestions above or an idea of your own to share your narrative.

 Reflecting on Your Writing

If you want to put your personal narrative in your **portfolio,** date it and include a brief reflection by responding to the questions below.

- What factors made you choose this subject over others to write about in your personal narrative?
- Which techniques did you use to spur your memory about specific details? How helpful were they?
- Did you learn anything about yourself in the process of writing the narrative?

A STUDENT MODEL

Going through a tough experience can sometimes teach us something important. Lindi Martin, who attends Jenks East Middle School in Tulsa, Oklahoma, describes such an experience in the following passages from her personal narrative.

Conquering Your Fears
by Lindi Martin

I was only eight, but I remember it like yesterday. I was sitting in the doctor's office when they gave my parents and me the shocking news. "I'm sorry to tell you this, but your daughter's condition is getting worse. The only way to fix it is by surgery."

Those words ripped into me like a serrated knife into a crisp, cold apple. It was a horrible sinking feeling that seemed to possess my whole body—a feeling so terrifying, even the bravest person alive could not possibly endure it.

I knew I had been "sick" and I knew it had been serious, but never, even in my nightmares, did I think of surgery. You see, I was born with a condition that affects your kidneys; it is called Bilateral Reflux. The only way I would live was to have reconstructive surgery.

. . . It was now time for surgery. They sent a surgical nurse down to my room with a gurney. Being the scared little girl that I was, I thought the moment I got up on it, they would hurt me. So I decided that my teddy bear, Rainbow, and I would follow along behind it, very defiantly, with my parents. When the doctors saw me walk in, they started to laugh, and I realized that everyone else who had seen me probably had laughed too. What was comic relief to them was no comedy at all to me. So I simply put my nose into the air and kept walking.

The nurse prepped me and had me lie down on the operating table. The doctor asked me what "flavor" of anesthesia I wanted; I thought for a while and answered, "Strawberry." He then asked me to count backward from one hundred as he lifted the mask over my face. I woke up a few hours later, feeling woozy and very sore. I saw my parents and drifted back to sleep. . . .

My experience has taught me a lot. I discovered that in order to conquer your fears, you must face them first. In a way I am thankful for my surgery, because I conquered a lot of my fears.

WRITING WORKSHOP

A Personal Journal

A personal narrative is meant to be shared with others—perhaps your classmates or a trusted adult. But some kinds of expressive writing are more private. The personal journal, for example, is usually written for yourself alone. You can use it to discover and to explore important things about your thoughts and feelings.

One woman who kept a personal journal is Beatrix Potter, who wrote and illustrated *Peter Rabbit* and other famous stories for children. One unusual thing about Potter's journal was that she kept it in code, which made it absolutely private. She started keeping the journal in 1881, when she was fifteen years old, and the code wasn't even translated until 1958. Here's what the journal looked like before it was translated.

All her life, Beatrix Potter was interested in animals, especially rabbits. Her pet rabbit was named Mr. Benjamin Bunny. She writes about him in this translated entry from her journal.

> Rabbits are creatures of warm volatile temperament but shallow and absurdly transparent. It is this naturalness, one touch of nature, that I find so delightful in Mr. Benjamin Bunny, though I frankly admit his vulgarity. At one moment amiably sentimental to the verge of silliness, at the next, the upsetting of a jug or tea-cup which he immediately takes upon himself, will convert him into a demon, throwing himself on his back, scratching and spluttering. If I can lay hold of him without being bitten, within half a minute he is licking my hands as though nothing has happened.
>
> * * *
>
> Benjamin once fell into an Aquarium head first, and sat in the water which he could not get out of, pretending to eat a piece of string. Nothing like putting a face upon circumstances.
>
> from *The Journal of Beatrix Potter, 1881–1897*

Thinking It Over

1. What does Beatrix Potter like about Mr. Benjamin Bunny?
2. What details tell you that Benjamin isn't the easiest pet in the world to get along with?
3. What does Beatrix Potter mean by "Nothing like putting a face upon circumstances"? How would people today express the same idea?

Writing a Personal Journal

Prewriting. Animals and drawing were Beatrix Potter's greatest interests through her whole life. What are yours? Music? Computer games? Books? Write a journal entry where you, like Beatrix Potter, describe an experience about your greatest interest. You might want to write your journal in a code, like Beatrix Potter's. The following diagram shows a "translation" of that code. You can use her code or make up one of your own.

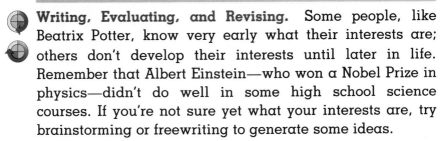

The Code Alphabet

ɑ	a	ɧ	k	ᴜ	u
ʟ	b	t	l	ɳ	v
ʒ	c	ɳ	m	ɱ	w
ơ	d	m	n	x	x
k	e	ℓ	o	ɳ	y
c	f	ℓ	p	ʒ	z
ơ	g	q	q	2	to, too, two
ℓ	h	ɯ	r	3	the, three
ʟ	i	୪	s	4	for, four
ʟ	j	1	t	✢	and

Writing, Evaluating, and Revising. Some people, like Beatrix Potter, know very early what their interests are; others don't develop their interests until later in life. Remember that Albert Einstein—who won a Nobel Prize in physics—didn't do well in some high school science courses. If you're not sure yet what your interests are, try brainstorming or freewriting to generate some ideas.

Proofreading and Publishing. If you don't intend to share your journal, especially if it's written in code, there's no need to proofread it, since it's written just for you. If you do want to share it, it might be interesting to see if a friend can break your code and understand what you've written.

You may also want to include your journal entry in your **portfolio.** If so, date the entry and attach a note of reflection on your writing. How does this piece differ from the other writings you have put in your portfolio so far? Did writing this journal entry make you want to keep a journal on a regular basis?

MAKING CONNECTIONS

SPEAKING AND LISTENING

Dramatizing a Personal Experience

Have you ever thought of a television comedy as a form of personal expression? Many sitcoms are just that. They're based on things that actually happened to the writer or to people the writer knew. Of course, the writer stretches the truth—and then stretches it some more.

With a partner, think of a personal experience that could be the basis for a comic scene. Perhaps one of you did something that had unexpected results. Or maybe you made a mistake that now seems amusing. Write the scene with your partner. Add humorous elements. Make the dialogue funny. Exaggerate! You'll probably find it helpful to act out the scene with your partner as you write. If you like, present your comic scene to the class. Here are some practical suggestions to get you started.

1. Your dog—who eats shoes, plants, and books—ate the science project that's due today from you and your partner. Explain the problem to your teacher.
2. You've just started helping out in your family's fast-food restaurant. You're slow because it's your first day, and a long line of customers stretches before you. Now you're faced with an angry customer who claims you gave him the wrong change.
3. Reluctantly, you agreed to play the role of Abraham Lincoln in the class play. Your first lines are, "Four score and seven years ago our fathers brought forth on this continent a new nation, conceived in liberty, and dedicated to the proposition that all men are created equal." On opening night, you can't remember a single word. A friend prompts you from the wings.

PERSONAL EXPRESSION ACROSS THE CURRICULUM

Social Studies

Different forms of personal expression—letters, journals, speeches, narratives—may become important historical documents. This happens when they leave a record of some important moment in history. For example, on July 2, 1881, President James Garfield was shot; he died eighty days later. His teenage daughter kept a journal describing what happened after his death. Now, more than one hundred years later, readers can relive this moment in history. Imagine that you were a witness to the scene that Mary Garfield describes. What might you have thought or felt?

It is beautiful to see how much the people got to love Papa through all his sickness. While we were carrying Papa's remains to Washington we came past Princeton. The whole college was down at the depot and had strewn flowers all along the tracks, and after the train had passed, the boys rushed on the tracks and gathered up the flowers to keep as mementos. At every town and crossing the people were standing, some bareheaded. In Baltimore people had come from miles around with their children, even their babies, hardly expecting to see anything but the train. . . . him to the main

Now, imagine that you have been taken forward or backward in time to one of the following historical moments. Or, if you like, you can choose your own historical moment. Then, write a brief speech, journal entry, or narrative about the experience. Before you write, you might want to do some research on the topic.

1. You're John Glenn, the first U.S. astronaut to orbit the earth. Alone in space, you look back and see the earth hanging in its beauty below you.

2. The year is 2005, and the first woman President of the United States is being sworn in to office. You're in the audience, witnessing the event.

3. The year is 1974. You're Hank Aaron, and you've just broken the home run record Babe Ruth set in 1935. (Babe Ruth hit his 714th home run that year.) The crowd goes wild.

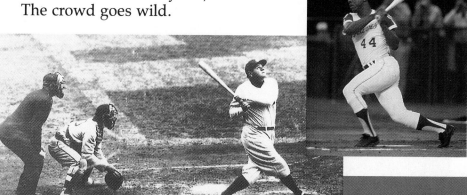

Creating Pictures and Images

Have you ever read or heard a story so scary that you couldn't sleep that night? You never actually saw them, but you have a very clear **image** of the horrors. The **pictures** you imagine were created with words—words that grabbed and played on your senses.

Writing and You. Writers often use words to paint a picture in your mind. Their words cause you to imagine sights, sounds, smells, textures, and tastes. Their vivid language helps you "see" what they want you to see—a woman's face, a crumbling building, a boat in a swirling, stormy sea. What kind of words might a writer use to describe you?

As You Read. As you read the following poem, look for the words that help you "see" the beginning of winter in the mountains.

Clifford Faust, *Jamaica* (1989).

October

by Gary Soto

A cold day, though only October,
And the grass has grayed
Like the frost that hardened it
This morning.

   And this morning
After the wind left
With its pile of clouds
The broken fence steamed, sunlight spread
Like seed from one field
To another, out of a bare sycamore
Sparrows lifted above the ridge.

In the ditch an owl shuffled into a nest
Of old leaves and cotton,
A black tassel of lizard flapping
From its beak. Mice
And ants gathered under the flat ground
And slipped downward like water,
A coyote squatted behind granite,
His ears tilting
Toward a rustle, eyes dark
With winter to come.

READER'S RESPONSE

1. After reading the poem, what feeling do you have about the coming of winter in the mountains?
2. Write a short journal entry about an especially hot or cold day where you live. Tell how the animals behave.

WRITER'S CRAFT

3. In this poem, Gary Soto uses many sight words to describe how the animals move as winter comes on. What are some of these words?
4. Writers of description sometimes compare a familiar object with an unfamiliar one. What does Soto compare the way sunlight spreads across the field with? What does he compare mice and ants going underground with?

Uses of Description

Writers of description want you mentally to see, hear, touch, taste, and smell what they describe. However, they may have different purposes for their descriptions. Here are some examples of possible uses of description.

- in a postcard, describing the mountain town you are visiting
- in a journal entry, describing your reaction to a friend's comment
- in an electronic bulletin board posting, describing some guinea pigs that you want to give away
- in a newspaper ad, describing a summer internship available to students
- in a police report, giving a detailed description of your stolen bicycle
- in a recipe, telling how to make enchiladas
- in an office memo, describing a photocopier that needs to be repaired
- in a poem, re-creating the sound of water splashing in a pool
- in a play, describing the setting of a scene

If you read a travel brochure about China or a history chapter about the ancient Maya, you'll find description. You'll also find it in ads on buses and in magazines and enjoy it in stories, poems, plays, and novels. No matter what the writer's purpose or where you find it, all good description forms pictures and images in the reader's mind.

LOOKING AHEAD

In this chapter, you'll use the writing process to write a description. Your basic purpose will be literary. Keep in mind that a good description

- has sensory details that help the reader form clear images of the subject
- uses precise words
- is clearly organized and easy to follow

Writing a Description

Finding a Focus

"Focus your attention on the hat," the magician says, and before your eyes a rabbit appears!

In writing a good description, you become a magician of sorts, too. Focusing your attention on a specific subject, a particular audience, and a clear purpose is the first step in making the subject you are writing about "appear like magic" in print before the very eyes of your readers.

Thinking About Subject, Purpose, and Audience

Description is part of almost every kind of writing you do. You usually don't have to think of a subject to write about. The subject is just a natural part of the writing you're doing. For example, you might describe last week's pep rally to a friend in a letter. And, if your collie wanders away, you'll describe it in notices that you put up around the neighborhood.

When the choice of a subject is yours, however, select something or someone familiar. For example, a teacher might ask you to write a description of a person. A good choice might be your favorite neighbor or your best friend. It's also a good idea to limit your subject. You can describe the Statue of Liberty more thoroughly than you could describe all of New York City.

Your purpose for writing helps you to decide whether to write an objective or subjective description. When your purpose is to inform, you usually write an *objective description.* An objective description gives a factual, realistic picture of a subject without revealing your feelings about it. Notice the factual, realistic details in this objective description of a dragon.

> A dragon is a large, imaginary, cold-blooded creature that has a bony skeleton and a body covered with scales or horny plates. It usually has a large tail, claws, and wings that enable it to fly. It also has the ability to breathe fire and smoke.

When your purpose is to be creative, you'll usually write a *subjective description.* This type of description creates a clear picture of the subject with details that also reveal your thoughts and feelings about it. Its details may also create a mood, or main feeling. In this subjective description of a dragon, a boy named Keevan learns that a newly hatched dragon will be his. As you read, compare this description with the objective description of the dragon above. How do you think Keevan feels about his dragon?

Why? asked the dragon again. *Don't you like me?* His eyes whirled with anxiety, and his tone was so piteous that Keevan staggered forward and threw his arms around the dragon's neck, stroking his eye ridges, patting the damp, soft hide, opening the fragile-looking wings to dry them, and assuring the hatchling wordlessly over and over again that he was the most perfect, most beautiful, most beloved dragon in the entire weyr, in all the weyrs of Pern.

Anne McCaffrey, "The Smallest Dragonboy"

WRITING NOTE   In subjective description, you may want to speak directly to your reader, using the words *I* and *me.* And you usually write in a relaxed way, as though you were speaking with good friends.

No matter what kind of description you're writing, think about your audience. Ask yourself these questions:

1. What details do my readers already know about my subject?
2. What details do my readers need to know about my subject?
3. How do I want my readers to feel about my subject?

PART 1

Starting Your Description

Who or what stands out in your mind? a grandparent? a pop star? a stuffed animal from long ago? a favorite pair of tennis shoes? In this chapter, you'll write a subjective description. To begin, choose a subject (a specific person, place, or object). Then, focus your writing by filling out a chart like the one below.

A pop star?

A stuffed animal?

SUBJECT: my tennis shoes
PURPOSE: to express my feelings
TYPE: subjective
AUDIENCE: my classmates and teacher

A grandparent?

Prewriting

Planning Your Description

To explore your subject further, you'll need to gather specific details. This means you'll need to know what to look for, where to look, and how to use what you find.

Identifying Descriptive Details

As you describe your subject, look for different kinds of specific details. These include both sensory details and factual, realistic details.

Sensory Details.   You gather information through all five of your senses—sight, hearing, touch, smell, and taste. Include details that appeal to all your senses. The fastest way to create a clearer description is to add more sensory details. For example, you can write that the dog *whimpered pleadingly* (sound) and that it had a *soft, silky coat* (touch) and a *faint, perfumy scent* (smell) after its bath.

Factual, Realistic Details.  Sometimes your sensory details will need to be very precise. These factual, realistic details create an exact image that can't be misunderstood. They can be tested or checked for accuracy by your readers. For example, you can write about a missing dog that it's a *cream-colored collie, thirty inches high.*

E X E R C I S E 1 ▶ **Gathering Sensory and Factual Details**

How many sensory and factual details can you imagine about a subject? With two or three classmates, choose one of the subjects below. Then make two lists. Label them *Sensory Details* and *Factual Details.* Now brainstorm with your classmates, and write down as many sensory and factual details as you can think of about your subject.

1. a school assembly
2. the beach or the woods
3. a thunderstorm
4. a frog or snake
5. a new car
6. a baseball or soccer game

Collecting Details

Depending upon your subject, you can collect specific details for your description in one or more ways. You can *observe, recall, research,* or *imagine* details.

Observing.   Real observation requires planting yourself in front of your subject and tuning up all your senses. As you observe, ask yourself, "What sensory details do I notice?" "What factual, realistic details can I include?"

Recalling.   You can collect details by tapping into your memories. Close your eyes and try to recall how your subject looked, smelled, felt, sounded, or tasted. Check your details with others who shared the experience with you. Try to remember if your subject reminded you of something else. What was it? Why did you make the connection?

Researching.   Books, magazines, pictures, audiovisual materials, online sources, and knowledgeable people ex-

pand your horizons. They give you a way to go beyond the limits of your specific time and place. You may live in a warm climate, but by searching the Internet for images of and information on Alaska, you can gather details about a blizzard.

Imagining.   To imagine your subject, close your eyes and focus on it. Ask the same kinds of questions you ask when you observe directly. Whether your subject is real or imaginary, your readers will need specific details to re-create it in their "mind's eye." (For more on imagining, see page 31.) For real subjects, you might imagine how you'd *like* the subject to be.

As you collect details, a chart can help you keep track of them. For example, if you're collecting details about your school bus, you might make a chart like the following one. This writer focused on recalling, observing, and imagining details. For other subjects, you might find it helpful to use different methods of collecting details.

> <u>What I recall:</u> Face of Mr. Deal—the driver—scowls and smiles; 25 rows of torn brown vinyl seats; litter on floor; number 672 on bus; laughter; squealing brakes; bounces on bumpy roads; hot seats in summer; wet wool coats
>
> <u>What I observe:</u> Mr. Deal's county bus license; safety rules and fire extinguisher; squishy feel of foam under ripped vinyl; sticky seats; strong smell of cleaner used on floors every Monday
>
> <u>What I imagine:</u> Small TVs and CD players installed on seat backs; soft, padded seats that recline; air conditioning; bus attendants serving snacks

EXERCISE 2 ▶ **Speaking and Listening: Collecting Details**

In groups of four, practice using different methods of collecting details. Have one person, the speaker, choose one of the following situations and describe which method (or methods) of collecting details is best. Then use that method to gather details for your group. The rest of the group—the listeners—should try to think of details to add to the speaker's description. Take turns until each group member has had a chance to be speaker. Have a volunteer list the details.

1. Look out the window, wherever you are. Describe the view to a movie director who's looking for a place to film a new movie.
2. You're talking on an intergalactic phone hookup to an alien teenager. Describe the nearest shopping mall on a Saturday afternoon.
3. You've been asked to design a float that would represent your school in a national parade. Describe how it would look.
4. Describe Mount Rushmore to an exchange student from India.

PART 2:
Collecting Details

Have a contest with yourself. See how many details you can collect for the subject you chose in Writing Assignment, Part 1. Make a chart such as the one on page 161. Collect as many details as you can, although you probably won't use all of them in your description.

Selecting and Organizing Details

Movie directors control what their audience "sees." To create a main feeling for readers, you'll include certain details and leave out others. For example, if you're describing the "chaos" of your afternoon bus ride, you'd include "litter on floor," "laughter," and "squealing brakes." But you might omit "safety rules" and "fire extinguisher."

After you've selected your details, think about arranging them in a way that makes sense to readers. You usually arrange details in a description in one of two ways:

- *spatial order*—arranges details in the way you see them
- *order of importance*—puts the most important details either first or last

 REFERENCE NOTE: For more on arranging details, see pages 36–39.

To develop your subject for description

- think about your purpose and your audience
- collect both sensory and realistic details by observing, recalling, researching, or imagining
- choose details that create a main feeling
- arrange details in a way that makes sense

| WRITING ASSIGNMENT | PART 3: **Selecting and Arranging Details** |

What do you want your readers to feel about your subject? Suspense—like on a stormy night when the lights go out? Excitement—like during a Chinese New Year's celebration? Review your lists of details for your subject. Select details that create one main feeling. Then, arrange your details in a reasonable order, and number them.

Writing Your First Draft

Exact Words and Figures of Speech

The basic elements of good description that you've studied so far are

- sensory and factual details
- a main feeling, or main impression
- an arrangement of details that makes sense

When you add *exact words* and *figures of speech* as you write your first draft, your description will leap off the pages into your reader's mind.

Exact Words.   What's the difference between *walking* or *slithering* across the room? *Walking* is such a general word that it gives a weak, fuzzy picture. *Slithering,* on the other hand, is precise—slinky, sneaky, snaky.

In your descriptions, avoid vague, general words. Choose precise nouns, verbs, adjectives, and adverbs. Add to your supply of precise words by developing your own **word bank.** As you read or hear vivid, specific words, collect them. Write them down in a special section of your notebook or journal. Organize them into useful groups, as in the following word bank.

A SENSORY WORD BANK			
SIGHT WORDS			
oblong	twisted	aqua	vivid
four-sided	flat	mulberry	canary
SOUND WORDS			
roar	hum	rasp	thunder
twitter	blast	scrape	rumble
TASTE WORDS			
sour	bitter	nutty	bland
spicy	sweet	salty	hot

(continued)

A SENSORY WORD BANK *(continued)*			
SMELL WORDS			
sweet	rotten	mildewed	moldy
spicy	stale	musty	fresh
TOUCH WORDS			
smooth	icy	slippery	cool
slimy	wet	dry	rough

Figures of Speech. Figures of speech are "special-effects" language that is not meant to be taken literally. When you say, for example, that it's raining cats and dogs, you don't *really* mean that animals are falling from the sky. *Figures of speech* (*similes, metaphors,* and *personification*) are imaginative comparisons that create striking images. (See pages 178–181 for more about using figurative language in writing poems.)

- A *simile* compares two basically unlike things, using the word *like* or *as.*
  The pep band's *sound* hit us *like a tidal wave.*

- A *metaphor* makes a direct comparison without using the word *like* or *as.* A metaphor says that something *is* something else.
  The missing dog's *wagging tail was a white flag of surrender.*

■ *Personification* gives human characteristics to nonhuman things.

> The *heat swallowed* my energy.

When used well, figures of speech can make your subject come alive for readers.

WRITING NOTE

Clichés are overused and worn-out figures of speech. You probably know hundreds: "fresh as a daisy," "cold as ice," "eager beaver." Try to avoid clichés when you write. Instead, use your imagination to think of a new comparison.

In the following passage, a character named Ichiro Terada describes a Japanese Brazilian farming community, Esperança, established by pioneers in the 1920s. Look for the precise details that bring an imaginary scene to life.

A PASSAGE FROM A NOVEL

from **Brazil-Maru**
by Karen Tei Yamashita

Realistic details

When Okumura first went out to show my father the boundaries of our new land, I went along. He pointed out the measurements across the front of the land along the road. The lots were all measured out in long strips of sixty acres, each lot having access to one of several roads which crisscrossed Esperança. Now we were only a handful of families, but soon there would be over two hundred of us. Our lot was several miles from the long house which marked what became the center of Esperança with its co-op offices, store, warehouses, and eventually a school and church. Okumura's house was located in this center, and soon, so were the houses of others who worked at the co-op.

My father and I looked at the acreage. It was a green wall of dense forest, trees and vines and brush rising high into the sky. We could not see farther than several meters in from the road. What might be behind that wall of green life, we could not say. When we set fire to the forest, droves of yellow and green parakeets and clattering orange-beaked toucans swept up in great clouds above the flames, while small animals, armadillos, snakes, and lizards stumbled and scurried from the smoke. From time to time, wild boars and even a panther might be seen. When the fires died down and the earth was only warm to the touch, the men took long saws and hatchets and cut down the large trees that had not succumbed to the fire. Across the road could be seen the results of the labor of other settlers further along in this enterprise — the charred stumps of enormous trees now hidden in a field of green rice. Soon everything would be very different.

When I think about the old forest, I invariably think about the incredible variety of insects in those days. Along with the occasional appearance of some unusual bird, the great variety of insects that yet remain are a reminder of the wonderfully complex living space the forest once was. When the forest was still intact, you could not light a candle or a lamp at night without being visited by a small dense cloud of moths, butterflies, beetles, mosquitoes, flies, crickets, and spiders of every color and description. They flew and crept through our open windows and doors in

Sensory details— sight

Sensory detail— sound

Sensory detail— touch

Realistic details

Sensory
details—
touch and
sound

the hot evenings or congregated near the seeping lights on the walls of our houses. They seemed to us a terrible nuisance, lighting on our bodies to suck our blood or buzzing frantically around, falling into our food and clothing. In the mornings, my mother was forever sweeping out their brittle carcasses. As more and more of the forest was cleared, the number and variety of insects slowly diminished....

Realistic
details

Sensory
details—
sight and
touch

It's not possible here to name all the strange bugs we had never before seen. There were the giant *sauva* ants, who came in small armies and could destroy in one evening an entire crop of anything we might have planted. There were poisonous caterpillars whose furry bodies burned our skin. There were giant hairy spiders, sometimes as large as fifteen or twenty centimeters across. There were large ticks whose hard bodies were the size of large watermelon seeds. Those insects that could find food despite the clearing of the forest can still be encountered today, but the strangest and most interesting of them have disappeared with the trees.

EXERCISE 3 ▶ **Analyzing a Description**

After reading the passage from *Brazil-Maru,* discuss the following questions with your class or in a small group.

1. What type of order does the writer use in the description of the settlement in the first paragraph?
2. Identify three words in this passage that appeal to the sense of touch. What do these images have in common?
3. How do the factual and sensory details in the third and fourth paragraphs contribute to the portrait of the forest? How do the sensory details make you feel?
4. What is the narrator's main feeling about the place he describes? Which words convey this feeling?

A Writer's Model for You

In the passage from *Brazil-Maru*, Karen Tei Yamashita imagines the sensory details—of sight, touch, and sound —in an unusual community. When you write, your subject may be closer to home than hers. Whatever your subject, it can become "real" for your readers if it has the elements of good description.

Notice how the writer in the following model states her subject and main feeling near the beginning. Then she develops these with specific details presented in a clear order. By the end, readers would recognize these shoes anywhere. You may want to follow this writer's model as you write your own description.

A WRITER'S MODEL

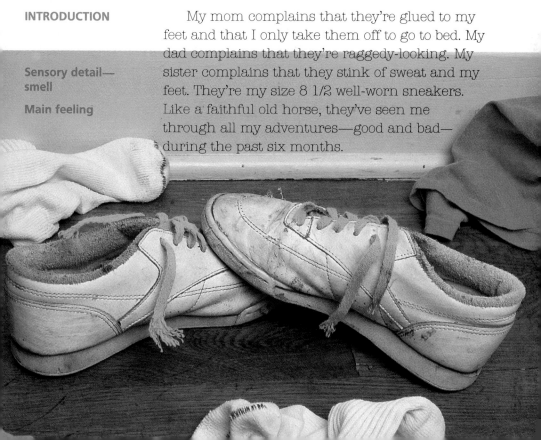

INTRODUCTION

My mom complains that they're glued to my feet and that I only take them off to go to bed. My dad complains that they're raggedy-looking. My

Sensory detail— smell

sister complains that they stink of sweat and my feet. They're my size 8 1/2 well-worn sneakers.

Main feeling

Like a faithful old horse, they've seen me through all my adventures—good and bad— during the past six months.

BODY
Spatial order—
top to bottom

Once when they were new, the tops of my sneakers used to be sparkling white leather with crisply rolled, neatly stitched trim. Now they're dim and gray with dirt in all the crinkles. The top

Sensory detail—
touch

stitching's coming unstitched in parts, and there are rough places where the shiny, soft leather's been totally scuffed off. My glow-in-the-dark orange shoelaces were once bright and cheerful, but now they're all dirty with frayed edges. Their shiny plastic tips are long gone, which makes it hard for me to lace the shoes if they ever get unlaced.

Realistic
details

Simile

If you turn them over, you'll see that the sneakers' thick gray soles are made up of hundreds of raised dots. They're huddled together like a crowd squeezed into a subway car at rush

Sensory detail—
touch

hour. The dots on the heel and front of the sole are worn totally smooth. And where I drag my right foot when I serve in tennis, the sole is

Sensory detail—
sight

completely worn through. This one-inch hole goes from the bottom of the shoe under my right big toe all the way through to the inside of my

CONCLUSION

shoe. I'd be able to recognize my sneakers anywhere because of this hole.

PART 4:
Writing a First Draft

You have a list of details about your subject, and you've put them in the order you want to use them. Now write a first draft of your description. As you turn your notes into sentences and paragraphs, concentrate on using sensory and factual details, precise words, and figures of speech. To create a main feeling for readers, carefully choose suitable details.

Evaluating and Revising

Revising is cleaning up after yourself, but it means more than just correcting mechanical errors in your writing. It means finding weaknesses in content and organization and then correcting them.

To help you evaluate and revise your own description, use the chart on the following page. Begin by asking yourself each question in the left-hand column. If you find a weakness, use the revision technique suggested in the right-hand column. You can use these guidelines for your own or for a classmate's writing.

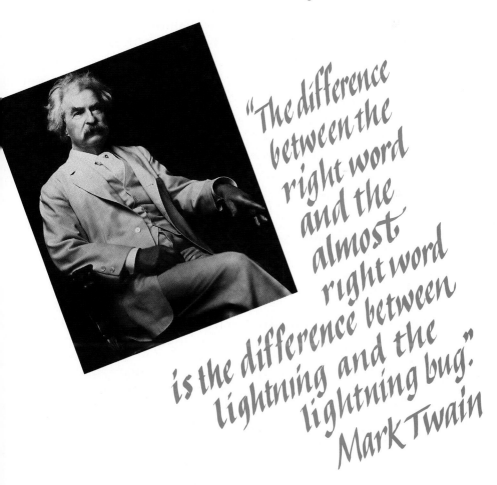

"The difference between the right word and the almost right word is the difference between lightning and the lightning bug."
Mark Twain

EVALUATING AND REVISING DESCRIPTION

EVALUATION GUIDE	REVISION TECHNIQUE
1 Is the subject clearly identified?	**Add** an opening sentence that clearly identifies the subject.
2 Do sensory and factual details create a clear picture of the subject? Are figures of speech and precise words included?	**Add** figures of speech and details, especially those appealing to senses other than sight. **Replace** general words with precise ones.
3 Are the writer's thoughts and feelings a part of the description?	**Add** sentences that express the writer's thoughts and feelings.
4 Do all specific details help create the main feeling?	**Cut** details that don't support the main feeling. **Add** some that do.
5 Are the details organized in a way that makes sense?	**Reorder** details in a way that makes sense to the reader.

E X E R C I S E **4** ▶ **Analyzing a Writer's Revisions**

Here's part of an early draft of the description on page 170. Study the writer's revisions, then answer the questions.

If you turn them over, you'll see that the

sneakers' thick soles are made up of ~~lots~~ of

       gray   *hundreds*   **add/replace**

raised dots. They're huddled together like a

crowd squeezed into a subway car at rush

hour. The dots on the heel and front of the

(totally smooth)

sole are worn. And where I drag my right   **add**

foot when I serve in tennis, the ~~sturdy,~~   **cut**

~~cushioned~~ sole is completely worn through.

I'd be able to recognize my sneakers   **reorder**

anywhere because of this hole. This

one-inch hole goes from the bottom of the

shoe under my right big toe all the way

through to the inside of my shoe.

1. Why did the writer add *gray* to the first sentence and *totally smooth* to the third sentence? How do these changes improve the paragraph?
2. Why did the writer replace *lots* with *hundreds* in the first sentence?
3. Why did the writer cut *sturdy, cushioned* from the fourth sentence? [Hint: What main feeling does the writer want to give about the sneakers?]
4. Why did the writer rearrange the order of the last two sentences?

CRITICAL THINKING

Evaluating Word Choice

Is your precise word the right word? No two words have exactly the same meaning.

Some words are used with specific situations. For example, *shift* and *transfer* both mean "move." *Shift* usually suggests changing position. But *transfer* more often describes changing from something like one vehicle to another. You might *shift* nervously from one foot to the other, but you would *transfer* from one bus to another.

Specific words may also call up specific feelings. *Murmur* and *mutter* both mean "a low flow of words or sounds," but *mutter* usually suggests anger. An unhappy customer would probably *mutter* about a bill, but a happy mother would *murmur* (not *mutter*) to her baby.

To help you decide if you've got the right word, check a dictionary. After a word's definitions, look for a list of synonyms. There you'll find the differences between the closely related words.

 CRITICAL THINKING EXERCISE:
Evaluating Word Choice

What's your choice for the most precise word? For each of the following sentences, select the word in parentheses that best fits the situation and the feeling. Explain your choice. Use a dictionary to help you if you wish.

1. In the middle of watching her favorite television program, my sister (*roosted, perched*) on the sofa.
2. Unable to contain her ideas any longer, she (*sputtered, blurted*) out her plan.
3. Totally exhausted, he (*slumped, slouched*) into the chair.
4. Fashioned from discarded car parts, his invention was a(n) (*ingenious, cunning*) solution to our problem.
5. Without salt, the stew left a (*bland, dull*) taste in my mouth.

PART 5:
Evaluating and Revising Your Description

You've learned that revision is a natural part of writing. Now apply the guidelines on page 172 to your first draft. Exchange papers with a partner and comment on each other's descriptions. Based on your evaluation and your partner's, make any changes you feel are needed. Evaluate and revise your word choice where necessary.

Proofreading and Publishing

Proofreading. Before you consider your paper finished, read it again for mistakes in spelling, capitalization, grammar, and usage. When others read your description, you want them to *see* your subject, not your careless errors!

GRAMMAR HINT

Misplaced Modifiers

As you write description, you'll often include phrases that describe words in your paper. When a sentence has a modifying phrase, you should usually place the phrase right next to the word it modifies. A misplaced modifier may have comic results.

MISPLACED   Buried beneath a huge pile of oak leaves, Elena found a five dollar bill.

CORRECTED   Elena found a five dollar bill buried beneath a huge pile of oak leaves.

☞ REFERENCE NOTE: For more information on placement of modifiers, see pages 668–673.

Publishing. Here are two suggestions for sharing descriptions with an audience:

- Take turns reading your descriptions aloud in class. Keep a list of vivid, precise words that you hear. Use your lists to create a class word bank.
- Make a class anthology. Illustrate your description with a photo, cartoon, or drawing. Collect the illustrated descriptions in a special notebook. Save your class anthology to be used as a model for a similar project that can be compiled by later classes.

 COMPUTER NOTE: You can use your word-processing program's Border and Box tools to create eye-catching pages when preparing to publish your description.

 PART 6:
Proofreading and Publishing Your Description

Proofread your description carefully, correcting any errors you discover. Publish or share your final version with your classmates.

 Reflecting on Your Writing

If you plan to include your description in your **portfolio,** date it and use the following questions to write a brief reflection to accompany your description.

- Which method of collecting details—observing, recalling, researching, or imagining—did you find most helpful?
- Were you able to convey the feeling you wanted about your subject? What might you do differently the next time you write a description?
- In writing this description, did you learn anything new about your feelings or attitude toward your subject?

A STUDENT MODEL

Sometimes, descriptions of the people or places closest to you turn out to be especially memorable. Alyssa Reynolds, who attends Paris Gibson Middle School in Great Falls, Montana, paints a vivid picture of her brother David.

The Thing That Lives in My House
by Alyssa Reynolds

"Oh, how sweet he looks. You are so lucky to have a brother like him," they tell me. I suppose he looks sort of sweet and innocent. Strawberry-blond hair and blue eyes with dirty shoes and holey jeans certainly don't hurt his impression on people. He might even come across . . . cute?

When I see the dirt, I know better. He has either dug up the flower garden or buried my TV. To me his smile looks sneaky and superficial, and his answers to questions sound guilty and evasive. I grab him and pull him from the room. His arm feels gritty and sweaty. "David, what did you do this time?" I ask.

"Nothing . . . except dig a few holes for Jack." He turns and goes back into the living room. (Jack is our neighbor boy.)

David whines a little more to my mother and then goes back outside, slamming the door loudly. I know him. He is a sneaky little liar who plays up to anyone who listens. If he doesn't get his way, he runs to his room, slams the door at least twice, and then cries like a baby. He is obstinate and does anything he wants, no matter what the consequences. Sometimes, it's true, he can be pretty decent and usually isn't as bad as I've just described. I still am going to look for my television set.

WRITING WORKSHOP

A Free Verse Poem

The writer of the model on pages 169–170 includes many specific details in her description. For example, she mentions details that tell you about her old tennis shoes' size, their smell, what material they're made of, and how they looked when they were new contrasted with how they look now.

But notice that these details are not what make the writer's tennis shoes distinctly individual. Although the writer's description of these general details help give us a clear picture of her well-worn sneakers, there is one special detail that she mentions that she believes makes her shoes unique—the hole in the sole underneath the big toe of the right shoe. This special detail about her shoes makes the writer feel that she could recognize them anywhere.

Sometimes when you are writing a shorter description, such as a short free verse poem, you may decide to focus only on those special details that make your subject "stand out from the crowd." While they may not give your readers a complete picture, these few details can still create a powerful image.

In "grandmother," Ray Young Bear uses only a few details to describe his subject. Still, these details are enough to give readers a unique feeling about her. Like other free verse poetry, this poem doesn't have a regular pattern of rhyme or rhythm. Instead, it creates a pattern with repeated phrases and uses the rhythms of everyday speech.

grandmother

by Ray Young Bear

if i were to see
her shape from a mile away
i'd know so quickly
that it would be her.
the purple scarf
and the plastic
shopping bag.
if i felt
hands on my head
i'd know that those
were her hands
warm and damp
with the smell
of roots.
if i heard
a voice
coming from
a rock
i'd know
and her words
would flow inside me
like the light
of someone
stirring ashes
from a sleeping fire
at night.

Thinking It Over

1. What two details of sight would make it possible for the person who speaks in the poem to recognize his grandmother from a great distance?
2. A *simile* uses the word *like* or *as* to compare two different things. What is the simile in this poem?
3. How do you think the speaker in this poem feels about his grandmother?
4. The poem begins "if i were to see." Where else in the poem does Ray Young Bear repeat this pattern of words? How does the pattern change each time?

Writing a Free Verse Poem

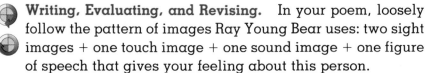 **Prewriting.** Now you try it. Write a free verse poem describing a person you know well, perhaps a relative, a neighbor, or a friend. After you've chosen a subject, jot down your answers to these questions.

1. How would you recognize this person from a great distance? List two or three details of sight that would cause you to recognize him or her.
2. How would you recognize this person's touch? List two or three details of touch.
3. How would you recognize the person by sound? List two or three sound details.
4. What main feeling does this person give you? What else gives you the same feeling?

Writing, Evaluating, and Revising. In your poem, loosely follow the pattern of images Ray Young Bear uses: two sight images + one touch image + one sound image + one figure of speech that gives your feeling about this person.

Use repeated phrases to introduce and develop each image. Begin your poem with "When I see (the person)/I recognize (two sight images)." Then, repeat "When I" and "I recognize" as you introduce the other images in your poem. Or, if you wish, use other repeated phrases.

To decide where lines should end, read your poem aloud. Listen for places where the thought seems to break naturally.

Proofreading and Publishing. Make sure that your poem looks as good as it sounds. Proofread carefully before making your final copy. With your classmates, create a bulletin board display showcasing your work. Include a photograph or drawing of your subject with your poem.

If you want to add your poem to your **portfolio,** first date it. Then, reflect on your writing process by answering the following questions, remembering to save your answers in your portfolio. Which type of sensory detail—sight, touch, or sound—was the hardest to come up with? Why? Did reading your poem aloud help you to decide where lines should end? Was writing a poem about this particular person the best way to describe her or him? Or would you prefer to write a story or essay about this person instead?

MAKING CONNECTIONS

MASS MEDIA

A Classified Ad

PUPS! Boston terriers, 6 mos., all shots. Need loving home. $10! 555-0098

Two-person tent, excel cond, blue, mesh window and door. $25. Mike—555-3379 eves.

Ordinary people trying to sell cars, houses, furniture, bicycles, and pets sometimes place a classified advertisement in a newspaper. Because newspapers charge by the line, sellers try to give information in just a few lines. A classified ad gives realistic details about the object (such as its price, size, and age) and tells how to reach the seller. Advertisers may also try to attract buyers by expressing their feelings about an object's appearance or condition.

How good a salesperson or advertiser are you? Work with two or three classmates and write a three-line (twenty-two letters per line) classified ad for three of the following objects. Make up any details you need and use abbreviations to save space. Remember that you want to sell the item. Make it appealing to readers!

1. a skateboard
2. a ten-speed bicycle
3. a CD player
4. a pet python
5. a collection of baseball cards
6. a Siamese kitten

WRITING ACROSS THE CURRICULUM

Biology Riddles

What living creature does this riddle describe?

> RIDDLE
>
> It lives in the water and breathes through gills. With no legs, it moves from place to place by moving its tail. It feeds on algae. In the spring, it hatches from an egg. By fall, it has disappeared into something else. What is it?

The riddle describes a tadpole, the early stage of a frog.

Riddles like these are a fun way to review or learn about plants and animals. With your classmates, create a set of riddles on index cards. Write a riddle like the tadpole example on one side of a card and your answer (the name of the plant or animal you're describing) on the back. You may need to do some research on your animal in an encyclopedia or field guide.

6 CREATIVE WRITING: NARRATION

Imagining Other Worlds

Living in this **world** is often fun and exciting. But when it isn't, all we have to do is open the escape hatch of our imagination. Our **imaginations** can take us to past worlds, future worlds, or worlds that can never be.

Writing and You.   Writers use their imaginations to come up with ideas for stories, novels, poems, plays, and movie and TV scripts. They create hairy monsters in horror movies, domed cities in science fiction stories. They write poems that look at parrots, or snow, or spiders in imaginary ways. They imagine people and places so real that you feel you know them. Imagine a world of your own. What would it be like?

As You Read.   As you read this story, notice how people can also use their imagination to explain the world around them.

John Ross, detail of *Homage to the City* (1984).

185

f r o m

The Sound of Flutes

told by Henry Crow Dog

Once, untold generations ago, the people did not know how to make flutes. Drums, rattles, bull-roarers, yes—but no flutes. In these long-past days, before the white man came with his horse and firestick, a young hunter went out after game. Meat was scarce, and the people in his village were hungry. He found the tracks of an elk and followed them for a long time. The elk is wise and swift. It is the animal that possesses the love-charm. If a man has elk medicine, he will win the one he loves for his wife. He will also be a lucky hunter.

Our poor young man had no elk medicine. After many hours, he finally sighted his game. The young hunter had a fine new bow and a quiver made of otterskin full of good, straight arrows tipped with points of obsidian—sharp, black, and shiny like glass. The young man knew how to use his weapon—he was the best shot in the village—but the elk always managed to stay just out of range, leading the hunter on and on. The young man was so intent on following his prey that he hardly took notice of where he went.

At dusk the hunter found himself deep inside a dense forest of tall trees. The tracks had disappeared, and so had the elk. The

"He dreamed that a bird
called *Wagnuka*, the
redheaded woodpecker,
appeared to him, singing
the strangely beautiful
new song, saying, 'Follow
me and I will teach you.' "

young man had to face the fact that he was lost and that it was now too dark to find his way out of the forest. There was not even a moon to show him the way. Luckily, he found a stream with clear, cold water to quench his thirst. Still more luckily, his sister had given him a rawhide bag to take along, filled with *wasna*—pemmican—dried meat pounded together with berries and kidney fat. Sweet, strong wasna—a handful of it will keep a man going for a day or more. After the young man had drunk and eaten, he rolled himself into his fur robe, propped his back against a tree, and tried to get some rest. But he could not sleep. The forest was full of strange noises—the eerie cries of night animals, the hooting of owls, the groaning of trees in the wind. He had heard all these sounds before, but now it seemed as if he were hearing them for the first time. Suddenly there was an entirely new sound, the kind neither he nor any other man had ever experienced before.

It was very mournful, sad, and ghostlike. In a way it made him afraid, so he drew his robe tightly about him and reached for his bow, to make sure that it was properly strung. On the other hand, this new sound was like a song, beautiful beyond imagination, full of love, hope, and yearning. And then, before he knew it, and with the night more than half gone, he was suddenly asleep. He dreamed that a bird called *Wagnuka,* the redheaded woodpecker, appeared to him, singing the strangely beautiful new song, saying, "Follow me and I will teach you."

When the young hunter awoke, the sun was already high, and on a branch of the tree against which he was leaning was a redheaded woodpecker. The bird flew away to another tree and then to another, but never very far, looking all the time over its shoulder at the young man as if to say "Come on!" Then, once more the hunter heard that wonderful song, and his heart yearned to find the singer. The bird flew toward the sound, leading the young man, its flaming red top flitting through the leaves, making it easy to follow. At last the bird alighted on a cedar tree and began tapping and hammering on a dead branch, making a noise like the fast beating of a small drum. Suddenly there was a gust of wind, and again the hunter heard that beautiful sound right close by and above him.

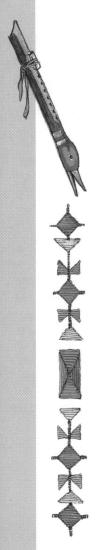

Then he discovered that the song came from the dead branch which the woodpecker was belaboring with its beak. He found, moreover, that it was the wind which made the sound as it whistled through the holes the bird had drilled into the branch. "*Kola,* friend," said the hunter, "let me take this branch home. You can make yourself another one." He took the branch, a hollow piece of wood about the length of his forearm, and full of holes. The young man walked back to his village. He had no meat to bring to his tribe, but he was happy all the same.

Back in his tipi, he tried to make the dead branch sing for him. He blew on it, he waved it around—but no sound came. It made the young man sad. He wanted so much to hear that wonderful sound. He purified himself in the sweatlodge and climbed to the top of a lonely hill. There, naked, resting with his back against a large rock, he fasted for four days and four nights, crying for a dream, a vision to teach him how to make the branch sing. In the middle of the fourth night, Wagnuka, the bird with the flaming red spot on his head, appeared to him, saying, "Watch me." The bird turned into a man, doing this and that, always saying, "Watch me!" And in his vision the young man watched—very carefully.

When he awoke he found a cedar tree. He broke off a branch, and working many hours hollowed it out delicately with a bowstring drill, just as he had seen Wagnuka do it in his vision. He whittled the branch into a shape of a bird with a long neck and an open beak. He painted the top of the bird's head red with *washasha,* the sacred vermilion color. He prayed. He smoked the branch with incense of burning sage and sweet grass. He fingered the holes as he had watched it done in his dream, all the while blowing softly into the end of his flute. Because this is what he had made—the first flute, the very first *Siyotanka.* And all at once there was the song, ghostlike and beautiful beyond words, and all the people were astounded and joyful.

In the village lived an *itancan,* a big and powerful chief. This itancan had a daughter who was beautiful, but also very haughty. Many young men had tried to win her love, but she had turned them all away. Thinking of her, the young man made up a special song, a song that would make this proud *winc-*

incala fall in love with him. Standing near a tall tree a little way from the village, he blew his flute.

All at once the wincincala heard it. She was sitting in her father's, the chief's, tipi, feasting on much good meat. She wanted to remain sitting there, but her feet wanted to go outside; and the feet won. Her head said, "Go slow, slow," but her feet said, "Faster, faster." In no time at all she stood next to the young man. Her mind ordered her lips to stay closed, but her heart commanded them to open. Her heart told her tongue to speak.

"*Koshkalaka, washtelake,*" she said. "Young man, I like you." Then she said, "Let your parents send a gift to my father. No matter how small, it will be accepted. Let your father speak for you to my father. Do it soon, right now!"

And so the old folks agreed according to the wishes of their children, and the chief's daughter became the young hunter's wife. All the other young men had heard and seen how it came about. Soon they, too, began to whittle cedar branches into the shapes of birds' heads with long necks and open beaks, and the beautiful haunting sound of flutes traveled from tribe to tribe until it filled the whole prairie. And that is how Siyotanka the flute came to be—thanks to the cedar, the woodpecker, the wind, and one young hunter who shot no elk but who knew how to listen.

transcribed and edited by Richard Erdoes

READER'S RESPONSE

1. What other stories have you heard or read that explain something in the world—questions about nature, the earth, early inventions? In a small group, share the stories you remember. What's the most unusual or the most interesting one?
2. The hunter and the chief's daughter are strongly affected by the music they hear. In your journal, write about a time music affected you.

WRITER'S CRAFT

3. Legends and myths tell stories to explain the world. What is explained in this legend?
4. In most stories, a problem or conflict sets the characters in motion. What is it in this story?
5. A good story has many specific details. What details can you find about the hunter's arrows? his food? the sound of the music?

Ways to Write Creatively

A story, the main kind of writing you're going to do in this chapter, is one kind of creative writing. A poem, which you may also write in this chapter, is another kind of creative writing. When people write creatively, they use their imagination and their skill with language to make something unique. They might write novels, plays, television scripts, or song lyrics. Here are some specific ways writers develop their creative writing.

- in a poem, telling about a girl who hits her first home run
- in a story, telling what happens to astronauts lost in space
- in a science fiction story, describing what a town would look like twenty years from now
- in a play, describing how a character acts during her first day at a new job
- in a poem, recalling the memory of a favorite meal
- in a children's story, telling about an otter that tries to figure out what a pomegranate is
- in a movie script, showing how two brothers are alike yet different
- in a story, telling how a fourteen-year-old helps his Danish cousin learn English
- in a novel, having a character decide whether an action would help others

LOOKING AHEAD

In the main assignment in this chapter, you'll use narration to create a story. Keep in mind that an effective short story

- entertains the reader
- develops a conflict, or problem
- holds the reader's interest through well-developed characters, setting, and plot

Writing a Short Story

Finding a Story Idea

Some scientists actually study creative people, and they've learned some things about how creativity works. Big ideas often come to artists and thinkers when they're relaxed and *not* searching for brilliant thoughts. So relax. Let your imagination react to the people, places, and events around you.

Shoe reprinted by permission: Tribune Media Services.

Thinking About Purpose and Audience

Your main *purpose* in writing a story is to give your imagination some exercise—to be creative. But your purpose is also to entertain your readers, whether with humor, suspense, exciting action, or a heartbreaking drama. Your story may even have a message, or theme. For instance, the story of an injured hockey star will really hold readers in suspense. Yet it may also show them that dealing with a physical disability takes courage and patience.

Who will be your *audience*? You may write a story for very young readers, your classmates, or adults. Keep your audience in mind as you plan your story. A story about cheating on final exams just won't work for preschoolers, and fairy tales probably won't interest your classmates.

Starting with Characters and Situations

What do all good stories have in common? Two things: a main character (an interesting one, of course!) and a *conflict,* or problem, to be solved. The character has to want something, or be confused, or face a threat—any *situation* that makes the reader wonder what's going to happen.

Characters.   Sometimes the character suggests the conflict. Maybe a girl gets on your bus—a girl who has the longest hair you've ever seen. Does someone else have to untangle it? Doesn't it get caught in things? You're on your way to a situation with conflict.

Situations.   Sometimes a situation, or conflict, suggests a character. Maybe you come across a newspaper article on spelunking (cave exploring). Don't people get afraid in caves—or lost? How could it happen? What kind of person would get into that fix? You're on your way to a main character with a definite problem.

Here are some examples of story ideas that include characters in situations with conflict.

STORY IDEAS

■ Alicia, who came to the United States from Mexico when she was nine, has to go to a school where no one speaks Spanish.

- A boy discovers that a visitor from outer space has eaten his bicycle.
- An eighth-grader's chess team, the Rooks, wins the city championship, but the school doesn't have enough money to send the team to the state finals.
- A girl must decide what to do when she sees a friend cheat on a test.

As you search for story ideas, try

- brainstorming story ideas in a small group
- using your own experience, newspapers, and TV
- asking yourself some "What if?" questions (See pages 24–31 for more help with these prewriting techniques.)

EXERCISE 1 ▶ **Exploring Story Ideas**

Who would be fun to write about? What real or imaginary situations might make good stories? With a small group, brainstorm ideas for characters and situations with a conflict. Have one person take notes, keeping two separate lists for characters and situations.

PART 1:
Finding a Story Idea

Loosen up and let your imagination soar. You can use ideas from Exercise 1 or think up an altogether different main character and situation. In two or three sentences, write your idea for a story. Identify the main character and the story situation. Be sure the situation involves a conflict.

Prewriting

Planning Your Story

As you gather material for your story, you'll need to develop your characters, setting, and plot.

Thinking About Characters, Setting, Plot

Characters. A story holds the reader's interest when the *characters* seem so real they could walk right off the page. To get them walking, you can use realistic details from the people around you as well as from your imagination. One character may have your brother's curly hair and your next-door neighbor's funny laugh. Another character may sneeze like your science teacher or walk like your Aunt May. To develop your characters, you might make a list, a cluster, or a chart of details. Start by asking yourself these questions:

- How old is the character? What does he or she look like?
- How does the character dress? move?
- What are the character's personality traits (patient, bossy, stubborn, kind, and so on)?

Setting. The time and place of your story is its **setting.** Setting can be just a backdrop for the action, or it can be very important. Henry, for example, may be descending in a hot-air balloon right into a Civil War battle.

Setting can also help create a mood, or atmosphere. As Jem walks alone through misty woods, the darkness and forest noises create a mood of mystery and suspense. To think about your story's setting, try listing, clustering, or using a chart to gather details. Use the following questions to get started.

- How important is the setting to the story's action? Is it just a backdrop that helps create a feeling? Or does the setting help put events in motion?
- Can I use the setting to create a mood?
- What places, weather, or times of day will I need to describe? What sensory details (smells, sights, and sounds) will I use?

 COMPUTER NOTE: Use your word-processing program's thesaurus to help you brainstorm ideas and generate words to describe your characters, setting, and plot.

 **WRITING ASSIGNMENT**

PART 2:
Gathering Details for Characters and Setting

Can you see your characters in your mind's eye? Can you hear them? Are they short, muscle-bound, fidgety, or loud? And *where* are they? Are they seeking shelter from a sandstorm or snorkeling underwater? Is it the year 4002 or a winter night in the present? Use the questions on pages 197 and 198 to spark your imagination, and jot down your ideas.

Plot. What happens in the story is its *plot.* Some stories are fast-moving and action-packed. Others focus on one or two important events. To develop an effective plot, think about the following main elements.

- **Conflict.** Your story situation must hold a conflict or problem. Does the main character want something badly or face a tough decision? Or must the character struggle against something—nature or another person?

- **A Series of Events.** One action should lead to another as the character struggles to solve the problem or conflict. Do you have a chain of events that keeps the action moving?
- **High Point.** You need a moment in the story, the high point, when the reader feels great interest and suspense about how the problem will be settled. Do you have a scene in your story when things will be decided, one way or another?
- **Outcome.** Following the high point, there are usually a few final details to work out. Do you tie up loose ends so that readers aren't left with questions?

Creating a Story Map. When you plan your story plot, you can put it into a story map. A *story map* outlines your characters, setting, and plot all at once.

HERE'S HOW

CHARACTERS:	Letasha, 14, who's afraid of heights, curious, determined, quick thinking Letasha's mother, who nags Letasha about homework two scary creatures
SETTING:	A very high mountaintop, a blizzard, a dark cave, home; time—modern
PLOT:	Conflict: Letasha finds herself alone on a dangerous mountaintop and wants to get down. Events: (1) She starts down the mountain. (2) She seeks shelter from a blizzard. (3) She shares a cave with a mountain lion. High point: (4) She faces a red-eyed monster. Outcome (surprise ending): It's all a video game.

PART 3:
Creating a Story Map

Pull your ideas together and create a story map like the one on page 199. Take time to flesh out your plot. What will be your story's events, conflict, and outcome? Be sure to include characters and the setting, too.

Choosing a Point of View

Who will tell your story? If you use the *first-person point of view,* the narrator (or storyteller) is a character in the story. The narrator uses the first-person pronoun *I* and speaks directly to the reader. First-person can make a story more believable.

If you use the *third-person point of view,* the narrator is *not* a character in the story. Characters are referred to with third-person pronouns, such as *he, she,* and *they.*

Be sure to use the same point of view throughout the story. The two points of view make a difference in how you tell the story, and you don't want to mix them up.

FIRST PERSON   **I** really needed to keep that job in the cafe, but **I** made mistakes all the time because the owner, grouchy Mrs. Yu, kept staring at **me**. **I** was sure she didn't like **me**.

THIRD PERSON   Wing dropped another cup, as Mrs. Yu watched from the corner. **She** sighed. **He** looked so much like Arlan, **her** only son—**her** lost son. How could **she** fire **him**?

PART 4:
Speaking and Listening: Choosing a Point of View

Which point of view is better for your story? Write your story's first paragraph using third-person. Then rewrite the same paragraph using first-person with the main character as narrator. After reading both paragraphs aloud to a small group, ask them which version they like better.

Writing Your First Draft

Keep your story map in front of you as you write your first draft. But let your imagination take charge. As your story takes shape, feel free to make changes.

Combining the Basic Elements of a Story

Professional writers know the essential ingredients of a good short story: a strong beginning and ending, interesting characters, dialogue, and suspense.

Making the Plot Interesting.   Use a zesty or teasing beginning to hook your reader's attention. Here's Edgar Allan Poe's first sentence in "The Tell-Tale Heart": "True!—nervous—very, very dreadfully nervous I had been and am; but why *will* you say that I am mad?"

A suspenseful story keeps the readers guessing about what will happen next. Give your story a strong high point and resolve the conflict in a satisfying and believable way.

Making Your Characters Seem Real.   You can *tell* the reader directly what a character is like. (For example, "María is determined and hard-working.") But it's always better to *show*, not tell.

- **Show what the character says.** "No matter what you say," María repeated, "I won't give up. I'm sure I have a chance to win this meet."

- **Show what the character does.** María got to the gym at 6 A.M., just as she had every day for a year. She dove into the water and started swimming laps— 10, 25, 40, 75, 100. After school she was back at the gym swimming another 50 laps.

- **Show what others say about the character.** "Poor María," Janice sighed. "She hasn't got a life. All she does is practice, practice, practice."

Good storytellers use vivid word pictures so their readers can "see" the story's characters and events in their mind's eye. Be sure to make the verbs and sensory details in your story as specific and lively as possible.

VAGUE (telling) For a long time Jim didn't write anything. He just listened to noises in the room and felt sick.

SPECIFIC (showing) Jim stared at his paper. Around him, he could hear the other students coughing, turning pages, scratchily writing. His stomach felt knotted, and his hands were sweaty. But his brain stayed horribly empty.

 REFERENCE NOTE: See pages 457–468 for more about verbs and page 66 for help with using sensory details.

Creating Dialogue. Which of these two sentences would you rather read in a story?

SUMMARY Angela hates her new haircut.

DIALOGUE "I look like I was just attacked by a crazy lawn mower!" Angela hollered.

Writers use *dialogue* (the words that characters say) to help reveal a character's personality. To make your dialogue sound natural, use short sentences, fragments, and contractions. Use informal language, the kind people actually use when they talk. And don't always write *he said* or *she said*. Try to use dialogue tags that give a better idea of *how* a character speaks (*she murmured, yelled, complained, laughed,* and so on).

Looking at a Short Story

No two stories emphasize exactly the same elements. The writer of a mystery may choose to emphasize plot. The writer of a love story may devote more time to character. Notice how the writer of the following story gets right into the action—bam!—and also creates a memorable character.

A SHORT STORY

Thank You, M'am
by Langston Hughes

BEGINNING
Character and setting details

Event 1/ Conflict

Appearance and action details

Event 2

Dialogue— character development

She was a large woman with a large purse that had everything in it but hammer and nails. It had a long strap and she carried it slung across her shoulder. It was about eleven o'clock at night, and she was walking alone, when a boy ran up behind her and tried to snatch her purse. The strap broke with the single tug the boy gave it from behind. But the boy's weight, and the weight of the purse combined, caused him to lose his balance so, instead of taking off full blast as he had hoped, the boy fell on his back on the sidewalk, and his legs flew up. The large woman simply turned around and kicked him right square in his blue-jeaned sitter. Then she reached down, picked the boy up by his shirt front, and shook him until his teeth rattled.

After that the woman said, "Pick up my pocketbook, boy, and give it here."

She still held him. But she bent down enough to permit him to stoop and pick up her purse. Then she said, "Now ain't you ashamed of yourself?"

Firmly gripped by his shirt front, the boy said, "Yes'm."

The woman said, "What did you want to do it for?"

The boy said, "I didn't aim to."

She said, "You a lie!"

By that time two or three people passed, stopped, turned to look, and some stood watching.

Appearance—
details

MIDDLE

Event 3

Appearance—
details

Dialogue—
character
development

"If I turn you loose, will you run?" asked the woman.

"Yes'm," said the boy.

"Then I won't turn you loose," said the woman. She did not release him.

"I'm very sorry, lady, I'm sorry," whispered the boy.

"Um-hum! And your face is dirty. I got a great mind to wash your face for you. Ain't you got nobody home to tell you to wash your face?"

"No'm," said the boy.

"Then it will get washed this evening," said the large woman starting up the street, dragging the frightened boy behind her.

He looked as if he were fourteen or fifteen, frail and willow-wild, in tennis shoes and blue jeans.

The woman said, "You ought to be my son. I would teach you right from wrong. Least I can do right now is to wash your face. Are you hungry?"

"No'm," said the being-dragged boy. "I just want you to turn me loose."

"Was I bothering *you* when I turned that corner?" asked the woman.

"No'm."

"But you put yourself in contact with *me,*" said the woman. "If you think that that contact is not going to last awhile, you got another thought coming. When I get through with you, sir, you are going to remember Mrs. Luella Bates Washington Jones."

Action details/
Suspense

Sweat popped out on the boy's face and he began to struggle. Mrs. Jones stopped, jerked him around in front of her, put a half-nelson about his neck, and continued to drag him up the street. When she got to her door,

Setting details

she dragged the boy inside, down a hall, and into a large kitchenette-furnished room at the rear of the house. She switched on the light and left the door open. The boy could hear other roomers laughing and talking in the large house. Some of their doors were opened, too, so he knew he and the woman were not alone. The woman still had him by the neck in the middle of her room.

She said, "What is your name?"

"Roger," answered the boy.

Action and
setting details/
Suspense

Event 4

"Then, Roger, you go to that sink and wash your face," said the woman, whereupon she turned him loose—at last. Roger looked at the door—looked at the woman—looked at the door—*and went to the sink.*

Dialogue—
character
development

"Let the water run until it gets warm," she said. "Here's a clean towel."

"You gonna take me to jail?" asked the boy, bending over the sink.

"Not with that face, I would not take you nowhere," said the woman. "Here I am trying to get home to cook me a bite to eat and you snatch my pocketbook! Maybe you ain't been to your supper either, late as it be. Have you?"

"There's nobody home at my house," said the boy.

"Then we'll eat," said the woman. "I believe you're hungry—or been hungry—to try to snatch my pocketbook."

"I wanted a pair of blue suede shoes," said the boy.

"Well, you didn't have to snatch *my* pocketbook to get some suede shoes," said Mrs. Luella Bates Washington Jones. "You could of asked me."

"M'am?"

Action and setting details

The water dripping from his face, the boy looked at her. There was a long pause. A very long pause. After he had dried his face and not knowing what else to do dried it again,

HIGH POINT

the boy turned around, wondering what next. The door was open. He could make a dash for it down the hall. He could run, run, run, run, *run!*

The woman was sitting on the daybed. After a while she said, "I were young once and I wanted things I could not get."

There was another long pause. The boy's mouth opened. Then he frowned, but not knowing he frowned.

Dialogue—character development

The woman said, "Um-hum! You thought I was going to say *but,* didn't you? You thought I was going to say, *but I didn't snatch people's pocketbooks.* Well, I wasn't going to say that." Pause. Silence. "I have done things, too, which I would not tell you, son—neither tell God, if He didn't already know. So you set down while I fix us something to eat. You might run that comb through your hair so you will look presentable."

Setting details

In another corner of the room behind a screen was a gas plate and an icebox. Mrs.

Event 5

Jones got up and went behind the screen.

The woman did not watch the boy to see if he was going to run now, nor did she watch her purse which she left behind her on the daybed. But the boy took care to sit on the far side of the room where he thought she could easily see him out of the corner of her eye, if she wanted to. He did not trust the woman *not* to trust him. And he did not want to be mistrusted now.

OUTCOME
Dialogue—
character
development

"Do you need somebody to go to the store," asked the boy, "maybe to get some milk or something?"

"Don't believe I do," said the woman, "unless you just want sweet milk yourself. I was going to make cocoa out of this canned milk I got here."

"That will be fine," said the boy.

Action and
setting details

She heated some lima beans and ham she had in the icebox, made the cocoa, and set the table. The woman did not ask the boy anything about where he lived, or his folks, or anything else that would embarrass him. Instead, as they ate, she told him about her job in a hotel beauty shop that stayed open late, what the work was like, and how all kinds of women came in and out, blondes, redheads, and Spanish. Then she cut him a half of her ten-cent cake.

"Eat some more, son," she said.

**Event 6/
Final details**

When they were finished eating she got up and said, "Now, here, take this ten dollars and buy yourself some blue suede shoes. And next time, do not make the mistake of latching onto *my* pocketbook *nor nobody else's* — because shoes come by devilish like that will burn your feet. I got to get my rest now. But I wish you would behave yourself, son, from here on in."

She led him down the hall to the front door and opened it. "Goodnight! Behave yourself, boy!" she said, looking out into the street.

**Character
development**

Action details

The boy wanted to say something else other than, "Thank you, m'am," to Mrs. Luella Bates Washington Jones, but he couldn't do so as he turned at the barren stoop and looked back at the large woman in the door. He barely managed to say, "Thank you," before she shut the door. And he never saw her again.

| EXERCISE 2 ▶ | **Analyzing the Elements of a Short Story** |

Think about the basic elements of "Thank You, M'am," and answer the following questions with a partner.

1. Did this story hold your interest? make you laugh? keep you guessing? What was your reaction? Why?
2. In this story Roger and Mrs. Jones have a conflict with each other: He wants to steal her purse and escape. She doesn't want him to. How is the conflict settled?
3. Both Roger and Mrs. Jones are vivid characters. For each one, find an example of actions and dialogue that helps make the character seem real.
4. Setting details in Mrs. Jones's apartment are sometimes very important in this story. Explain with an example.
5. After Roger decides he wants to stay with Mrs. Jones, there's quite a bit of story left. What do you learn in the outcome?

Using a Story Framework

Your story won't be exactly like Langston Hughes's. It may have less dialogue. It may have a more suspenseful high point or more action. But even with these differences, your story can be just as entertaining.

As a beginning story writer, you may find it helpful to use a framework like the one the writer used in the following story. Notice how the story gets right to a conflict and has a clear chronological framework.

"It's the little details that do it, that bring a character or a scene alive in the reader's mind."

Jean Auel

A WRITER'S MODEL

The Final Problem

BEGINNING

Conflict and setting

Background/ Setting

For someone afraid of heights, I'm in a fine mess. Here I am alone on a mountaintop who-knows-how-many miles high. Last night I went to bed in the room I share with my sister. And now, suddenly, I'm thousands of miles from nowhere, and it's twenty below zero—at least.

Dialogue— character development

"Now calm down, Letasha." (I always talk to myself when I'm nervous.) "You have two choices. You can try to get down off this mountain. Or you can stay here and just wait for everything to get better." ("Are you crazy?" the other voice inside me shouts. "If you don't <u>act</u>, there's no hope.")

Event 1

What's this? Mountain-climbing stuff! And a backpack with a tent! OK. I'm going down.

MIDDLE

Setting

My heart's thumping and my knees feel squishy, but I inch myself downward. Suddenly an angry-looking black cloud surrounds me, and the wind picks up like in <u>The Wizard of Oz</u>.

Dialogue— character development

"Now, think, Letasha, think," I say to myself as I try to come up with a plan. I can't pitch the tent in this wind, but I <u>can</u> go into that cave.

Event 2

So I hurry into the cave. It's so dark I can't see a thing, but I'm safe from that storm . . . I think.

Suspense

Whose yellow eyes aren't blinking at me from over there on the far side of the cave? And—oh, oh—what's that roar?

Dialogue

"Now, Letasha. You can either run out of this cave into the worst blizzard you've ever imagined, or you can stay here and hope your cave buddy is already full and feeling friendly." (Right.)

Suspense

Event 3

I stay, staring at those yellow eyes that stare right back at me. Finally, the storm stops, and I rush outside.

Suspense

Dialogue

Character development/ Suspense

HIGH POINT

OUTCOME Dialogue

Surprise ending

I gasp. Right there in the fresh snow gigantic footprints walk past my cave and around a curve. "OK, Letasha, do you follow these footprints to see who made them? Or do you run for it in the opposite direction—and down? Or is it back to the cave with the Yellow-Eyed Roaring Thing?"

Mom always says I'm too curious for my own good. Scared to death, I follow the footprints round the curve. Suddenly, a huge monster with an ugly head, angry red eyes, and hairy arms with sharp claws is reaching toward me—

"Letasha, haven't you finished your math yet?" Mom yells from the kitchen.

Hurriedly I switch off the video game. "Almost, Mom. This last problem is kind of hard."

WRITING ASSIGNMENT

PART 5:
Writing Your First Draft

Both "Thank You, M'am" and "The Final Problem" give you good ideas for writing. But don't think that you have to make your story like them. Just begin following your story map—but, of course, feel free to make changes. Start writing now, and see what happens.

Evaluating and Revising

The hardest part is over, but you've still got important work to do. How can you make your story better? Is the conflict really interesting? Are the characters believable? If something doesn't work, either fix it or get rid of it. Here's what writer Pat Mora has to say about revising.

Do you know the quotation that says that learning to write is like learning to ice-skate? You must be willing to make a fool of yourself. Writers are willing to try what they can't do well so that one day they can write a strong poem or novel or children's book.

After writers gain some confidence, writers begin to spend more and more time revising just as professional ice-skaters create and practice certain routines until they have developed their own, unique style. You probably don't like rewriting now. I didn't either until a few years ago. . . .

It's important . . . not to fall in love with the words you write. Pick your words or phrases, and then stand back and look at your work. Read it out loud.

Pat Mora, "A Letter to Gabriela, A Young Writer"

The following guidelines will help you pinpoint weak spots in your draft. If you answer *no* to any question in the left-hand column, use the revision technique suggested in the right-hand column.

EVALUATING AND REVISING SHORT STORIES

EVALUATION GUIDE	REVISION TECHNIQUE
1 Does the beginning present a main character in an interesting conflict?	**Add** sentences that show the main character and a clear conflict or problem.
2 Does the plot have a strong high point and satisfying outcome?	**Add** a tense scene that solves the conflict. **Add** details that explain how everything works out.
3 Are the characters lifelike and believable?	**Add** details about what the characters look like, what they do, and how they feel. **Add** dialogue that sounds natural.
4 Is the setting clear? If possible, does it help set a mood?	**Add** specific details of time and place. **Add** vivid sensory details.
5 Is the point of view the same throughout the story?	**Cut** or **replace** statements that change the point of view.

CRITICAL THINKING
Analyzing the Parts of a Short Story

When you *analyze* something, you look closely at its separate parts and see how they work together. That's just what writers do when they revise. They look at characters, plot, setting, and dialogue to see if changes can make them stronger and more entertaining for the reader. When the writer of "The Final Problem" analyzed one paragraph of her story, she made these revisions.

> ^fresh ^gigantic
> ^Right there in the snow footprints   **add**
>
> walk past my cave and around a curve.
>
> ~~Letasha gasps.~~ "OK, Letasha, do you follow   **replace/reorder**
>
> these footprints to see who made them?
>
> Or do you run for it in the opposite
>   *is it back*
> direction—and down? Or ~~would you prefer~~   **replace**
>   *Yellow-Eyed Roaring Thing*
> ~~to return~~ to the cave with the animal?"   **replace**

CRITICAL THINKING EXERCISE:
Analyzing a Writer's Revisions

Analyzing the changes the writer made can help you with your own revision. Working with a partner, first read aloud the draft paragraph and then the revision. Then, use the following questions to guide your analysis.

1. Why does the writer change *Letasha* to *I*?
2. What's the effect of moving *I gasp* to the beginning?
3. Are the words *fresh* and *gigantic* good additions? Why?
4. Why does the writer replace *would you prefer to return* with *is it back*? [Hint: See page 202.]
5. Is *Yellow-Eyed Roaring Thing* better than *animal*? Why?

WRITING ASSIGNMENT

PART 6:
Evaluating and Revising Your Story

Now evaluate and revise your own story, using the guidelines on page 213. Swap drafts with a classmate for feedback and additional suggestions.

Proofreading and Publishing

Proofreading. Double-check your story carefully to correct errors in spelling, usage, and mechanics.

MECHANICS HINT

Punctuating Dialogue

Punctuating dialogue can be especially tricky. Here are some rules that will help you figure out two things: what to put in quotation marks and how to punctuate what your characters say.

1. Enclose a character's words in quotation marks.

EXAMPLE **"Get off that phone!" Mark demanded.**

2. Commas and periods always go inside a quotation mark. Question marks and exclamation marks go inside when the quotation itself is a question or an exclamation.

EXAMPLES "OK, Mark. The phone's all yours."
"It's about time, Larry," Mark scowled.
"Don't snap at me!" Larry barked.
"How would you like to wait so long?" Mark grumbled.

☞ REFERENCE NOTE: For more information on punctuating dialogue, see pages 772–777.

Publishing. With two or three classmates, brainstorm some ideas for publishing your stories or sharing them with others. Here are two possibilities.

- Illustrate your story with drawings or magazine photos, make a classroom short story collection, and give it to the school library.
- Volunteer to read your story aloud to someone who does not read or see well.

PART 7:

Proofreading and Publishing Your Story

Carefully proofread your revised story, and give your final copy a once-over, too. Share your story with friends and family, or find another way to publish it.

 Reflecting on Your Writing

Your story will make a good addition to your **portfolio.** To include it, write a brief reflection by responding to the questions below. Remember to date your story and reflection.

- Which aspect of your story did you decide on first: characters, setting, or plot? Why?
- Did you use a story map? Why or why not?
- Which techniques did you use to make your characters seem real? What else could you do to make the characters more realistic?

A STUDENT MODEL

Imagining can get you everywhere and anywhere, as Amey Horse Looking shows in the following passages from her story. A student at Dakota Junior High School in Rapid City, South Dakota, Amey says her ideas come from her imagination and that "once I get started I can't stop."

The Dream
by Amey Horse Looking

The wind blew through her hair while she was walking in the meadow. The flowers were so irresistible that she picked some and then she heard a sound like someone saying something but the person was running. She could hear the heavy footsteps coming. She looked around frantically and started to run until she entered the forest and looked around her.

. . . As she ventured deeper and deeper in the forest, she saw a little cabin with a light on and smoke coming out of the chimney. She knew she must go somewhere safe because she felt that something or someone was following her.

Just then, she felt cold, cold hands running up her shoulders. She was so horrified she did not think to look around and she fainted. It was hours before she awoke; she was not harmed or hurt—she was lying in a strange bed. . . . As she turned around, she saw a kind old man sitting in a rocking chair. His hair was very stringy with streaks of gray. The wrinkles of his face were like ripples of water. His eyes were a majestic gray. The lips of his face were faded pink. The weird thing that she could not understand was what a kind old man was doing in the deep part of the forest.

As the day passed, she decided to stay with the man until he drove into town the next day. That night, she lay in her bed. Suddenly, she heard a chopping sound, the strange noise she had heard in the meadow. Then she heard a lot of racket and the sound of heavy feet walking toward the door, frightening her. She called for the old man but could not find him. When she opened the back door, she was surprised because she saw the old man moving toward her in a fierce way. Just then, she woke up from her dream as her mother called her for breakfast.

As she was eating, she pushed the bowl of oatmeal back and looked out the window and saw the same man walking by and looking at her while laughing. She figured her dream was true.

WRITING WORKSHOP

A Narrative Poem

Poems can tell stories, too, and when they do, they're called **narrative poems.** In fact, narrative poems may be one of the first ways stories were passed around—before writing and books—because poetry's rhythms make memorization easier. (Have you noticed how people say even the Pledge of Allegiance in a singsong way?)

Like stories, narrative poems can have characters, conflict, setting, and theme. Unlike stories, poems may have musical rhythm (whether a regular or loose beat) and rhyme (but poems don't have to rhyme). Poems also usually have very strong word-pictures (poets love sensory words!).

Here's a narrative poem that builds, line by line, an unusual picture. Where do you think the poet got his idea for this story?

Jimmy Jet and His TV Set
by Shel Silverstein

I'll tell you the story of Jimmy Jet—
And you know what I tell you is true.
He loved to watch his TV set
Almost as much as you.

He watched all day, he watched all night
Till he grew pale and lean,
From "The Early Show" to "The Late Late Show"
And all the shows between.

He watched till his eyes were frozen wide,
And his bottom grew into his chair.
And his chin turned into a tuning dial,
And antennae grew out of his hair.

And his brain turned into TV tubes,
And his face to a TV screen.
And two knobs saying "VERT." and "HORIZ."
Grew where his ears had been.

And he grew a plug that looked like a tail
So we plugged in little Jim.
And now instead of him watching TV
We all sit around and watch him.

Thinking It Over

1. Well, Jimmy Jet is certainly a character with a problem. What is it? (What causes the narrative's events?) What do you think of the poem's outcome?
2. At which line did you suspect something fantastic was happening?
3. In each group of lines (called a **stanza**), which lines rhyme? How many beats do you hear in each line? How would you describe the feeling, or tone, that the rhyme and rhythm give the poem?
4. In this poem, the narrator is a character. How can you tell? Make a guess about who he (or she) is.
5. Does this funny poem have a message? Explain.

Writing a Narrative Poem

Prewriting. What you learned about story ideas holds true for narrative poems. They can be fantastic or about everyday life. Choose a story about yourself or someone you know or have heard or read about. Then, in a small group, brainstorm narrative poem ideas. Choose the idea you like best, and jot down details to develop your plot and characters.

Writing, Evaluating, and Revising. You can write with rhyme or without it—whichever seems comfortable. And you also have choices in rhyme patterns (look at a few different poems). The rhythm can use regular beats or be more free: Just make it pleasing to your ears.

Remember to show rather than tell, using specific nouns, lively verbs, and descriptive modifiers. Break your poem into lines and stanzas where breaks seem natural.

Read your poem aloud to see how it sounds. Then, swap poems with a classmate, and give each other suggestions.

Proofreading and Publishing. Correct all spelling, and check to see that your punctuation helps readers pause and stop in the right places. Hold a "Storyteller's Day" in class, but practice reading aloud first.

To add your narrative poem to your **portfolio,** date it and attach a note of reflection that answers the following questions. Did you write a fantastic poem or a realistic one? Why? How did you choose the rhyme and rhythm patterns you used?

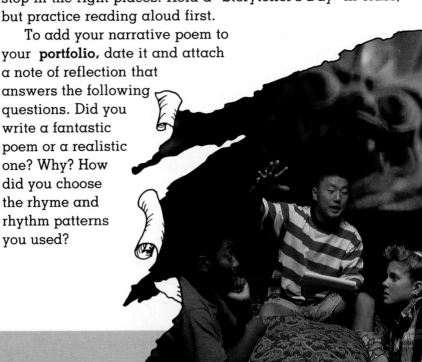

MAKING CONNECTIONS

A Legend or Myth

Myths and *legends* are traditional stories that explain something about the world. They usually involve gods or other supernatural beings. For example, because people everywhere have similar questions about nature, most cultures have myths that explain the cycles of sun and moon, the presence of stars in the sky. "The Sound of Flutes" (pages 186–192) is a traditional Native American legend. It has a bird that communicates with a man, and it explains how the Plains Indians invented the flute.

Try writing a myth that explains why something is the way it is. Start by thinking about the world around you, and brainstorm some questions you'd like to explain in a fun and imaginative way. For example:

- Why do cats chase mice?
- Why do flowers smell sweet?
- Why do people kiss?

Visual Stories

There is an old saying that one picture is worth a thousand words. But maybe that isn't so—maybe one picture can *stimulate* a thousand words! For this activity, begin by finding a photograph or a painting that grabs your imagination. (The photograph can be one you've taken yourself or one you find in a newspaper or magazine.) What story can you write about the moment captured in the picture? Here are some questions to help you plan.

- Who is in the picture? And why?
- What can you tell about the character(s) from the setting?
- What happens to the character(s)? What's the conflict?

7 WRITING TO INFORM: EXPOSITION

Working and Playing

When was a big INFORMATION sign a great relief for you? Were you in a subway station, a sports arena, a museum? People couldn't get through life without information, and that's why we're always sharing it—everything from world news to baseball scores. And because **working and playing** are such big parts of life, we often give instructions for how to use something or how to do something.

Writing and You. Everywhere you look, writers are giving you instructions. In a magazine, you learn how to save money on clothes. On television, you learn how to build a birdhouse. Have you followed any instructions today?

As You Read. In the following essay, humorist Dave Barry tells you how to deal with a medical emergency in the wilderness. Do you think he wants you to take his directions seriously?

Jacob Lawrence, *The Builders No.1* (1970). Henry Art Gallery, University of Washington, Seattle. Gift of the artist.

What to Do in a
Wilderness
Medical
Emergency

by Dave Barry

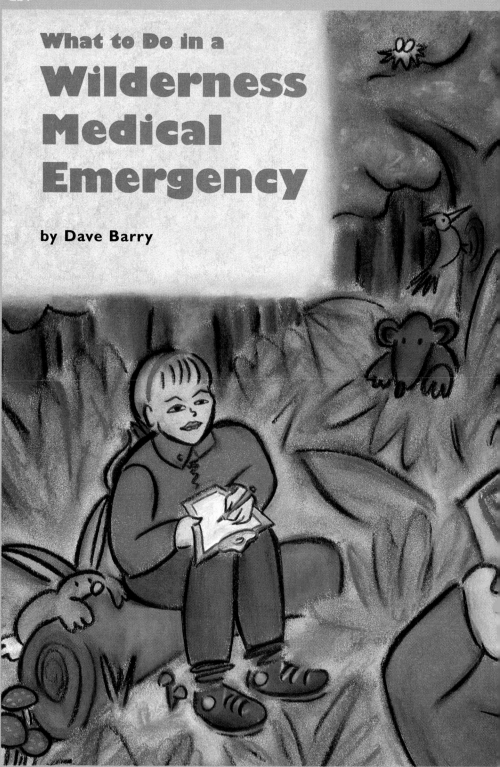

Experts agree that the most important rule in a wilderness medical emergency is: *Keep your head down on the follow-through.* No! My mistake! That's the most important rule in *golf.* The most important rule in a wilderness medical emergency is: *Don't panic.* To prevent the victim from going into shock, you must reassure him, as calmly as possible, that everything's going to be fine:

> VICTIM *(clearly frightened)*: Am I going to be okay?
>
> YOU *(in a soothing voice)*: Of course you are! I'm sure we'll find your legs around here someplace!
>
> VICTIM *(relieved)*: Whew! You got any Cheez-Its?

Once the victim has been calmed, you need to obtain pertinent information by asking the following Standard Medical Questions:

1. Does he have medical insurance?
2. Does his spouse have medical insurance?
3. Was he referred to this wilderness by another doctor?
4. How much does he weigh?
5. Does that figure include legs?

Write this information down on a medical chart; then give the victim a 1986 copy of *Fortune* magazine to read while you decide on the correct course of treatment. This will depend

on the exact nature of the injury. For example, if it's mushroom poisoning or a broken limb, you'll need to apply a tourniquet. Whereas if it's a snake bite, then you need to determine whether the snake was poisonous, which will be indicated by tiny markings on the snake's stomach as follows:

WARNING: POISON SNAKE!

ACHTUNG! SCHLANGE SCHNAPPENKILLEN!

In this case, you need to apply a tourniquet to the snake, as shown in Figure 1.

Figure 1. Putting a tourniquet on a snake

1. Have snake lie down.

wrong

right

2. Apply tourniquet to snake's body.

wrong

right

from *Dave Barry's Only Travel Guide You'll Ever Need*

READER'S RESPONSE

1. Which step in "What to Do in a Wilderness Medical Emergency" do you think is the funniest? the least funny? Why?
2. What other situations or settings can you think of that could be turned into a funny story?

WRITER'S CRAFT

3. Dave Barry's purpose isn't really to inform, but to use his imagination to entertain you. How does Barry's first sentence signal that he is not going to provide serious instructions?
4. Although you know early on that Barry is not being serious, what words and phrases does he use that make his instructions sound like real ones you have read?

Ways to Inform

In this chapter, you'll focus on a way of writing to inform:
giving instructions. But this is only one of many ways to
share information. Here are some examples of how you
can write to inform.

- in a presentation to a photography club, telling how
  to take good pictures with a specific camera model
- in a note to your younger brother, telling how to
  buy clothes on a budget
- in a notice on a bulletin board, describing your lost
  jacket so that teachers and fellow students will
  recognize it
- in a paper for science class, describing the inside
  of a beehive
- in a letter to a friend, explaining the differences
  between writing with a word processor and writing
  with a typewriter
- in an essay, writing about the meaning of *self-reliance*
- in a movie review, evaluating how well a film's
  music fits the action
- in a report to the school board, explaining how a
  computer lab will benefit students

OOKING
HEAD

In this chapter's main assignment, you'll use
narration to give instructions. You will write
about how to use or do something. As you
work, keep in mind that a paper giving
instructions

- tells readers how to use a product or follow
  a procedure
- discusses all necessary materials and steps
- defines any terms the audience may not
  understand

Writing Instructions

 *Prewriting*

Choosing a Product or Procedure to Explain

Instructions explain a process—how to use something or how to do something. A set of instructions may be a few lines on a package of frozen food that explain how to cook it. Or they may form a thousand-page manual that accompanies a powerful computer. For many people in the workplace, writing instructions is a regular part of the job. But you don't have to be an expert to write instructions. Do you know how to perform basic dives from a springboard, operate a VCR, or use a computer? Can you take especially good pictures, make spaghetti, or change a bicycle tire? Brainstorm a list of things you know how to do, or products you know how to use. Then, to narrow down your list, think about your purpose and audience.

Thinking About Purpose

Remember that your purpose is to inform readers about how to use a product or perform a procedure. If your paper succeeds, your readers will learn a new skill. If you explain how to whittle a duck out of wood, for instance, your readers should come away knowing how to make a wooden duck.

Thinking About Audience

Make sure your topic fits your audience. If you're writing for wilderness explorers, don't waste time telling them how to follow trail markers. Think of something your audience might not know and may want to learn how to do.

To choose a topic for your set of instructions

- brainstorm (see page 27) a list of products you know how to use or things you like to do
- pick something you know or do well
- make sure your topic and your audience are a good match

E X E R C I S E 1 ▶ **Matching Topic and Audience**

Decide which topics are suitable or unsuitable for each audience. (More than one topic may work for some of the audiences.) Be ready to explain your choices.

1. Audience: Eighth-grade students
   Topics: How to repair a machine that stamps out
             plastic forks
             How to get ready for school quickly
             How to fix a flat bicycle tire
             How to tell time

2. Audience: Readers of a science fiction magazine
   Topics: How to arrange flowers
             How to predict advances in transportation
             technology
             How to join the Loyal Order of Moose
             How filmmakers create fantasy characters
             and settings for movies

E X E R C I S E 2 ▶ **Exploring Possible Topics**

Get together with three or four classmates to talk about what each of you might teach the others. Using the prompt, "One thing I do really well is ____," try to come up with at least three ideas for each person in the group. Now review your ideas: Which ones would you most like to learn? Which ones could you explain in a paragraph or short paper?

WRITING ASSIGNMENT	PART 1:
	Choosing a Topic to Explain

You can explain how to use a product or to do a procedure that your group listed, or you can choose another one that you know or do well. Can you apply clown makeup? Can you tell young children how to use basic computer functions? Can you explain how to give a party? After you've picked your topic, write a sentence telling what you will explain. Also identify the audience for your paper.

Prewriting

Gathering and Organizing Your Information

Before you start writing, plan what you will say. Organized notes make writing much easier.

Listing Steps and Materials

A set of instructions gives two kinds of information. It tells readers, step by step, how to use a product or do a procedure; and it tells them what materials and equipment they need.

The amount and kind of information you give depend on your audience. Suppose that you want to explain how to make quesadillas. Are you writing for classmates preparing food for a school fair? Are you writing for people who think that cooking means microwaving a frozen dinner? Or are you writing for experienced cooks? Each audience knows different things about cooking and will need different information.

Drawing from Experience. Since you've done the process, you can draw most of your information from experience. Picture yourself going through the procedure or using the product. In your mind, break the task down into specific steps. What do you do first, second, and so on? What is the result of going through the process?

As you mentally "do" each step, think about the materials you're using. Take notes about any tools and supplies that you need. Also, jot down special terms—for example, *joystick, greasepaint, Phillips screwdriver*—so you'll remember to define them later.

You can use a three-column chart to record your information. Write each step in the first column, materials in the second, and terms in the third. Here's a chart one writer made for a paper giving instructions.

HERE'S HOW

How to Compost Garbage		
Steps	Materials	Terms
1. Collect garbage	Plastic jug	Organic garbage
2. Dig hole	Spade	
3. Dump garbage in hole		
4. Cover with fertilizer	Fertilizer	
5. Cover with dirt		
6. Spray with water	Garden hose	

Using Other Information Sources. As you take notes, you may find gaps in your knowledge. The library is the best place to do research. You may even find a "how-to" video on your topic. People can help, too. If you don't know anyone who can answer your question, look for an expert in the Yellow Pages. A plumber, for example, can tell you what tools to use to fix a leaky faucet.

Drawing Pictures to Show Steps. You can make some activities clearer by drawing diagrams of important steps. Look at common instructions (for model building or sewing, for instance), and you'll see how diagrams can help. As you go through your steps, decide whether pictures would help readers. (And if your procedure needs many pictures to be clear, pick another one. It's too hard!) Here's a diagram on performing a horse vault.

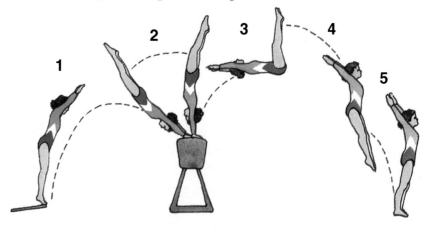

EXERCISE 3 ▶ **Listing Steps and Materials**

You breeze through dozens of everyday procedures on automatic pilot. It sounds easy, right? But can you break them into clear steps? Get together with a group of classmates and break each of the following procedures into steps. Also list materials and any necessary equipment, and decide if you need drawings.

1. blow-drying or moussing your hair
2. changing a bicycle tire
3. making a grilled cheese sandwich
4. packing clothes and personal belongings for a move

Organizing Your Information

What's wrong with these directions for painting a room?

Paint the ceiling first. Then do the walls. Keep the floor from getting paint on it. Use dropcloths to protect the furniture. Move the furniture away from the walls. Wear old clothes that you don't mind getting paint on.

Readers who followed these steps in order would have as much paint on floors, furniture, and clothes as on the walls. To keep readers on the right track (and clean), plan how you'll arrange your information—before you begin to write. To explain most processes, you begin by telling what materials will be needed. Then you put the steps in *chronological order*—the order in which the steps occur in time.

And once you start explaining how to do something, stay focused on the task. Include only the information that your audience needs to do the procedure or use the product. Unnecessary details distract and confuse readers. Cross out facts, examples, and descriptions that don't relate to the procedure or product.

To plan a set of instructions

- list the steps readers should follow
- as you list steps, jot down materials and/or equipment, and terms to explain
- put the steps into chronological order
- cross out unnecessary information

EXERCISE 4 ▶ **Arranging Information in Chronological Order**

A ranger made some quick notes for campers about how to build a campfire. See if you can put these steps in the most efficient chronological order.

> Set fire to newspaper.
>
> Gather dead twigs for kindling.
>
> Buy newspaper at camp store.
>
> Make twigs lean together like tepee poles over
>
>   newspaper.
>
> Crumple newspaper.
>
> Sweep ground clear of anything that might burn.
>
> Buy wood at camp store.
>
> When fire gets going, lay wood over kindling.

CRITICAL THINKING
Evaluating Details

Sometimes, too much detail in a set of instructions can overwhelm and confuse the reader. To decide if a detail is necessary in your instructions, ask yourself *Is this information that my audience already knows? Without this detail, could readers make a mistake?*

CRITICAL THINKING EXERCISE:
Evaluating Details

Here are some notes a writer jotted down about recording a message for a telephone answering machine. The audience is a class of eighth-graders. What information isn't needed in the instructions?

A telephone answering machine answers the telephone for you.
My brother taught me how to use my answering machine.
These instructions will show you how to record an outgoing message on your answering machine.
First, press and hold the ANNOUNCE button.
The ANNOUNCE button is located on the inside compartment of your machine.
As you record the message, do not pause more than two seconds.
The president signed a new bill that affects the telephone, TV, and cable industries.

PART 2:
Planning Your Instructions

Make a chart like the one on page 232, and list steps, materials, equipment, and terms to define. Make sure steps are chronological, and cross out unnecessary information.

Writing Your First Draft

The Parts of a Set of Instructions

A set of instructions includes these parts:

- an introduction that catches the reader's attention
- a body that includes a description of the product, a list of materials and equipment, and the steps in the procedure
- a conclusion that summarizes the steps or discusses problems and what to do about them

With some instructions, you do not need every one of these parts. For example, if you are explaining how to use a digital clock radio, you will not have to describe materials and equipment other than the radio itself.

The Introduction.   How many times have you put down a set of instructions after reading only a sentence or two? A good introduction catches your readers' attention and motivates them to read the instructions. The introduction tells what the instructions will help them to achieve, for example: *This manual explains in simple steps how to install, use, and care for your new telephone answering system.*
   The introduction may also state

- how the product or procedure benefits you
- how the instructions are organized
- what you'll need to know in order to follow the instructions

The Body.   If you are explaining how to use a product— for example, how to program a remote control or how to use an electronic "invisible fence" to keep your dog in the yard—include a description of the product. Tell how it works and what its special features are. If, on the other hand, your instructions explain how to do something— how to be a champion in-line skater or how to deflea a dog, for example—you do not have to describe a product.

The body also includes a list of materials and equipment. In this part, you describe the items the reader will need to use the product or do the procedure, for example: *To program this remote-control device, you will need the all-in-one remote-control device and 4 AAA alkaline batteries.*

The steps are the heart of the body in a set of instructions. They explain the sequence for carrying out the process—how to use the product or perform the procedure. As you list steps in the instructions, remember to

- list steps in the order they're actually done
- supply background information and helpful hints
- include warnings with steps that might be unsafe
- define unfamiliar terms

As you write, remember that you're a guide, not a drill sergeant. A friendly tone will be helpful to your audience.

The Conclusion. The conclusion usually sums up the steps the reader follows to use the product or do the procedure. It may also include a trouble-shooting guide to help readers with problems that might arise. Trouble-shooting guides typically appear in chart form, as illustrated by the following example.

PROBLEM	CAUSE	SOLUTION
TV does not respond to remote control.	Remote control batteries might be weak.	Replace batteries.

Calvin & Hobbes copyright 1986 Watterson. Distributed by Universal Press Syndicate. Reprinted with permission. All rights reserved.

To write a set of instructions

- tell readers what the instructions will do for them
- describe the product or procedure
- list materials and equipment readers will need
- give directions in the order the steps should be completed
- tell readers what to do if things go wrong

The writers of the following instructions explain how to build a hot air balloon. As you read, ask yourself if you would be able to follow their instructions.

A PASSAGE FROM A BOOK

from **Science Crafts for Kids**

by Gwen Diehn and Terry Krautwurst

Hot Air Balloon

INTRODUCTION

This is a tricky project but well worth the fine-tuning it takes to get your balloon aloft. The trick is to be sure the air outside the balloon is much cooler than the air you put into the balloon.

LIST OF EQUIPMENT AND MATERIALS

What You'll Need

12 pieces of colored tissue paper, each 20 by 30 inches
White craft glue
A stapler
A marker

A ruler or yardstick
Sharp scissors
Old newspaper
A hair dryer

What to Do

BODY
Steps

Figure 1

1. Run a thin bead of glue along the short edge of a piece of tissue paper, 1/4 inch from the edge. Overlap a second piece of paper over the glue so that the two pieces are joined and make one long piece of tissue paper 20 inches wide and about 5 feet long.

2. Repeat Step 1 five more times until you have six long sheets of paper.

3. Fold each long sheet of paper in half lengthwise, and stack the six sheets exactly on top of one another. Keep all folded edges on the same side.

4. Be sure all edges are even; then, staple the stack together along the unfolded edges and at the top and bottom. (See Figure 1.) Put the staples about 10 inches apart, and be sure not to put any staples on the folded edge. (The staples will make it easier to cut the pieces of paper all at one time.)

Explanation

Make dots 5" apart.   3³/₄

9¹/₈

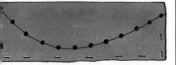

Figure 2

5. Use the marker and ruler to mark the top sheet of tissue paper like Figure 2.

6. Join the dots with a curving line. (See Figure 3.) You should have a gentle curve. Carefully cut through the whole stapled stack of paper at once along the curved line. You will have cut off the stapled pieces and will be left with a stack of folded papers.

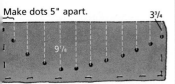

Figure 3

7. Put the first folded piece of paper on top of some sheets of old newspaper. Put a piece of newspaper between the two layers of tissue, to keep the glue from seeping through. Run a thin bead of glue along the curved edge of the top sheet. (See Figure 4.)

8. Place the second piece of folded tissue paper on top of the first, gluing the curved edges together.

Figure 4

Figure 5

Hint

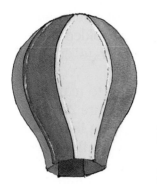

Figure 6

Figure 7

9. Slip newspaper between the two layers of tissue paper on piece number two.

10. Repeat Steps 7, 8, and 9 for the rest of the six sheets of tissue paper. You should end up with a stack of tissue paper sheets folded on one edge and glued together like an accordion on the other, curved edge. (See Figure 5.)

11. When the glue is dry, carefully take out all of the newspaper. Some of it will be stuck to the tissue paper, and you will have to peel it away in the stuck spots.

12. Open the bottom piece of tissue.

13. Put a thin bead of glue all along the curvy edge, just as you did in Step 7.

14. Unfold the top piece of tissue paper, and press its curvy edges all along the bead of glue. (See Figure 6.) The balloon pieces are now all joined.

15. Wait for the glue to dry completely before inflating the balloon. (See Figure 7.) While you are waiting for the glue to dry, you can glue tissue paper streamers to the bottom edge for decoration if you like.

16. Ask a friend to help you hold the balloon upright while you carefully place a hair dryer just inside the open bottom of the balloon. When the balloon is inflated and all puffed out, it should rise to the ceiling.

Tip to avoid
problems

CONCLUSION

17. If you want to fly your balloon outside, you can do so successfully only on dry,
cool or cold days when there is no breeze.

When you fly your balloon inside, try to
find a cool room with a high ceiling so you
can watch the balloon lift as if by magic.
Happy flying!

**WRITING
NOTE** Notice that the writers of this essay keep
their sentences short and to the point. Simple,
straightforward language will help readers
understand and follow your instructions.

EXERCISE 5 ▶ **Analyzing a Set of Instructions**

1. How do the authors introduce their set of instructions?
   Does their introduction make you want to construct a
   balloon? Explain.
2. Where is the list of equipment and materials? Why do
   you think it appears here rather than in the body of
   the essay?
3. What determines the order in which the authors give
   steps?
4. Could you follow the authors' instructions and create
   your own balloon? Explain.
5. The authors' last step hints at one problem the reader
   might have. What do you think are some other problems
   a reader might have building or flying a hot air balloon?

A Basic Framework for a Set of Instructions

Building a hot air balloon—even one that can't carry people—is a complicated project. Your instructions will probably require fewer steps. Here is a writer's model that
shows you a basic framework for a set of instructions.

A WRITER'S MODEL

Isn't it time you gave something back to Mother Earth? Here's a gift she'll really appreciate: a compost pile that turns your household garbage into rich soil. And you can make it yourself.

Just think how much garbage goes out of your house every year. If your family is like most in America, in a year's time your garbage can be measured in tons! We're even running out of places to put our garbage. Composting is one little thing you can do to help. These instructions will teach you how to make your own compost.

To compost garbage, you need a yard, and it has to have a corner that you don't use. You also need a plastic jug, a shovel, a bag of fertilizer, and a garden hose. You can use a one-gallon milk jug, but cut off the top to make a wider opening. You'll find fertilizer at garden stores.

Composting is pretty simple. Begin by collecting your organic garbage in the plastic jug. What is organic garbage, you ask? It's anything that comes from a plant or many other living things. You can put egg shells, coffee grounds, and vegetable peels into your compost jug. But

Helpful hint

you can't put cans, bottles, and paper in there. Also, don't put meat or fat into your compost, because they will attract unwanted animals and insects.

Step 2

Explanation

Step 3

Step 4

Step 5

As soon as you begin to collect organic garbage, go out to your yard and dig a hole where you want your compost. Make it about two feet deep and three feet across. Then, when your jug is full, empty it into the hole and pour a thin layer of fertilizer over it. Shovel a layer of dirt over the fertilizer. Wet it down with the hose, and you're finished for the day. The next time your jug is full, repeat the process.

CONCLUSION

Restatement of benefits

New benefit

That's all there is to it: a layer of organic garbage, a thin layer of fertilizer, a layer of dirt, and a little water. In a year or so, the hole in your yard will be full of rich, crumbly brown garden soil. You'll have the satisfaction of knowing you've done something that helps the earth. And when you taste the vegetables grown in the soil you've made, you'll know it was worth the trouble.

WRITING NOTE The writer of the essay about composting uses transitional words and phrases like *after, then,* and *in a year or so.* These words help the reader know when each step takes place. (For more information on transitions, see pages 71–73.)

You may find it helpful to use this framework for your essay. The essay about composting describes a procedure, not a product. Otherwise, it follows the framework.

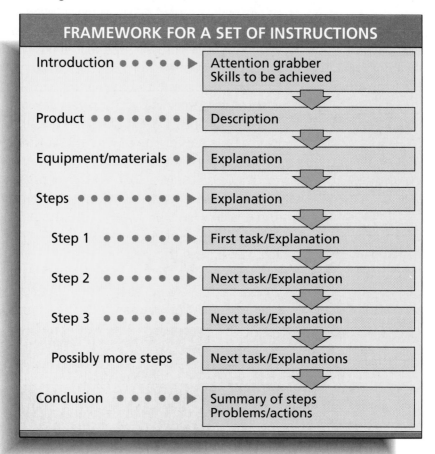

FRAMEWORK FOR A SET OF INSTRUCTIONS

Introduction ▶	Attention grabber Skills to be achieved
Product ▶	Description
Equipment/materials ▶	Explanation
Steps ▶	Explanation
Step 1 ▶	First task/Explanation
Step 2 ▶	Next task/Explanation
Step 3 ▶	Next task/Explanation
Possibly more steps ▶	Next task/Explanations
Conclusion ▶	Summary of steps Problems/actions

WRITING ASSIGNMENT

PART 3:
Writing a Draft of Your Set of Instructions

You've got all the information you need to write a first draft of your set of instructions. To help you stay on track as you write, keep looking back at the basic framework on this page. Also, be sure to use the chart you made in Writing Assignment, Part 2 (page 235).

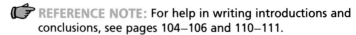

REFERENCE NOTE: For help in writing introductions and conclusions, see pages 104–106 and 110–111.

Evaluating and Revising

Use the following chart to evaluate and revise your paper. If you answer no to a question in the left-hand column, use the revision technique in the right-hand column.

EVALUATING AND REVISING INSTRUCTIONS

EVALUATION GUIDE	REVISION TECHNIQUE
1 Does the introduction catch the reader's interest and tell what skills the instructions teach?	**Add** interesting details in your opening sentence. **Add** a sentence that tells what skills readers will learn.
2 If the essay involves a product, is the product described?	**Add** descriptive details about the product.
3 Does the essay list needed equipment and materials before giving the steps?	**Add** a list of all the necessary equipment and materials before giving the steps.
4 Are the steps given in the order in which they should be done? Are all the details related to the process?	**Reorder** the steps so they are in chronological order. **Cut** unnecessary details.
5 Are all unfamiliar terms clearly defined?	**Add** definitions of terms the audience may not know.
6 Does the conclusion summarize the steps? Does it discuss problems and possible solutions for readers to try?	**Add** a sentence that summarizes the steps. **Add** information on possible problems and possible solutions for readers to try.

| **E X E R C I S E 6** ▶ | **Analyzing a Writer's Revisions** |

Study the writer's revisions of a paragraph from the model on pages 242–243. Then, answer the questions that follow the paragraph.

> To compost garbage, you need a yard, and it has to have a corner that you don't use. ~~You might want to put a fence~~ ~~around the corner that you're going to use~~ ~~for composting. A picket fence or one~~ ~~made out of wire mesh would look nice;~~ ~~but you don't really need one.)~~ However, *also* you ~~do~~ need a plastic jug, a shovel, a bag of fertilizer, and a garden hose. ~~Watering~~ ~~is the last step.~~ You can use a one-gallon milk jug, but cut off the top to make a wider opening. *You'll find fertilizer at garden stores.*

         cut
         cut
         replace
         cut
         add

1. Why did the writer cut the second and third sentences?
2. Why did the writer change the beginning of the fourth sentence?
3. Why did the writer remove the sentence about watering?
4. Why did the writer add the sentence about fertilizer?

| **E X E R C I S E 7** ▶ | **Speaking and Listening: Explaining Instructions Orally** |

Here's a way to find out if your instructions make sense to other people. Work in groups of three. Read your draft to one person only. Then, listen as he or she explains the instructions to the third student. Does the speaker understand your instructions? Take notes about any problems. Keep trading places so that everyone has a turn as reader, speaker, and listener.

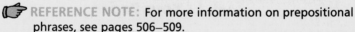

GRAMMAR HINT

Using Prepositional Phrases

When you write instructions, it's often very important to show clear relationships between objects. Otherwise your instructions could be very confusing. Prepositional phrases can help you show those relationships.

UNCLEAR   Move the candle.
   CLEAR   Move the candle **to the table.**

UNCLEAR   Twist the cap.
   CLEAR   Twist the cap **off the bottle.**

UNCLEAR   Pack essential repair tools and mount the bag securely.
   CLEAR   Pack essential repair tools **in a saddlebag** and mount the bag securely **under the bicycle seat.**

REFERENCE NOTE: For more information on prepositional phrases, see pages 506–509.

WRITING ASSIGNMENT

PART 4:

Evaluating and Revising Your Set of Instructions

Build on the notes you took for Exercise 7 by trading your written instructions with another student. Use the questions from the chart on page 245 to evaluate each other's paper. Listen without arguing to your partner's evaluation of your work. Now it's up to you to evaluate your own paper and revise the weaknesses you find.

Proofreading and Publishing

Proofreading.   A tiny error can ruin a set of instructions. If you write about how to get into *The Guinness Book of World Records,* an incorrect address could mean that readers would never see their new records published!

COMPUTER NOTE: Spell-checking programs can be real time-savers. Remember, though, that they can't tell the difference between homonyms such as *their, there,* and *they're.*

Publishing.   Now you need to communicate your instructions to the audience you had in mind. Here are two suggestions.

- Glue your essay on cardboard, framed with a border. Hang it in a workshop or other place suitable to your topic.
- Send your paper to a hobby magazine. You can find addresses in directories at your local library.

**WRITING
ASSIGNMENT**

PART 5:
**Proofreading and Publishing
Your Paper**

Correct any errors you find in your essay. Use one of the ideas above or one of your own to share your paper.

 Reflecting on Your Writing

If you want to put your instructions in your **portfolio,** date them. Include the answers to these questions.

1. How did you choose a product or procedure to explain?
2. How did you grab your readers' attention at the beginning of the instructions?
3. Did you have problems in giving step-by-step directions? Explain.

A STUDENT MODEL

Michael Hutchison's paper offers what nearly every student needs at one time or another: instructions on how to get organized for school in the morning. Michael, who is a student at North Middle School in O'Fallon, Missouri, suggests that writers of instructions "just think of how you would normally go about doing" a procedure. Here is the first part of Michael's paper.

Starting the School Day Right
by Michael Hutchison

Are you tired of always rushing around trying to get ready for school in the mornings? Would you like to know how to get to school without missing your bus or panicking because you did not wake up early enough? Just follow this simple plan and you will never be late again.

The first thing you might want to do is take your bath or shower the night before, instead of in the morning. This can save a lot of time! Also, go ahead and decide what you are going to wear the following day and lay it out so you won't have to spend time looking for your belt or shoes.

Finally, gather all your books and anything else you need to take to school the next morning and place it close to the door along with your coat. If you have to look for these things, it takes up valuable time. You will be in a good mood in the morning, because you have not had to rush around looking for your things.

WRITING WORKSHOP

The Cause-and-Effect Essay

Instructions are a kind of informative writing that answer the question *How do you do or use that?* A similar kind of informative writing is the *cause-and-effect essay*. It answers the question *Why does that happen?* or *What is the result?* A cause-and-effect essay begins with an event or situation and then helps readers understand its causes (*Why?*) or its effects (*What's the result?*).

Let's suppose a new school fad is wearing banana necklaces. You could explore its causes (someone really cool did it for a joke). Or you could write about its effects (a new club—the Necklace Squashers).

Sometimes causes and effects are very clear and simple, but events worth writing about usually aren't. They may have more than one cause or effect—and sometimes we simply can't know them all. Here's an essay about a mysterious decline in frogs and toads. Notice how the writer first discusses possible causes but then focuses on effects.

A Cautionary Tale
by Billy Goodman

In many parts of the United States, and indeed the world, frogs and toads are becoming less and less common. The once-loud chirping and croaking of huge numbers of these animals is getting quieter, as their numbers decline. Why?

Scientists don't have an answer. It probably has something to do with the destruction of frogs' habitats. Some scientists have suggested that acid rain—rain that's more acidic than normal because of air pollution—might be the culprit. Many frogs and toads are easily harmed by acidity in water where they lay their eggs. The decline may have nothing to do with humans.

Whatever the reason, a decline in frog and toad populations could have far-reaching effects. Since frogs and toads normally eat lots of insects, fewer of the amphibians could lead to an insect population explosion. The larger number of insects will devour more plant food—including crops—than usual. In response, farmers may increase their use of pesticides.

Many fish eat tadpoles. So if there are fewer tadpoles, there will be less food for some fish. So fish populations might decline. That would be bad news for fish-eating birds or for people who like to fish.

The moral of this story is "You can't do just one thing." Something that affects one species is bound to affect others up and down the food chain.

from A Kid's Guide to How to Save the Planet

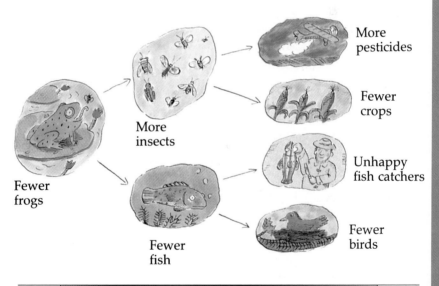

More pesticides

Fewer crops

More insects

Unhappy fish catchers

Fewer frogs

Fewer birds

Fewer fish

Thinking It Over

1. What does the writer say about possible causes for the decline in frogs and toads?
2. The writer tells about effects that go on to produce other effects. This is called a **cause-and-effect chain.** What are all the effects of fewer frogs?
3. A "cautionary tale" is a story that gives a warning. What is the writer's warning?

Writing a Cause-and-Effect Essay

Prewriting. For this paper, just focus on the causes or the effects of an event. You don't have to explain both. Think of something that makes you want to explore *Why?* or *What's the result?*—perhaps a real fad at your school or being the oldest child in your family. Don't tackle a vast question such as *What caused the Vietnam War?* Use a diagram like the one on page 251 to map your paper. Write your event in a circle (you don't have to draw), and then use more circles and arrows to connect causes and effects.

Writing, Evaluating, and Revising. In your introduction, clearly identify the event or situation. Then you can use order of importance—from most to least important, or the opposite—to organize causes or effects. For a cause-and-effect chain, use chronological order. Make sure you have some facts and examples that help support your explanation.

Proofreading and Publishing. Check for errors in your final copy, and think about who might want to read your paper. A paper on teen centers could go to the city council, one on reducing concert ticket prices to the newspaper, and one on fads to the school paper.

If you want to include your cause-and-effect essay in your **portfolio,** date it. Then, include the essay with a reflection on your writing based on these questions. How did you choose the topic for your essay? How difficult (or easy) was it to find facts and examples to support your explanation?

Fox Trot copyright 1989 Bill Amend. Reprinted with permission of Universal Press Syndicate. All rights reserved.

SPEAKING AND LISTENING

Health: Emergency Directions

Workers who answer the 911 emergency number operate under a great deal of stress. They often have to explain a complicated procedure over the phone to someone who's in a panic and screaming for help. Could you give life-saving instructions over the phone? You never know until you try. Get together with a group of four or more class-mates. Each group member should learn a separate emer-gency medical procedure from a first-aid manual. For example, you might learn how to deal with a bad cut or what to do if someone's choking on a piece of food.

Then, take turns being the 911 emergency worker, the injured person, the helper, and an observer. Position yourselves so that the 911 speaker can't see or be seen by the others. As the helper tries to follow the speaker's directions, the observer should take notes. After each "emergency," discuss what happened, especially any-thing that went wrong and how to correct it.

Taking a Stand

Taking a stand is our way of telling people that we feel strongly about something. Persuasion means trying to bring others around to our way of thinking.

Writing and You. Someone is always trying to persuade someone else to act or think a certain way. Advertisers do whatever they can to get you to buy everything from T-shirts to tennis rackets. Your parents try to convince you to do more homework. You do it yourself. You try to persuade your best friend to go to a ballgame. Do you think it's important to take a stand when you feel strongly about something?

As You Read. Here is an excerpt from a book that takes a stand on recycling. As you read, think about what you are being asked to do. Are you convinced you should do it?

Bernie Boston, *Flower Power* (1967).

USE IT AGAIN AND AGAIN AND AGAIN

by The EarthWorks Group

Take A Guess.

How many disposable plastic bottles do we use in four days?
A) Enough to fill a truck B) Enough to fill a warehouse
C) As many as there are people in the whole U.S.

Long before you were born, back when your grandparents were kids, there was no such thing as a paper towel or a paper napkin. People used cloth. Back then, everything was used again and again. In fact, most people would never have imagined throwing something away after using it just once.

But today, we have lots of things that are made especially to be tossed in the garbage after one use; we call them "disposable." Aluminum foil, plastic bags, paper bags, plastic food wrap, and other products are all considered "disposable."

What's going on? Our Earth's treasures are being thrown out as trash. Wouldn't it be wonderful if everyone did a little something to stop this waste? Just imagine what a difference it would make!

Did You Know

- We use millions of feet of paper towels every year. That's a lot of trees!
- Americans use 35 million paper clips every day.
- Americans buy 500 million disposable lighters every year. That's millions of pounds of plastic made by factories just so grown-ups can throw it away.

What You Can Do

- Keep a cloth towel by the sink. Next time you rinse your hands or need to wipe up a spill, grab the cloth towel instead of a paper one.
- Keep a "rag bag" handy. Put your old, torn clothes in it, and you'll have a supply of rags to help you out with messy chores or art projects.
- Save plastic bags—you can use them again. If they're dirty, turn them inside out, rinse them and hang them up to dry.
- Aluminum foil is reusable. Wash it off, let it dry, and put it away. When it can't be used again, recycle it.

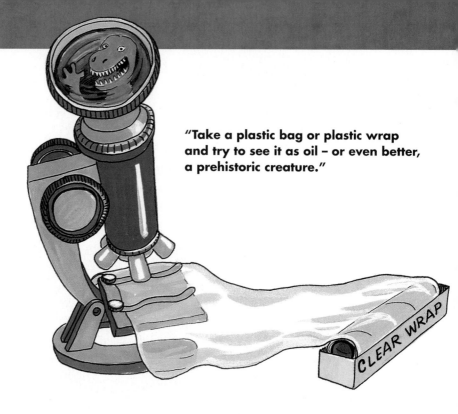

"Take a plastic bag or plastic wrap and try to see it as oil – or even better, a prehistoric creature."

- Have you got some reusable food containers in your kitchen? (You know, the kind with snap-on tops.) Use them instead of just covering or wrapping food with plastic wrap.
- Start an Earth-positive lunchtime trend—use a lunchbox to carry your food to school. Or if you take a bag lunch, bring home the paper and plastic bags so you can reuse them.

See For Yourself

Look around your house for some "disposable" things. Try to picture where they come from. Hold up a roll of paper towels and imagine it's a tree. Take a plastic bag or plastic wrap and try to see it as oil—or even better, a prehistoric creature. See aluminum foil as a precious metal from underground. They seem a lot more important now, don't they? They are!

from *50 SIMPLE THINGS KIDS CAN DO TO SAVE THE EARTH*

Answer: C. 240 million! Incredible!

READER'S RESPONSE

1. The writers want to convince you that people are wasteful *and* to change your behavior. Will you try any suggestions listed under "What You Can Do"? Which ones, and why?
2. What do you think is the most convincing part of this piece of writing? Why? Take a few minutes to respond in your journal. Do you feel you should try any of the writers' suggestions?

WRITER'S CRAFT

3. The writers give one main reason why we should use things again and again. What is it?
4. What is some of the evidence—proof—that supports this reason?
5. Where do you think the writers are appealing to your emotions, not just to your mind?

"You have to figure out what you think because you're taking a stand."

—ELLEN GOODMAN

Ways to Persuade

Any writer trying to persuade has the same goal as the writers of "Use It Again . . .": to make readers believe or act in a certain way. But writers can present their persuasive messages in many ways. Here are some examples.

- in a personal essay, writing about your experiences to persuade more girls to study science
- in a poster, describing a Cinco de Mayo celebration to encourage people to come to it
- in a newspaper opinion piece, describing your local library to convince readers that it's not truly accessible to people who use wheelchairs
- in an office memo, contrasting two types of software to persuade your supervisor that one type is better
- in a letter to the city council, defining the word *compassion* to convince council members to support a program to help people who are homeless
- in a multimedia review, evaluating a World Wide Web site to encourage people to visit it
- in a letter to school administrators, weighing the pros and cons of a lunch policy to persuade them to change it
- in an e-mail message to a friend, describing a band to convince him to go to a show

LOOKING
AHEAD

In this chapter, you'll use evaluation to develop a persuasive composition and a campaign speech. As you work on your writing in this chapter, keep in mind that effective persuasion

- states a clear opinion on the topic
- gives convincing support for the opinion
- may appeal to the reader's emotions

Writing a Persuasive Paper

Prewriting

Choosing a Topic

You've learned that your old elementary school is about to be renamed. Its present name is the Shady Lawn School. The Board of Education wants to call it the Roderick O. Terwilliger School, after a former principal. You don't know much about Mr. Terwilliger, since he retired before you attended. But you think that changing the name of the school would be a mistake.

If you decide to say what you think, you'll be trying to persuade. And the school name is an ideal persuasion topic: an issue you feel strongly about, and one that matters to others.

Finding an Issue That Matters. When you write persuasion, you focus on issues you really care about. After all, if you're not interested, how can you be convincing? But your own interest is just the starting point. The issue (the topic or problem you're concerned about) shouldn't matter *only* to you. It should also be an issue that your audience will find of interest and importance.

Identifying and Stating Your Opinion. Obviously, you have to know what you think before you can write about it. That requires asking, "What is my opinion about this issue?" An *opinion* is how you feel or what you think about a topic. It's what you believe. Of course, someone else may have an opposing opinion on the issue.

An opinion is not the same as a *fact.* You can check the truth of a fact. For example, it's a fact that the northern spotted owl is on the endangered species list. But whether the government should ban logging in certain areas to protect the spotted owl is a matter of opinion.

When you choose an issue to write about, it's a good idea to write a *statement of opinion.* That's a single sentence expressing your opinion about the topic. For example, here are some statements of opinion you might write on a variety of topics.

HERE'S HOW

Statements of opinion:

• Professional football should be played according to college rules.

• The volume of TV ads should be no louder than that of regular programs.

• Home economics should be a required course for all eighth-grade students.

Reminder

When choosing a topic for a persuasive composition

- find an issue that concerns you by brainstorming, talking to other people, listening to radio and television, or looking through newspapers and magazines
- recognize opposing opinions, and be ready to deal with them
- write a sentence that clearly states your topic and your opinion about it

---

EXERCISE 1 ▶ **Distinguishing Fact from Opinion**

With a small group, identify each of the following statements as either a *fact* or an *opinion.* Remember that a fact can be checked for truth, while an opinion is a belief or an attitude.

1. Persian cats have longer hair than Siamese cats.
2. Horror movies are a waste of money.
3. The sport of baseball is so well liked by Americans that it is often called the "national pastime."
4. John F. Kennedy deserves a national holiday in his honor.

 **EXERCISE 2** ▶ **Exploring Possible Issues**

Working with a small group, make a list of five issues you think you could write about. Use your imagination, but discuss whether the topics will work for short papers. You can suggest issues involving your school, your community, your state, the nation, or the world.

WRITING ASSIGNMENT

PART 1:
Choosing an Issue to Write About

To choose an issue, remember: How much you care really counts. You can choose an issue from Exercise 2 or make up a new one. If an item in today's news caught your attention—and you have a definite opinion about it—you may have a ready-made topic. When you've decided, write a statement of opinion: a sentence that names the topic or issue and tells your opinion about it.

Planning for Persuasive Writing

"True ease in writing," wrote the poet Alexander Pope, "comes from art, not chance." Part of the art lies in careful planning. Let's take a look at how to plan a paper that will persuade your readers.

Thinking About Purpose and Audience

Purpose is clear and strong in a persuasion paper: You want to convince your readers to think as you do—and perhaps to make them act. To succeed, you'll have to understand the people you're writing for: your audience. Who are they? What do they already know about your topic? And, most important, what are *their* opinions on it? If you can answer those questions, you're off to a solid start.

Suppose, for example, you belong to a club that would like to hold a hayride. You'll probably have to convince several different groups that a hayride is a good idea. Think about the interests and concerns of these people.

AUDIENCE	INTERESTS AND CONCERNS
Other club members	Having fun, having a long ride in a wagon pulled by a horse
Parents of club members	Transporting members to the hayride, having chaperones, ensuring safety
Club sponsor	Figuring costs, organizing the hayride, finding chaperones, preventing accidents

HERE'S HOW

WRITING NOTE

You don't have to be the ultimate expert on your topic. However, you should know enough about it to make a persuasive case. If you don't have all the information you need, make sure you can get it from the library or from other people.

EXERCISE 3 ▶ **Speaking and Listening: Analyzing Audience**

Two questions will help you analyze your audience: (1) *What person or group in my audience will disagree most strongly with my opinion?* (2) *Why will they disagree?* Practice using these questions in a small group. Here's how to do it.

- One person chooses one of the following opinions.
- He or she names an audience that might disagree with it (like the club sponsor for the hayride).
- The other group members become the "disagreers." They each give one reason for disagreeing. (The sponsor might say, "It's just too dangerous.")

1. Our school week should be four days instead of five.
2. Our community should create one or more parks entirely for the use of teenagers.
3. The United States should ban professional boxing.

Supporting Your Opinion

Few readers will accept your opinion merely because you tell them you're right. To be convincing, you have to give your readers *reasons* and *evidence.*

Reasons.   *Reasons* answer the question "Why?" If you write "We need a larger budget for the school library," the question "Why?" immediately arises. You give reasons: "Many books need to be replaced. Students can't always find the materials they need."

But reasons alone aren't always enough to persuade your audience. Readers usually want proof that your reasons are good ones.

Evidence.   *Evidence* is the proof that your opinion and reasons for it are sound. It can consist of facts or expert opinion. A *fact* is information that can be checked by testing, by observing firsthand, or by reading reference materials. Some facts consist of **data,** or information that may lead to conclusions. Facts may also consist of **statistics,** or numerical information. For example, you examine fifty books in the school library. You find that fourteen have pages missing and three have no covers. These are facts—in the form of statistics—that you can use to support your opinion that the library needs more money.

Expert opinion consists of statements by people who are recognized as authorities on the subject. You ask your school librarian about the budget. She replies, "Yes, we need more money if we're going to provide students with the services they need." That's an expert opinion.

Using Appeals to the Emotions

You know what an emotion is. It's a lump in your throat, a sense of belonging, a rush of sympathy. When you make an emotional appeal, you try to cause such feelings.

Writers often make powerful emotional appeals through examples. For instance, you may want to persuade readers to give money for the relief of flood victims.

A vivid description of one suffering family—their home destroyed, their belongings washed away—will pull strongly at your readers' sympathy.

So consider how you want your audience to *feel* about your topic. If you do, then you can choose an example that appeals to their emotions. Your own experiences can help. An experience that made you angry will probably make your readers feel the same way. But remember: Don't overdo it—you need to balance your emotional appeals with reasons and evidence. Most people will want to see data, statistics, or expert opinions backing up a passionate statement before they accept it as being true.

CRITICAL THINKING

Evaluating Your Reasoning

Emotional appeals can be powerful. They're important in persuasion. But watch out! They can be used in ways that weaken your case instead of strengthening it. As you plan your paper, it's good to know some common types of appeals so that you can *evaluate,* or judge, the support you'll use.

EMOTIONAL APPEALS THAT MAY BACKFIRE		
APPEAL	EMOTION/NEED	EXAMPLE
Bandwagon	Desire to join the crowd, to be on the winning side	Buy Apple Zingers cereal! Everyone is eating Apple Zingers— for breakfast and for healthful snacks.
Flattery	Desire to think highly of oneself	You're young, stylish, practical—so of course you shop at Uchida's.

EMOTIONAL APPEALS THAT MAY BACKFIRE *(continued)*		
APPEAL	EMOTION/NEED	EXAMPLE
Testimonial	Desire to identify with those who seem more important, more knowledgeable, or more famous than we are	As a pro football coach, I know how important a healthful diet is. That's why I start every day with Health-Aid Orange Juice.

 CRITICAL THINKING EXERCISE:
Evaluating Support

You've seen and heard many emotional appeals like the three in the chart. Now you know their names and what they're supposed to do. With a small group, read the following opinion and the three emotional appeals that support it. Identify each appeal as *bandwagon, flattery,* or *testimonial.* Discuss whether you think the appeal works well or backfires. Be sure you can explain your answers to other groups.

Opinion: All baseball stadiums should have playing fields of real grass.

Emotional Appeals
1. "You're a real baseball fan—not one of those people who watch the World Series and nothing else. So you *know* that real grass is the only surface for baseball."
2. "As Phillies star Dick Allen put it, 'If my horse can't eat it, I don't want to play on it.'"
3. "Artificial turf has few defenders. Everybody from the baseball commissioner on down prefers green grass to a green rug."

PART 2:
Finding Support for Your Opinion

Read over your opinion statement, and ask yourself "Why?" That's what readers will do. Start listing reasons *and* evidence to support the reasons. Remember that facts, data, statistics, and expert opinions make the best evidence, but also consider emotional appeals that could help. A chart like this one is a good organizer.

OPINION:	
AUDIENCE:	
REASONS	EVIDENCE
1.	1.
2.	2.
EMOTIONAL APPEALS:	

Writing Your First Draft

Now that you've gathered support for your opinion, it's time to put everything together and write.

Combining the Basic Elements of Persuasion

Always keep in mind what a persuasive paper does. It

- states an opinion about a topic
- aims to convince an audience to think or act as the writer suggests
- uses reasons, evidence, and sometimes emotional appeals to convince the audience

But how do you get this onto paper? Here are some guiding ideas for writing your draft.

A Good Beginning.   You have to grab your readers' attention right away. Perhaps you can begin with a startling fact: "Texas has the legal right to divide itself into five states." That's exactly what your paper recommends doing—but the fact itself is eye-catching enough to be a good beginning. Or you might start with an interesting anecdote. Then, when you have your readers' attention, state your opinion clearly.

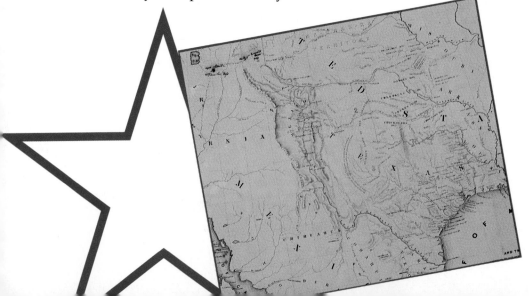

You might need to include some background information in your introduction. This will help your readers understand what's behind the issue—what all the excitement is about. For example, you might believe that people in your neighborhood should donate money to help your local animal shelter to expand. Some background information is that your neighborhood has doubled in size in the last five years. That will help readers understand your opinion.

Clearly Organized Support. In a persuasive paragraph, you might have a sentence to support each reason. In a composition, you might need a paragraph for each reason. In arranging reasons, you may want to put them in order of importance: from the most important to the least important or vice versa.

A Good Ending. A persuasive paper needs a strong ending. You may find that a summary of reasons works well. Or you may want to repeat your opinion in forceful words. Or you may end with a call to action. You tell readers what they should do as a result of being persuaded.

Here's a chance to see how a professional writer combines the basic elements of persuasion.

A MAGAZINE EDITORIAL

from Ban Dogs from Trails?
by Kent Dannen

Emotional
appeal

Issue

The "dogs-shouldn't-be-allowed" people are pressuring the U.S. Forest Service to ban all dogs from Indian Peaks Wilderness in Colorado for two reasons: A significant

Background/
Emotional
appeal

minority of dog owners do not obey the rule to leash their dogs on wilderness trails; and some people just do not like dogs. . . .

Reason

Explanation/
Emotional
appeal

Banning dogs from Indian Peaks trails affects me and every other responsible American dog owner because these national paths through unsurpassed beauty belong to us. Even if you do not or cannot use your right to enjoy Indian Peaks with your dog at present, do you want this right taken away

Emotional
appeal

from you? Don't you want this right preserved for other dog owners? . . .

Statement of
opinion

Banning dogs from wilderness trails is a remedy far worse than the ailment. . . .

Reason

Evidence/
Facts

Numerical
data

Wilderness managers and users need to recognize that dogs greatly enhance the wilderness experience for humans. As burden bearers and companions, domestic dogs have been in Indian Peaks and other North American wilderness areas for some 10,000 years. Dogs share their senses with humans to point out things we otherwise would over-

Emotional appeal

look. Dogs are the best bridge between humans and the nonhuman aspects of nature and, thus, greatly broaden our viewpoint of the world. Hiking with dogs is fun.

Evidence/ Expert opinion

Call to action

Many famous writers about the wilderness, such as John Muir, Aldo Leopold and Bob Marshall, have testified to the value of dogs on the trail. Now you need to do the same. Please write to the Forest Service in Colorado.

Dog Fancy

EXERCISE 4 ▶ **Analyzing a Persuasive Editorial**

After you have read Kent Dannen's editorial, discuss it with some other students. How would you answer these questions?

1. How does the author grab your attention at the beginning of the editorial? Do you learn the author's opinion in the first paragraph? Explain.
2. What two reasons does Dannen give for opposing the ban on dogs on the trail? What specific evidence does he offer to support his second reason?
3. Kent Dannen's audience is readers of *Dog Fancy* magazine. Do you think his support fits this audience? Explain.
4. Dannen ends with a call to action. Does he persuade you to write to the Forest Service? Why?

A Simple Framework for a Persuasive Paper

The editorial on pages 271–273 shows you that persuasion doesn't have to be organized in a single way. But until you're a professional persuader (as an editor is), you'll find the following framework useful for your own writing.

A WRITER'S MODEL

Video Games Yes, Violence No

INTRODUCTION
Attention grabber

"Explosions so real you should warn the neighbors!" "Smash somebody's face in the comfort of your own home!" "The most violent karate game available!" Those are real quotes from the boxes of real video games. No wonder parents think video games are all violence and death-defying danger. Fortunately, they're wrong.

Statement of opinion

Plenty of exciting, nonviolent video games exist. Those are the ones worth playing.

Reason
Evidence/Facts

Violence in video games is just as wrong as violence anywhere else. It's true that on-screen guided missiles don't kill real people. And some studies have concluded that video games don't breed violence among kids. But even makers of video games have acknowledged that video-game violence can have harmful effects like frightening young children. For instance, in 1993, video-game companies began rating games for violence to warn consumers about violent content.

Data

Reason
Explanation
Evidence/Facts

With violent games, the violence is all there is. You don't have to use your brain, only your reflexes. You don't have to know anything except the game's basic rules. Despite all the explosions and phony danger and near-disasters, these games are boring to people who want mental challenge. Give me a quest or a mystery any day.

Emotional appeal

CONCLUSION
Statistics

Violence in video games affects many people. Half the households in the United States—and 80 percent of those with eight- to fourteen-year-old boys—have video games. Let's not spend any more money on death and destruction packaged as fun. The next time you play a video game, why not choose a brainteaser over brute force?

Restatement of opinion and call to action

Here is the writer's framework in visual form.

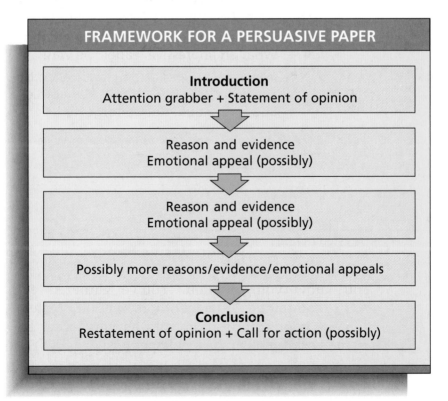

FRAMEWORK FOR A PERSUASIVE PAPER

Introduction
Attention grabber + Statement of opinion

Reason and evidence
Emotional appeal (possibly)

Reason and evidence
Emotional appeal (possibly)

Possibly more reasons/evidence/emotional appeals

Conclusion
Restatement of opinion + Call for action (possibly)

GRAMMAR HINT

Types of Sentences

Part of being persuasive is keeping your audience's attention. One way to do that is by writing interesting sentences—by using sentence variety. There are four basic types of sentences: *declarative, interrogative, imperative,* and *exclamatory.* For instance, to convince your readers that Mary McLeod Bethune should be studied in history class, you could use sentences like these.

EXAMPLES   ***Declarative* (makes a statement):** Mary McLeod Bethune was an early leader in the struggle for racial justice.

***Interrogative* (asks a question):** Have you ever heard of Mary McLeod Bethune?

***Exclamatory* (expresses strong emotion):** What an impressive leader she was!

***Imperative* (gives a command):** Sign the petition today if you think Mary McLeod Bethune should not be forgotten.

 REFERENCE NOTE: For more information about types of sentences, see pages 422–423.

WRITING ASSIGNMENT

PART 3:
Writing a Draft of Your Persuasive Paper

You know your opinion. You've gathered evidence. You're committed! Now let others know it. Write the first draft of your composition, and as you write, keep the **Framework for a Persuasive Paper** (see page 275) in mind.

Evaluating and Revising

You know what the word *incredible* means. In persuasive writing, you want to be the opposite of incredible. You want to be *credible*, or believable. Credibility is something you should evaluate carefully in your draft. One professional writer has made this point clear:

> Credibility is just as fragile for a writer as for a President. Don't inflate an incident to make it more outlandish than it actually was. If the reader catches you in just one bogus [phony] statement that you are trying to pass off as true, everything you write thereafter will be suspect. It's too great a risk, and not worth taking.
>
> William Zinsser, *On Writing Well*

That's good advice, and the chart on the following page gives you more. Answer the questions in the left-hand column. If you find a weakness, use the revision technique suggested in the right-hand column.

Peanuts reprinted by permission of United Feature Syndicate, Inc.

EVALUATING AND REVISING PERSUASIVE PAPERS

EVALUATION GUIDE	REVISION TECHNIQUE
1 Do the first one or two sentences grab the reader's attention?	**Add** a startling fact or **replace** the present sentences with an anecdote.
2 Is the writer's opinion stated clearly and quickly?	**Add** a sentence (or **replace** an existing sentence) to make your opinion clear.
3 Are there enough reasons and evidence to make the opinion convincing?	**Add** more reasons, facts, data, statistics, or expert opinions to the paper.
4 Are the emotional appeals effective?	**Cut** any statements that rely too much on the band-wagon approach, flattery, or nonexpert testimonials.
5 Is the conclusion strong?	**Add** a sentence that restates your opinion in strong words, or **add** a call to action.

When you evaluate and revise your persuasive paper, make sure you have

- clearly connected your ideas by using transitions
- arranged your ideas logically so your readers can follow your thinking
- used sentence variety to keep your readers' attention

E X E R C I S E 5 ▶   **Analyzing a Writer's Revisions**

Study the revisions of the paragraph from the composition on page 274. Then, answer the questions that follow.

With violent games, the violence is all
(∧only your reflexes⊙)
there is. You don't have to use your brain.   **add**

~~These are games for the stupid.~~ You don't,   **cut**
the game's basic rules⊙
have to know anything except ~~what the~~   **cut/replace**

~~game is about.~~ Despite all the explosions

and phony danger and near-disasters,
(to people who want mental challenge⊙)
these games are boring. Give me a quest,   **add/cut**

~~or a great battle,~~ or a mystery any day.   **cut**

1. Why did the writer add *only your reflexes* to the second sentence?
2. Why did the writer cut the third sentence?
3. Why is *the game's basic rules* better support than *what the game is about*?
4. Why would adding *to people who want mental challenge* help the writer convince the audience?
5. Why did the writer cut *or a great battle*?

COMPUTER NOTE: Use your word-processing program's Find command to help you look for overused words to replace.

WRITING ASSIGNMENT

PART 4:
Evaluating and Revising Your Persuasive Paper

Exchange papers with a classmate, and use the questions from the chart on page 278 to evaluate your classmate's paper. Then, make any changes you have decided are necessary.

Proofreading and Publishing

Proofreading.   When your purpose is to persuade, you want your paper to be convincing in every way. That means careful proofreading—getting rid of any errors you've made in spelling, capitalization, punctuation, and usage. Check to be sure you haven't overused exclamation marks. Strong feelings about a topic can lead to too many *!!!!!!!*'s.

Publishing.   Finally the time has come to reach out to your audience. They won't be persuaded if they don't know about your paper. Here are some possible ways to publish it.

- If you've written on a school issue or an issue of concern to teens, ask for permission to photocopy and hand out your paper before school.
- If you've written on a broader issue, send your paper to the local newspaper as a letter to the editor.
- If several members of your class have written on the same issue, have a debate. Each person can present his or her side, and your classmates can discuss both sides of the issue. Or, you can just have an "opinion forum," in which everyone has a chance to present his or her paper to the class.

PART 5:
Proofreading and Publishing Your Paper

You've worked hard on your paper. You don't want any errors to distract your readers. Take care now to proofread your paper and to correct any errors. Then publish or share your paper with others. You can use one of the ideas given above.

Reflecting on Your Writing

To add your paper to your **portfolio,** date it and use the following questions to write a reflection to accompany your paper.

- Did you use evidence such as statistics to support your opinion? What type of evidence might you add to make the paper more persuasive?
- Do your ideas seem to flow in a natural manner? Could you rearrange and reword your sentences to express your ideas more smoothly?
- What did you learn about your ability to persuade by writing this paper?

A STUDENT MODEL

LaKeesha Fields, a student at Nottingham Middle School in St. Louis, Missouri, takes a stand on a personal issue in her persuasive paper. As you read LaKeesha's persuasive paragraph, notice how naturally she presents her reasons for owning a pet.

Everyone Should Own a Pet
by LaKeesha Fields

Loneliness is a painful state of being. This is why people need the companionship of animals when there is no one else around. For example, you can talk to pets. Although they don't respond, it seems as if they always understand. You can snuggle up with your pet to watch TV. When you go for a walk, your pet can protect you from danger, and your pet can also be a friend when you're in need of one. Pets can be very helpful when you're home alone, because they can be very alert and sense things that you can't. Although pets can't talk or respond, they give unconditional love. They're an antidote for loneliness, because they can cure your desire for company.

WRITING WORKSHOP

A Campaign Speech

Politics is the art of persuasion. New laws need backers. Candidates need supporters. One key goal of a politician is to attract votes, and a good campaign speech can go a long way toward doing that.

Why not use what you've learned about persuasion to write a campaign speech for someone in your class? Read the following speech, and then answer the questions.

When next Friday's election is over, Latricia Gonzalez will be our new vice-president. Yes, Latricia will win the second-highest office in our student government at Montoya Middle School. She'll win because she clearly deserves to. She knows that the vice-presidency is more than just a title. It's a challenge she can meet.

The vice-president has a job to do. She has to step in when the president is absent. That happened four times last year. It's likely to happen again this year. In addition, the vice-president has a major responsibility for fund-raising for student projects.

Who could handle this job better than Latricia Gonzalez? No one. Period. That's because Latricia is a take-charge person--a born leader. Last year she co-chaired the program for Health Awareness Month. She has served as co-captain of the Glee Club and as president of the Girls Sports Club. And fund-raising is one of her specialties. Last year she helped raise nearly a thousand dollars for the all-club banquet.

Latricia Gonzalez is well qualified for the vice-presidency--as she's proved again and again. She's eager to serve, and she'll make things happen. Vote for Latricia Gonzalez on May 4. Latricia for Leadership!

Thinking It Over

1. Why does the writer begin by saying that Latricia is going to win?
2. What two specific duties of the vice-presidency does the writer name?
3. What reasons does the writer give for thinking Latricia will be a good vice-president?
4. What specific evidence does the writer give to support the reasons?
5. Are any of the writer's appeals emotional? Explain.

Writing a Campaign Speech

Prewriting. What elections go on at your school? Choose one (and if it's happening now that's even better), and write a campaign speech for someone you really believe would do a good job. Like the writer of the sample speech, you need to know the duties of the office. Then list all the reasons you can think of why someone would support your candidate. Also think about the voters (people at your school). Which of the reasons will they find most convincing? What do they care about? Choose the two or three reasons most likely to persuade the audience.

Writing, Evaluating, and Revising. Most people like speeches to be brief and to the point. Think of a way to grab the audience's attention and to hold it while you make your points. Short sentences are usually more forceful than long sentences.

When evaluating the speech, be sure to read it aloud. A speech is written to be spoken, so pay attention to rhythm and word choice. The speech should be clear, convincing, and lively. You may even want to invent a slogan like *Latricia for Leadership!*

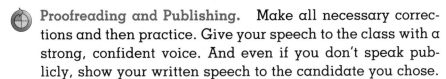

Proofreading and Publishing. Make all necessary corrections and then practice. Give your speech to the class with a strong, confident voice. And even if you don't speak publicly, show your written speech to the candidate you chose.

If you want to include your speech in your **portfolio,** date it and attach a note of reflection on your writing. Did you keep your audience of peers in mind when you were writing your speech? How might you change the speech to emphasize the concerns of people in your school? Which part of your speech do you think delivers the most impact?

MAKING CONNECTIONS

PERSUASION IN ACTION

Persuasive Letters

When you want to persuade someone, a letter can be the best way. Teachers write letters of recommendation, consumers write letters of complaint, and many people write persuasive letters to the editors of newspapers and magazines. Here's an example of a letter to the editor.

Dear Editor:

As one who has used a wheelchair all my life, I have seen the vast increases in educational opportunities for children and youth with disabilities since passage of the Individuals with Disabilities Education Act (IDEA). Contrary to alarmist views, in its twenty years IDEA has brought students with disabilities out of the scholastic Dark Ages. Before IDEA, most such students—including myself—were either excluded from public schools or received an inadequate education. Too many of us were ill-prepared for employment and had to depend on public funds. With IDEA, more students with disabilities are graduating from high school, entering college, getting jobs, and paying taxes.

The IDEA does not require that children with disabilities get a "better" or "fancier" education than others. It does guarantee they will receive the education they need to fulfill their potential. America can't afford to go back to pre-IDEA days when the contributions of those with disabilities were wasted through the lack of granting them an adequate education.

Judith E. Heumann
Washington, D.C.

Look through a magazine or newspaper that you read regularly. Starting with a topic or issue that interests you, find an article with which you strongly agree or disagree. Then, write a persuasive letter to the editor about it. Send or e-mail your letter to the magazine or newspaper. If it's published, bring the clipping to class.

WRITING ACROSS THE CURRICULUM

Presenting Solutions for Problems

Sometimes persuasion involves offering solutions to problems. For example, you think that you have a solution for the problem of tardiness to classes in your junior high school. You could write a letter or essay to persuade the school administration that your solution is a good one. When you need to persuade someone to accept your solution to a problem, you can follow these steps:

- **Identify and explain the problem.** For example, you might explain how many students are late to class in a typical day and how long it takes to get from a first-floor class to a second-floor class.
- **Explain the solution you are recommending.** For example, you could explain that adding ten minutes to the school day would allow the time students have between classes to be increased from three minutes to five minutes.
- **Show why your solution will work. Use reasons, facts, data, statistics, and examples.** For example, you could explain that 80 percent of teachers, parents, and students support this solution.

Now, think of a problem in your school or community. If you haven't already thought of a solution, brainstorm or research ideas. Then, write an essay or letter to persuade your audience to accept your solution to the problem.

SPEAKING AND LISTENING

Persuasion in Advertising

Television advertising shows you that words *and* images are tools of persuasion. Most ads use emotional appeals, but they may also refer to facts or statistics. Here are two examples:

- A narrator explains that a man with a stomach-ache who has used the wrong antacid could have gotten relief in "2.2 seconds."
- A pink, drum-beating, mechanical bunny wanders across the screen because its batteries keep on "going and going and going."

Can you use words and images to persuade someone to buy a product in *30 seconds*? First, watch some TV ads, making notes about visuals, words, and the audience you think the ads are meant for.

Then, work with a partner to make up an ad for a real or invented product. Write and sketch your ad idea in two columns: **Words** and **Images.** Be ready to present your ad to the class or—if you can—videotape it.

9 WRITING ABOUT LITERATURE: EXPOSITION

Reading and Responding

Do you like every book, every comic strip, every magazine article you **read?** Of course not. Nobody does. But, whether you like them or not, chances are you'll **respond.** Reading does that to us. It makes us laugh, fires us up, gives us gooseflesh, or makes us yawn.

Writing and You. Some writers make a living by telling us what they think about books, movies, plays, and TV shows. Their opinions have turned so-so movies into blockbusters. Their discoveries of little known authors have led to delightful hours of reading for the rest of us. Have you ever read a book that you liked so much you couldn't wait to tell a friend about it?

As You Read. Here's a response to Katherine Paterson's book *Lyddie.* As you read, think about the reviewer's opinion. Do you think she likes the book?

Roger de la Fresnaye, detail of *Emblems* (c. 1913). © The Phillips Collection, Washington, D.C.

A Review of Katherine Paterson's

LYDDIE

by Kathleen Odean

I n this superb novel, Paterson deftly depicts a Lowell, Massachusetts fabric mill in the 1840s and a factory girl whose life is changed by her experiences there. Readers first meet 13-year-old Lyddie Worthen staring down a bear on her family's debt-ridden farm in the Vermont mountains. With her fierce spirit, she stares down a series of metaphorical bears in her year as a servant girl at an inn and then in her months under grueling conditions as a factory worker. Lyddie is far from perfect, "close with her money and her friendships," but she is always trying. She suffers from loneliness, illness, and loss at too early an age, but she survives and grows. An encounter with a runaway slave brings out her generosity and starts her wondering about slavery and inequality. Try as she might to focus on making money to save the farm, Lyddie cannot ignore the issues around her, including the inequality of women. One of her roommates in the company boarding house awakens Lyddie to the wonder of books. This dignity brought by literacy is movingly conveyed as she improves her reading and then helps an Irish fellow worker learn to read. The importance of reading is just one of the threads in this tightly woven story in which each word serves a purpose and each figure of speech, drawn from the farm or the factory, adds to the picture. Paterson has brought a troubling time and place vividly to life, but she has also given readers great hope in the spirited person of Lyddie Worthen.

READER'S RESPONSE

1. Does *Lyddie* sound like a book you'd like to read? Explain why or why not.
2. If you've already read this book, tell why you think it's a good story.

WRITER'S CRAFT

3. What does the reviewer think of *Lyddie*? What sentences tell you her opinion?
4. What examples does the reviewer use to support her opinion? In other words, what evidence does she give for liking or disliking the book?

Purposes for Writing About Literature

A review discusses the strengths and weaknesses of a book or film or other creative work. Sometimes a review's purpose is just to inform the reader. At other times, the purpose is to persuade the reader that a work is or is not worth reading or seeing. Remember, though, that reviews are not the only way to write about literature. You can write about books and other creative works in many other ways, for a variety of purposes. Here are a few examples.

- in your journal, writing about a monster movie that kept you from sleeping
- in a letter, telling a friend about your favorite movie
- in a letter to television network executives, trying to persuade them not to cancel your favorite show
- in a book jacket blurb, describing the book in order to persuade people to read it
- in a message for a company bulletin board, telling your coworkers about a book you think they'd enjoy
- in a script, recording a dialogue between similar characters from stories by two different authors
- in an epilogue for a novel you've read, imagining what happens to the characters after the novel ends

LOOKING AHEAD

In this chapter, you will be writing an informative evaluation of a story. Keep in mind that an effective evaluation

- evaluates at least one element from the story
- gives quotations and details from the story to support the evaluation

Writing a Story Evaluation

 *Prewriting*

Starting with Personal Response

No one feels and thinks exactly the way you do about a piece of literature. You may laugh out loud when a character does something silly. At the same time, your friend may be annoyed because he thinks the character is dumb. You may find a scene so spooky you forget to breathe, but someone else may think it's boring. There is no right or wrong personal response to a story or poem. Each person responds differently. That's why anyone's response is called a *personal* response.

WAYS TO RESPOND PERSONALLY

- Write a journal entry about how a poem or story makes you feel. Is it scary like the one you tell around a campfire right before bedtime? Do you feel it says something about you and your life? Is it fun just because it leads you to imagine fantastic people, places, and situations?

- Imagine what happens to a character after a story or poem ends. What's going on in the character's life a year later? five years later?

- Pretend you're a character in the story or poem. As this character, write a letter to a friend. Tell about something that's important to the character.

Here's a story about a boy who is sick with the flu. Before the story begins, the boy has lived in France and gone to school there. As you read, start with your personal response. Can you understand the boy's feelings?

A SHORT STORY

A Day's Wait
by Ernest Hemingway

He came into the room to shut the windows while we were still in bed and I saw he looked ill. He was shivering, his face was white, and he walked slowly as though it ached to move.

"What's the matter, Schatz?"

"I've got a headache."

"You better go back to bed."

"No. I'm all right."

"You go to bed. I'll see you when I'm dressed."

But when I came downstairs he was dressed, sitting by the fire, looking a very sick and miserable boy of nine years. When I put my hand on his forehead I knew he had a fever.

"You go up to bed," I said, "you're sick."

"I'm all right," he said.

When the doctor came he took the boy's temperature.

"What is it?" I asked him.

"One hundred and two."

Downstairs, the doctor left three different medicines in different colored capsules with instructions for giving them. One was to bring down the fever, another a purgative, the third to overcome an acid condition. The germs of influenza can only exist in an acid condition, he explained. He seemed to know all about influenza and said there was nothing to worry about if the fever did not go above one hundred and four degrees. This was a light epi-

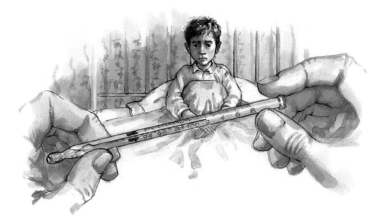

demic of flu and there was no danger if you avoided pneumonia.

Back in the room I wrote the boy's temperature down and made a note of the time to give the various capsules.

"Do you want me to read to you?"

"All right. If you want to," said the boy. His face was very white and there were dark areas under his eyes. He lay still in the bed and seemed very detached from what was going on.

I read aloud from Howard Pyle's *Book of Pirates;* but I could see he was not following what I was reading.

"How do you feel, Schatz?" I asked him.

"Just the same, so far," he said.

I sat at the foot of the bed and read to myself while I waited for it to be time to give another capsule. It would have been natural for him to go to sleep, but when I looked up he was looking at the foot of the bed, looking very strangely.

"Why don't you try to go to sleep? I'll wake you up for the medicine."

"I'd rather stay awake."

After a while he said to me, "You don't have to stay in here with me, Papa, if it bothers you."

"It doesn't bother me."

"No, I mean you don't have to stay if it's going to bother you."

I thought perhaps he was a little light-headed and after giving him the prescribed capsules at eleven o'clock I went out for a while.

It was a bright, cold day, the ground covered with a sleet that had frozen so that it seemed as if all the bare trees, the bushes, the cut brush and all the grass and the bare ground had been varnished with ice. I took the young Irish setter for a little walk up the road and along a frozen creek, but it was difficult to stand or walk on the glassy surface and the red dog slipped and slithered and I fell twice, hard, once dropping my gun and having it slide away over the ice.

We flushed a covey of quail under a high clay bank with overhanging brush and I killed two as they went out of sight over the top of the bank. Some of the covey lit in trees, but most of them scattered into brush piles and it was necessary to jump on the ice-coated mounds of brush several times before they would flush. Coming out while you were poised unsteadily on the icy, springy brush they made difficult shooting and I killed two, missed five, and started back pleased to have found a covey close to the house and happy there were so many left to find on another day.

At the house they said the boy had refused to let any one come into the room.

"You can't come in," he said. "You mustn't get what I have."

I went up to him and found him in exactly the position I had left him, white-faced, but with the tops of his cheeks flushed by the fever, staring still, as he had stared, at the foot of the bed.

I took his temperature.

"What is it?"

"Something like a hundred," I said. It was one hundred and two and four tenths.

"It was a hundred and two," he said.

"Who said so?"

"The doctor."

"Your temperature is all right," I said. "It's nothing to worry about."

"I don't worry," he said, "but I can't keep from thinking."

"Don't think," I said. "Just take it easy."

"I'm taking it easy," he said and looked straight ahead. He was evidently holding tight onto himself about something.

"Take this with water."

"Do you think it will do any good?"

"Of course it will."

I sat down and opened the *Pirate* book and commenced to read, but I could see he was not following, so I stopped.

"About what time do you think I'm going to die?" he asked.

"What?"

"About how long will it be before I die?"

"You aren't going to die. What's the matter with you?"

"Oh, yes, I am. I heard him say a hundred and two."

"People don't die with a fever of one hundred and two. That's a silly way to talk."

"I know they do. At school in France the boys told me you can't live with forty-four degrees. I've got a hundred and two."

He had been waiting to die all day, ever since nine o'clock in the morning.

"You poor Schatz," I said. "Poor old Schatz. It's like miles and kilometers. You aren't going to die. That's a different thermometer. On that thermometer thirty-seven is normal. On this kind it's ninety-eight."

"Are you sure?"

"Absolutely," I said. "It's like miles and kilometers. You know, like how many kilometers we make when we do seventy miles in the car?"

"Oh," he said.

But his gaze at the foot of the bed relaxed slowly. The hold over himself relaxed too, finally, and the next day it was very slack and he cried very easily at little things that were of no importance.

E X E R C I S E 1 ▶ **Responding to a Story**

What was your personal response to the story? Were you surprised at the end? Did you know that Schatz thought he was going to die? Do you think you would act the same way Schatz did? Choose one of the personal response ideas on page 293. Write your thoughts in your journal or share them with a classmate.

E X E R C I S E 2 ▶ **Speaking and Listening: Acting Out a Story**

Think about what Schatz might do a week after this story ends. Get together with a classmate or two and write a scene that might happen one week later. Here are some suggestions for writing your scene.

1. Decide where Schatz will be and who will be with him.
2. Decide what actions will take place. Will Schatz still think he's going to die? Will he be proud of his experience or embarrassed by it? Will he want to play all the time or just sit and think?
3. Write down what Schatz and any other characters will say.

After you've written your scene, act it out for the rest of your class.

WRITING ASSIGNMENT

PART 1:
Choosing a Story for Response

Find a story in your literature book or ask your teacher or media center specialist for a suggestion. Read the story for fun and then write your personal response to it in your journal. In addition to writing about your feelings, try writing a new ending for the story. How else might it have turned out?

Prewriting

Looking at a Story More Closely

When you read for fun, your personal response is all that really counts. But sometimes you'll need to read more seriously. You may have to give an oral report or write a paper for your English class. Then you will have to have some knowledge about the general characteristics, or elements, of literature.

The following chart explains the main elements, or features, of stories.

ELEMENTS OF STORIES
CHARACTERS: *Characters* are the individuals in the story. They may be people, animals, or even things. For example, in a folk tale the characters may be animals. In a science fiction fantasy, they may be robots.
SETTING: The *setting* is where and when a story takes place. It may be the sidewalks and streets of Harlem, or it may be the muddy waters of a creek in the South. It may even be an imaginary city in a distant galaxy.

(continued)

ELEMENTS OF STORIES *(continued)*

PLOT: *Plot* is what happens in the story. It's a chain of events. One thing causes another thing to happen, and so on. A plot is centered around a *conflict* that must be resolved (solved or ended) by the end of the story.

THEME: *Theme* is the meaning of the story. Some stories are meant purely to entertain. The writer is not trying to make a point about life or human nature. In other stories, however, the actions and the way they turn out have some meaning or messages for the reader.

E X E R C I S E **3** ▶ **Thinking About Story Elements**

Review the story "A Day's Wait." This time, think about the elements of stories. Then, use your knowledge about stories to answer these questions.

1. Who is the main character?
2. Where does the story take place?
3. What is the basic plot of the story? How does one event lead to another?
4. What is the conflict in this story? How is the conflict resolved at the end of the story?
5. Does this story have a theme or message? If so, how would you state it in your own words?

WRITING
ASSIGNMENT

PART 2:
Looking at a Story Closely

Now that you've given yourself a chance to respond personally to your story, take a closer look. Try to see how it works and what makes it work that way. Use the questions in Exercise 3 as a guide for your thinking. Write down your answers to the questions and save them to use later.

Planning a Story Evaluation

Movie critics evaluate movies. Experts on video games evaluate new games. (Perhaps you've read evaluations of movies and video games in magazines or seen them on television.) And people who know literature evaluate stories, poems, and novels. When you evaluate literature, you start with two things: your personal response and your understanding of the elements of literature. Then you plan your evaluation.

Evaluating a Story

You evaluate things all the time. When you evaluate, you judge something against a set of standards. Standards are the characteristics that a good story or movie or video game will have. For example, all video games have graphics, but not all graphics are alike. They may be terrific, terrible, or somewhere in between. Here are some standards that are often used to make judgments about stories. Notice that they're based on the elements you reviewed on pages 300–301.

CHARACTERISTICS OF A GOOD STORY
1. The **characters** are believable. Even when the characters are animals or fantasy creatures, they seem natural and real.
2. The **setting** seems realistic. It helps the story along and doesn't get in the way.
3. The chain of events (**plot**) seems natural and possible but includes some surprises.
4. The story presents a **theme** or message that many readers care about.

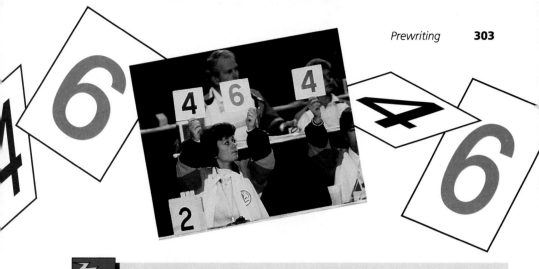

CRITICAL THINKING
Drawing Conclusions

You know what the conclusion to a story or movie is. It's the ending. But a *conclusion* can also be a way of thinking. After you evaluate something, you have to make a judgment about the meaning of your evaluation. That's called *drawing a conclusion.*

You draw conclusions from your evaluations all the time. You look at a pair of jeans you might buy and ask questions about them. Are they in style? Are they made well? Do they cost too much? After you've finished the evaluation, you draw a conclusion. *I shouldn't buy these jeans because they aren't made well and they're too expensive.*

You evaluate and draw conclusions about a story the same way. You look at the elements and decide whether they're working well. Then you draw a conclusion— whether or not it's a good story. Usually your conclusion will determine whether you recommend the story to anyone else.

Here are some questions that will help you evaluate stories. (You'll see that these questions are related to the characteristics of a good story, page 302). Your answers will enable you to draw your own conclusion.

- Are the characters believable? Does what they say and do seem natural and real?

- Does the setting seem realistic? Is it important to the plot and the conflict?
- Does the plot seem possible? Does it include at least one surprise?
- Does the story have meaning for you? Will you remember anything about it a few weeks or months from now?

If you answer *yes* to all the questions, your conclusion is that the story is good—one you'd recommend. If you answer *no*, you wouldn't recommend it. If your answers are mixed, you may be able to recommend just parts of it.

CRITICAL THINKING EXERCISE:
Drawing a Conclusion About a Story

Look at "A Day's Wait" again and use the questions above and on page 303 to evaluate it. Then, draw a conclusion about the story. Now, get together with some classmates and compare your conclusions. Would you recommend this story? Why?

WRITING NOTE   The conclusion you draw about a story may be based on one or more of the elements. For example, here's a sample conclusion about one story element.

> In the story "____," the main character's words, thoughts, and actions make her seem like a real person facing real problems.

Here's an example of a conclusion about all four of the elements you've studied.

> In the story "____," the elements of character, setting, plot, and theme work together to create a lively and meaningful story.

Of course, your conclusion doesn't have to be positive. Here's one for a story that's not very good.

> In the story "_____ ," the plot is a series of dull actions that have no suspense or meaning.

WRITING ASSIGNMENT

PART 3:
Evaluating and Drawing a Conclusion

Now you're ready to evaluate the story you're going to write about. Evaluate it by writing down the answers to the questions listed under Critical Thinking (pages 303–304). What conclusion can you draw from your answers? Write a sentence or two stating your conclusion. Here's an example conclusion about "A Day's Wait": *"A Day's Wait" is a good story because the plot is believable yet surprising, and the characters seem like real people.*

Finding Support for Your Conclusion

You could just tell your readers your conclusion and stop there. But they might not accept it. They might say, "I'm not going to read this story unless you show me that the plot is surprising." You need to give your readers some evidence to prove your conclusion is true.

The place to find evidence is in the story itself. You need to read the story again. This time look for details that will prove your conclusion is right.

The kinds of details you can use are description, actions, and dialogue. Here are some examples of these kinds of details from "A Day's Wait."

Description:	"His face was very white and there were dark areas under his eyes."
Actions:	"At the house they said the boy had refused to let any one come into the room."
Dialogue:	"'You don't have to stay in here with me, Papa, if it bothers you.'"

Here's the way one writer took notes on details to support her conclusion about the story.

> <u>Characters</u>
>
>   *p. 295* "His face was very white and there were dark areas under his eyes." Schatz acts and looks like he's really sick.
>
>   *p. 295* Schatz tells his dad, "You don't have to stay in here with me...." Shows he doesn't want to worry his dad.
>
>   *p. 297* Schatz won't let anyone come in his room. Shows he's frightened and worried.

WRITING ASSIGNMENT

PART 4:
Gathering Support for Your Conclusion

Read your story again. Look for descriptions, actions, or dialogue to support the conclusion you wrote in Writing Assignment, Part 3 (page 305). Keep reading until you find at least three pieces of evidence.

To plan a story evaluation

- look closely at the story
- judge the elements of the story against the characteristics of a good story
- draw a conclusion about one or more elements of the story
- find details in the story to support your conclusion

Writing Your First Draft

You've done quite a bit. You've evaluated a story, drawn a conclusion about it, and found evidence to support your ideas. Now it's time to create a written evaluation.

The Basic Parts of a Story Evaluation

An evaluation paper is one kind of composition. It has three basic parts.

The Introduction. The introduction is usually one paragraph and it contains three things:

- **The Author and Title of the Story**—Your readers need to know what you're writing about.
- **A Brief Summary of the Story**—You just need a tiny bit of information to help the reader understand what you'll say later.
- **The Main Idea**—You already have your paper's main idea: It's the conclusion you drew when you evaluated your story.

The Body. This is where you put the evidence you've gathered to support your conclusion, or main idea. You might have one or two paragraphs on each story element you're evaluating. For example, you might have one paragraph about character and another about theme.

The Ending. The last part of your paper has to bring things to a close. All you have to do is restate your main idea in slightly different words. For more information on composition form, look at Chapter 3.

A Writer's Model for You

Here's a model paper based on the writer's conclusion about the plot and characters of "A Day's Wait." The writer could have drawn a conclusion about the story's theme and written a different paper.

A WRITER'S MODEL

Evaluation of "A Day's Wait"

Information about story, author, title, main idea

In Ernest Hemingway's "A Day's Wait," a young boy is convinced that he's going to die. He has confused American and French thermometers and thinks his temperature is extremely high. This is a good story because the plot is believable and the characters seem like real people.

Evaluation of plot

Details from story

Quotations from story

One reason the plot works so well is that Schatz's conflict could have really happened. Schatz has heard the doctor say he has a temperature of one hundred two degrees, but he didn't hear the doctor explain "there was no danger." Also, in France, Schatz had heard " 'you can't live with forty-four degrees.' " It seems natural that he would worry about dying from a fever of one hundred two degrees. Also, the conflict is solved in a believable way. " 'About how long will it be before I die?' " Schatz asks. Then the father realizes what has been bothering Schatz and explains the difference between the thermometers. That solves Schatz's problem.

Quotation from story

Details from story

Evaluation of character

Quotation from story

Details from story

Hemingway makes Schatz and the father seem like real people. The reader can really "see" that Schatz is sick. "He was shivering, his face was white, and he walked slowly as though it ached to move." Schatz also has a headache and a fever. The father acts real. He puts his hand on Schatz's forehead to see if he has a fever and gives him his medicine. At the end, he realizes what's been bothering Schatz and feels sorry about it. He says, " 'You poor Schatz.' " Then, without making Schatz feel dumb, he explains about the thermometers.

Quotation from story

Restatement of main idea

The realistic characters and plot of "A Day's Wait" work well together. They make this story both memorable and enjoyable.

A Basic Framework for a Story Evaluation

It may be helpful for you to follow a framework when you're writing an evaluation. Here's the framework for the model evaluation of "A Day's Wait."

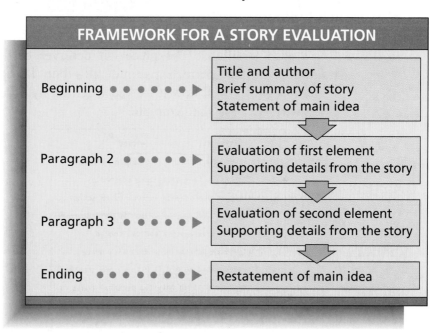

FRAMEWORK FOR A STORY EVALUATION

Beginning ➤ Title and author
Brief summary of story
Statement of main idea

Paragraph 2 ➤ Evaluation of first element
Supporting details from the story

Paragraph 3 ➤ Evaluation of second element
Supporting details from the story

Ending ➤ Restatement of main idea

WRITING ASSIGNMENT

PART 5:
Writing a Draft of Your Story Evaluation

Now it's time for you to try to pull it all together. Write your first draft of your story evaluation. You might follow the framework above. Don't worry about making this draft perfect. You'll get another chance to make it better.

Evaluating and Revising

Stephen King has become one of our most popular writers. One of his first experiences as a writer happened when he was a sports writer for a small-town newspaper. King says that John Gould, an editor who worked on his first piece, taught him all he ever needed to know.

I wish I still had the piece—it deserves to be framed, editorial corrections and all—but I can remember pretty well how it looked when he had finished with it. Here's an example:

> Last night, in the ~~well-loved~~ gymnasium ~~of~~ [Lisbon High School], partisans and Jay Hills fans alike were stunned by an athletic performance unequalled in school history: Bob Ransom, ~~known as "Bullet" Bob~~ ~~for both his size and accuracy,~~ scored thirty-seven points. He did it with grace and speed...and he did it with an odd courtesy as well, committing only two personal fouls in his ~~knight-like~~ quest for a record which *as basketball team* has eluded Lisbon ~~thinclads~~ since 1953...

When Gould finished marking up my copy in the manner I have indicated above, he looked up and must have seen something on my face. I think *he* must have thought it was horror, but it was not: it was revelation.

"I only took out the bad parts, you know," he said. "Most of it's pretty good."

"I know," I said, meaning both things: yes, most of

it was good, and yes, he had only taken out the bad parts. "I won't do it again."

"If that's true," he said, "you'll never have to work again. You can do *this* for a living."

> Stephen King, "Everything You Need to Know About Writing Successfully in Ten Minutes"

Like Stephen King, it's time to take out the bad parts of your paper and leave the good. To begin, ask yourself the questions in the left-hand column of the chart below. Then use the revision ideas suggested in the right-hand column to correct any problems.

EVALUATING AND REVISING STORY EVALUATIONS

EVALUATION GUIDE	REVISION TECHNIQUE
1 Does the beginning give the author and title of the story and summarize the plot?	**Add** the author and title of the story. **Add** a sentence or two summarizing the story.
2 Does the beginning state the main idea of the paper?	**Add** a sentence or two stating your main idea (the conclusion you drew from your evaluation of the story).
3 Does the writer support the main idea with evidence from the story?	**Add** information from the story to show why you drew your conclusion. Use descriptive details, action details, and dialogue to prove your main idea.
4 Does the ending bring the paper to a close without leaving the reader hanging?	**Add** a sentence or sentences (or **replace** one you have) that restate your main idea in different words.

| E X E R C I S E   **4** ▶ | **Analyzing a Writer's Revisions** |

Here's the rough draft of the first two paragraphs from the evaluation of "A Day's Wait" (page 308). Work with one or two classmates to try to figure out why the writer made the changes shown here. Then, answer the questions that follow. The evaluating and revising chart on page 311 may help you decide.

In Ernest Hemingway's "A Day's Wait,"

~~A~~ young boy is convinced that he's   **add**

going to die. He has confused American

and French thermometers and thinks his

temperature is extremely high. This is a

good story because the plot is believable

and the characters seem like real people.

One reason the plot works so well is

that Schatz's conflict could have really

happened. Schatz has heard the doctor

say he has a temperature of one hundred

two degrees, but he didn't hear the doctor

("there was no danger.")

explain ~~it~~. Also, in France, Schatz had   **replace**

heard " 'you can't live with forty-four

degrees.' " It seems natural that he would

worry about dying from a fever of one

hundred two degrees. Also, the conflict is

solved in a believable way. " 'About how

long will it be before I die?' " Schatz asks.

Then the father realizes what has been

(and explains the difference between the thermometers.)

bothering Schatz ∧ That solves Shatz's   **add**

problem. ~~Then the father goes out~~   **cut**

~~hunting.~~

1. In the first sentence, why did the writer add the words *In Ernest Hemingway's "A Day's Wait"*?
2. In the fifth sentence, why did the writer replace *it* with *"there was no danger"*?
3. Why did the writer add *and explains the difference between the thermometers* to the next-to-last sentence?
4. Why did the writer cut the last sentence? [Hint: Does this line give evidence to support the writer's main idea? Is it true to the story?]

Calvin & Hobbes copyright 1987 Watterson. Distributed by Universal Press Syndicate. Reprinted with permission. All rights reserved.

WRITING ASSIGNMENT

PART 6:
Evaluating and Revising Your Story Evaluation

You've seen one writer's evaluation and revision. Now, exchange papers with a classmate and use the questions from the evaluating and revising chart on page 311 to evaluate each other's papers. (See the Peer-Evaluation Guidelines on page 44 for help.) Be ready to suggest ways of fixing any problems you find. Then, use your partner's comments and your own evaluation to revise your paper.

Proofreading and Publishing

Proofreading.   You're ready to share your evaluation with the world. Proofread it carefully for errors in spelling, grammar, punctuation, or capitalization.

 COMPUTER NOTE: Your word-processing program may allow you to add character names from the story to a user dictionary so the names won't be flagged as errors during a spelling check.

MECHANICS HINT

Using Quotation Marks

Be sure to put double quotation marks around any words taken directly from the story. If the words you quote include dialogue, enclose the dialogue in a set of single quotation marks within the existing double quotation marks.

EXAMPLES   *Words from Story.* **"He was shivering, his face was white, and he walked slowly as though it ached to move."**

Dialogue from Story. **" 'You go up to bed,'** I said, **'you're sick.' "**

 REFERENCE NOTE: For more information about using quotation marks, see pages 772–777.

Publishing.   Plan a way to share your story evaluation with your classmates. Here is one idea.

■ Get together with your classmates and gather your evaluations into booklets, organized by story titles. File the booklets in your classroom or library.

PART 7:
Proofreading and Publishing Your Story Evaluation

You've just about completed your assignment. Now, proofread your final draft carefully, make changes to improve it, and then share it with others.

 ## Reflecting on Your Writing

If you plan to add your evaluation to your **portfolio,** date it and attach your answers to the following questions.

- What kinds of changes did you make during the revision stage? Why did you make the changes?
- Was it harder to express your main idea or to find story details to support it? Why?

A STUDENT MODEL

Nicci Ferrari, a student at Andrew Jackson Junior High School in Cross Lanes, West Virginia, offers some good ideas for writing about literature. She says, "I would take my time reading the story. I would make sure I understood the story first before I wrote anything."

"Up the Slide"
by Nicci Ferrari

Jack London's short story "Up the Slide" is an exciting and mysterious story about a young man named Clay who has to climb an almost impossible snow-covered slope. Clay and Swanson, his traveling partner, are headed down the Yukon Territory to get the mail. While Swanson is cooking dinner, Clay goes after firewood. What he thinks is going to be a half hour trip turns out to be much more than that. Clay finds just the wood he wants, but it is up high on a snow-covered slide. He studies the cliff and decides on the correct way to reach the tree. He climbs up and slides many times, but he does manage to get to the tree and cut it down. When Clay is ready to leave, he realizes he cannot make it down the same way. It is too steep and his shoes are so slick that he cannot depend on them to dig in the snow. He decides on another route down the slide. When he starts out, he falls, slides, and even rolls many times before he reaches the bottom. At times the reader isn't sure he will make it down alive. When he is down, he is a long way from where he left the sled dogs, but he takes the river trail back. Here he also finds Swanson, who has a fire going, waiting for him to come down. Even though Swanson laughs at Clay, they have firewood to sell a week later. The excitement and mystery in "Up the Slide" is not knowing if Clay will actually make it down the slope.

WRITING WORKSHOP

Comparing and Contrasting Stories

Just as you've evaluated one story, you can evaluate two stories. Then you have a basis to compare or contrast them. When you *compare*, you show how things are alike. When you *contrast*, you show how they are different. Usually you compare or contrast only one element in the stories. For example, you might compare the characters or the setting, but probably not both.

Depending upon what you find when you evaluate, you may compare the two stories, contrast them, or both compare and contrast. Here's a paper that compares and contrasts the way the main characters from two different stories deal with a similar conflict—a poisonous snake. Notice that the writer begins by naming the author and title of each story and by stating the main idea. As you read, look for reasons and evidence the writer uses to support the likenesses and differences.

Roald Dahl's story "Poison" and Mona Gardner's story "The Dinner Party" both take place in India, where the main characters have to deal with the same conflict—the threat of a poisonous snake. The way they deal with this conflict is very different. In "Poison," a man named Harry Pope thinks that a deadly poisonous snake is in his bed. Harry's terror makes him sweat horribly. He depends on his friend Timber to save him. But, because of his fear, Harry treats Timber rudely, saying things like " 'Don't be a fool' " and " 'Why don't you shut up then?' " At the end, the characters discover there actually wasn't a snake in the bed after all. In "The Dinner Party," a cobra is crawling across the foot of Mrs. Wynnes, the hostess of a dinner party. Only one other guest at the dinner table realizes a snake is present. The other guests remain unaware.

Unlike Harry, Mrs. Wynnes does not sweat and snap at her friends. Instead she stares "straight ahead, her muscles contracting slightly." Calmly, and in perfect control, she instructs a servant to put a bowl of milk, bait for the snake, on the veranda. Her reaction is brave and unexpected, because earlier in the story, the colonel says that a woman's " 'unfailing reaction in any crisis is to scream.' "

Thinking It Over

1. Where does the writer state the main idea of the paper? What is it?
2. What does the paper compare? What details does the writer give from each story to support this comparison?
3. What does the paper contrast? What details does the writer give to show these differences?
4. This paper doesn't have an ending, or conclusion. Try writing a one- or two-sentence ending. Share it with two or three of your classmates and decide which one is best.

Writing a Paragraph About Two Stories

Prewriting. Find a story that has something in common with the story you evaluated in this chapter. Perhaps the characters face similar struggles (like the stories compared above), or perhaps both stories have settings that create suspense. Look for key elements that the stories share. Next, jot down differences. Use a Venn diagram like the one below to record your notes. Notice how the similarities fall in the area where the ovals overlap.

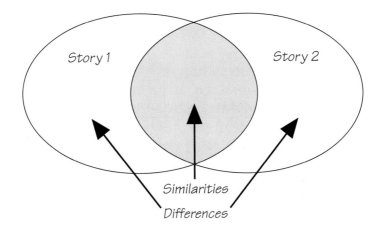

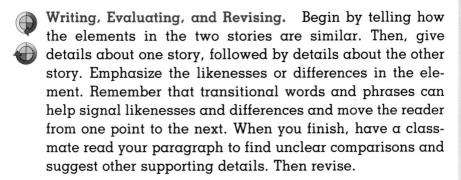

Writing, Evaluating, and Revising. Begin by telling how the elements in the two stories are similar. Then, give details about one story, followed by details about the other story. Emphasize the likenesses or differences in the element. Remember that transitional words and phrases can help signal likenesses and differences and move the reader from one point to the next. When you finish, have a classmate read your paragraph to find unclear comparisons and suggest other supporting details. Then revise.

Proofreading and Publishing. Proofread to find mistakes in spelling, grammar, and punctuation. Then, share your paragraph with classmates. Get together with students who are familiar with both stories to discuss similarities and differences you may have missed.

You may decide to include this paper in your **portfolio.** If you do, date the paper and write a brief reflection that responds to these questions: Which was more interesting—comparing and contrasting two stories, or evaluating one story at a time? Why? Which took more time? Why?

MAKING CONNECTIONS

Responding to Poetry

Here is a poem that asks two questions. The questions may be addressed to an actual person named Robert, to all of the poem's readers, or to both. Read the poem, and then think about your own personal response.

Robert, Who Is Often a Stranger to Himself
by Gwendolyn Brooks

Do you ever look in the looking-glass
And see a stranger there?
A child you know and do not know,
Wearing what you wear?

What do you think of this poem? Did you like it? Have you ever looked in the mirror and been surprised at what you saw? Here are some ways you can respond to this poem. Try one of them.

- Write a journal entry describing what you see when you look at your reflection in a mirror.
- In a paragraph, explain how a person's self-image can sometimes differ from his or her outward appearance.
- Using the form of a poem, write a few questions that you would like to ask one of your friends, or someone you don't know very well. Give your poem a title that says something about the person to whom the questions are addressed.

A Character Analysis

When you evaluate story characters, like Schatz and his father or Harry Pope and Mrs. Wynnes, you look closely at the details that the writer uses to make the characters seem real. You study what the characters say, think, and do. You study the way the characters look and how other characters respond to them. But besides helping you to evaluate a character, these details also suggest the kind of person the character is.

You can use the same kind of information to analyze the character or personality of a real person. For example, here's a character analysis of Joseph, chief of the Nez Perce.

Chief Joseph of the Nez Perce was an outstanding leader of his people. He was a brave, fierce warrior when he had to be, but also gentle and kind and loved by his people. He cared deeply for their individual welfare, showing concern when one of his people was sick. Each morning, he rode through the camp shouting a speech, giving thanks that the men, women, and children were alive and well. He tried all peaceful means to gain justice for his people before having to fight the soldiers. When he did fight the U.S. cavalry, he surrendered for the good of his people with the famous words, "I will fight no more forever."

Choose a character to analyze. It may be a character from a novel or a story. It may be a movie character or a character from a favorite television program. Or it may be a real person—a friend, a relative, or even yourself.

Jot down notes about how the person looks, talks, and acts. Do any of these things give you a clue about the kind of person this is? Write a character analysis of the person. Begin with a statement that gives the overall qualities of the person and then list details and examples to support your statement. The notes you jotted down should help you.

WRITING ACROSS THE CURRICULUM

Comparing and Contrasting Historical Figures

History tests often have essay questions that ask you to compare two historical figures. Here, for example, is a comparison of two famous African American women who fought against the practice of slavery.

> Sojourner Truth and Harriet Tubman were coura-geous African American women who devoted their lives to the fight against slavery during the 1800s. Both women were born as enslaved people; but their different back-grounds and distinct personalities led them to separate paths. Sojourner Truth was raised in New York and freed from slavery under a New York law. She had a deep, unshakable faith in God. Her quick wit and deep voice became famous as she preached against slavery through-out New England and the Midwest. Harriet Tubman was a bold, brave woman from Bucktown, Maryland. Her deter-mination and resourcefulness helped her escape slavery. She also became the most famous leader of the Under-ground Railroad, guiding many slaves to freedom.

Use the skills that you learned in the Writing Workshop on pages 317–319 to compare and contrast two people from history. First, select two people that you have studied who have something in common. Then, use what you know about their thoughts, actions, and words to compare and contrast them. (You may want to do some research first.) Here are some suggestions.

- General Robert E. Lee and General Ulysses S. Grant
- The writers Maya Angelou and Alice Walker
- The conductors Seiji Ozawa and Leonard Bernstein

10 WRITING A RESEARCH REPORT: EXPOSITION

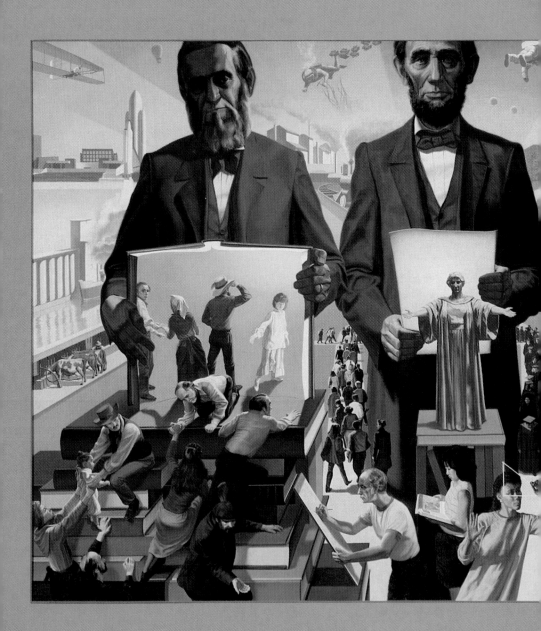

Exploring Your World

There are many ways to explore your world. You can travel by rickshaw in China or by camel in Saudi Arabia. You can explore the sea from a submarine, or view the earth from a spaceship. But you can also **explore your world** without ever leaving home.

Writing and You. Written reports help you explore the world through the writer's eyes. Employees share information with their co-workers in workplace reports. Historians let you visit the exciting people and events of yesterday. Magazine, newspaper, and TV writers explore the world of today. Can you think of other kinds of reports?

As You Read. Use your imagination as you read the following report about the rain forests of the equator. You can explore a world you've probably never seen.

Billy Morrow Jackson, *We the People: The Land-Grant College Heritage* (1986–1987). Krannert Museum of Art, University of Illinois, Champaign.

F   R   O   M

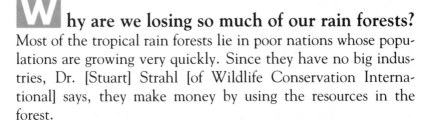

Why are we losing so much of our rain forests?
Most of the tropical rain forests lie in poor nations whose populations are growing very quickly. Since they have no big industries, Dr. [Stuart] Strahl [of Wildlife Conservation International] says, they make money by using the resources in the forest.

"It takes minutes for a chain saw to topple a seven-foot-wide tree, but it will take five centuries for another tree to grow to the same size," says Matthew Hatchwell. He works to help save the Earth's rain forests. The crashing timber destroys small trees lying in its path. Tractors flatten more forest when they drag the trunks to loading areas.

As roads are cut to get the logs to market, it opens up the area to a flood of people who burn parts of the jungle to make room for farms and ranches. The problem is that most of the nutrients are in the living trees—not in the topsoil. So if the forest is cut down and burned, there is a very thin layer of rich

L O S T

BY ELIZABETH VITTON

ash which can grow crops for a few years. But once the nutrients have been used up by the crops or been washed away by the warm rains, the land becomes almost worthless. "When the soil gives out," according to Hatchwell, "it forces farmers to clear more and more land."

RAIN FORESTS ARE THE "LUNGS" OF THE PLANET.

Destroying rain forests as far away as Brazil and Indonesia has serious consequences for all of us. For example, the world needs trees to recycle carbon dioxide (CO_2), an odorless gas. Rain forests are the "lungs" of the planet. They suck the CO_2 out of the atmosphere through their leaves. The trees then "breathe" oxygen back into the atmosphere and pump it with moisture that falls as rain.

But trees are about 50 percent carbon. If they are burned, the CO_2 trapped inside them is released. "It's a double whammy," explains Dr. Russell Mittermeier, a conservationist. "The burning itself releases huge amounts of CO_2. And it reduces the trees available to absorb the gas."

"WE NEED RAIN FORESTS TO HELP CONTROL OUR CLIMATE."

Carbon dioxide is a "greenhouse" gas. Like a greenhouse, carbon dioxide lets the sun's incoming rays through, but blocks reflected rays from leaving the atmosphere. It traps the sun's heat. But many scientists believe that too much carbon dioxide could cause the Earth to heat up. The "greenhouse effect" would do more than just cause the temperature to rise, says Dr. Strahl. "It would also affect winds, rainfall, sea levels and storms. We need rain forests to help control our climate."

READER'S RESPONSE

1. Do you think that destroying rain forests is a bad idea? If so, what do you think we should do about it?
2. What did you learn from this report? In your own words, summarize or explain an interesting statement or fact from the report to a small group of your classmates.

WRITER'S CRAFT

3. The purpose of a report may be to inform or persuade. What do you think the purpose of this report was? Why?
4. Reports should contain facts that are new to the audience. What facts in this report were new to you?
5. The writer tells us the sources of some of her information. What are they?

Ways to Develop a Report

Each year, publishers release hundreds of books reporting on everything from popular video games to new exercise trends. Monthly and weekly magazines offer reports on new products and current topics of interest. Newspapers and TV networks provide daily news. And reports of all kinds are posted continuously on the Internet.

What all these reports have in common is that they give information. But they may be developed in different ways. The report on the rain forest was developed mostly by description. Here are some other ways to develop a report.

- in a history report, explaining how the Iroquois League of American Indian nations was formed
- in a report on a museum exhibit, describing how Egyptian mummies were prepared
- in a report for hikers, describing the plants on Mount Washington
- in a report for a life science class, describing how a giant anaconda snake feeds
- in a report on the need for recycling, classifying the types of garbage that make up a typical landfill
- in a workplace report, estimating how long it will take to complete a project, and explaining possible delays

LOOKING AHEAD

In the main assignment for this chapter, you'll choose a subject, gather information on it from several sources, and then write a short report. Your report should

- draw on information from a variety of sources
- present the information in an interesting way
- list all of the sources you used

Writing a Report

 *Prewriting*

Choosing and Narrowing a Subject

How do hurricanes form? Do electric eels really give off shocks? Is it true cats were treated like royalty in ancient Egypt? Writing a report gives you a chance to find the answers to interesting questions.

Choosing Your Subject

What do you wonder about? What's important to you? Do you like to climb rocks or collect them? Do you play a musical instrument or a sport? What have you read or seen lately that you'd like to know more about? Answering these questions can help you decide on a subject for a report.

Here are some broad subjects. Think of some others that interest you.

snakes	Cuba	space labs
hairstyles	animals	holiday customs
robots	games	lasers

Narrowing Your Subject

You can find information on these subjects in books and articles, on videotapes, and on the World Wide Web. In fact, you'll find far too much information for a short report. But each broad subject contains many smaller *topics*, or parts, that are suitable for short reports. So you can narrow your subject by focusing on just one part of it. You may need to narrow your subject more than once, depending on the length of your report and how much information is available. Here's how the subjects you've just read about can be narrowed.

rattlesnakes
men's hairstyles
  of the past sixty
  years
robots for the home

Havana
greyhounds
the origins
  of lacrosse

space labs in
  the year 2000
Cinco de Mayo
lasers for dentistry

Remember that each subject contains many topics. For example, here's a map of the subject "holidays."

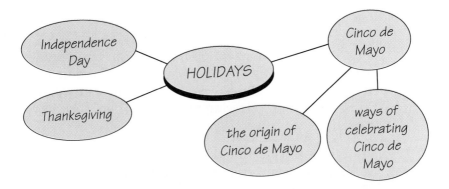

Before deciding on your topic, ask yourself these questions:

1. Can I find enough facts about this topic? Where?
2. Is my topic too broad for a short report? (Or, if the topic is too narrow, you won't be able to find enough information.)
3. Do I have time to get the information I need? (If you have to send away for information, how long will it take to get it?)
4. How can I make the topic interesting?

PART 1:
Choosing a Topic for Your Report

What would you like to know about? Think of a subject that interests you. Then, narrow it to a topic for your report. Before making a final decision, review the questions on page 331.

A well-written report can't be done in just a day or two. Think about the time you have, and make out a schedule that will give you time to do the following six things. Then, stick to your schedule.

1. Find information about your topic.
2. Take notes about the information.
3. Organize your information.
4. Write a first draft.
5. Evaluate and revise your first draft.
6. Proofread and publish your report.

Shoe reprinted by permission: Tribune Media Services.

 *Prewriting*

Planning Your Report

Have you ever gone camping or helped to give a party for someone? You probably planned ahead so that you'd have everything you needed. Planning ahead for your report will help you have what you need for it, too.

Thinking About Audience and Purpose

Why are you writing a report? The main *purpose* of a report is to give information. The information consists mostly of facts and the opinions of experts.

Who is your audience? Probably your first *audience* will be your teacher and classmates, but reports might be for different audiences. (On pages 33–35, you'll find suggestions for other audiences.) Always ask yourself these questions about your audience:

- What does my audience already know about my topic?
- What does my audience need to know?
- What new or unusual information will interest my audience? What will surprise them?

You don't want to bore your readers by telling them what they already know. But you don't want to confuse them by not telling enough, either. If you use a word they may not know, define it. If they need to know how or why about something, explain it.

EXERCISE 1 ▶ **Thinking About Audience and Purpose**

You're planning a report on killer whales to read to your class. Here are some sentences about whales. Which information would you use in your report? Why wouldn't you use the rest of the information?

1. Whales live in water.
2. Killer whales are the fastest members of the dolphin family and can swim for short distances at 25 knots.
3. A knot is a measure of speed, equal to 1.15 miles per hour.
4. A friend of mine saw a killer whale in a marine park.
5. Killer whales travel in groups, called pods.

Making an Early Plan

What do you want to know about your topic? What does your audience need to know? Before you begin your research, make an *early plan* for your report by listing the main ideas that you want to cover. An **early plan,** sometimes called an *informal outline,* is a list of headings that will guide your research. Here is a writer's early plan for a report on men's hairstyles.

HERE'S HOW

Report topic: men's hairstyles of the past sixty years

when hairstyles have changed the most

what these hairstyles were like

people who influenced the hairstyles

what the hairstyles have meant

Asking Questions

The next step is to ask yourself questions that will help you find the information in your early plan. Like your early plan, the questions will help to guide your research and keep you focused on your topic.

You can start with the *5W-How?* questions: *Who? What? When? Where? Why? How?* These questions will often make you think of other questions you can ask. For the report on "men's hairstyles of the past sixty years," the writer began research with the following questions:

> *Who* has influenced hairstyles?
> *What* have been some of the most popular hairstyles?
> *What* have different hairstyles meant to men?
> *When* have hairstyles changed the most?
> *Where* do styles change first?
> *Why* do styles change?
> *How* are men wearing their hair now?

| WRITING ASSIGNMENT | PART 2: **Making an Early Plan and Asking Questions** |

What do you and your readers want to know about your topic? Write down the main points you want to cover in your report. This is your early plan. Then, make a list of *5W-How?* questions that will help you to find the information you need. Save your early plan and questions to guide your later research.

If you don't know much about your topic, you may want to do some general reading first. Then you can make your early plan. Encyclopedia articles or magazines or World Wide Web sources can give you a good overview of your topic. You might also talk to people who know about the topic.

Finding Sources

Use at least three sources of information for your report. Check the library for both print sources (encyclopedias, books, magazines, newspapers, booklets, pamphlets) and nonprint sources (videotapes, audiotapes, CD-ROMs).

Also, search the World Wide Web for pages or sites containing keywords associated with your topic, and check radio and TV guides for related programs. Depending on your topic, you might also ask for information at museums, bookstores, colleges, or government offices.

☞ REFERENCE NOTE: For help with finding information using online catalogs, online databases, and the Internet, see pages 882–886.

Interviewing. If you know of an expert on your topic, arrange to talk with him or her. The expert might be a teacher, a parent, a businessperson, or another student. For example, if your topic is the effect of the Beatles on later music, you might talk with a music teacher who knows about the group's history and influence.

☞ REFERENCE NOTE: For information on interviewing, see pages 873–874.

EXERCISE 2 ▶ **Speaking and Listening: Interviewing**

Practice interviewing with a classmate. Give each other a topic of interest: a favorite sport, hobby, movie, and so on. Then, write some *5W-How?* questions for gathering information when you interview your classmate about this interest. After the interview, organize your notes and prepare a two- or three-minute oral report. Tell the class about the person you interviewed.

CRITICAL THINKING

Evaluating Sources

When you evaluate, you make judgments about quality or value. When you're researching a topic, it's important to evaluate the sources of information. Not all your sources will be equally useful. Here are some questions that will help you evaluate, or judge, the usefulness of a source.

1. Is the source nonfiction? You're looking for facts, so don't use print or nonprint sources that are fiction, such as stories and novels.
2. Is the information current? Some topics, such as those about modern science, technology, and medicine, need the latest available information. However, if your topic is "the origin of hot-air balloons," your information doesn't need to be as up-to-date. You can find the publication date on the copyright page of a book or magazine.
3. Can you trust the information? Some sources can be trusted more than others. Usually, reference books, textbooks, books by experts, and respected magazines and newspapers are reliable. Papers and magazines that focus on scandals or bizarre events probably aren't. Evaluate TV programs, videotapes, and World Wide Web sources the same way. Use only those that actually present verifiable facts about your topic.

4. Is the information objective? Sometimes information is biased. That is, only one side of a topic is presented, and you don't get a realistic view.

CRITICAL THINKING EXERCISE:
Evaluating Sources

How good are you at evaluating sources? With a classmate or a small group, evaluate the sources for each topic in the left-hand column by choosing the best source in the right-hand column. Use the four evaluation questions on page 337 and above. Discuss why the sources in the right-hand column should or should not be used.

Topic

1. Harmful and helpful spiders

Sources

a. *Arachnophobia*, a movie about spiders that invade a town
b. An article about spiders in the latest edition of *The World Book Encyclopedia*
c. A book, written by a medical doctor in 1915, on the treatment of spider bites

2. Recent trends in video games

a. An article on video games in the latest issue of *Scientific American*
b. A TV interview with the inventor of a video game
c. An article in a newspaper on sale at the supermarket checkout stand about someone who was captured by a video game and taken to Mars

Listing Sources

Finding sources is like going on a treasure hunt. Start your search at the library or at one of the other places mentioned on page 336. To keep track of the sources you find, create *source cards*. Source cards are index cards, half-sheets of paper, or computer files. Use a separate card, sheet, or computer file for each source. Put a *source number* at the top right of each source card. If you have four sources, for example, number them 1, 2, 3, 4. Source cards save you time, and you'll use the information from them at the end of your report.

There are several ways to list sources. The following way is recommended by the Modern Language Association (MLA). You should use whatever form your teacher recommends. No matter what form you use, follow the capitalization, punctuation, and order of information exactly. (Notice that the author's last name is first, followed by a comma and his or her first name.)

MLA Guide for Listing Sources

1. **Books:** author, title, city, publisher, and year.
   Nunn, Joan. Fashion in Costume, 1200–1980.
   New York: Schocken, 1984.

2. **Magazines and Newspapers:** author (if any), title of article, name of magazine or newspaper, date, and page numbers.
   Katz, Jane. "The Haircut That Changed My Life."
   Redbook July 1996: 25.

3. **Encyclopedia Articles:** author (if any), title of article, name of encyclopedia, year and edition (ed.).
   Sassoon, Vidal. "Hairdressing." The World Book
   Encyclopedia. 1995 ed.

4. **Interviews:** expert's name, the words *Personal interview* or *Telephone interview,* and date.
   Mullens, Sean. Telephone interview. 19 June 1996.

(continued)

MLA Guide for Listing Sources *(continued)*

5. **Television or Radio Programs:** title, network, station call letters and city (if any), and date of broadcast.
   The Beatles Anthology. ABC. KVUE, Austin.
        19, 22, 23 Nov. 1995.

6. **Electronic Materials:** author (if any), title (include print publisher, date of print publication, and page numbers if material was originally in a print source), date of electronic posting or publication (if given, for online sources), title of CD-ROM or title of database (if any, for online sources), type of source (*CD-ROM* or *Online*), location of source (*Internet,* online service, or city, if given, for CD-ROMs), name of vendor or distributor (CD-ROMs), date of publication (CD-ROMs) or date of access, and Internet address (if any).
   "50 Years of Hairstyles." Ebony Magazine
        Nov. 1995: 222B. Middle Search. CD-ROM.
        EBSCO Publishing. May 1996.

1

Nunn, Joan. Fashion in Costume, 1200–1980.
     New York: Schocken, 1984.

2

HairNet Hot Line. 1997. Online. Internet.
     12 Dec. 1997. Available http://www
     .hairnet.com/hotline/hotline.html.

PART 3:
Finding and Listing Sources for Your Report

Where can you find the information you need? Start with a library, but check other places as well. Do you know of someone you can interview? Try to find at least one non-print source. Find three or four sources of information, and then create your source cards.

Taking Notes

You've found your information, but you can't use it all. How do you decide what to use? Let your early plan and questions about your topic guide you (see pages 334–335). Scan through your sources for information that relates to your headings and your questions. Don't be afraid to add new, interesting information you find, but add headings to your early plan that reflect these new ideas. These tips can help you take efficient notes:

- Use a separate 4″ × 6″ note card, sheet of paper, or computer file for each source and for each note.
- Use abbreviations and short phrases. You can also make lists of ideas. You don't need to write complete sentences.
- Put quotation marks around exact words from sources, and name your sources. *Plagiarism*—copying without using quotation marks or naming sources—is a type of cheating or lying, as bad as stealing answers for a test.
- Label the top of each card, sheet, or file with a key word or phrase that tells what it is about. These words and phrases can come from your early plan.
- Put the source number at the top, also.
- At the bottom of each card, sheet, or file, write the page number where you found the information.
- Take notes from each of your sources.

On the following page you'll find an example of a note taken from *Fashion in Costume, 1200–1980* by Joan Nunn.

1	source number
Who influenced	label
The new fashion—set by messy hair	note written
of hippies or neat, round Beatles	in your own
haircut with long bangs—caught on	words
1st in Brit., later Am.	
p. 220	page number

 REFERENCE NOTE: For more information on taking notes, see pages 917–918.

WRITING ASSIGNMENT

PART 4:

Taking Notes for Your Report

What interesting things have you found out about your topic? Using note cards, half-sheets of paper, or computer files, take notes from the sources you listed in Writing Assignment, Part 3 (page 341). You'll use your notes when you write your paper.

Organizing and Outlining Your Information

Now that you have most of your information, you need to organize it. You may make some changes as you write and revise, but the outline you make now will be a useful guide. Here are some steps you can take to organize your information.

1. Separate your note cards, sheets, or computer files into sets with the same or similar labels.
2. Think of a heading to identify each set. It will be similar to the labels on your cards, sheets, or files.
3. Decide on the order of your main headings—perhaps order of importance or chronological (time) order.

4. Sort the cards, sheets, or files in each set to make subheadings for your outline.
5. Create an outline from your main headings and subheadings.

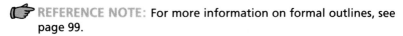

REFERENCE NOTE: For more information on formal outlines, see page 99.

Below is an example of a formal outline. After you've finished organizing your notes, you can create an outline like this and use it as a plan for writing your first draft.

Sixty Years of Haircuts

I. Changes in the forties and fifties
    A. Forties: crew cuts
    B. Fifties: ducktails
        1. Influence of Tony Curtis
        2. Influence of Elvis Presley
II. Changes in the sixties and seventies
    A. Sixties: long hair
        1. Influence of the Beatles
        2. Influence of African ancestry
    B. Seventies: group identification
        1. Shaved heads
        2. Mohawks: now and long ago
III. Changes in recent decades
    A. Eighties: outrageous statements
    B. Nineties and today: personal style

PART 5:
Writing an Outline for Your Report

Now, use the information from your notes to write your outline. You don't have to put everything in the notes into the outline. Use just the headings and subheadings that will guide you when you write your report.

Writing Your First Draft

Is writing a report different from writing other compositions? It isn't in some ways. A report has an introduction, a body, and a conclusion, just like much of the other writing you've done. But the information in a report consists of facts from outside sources. At the end of a report you list your sources so that your readers know where your information comes from.

Understanding the Parts of a Report

Introduction.   The *introduction* of a report isn't mentioned in the outline, so what's it doing in your paper? It's a short beginning paragraph that's there to grab your reader's attention. It tells in an interesting way what your report is about. In the model report on page 345, the writer uses startling facts about what people do to their hair, followed by a surprising statement, to catch the reader's interest. The reader can tell what the main idea (or point) of the report is from this statement.

Body.   The *body* of the report is where the information from your note cards goes. Each of the main headings from your outline can be discussed in one or more paragraphs. Some of your subtopics may need separate paragraphs, too, if you have enough information about them. Or, you may combine some subtopics in a single paragraph. Just make sure each paragraph tells enough to make its main idea clear.

Conclusion.   The *conclusion* of a report sums up your main points in an interesting way. Your conclusion may be short, but it should give a finished feeling to your paper. Notice that the model report ends with a question, yet lets the reader know that it's the end.

If your readers want to know more about your topic, they can refer to your list of sources. Here's the way to make your list of sources.

1. Put the title *Works Cited* at the top of a new page. (You might use *Bibliography* instead, but most style guides suggest using that word for a list of print sources only.)
2. List your sources in alphabetical order by the author's last name. (When there is no author, alphabetize by the first word of the title.)
3. Use the same style you used for your source cards.

Use the sample Works Cited list on page 348 as a model.

COMPUTER NOTE: Most word-processing programs have features to help automatically format and alphabetize a Works Cited list.

Writing Your Report

Except for direct quotations, write your report in your own words. Although your outline helps to guide you, you don't have to follow it strictly. As you're writing, you may decide to rearrange parts of your draft, or to cut or add something. Keep referring to your notes and go back to your sources if you need more information.

You can use the following sample report as a model. As you read, notice how the report follows the outline on page 343. Remember that your report may not be this long. Writing a good report is what's important.

A WRITER'S MODEL

Sixty Years of Haircuts

INTRODUCTION

Interest grabber

Main idea

During the past sixty years, men's haircuts have gone through big changes--from crew cuts and moptops to Mohawks, flattops, and beyond. Over the decades, though, one thing has stayed the same: Hairstyles have been a way for men to show who they are and what they stand for.

BODY

1940s and 1950s

For many years before 1940, most men wore a standard hairstyle. It was parted on the

**Influence of
Tony Curtis**

**Influence of
Elvis Presley**

1960s

**Influence of
the Beatles**

left and tapered at the back. With the outbreak of the Second World War, U.S. Army and Navy men adopted the crew cut. It was a short-all-over style that was easy to keep clean. During the early fifties, the crew cut became the "in" fashion on college campuses. Whether men knew it or not, their crew cuts announced that they were clean-cut, athletic, and patriotic.

Crew-cut men laughed at men brave enough to try a new style, the ducktail, but many eventually wore it. The film star Tony Curtis was one of the first to comb and oil his curly hair to a flipped-up point at the back. A ducktail suggested that its wearer was romantic, healthy (so much hair!), and carefree.

Elvis Presley copied the Tony Curtis look and took it to new heights. Elvis's own hair was mousy brown, but he dyed it blue-black. Then he teased it into a high wave in front and used gel and spray to make it look as lush as possible on top. Elvis attracted attention by combing and stroking his long wooly sideburns on stage.

The true revolution in hairstyles began in the sixties with the Beatles. Their haircut, the "moptop," was cut in a bowl shape, with bangs over the eyebrows. The moptop looked completely different from other styles because it was so natural and childlike. Many American men

quickly copied the Beatles. It was the first time they had let their hair grow long and natural since the 1780s.

Influence of African ancestry

In the late sixties, a hairstyle became a symbol of racial pride and the civil rights movement. To emphasize their African ancestry and distinctive culture, black men and women let their hair grow out in an "Afro." It was a round, naturally curly hairstyle.

1970s

Men's hairstyles during the seventies continued to identify the groups men belonged to. Men who wanted to look responsible returned to shorter hairstyles. To show their scorn of long-haired "idealists," some people shaved off all their hair.

Shaved heads

Mohawks

Wild-looking, spiked hair saw a rebirth in the seventies. Some versions of this were called "Mohawks," but it was more like a style worn long ago by the Huron, Osage, and Omaha nations. As a way of daring their enemies to scalp them, some Native Americans used to arrange their hair in a row of long spikes. They used bear grease to stiffen the spikes and shaved the rest of their heads to emphasize the frightening effect.

1980s

In the eighties and early nineties, trendsetters wanted to look different from everyone else. They thought the more outrageous the better. One unisex style, called the "buzz" or "flattop," had closely cut or shaved sides like a Mohawk. However, the top hair of a flattop was clipped into a geometric shape and stood up straight--like Bart Simpson's hair. Neon colors emphasized the effect.

Styles today

Professional hairstylist Sean Mullens says that most men today want a short, easy-to-care-for hairstyle. He adds that many of his customers ask for a style that allows them to "get out of the shower, run their fingers through their hair, and be done with it."

Direct quotation

CONCLUSION
Summary of main ideas

As you have seen, men's hairstyles can have political, social, and personal meanings. The journey from crew cut to flattop and beyond has taken sixty years. As the journey continues, what new hairstyles will men wear to show who they are and what they stand for?

Works Cited

The Beatles Anthology. ABC. KVUE, Austin. 19, 22, 23 Nov. 1995.

Corson, Richard. *Fashions in Hair: The First Five Thousand Years.* London: Owen, 1971.

"50 Years of Hairstyles." *Ebony Magazine* Nov. 1995: 222B. *Middle Search.* CD-ROM. EBSCO Publishing. May 1996.

Mullens, Sean. Telephone interview. 19 June 1996.

Sassoon, Vidal. "Hairdressing." *The World Book Encyclopedia.* 1995 ed.

PART 6:
Writing Your First Draft

You've done a great deal of preparation, and now it's time to write your first draft. Use your notes and outline as guides. Remember to list your sources on a separate Works Cited page at the end of your report.

Evaluating and Revising

Sometimes it's surprising to learn how much time published writers spend revising their work. Marjorie Kinnan Rawlings, for example, worked on *The Yearling* for a year and then started all over again. Rawlings even spent a great deal of time revising the title itself. A book about her editor (a man named Maxwell Perkins) tells how the title of the novel changed.

> Six months into the writing, Marjorie Rawlings was still hunting for a title. She sent a list of alternatives to Perkins and asked for his opinion. He did not care much for *The Flutter Mill.* Of *Juniper Island* he said: "I do not think place names are good for a book. There is not enough human suggestion in them." Of her third title he wrote, "I would think one which carried the meaning of *The Yearling* was probably right." The more he spoke of it, the better it sounded to him. He wrote her in the spring of 1937, "It seems to have a quality even more than a meaning that fits the book." It stuck.
>
> A. Scott Berg, *Max Perkins: Editor of Genius*

You may like your title as it is, but every piece of writing can benefit from revision. After you write the first draft of your report, set it aside. After a day or two, use the following chart to help you evaluate and revise your writing. Begin by asking yourself the questions in the left-hand column. If your answer to any question is *no,* use the technique on the right to correct the problem.

EVALUATING AND REVISING REPORTS

EVALUATION GUIDE	REVISION TECHNIQUE
1 Does the report use several different sources?	**Add** sources. Try to find and use at least one nonprint source.
2 Does the report consist of facts and the opinions of experts?	**Add** facts or an expert's opinion. **Cut** your own thoughts and feelings.
3 Is the report in the writer's own words? If someone else's words are used, are they in quotation marks?	**Replace** with your own words, or **add** quotation marks where you've used someone's actual words.
4 Is the information well organized?	**Reorder** sentences or paragraphs in order of importance or chronological order.
5 Is the introduction interesting? Does it tell what the report is about?	**Add** attention-getting details. **Add** a sentence that tells the main idea.
6 Does the conclusion bring the report to a close?	**Add** a sentence that summarizes the main idea.
7 Is the list of sources on a separate sheet at the end of the report? Is the form correct?	**Add** the list of sources in the correct form.

EXERCISE 3 ▶   **Analyzing a Writer's Revisions**

Here are the changes the writer made in one paragraph while revising "Sixty Years of Haircuts." Look at the changes carefully. Then answer the questions that follow.

> In the eighties and early nineties,
>
> trendsetters wanted to look different from
>
> everyone else. They thought the ~~funnier~~ *more outrageous*   **replace**
>
> the better. Neon colors emphasized the   **reorder**
>
> effect. One unisex style, called the "buzz"
>
> or "flattop," had closely cut or shaved sides
>
> like a Mohawk. ~~It's my favorite style.~~   **cut**
>
> However, the top hair of a flattop was
>
> clipped into a geometric shape and stood
>
> up straight, *– like Bart Simpson's hair.*   **add**

1. Why did the writer replace the word *funnier* with the words *more outrageous* in the second sentence? [Hint: Which word expresses the correct fact?]
2. Why did the writer move (reorder) the third sentence to the end of the paragraph? How does this change help the organization of the paragraph?
3. Why did the writer cut the sentence *It's my favorite style*? [Hint: Review page 333.]
4. Why did the writer add the phrase *like Bart Simpson's hair* to the last sentence?

WRITING ASSIGNMENT

PART 7:
Evaluating and Revising Your Report

Read your report to two or three classmates. Listen to their suggestions and take notes on what seems helpful. Then go over your draft, using the evaluating and revising chart (page 350) and your classmates' suggestions.

Proofreading and Publishing

Remember, **proofreading** is reading carefully and correct-ing mistakes. **Publishing** is sharing your work. Here's a publishing idea: Offer your report to your school librarian as a resource that other students can consult later.

MECHANICS HINT

Capitalizing Titles

In titles, capitalize the first word and all important words. Unless one of them is the first word of a title, do not capitalize *a, an, the,* coordinating conjunctions, or prepositions with fewer than five letters.

EXAMPLES Book: *Ambush in the Amazon*
Story: "Beware of the Dog"
Poem: "The Boy and the Wolf"

 REFERENCE NOTE: See pages 726–727 for more help.

PART 8:
Proofreading and Publishing Your Report

Proofread your revised paper, and share it with others. Give a copy to anyone you interviewed, too.

Reflecting on Your Writing

To add your report to your **portfolio,** date it and include your answers to the following questions.

- How did you choose your topic?
- If you were just starting a report on the same topic, what would you do differently? Why?

A STUDENT MODEL

Alexis M. Webster attends school in Kinston, North Carolina. Notice the specific facts she provides in the following excerpt from her report on carnivorous plants.

Carnivorous Plants
by Alexis M. Webster

Carnivorous plants are plants that eat insects or animals to get their nutrients. These plants are most likely to be found in very moist or very nutrient-poor places. Unlike other plants, these plants capture their food. While the green leaves on the plants produce carbohydrates, the insects and animals they catch provide nutrients such as nitrogen.

Carnivorous plants have special organs that capture the insects. Some carnivorous plants have flowers that look or smell from a distance like old smelly meat. This smell and color attracts the insects and animals. Pitcher plants, sundews, bladderworts, butterworts, and Venus's-flytraps all are types of carnivorous plants.

Pitcher plants capture insects in order to get enough nutrients to stay alive. They have interesting ways of trapping their own insects. The pitcher plants grow leaves that look like pitchers with open lids (the pitchers are leaves, not flowers). The inner part of the pitcher has a sweet juice that attracts lots of insects. Once an insect gets into the pitcher, it cannot climb its way out. Therefore the prey is most likely to drown in the pool of digestive liquid inside the pitcher.

Some types of pitcher plants are found in the wilds of tropical Asia, Malaysia, New Caledonia, and northern Australia. Also, the American pitcher plant, which belongs to the genus Sarracenia, is found in North America, mainly in swampy places in the east. The pitchers of some of these plants contain downward pointing hairs. This makes it even more difficult for the insect to crawl out of the pitcher.

WRITING WORKSHOP

A Book Report

You've already written one kind of report: a research report in which you presented information from a number of sources. Here's a chance for you to write another kind of report: a book report in which you evaluate a single work.

A book report is a lot like a movie review. The writers of both—often following a standard outline—evaluate a work, describe what they like or dislike about it, and give reasons for their opinions. A book report about a novel, for example, should include the features outlined below.

- the title of the book and the author's name
- an introduction that gets the reader interested
- a brief description of the setting and main character(s)
- a brief summary of the plot that doesn't ruin the suspense for the reader
- an evaluation of the book—why the audience should or should not read it

The following book report is an evaluation of the novel *I, Juan de Pareja*. Does the writer think the book is worth reading? What does the writer say is good or bad about the book? Does the writer give enough information about the book for you to understand the evaluation?

The Secret Artist

Juan de Pareja's mother dies when he is just five. A young black boy, Juan is a slave and totally dependent on the kindness of his owners. Then they both die, and he finds himself in the cruel grip of a muleteer (a person who drives mule teams). He runs away, but the muleteer finds him. Will his life now be one of slavery and cruelty?

The answer is both yes and no. The life story of the young boy is told in the novel <u>I, Juan de Pareja</u> by Elizabeth Borton de Treviño. Juan's story is set in Spain during the 1600s. After his owners die, he is sent to Madrid to become the slave of Diego Velázquez, the great artist.

Velázquez trains Juan to be his assistant, and soon Juan is caught up in the beauty of his art. He learns to stretch a canvas, mix paints, clean brushes, and adjust the light. He watches and admires Velázquez, a quiet, hard-working man who is dedicated to his art. Juan yearns to paint, too, but Spanish law forbids slaves to learn the arts. Velázquez's fame grows, and Juan goes with him on trips to Italy. There Juan can no longer resist his yearning to paint. He paints in secret, learning and improving.

Through the years both Juan and his master's talent and their friendship grow. But still Juan hides his secret from the great artist. On one trip to Italy, he vows he will not keep his painting a secret any longer. The surprise ending is both sad and joyful.

This is a historical story of two painters, one the master, the other his slave. But the real enjoyment comes from seeing how the affection and kindness between the two men changes both of their lives. It's a story you won't easily forget.

I, Juan de Pareja

Elizabeth Borton de Treviño

Thinking It Over

1. How does the writer try to get you interested in reading the report? Does the writer succeed?
2. Why doesn't the writer reveal the ending of the book?
3. Is the writer's evaluation positive? How do you know?
4. Does the report inspire you to read the book? Explain.

Writing a Book Report

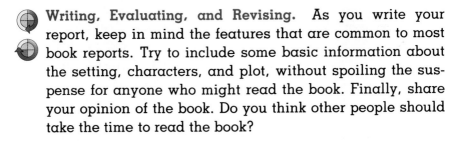

Prewriting.　If your teacher hasn't assigned one, ask friends for suggestions for a book to write about. After you've chosen a book, read it just for pleasure. Then, go back over it, reading some parts more carefully. Jot down notes or insert slips of paper into pages where you learn about the main details of the characters, plot, conflicts, or setting. Decide what parts will help you explain the book and your opinion about it. Decide whether to recommend the book to others.

Writing, Evaluating, and Revising.　As you write your report, keep in mind the features that are common to most book reports. Try to include some basic information about the setting, characters, and plot, without spoiling the suspense for anyone who might read the book. Finally, share your opinion of the book. Do you think other people should take the time to read the book?

Proofreading and Publishing.　Since other people will be reading your book report, take the time to proofread it carefully. Clean up any errors in spelling, mechanics, and capitalization. If your school newspaper has a book review section, think about submitting your report for publication.

　　If you decide to include your book report in your **portfolio,** date it and attach a note responding to these questions: How did you decide which information from the book to include, and which to leave out? How was this paper different from others you've written?

MAKING CONNECTIONS

RESEARCH ACROSS THE CURRICULUM

Biographical Report

Would you like to know more about some historical person or someone in your family? You can use your research and report-writing skills to prepare a biographical report.

For a biographical report, you'll need at least three sources. If books and articles have been written about the person, use them. If you research the life of a family member, interview the person and people who know him or her. Here are some things you'll want to find out.

1. When and where was the person born? If the person is no longer living, when and where did he or she die?
2. What is interesting and special about the person?
3. What are the person's achievements? Has the person received special recognition for something?

The following is an example of a biographical report written for a book. Notice how the writer uses facts and quotations that emphasize the uniqueness of his subject.

Alta Weiss

Alta Weiss was a doctor's daughter from Ragersville, Ohio, who began to pitch for boys' teams at the age of fourteen. At sixteen, she joined a men's semiprofessional team, the nearby Vermilion Independents. Twelve hundred people turned out to see her make her debut: she gave up only four hits and a single run in five innings. "Miss Weiss," said the Lorain *Times Herald* in 1907, "can easily lay claim to being the only one who can handle the ball from the pitcher's box in such style that some of the best semi-pros are made to fan the atmosphere."

Soon, special trains were being run out from Cleveland whenever she pitched. When she appeared in the Cleveland Naps' park, more than 3,000 people paid their way in to see her. "I found that you can't play ball in skirts," she told reporters. "I tried. I wore a skirt over my bloomers—and nearly broke my neck. Finally I was forced to discard it, and now I always wear bloomers—but made so wide that the fullness gives a skirtlike effect."

Her baseball skills were good enough to put her through medical school. Even after she began to practice as a physician, she continued to play off and on into the 1920s.

Geoffrey C. Ward and Ken Burns,
from *Baseball: An Illustrated History*

Choose a person to write about, just as you chose a topic earlier for your report. Take careful notes as you read or interview. Then follow the same steps you followed for your research report.

SPEAKING AND LISTENING

Studying the Influence of the Mass Media

On the radio, you listen to an interview of the coach of the Buffalo Bills ten minutes after the Super Bowl is over. On television, you watch the president's State of the Union speech and, five minutes later, a comedian pretending he is the president.

Today the mass media bring information and entertainment to us the moment it happens, no matter where it occurs around the world. Have you ever thought about how the mass media affect your life? how much they influence you and your world? To find out, try one of the following research projects. Then share what you have discovered about the media in an oral report to your class.

A. Think of something, a product you have seen or heard advertised, that you or your family has bought recently. It might be sneakers, a CD or audiotape, a television, or even a food item you bought in a grocery store or at a health food restaurant. After you've thought of the product, you can use the following questions to study the influence of the media.

- Where was this product advertised—TV? radio? newspapers? magazines?
- What technique did the ad(s) use to sell the product—humor? a famous personality? facts? a comparison with another product?
- Would you or your family have purchased this product if it had not been advertised? Why?
- What does this research tell you about the way the media influence your buying habits?

B. Study how the media's handling of the news influences you and your world.

1. Begin by watching the evening edition of a nationally televised news program. Note one or two stories that the program highlights. What facts are given? How much time does the program give to each story?
2. Look for the same stories in your local newspaper the next day. How much space are they given? Are they on the front page or further back in the paper? Is the information the same, or has it been changed? How?
3. Check the paper's editorial page several days in a row. If you find the story, what's the writer's point of view? If there is more than one editorial about the story, how are they different?
4. Look for the story in the next issue of a weekly newsmagazine like *Time* or *Newsweek.* Is there more or less information? different information?
5. How do you think the media affected your thinking about this story? the thinking of other people you know?

11 WRITING EFFECTIVE SENTENCES

LOOKING
AHEAD

This chapter will give you some practice at writing clear, effective sentences. As you work through the chapter, you will learn how to

- write complete sentences
- combine sentences
- revise sentences for style

Writing Clear Sentences

Whether you are writing for school or for the workplace, you want your writing to be clear and understandable. One of the easiest ways to make your writing clear is to use complete sentences. A complete sentence is a word group that

- has a subject
- has a verb
- expresses a complete thought

EXAMPLES   Dolphins communicate with one another by
                    making clicking and whistling sounds.
                 When a dolphin is in trouble, it can give off a
                    distress call.
                 Help!

Each of these examples meets all the requirements of a sentence. At first glance, the third example may not appear to have a subject. The subject, *you*, is understood in the sentence even though it isn't stated: "(You) help!"

There are two stumbling blocks to the development of clear sentences: *sentence fragments* and *run-on sentences*. Once you learn how to recognize fragments and run-ons, you can revise them to create clear, complete sentences.

Sentence Fragments

A **sentence fragment** is a part of a sentence that has been punctuated as if it were a complete sentence. Like a fragment of a painting or photograph, a sentence fragment is confusing because it doesn't give the whole picture.

FRAGMENT   **Looked something like a sewing machine.** [The
                   subject is missing. *What* looked like a sewing
                   machine?]
SENTENCE   **The first typewriter looked something like a
                   sewing machine.**

FRAGMENT   **Christopher Sholes the typewriter in 1867.** [The
                   verb is missing. What did Sholes *do* in 1867?]
SENTENCE   **Christopher Sholes helped design the typewriter
                   in 1867.**

FRAGMENT	After Mark Twain typed one of his manuscripts on a Sholes typewriter. [This group of words has a subject and a verb, but it does not express a complete thought. *What happened* after Mark Twain typed one of his manuscripts on a Sholes typewriter?]
SENTENCE	After Mark Twain typed one of his manuscripts on a Sholes typewriter, the invention began to attract public attention.

WRITING NOTE Often, fragments are the result of writing in a hurry or being a little careless. For example, you might accidentally chop off part of a sentence by putting in a period and a capital letter too soon. In the following example, notice that the fragment in dark type is actually a part of the sentence that comes before it.

We laughed at the clowns. **When they rode around on gigantic tricycles.**

You can correct the fragment by attaching it to the sentence it belongs with.

We laughed at the clowns when they rode around on gigantic tricycles.

| EXERCISE 1 ▶ | **Identifying Sentence Fragments** |

Use this simple three-part test to find out which of the following word groups are sentence fragments and which are complete sentences.

1. Does the group of words have a subject?
2. Does it have a verb?
3. Does it express a complete thought?

If the group of words is a complete sentence, write *S.* If it is a fragment, write *F.* [Remember: A complete sentence can have the unstated subject *you.*]

1. The English clown Lulu was one of the first female clowns to gain attention in the United States.
2. When John Ringling North discovered her.
3. Performed for the Ringling Brothers and Barnum & Bailey Circus.
4. Lulu had entertained the British royal family in England.
5. Lulu's grandmother a tightrope walker.
6. While she and her husband performed as a clown team.
7. Lulu used a gigantic fake hand to shake hands with children.
8. The funny handshake Lulu's special trick.
9. Lulu in this country in 1939.
10. Was the wife of clown Albertino Adams.

| EXERCISE 2 ▶ | **Finding and Revising Fragments** |

Some of the following groups of words are sentence fragments. Revise each fragment by (1) adding a subject, (2) adding a verb, or (3) attaching the fragment to a complete sentence. You may need to change the punctuation and capitalization, too. If the word group is already a complete sentence, write *S*.

EXAMPLE   **1.** After the sun rose.
              1. *We walked to the beach after the sun rose.*

1. People near the water.
2. Two little children were playing in the wet sand.
3. Whenever the waves broke.
4. My sister and I on a red inflatable raft.
5. Tried to ride the waves as they came in.
6. A huge wave flipped over the raft.
7. Because we were good swimmers.
8. We were ready to go back in the water after we rested in the sun for a while.
9. Ran by and kicked sand on our blanket.
10. The family next to us a sand sculpture of a dragon.

Run-on Sentences

If you run together two complete sentences as if they were one sentence, you get a *run-on sentence*. Run-ons are confusing because the reader can't tell where one idea ends and another one begins.

RUN-ON   Margaret Bourke-White was a famous news photographer she worked for *Life* magazine during World War II.

CORRECT   Margaret Bourke-White was a famous news photographer. She worked for *Life* magazine during World War II.

RUN-ON   Bourke-White traveled all over the world taking photographs, she went underground to photograph miners in South Africa.

CORRECT   Bourke-White traveled all over the world taking photographs. She went underground to photograph miners in South Africa.

To spot run-ons, try reading your writing aloud. A natural, distinct pause in your voice usually marks the end of one thought and the beginning of another. If you pause at a place where you don't have any end punctuation, you may have found a run-on sentence.

MECHANICS HINT

Using Correct End Punctuation

A comma does mark a brief pause in a sentence, but it does not show the end of a sentence. If you use just a comma between two complete sentences, you create a run-on sentence.

RUN-ON   Our dog finally came home late last night, she was dirty and hungry.
CORRECT   Our dog finally came home late last night. She was dirty and hungry.

☞ REFERENCE NOTE: For more about commas, see pages 741–755.

Revising Run-on Sentences

There are several ways you can revise run-on sentences. Here are two of them.

1. You can make two sentences.

RUN-ON   Kite building is an ancient art the Chinese made the first kites around three thousand years ago.
CORRECT   Kite building is an ancient art. The Chinese made the first kites around three thousand years ago.

2. You can use a comma and the coordinating conjunction *and*, *but*, or *or*.

RUN-ON   The Chinese sometimes used kites in religious ceremonies, they usually used them for sport.

CORRECT   The Chinese sometimes used kites in religious ceremonies, **but** they usually used them for sport.

COMPUTER NOTE: Use your word-processing program when you revise your draft for fragments, run-on sentences, or style. The Cut and Paste commands can help you find the best place for words or phrases within a sentence and for sentences within your draft.

EXERCISE 3   **Identifying and Revising Run-ons**

Decide which of the following groups of words are run-ons. Then, revise each run-on by (1) making it into two separate sentences or (2) using a comma and a coordinating conjunction. If the group of words is already correct, write *C*.

1. The Louvre is the largest museum in the world it is also one of the oldest.
2. The first works of art in the Louvre were bought by the kings of France each ruler added more treasures.
3. King Francis I was a great supporter of the arts he bought the *Mona Lisa.*
4. As other French rulers made additions, the collections grew.
5. The Louvre is now a state-owned museum, its new pieces are either bought or received as gifts.

6. Each year, about one and a half million people from all over the world come to see the artwork at the Louvre.
7. The buildings of the Louvre form a rectangle there are courtyards and gardens inside the rectangle.
8. The Louvre covers about forty acres, it has about eight miles of gallery space.
9. Over one million works of art are exhibited in the Louvre.
10. Many of the buildings of the Louvre have been expanded and modernized, this photograph shows how the Louvre looks today.

REVIEW A ▶ **Revising to Correct Fragments and Run-ons**

The following paragraph is confusing because it contains some fragments and run-ons. First, identify the fragments and run-ons. Then, revise each fragment and run-on to make the paragraph clearer.

Godzilla a movie about a huge reptile. Godzilla looks like a dinosaur he breathes fire like a dragon. He comes up out of the ocean. After an atomic bomb wakes him up. Godzilla can melt steel with his atomic breath he is big enough to knock down huge buildings. In the film he destroys the city of Tokyo he gets killed at the end.

Combining Sentences

Sometimes a short sentence can express your meaning perfectly. But a long, unbroken series of short sentences will make your writing sound choppy. For example, read the following paragraph, which is made up of short sentences:

> George Lucas's films are famous. They are famous for their plots and special effects. The plots are suspenseful. The special effects are thrilling. Star Wars became a success in the late 1970s. Lucas wrote and directed it. Its success was international. Lucas later teamed up with director Steven Spielberg. They created Raiders of the Lost Ark. The movie was popular.

Now read the revised version. To make the paragraph more interesting, the writer combined some of the short, choppy sentences into longer, smoother ones. Notice how *sentence combining* has helped to eliminate some repeated words and ideas.

> George Lucas's films are famous for their suspenseful plots and thrilling special effects. Star Wars, which Lucas wrote and directed, became an international success in the late 1970s. Lucas later teamed up with director Steven Spielberg to create the popular Raiders of the Lost Ark.

Combining by Inserting Words

One way to combine short sentences is to pull a key word from one sentence and insert it into the other sentence. Sometimes you'll need to change the form of the key word before you can insert it.

INSERTING WITHOUT A CHANGE	
ORIGINAL	Louis Armstrong was a famous musician. He was a jazz musician.
COMBINED	Louis Armstrong was a famous **jazz** musician.
INSERTING WITH A CHANGE	
ORIGINAL	Armstrong was an easygoing person. He was a friend to many people.
COMBINED	Armstrong was an easygoing, **friendly** person.

WRITING NOTE — When you change the forms of words, you often add endings such as *–ed, –ing,* and *–ly* to make adjectives and adverbs.

EXAMPLES
need   ⟹   needed
sing   ⟹   singing
fortunate   ⟹   fortunately

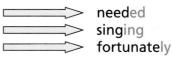

EXERCISE 4 — **Combining Sentences by Inserting Words**

Combine each of the following sentence pairs by taking the italicized word from the second sentence and inserting it into the first sentence. Follow the hints in parentheses for changing the forms of words.

EXAMPLE   **1.** Young Louis Armstrong first showed his talent on the streets of New Orleans. His talent was for *music.* (Add *–al.*)

         1. *Young Louis Armstrong first showed his musical talent on the streets of New Orleans.*

1. He became a jazz musician. He received *acclaim* for his music. (Add *–ed* and change *a* to *an*.)
2. Louis Armstrong had a deep voice. His voice was *rough*.
3. Louis Armstrong sang jazz. His jazz singing was *brilliant*. (Add *–ly*.)
4. Louis started playing at a New Orleans night spot. He played *cornet*.
5. He became famous as a solo trumpet player. He was famous on an *international* level. (Add *–ly*.)

Combining by Inserting Phrases

A ***phrase*** is a group of words that doesn't have a subject and a verb. You can combine sentences by taking a phrase from one sentence and inserting it into the other sentence.

ORIGINAL   Brown bears gather in groups. They gather around river banks.

COMBINED   Brown bears gather in groups **around river banks.**

Sometimes you will need to put commas around the phrase you are inserting. Ask yourself whether the phrase renames or explains a noun or pronoun in the sentence. If it does, use a comma or commas to set off the phrase from the rest of the sentence.

ORIGINAL   Alaska is home to the big brown bears. The big
           brown bears are the largest kind of bear.
COMBINED   Alaska is home to the big brown bears, **the
           largest kind of bear.**

Often, you can change the verb in a sentence to make
a phrase. You change the verb by adding *–ing* or *–ed* or by
putting the word *to* in front of it. You can then use the
phrase to modify a noun or pronoun in another sentence.

ORIGINAL   The bear prepares his winter retreat. He digs a
           burrow in a bank.
COMBINED   **Digging a burrow in a bank,** the bear prepares
           his winter retreat.

ORIGINAL   Bears dig in the ground. This is how they find
           roots and sweet bulbs.
COMBINED   Bears dig in the ground **to find roots and
           sweet bulbs.**

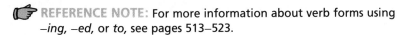 REFERENCE NOTE: For more information about verb forms using
–ing, –ed, or *to,* see pages 513–523.

| EXERCISE 5 ▶ | **Combining Sentences by Inserting Phrases** |

Combine each pair of sentences by taking the italicized
words from the second sentence and inserting them into
the first sentence. The hints in parentheses tell you when
to change the forms of words. Add commas where needed.

EXAMPLE   **1.** Television networks have made professional
          tennis a popular sport. They *show all the
          major tournaments.* (Change *show* to *showing.*)
          1. *Showing all the major tournaments, television
          networks have made professional tennis a
          popular sport.*

1. During the first fifty years of its history, tennis was
   largely a pastime. It was a pastime *of the wealthy.*
2. Prominent players competed in professional promo-
   tions. They *toured with their managers.* (Change *toured*
   to *touring.*)

3. Rod Laver won the Wimbledon men's singles title in 1961. Rod Laver was *an Australian.*
4. Nonprofessional tennis declined as a major attraction. It declined *in a short time.*
5. Women players organized themselves. They did this so they could *demand equal prize money.* (Add *to* in front of *demand.*)

Combining by Using *And, But,* or *Or*

You can also combine sentences by using the conjunctions *and, but,* or *or.* With one of these connecting words, you can form a *compound subject,* a *compound verb,* or a *compound sentence.*

Compound Subjects and Verbs

Sometimes two sentences have the same verb with different subjects. You can combine the sentences by linking the two subjects with *and* or *or.* When you do this, you create a *compound subject.*

ORIGINAL   Kangaroos carry their young in pouches. Koalas carry their young in pouches.
COMBINED   **Kangaroos and koalas** carry their young in pouches.

If two sentences have the same subject with different verbs, you can link the verbs with *and, but,* or *or* to form a *compound verb.*

ORIGINAL   Kangaroos can hop on their hind legs. They can walk on all four legs.

COMBINED   Kangaroos **can hop** on their hind legs **or walk** on all four legs.

GRAMMAR HINT

Checking for Subject–Verb Agreement

When you form a compound subject, make sure that it agrees with the verb in number.

ORIGINAL   Tasmania is in Australia. Queensland is in Australia.

REVISED   **Tasmania and Queensland are** in Australia. [The plural subject takes the verb *are.*]

☞ REFERENCE NOTE: For more information about agreement of subjects and verbs, see pages 575–588.

EXERCISE 6 ▶ **Combining by Forming Compound Subjects and Compound Verbs**

Combine each of the following sentence pairs by forming a compound subject or a compound verb. Make sure your new subjects and verbs agree in number.

1. Australia produces many cattle products. Australia consumes many cattle products.
2. Beef is popular in Australia. Lamb is popular in Australia.
3. Australians grill their meat. Australians also roast their meat.
4. Potatoes are often served with the meat. Other vegetables are often served with the meat, too.
5. Italian cooking is becoming popular in Australia. Greek cooking is also becoming popular.

Compound Sentences

Sometimes you may want to combine two sentences that express equally important ideas. You can connect the two sentences by using a comma and the conjunction *and, but,* or *or.* When you link sentences in this way, you create a *compound sentence.*

ORIGINAL   Many nations throughout the world use the metric system. The United States still uses the old system of measurement.

COMBINED   Many nations throughout the world use the metric system, **but** the United States still uses the old system of measurement.

WRITING
NOTE

Before you create a compound sentence out of two simple sentences, make sure the thoughts in the sentences are closely related to each other. If you combine two sentences that are not closely related, you will confuse your reader.

UNRELATED   Kim chopped the vegetables, and I like soup.

RELATED   **Kim chopped the vegetables,** and **I stirred the soup.**

EXERCISE 7   **Combining Sentences by Forming a Compound Sentence**

The sentences in each of the following pairs are closely related. Make each pair into a single compound sentence by adding a comma and the connecting word *and, but,* or *or.*

EXAMPLE   **1.** The kilogram is the basic unit of weight in the metric system. The meter is the basic unit of length.

1. *The kilogram is the basic unit of weight in the metric system, and the meter is the basic unit of length.*

1. The metric system was developed in France. It became popular in many countries.
2. We can keep the old system of measurement. We can switch to the metric system.
3. The old system of measurement has more than twenty basic units of measurement. The metric system has only seven.
4. A meter equals ten decimeters. A decimeter equals ten centimeters.
5. Counting by tens is second nature to most people. Many people still find the metric system difficult to learn.

Combining by Using a Subordinate Clause

A *clause* is a group of words that contains a verb and its subject. An *independent clause* can stand alone as a sentence. A *subordinate clause* can't stand alone as a sentence because it doesn't express a complete thought.

INDEPENDENT CLAUSE **Henry David Thoreau was living alone in the woods.** [can stand alone as a sentence]

SUBORDINATE CLAUSE **when he wrote *Walden*** [can't stand alone as a sentence]

If two sentences are closely related but unequal in importance, you can combine them by using a subordinate clause. Just turn the less-important idea into a subordinate clause and attach it to the other sentence (the independent clause). The subordinate clause will give additional information about an idea expressed in the independent clause.

ORIGINAL **For two years, Thoreau lived in a simple hut. He built the hut at Walden Pond.**

COMBINED **For two years, Thoreau lived in a simple hut that he built at Walden Pond.**

☞ REFERENCE NOTE: For more information about sentences that contain subordinate clauses, see pages 562–565.

Clauses Beginning with *Who, Which,* or *That*

You can make a short sentence into a subordinate clause by inserting *who, which,* or *that* in place of the subject.

ORIGINAL   The Aztecs were an American Indian people. They once ruled a mighty empire in Mexico.

COMBINED   The Aztecs were an American Indian people **who once ruled a mighty empire in Mexico.**

Clauses Beginning with Words of Time or Place

You can also make a subordinate clause by adding a word that tells time or place. Words that tell time or place include *after, before, where, wherever, when, whenever,* and *while*.

ORIGINAL   The capital city of the Aztec empire was in central Mexico. Mexico City stands in that spot today.

COMBINED   The capital city of the Aztec empire was in central Mexico, **where Mexico City stands today.**

MECHANICS HINT

Using Commas with Introductory Clauses

If you put your time or place clause at the beginning of the sentence, you'll need to put a comma after the clause.

ORIGINAL   The Aztec empire grew. Aztec warriors conquered nearby territories.

COMBINED   **When Aztec warriors conquered nearby territories,** the Aztec empire grew.

👉 REFERENCE NOTE: For more information about using commas after time or place clauses, see pages 752–753.

EXERCISE 8 ▶ **Combining Sentences by Using a Subordinate Clause**

Combine each of the following sentence pairs by making the second sentence into a subordinate clause and attaching it to the first sentence. The hints in parentheses will tell you what word to use at the beginning of the clause. To make a smooth combination, you may need to delete one or more words in the second sentence of each pair.

1. The Aztecs practiced a religion. It affected every part of their lives. (Use *that.*)
2. Aztec craftworkers made drums and rattles. Drums and rattles were their main musical instruments. (Use a comma and *which.*)
3. Aztec cities had huge temples. The people held religious ceremonies there. (Use *where.*)
4. Their empire was destroyed by the Spanish. The Spanish conquered it in 1521. (Use *who.*)
5. There was very little left of the Aztec civilization. The Spanish invaders tore down all the Aztec buildings. (Use *after.*)

e Granger Collection, ew York.

| R E V I E W **B** ▶ | **Revising a Paragraph by Combining Sentences** |

The following paragraph sounds choppy because it has too many short sentences. Use the methods you've learned in this section to combine some of the sentences. You'll notice the improvement when you're finished.

> The Arctic is a cold region. It is around the North Pole. The Arctic seems like a barren place. But berries actually grow in a few places. Vegetables actually grow in a few places. The area also has rich mineral deposits. These deposits have attracted people to the region. Mines in Alaska and Canada produce gold and copper. Mines in arctic Russia produce tin. Early explorers revealed that the Arctic is far from worthless. They discovered many natural resources in the area.

Improving Sentence Style

You've learned how to improve choppy sentences by combining them into longer, smoother sentences. Now you'll learn how to improve *stringy* and *wordy sentences* by making them shorter and more precise.

Revising Stringy Sentences

Stringy sentences just ramble on and on. They have too many independent clauses strung together with words like *and* or *but.* If you read a stringy sentence out loud, you'll probably start to run out of breath. You won't have a chance to pause before each new idea.

> I dreamed I was in a big castle and I turned a corner and I could see a young princess and she waved at me but then she ran up the stairs and she ran into the darkness.

As you can see, stringy sentences are confusing because they don't show the relationships between the ideas. To fix a stringy sentence, you can

- break the sentence into two or more sentences
- turn some of the independent clauses into phrases or subordinate clauses

Now read the revised version of the stringy sentence. Notice how the writer turned one independent clause into a subordinate clause and another into a phrase.

> I dreamed I was in a big castle. When I turned a corner, I could see a young princess. She waved at me, but then she ran up the stairs into the darkness.

MECHANICS HINT

Punctuating Compound Sentences

When you revise a stringy sentence, you may decide to keep *and* or *but* between two independent clauses. If you do, be sure to add a comma before the *and* or *but* to show a pause between the two thoughts.

ORIGINAL   She waved at me but then she ran up the stairs into the darkness.

REVISED   She waved at me, but then she ran up the stairs into the darkness.

EXERCISE 9 ▶ Revising Stringy Sentences

Some of the following sentences are stringy and need improving. First, identify the stringy sentences. Then, revise them by using the methods you've learned. If a numbered item doesn't need to be improved, write *C*.

1. Harriet Ross grew up as a slave in Maryland, and she worked on a plantation there, but in 1844 she married John Tubman, and he was a freed slave.
2. Harriet Tubman did not believe that people should be slaves, and she decided to escape, and late one night she began her dangerous trip to the North.
3. Traveling at night, she made the long journey to Philadelphia, Pennsylvania.
4. New friends told her about the Underground Railroad, and it was a secret group of people, and they helped runaway slaves get to the North.
5. Tubman decided she would rescue more slaves from the South, and she used the North Star as her guide, and she led groups of slaves along the road to freedom, and she made nineteen trips in twelve years.
6. The slaves hid during the day and continued their journey at night.
7. Tubman never learned to read or write, but she was a powerful speaker, and she spoke at many anti-slavery meetings.
8. The Civil War broke out, and Tubman volunteered to help the Union army, and she served as a cook and a nurse, and later she became a spy.
9. The war ended, and Tubman settled in Auburn, New York, and she started a home for elderly black men and women.
10. The people of Auburn built Freedom Park in memory of Tubman.

HARRIET TUBMAN

Revising Wordy Sentences

Sometimes you may use more words than you really need. Extra words don't make writing sound better. They just get in the reader's way. You can revise *wordy sentences* in three different ways.

1. Replace a group of words with one word.

WORDY   Our snowman was the biggest and best on the block due to the fact that we had spent over three hours making it.

REVISED   Our snowman was the biggest and best on the block **because** we had spent over three hours making it.

WORDY   With great suddenness, our beautiful snowman began to melt.

REVISED   **Suddenly,** our beautiful snowman began to melt.

2. Replace a clause with a phrase.

WORDY   When the play had come to an end, we walked to a restaurant and treated ourselves to pizza.

REVISED   **After the play,** we walked to a restaurant and treated ourselves to pizza.

WORDY   I ordered a slice with mozzarella cheese, which is my favorite topping.

REVISED   I ordered a slice with mozzarella cheese, **my favorite topping.**

3. Take out a whole group of unnecessary words.

WORDY   What I mean to say is that Carlos did not go to the movie with us.

REVISED   Carlos did not go to the movie with us.

WORDY   We all liked the movie because it had some very funny scenes that were the kinds of scenes that make you laugh.

REVISED   We all liked the movie because it had some very funny scenes.

Extra words and phrases tend to make writing sound awkward and unnatural. As you revise your writing, try reading your sentences aloud to check for wordiness or a stringy style. If a sentence sounds like a mouthful to you, chances are it is stringy, wordy, or both.

E X E R C I S E **10**   **Revising Wordy Sentences**

Decide which of the following sentences are wordy and need improving. Then revise each of the wordy sentences. You can (1) replace a phrase with one word, (2) replace a clause with a phrase, or (3) take out an unnecessary group of words. If the sentence is effective as it is, write C.

1. Most wasps are helpful to humanity because of the fact that they eat harmful insects.
2. What I want to say is that wasps do far more good than harm.
3. Social wasps are the type that live together as groups and work as a team to build their nests.
4. Social wasps make their nests from old wood and tough plant fibers.
5. They chew and chew the wood and fiber until the mixture becomes pasty and mushy.
6. The mixture becomes a material that is called wasp paper.
7. According to some historians, the Chinese invented paper after watching wasps make it.
8. A wasp colony lasts only through the summer.
9. The queen wasp, being the only member of the colony to survive the winter, comes out of hibernation in the spring.
10. The queens start new colonies by means of building nests and laying eggs.

REVIEW C ▸ Revising Stringy and Wordy Sentences

The following paragraph is hard to read because it contains stringy and wordy sentences. First, identify the stringy and wordy sentences. Then, revise them to improve the style of the paragraph.

On Halloween night in 1938, an amazing event took place that was very surprising. Many families were gathered around their radios, and they were listening to music, and then they heard that Martians had invaded Earth. Actually, the fact is that the news report was a radio version of H. G. Wells's novel The War of the Worlds. But Orson Welles, who was the producer of this famous hoax, made the show very realistic. Thousands of Americans were frightened and upset, and many people jumped in their cars to escape from the aliens, and some people even reported seeing the Martians and their spaceships.

1982

"Yeeeeeeeeeeeha!"

MAKING CONNECTIONS

Filling in the Missing Pieces

You're searching through an old trunk in an attic, hoping to find some treasures from the past. In a string-tied bundle of papers, you discover a yellowed newspaper that's dated exactly one hundred years from the day you were born. What luck! You anxiously unfold the front page and begin reading. However, every time you get really excited about an article, a tear or smudge in the newspaper keeps you from finding out what happened.

Read through each article a few times, and try to guess what words are missing. Rewrite the fragments in complete sentences to reconstruct the original articles. [Hint: If you can't puzzle out the original sentences, use your imagination.]

The Lincoln Reporter

LIMITS ON TEXAS CATTLE

Western ranchers are trying to improve their herds with breeding stock from the East. However, a dreaded Texas fever among cattle ⬚⬚⬚ some herds. Northern plains ranchers are demanding that limits be set on the number of cattle being brought in from Texas. ⬚⬚⬚ have begun to lobby in both state and national legislatures.

Cowboys' wages continue to grow

There may be no such thing as a rich cowboy. However, ⬚⬚⬚ continue to grow. Last month's survey ⬚⬚⬚ the average cowhand's wages at $25 to $30

WESTWARD HO!

Eastern ⬚⬚⬚ are continuing to homestead on the high plains. Last month record numbers of farmers ⬚⬚⬚ near Dodge City, Kansas, an area previously reserved for ranchers. Settlers ⬚⬚⬚ with equal speed into Nebraska.

Billy the Kid ⬚⬚⬚ at the hand of Pat Garrett
(Story on page 2)

RAILROAD STATIONS PROVIDE MANY SERVICES

Railroad stations from South Dakota to Missouri ⬚⬚⬚ the center for town activity and business. Union Station in St. Louis now ⬚⬚⬚ telegraph and mail service as well as a full schedule of passenger and freight trains. The station has also recently added a cafe and a saloon.

12 ENGLISH: ORIGINS AND USES

LOOKING AHEAD

As you work through this chapter, you will learn

- where English comes from
- how English has grown and changed
- what varieties of English people use today
- how to choose appropriate words when you speak and write

A Changing Language

Did you know that the word *nice* originally meant "foolish," or that the word *prince* comes from French? Have you ever wondered how "teddy" bears got their name? Like people, words have histories. The story behind each English word is part of a much larger history—the history of English itself.

A Family of Languages

If you look at photographs in a family album, you can usually see a resemblance among people from different generations. Languages show family resemblances, too. English and dozens of other languages have the same ancestor, a language that was spoken over six thousand years ago in Europe. You can still see similarities among languages that come from this early language.

ENGLISH	FRENCH	GERMAN	SPANISH
mother	mère	Mutter	madre

The Growth of English

No one can say exactly when English began. But we do know that it was being written about 1,300 years ago and was being spoken long before that. Over the centuries, the language has gradually grown and changed along with the people who use it. This change and growth is divided into three major stages: *Old English, Middle English,* and *Modern English.*

Following are Old, Middle, and Modern English versions of a line from the Lord's Prayer (Matthew 6:9–13). Notice how the language gradually developed into the English we use today.

OLD ENGLISH	Urne gedæg hwamlican hlaf syle us to dæg.
MIDDLE ENGLISH	Oure iche-dayes-bred gif us to-day.
MODERN ENGLISH	Give us this day our daily bread.

   English has changed so much in 1,300 years that only language scholars can understand Old English without a translation. Yet we can still see the resemblance between present-day English words and their Old English ancestors.

OLD ENGLISH	modor	sunne	steorra	meolc
MODERN ENGLISH	mother	sun	star	milk

EXERCISE 1 ▶ **Matching Present-Day and Old English Words**

See if you can match each present-day English word in the left-hand column with its Old English ancestor in the right-hand column. [Hint: Look at the beginning consonants, and use the process of elimination.]

1. blue
2. green
3. cat
4. bright
5. black
6. lip
7. white
8. mouth
9. rain
10. dog

a. catt
b. blaewen
c. docga
d. muth
e. blaec
f. regn
g. bryht
h. grene
i. hwit
j. lippa

Changes in English

   As you can see from the examples at the top of this page, the spellings of words have changed since Old English times. English has changed in other ways, too. Pronunciations of words have changed, and some words have taken on meanings different from their original ones. English also has a much larger and richer vocabulary than it did 1,300 years ago.

Changes in Pronunciation

Users of Old and Middle English pronounced words differently from the way we do. Pronunciation changes help explain why many present-day English words aren't spelled as they sound. For example, the word *knight* used to be pronounced with a *k* sound at the beginning. The *k* eventually became silent, but the spelling never caught up with the pronunciation.

The major pronunciation changes have been changes in vowel sounds. In the 13th century, *meek* would have sounded like *make*, *boot* like *boat*, and *mouse* like *moose*.

E X E R C I S E **2** ▶   **Spelling Words As They Sound**

You've been elected to a committee to update the spellings of English words. Choose ten words that aren't spelled as they sound. Then respell each word to reflect the way you pronounce it. Do you think your new spellings could catch on? Why or why not?

Changes in Meaning

Over time, words take on new meanings as people use them in different ways. Here are some examples of gradual changes in the meanings of words.

CHANGES IN MEANING

	Old English	Middle English	Modern English
	450 1100	1500	PRESENT
SILLY . . . . . happy, blessed		harmless	foolish
GLAMOUR		enchantment	charm, fascination
COMPUTER		a person who computes or calculates	an electronic machine

The Glamour of Grammar

Glamour and *grammar* may not seem to have much in common, but the two words are actually close cousins. Both come from the Middle English word *gramer*, which had two very different meanings: "grammar" and "enchantment." Eventually *glamour* was used only with the second meaning. As shown in the time line on the previous page, the meaning of *glamour* has changed over time to the one we're familiar with today.

English Builds Its Vocabulary

The large vocabulary of English (over 600,000 words!) makes it a rich and flexible language. But English wasn't always as expressive as it is today. For example, users of Old English never heard of the words *beauty*, *sketch*, or *key*. Only about 15 percent of the words we use come from Old English. The rest have been borrowed or invented over the centuries.

Borrowed Words

Thousands of our everyday words were borrowed from the vocabularies of other languages. Norse, Latin, French, and Spanish are just a few of the languages that have left their mark on English.

NORSE	*sky*	ENGLISH	*sky*
LATIN	*papyrus*	ENGLISH	*paper*
FRENCH	*faceon*	ENGLISH	*fashion*
SPANISH	*cañón*	ENGLISH	*canyon*

Words from Names

Proper names are another source of new words in English. Many objects are named after the people who invented or inspired them. Others are named after the places they come from.

EXAMPLES   *graham cracker:* from Sylvester Graham, the
                      American clergyman who invented this type
                      of cracker
                  cologne: from Cologne, a city in Germany
                  sardines: from Sardinia, an island in the
                      Mediterranean Sea
                  teddy bear: from Theodore ("Teddy")
                      Roosevelt, twenty-sixth President of the
                      United States

E X E R C I S E 3 ▶   **Researching Word Origins**

Using a dictionary that gives word origins, find out what language each of the following words was borrowed from. Give the meaning of the original foreign word if your dictionary lists it.

1. noble
2. chigger
3. jungle
4. ghoul
5. tortilla

E X E R C I S E 4 ▶   **Researching Words from Names**

Use a dictionary to find out what name each of the following words comes from. Then choose one of the words and research it further in an encyclopedia. In two or three sentences, explain how and when the word came into English.

1. cashmere
2. sandwich
3. diesel
4. pasteurize
5. watt

American English

When English colonists first settled in the New World, they used the same form of English that their relatives in England used. But the colonists began to develop their own form of English—*American English.* Gradually, colonists and settlers adopted new pronunciations and spellings of words. They also kept some old forms of words that people in England began to change.

Speakers of American English have borrowed words from many different languages. The languages of American Indian peoples, of African peoples, and of immigrants from around the world have helped shape the American English we use today. Here are just a few examples of words American English has borrowed from other languages.

AMERICAN INDIAN	chipmunk, moose, totem
AFRICAN	gumbo, okra
SPANISH	avocado, patio, tamale
DUTCH	boss, sleigh, waffle

The Granger Collection, New York.

Dialects of American English

Different groups of people speak different forms of American English. These special forms are called *dialects.* Dialects vary from one another in vocabulary, grammar, and pronunciation. You are already familiar with standard American English, the variety of English most often used in books and newspapers, in schools and businesses, and on radio and television. In addition to standard English, Americans speak two kinds of dialects: *regional dialects* and *ethnic dialects.*

Regional Dialects

You've probably noticed that people from a particular region of the country tend to talk alike. That's because they use the same *regional dialect.* There are three major regional dialects in the United States: *Northern, Midland,* and *Southern.* Here are some examples of the differences between them.

	NORTHERN	MIDLAND	SOUTHERN
Vocabulary	johnnycake	corn bread	corn pone
Grammar	ten pound	ten pounds	ten pound
Pronunciation	*greasy* with an *s* sound	*greasy* with an *s* or a *z* sound	*greasy* with a *z* sound

It's important to know that not everyone in a region must use that region's dialect. Also, people in one region may use words and expressions that are considered part of another group's dialect.

Ethnic Dialects

Your cultural heritage can also make a difference in how you speak. The English used by a particular cultural group is called an ***ethnic dialect.*** Like a regional dialect, an ethnic dialect is a shared language that many (but not all) members of a group have in common.

The most widely spoken American ethnic dialects are the Black English of many African Americans and the Spanish-influenced English of many people from Mexico, Central America, Cuba, and Puerto Rico. Many words from these dialects have become part of the general American vocabulary. For example, *jazz* and *jukebox* come from African American dialect, and *bronco* and *mesa* come from Hispanic English.

| EXERCISE 5▶ | **Hearing a Dialect** |

When writers use dialect, they help you hear a character's speech. In the following passage, the speaker is an African American girl who is riding in a car with her family. She decides to ask her uncle a straightforward question—whether or not he is going to get married. In this passage, she explains why she is inclined to "speak-up" about what's on her mind. Read the passage aloud, pronouncing the words as the author has spelled them. Is the character's dialect different from the way you speak? How would you express the same thoughts in your own dialect?

So there I am in the navigator seat. And I turn to him and just plain old ax him. I mean I come right on out with it. No sense goin all around that barn the old folks talk about. And like my mama say, Hazel—which is my real name and what she remembers to call me when she bein serious—when you got somethin on your mind, speak up and let the chips fall where they may. And if anybody don't like it, tell em to come see your mama. And Daddy look up from the paper and say, You hear your mama good, Hazel. And tell em to come see me first. Like that. That's how I was raised.

Toni Cade Bambara, "Gorilla, My Love"

Standard American English

Many Americans use more than one variety of English. They speak a regional or ethnic dialect at home and use *standard American English* at school or work. Standard English is the most widely used and accepted variety of American English. Because it's commonly understood, it allows people from many different regions and cultures to communicate with one another clearly. It is the variety of English you read and hear most often in books and magazines, on radio and television. It is the kind of English people are expected to use in most school and business situations.

Standard English has rules and guidelines that help you to recognize and use it. Some of these rules and guidelines are presented for you in the **Handbook** in this textbook. To identify the differences between standard American English and other varieties of English, the **Handbook** uses the labels *standard* and *nonstandard*. *Nonstandard* doesn't mean wrong language. It means language that is inappropriate in situations where standard English is expected.

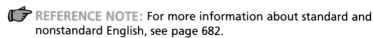 **REFERENCE NOTE:** For more information about standard and nonstandard English, see page 682.

Choosing Your Words

Because English has such a large vocabulary, you can say the same thing in many different ways. For example, the following sentences have basically the same meaning:

> I am leaving, but I will return in a short period of time.
> I'm going out, but I'll be back in a spell.

Words communicate much more than basic meanings. They also express attitudes and feelings. That's why it's important to choose your words with care, adapting your language to suit different purposes, audiences, and situations.

Formal and Informal English

Look again at the example sentences on page 394. Just a few words have been changed from the first sentence to the second, but the effect of each sentence is different. One is written in *formal English* and the other in *informal English*.

Formal English is the language you would use for dignified occasions such as public speeches, graduation ceremonies, and serious papers and reports. It often includes long sentences and extremely precise words. It usually doesn't include contractions such as *don't* or *isn't*.

The following paragraph about cowboys is written in formal English. Notice the author's word choice and the length of the sentences.

> Many a cowboy has spread his bandanna, perhaps none too clean itself, over dirty, muddy water and used it as a strainer to drink through; sometimes he used it as a cup towel, which he called a "drying rag." If the bandanna was dirty, it was probably not so dirty as the other apparel of the cowboy, for when he came to a hole of water, he was wont to dismount and wash out his handkerchief, letting it dry while he rode along, holding it in his hand or spread over his hat. Often he wore it under his hat in order to help keep his head cool. At other times, in the face of a fierce gale, he used it to tie down his hat. The bandanna made a good sling for a broken arm; it made a good bandage for a blood wound.
>
> J. Frank Dobie, *A Vaquero of the Brush Country*

Informal English is used in most everyday speaking and writing. For example, you probably use informal English when you talk with family members or friends and when you write personal letters or journal entries. Informal English usually has short sentences that are easy to understand. It also includes contractions and conversational expressions.

In the following passage, a teenage girl is speaking. How does the writer's language differ from J. Frank Dobie's?

> The first time I visited Meg's house, she took me upstairs to her room, and I wound up trying on her clothes. We were pretty much the same size, since Meg was shorter and thinner than average. Maybe that's how we became friends in the first place. Wearing Meg's jeans and T-shirt, I looked at myself in the mirror. I could almost pass for an American—from the back, anyway.
>
> Lensey Namioka, "The All-American Slurp"

Uses of Informal English

There are two uses of informal English that you should be familiar with: *colloquialisms* and *slang*.

Colloquialisms are the colorful, widely used expressions of conversational language.

EXAMPLES   That movie **gave me the creeps.**
Bernice is a **real sport.**
The children were **acting up** at bedtime.

Slang consists of made-up words and old words used in new ways. Most slang expressions are a special vocabulary for a particular group of people, such as teenagers, musicians, or military recruits. Because slang has a limited use, it usually lives a short life.

The following words, when used with the given meanings, are all considered slang. Although these expressions were once current, they probably seem out-of-date to you now. What slang words do you and your friends use to express the same meanings?

cool: pleasing, excellent
hang out: spend time at a place
get into: enjoy, be interested in
grub: food

Luann reprinted by permission of United Feature Syndicate, Inc.

STYLE NOTE You may want to use slang sometimes in journal entries, letters to friends, and other writing that's highly informal. However, don't use slang in formal writing such as essays, test answers, or reports. Notice how inappropriate slang sounds in an otherwise formal sentence:

> We toured the elegant, stately rooms of Monticello, Thomas Jefferson's *cool pad.*

E X E R C I S E 6 ▶ **Using Formal or Informal English**

What kind of language would you use in each of the following situations? Choose one of the situations and do the writing described. Use the formal or informal English that you think is appropriate for the situation.

1. a letter to a mail-order company complaining about a faulty product
2. a note to a friend's parents thanking them for taking you on a weekend trip
3. a journal entry describing something funny that happened at school
4. a conversation between two teenagers in a mall

Denotation and Connotation

Would you rather be described as *thrifty* or *stingy*? The words have the same basic meaning, or **denotation,** but they have very different effects on a reader or listener. They have different emotional associations, or **connotations.** You might be pleased if someone described you as *thrifty*, since the word suggests the positive quality of being economical. But you would probably be offended if someone described you as *stingy*, since the word has negative associations of selfishness and penny-pinching.

Think about the connotations of a word before you use it. If you use a word without taking into account its emotional effect, you may send the wrong message to your audience.

STYLE NOTE It's especially important to think about connotations when you are choosing among *synonyms*—words that have similar meanings. For example, suppose you've written the following sentence in a classified advertisement for a yard sale. You decide that you need to replace the word *selective.* Which of the words in parentheses is the best replacement?

> Attention, selective shoppers: we have a great selection of records, clothing, lawn tools, and toys. (*picky, choosy*)

Picky and *choosy* are both synonyms for *selective,* but they have very different connotations. *Picky* is a negative word that suggests your customers are overly fussy. *Choosy* is a positive word that suggests they are particular about what they buy. Which word is appropriate for your ad?

Tired Words and Expressions

You would probably get annoyed if you heard the same song being played every time you turned on the radio. After a while, the song would lose its appeal. The same thing happens to words when they are overused. They become tired, and they lose their freshness and force. *Nice, fine, great,* and *wonderful* are good examples of tired words. They may be acceptable in conversation, but they are too vague to be effective in writing.

Tired expressions, or *clichés,* are also vague and bland. Here are some examples of clichés.

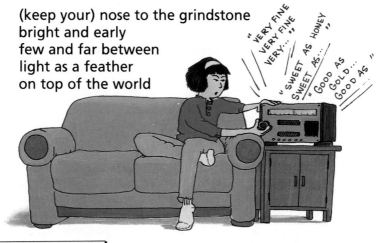

(keep your) nose to the grindstone
bright and early
few and far between
light as a feather
on top of the world

EXERCISE 7 ▶   **Identifying Tired Words and Clichés**

Make a list of all the tired words and expressions you can think of. Spend a few days watching and listening for them, jotting down words and expressions in a notebook as you hear them. Then, compare your list with those of your classmates. By combining lists, you'll have a handy collection of words and expressions to avoid when you write.

COMPUTER NOTE: Once you have made a list of tired words and clichés, use your word-processing program's Find command to search for each of them in your draft. Then, use the thesaurus tool to choose appropriate synonyms.

Jargon

Jargon is special language that is used by a particular group of people, such as people who share the same profession, occupation, sport, or hobby. A word can be used as jargon by several groups, with each group giving it a different meaning. For example, the word *hold* is used by lawyers to mean "to bind by contract" and by musicians to mean "a pause" or "to prolong a tone or rest."

Jargon can be practical and effective because it reduces many words to just one or two. However, jargon is inappropriate for a general audience, who may not be familiar with the special meanings of the words.

👉 REFERENCE NOTE: For an example of how dictionaries label special uses of words, see pages 890–891.

EXERCISE 8 ▶ **Translating Jargon**

Like many other groups, television and movie crews have their own jargon. Look up each of the following words in a dictionary to find out what special meaning it has for filmmakers.

1. cut
2. dolly
3. dub
4. fade
5. frame

6. pan
7. scene
8. tracking shot
9. wipe
10. zoom

MAKING CONNECTIONS

Writing Original Autographs

It's the last day of the school year, and your classmates are passing around autograph books in the cafeteria. You're about to sign a friend's book when you notice that everyone has written the same tired, boring expressions around the page. Instead of saying the same things everyone else has, you decided to write a lively, original message for each of your friends to remember you by.

Here are some of the autographs that you *don't* want to write. Use your imagination to express the same thoughts and feelings in more interesting ways. Write each autograph in any form you like—as a poem, a short letter, or just an attention-grabbing sentence or two.

Have a terrific summer!
Lian

Take it easy over the summer.
Angelo

You're a great friend
Hope to see you next year!
John

Roses are red,
violets are blue.
It's great to have
a friend like you.
Paula

Nice knowing you,
Dolores

Hope you have a good time on vacation
Chet

PART TWO

HANDBOOK

13 THE SENTENCE

Subject and Predicate, Kinds of Sentences

Diagnostic Test

A. Identifying Sentences and Sentence Fragments

Identify each group of words as a *sentence* or a *sentence fragment*. If the word group is a sentence fragment, correct it by adding words to make a complete sentence.

EXAMPLES
1. Although I know your first name.
1. *sentence fragment—Although I know your first name, I don't know your last name.*

2. You may call me by my given name or by my surname.
2. *sentence*

1. While it may seem strange to go by one name.
2. People had only first names for thousands of years.
3. Calling people by one name.

4. The ancient Romans sometimes gave people second names.
5. Last names became common in the thirteenth century in Italy.

B. Identifying Subjects and Predicates

Label each italicized group of words as the *complete subject* or the *complete predicate* of the sentence. Then, identify the simple subject or the verb in each word group.

EXAMPLES **1.** *The mean dog next door* barks fiercely.
        1. *complete subject; simple subject—dog*

        2. The mean dog next door *barks fiercely.*
        2. *complete predicate; verb—barks*

6. Mr. Adams *gave me his old croquet set.*
7. Why did *that large new boat* sink on such a clear day?
8. *Trees and bushes all over the neighborhood* had been torn out by the storm.
9. Walking to school, Bill *was splashed by a passing car.*
10. *My old bicycle with the ape-hanger handlebars* is rusting away in the garage now.
11. *The creek behind my house* rises during the summer rains.
12. Sandy's little sister *bravely dived off the high board at the community pool.*
13. *Does* Max *want another serving of pie?*
14. My cousins and I *played basketball and walked over to the mall yesterday.*
15. *Fridays and other test days* always seem longer than regular school days.

C. Classifying Sentences

Classify each of the following sentences as *declarative, interrogative, imperative,* or *exclamatory.* Then, write the last word of each sentence and supply the correct end punctuation.

EXAMPLE   **1.** Please tell me if the seahorse is a fish
              1. *imperative—fish.*

16. The sea horse is a very unusual kind of fish
17. What a beautiful butterfly that is
18. Can you believe that most polar bears don't hibernate
19. Daniel, find out how many miles per hour a rabbit can hop
20. Some jack rabbits can hop forty miles per hour

The Sentence

13a. A *sentence* is a group of words that expresses a complete thought.

A sentence begins with a capital letter and ends with a period, a question mark, or an exclamation point.

EXAMPLES   Sean was chosen captain of his soccer team.
           Have you read the novel *Shane*?
           What a dangerous mission it must have been!

When a group of words looks like a sentence but does not express a complete thought, it is a *sentence fragment.*

SENTENCE FRAGMENT   The music of Scott Joplin. [This is not a complete thought. What about the music of Scott Joplin?]

SENTENCE   The music of Scott Joplin has been recorded by many musicians.

SENTENCE FRAGMENT   After watching Rita Moreno. [The thought is not complete. Who watched Rita Moreno? What happened afterward?]

SENTENCE   After watching Rita Moreno, Carol decided to become an entertainer.

SENTENCE FRAGMENT	**Even though she had worked a long time.** [The thought is not complete. What happened even though she had worked a long time?]
SENTENCE	**Louise Nevelson had not completed the sculpture even though she had worked a long time.**

☞ REFERENCE NOTE: For more information about sentence fragments, see pages 361–362.

▶ EXERCISE 1 **Identifying Sentences and Revising Sentence Fragments**

Tell whether each group of words is a *sentence* or a *sentence fragment*. If the word group is a sentence, correct it by adding a capital letter and end punctuation. If the word group is a sentence fragment, correct it by adding words to make a complete sentence.

EXAMPLES **1.** classes in mountain climbing will begin soon
1. *sentence—Classes in mountain climbing will begin soon.*

2. living alone in the mountains
2. *sentence fragment—Living alone in the mountains, the couple make their own furniture and clothes.*

1. catching the baseball with both hands
2. in the back of the storeroom stands a stack of boxes
3. a long, narrow passage with a hidden trapdoor at each end
4. after waiting for six hours
5. the gymnasium is open
6. last night there were six television commercials every half-hour
7. instead of calling the doctor this morning about her sore throat
8. beneath the tall ceiling of the church
9. are you careful about shutting off unnecessary lights
10. doing the multiplication tables

EXERCISE 2

Identifying Sentences and Sentence Fragments

Tell whether each group of words is a *sentence* or a *sentence fragment*.

EXAMPLES   [1] Can you name the famous American woman in the picture below?
1. *sentence*

[2] A woman who made history.
2. *sentence fragment*

[1] One of the best-known women in American history is Sacagawea. [2] A member of the Lemhi band of the Shoshones. [3] She is famous for her role as interpreter for the Lewis and Clark expedition. [4] Which was seeking the Northwest Passage.

[5] In 1800, the Lemhis had encountered a war party of the Hidatsa. [6] Who captured some of the Lemhis, including Sacagawea. [7] Later, with Charbonneau, her French Canadian husband, and their two-month-old son. [8] Sacagawea joined the Lewis and Clark expedition in what is now North Dakota. [9] Her knowledge of many languages enabled the explorers to communicate with various peoples. [10] Sacagawea also searched for plants that were safe to eat. [11] And once saved valuable instruments during a storm. [12] As they traveled farther. [13] The explorers came across the Lemhis. [14] From whom Sacagawea had been separated years before. [15] The Lemhis helped the explorers. [16] By giving them guidance.

The Granger Collection, New York.

[17] After they returned from the expedition. [18] Clark tried to settle Sacagawea and Charbonneau in St. Louis. [19] However, the couple moved back to Sacagawea's native land. [20] Where this famous woman died in 1812.

▶ EXERCISE 3　**Writing Interesting Sentences**

Revise each sentence fragment by adding words to make an interesting sentence.

EXAMPLE　**1.** At the last minute.
　　　　　1. *At the last minute, her parachute opened.*

1. on the last day of summer
2. found only in the country
3. a graceful ballerina
4. burning out of control
5. the old building by the lake

The Subject and the Predicate

A sentence consists of two parts: a *subject* and a *predicate*.

13b. A *subject* tells whom or what the sentence is about. The *predicate* tells something about the subject. A complete subject or a complete predicate may be only one word or more than one word.

EXAMPLES
comp. subj. | comp. pred.
Christopher | ran the mile in record time.

comp. subj. | comp. pred.
Three jars on the shelf | exploded.

comp. subj. | comp. pred.
A large silver poodle | won first prize.

Usually, the subject comes before the predicate. Sometimes, however, the subject may appear elsewhere in the sentence. To find the subject of a sentence, ask *Who?* or *What?* before the predicate.

EXAMPLES   **A bird's nest** sat at the top of the tree. [What sat at the top of the tree? A bird's nest sat there.]

Laughing and running down the street were **two small boys.** [Who were laughing and running down the street? Two small boys were.]

Can **horses** and **cattle** swim? [What can swim? Horses and cattle can swim.]

▶ EXERCISE 4   Identifying Subjects and Predicates

Write the following sentences. Separate the complete subject from the complete predicate with a vertical line.

EXAMPLE   [1] Legends and folk tales have been repeated and enjoyed throughout the Americas.

   1. *Legends and folk tales | have been repeated and enjoyed throughout the Americas.*

[1] The Chorotega people lived in Nicoya, Costa Rica, hundreds of years ago. [2] One Chorotega folk tale tells the story of the Chorotegan treasure and praises Princess Nosara for protecting it from the Chirenos. [3] Chireno warriors landed, according to the story, on the Nicoya Peninsula and attacked the Chorotegas. [4] The Chorotegas were surprised but reacted quickly. [5] Princess Nosara grabbed the treasure and ran to her friend's house for help. [6] Nosara and he took a bow and some arrows and fled into the woods. [7] The couple ran from the enemy all night and at last reached a river. [8] The brave girl dashed into the mountains alone, hid the treasure, and returned to the river. [9] Chireno warriors attacked shortly after her return, however, and killed the princess and her friend. [10] The murderous Chirenos searched for the treasure but never found it.

▶ EXERCISE 5   Identifying Complete Subjects and Complete Predicates

When you were younger, did you ever play mix-and-match animal games? In those games, players combine

GRAMMAR

pictures of the head and upper body of one animal with the lower body and feet of another animal to make funny-looking creatures. You can play the same kind of mix-and-match game with sentence parts. Here are five complete subjects and five complete predicates that are all mixed up. Match each subject with a predicate to create sentences. Use any combination you want, but use each one only once. Be sure to capitalize and punctuate each sentence correctly. Then, draw a line between the complete subject and the complete predicate.

EXAMPLE   **1.** a blue whale feeling happy
                  likes to sing and dance
            1. *A blue whale feeling happy* | *likes to sing and dance.*

the purple elephant in the airport
screeched to a stop in front of the school
looked at my brother and sneezed
three opossums standing perfectly still
ate our telephone book and asked for more
a bird with wings twice as long as your arms
a noisy snail named Speedy
is sitting on my sandwich
the red and black frogs on the table
was reading the Help Wanted ads in the newspaper

The Simple Subject

13c. A *simple subject* is the main word in the complete subject.

EXAMPLES   My **date** for the dance | arrived late. [The complete subject is *My date for the dance.*]
                  The long, hard **trip** across the desert | was finally over. [The complete subject is *The long, hard trip across the desert.*]
                  Pacing back and forth in the cage was | a hungry **tiger.** [The complete subject is *a hungry tiger.*]

GRAMMAR

The simple subject may consist of more than one word.

EXAMPLES **Stamp collecting** | is my father's hobby.
Looney Tunes | is my favorite cartoon show on television.
Ann Richards | was elected governor of Texas.

The simple subjects in these examples are all compound nouns.

☞ REFERENCE NOTE: For more information on compound nouns, see page 432.

NOTE: In this book, the term *subject* refers to the simple subject unless otherwise indicated.

▶ EXERCISE 6 **Identifying Complete Subjects and Simple Subjects**

Identify the *complete subject* and the *simple subject* in each sentence of the following paragraph.

EXAMPLE [1] The teams in the picture on the next page compete in the Caribbean Baseball Leagues.

1. complete subject—*The teams in the picture on the next page;* simple subject—*teams*

[1] People throughout Latin America enjoy going out to a ballgame. [2] The all-American sport of baseball has been very popular there for a long time. [3] In fact, fans in countries such as Cuba, Panama, and Venezuela go wild over the game. [4] As a result, the Caribbean Baseball Leagues were formed more than fifty years ago. [5] Each year the teams in Latin America play toward a season championship. [6] That championship is known as the Caribbean World Series. [7] A total of more than one hundred players compete in the series. [8] Many talented Latin American players are recruited by major United States teams each year. [9] The list of these players includes such baseball greats as Fernando Valenzuela, Ramón Martinez, and José Canseco. [10] In addition, a number of U.S. players train in the Latin American winter leagues.

The Simple Predicate, or Verb

13d. A *simple predicate,* or *verb,* is the main word or group of words in the complete predicate.

In the following examples, the vertical lines separate the complete subjects from the complete predicates.

EXAMPLES   comp. subj.   comp. pred.
The popular movie star | **signed** autographs for hours.

comp. subj.   comp. pred.
The trees | **sagged** beneath the weight of the ice.

    A simple predicate may be a one-word verb, or it may be a verb phrase. A *verb phrase* consists of a main verb and its helping verbs.

EXAMPLES   comp. subj.   comp. pred.
Our class | **is reading** the famous novel *Frankenstein.*

comp. subj.   comp. pred.
The musicians | **have been rehearsing** since noon.

comp. subj.   comp. pred.
Those books | **will** not **be** available in the media center until next week.

The words *not* and *never*, which are frequently used with verbs, are not part of a verb phrase. Both of these words are adverbs.

EXAMPLES   She | **did** not **believe** me.
The two cousins | **had** never **met.**

☞ REFERENCE NOTE: For more information about verb phrases, see pages 464–465.

A ***complete predicate*** consists of a verb and all the words that describe the verb and complete its meaning. Sometimes the complete predicate can appear at the beginning of a sentence.

                   comp. pred.   comp. subj.
EXAMPLE   **On the tiny branch perched** | a chickadee.

Part of the predicate may appear on one side of the subject and the rest on the other side.

EXAMPLE   **Before winter** many birds **fly south.**

NOTE: In this book, the term *verb* refers to the simple predicate unless otherwise indicated.

▶ EXERCISE 7   **Identifying Complete Predicates and Verbs**

Identify the *complete predicate* and the *verb* in each of the following sentences. Keep in mind that parts of the complete predicate may come before and after the complete subject.

EXAMPLE   **1.** A ton and a half of groceries may seem like a big order for a family of five.
1. *complete predicate—may seem like a big order for a family of five; verb—may seem*

1. Such a big order is possible in the village of Pang.
2. This small village is located near the Arctic Circle.
3. The people of Pang receive their groceries once a year.
4. A supply ship can visit Pang only during a short time each summer.

GRAMMAR

5. In spring, families order their year's supply of groceries by mail.
6. The huge order is delivered to Pang a few months later.
7. The people store the groceries in their homes.
8. Frozen food is kept outdoors.
9. Too costly for most residents is the air-freight charge for a grocery shipment to Pang.
10. Villagers also must hunt and fish for much of their food.

▶ EXERCISE 8   **Identifying Verbs and Verb Phrases**

Identify the *verb* or *verb phrase* in each of the following sentences.

EXAMPLE   [1] **Samuel Pepys (pēps) was an English government worker.**
   1. *was*

[1] Between 1660 and 1669, Samuel Pepys kept a diary. [2] He wrote the diary in a secret shorthand. [3] This secret shorthand was finally decoded after many years of hard work. [4] In 1825, *The Diary of Samuel Pepys* was published. [5] Presented in the diary is a personal look at life in England during the seventeenth century. [6] In many entries Pepys told about his family and friends. [7] Some of these accounts are quite humorous. [8] In other entries Pepys described very serious events. [9] For example, in entries during 1666, Pepys gave a detailed account of the Great Fire of London. [10] What other events might be described in the diary?

▶ REVIEW·A   **Identifying Subjects and Verbs**

Identify the *subject* and the *verb* in each of the following sentences.

EXAMPLE   [1] **In Greek mythology, Medusa was a horrible monster.**
   1. *subject—Medusa; verb—was*

[1] On Medusa's head grew snakes instead of hair. [2] According to Greek myth, a glance at Medusa would turn a mortal into stone. [3] However, one proud mortal, named Perseus, went in search of Medusa. [4] Fortunately, he received help from the goddess Athena and the god Hermes. [5] From Athena, Perseus accepted a shiny shield. [6] With Hermes as his guide, Perseus soon found Medusa. [7] He knew about Medusa's power. [8] Therefore, he did not look directly at her. [9] Instead, he saw her reflection in the shiny shield. [10] The picture below shows Perseus's victory over the evil Medusa.

▶ REVIEW B **Writing Sentences**

Some of the following word groups are complete subjects and some are complete predicates. Write each word group, adding the part needed to make a sentence. Then, underline the subject once and the verb twice.

EXAMPLE **1.** marched for five hours
1. *The members of the band marched for five hours.*

1. should not be left alone
2. the vacant lot down the street
3. danced across the floor
4. looked mysteriously at us
5. their best player
6. the famous movie star

7. is going to the game
8. one of the Jackson twins
9. could have been left on the bus
10. the neighborhood watch group

The Sentence Base

Because a subject and a verb are the essential parts of a sentence, they are called the *sentence base.* All the other words in a sentence are attached to the sentence base.

Sentence base: **Dogs play.**
Sentence base with other words attached: Every day two frisky **dogs** named Bison and Stark **play** for hours on our lawn.

The additional words give informative details, but they would be meaningless without the sentence base.

EXERCISE 9   **Using the Sentence Base to Write Complete Sentences**

How would you send an urgent message to someone? Today, you might use a facsimile (fax) machine, a telephone, or a computer. You could also send a telegram. In 1837, Samuel F. B. Morse invented the first telegraph machine for sending messages electronically. Telegraph messages, called telegrams, are usually short because the number of words in a message determines the cost of sending it.

Your family has just received this telegram from your uncle who is coming to visit. Add words to each sentence base in this message to fill in details about what happened.

CAR BROKE DOWN. DOG FAINTED. HELP ARRIVED. CAR REPAIRED. WE ARRIVE SUNDAY.

EXAMPLE   **1. BAD LUCK CONTINUES.**
1. *Our bad luck on this vacation continues to cost us time and money.*

The Compound Subject

13e. A *compound subject* consists of two or more connected subjects that have the same verb. The usual connecting words are *and* and *or*.

EXAMPLES **Keshia** and **Todd** worked a jigsaw puzzle.
Either **Carmen** or **Ernesto** will videotape the ceremony tomorrow.
Among the guest speakers were an **astronaut,** an **engineer,** and a **journalist.**

EXERCISE 10 **Identifying Compound Subjects and Their Verbs**

Identify the *compound subject* and the *verb* in each of the following sentences.

EXAMPLE **1.** Festivals and celebrations are happy times throughout the world.
1. *compound subject—Festivals, celebrations; verb—are*

1. Children and nature are honored with their own festivals in Japan.
2. Among Japanese nature festivals are the Cherry Blossom Festival and the Chrysanthemum Festival.
3. Fierce dragons and huge ships fly in the sky during Singapore's Kite Festival.
4. Elaborate masks and costumes are an important part of the Carnival Lamayote in Haiti.
5. Flowers and other small gifts are presented to teachers during Teacher's Day in the Czech Republic.
6. Brave knights and their ladies return each year to the medieval festival at Ribeauvillé, France.
7. During Sweden's Midsommar (midsummer) Festival, maypoles and buildings bloom with fresh flowers.
8. Wrestling and pole climbing attract crowds to the Tatar Festival of the Plow in Russia.

9. Games, dances, and feasts highlight the Green Corn Dance of the Seminole Indians of the Florida Everglades.
10. In Munich, Germany, floats and bandwagons add color to the Oktoberfest Parade.

The Compound Verb

13f. A *compound verb* consists of two or more verbs that have the same subject.

A connecting word—usually *and, or,* or *but*—is used between the verbs.

EXAMPLES   The dog **barked** and **growled** at the stranger.
We **can go** forward, **go** back, or **stay** right here.
The man **was convicted** but later **was found** innocent of the crime.

 EXERCISE 11   **Identifying Subjects and Compound Verbs**

Identify the *subject* and the *compound verb* in each of the following sentences.

EXAMPLE   **1.** The hikers loaded their backpacks and studied the map of the mountain trails.
1. *subject—hikers; compound verb—loaded, studied*

1. Linda wrote her essay and practiced the piano last night.
2. Miami is the largest city in southern Florida and has been a popular resort area since the 1920s.
3. According to Greek mythology, Arachne angered Athena and was changed into a spider.
4. Martina Arroyo has sung in major American opera halls and has made appearances abroad.
5. This year the Wildcats won seven games and lost five.

6. During special sales, shoppers arrive early at the mall and search for bargains.
7. Maria Montessori studied medicine in Italy and developed new methods for teaching children.
8. Jim Rice autographed baseballs and made a short speech.
9. General Lee won many battles but lost the war.
10. In the summer many students go to music camps or take music lessons.

Both the subject and the verb of a sentence may be compound. In such a sentence, each subject goes with each verb.

$$\overset{S}{} \qquad \overset{S}{} \ \overset{V}{}$$
EXAMPLE The **captain** and the **crew battled** the storm and

$$\overset{V}{}$$
hoped for better weather. [The captain battled and hoped, and the crew battled and hoped.]

▶ EXERCISE 12   **Identifying Compound Subjects and Compound Verbs**

Identify the *subjects* and the *verbs* in each sentence in the following paragraph.

EXAMPLE [1] In the picture on the next page, Aaron Neville and his brothers are performing at the New Orleans Jazz Festival.
1. *subjects—Aaron Neville, brothers; verb—are performing*

[1] Aaron and his brothers (Art, Charles, and Cyril) make up the Neville Brothers. [2] The four brothers play different instruments and have their own individual styles. [3] They formed their act and started singing together in 1977. [4] Before then, the brothers performed and toured separately. [5] New Orleans is their hometown and has influenced their music. [6] They grew up hearing music at home and found it everywhere. [7] New Orleans gospel sounds and jazz rhythms fill the brothers' songs. [8] The four brothers have strong opinions and often sing

about social issues. [9] *Yellow Moon* and *Brother's Keeper* are two of their most popular albums. [10] The children and grandchildren of the Neville Brothers have now joined in this family's musical tradition.

 EXERCISE 13 **Writing Sentences and Identifying Subjects and Verbs**

Write ten sentences describing the major characters and actions in your favorite book or movie. Include at least two compound subjects and two compound verbs. Underline each subject once and each verb twice.

EXAMPLE **1.** *Bilbo Baggins* and the *dwarves* <u>travel</u> to the *Lonely Mountain in* The Hobbit.

WRITING APPLICATION

Using Subjects and Predicates to Express Whole Thoughts

Peanut butter and jelly, socks and shoes—what do they have in common? They are pairs of things that work together. A subject and a predicate are another working pair. You've got to use both of them to form a sentence that clearly expresses a whole thought.

SUBJECT   Alvin's new hamster
PREDICATE ran in its exercise wheel all night long.
SENTENCE   Alvin's new hamster ran in its exercise wheel all night long.

WRITING ACTIVITY

Your best friend is on vacation, and you are pet-sitting. Write a paragraph in your journal about your experiences taking care of your friend's pet.

Prewriting You could write about a pet you know or one that is unfamiliar to you. Jot down notes about the pet you choose. Then, think about what you might do or what might happen while you're taking care of the pet.

Writing As you write your first draft, think about how to organize your notes and your thoughts. Tell about your experiences in a logical order, and use complete sentences. Your tone can be humorous or serious.

Evaluating and Revising Read through your paragraph to be sure that each sentence has a subject and a predicate. Does your paragraph tell about your experience in an interesting way? Add, delete, or rearrange details to make your paragraph more entertaining or informative.

Proofreading Read over your paragraph once more, looking for errors in punctuation, spelling, and capitalization. The names of kinds or breeds of domestic animals aren't capitalized unless they contain a proper noun or adjective, as in *English setter*.

Kinds of Sentences

13g. A *declarative sentence* makes a statement. It is followed by a period.

EXAMPLES   Miriam Colón founded the Puerto Rican
                    Traveling Theatre.
            Curiosity is the beginning of knowledge.

13h. An *interrogative sentence* asks a question. It is followed by a question mark.

EXAMPLES   What do you know about glaciers**?**
Was the game exciting**?**

13i. An *imperative sentence* gives a command or makes a request. It is followed by a period. A strong command is followed by an exclamation point.

EXAMPLES   Do your homework each night**.**
John, please close the door**.**
Watch out**!**

If an imperative sentence does not have a subject, the "understood" subject is always *you*.

(You) Do your homework each night.
John, (you) please close the door.
(You) Watch out!

13j. An *exclamatory sentence* shows excitement or expresses strong feeling. It is followed by an exclamation point.

EXAMPLES   What a sight the sunset is**!**
Sarah won the VCR**!**

NOTE: Many people overuse exclamation points. In your own writing, save exclamation points for sentences that really do show strong emotion. When it is overused, this mark of punctuation loses its impact.

▶ EXERCISE 14   **Classifying Sentences**

Classify each of the following sentences according to its purpose.

EXAMPLE   **1.** Let no man pull you so low as to make you hate him.

Booker T. Washington, from *I Have a Dream*
1. *imperative*

1. If all the beasts were gone, men would die from great loneliness of spirit, for whatever happens to the beasts also happens to the man.

   Chief Seattle, from his statement of surrender

2. No one can make you feel inferior without your consent.

   Eleanor Roosevelt, *This Is My Story*

3. What happens to a dream deferred?

   Langston Hughes, "Harlem"

4. I know not what course others may take; but as for me, give me liberty or give me death!

   Patrick Henry, speech in the Virginia Convention of 1775

5. Look! Up in the sky! It's a bird! It's a plane! It's Superman!

   ™DC Comics Inc. All rights reserved. Used by permission of DC Comics Inc.

6. Join the union, girls, and together say *Equal Pay for Equal Work.*

   Susan B. Anthony, *The Revolution* (October 8, 1868)

7. Why must everything work the same way for everybody?

   Denise Chávez, *The Flying Tortilla Man*

8. Peace is respect for the rights of others.

   Benito Juárez, from *The Kaleidoscopic Air*

9. The history of every country begins in the heart of a man or woman.

   Willa Cather, *O Pioneers!*

10. He who has courage and faith will never perish in misery!

    Anne Frank, *Anne Frank: The Diary of a Young Girl*

▶ REVIEW C   **Classifying Sentences**

Choose the appropriate end punctuation for each sentence. Classify each sentence according to its purpose.

EXAMPLE   **1.** Turn left at the corner
            1. *period—imperative*

1. Alana bought some angelfish for her aquarium

2. How many times has our track team won the state championship
3. Imagine a ride in the space shuttle
4. Because of its ruffled "collar," the frilled lizard looks like a comical monster
5. Can you give me directions to the post office
6. How fresh the air feels after a storm
7. Think about both sides of the problem
8. Many large museums in the United States display pottery made by Maria Martinez
9. What teams are playing in the World Series
10. What a fantastic world lies beneath the waves

PICTURE THIS

You are a member of the City Improvement Committee. Each month the committee awards a prize to the person who has done the most to improve the city's appearance. Your job is to rate this sculpture and report back to the rest of the committee. Miriam Schapiro designed this large, outdoor sculpture called *Anna and David*. The two dancing figures are made of painted stainless steel and aluminum. Write five sentences about the sculpture, giving your opinion of it. Use each of the four kinds of sentences at least once, and punctuate them correctly.

Miriam Schapiro, *Anna and David* (1987). Painted stainless steel and aluminum, 35' × 31' × 9". Courtesy Steinbaum-Krauss Gallery, NYC.

Subject: outdoor sculpture
Audience: City Improvement Committee members
Purpose: to give your comments and opinions

Review: Posttest 1

A. Identifying Sentences and Sentence Fragments

Identify each group of words as a *sentence* or a *sentence fragment.* If the word group is a sentence fragment, correct it by adding words to make a complete sentence.

EXAMPLES   **1.** Do you like the U.S. Postal Service's special postage stamps?
1. *sentence*

2. When my parents buy stamps.
2. *sentence fragment—When my parents buy stamps, they ask for new commemorative ones.*

1. Commemorative stamps are issued to give special recognition to someone or something.
2. Stamps with pictures of animals or famous people.
3. A block of four different stamps that commemorate Earth Day.
4. All four of the winning designs for the Earth Day 1995 stamp were created by young people.
5. Since I like "Love" stamps and holiday stamps.

B. Identifying Subjects and Predicates

Label each italicized group of words as the *complete subject* or the *complete predicate* of the sentence. Then, identify the simple subject or the verb in each word group.

EXAMPLES **1.** *Anyone searching for the world's highest mountains* must look on land and in the sea.
1. *complete subject; simple subject—Anyone*

2. Anyone searching for the world's highest mountains *must look on land and in the sea.*
2. *complete predicate; verb—must look*

6. *Much of the earth's surface* is mountainous.
7. *Can* you *name the world's highest mountain?*
8. *Mount Everest, which is in the Himalayas,* claims that title.
9. In fact, *seven of the world's highest mountains* are in the Himalayan mountain range.
10. Mount Everest *towers to a height of 29,028 feet above sea level.*
11. *The Alps in Europe, the Rockies in North America, and the Andes in South America* are other high mountain ranges.
12. Many high mountains *also have been discovered under the ocean.*
13. Down the middle of the Atlantic Ocean floor runs *the earth's longest continuous mountain range.*
14. The peaks of some undersea mountains *rise above the surface of the water and form islands.*
15. In the Pacific Ocean, *the islands of Hawaii* are actually the peaks of submerged mountains that are part of a 1,600-mile-long chain.

C. Classifying Sentences

Classify each of the following sentences as *declarative, interrogative, imperative,* or *exclamatory.* Then, write the last word of each sentence and provide the appropriate end punctuation.

EXAMPLE **1.** Write your name and the date at the top of your paper
1. *imperative—paper.*

16. Juana plans to study architecture at the state university after she graduates
17. This isn't the right answer, is it
18. No, it definitely is not
19. Clean up your room this morning, and be sure to put your dirty clothes in the laundry hamper
20. I can't right now, Mom, because everybody is waiting for me at Andy's house

Review: Posttest 2

Writing a Variety of Sentences

Write your own sentences according to the following guidelines. Make the subjects and verbs different for each sentence.

EXAMPLE **1.** an interrogative sentence with a single subject and a single verb
1. *Is Danielle bringing dessert?*

1. a declarative sentence with a compound subject
2. an imperative sentence with a compound verb
3. a declarative sentence with a single subject and a single verb
4. an interrogative sentence with a compound subject
5. an interrogative sentence with a compound verb
6. an exclamatory sentence with a single subject and a single verb
7. an imperative sentence with a single subject and a single verb
8. a declarative sentence with a compound verb
9. an exclamatory sentence with a compound verb
10. a declarative sentence with a compound subject and a compound verb

14 THE PARTS OF SPEECH

Noun, Pronoun, Adjective

Diagnostic Test

Identifying Nouns, Pronouns, and Adjectives

Identify each italicized word in the following sentences as a *noun*, a *pronoun*, or an *adjective*.

EXAMPLE **1.** The biplane had two *wings* and a *wooden* propeller.
1. *wings—noun; wooden—adjective*

1. Sometimes I don't feel well when *it* gets cloudy and the *dark* sky threatens rain.
2. My little sister, *afraid* of *thunder* and lightning, hid under the bed.
3. Inger's mother gave *each* of us a glass of *cold* milk.
4. One by one, *each* husky ventured out into the *cold*.
5. *Who* went to the movie *Saturday* night?
6. When the *Neville Brothers* came to town, we went to *their* concert.

7. The house across the street has been up for *sale* since *Tuesday*.
8. *Diego Rivera* painted many *large* murals.
9. *That* rifle doesn't belong to *anyone*.
10. *That* is an *Aleut* mask.
11. Give me *some* iced *tea*, please.
12. *Somebody* said that there would be no more *discount* movie tickets.
13. I got a *discount* on *our* tickets, though.
14. *Mr. Taylor* donated the *sports* equipment.
15. In high school, Carl Lewis excelled in *track* and several *other* sports.
16. *Everyone* liked one painting or the *other*.
17. Juana went to the *mall* by *herself*.
18. Hobbies take up so *much* time that they often become *work*.
19. My aunt's *work* schedule often takes *her* out of town.
20. *This* parakeet screeches if he doesn't get *enough* seed.

The Eight Parts of Speech

| noun | pronoun | verb | conjunction |
| adverb | adjective | preposition | interjection |

The Noun

14a. A ***noun*** is a word used to name a person, a place, a thing, or an idea.

PERSONS	Alice Walker, Dr. Lacy, children, architect, team
PLACES	desert, neighborhood, outer space, New York City
THINGS	money, wind, animals, *Voyager 2*, Statue of Liberty
IDEAS	courage, love, freedom, luck, equality

GRAMMAR

▶ EXERCISE 1   **Identifying Nouns**

Identify all of the nouns in each of the following sentences.

EXAMPLE   **1.** Many Native American chiefs are known for their courage and wisdom.
1. *chiefs, courage, wisdom*

1. Chief Joseph of the Nez Perce was a wise leader whose American Indian name means "Thunder Traveling over the Mountains."
2. He was an educated man and wrote that his people believed in speaking only the truth.
3. In this photograph, Satanta, a Kiowa chief, wears a silver medal with the profile of President James Buchanan on it.
4. He wore the medal during a famous council for peace at Medicine Lodge Creek in Kansas.
5. In a moving speech, Satanta described the love that his people had for the Great Plains and the buffalo.
6. *The Autobiography of Black Hawk* is an interesting book by the Sauk chief who fought for lands in the Mississippi Valley.
7. Sitting Bull's warriors soundly defeated General George A. Custer and his troops at the Battle of the Little Bighorn.

8. After years of leading the Sioux in war, Sitting Bull toured with Buffalo Bill and his Wild West Show.
9. Red Cloud of the Oglala Sioux and Dull Knife of the Cheyennes were other mighty chiefs.
10. Chief Washakie received praise for his leadership of the Shoshones, but he was also a noted singer and craftsman.

Compound Nouns

A *compound noun* is two or more words used together as a single noun. The parts of a compound noun may be written as one word, as separate words, or as a hyphenated word.

ONE WORD	seafood, filmmaker, footsteps, videocassette, grasshopper, daydream, Passover, Iceland
SEPARATE WORDS	compact disc, police officer, John F. Kennedy, House of Representatives, *The Call of the Wild*
HYPHENATED WORD	self-esteem, great-grandparents, fund-raiser, fourteen-year-old, sister-in-law

NOTE: When you are not sure how to write a compound noun, look in a dictionary.

▶ EXERCISE 2   **Identifying Compound Nouns**

Identify the compound noun in each sentence of the following paragraph.

EXAMPLE   [1] Did you know that the most famous alphabet used by people with visual impairments was invented by a fifteen-year-old?
    1. *fifteen-year-old*

[1] In 1824, Louis Braille, a visually impaired French boy, decided to create an alphabet. [2] With talent, hard

work, and self-discipline, Braille developed the basics of his alphabet by the time he was fifteen years old. [3] His first version used a series of dots and dashes, but that system had drawbacks. [4] As a young teacher at the National Institute for Blind Children in Paris, Braille perfected an alphabet of raised dots. [5] Today, a machine called the braillewriter is used to write braille.

Collective Nouns

A *collective noun* is a word that names a group.

EXAMPLES   faculty   family herd team congress
             audience flock crew jury committee

Common Nouns and Proper Nouns

A *common noun* names any one of a group of persons, places, things, or ideas. A *proper noun* names a particular person, place, thing, or idea. Proper nouns always begin with a capital letter. Common nouns begin with a capital letter only at the beginning of a sentence.

COMMON NOUNS	PROPER NOUNS
poem	"The Raven," *I Am Joaquín*
nation	Mexico, United States of America
athlete	Joe Montana, Zina Garrison-Jackson
ship	*Mayflower*, U.S.S. *Constitution*
newspaper	*The New York Times*, *USA Today*
river	Rio Grande, Congo River
street	Market Street, University Avenue
day	Friday, Independence Day
city	Los Angeles, New Delhi
organization	National Forensic League, Girl Scouts of America

EXERCISE 3   Identifying Nouns

Identify the nouns in each numbered sentence in the following paragraph.

EXAMPLE   [1] Forests provide a home for insects, mammals, birds, and reptiles.

    1. *Forests, home, insects, mammals, birds, reptiles*

[1] Forests exist in many shapes, sizes, and kinds. [2] Boreal forests grow in regions that have cold winters and short springs. [3] The word *boreal* means "located in northern areas." [4] For example, the boreal forests in Canada contain mostly evergreens, which grow well in a cold climate. [5] Rain forests, on the other hand, are usually located in tropical regions. [6] However, one rain forest is found on a peninsula in the northwestern state of Washington. [7] This rain forest is able to grow in a northern climate because the area is extremely damp. [8] Forests throughout most areas of the United States have both evergreens and deciduous trees, such as oaks, beeches, and maples. [9] Pacific coastal forests extend from central California to Alaska. [10] Two types of trees that grow in these forests are the famous redwoods (the tallest trees in the world) and the giant Douglas fir.

REVIEW A   Classifying Nouns

Identify the nouns in the following paragraph. Classify each noun as *common* or *proper*.

EXAMPLE   [1] One of the most popular tourist attractions in the United States is the monument that commemorates Abraham Lincoln.

    1. *attractions—common; United States—proper; monument—common; Abraham Lincoln—proper*

[1] Each day huge crowds of people visit the Lincoln Memorial in Washington, D.C. [2] The monument was designed by Henry Bacon and was dedicated on Memorial

Day. [3] As you can see in the photograph, the Lincoln Memorial consists of a large marble hall that encloses a gigantic lifelike statue of Abraham Lincoln. [4] The figure, which was carved out of blocks of white marble, is sitting in a large armchair as if in deep meditation. [5] On the north wall is found a famous passage from an inaugural address by Lincoln, and on the south wall is inscribed the Gettysburg Address.

Concrete Nouns and Abstract Nouns

A *concrete noun* names a person, place, or thing that can be perceived by one or more of the senses (sight, hearing, taste, touch, or smell). An *abstract noun* names an idea, a feeling, a quality, or a characteristic.

CONCRETE NOUNS	hummingbird, telephone, teacher, popcorn, ocean, Golden Gate Bridge, Jesse Jackson
ABSTRACT NOUNS	knowledge, patriotism, love, humor, beliefs, beauty, competition, Zen Buddhism

The Pronoun

14b. A *pronoun* is a word used in place of one noun or more than one noun.

EXAMPLES   When Kelly saw the signal, Kelly pointed the signal out to Enrique.
When Kelly saw the signal, **she** pointed **it** out to Enrique.

Lee and Pat went fishing. Lee and Pat caught six bass.
Lee and Pat went fishing. **Both** caught six bass.

The word that a pronoun stands for is called its *antecedent.*

                        antecedent   pronoun
EXAMPLES   Elena read the **book** and returned **it** to the library.

               antecedent   pronoun
The **models** bought **themselves** new dresses.

             antecedent   pronoun   pronoun
Catherine told **her** father **she** would be late.

          pronoun   antecedent
"Do **you** know the answer?" Ms. Rios asked **Chen.**

Sometimes the antecedent is not stated.

         pronoun
EXAMPLES **Who** invented the telephone?

         pronoun
No one could solve the riddle.

  pronoun   pronoun   pronoun
I thought **you** said that **everybody** would help.

▶ EXERCISE 4   **Identifying Pronouns**

Identify the pronoun or pronouns in each sentence in the following paragraphs. After each pronoun, write the antecedent that the pronoun refers to. If a pronoun does not refer to a specific antecedent, write *unidentified.* [Note: The antecedent may appear before or after the pronoun or even in a previous sentence.]

EXAMPLE   [1] When the luggage cart fell on its side, the bags and their contents scattered everywhere.
    1. *its—cart; their—bags*

[1] The passengers scrambled to find their luggage and even got down on hands and knees to pick up their belongings. [2] In no time, the travelers found themselves quibbling over toothbrushes, combs, and magazines.

[3] One salesperson shouted, "The brown bag belongs to me! [4] It has my name on it."

[5] "Are you sure the blue socks are yours?" asked another traveler. [6] "I have a pair just like them."

[7] A young couple asked, "Who owns a pink and yellow shirt? [8] This isn't ours."

[9] "Those are the birthday presents I bought for a friend of mine!" yelled an angry man in a blue suit.

[10] As a crowd of people gathered, many just laughed, but several offered to help.

Personal Pronouns

A *personal pronoun* refers to the one speaking (*first person*), the one spoken to (*second person*), or the one spoken about (*third person*).

PERSONAL PRONOUNS	
FIRST PERSON	I, me, my, mine, we, us, our, ours
SECOND PERSON	you, your, yours
THIRD PERSON	he, him, his, she, her, hers, it, its, they, them, their, theirs
FIRST PERSON	During spring break, **I** visited **my** relatives.
SECOND PERSON	Did **you** say that this pen is **yours**?
THIRD PERSON	The coach gathered the players around **her** and gave **them** a pep talk.

NOTE: Some authorities prefer to call possessive forms of pronouns (such as *my, his,* and *their*) adjectives. Follow your teacher's instructions regarding possessive forms.

Reflexive and Intensive Pronouns

A *reflexive pronoun* refers to the subject and directs the action of the verb back to the subject. An *intensive pronoun* emphasizes a noun or another pronoun. Notice that reflexive and intensive pronouns have the same form.

REFLEXIVE AND INTENSIVE PRONOUNS	
FIRST PERSON	myself, ourselves
SECOND PERSON	yourself, yourselves
THIRD PERSON	himself, herself, itself, themselves

REFLEXIVE   Juan wrote **himself** a note as a reminder.
The rescuers did not consider **themselves** heroes.
INTENSIVE   Amelia designed the costumes **herself.**
I **myself** sold more than fifty tickets.

If you are not sure whether a pronoun is reflexive or intensive, try omitting the pronoun. If the meaning of the sentence stays the same, the pronoun is intensive. If the meaning changes, the pronoun is reflexive.

EXAMPLES   Rachel painted the fence herself.
Rachel painted the fence. [Without *herself*, the meaning stays the same. The pronoun is intensive.]

They treated themselves to a picnic.
They treated to a picnic. [Without *themselves*, the sentence doesn't make sense. The pronoun is reflexive.]

▶ EXERCISE 5   **Identifying Pronouns and Antecedents**

Identify the pronoun or pronouns in each of the following sentences as *personal, reflexive,* or *intensive.* After each pronoun, write the antecedent that the pronoun refers to. If a pronoun does not refer to a specific antecedent, write *unidentified.* [Note: The antecedent may appear before or after the pronoun or even in a previous sentence.]

EXAMPLE **1.** Italian explorer Marco Polo traveled to China, where he and Emperor Kublai Khan became friends.
   1. *he—personal—Marco Polo*

1. British explorer Sir Richard Burton himself wrote many books about his adventures in Africa.
2. We watched the movie about Robert O'Hara Burke's trip across Australia in the 1800s.
3. Queen Isabella of Spain herself gave approval for the famous voyages of Christopher Columbus.
4. Matthew Henson prided himself on being the first person actually to reach the North Pole.
5. He wrote *A Negro Explorer at the North Pole* about his expeditions with Commander Robert E. Peary.
6. I myself just read about Dutch explorer Abel Tasman's voyages on the South Seas.
7. Lewis and Clark surely considered themselves lucky to have Sacagawea, a Shoshone woman, as their guide.
8. President Thomas Jefferson sent them to explore the land west of the Mississippi River.
9. Do you think that the Spanish explorer Francisco Coronado really pictured himself finding the Seven Cities of Gold?
10. Our teacher told us about Samuel de Champlain's founding of the colony of Quebec.

Demonstrative Pronouns

A *demonstrative pronoun* points out a person, a place, a thing, or an idea.

Demonstrative Pronouns
this   that   these   those

EXAMPLES   **This** is the most valuable baseball card I have.
These are the names of **those** who volunteered.

NOTE: When the words *this, that, these,* and *those* are used before a noun, they are adjectives, not pronouns.

Interrogative Pronouns

An *interrogative pronoun* introduces a question.

Interrogative Pronouns
what   which   who   whom   whose

EXAMPLES   **What** is the largest planet in our solar system?
Who scored the most points in the game?

Relative Pronouns

A *relative pronoun* introduces a subordinate clause.

Relative Pronouns
that   which   who   whom   whose

EXAMPLES   The Bactrian camel, **which** has two humps, is native to central Asia.
Ray Charles is one of several blind performers **who** have had a number of hit recordings.

☞ REFERENCE NOTE: For more information about subordinate clauses, see pages 535–548.

GRAMMAR

EXERCISE 6 **Identifying Demonstrative, Interrogative, and Relative Pronouns**

Identify the demonstrative, interrogative, and relative pronouns in each of the following sentences.

EXAMPLE   **1.** Which of you has heard of *The Mustangs of Las Colinas,* a sculpture that is located in Irving, Texas?
     1. *Which—interrogative; that—relative*

1. This is a picture of the sculpture, which suggests its larger-than-life size.
2. The nine mustangs that make up the work appear to gallop across Williams Square in the Las Colinas Urban Center.
3. The horses, whose images are cast in bronze, form the world's largest equestrian (horse) sculpture.
4. That is an amazing sight!
5. What is the name of the sculptor who created the mustangs?
6. Robert Glen, who was born in Kenya, is the artist whom you mean.
7. Looking at this work, you can imagine the amount of time that Glen has spent studying wildlife.
8. The Mustang Sculpture Exhibit, which is housed in a building near the statue, provides more information about Glen and the mustangs.
9. Who told me mustangs are descended from horses brought to the Americas by the Spanish?
10. Horses like these roamed wild over Texas and other western states in the 1800s.

EXERCISE 7 **Writing Sentences with Pronouns**

Write a paragraph about a well-known person from public life, the entertainment field, or sports. By using pronouns, describe this person without revealing his or her name until the end of the paragraph. Read your paragraph aloud, and have the class guess who the person is.

Indefinite Pronouns

An *indefinite pronoun* refers to a person, a place, or a thing that is not specifically named.

Common Indefinite Pronouns				
all	both	few	nobody	several
another	each	many	none	some
any	either	more	no one	somebody
anybody	everybody	most	nothing	someone
anyone	everyone	much	one	something
anything	everything	neither	other	

EXAMPLES **Everyone** completed the test before the bell rang.
Neither of the actors knew what costume the **other** was planning to wear.

Many indefinite pronouns can also serve as adjectives.

EXAMPLES Look in **both** cabinets. [*Both* is an adjective modifying *cabinets.*]
Both contain winter clothing. [*Both* is an indefinite pronoun.]

Each player took **one** cap. [*Each* is an adjective modifying *player; one* is an adjective modifying *cap.*]
Each of the players took **one** of the caps. [*Each* and *one* are indefinite pronouns.]

GRAMMAR

 EXERCISE 8 **Using Indefinite Pronouns**

Have you ever thought about who writes billboards? What you read is written by advertising copywriters. Their goal is to persuade you to do something or to buy something. Try creating your own billboard ads. First, think up five products, services, or places to advertise on billboards (you can make up items if you wish). Then, write at least one sentence to advertise each one. In each ad, use an indefinite pronoun, and underline it. If you like to draw, you might sketch the layout of the billboard and show where your ad's slogan should go.

EXAMPLES Product: *Everybody should try new Super Comb Hair Styler Wand!*
Service: *No one likes to clean doghouses— except us!*
Place: *Be one of the few in your town to visit Zambia this year!*

WRITING APPLICATION

Using Pronouns in a Story

Just try writing about yourself or someone else without using pronouns! You'll soon find that it's awkward to keep using your own name or others' names over and over. That's where pronouns can help you.

AWKWARD Yoshi returned to get Yoshi's book.
CORRECTED Yoshi returned to get his book.

WRITING ACTIVITY

You've just read a magazine article describing a boy's wild adventure while camping with his family. His story sparks your imagination. Write your own personal adventure story. In it, use a variety of pronouns.

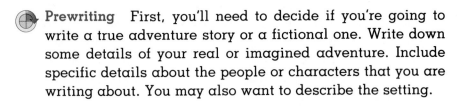

Prewriting   First, you'll need to decide if you're going to write a true adventure story or a fictional one. Write down some details of your real or imagined adventure. Include specific details about the people or characters that you are writing about. You may also want to describe the setting.

Writing   As you write your first draft, be sure that your story follows a logical order.

Evaluating and Revising   Ask a friend to read your first draft. Are the actions and characters clear? Revise any parts of your story that confuse your reader. Make sure that the antecedent for each pronoun is clear.

Proofreading   After revising your story, set it aside for a while. Read through it again later, looking for errors in grammar, punctuation, and spelling. The order of events is important in a story, so be sure that verbs are in the right tense. Also, check that pronouns are in the right form.

▶ REVIEW B   **Identifying Kinds of Pronouns**

Identify each of the pronouns in the following sentences as *personal, reflexive, intensive, demonstrative, interrogative, relative,* or *indefinite.*

EXAMPLE   **1.** Can you name some of the many famous Hispanic entertainers that have their stars on Hollywood's Walk of Fame?
   1. *you—personal; some—indefinite; that—relative; their—personal*

1. This is Tito Puente himself at the ceremony to install his star.
2. Many refer to him as the "King of Latin Music" or the "King of Salsa."
3. Who is the woman kneeling beside him?

4. She is Celia Cruz, the Cuban salsa singer, and you can see for yourself both of them are very happy and proud.
5. Everybody has heard of some of the entertainers honored with bronze stars on Hollywood Boulevard.
6. One musician whom you might know appeared on the old *I Love Lucy* TV show, which is still shown.
7. Of course, that was Desi Arnaz, who was a Cuban bandleader.
8. Which Hispanic singers can you name who have stars on the Walk of Fame?
9. All of the following singers have their stars there: Julio Iglesias, Tony Orlando, Ritchie Valens, and José Feliciano.
10. Actors José Ferrer, Cesar Romero, and Ricardo Montalbán are other Hispanics whose stars you will find there.

The Adjective

14c. An *adjective* is a word used to modify a noun or a pronoun.

To **modify** a word means to describe the word or to make its meaning more definite. An adjective modifies a word by telling *what kind, which one, how much,* or *how many.*

WHAT KIND?	WHICH ONE?	HOW MUCH? or HOW MANY?
tall woman	*another* one	*less* time
steep mountain	*this* year	*more* money
long hike	*last* answer	*many* mistakes
eager clerk	*those* people	*several* others
tired dog	*that* dress	*few* marbles
exciting story	*middle* row	*larger* share

Articles

The most frequently used adjectives are *a, an,* and *the.* These adjectives are called *articles.*

The adjectives *a* and *an* are *indefinite articles.* Each one indicates that the noun refers to someone or something in general. *A* is used before a word beginning with a consonant sound. *An* is used before a word beginning with a vowel sound.

EXAMPLES   How is **a** gerbil different from **a** hamster?
An accident stalled traffic for **an** hour.

The adjective *the* is a *definite article.* It indicates that the noun refers to someone or something in particular.

EXAMPLE   **The** key would not open **the** lock.

⬛▶ EXERCISE 9   **Using Appropriate Adjectives**

Revise the following sentences, replacing the italicized questions with adjectives that answer them.

EXAMPLE   **1.** They sold *how many?* tickets for the *which one?* show.
1. *They sold fifty tickets for the first show.*

1. Even though we had run *how many?* laps around the track, we still had to run *how many?* others.
2. *Which one?* weekend, *how many?* hikers went on a *what kind?* trip to the *what kind?* park.
3. We rode in a *what kind?* van that carried *how many?* people and drove *how many?* miles to the game.
4. There was *how much?* time left when I started to answer the *which one?* question on the test.
5. During the *what kind?* afternoon we washed more than *how many?* cars and earned *how many?* dollars.

Adjectives in Sentences

An adjective may come before or after the word it modifies.

Each one of us brought **used** books for the auction.

The map, although **old** and **worn,** proved to be **useful.**

These rare coins are extremely **valuable.**

▶ EXERCISE 10   **Identifying Adjectives and the Words They Modify**

Identify the adjectives and the words they modify in the following paragraph. Do not include *a, an,* and *the.*

EXAMPLE   **[1] Many people considered the old man unlucky.**
       1. *Many—people; old—man; unlucky—man*

[1] For eighty-four days, Santiago, an old Cuban fisherman, had not caught a single fish. [2] Despite his bad luck, he remained hopeful. [3] On the eighty-fifth day, he caught a ten-pound albacore. [4] Soon after this catch, he hooked a huge marlin. [5] For nearly two days, the courageous fisherman struggled with the mighty fish and finally harpooned it. [6] Exhausted but happy, Santiago sailed toward shore. [7] Within an hour, however, his bad

luck returned. [8] What happened to the old fisherman and his big catch? [9] Does the story have a happy ending? [10] You can find the answers in Ernest Hemingway's novel *The Old Man and the Sea*.

> EXERCISE 11 **Revising Sentences**

In each sentence, add interesting adjectives to modify the nouns and pronouns.

EXAMPLE **1. The children took a nap.**
   1. *The five grumpy children took a long nap.*

1. Carolyn gave a cat to her aunt.
2. Luís donated books and jeans for the sale.
3. We watched the parade pass under our window.
4. The fielder caught the ball and made a throw to the catcher.
5. The dancer leaped across the stage.
6. The hikers took shelter in the cabin.
7. The actor played the role of a detective.
8. The explorers could not find a way out of the cave.
9. The lawyer questioned the witness.
10. The knight fought the dragon and rescued the princess.

Proper Adjectives

A *proper adjective* is formed from a proper noun and begins with a capital letter.

PROPER NOUN	PROPER ADJECTIVE
Africa	**African** nations
China	**Chinese** calendar
Shakespeare	**Shakespearean** drama
Islam	**Islamic** law
Rio Grande	**Rio Grande** valley

▶ EXERCISE 12   **Identifying Proper Adjectives**

Identify the proper adjectives and the words they modify in the following sentences.

EXAMPLE   **1.** In recent years many American tourists have visited the Great Wall in China.
      1. *American—tourists*

1. The early Spanish explorers built several forts along the Florida coast.
2. The professor of African literature gave a lecture on the novels of Camara Laye, a writer who was born in Guinea.
3. Which Arthurian legend have you chosen for your report?
4. The program about the Egyptian ruins was narrated by an English scientist and a French anthropologist.
5. Aeolus was the god of the winds in ancient Greek mythology.
6. The society of Victorian England was the subject of many British novels in the late 1800s.
7. During last night's press conference, the president commented on the Mideast situation.
8. My friend from Tokyo gave me a Japanese kimono.
9. We saw a display of Appalachian crafts in the public library.
10. Marian McPartland, a jazz pianist from New York City, played several Scott Joplin songs.

PICTURE THIS

You are a scribe, an official writer, in ancient Egypt. The family in the painting on the next page has hired you to keep a record of their activities. Now your job is to record this scene of the children bringing gifts to their parents. Write a paragraph describing what you see. Use at least twenty adjectives to give an accurate description.

Subject: children bringing gifts to parents
Audience: a family in ancient Egypt
Purpose: to keep a family record

Egyptian Expedition of The Metropolitan Museum of Art, Rogers Fund, 1930.

Changing Parts of Speech

The way that a word is used in a sentence determines what part of speech it is. Some words may be used as nouns or adjectives.

NOUN	How often do you watch **television?**
ADJECTIVE	What is your favorite **television** program?

NOUN	Return these books to the **library.**
ADJECTIVE	These **library** books are overdue.

NOUN	Would you like to attend **school** year-round?
ADJECTIVE	The meeting will be held in the **school** cafeteria.

Some words may be used as pronouns or adjectives.

PRONOUN	**Each** did the assignment.
ADJECTIVE	**Each** person did the assignment.

PRONOUN **Some** have gone to their dressing rooms.
ADJECTIVE **Some** actors have gone to their dressing rooms.

PRONOUN **Whose** are these?
ADJECTIVE **Whose** gloves are these?

Shoe reprinted by permission: Tribune Media Services.

EXERCISE 13 **Identifying Adjectives**

Identify the adjectives in the following paragraph. Do not include the articles *a, an,* and *the.* [Note: If a word is capitalized as part of a name, it is part of a proper noun and is not an adjective, as in *New York* and *White House.*]

EXAMPLE [1] Have you heard of the Heidi Festival, a popular event in New Glarus, Wisconsin?
    1. *popular*

[1] For geography class, I wrote a short paper about New Glarus. [2] It was founded by adventurous Swiss settlers in 1845, and people call it "Little Switzerland." [3] As you can see on the next page, colorful reminders of the town's Swiss heritage are everywhere. [4] The special emblems of Switzerland's cantons, or states, are on street

signs and buildings. [5] Many of the women make beautiful lace, and there's even an embroidery factory. [6] Dairying is big business, too, and the townsfolk make delicious cheeses. [7] In a historical village, visitors can see reconstructed buildings, such as a schoolhouse, a blacksmith shop, a church, and the cheese factory shown below. [8] In this village, pioneer tools and belongings are on display. [9] New Glarus also has a museum in a mountain lodge, called a *chalet*. [10] Someday, I hope to see one of the summer festivals, such as the Heidi Festival, the Volksfest, or the Wilhelm Tell Pageant.

▶ REVIEW C **Identifying Nouns, Pronouns, and Adjectives**

Identify the italicized word in each sentence of the following paragraph as a *noun*, a *pronoun*, or an *adjective*.

EXAMPLE [1] Don't let *anyone* tell you that the age of exploration is over.
1. *pronoun*

[1] Two brothers, Lawrence and Lorne Blair, went on an amazing *adventure* that began in 1973. [2] For ten years they traveled among the nearly 14,000 *islands* of Indonesia. [3] *Each* of them returned with remarkable tales about the people, animals, and land. [4] Their *adventure* story began when some pirates guided them through the Spice

Islands. [5] There, they located *one* of the world's rarest and most beautiful animals—the greater bird of paradise. [6] Another *island* animal that the brothers encountered was the frightening Komodo dragon. [7] *Some* Komodo dragons are eleven feet long and weigh more than five hundred pounds. [8] *Each* day brought startling discoveries, such as flying frogs and flying snakes. [9] On *one* island, Borneo, they found a tribe of people thought to be extinct. [10] To *some*, the brothers' stay with the cannibals of West New Guinea is the strangest part of their trip.

▶ REVIEW D   **Identifying Nouns, Pronouns, and Adjectives**

Identify each *noun, pronoun,* and *adjective* in the following sentences. Do not include the articles *a, an,* and *the.*

EXAMPLE   **1.** Charles Drew was an American doctor.
    1. *Charles Drew—noun; American—adjective; doctor—noun*

1. Charles Drew developed techniques that are used in the separation and preservation of blood.
2. During World War II, Dr. Drew was the director of donation efforts for the American Red Cross.
3. He established blood bank programs.
4. His research saved numerous lives during the war.
5. Dr. Drew set up centers in which blood could be stored.
6. The British government asked him to develop a storage system in England.
7. Shortly before the beginning of World War II, Dr. Drew became a professor of surgery at Howard University.
8. After the war, he was appointed chief surgeon at Freedman's Hospital.
9. This physician and researcher made important contributions to medical science.
10. Many people who have needed blood owe their lives to his methods.

GRAMMAR

Review: Posttest 1

A. Identifying Nouns, Pronouns, and Adjectives

Identify each italicized word in the following sentences as a *noun*, a *pronoun*, or an *adjective*.

EXAMPLE **1.** *Each* student is required to take a foreign *language.*
1. *Each—adjective; language—noun*

1. *Each* of the clubs decorated a float for the Cinco de Mayo *parade.*
2. Jenna prepared breakfast *herself* this *morning.*
3. *Everybody* says that *high school* will be more work but more fun, too.
4. *This* is the greatest year the *team* has ever had.
5. *Who* can tell me *whose* bicycle this is?
6. That *German shepherd* puppy is a *lively* rascal.
7. This is their fault because *they* ignored all the *danger* signals.
8. We received word *that* they aren't in *danger.*
9. *That* drummer is the *best.*
10. Runner *Carl Lewis* won several Olympic *medals.*

B. Identifying Nouns, Pronouns, and Adjectives

Identify each numbered italicized word in the following paragraph as a *noun*, a *pronoun*, or an *adjective*.

EXAMPLE The [1] *president* has a [2] *private* airplane known as *Air Force One.*
1. *president—noun*
2. *private—adjective*

[11] *American* presidents have used many different types of transportation. President Thomas Jefferson's way of getting to his first inauguration was [12] *simple.* [13] *He* walked there and then walked home after taking the

[14] *oath* of office. President Zachary Taylor rode the **[15]** *same* horse throughout the **[16]** *Mexican War* and later during his term of office. James Monroe had the **[17]** *honor* of being the first president to ride aboard a steamship. In 1899, William McKinley became the **[18]** *first* president to ride in an automobile. President Theodore Roosevelt, **[19]** *whose* love of adventure is famous, rode in a submarine in 1905. Probably **[20]** *nobody* was surprised when the president himself took over the controls.

Review: Posttest 2

Writing Sentences with Nouns, Pronouns, and Adjectives

Write two sentences with each of the following words. Use each word as two different parts of speech—*noun* and *adjective* or *pronoun* and *adjective*. Write the part of speech of the word after each sentence.

EXAMPLE   **1.** this
      1. *This bicycle is mine.—adjective*
         This cannot be the right answer.—pronoun

1. game
2. some
3. American
4. right
5. that

6. green
7. more
8. Saturday
9. one
10. water

15 THE PARTS OF SPEECH

Verb, Adverb, Preposition, Conjunction, Interjection

Diagnostic Test

Identifying Verbs, Adverbs, Prepositions, Conjunctions, and Interjections

Write the italicized word or word group in each of the following sentences. Label each as an *action verb*, a *linking verb*, a *helping verb*, an *adverb*, a *preposition*, a *conjunction*, or an *interjection*.

EXAMPLE   **1.** That girl has *traveled* widely with her family.
            1. *traveled—action verb*

1. Rosie *hit* a home run and tied up the score.
2. *Wow*, that's the best meal I've eaten in a long time!
3. School can *be* fun sometimes.
4. Neither Carlos nor Jan wanted to go *very* far out into the water.

5. That dog looks mean *in spite of* his wagging tail.
6. *Have* you ever celebrated Cinco de Mayo?
7. If Ken will *not* help us, then he cannot share in the rewards.
8. My older sister was a cheerleader *during* her senior year.
9. The road that runs *close* to the railroad tracks is usually crowded.
10. Several of my friends *enjoy* the music of Quincy Jones.
11. No one could do much to help, *for* the damage had already been done.
12. *Where* have you been putting the corrected papers?
13. *Oh,* I didn't know he had already volunteered.
14. Jodie *was* taking in the wash for her mother.
15. Surely Ms. Kwan doesn't *expect* us to finish by today.
16. May I have a glass of milk and a combination sandwich *without* onions?
17. James *became* impatient, but he waited quietly.
18. My uncle always brings us presents *when* he visits during Hanukkah.
19. The car swerved suddenly, *yet* the driver remained in control.
20. The rose *smells* lovely.

The Verb

15a. A *verb* is a word used to express action or a state of being.

Action Verbs

An *action verb* may express physical action or mental action.

PHYSICAL ACTION   *jump, shout, search, carry, run*

Langston Hughes **wrote** volumes of poetry.

A distinguished cinematographer, James Wong Howe, **filmed** the movie.

MENTAL ACTION   *worry, think, believe, imagine, remember*

The scientist **studied** the ant colony.

Mario **knew** the answer to every question on the test.

▶ EXERCISE 1   **Identifying Action Verbs**

Identify the action verb in each sentence in the following paragraph.

EXAMPLE   [1] Dr. Antonia Novello visited with children at a hospital.

    1. *visited*

[1] President Bush named Dr. Novello Surgeon General of the United States in 1990. [2] This position made her the nation's chief medical officer. [3] It also gave her authority over many health programs. [4] Dr. Novello, the first female Surgeon General, trained as a pediatrician.

[5] As the Surgeon General, she directed much of her attention to children's well-being. [6] She has often referred to her own childhood experiences in a close-knit Puerto Rican family. [7] She believes strongly in the rights of all children. [8] Dr. Novello stresses the importance of children's home lives. [9] She urges adult involvement with children's daily activities. [10] She also promotes volunteer participation in all sorts of child welfare organizations.

Transitive and Intransitive Verbs

A *transitive verb* is an action verb that expresses an action directed toward a person or thing.

EXAMPLES   Joel **held** the baby. [The action of *held* is directed toward *baby.*]

Loretta **brought** flowers. [The action of *brought* is directed toward *flowers.*]

With transitive verbs, the action passes from the doer—the subject—to the receiver of the action. Words that receive the action of a transitive verb are called *objects.*

EXAMPLES   Our scout troop made a **quilt**. [*Quilt* is the object of the verb *made*.]

The voters elected **him**. [*Him* is the object of the verb *elected*.]

☞ REFERENCE NOTE: For more information about objects and their uses in sentences, see pages 491–493.

An *intransitive verb* expresses action (or tells something about the subject) without passing the action to a receiver.

EXAMPLES   Samuel Ramey **sang** beautifully in the opera *Don Giovanni.*

The Evans twins **played** quietly indoors the whole afternoon.

A verb may be transitive in one sentence and intransitive in another.

EXAMPLES   Janet **swam** ten laps. [transitive]
Janet **swam** well. [intransitive]

The teacher **read** a poem. [transitive]
The teacher **read** aloud. [intransitive]

☞ REFERENCE NOTE: Like intransitive verbs, linking verbs (*be, seem, feel,* etc.) never take direct objects. See page 461 for more information about linking verbs.

GRAMMAR

▶ EXERCISE 2 **Identifying Transitive and Intransitive Verbs**

In the following paragraph, identify each italicized verb as *transitive* or *intransitive*. Be prepared to identify the object of each transitive verb.

EXAMPLE Whether you [1] *know* it or not, about twenty percent of America's cowboys were African Americans.
1. *transitive*

During the years following the Civil War, thousands of African American cowboys [1] *rode* the cattle trails north from Texas. They [2] *worked* alongside Mexican, Native American, and Anglo trail hands. All the members of a cattle drive [3] *slept* on the same ground, [4] *ate* the same food, and did the same hard jobs. When day was done, they [5] *enjoyed* each other's company as they swapped stories and [6] *sang* around the campfire. When they finally [7] *reached* their destinations with their herds, they all [8] *celebrated* by having rodeos, parades, and shooting contests. Nat Love, one of the most famous African American cowboys, [9] *wrote* about his experiences on the range. In his book, he [10] *recalls* the times that he and his trailmates looked out for one another, regardless of skin color.

▶ EXERCISE 3 **Writing Sentences with Transitive and Intransitive Verbs**

For each verb given below, write two sentences. In one sentence, use the verb as a *transitive* verb and underline its object. In the other, use the verb as an *intransitive* verb. You may use different tenses of the verb.

EXAMPLE **1.** read
1. *For tomorrow, read the chapter about Taiwan that begins on page 441. (transitive)*
I think I'll read this evening instead of watching television. (intransitive)

1. win   **2.** help   **3.** play   **4.** run   **5.** freeze

Linking Verbs

A *linking verb* links, or connects, the subject with a noun, a pronoun, or an adjective in the predicate.

EXAMPLES   The star's name **is** Whoopi Goldberg. [name = Whoopi Goldberg]

Marie Curie **became** a famous scientist. [Marie Curie = scientist]

Tranh **is** one of the finalists. [Tranh = one]

Wild animals **remain** free on the great animal reserves in Africa. [free animals]

The watermelon **looks** ripe. [ripe watermelon]

COMMONLY USED LINKING VERBS				
Forms of *Be*	am are	be been	being is	was were
Other Verbs	appear become feel	grow look remain	seem smell sound	stay taste turn

NOTE: The forms of the verb *be* are not always used as linking verbs. When followed by a word or a group of words that tells *when* or *where*, a form of *be* is a *state-of-being verb*.

EXAMPLES   Geraldo **is** here now.
Your roller skates **are** in the attic.

▶ EXERCISE 4   **Using Linking Verbs**

Insert a different linking verb for each blank in the following sentences. Then, identify the words that each verb links.

EXAMPLE   **1.** Judith Jamison _____ calm during the première of the dance.

    1. *Judith Jamison remained calm during the première of the dance.*
    Judith Jamison—calm

1. The first day ____ long.
2. Your suggestion ____ good to me.
3. Our room ____ festive after we decorated it for the party.
4. The orange ____ a little too sweet.
5. In the novel the main character ____ a doctor, and he returns home to set up a clinic.
6. Before a storm the air ____ wet and heavy.
7. Did she ____ happy about living in Florida?
8. The diver ____ more confident with each dive she made.
9. They ____ quiet as the theater lights dimmed.
10. The lilacs ____ lovely.

All the linking verbs except the forms of *be* and *seem* may also be used as action verbs. Whether a verb is used to link words or to express action depends on its meaning in a sentence.

LINKING   The tiger **looked** tame.
ACTION   The tiger **looked** for something to eat.

LINKING   The soup **tasted** good.
ACTION   I **tasted** the soup.

LINKING   She **grew** tired of playing.
ACTION   She **grew** into a fine woman.

EXERCISE 5   **Identifying Action Verbs and Linking Verbs**

Identify the verb and its subject in each of the following sentences. If the verb is a linking verb, identify also the word or words that the verb links to its subject.

EXAMPLES   1. The people in the picture on the next page are enjoying the International Championship Chili Cook-off in Terlingua, Texas.
1. *are enjoying, people*

2. The event, first held in 1967, is extremely popular.
2. *is, event—popular*

1. Chili cook-offs throughout the Southwest attract devoted chili fans.
2. Real fans grow hungry at the mention of any dish containing chili peppers and chili powder.
3. These are important ingredients in Mexican cooking.
4. Chili cooks start with their favorite chili powder.
5. Basic chili powder consists of ground, dried chilies blended with other spices.
6. The most common chili is chili con carne.
7. This is a thick, spicy meat stew, often including beans.
8. Chili varies from somewhat spicy to fiery hot.
9. You also find many recipes for chili without meat.
10. Regardless of the other ingredients in a batch of chili, the chili powder smells wonderful to chili fans.

▶ EXERCISE 6   **Identifying Verbs**

Identify the verb or verbs in each sentence in the following paragraph. If the verb is a linking verb, identify also the words that the verb links.

EXAMPLE   [1] Do you know Tomás Herrera?
                1. *Do know*

                [2] He is a friend of mine, who lives next door to me.
                2. *is, He—friend; lives*

[1] Tomás is a young musician who loves all kinds of music. [2] No one knows how many hours he plays each week, although many people guess at least twenty. [3] His parents worry about him, yet he seems happy.

[4] One afternoon Tomás became restless. [5] The notes sounded wrong, and none of his music seemed right to him. [6] He grabbed several sheets of music paper and then wrote some notes. [7] After a little careful revision, he formed the notes into an original harmony.

[8] That night he performed his song for some of his friends. [9] Cristina exclaimed, "Tomás, that was excellent! [10] Is that really your first original song?"

Verb Phrases

A *verb phrase* consists of a main verb preceded by at least one *helping verb* (also called an *auxiliary verb*).

The following sentences contain verb phrases.

Seiji Ozawa **will conduct** many outstanding orchestras. [The main verb is *conduct.*]
He **has been praised** for his fine conducting. [The main verb is *praised.*]
His recordings **should be heard** by anyone interested in classical music. [The main verb is *heard.*]
He **will be leading** the orchestra tonight. [The main verb is *leading.*]

COMMONLY USED HELPING VERBS				
Forms of *Be*	am are	be been	being is	was were
Forms of *Do*	do	does	did		
Forms of *Have*	have	has	had		
Other Helping Verbs	can could	may might	must shall	should will	would

Some helping verbs may also be used as main verbs.

EXAMPLES   Did he **do** his homework?
She will **be** here soon.
We do not **have** enough time.

Sometimes the verb phrase is interrupted by another part of speech. In most cases, the interrupter is an adverb. In a question, however, the subject often interrupts the verb phrase.

EXAMPLES   People **may** someday **communicate** with
dolphins.
How much **do** you **know** about Lucy Stone, the
suffragist?
Because of the fog, we **could** not [*or* **couldn't**]
see the road.

Notice in the last example that the word *not* is never part of a verb phrase.

REFERENCE NOTE: For more information about contractions, see pages 783–784.

EXERCISE 7   **Identifying Verb Phrases**

Identify the verb phrases in the sentences in the following paragraph. Some sentences contain more than one verb phrase.

EXAMPLE   [1] What unusual jobs can you name?
1. *can name*

[1] Many people are earning a living at unusual jobs. [2] Even today people can find positions as shepherds, inventors, and candlestick makers. [3] It might seem strange, but these people have decided that ordinary jobs have become too boring for them. [4] Some people have been working as messengers. [5] You may have seen them when they were wearing clown makeup or costumes such as gorilla suits. [6] Other people have been finding work as mimes. [7] They can be seen performing at circuses, fairs, and festivals. [8] Chimney sweeps do still clean chimney flues for people. [9] Some chimney sweeps,

like the one in this picture, may even wear the traditional, old-time clothes of the trade. [10] With a little imagination, anyone can find an unusual job.

 REVIEW A

Labeling Linking Verbs and Action Verbs

Identify the verbs and the verb phrases in the following paragraph. Label each verb or verb phrase as an *action verb* or a *linking verb*.

EXAMPLE   **[1] Who were the Vikings, and where did they live?**
    1. *were—linking verb; did live—action verb*

[1] The Vikings were Norsemen who roamed the seas from A.D. 700–1000. [2] The term *Vikings* applies to all Scandinavian sailors, whether they were Norwegians, Swedes, or Danes. [3] People in other countries considered the Vikings the terror of Europe. [4] They worshiped such fierce gods as Thor and Odin. [5] Viking warriors hoped that they would die in battle. [6] They believed that when they died in battle, they went to Valhalla. [7] In Valhalla, they could always enjoy battles and banquets. [8] Each day, the warriors in Valhalla would go out to the battlefield and would receive many wounds. [9] Then, in spite of their injuries, at the end of the day they would all meet back at the banquet hall. [10] Their wounds would promptly heal, and they could boast about their great bravery in battle.

WRITING APPLICATION

Using Verbs to Make Your Writing Fresh and Lively

You've probably heard the old saying "Actions speak louder than words." In your writing, action verbs "speak louder" than many other words. Well-chosen action words help your reader picture what you're writing about. They make your writing lively and interesting and catch your readers' attention.

DULL   Mississippi State won the championship last night.
LIVELY   Mississippi State seized the championship last night.

What are some other verbs you could use instead of *won*?

▶ WRITING ACTIVITY

Your little sister likes for you to tell her exciting stories. You've told her so many stories that you've run out of new ones. To get ideas for new stories, you think about events you've read about or seen. Write a summary of an exciting incident from a book, a movie, or a television show. Use action verbs that are fresh and lively. Underline these verbs.

Prewriting   Think about books that you've read recently or movies and television shows that you've seen. Choose an exciting incident from one of these works. Freewrite what you remember about that incident.

Writing   As you write your first draft, think about how you're presenting the information. When telling a story, you should usually use chronological order (the order in which events occurred). This method would be easiest for your young reader to follow, too. Try to use fresh, lively action verbs.

Evaluating and Revising   Imagine that you are a young child hearing the story for the first time. Look over your summary and ask yourself these questions.

- Would I be able to understand what happened?
- Would the verbs I have used in the story help me picture what happened?
- Would I think the story is exciting?

Revise your summary if any of your answers is "no." Replace dull verbs with lively action verbs.

Proofreading Look over your summary to be sure that each verb you use is in the correct form and tense. (See pages 604–616.) Be sure that you have used action verbs rather than linking verbs.

▶ REVIEW B **Labeling Verbs**

Identify each verb in the following paragraph as an *action verb* or a *linking verb*. Treat verb phrases as single words. Some sentences contain more than one verb.

EXAMPLE [1] She dedicated her life to helping young people.
    1. *dedicated—action verb*

[1] Mary McLeod Bethune is a major figure in American history. [2] Bethune taught school after she completed her education in South Carolina. [3] In 1904, she moved to Florida and opened a school of her own. [4] This school eventually became Bethune-Cookman College, and Mary Bethune served as its president. [5] In 1930, Bethune was invited to a presidential conference on child health and protection. [6] Then, during Franklin Roosevelt's administration, she and others founded the National Youth Administration. [7] Her outstanding efforts impressed Roosevelt, and he established an office for minority affairs. [8] This office gave money to serious students so that they could continue their education. [9] In 1945, Bethune was an observer at the conference that organized

the United Nations. [10] Throughout her life, Bethune remained interested in education, and her efforts earned her national recognition.

The Adverb

15b. An *adverb* is a word used to modify a verb, an adjective, or another adverb.

An adverb tells *where, when, how,* or *to what extent (how much* or *how long).*

WHERE?	WHEN?
The forest fire started **here.** The couple was married **nearby.**	The police arrived **promptly.** **Then** the suspects were questioned.

HOW?	TO WHAT EXTENT?
The accident occurred **suddenly.** The prime minister spoke **carefully.**	We should **never** deceive our friends. She has **scarcely** begun the lesson.

Adverbs Modifying Verbs

Adverbs may come before or after the verbs they modify.

EXAMPLES **Slowly** the man crawled **down.** [The adverb *Slowly* tells how the man crawled, and the adverb *down* tells where he crawled.]
I **seldom** see you **nowadays.** [The adverb *seldom* tells to what extent I see you, and the adverb *nowadays* tells when I see you.]

Adverbs may come between the parts of verb phrases.

EXAMPLES   Keisha has **already** completed her part of the project. [The adverb interrupts and modifies *has completed.*]
Many students did **not** understand all of the directions. [The adverb interrupts and modifies *did understand.*]

Adverbs are sometimes used to ask questions.

EXAMPLES   **Where** are you going?
How did you do on the test?

▶ EXERCISE 8   **Identifying Adverbs That Modify Verbs**

Identify the adverbs and the verbs they modify in the following sentences.

EXAMPLE   **1.** How can I quickly learn to take better pictures?
1. *how—can learn; quickly—can learn*

1. You can listen carefully to advice from experienced photographers, who usually like to share their knowledge with beginners.
2. Nobody always takes perfect pictures, but some tips can help you now.
3. First, you should never move when you take pictures.
4. You should stand still and hold your camera firmly.
5. Some photographers suggest that you keep your feet apart and put one foot forward.
6. Many beginners do not move close to their subjects when they take pictures.
7. As a result, the subjects frequently are lost in the background, and the photographers later wonder what happened.
8. A good photographer automatically thinks about what will be in a picture and consequently avoids disappointment afterward.
9. Nowadays, cameras have built-in light meters, but you should still check the lighting.

10. You may already have heard the advice to stand with your back to the sun when taking pictures, and that tip is often a good one.

Adverbs Modifying Adjectives

EXAMPLES   An **unusually** fast starter, Karen won the race. [The adverb *unusually* modifies the adjective *fast,* telling *how fast* the starter was.]
Our committee is **especially** busy at this time of year. [The adverb *especially* modifies the adjective *busy*, telling *how busy* the committee is.]

EXERCISE 9   **Identifying Adverbs That Modify Adjectives**

Identify the adverbs and the adjectives they modify in the following sentences.

EXAMPLE   **1.** Because so many bicycles have been stolen, the principal hired a guard.
1. *so, many*

1. The team is extremely proud of its record.
2. All frogs may look quite harmless, but some are poisonous.
3. The class was unusually quiet today.
4. The Mardi Gras celebration in New Orleans is very loud and colorful.
5. The coach said we were too careless when we made the routine plays.
6. I waited nearly two hours to get tickets to *Sarafina.*
7. When kittens are with their mother, they look thoroughly contented.
8. Weekends are especially hectic for me when all of my teachers assign homework.
9. Those *fajitas* seem much spicier than these.
10. The new exchange student who comes from Norway is surprisingly fluent in English.

▶ EXERCISE 10 **Choosing Adverbs to Modify Adjectives**

The adverb *very* is used far too often to modify adjectives. Choose an adverb other than *very* to modify each adjective below. Use a different adverb with each adjective.

EXAMPLE **1.** strong
        1. *incredibly strong*

1. cheerful	4. messy	7. heavy	9. calm
2. sour	5. honest	8. long	10. graceful
3. wide	6. timid		

Adverbs Modifying Other Adverbs

EXAMPLES   Elena finished the problem **more** quickly than I did. [The adverb *more* modifies the adverb *quickly*, telling *how quickly* Elena finished the problem.]
Our guest left **quite** abruptly. [The adverb *quite* modifies the adverb *abruptly*, telling *how abruptly* our guest left.]

▶ EXERCISE 11 **Identifying Adverbs That Modify Other Adverbs**

For each of the following sentences, identify the adverb that modifies another adverb. Then write the adverb that it modifies.

EXAMPLE   **1.** Condors are quite definitely among the largest living birds.
        1. *quite—definitely*

1. The California condor and the Andean condor are almost entirely extinct.
2. Only very few California condors exist today, and nearly all of them live in captivity.
3. Andean condors are slightly more numerous, and more of them can still be seen in the wild.

4. You can see from this photograph why some people think that condors are most assuredly the ugliest birds.

5. Yet, once in the air, condors soar so gracefully that they can look actually beautiful.

▶ REVIEW C   **Identifying Adverbs**

Identify the adverbs in the order that they appear in each sentence in the following paragraph. After each adverb, write the word or phrase that the adverb modifies. Some sentences have more than one adverb.

EXAMPLE   [1] Sherlock Holmes solved the case very quickly.
    1. *very—quickly; quickly—solved*

[1] I have been a fan of mystery stories since I was quite young. [2] Some stories are incredibly exciting from start to finish. [3] Others build suspense very slowly. [4] If I like a story, I almost never put it down until I finish it. [5] In many cases, I can scarcely prevent myself from peeking at the last chapter to see how the story ends. [6] I never start reading a mystery story if I have tons of homework because then it is more tempting to read the story than to do my homework. [7] My favorite detectives are ones who cleverly match wits with equally clever villains. [8] I especially like detectives who carefully look around, hunting for clues. [9] The clues that they uncover are almost always found in unexpected, spooky places. [10] It's amazing how detectives can use these clues to solve the most complicated cases.

The Preposition

15c. A *preposition* is a word used to show the relationship of a noun or a pronoun to another word in the sentence.

Notice how a change in the preposition changes the relationship between *package* and *tree* in each of the following examples.

> The package **under** the tree is mine.
> The package **in** the tree is mine.
> The package **near** the tree is mine.
> The package **behind** the tree is mine.
> The package **next to** the tree is mine.
> The package **in front of** the tree is mine.

Prepositions that consist of more than one word, such as *in front of*, are called ***compound prepositions.***

Commonly Used Prepositions			
aboard	before	in	over
about	behind	in addition to	past
above	below	in front of	since
according to	beneath	inside	through
across	beside	in spite of	throughout
after	besides	instead of	to
against	between	into	toward
along	beyond	like	under
along with	but (meaning	near	underneath
amid	except)	next to	until
among	by	of	unto
around	down	off	up
aside from	during	on	upon
as of	except	on account of	with
at	for	out	within
because of	from	out of	without

▶ EXERCISE 12 **Identifying Prepositions**

Identify the prepositions in each sentence in the following paragraph. Be sure to include all parts of any compound prepositions you find.

EXAMPLE **[1] Throughout the centuries people have read about the legend of Romulus and Remus.**
   1. *Throughout, about, of*

[1] According to legend, Mars, the god of war in Roman mythology, was the father of the twin brothers Romulus and Remus. [2] When the twins were infants, an evil ruler had them placed in a basket and cast into the Tiber River. [3] Fortunately, they safely drifted to the bank of the river. [4] There they were rescued by a wolf. [5] Later they were found by a shepherd and his wife. [6] When the twins grew up, they wanted to build a city on the site where they had been rescued. [7] Instead of working together, however, the twins fought against each other. [8] During the quarrel Romulus killed Remus. [9] Then, the legend continues, Romulus founded the city of Rome about 753 B.C. [10] Out of hundreds of legends about the founding of Rome, this one has remained among the best known.

The Prepositional Phrase

A preposition is usually followed by a noun or a pronoun. This noun or the pronoun following the preposition is called the *object of the preposition.* All together, the preposition, its object, and the modifiers of the object are called a *prepositional phrase.*

EXAMPLE **The wagon train slowly traveled across the dusty prairie.** [The prepositional phrase consists of the preposition *across*, its object *prairie*, and two adjectives modifying the object—*the* and *dusty*.]

☞ REFERENCE NOTE: For more information about prepositional phrases, see pages 506–509 and 670.

> NOTE: Be careful not to confuse a prepositional phrase that begins with *to* (*to town, to her club*) with an infinitive that begins with *to* (*to run, to be seen*). Remember: A prepositional phrase always ends with a noun or a pronoun.

▶ EXERCISE 13 **Identifying Prepositional Phrases**

Identify the prepositional phrase or phrases in each sentence in the following paragraph. Then, underline each preposition.

EXAMPLE   [1] Walt Whitman wrote the very moving poem "O Captain! My Captain!" about Abraham Lincoln.
   1. *about Abraham Lincoln*

[1] In Whitman's poem, the captain directs his ship toward a safe harbor. [2] The captain represents Abraham Lincoln, and the ship is the ship of state. [3] The captain has just sailed his ship through stormy weather. [4] This voyage across rough seas symbolizes the Civil War. [5] On the shore, people joyfully celebrate the ship's safe arrival. [6] One of the ship's crew addresses his captain, "O Captain! my Captain! rise up and hear the bells." [7] Sadly, everyone except the captain can hear the rejoicing. [8] The speaker in the poem says that the captain "has no pulse nor will." [9] The captain has died during the voyage, just as Lincoln died at the end of the Civil War. [10] According to many people, "O Captain! My Captain!" is one of Whitman's finest poems.

PICTURE THIS

You and this cowboy are on night watch. It's a cool, quiet night. The cattle, however, seem extremely interested in the airplane flying over. Their behavior starts you thinking about a tall tale—a humorous, highly improbable story that stretches the facts. To amuse your companion,

GRAMMAR

write a tall tale about the cows watching the airplane. Use five similes expressed in prepositional phrases. To form a simile, use *like* or *as* to show how one thing is similar to another thing. For example: *The cows looked like an attentive movie audience.*

Subjects: cows watching an airplane
Audience: cowboy companion
Purpose: to entertain

Adverb or Preposition?

Some words may be used as either prepositions or adverbs. To tell an adverb from a preposition, remember that a preposition is always followed by a noun or pronoun object.

ADVERB   The plane circled **above.**
PREPOSITION   The plane circled **above** the field. [Note the object of the preposition—*field.*]

ADVERB   Can you come **over** to my house?
PREPOSITION   We saw a bald eagle fly **over** the treetops.
              [Note the object of the preposition—*treetops.*]

GRAMMAR

EXERCISE 14 **Writing Sentences with Adverbs and Prepositions**

Use each of the following words in two sentences, first as an adverb and then as a preposition. Underline the designated word.

EXAMPLE **1.** along
    1. *Do you have to bring your little brother along?*
    Wildflowers were blooming along the riverbank.

1. off   **2.** across   **3.** below   **4.** above   **5.** down

The Conjunction

15d. A *conjunction* is a word used to join words or groups of words.

Coordinating conjunctions connect words or groups of words used in the same way.

Coordinating Conjunctions						
and	but	or	nor	for	so	yet

EXAMPLES   Theo **or** Tyler [two nouns]
    small **but** comfortable [two adjectives]
    through a forest **and** across a river [two prepositional phrases]
    The stars seem motionless, **but** actually they are moving rapidly through space. [two complete independent clauses]

When *for* is used as a conjunction, it connects groups of words that are sentences. On all other occasions, *for* is used as a preposition.

CONJUNCTION   We wrote to the tourist bureau, **for** we
wanted information on places to visit.
PREPOSITION   We waited patiently **for** a reply.

NOTE: The conjunction *so* is often overused. Whenever possible,
reword a sentence to avoid using *so.*

EXAMPLE   You are new, so you'll probably get lost.
Because [*or* Since] you are new, you'll probably
get lost.

Correlative conjunctions are pairs of conjunctions that
connect words or groups of words used in the same way.

Correlative Conjunctions

| both . . . and | either . . . or | neither . . . nor |
| whether . . . or | not only . . . but also | |

EXAMPLES   **Both** horses **and** cattle were brought to North
America by the Spanish. [two nouns]
The student council will meet **not only** on
Tuesday **but also** on Thursday this week. [two
prepositional phrases]
Either leave a message on my answering
machine, **or** call me after 7:00 P.M. [two
complete ideas]

▶ EXERCISE 15   **Identifying Coordinating and
Correlative Conjunctions**

Identify the conjunctions in the following paragraph as
coordinating or *correlative*. Be prepared to tell what words
or groups of words the conjunctions join.

EXAMPLE   [1] The men and women in the picture on the
next page are wearing African clothes.
1. *and—coordinating*

[1] African clothing is fashionable today for both men
and women in the United States. [2] People wear not only
clothes of African design but also Western-style clothes
made of African materials. [3] American women have

GRAMMAR

worn modified African headdresses for years, but nowadays men are wearing African headgear, too. [4] Men and women sometimes wear *kufi* hats, which originated with Muslims. [5] Both women's dresses and women's coats are especially adaptable to African fashions. [6] Many women wear African jewelry or scarves. [7] Clothes made of such materials as *kente* cloth from Ghana, *ashioke* cloth from Nigeria, and *dogon* cloth from Mali have become quite popular. [8] These fabrics are decorated either with brightly colored printed designs or with stripes. [9] African-inspired clothes usually fit in whether you are at work or at play. [10] African styles are popular, for they show appreciation for ancient cultures.

The Interjection

15e. An *interjection* is a word used to express emotion. It does not have a grammatical relation to other words in the sentence.

EXAMPLES **Oh!** You surprised me.
Wow! Am I tired!
Well, I did my best.

▶ EXERCISE 16 **Identifying Interjections**

Some fairy tale characters are meeting to discuss their image. They're worried that the familiar fairy tales make them look stupid or silly. Identify the ten interjections used in the dialogue. Then try to guess who the four fairy tale speakers are.

EXAMPLE   **[1]** "Hooray! We're finally getting a chance to tell our side of the stories!"
   1. *Hooray!*

[1] "Beans! It's not fair what they say. I knew I was taking a giant step that day."

[2] "Well, it's not fair what they say about us, either. Don't you think Papa and Mama saw that little blonde girl snooping around our house?"

[3] "Yeah! And don't you think I intended to buy magic beans, anyway?"

[4] "You guys don't have it as bad as I do. Ugh! How dumb do people think I am? Of course I'd know my own grandmother when I saw her."

[5] "Pooh! I think your cloak was over your eyes, but how about me? I didn't go near those three pigs."

[6] "What! Next you'll probably tell me that I didn't see your brother at Grandmother's house."

[7] "Humph! I don't know what you really saw. It's difficult to tell sometimes in the woods."

[8] "Aw, let's not argue. We've got to put our best feet forward—all the way up the beanstalk if need be."

[9] "Yes! And I want to give people the real story about that kid who broke my bed."

[10] "Great! I'm ready to squeal on those three pigs!"

Determining Parts of Speech

The part of speech of a word is determined by the way the word is used in a sentence. Many words can be used as more than one part of speech.

GRAMMAR

EXAMPLES   **Each** cost three dollars. [pronoun]
            Each student baked a cake. [adjective]

            The tired shoppers sat **down** for a while.
            [adverb]
            The ball rolled **down** the hill. [preposition]

            A member of the crew has spotted **land**. [noun]
            The pilot can **land** here safely. [verb]

            Well, he seems to have recovered. [interjection]
            He doesn't look **well** to me. [adjective]

▶ REVIEW D   **Identifying Parts of Speech**

Identify the part of speech of the italicized word in each sentence. Be prepared to explain your answers.

EXAMPLES   **1.** The *ship* entered the harbor slowly.
            1. *noun*

            2. Did they *ship* the package to Dee and Seth?
            2. *verb*

  1. The English test was easy *for* him.
  2. He didn't go to the movies, *for* he wanted to practice on the drums.
  3. It was a steep *climb,* but we made it to the top of the hill.
  4. Kimiko and I *climb* the stairs for exercise.
  5. *Some* volunteered to sell tickets.
  6. We donated *some* clothes to the rummage sale.
  7. Looking for shells, the girl strolled *along* the shore.
  8. When we went sailing, Raúl and Manuel came *along*.
  9. I lost *my* book report!
 10. *My!* This is not a good day!

▶ REVIEW E   **Identifying Parts of Speech**

Identify the part of speech of each italicized word or group of words in the following paragraphs. Be prepared to explain your answers.

EXAMPLE   Dancing may be [1] *easy* for [2] *some*, but I have
[3] *always* had [4] *two* left [5] *feet*.

1. *adjective*   **2.** *pronoun*   **3.** *adverb*
4. *adjective*   **5.** *noun*

[1] *Yesterday* after [2] *school*, one of my friends [3] *tried* to teach [4] *me* some new dance steps. [5] *Well*, I was [6] *so* embarrassed I could have hidden [7] *in* the [8] *closet*. My feet [9] *seem* to have [10] *minds* of [11] *their* own [12] *and* do [13] *not* do what I want them to.

"You're [14] *too* tense when you dance, [15] *or* you're try-ing too hard. [16] *You* should [17] *relax* more," my friend told me.

[18] *"What!* [19] *How* can I relax?" I groaned. [20] *"No one* [21] *can relax* when his body goes [22] *left* and his feet go right!" At that point, I [23] *decided* to give up, but I know I'll try [24] *again* [25] *another* day.

▶ REVIEW F   **Using Different Parts of Speech**

Complete the following poem by adding words that are the parts of speech called for in the blank spaces.

EXAMPLE   Why [1] _(verb)_ Robin all alone?
[2] _(adverb)_ have all the others gone?
1. *Why sits Robin all alone?*
2. *Where have all the others gone?*

[1] _(interjection)_ , Robin thought her day was just fine.
She [2] _(verb)_ to the concert, and there wasn't a line.
[3] _(conjunction)_ when she got in and sat herself down,
People were leaving [4] _(preposition)_ rows all around.
You can see that Robin looks [5] _(adverb)_ dejected;
She thinks that she [6] _(verb)_ rejected.
If only she could have the chairs as her friends—
[7] _(interjection!)_ —she'd have friends without end.
She sat [8] _(adverb)_ and worried and pondered.
Was the problem with her [9] _(conjunction)_ the others?
    she wondered.
Then she [10] _(verb)_ at her ticket and saw she was late,
So she imagined the concert, and it was just great!

GRAMMAR

Review: Posttest 1

A. Identifying Different Parts of Speech

Identify each italicized word or word group in the following sentences as a *verb*, an *adverb*, a *preposition*, a *conjunction*, or an *interjection*. For each verb, indicate whether it is an *action verb*, a *helping verb*, or a *linking verb*. [Note: Keep in mind that correlative conjunctions and some prepositions have more than one word.]

EXAMPLE   **1.** I *am* reading a book *about* baseball cards.
      1. *am—helping verb; about—preposition*

1. We *watched* as the skywriter spelled out the words *carefully*.
2. *Both* the dog *and* the cat *are* dirty and need baths.
3. *Whoops*! I dropped my ring *under* the counter.
4. *Today* we studied the contributions that ancient North Africans made *to* mathematics.
5. Clever replies *never* occur to me until the situation is *long* past.
6. Sandy *does* not have enough granola *for* breakfast.
7. The girl *tried* again *in spite of* her previous difficulty.
8. *Well*, I really want to see *either* Key West *or* the Everglades when we go to Florida next summer.
9. *How did* the other team win so easily?
10. The beans with rice *tasted* good, *for* we were hungry.

B. Identifying Different Parts of Speech

Identify each italicized word or word group in the following paragraph as a *verb*, an *adverb*, a *preposition*, or a *conjunction*. [Note: Keep in mind that correlative conjunctions and some prepositions have more than one word.]

EXAMPLE   [1] You likely know that Christopher Columbus was a famous explorer, *but* do you know anything *about* his personal life?
      1. *but—conjunction; about—preposition*

[11] I've *learned* some interesting facts *about* Christopher Columbus. **[12]** He was born *into* a hard-working Italian family and *learned* how to sail as a boy. **[13]** He *became not only* a master sailor *but also* a mapmaker. **[14]** Although he had *barely* any formal education, he did *study* both Portuguese and Spanish. **[15]** The writings *of* ancient scholars about astronomy and geography *especially* interested him. **[16]** Columbus *apparently had* keen powers of observation. **[17]** These *served* him *well* on his expeditions. **[18]** On his voyages to find a sea route *to* the East Indies, Columbus *was* a determined, optimistic leader. **[19]** He let *neither* doubters *nor* hardships interfere *with* his plans. **[20]** Many people mistakenly think that Columbus was poor when he died in 1506, *but* he was actually *quite* wealthy.

Review: Posttest 2

Writing Sentences Using Different Parts of Speech

Write two sentences using each of the following words as the parts of speech given in parentheses. Underline the word in the sentence, and write its part of speech after the sentence.

EXAMPLE **1.** over (*adverb* and *preposition*)
          1. *The mob pushed on the statue of the defeated*
             tyrant until they tipped it <u>over</u>. (adverb)
             The horse jumped <u>over</u> the fence. (preposition)

  1. but (*conjunction* and *preposition*)
  2. like (*verb* and *preposition*)
  3. run (*noun* and *verb*)
  4. well (*adverb* and *interjection*)
  5. that (*pronoun* and *adjective*)
  6. more (*adjective* and *adverb*)
  7. last (*verb* and *adjective*)
  8. past (*noun* and *preposition*)
  9. near (*verb* and *preposition*)
 10. around (*preposition* and *adverb*)

SUMMARY OF PARTS OF SPEECH

Rule	Part of Speech	Use	Examples
14a	noun	names a person, a place, a thing, or an idea	Despite her **fear** of the **dark, Maya** enjoyed her **trip** through **Mammoth Cave**.
14b	pronoun	takes the place of a noun	**I myself** do not know **anyone who** saw **it**.
14c	adjective	modifies a noun or a pronoun	The **last stand-up** comedian, **talented** and **confident**, was **hilarious**.
15a	verb	shows action or a state of being	If we **had arrived** earlier, we **would have seen** many celebrities. We **were** upset. No one **was** there.
15b	adverb	modifies a verb, an adjective, or another adverb	I did **not** answer the last question **correctly**. It was **much more** difficult than the other questions.
15c	preposition	relates a noun or a pronoun to another word	**Because of** the storm the bridge **across** the bay was closed.
15d	conjunction	joins words or groups of words	Teachers **and** students will perform in the talent show. **Either** the principal **or** I will emcee the show.
15e	interjection	expresses emotion	**Ouch!** That hurts! **Aw**, that's too bad.

16 COMPLEMENTS

Direct and Indirect Objects, Subject Complements

Diagnostic Test

Identifying Complements

Identify each of the italicized words or word groups in the following sentences as a *direct object,* an *indirect object,* a *predicate nominative,* or a *predicate adjective.*

EXAMPLES
1. The rancher raised prizewinning *cattle.*
1. *cattle—direct object*

2. The rancher became a rich *man.*
2. *man—predicate nominative*

1. Pilar caught the *ball* and threw it to first base.
2. Your cousin seems *nice.*
3. I'm not the *one* who did that.
4. The sun grew *hotter* as the day went on.
5. Mrs. Sato gave *me* a failing grade.
6. Whoopi Goldberg is *famous* for comedy.
7. Amy's father and mother are both truck *drivers.*

8. Have you bought your *tickets* yet?
9. Did James ride his new *trail bike* to school today?
10. The irate customer sent the *store manager* a letter of complaint.
11. The nurse gave *Willie* a flu shot.
12. Josh often looks *tired* on Monday mornings.
13. With his calloused hands he cannot feel the *texture* of velvet.
14. My sister's room is always *neater* than mine.
15. Heather, who is new at our school, is the nicest *girl* I know.
16. The Algonquians used *toboggans* to haul goods over snow and ice.
17. Throw *Eric* a screen pass.
18. When left to dry in the sun, plums become *prunes*.
19. Dr. Charles Drew gave *science* a better way to process and store blood.
20. Ms. Rosada will be our Spanish *teacher* this fall.

Recognizing Complements

16a. A *complement* is a word or a group of words that completes the meaning of a verb.

Every sentence has a subject and a verb. Often a verb also needs a complement to make the sentence complete. Without a complement, each of the following subjects and verbs does not make a sentence.

```
              S        V
INCOMPLETE  Marlene brought [what?]
              S        V         C
  COMPLETE  Marlene brought sandwiches.

              S       V
INCOMPLETE  Carlos thanked [whom?]
              S       V     C
  COMPLETE  Carlos thanked her.
```

GRAMMAR

                S   V
INCOMPLETE   **We were** [*what?*]

                S   V   C
COMPLETE   **We were hungry.**

As you can see, a complement may be a noun, a pronoun, or an adjective. Complements complete the meanings of verbs in several ways.

EXAMPLES   **Jody painted her room.** [The noun *room* completes the meaning of the verb telling *what* Jody painted.]
                   My uncle sent me a postcard. [The pronoun *me* and the noun *postcard* complete the meaning of the verb by telling *what* was sent and *to whom* it was sent.]
                   The Ephron sisters are writers. [The noun *writers* completes the meaning of the verb *are* by identifying the sisters.]
                   This story is exciting. [The adjective *exciting* completes the meaning of the verb *is.*]

An adverb is never a complement.

     ADVERB   **The dog is outside.** [*Outside* modifies the verb by telling where the dog is.]
COMPLEMENT   **The dog is friendly.** [The adjective *friendly* modifies the subject by telling what kind of dog.]

A complement is never part of a prepositional phrase.

COMPLEMENT   Benjamin is studying his geography **notes.**
  OBJECT OF   Benjamin is studying for his geography **test.**
PREPOSITION

☞ REFERENCE NOTE: For more information on prepositional phrases, see pages 506–509.

▶ EXERCISE 1   **Identifying Subjects, Verbs, and Complements**

Identify the subject, verb, and complement in each sentence in the following paragraph. [Remember: A complement is never in a prepositional phrase.]

EXAMPLE [1] William Shakespeare was one of the owners of the Globe Theater.
1. *William Shakespeare—subject; was—verb; one—complement*

[1] During Shakespeare's time, plays were a common form of entertainment in England. [2] A great many people watched plays at the most popular playhouse in London—the Globe Theater. [3] Richard and Cuthbert Burbage built the Globe in 1599. [4] In this drawing, you can see many of the differences between the Globe and most modern theaters. [5] The Globe was a building with eight sides. [6] The building enclosed an inner courtyard. [7] The stage was a raised platform at one end of the courtyard. [8] Some of the audience watched the play from seats around the courtyard. [9] Many playgoers, however, did not have seats during a performance. [10] These people filled the courtyard in front of the stage.

 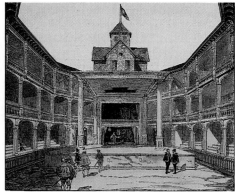 

The Granger Collection, New York.

EXERCISE 2 **Writing Sentences with Complements**

Write five sentences by adding a different complement to each of the following groups of words.

SUBJECT	VERB
1. men	asked
2. days	are
3. Pam	sent
4. runner	seemed
5. weather	will be

Direct Objects and Indirect Objects

The *direct object* and the *indirect object* are the two kinds of complements that complete the meaning of an action verb.

 REFERENCE NOTE: For more information about action verbs, see pages 457–459.

Direct Objects

16b. A *direct object* is a noun or a pronoun that receives the action of the verb or shows the result of the action. A direct object tells *what* or *whom* after an action verb.

EXAMPLES   Our history class built a **model** of the Alamo. [The noun *model* shows the result of the action verb *built* and tells *what* the class built.]
Has the freeze destroyed **some** of the crops? [The pronoun *some* shows the result of the action verb *Has destroyed* and tells *what* the freeze destroyed.]
Dorothea Lange photographed **farmers** in the Midwest during the Depression. [The noun *farmers* receives the action of the verb *photographed* and tells *whom* Dorothea Lange photographed.]

NOTE: A direct object may be compound.

EXAMPLE   The man wore a white **beard**, a red **suit**, and black **boots**.

EXERCISE 3   **Identifying Action Verbs and Direct Objects**

Identify the action verb and the direct object in each of the following sentences.

GRAMMAR

EXAMPLE   **1.** Volunteers distributed food to the flood victims.
      1. *distributed—food*

1. On the plains the Cheyenne hunted buffalo for food and clothing.
2. We watched a performance of Lorraine Hansberry's *A Raisin in the Sun.*
3. During most of its history the United States has welcomed refugees from other countries.
4. The leading man wore a hat with a large plume.
5. Are you preserving the environment?
6. After the game the coach answered questions from the sports reporters.
7. Did you see her performance on television?
8. The researchers followed the birds' migration from Mexico to Canada.
9. Mayor Fiorello La Guardia governed New York City during the Depression.
10. Have the movie theaters announced the special discount for teenagers yet?

Indirect Objects

16c. An *indirect object* is a noun or a pronoun that comes between the action verb and the direct object and tells *to what* or *to whom* or *for what* or *for whom* the action of the verb is done.

EXAMPLES   Dad gave the **horse** an apple. [The noun *horse* tells *to what* Dad gave an apple.]
Luke showed the **class** his collection of comic books. [The noun *class* tells *to whom* Luke showed his collection.]
Sarita bought **us** a chess set. [The pronoun *us* tells *for whom* Sarita bought a chess set.]

An indirect object, like a direct object, is never in a prepositional phrase.

INDIRECT OBJECT	She sent her **mother** some flowers.
OBJECT OF PREPOSITION	She sent some flowers to her **mother**.

NOTE: Like a direct object, an indirect object may be compound.

EXAMPLE Uncle Alphonso bought my **brother** and **me** an aquarium.

▶ EXERCISE 4 **Identifying Direct Objects and Indirect Objects**

Identify the direct objects and the indirect objects in the following sentences. [Note: Not every sentence has an indirect object.]

EXAMPLE **1.** They gave us their solemn promise.
1. *promise—direct object; us—indirect object*

1. They sent me on a wild-goose chase.
2. Gloria mailed the company a check yesterday.
3. The speaker showed the audience the slides of Zimbabwe.
4. Juan would not deliberately tell you and me a lie.
5. The coach praised the students for their school spirit.
6. I sent my cousins some embroidered pillows for their new apartment.
7. The art teacher displayed the students' paintings.
8. Sue's parents shipped her the books and the magazines she had forgotten.
9. Carly and Doreen taught themselves the importance of hard work.
10. In most foreign countries, United States citizens must carry their passports for identification.

▶ REVIEW A **Identifying Direct Objects and Indirect Objects**

Identify the direct objects and the indirect objects in the sentences in the following paragraph. [Note: Not every sentence has an indirect object.]

EXAMPLE [1] The spring rodeo gives our town an exciting weekend.

1. *weekend—direct object; town—indirect object*

[1] This year Mrs. Perez taught our class many interesting facts about rodeos. [2] She told us stories about the earliest rodeos, which took place more than a hundred years ago. [3] The word *rodeo,* she explained, means "roundup" in Spanish. [4] Mrs. Perez also showed us drawings and pictures of some well-known rodeo performers. [5] The Choctaw roper Clyde Burk especially caught our interest. [6] During Burk's career, the Rodeo Cowboys Association awarded him four world championships.

[7] For years, Burk entertained audiences with his roping skill. [8] He also bought and trained some of the best rodeo horses available. [9] This picture shows Burk on his horse Baldy. [10] Burk often gave Baldy credit for his success.

WRITING APPLICATION

Using Direct and Indirect Objects

Writers often use action verbs. Many of these action verbs require direct objects and indirect objects to make a complete statement. Without these objects, sentences are incomplete and cannot express your meaning to your readers.

INCOMPLETE	READER WONDERS
My favorite music store sells.	Sells what?
Mom gave five dollars.	Gave five dollars to whom?

Complete the meanings of the two incomplete statements above by adding a direct object and an indirect object where they are needed.

▶ WRITING ACTIVITY

You've just returned home from an interesting and enjoyable shopping trip. Write a letter to a friend telling about what happened on this trip. Use direct objects and indirect objects in your letter.

Prewriting   You may want to write about an actual shopping trip that you've made recently, perhaps to a shopping mall or a flea market. Or you can make up a shopping trip to another country or even another planet. Make a list of what you did, what you saw, and what you bought for whom.

Writing   As you write your first draft, think about describing your shopping trip in a way that will interest your friend. Use vivid action verbs and specific direct objects and indirect objects. Be sure to tell when and where your trip took place.

Evaluating and Revising   Read over your paragraph. Does it clearly tell why the shopping trip was so interesting and enjoyable? If not, you may want to add or change some details. Be sure that your paragraph follows a consistent and sensible order. For more about organizing ideas in a paragraph, see pages 74–83.

Proofreading   Check your paragraph for errors in grammar, punctuation, and spelling. Use a telephone book to check the spelling of names of stores, shopping malls, or shopping centers.

GRAMMAR

Subject Complements

A *subject complement* completes the meaning of a linking verb and identifies or describes the subject.

👉 REFERENCE NOTE: For more information about linking verbs, see page 461.

EXAMPLES **Alice Eng is a dedicated teacher.** [The noun *teacher* follows the linking verb *is* and identifies the subject *Alice Eng.*]
The lemonade tastes sour. [*Sour* follows the linking verb *tastes* and describes the subject *lemonade*—sour lemonade.]

There are two kinds of subject complements—*the predicate nominative* and the *predicate adjective.*

Predicate Nominatives

16d. A *predicate nominative* is a noun or a pronoun that follows a linking verb and identifies the subject or refers to it.

EXAMPLES **My aunt's dog is a collie.** [*Collie* is a predicate nominative that identifies *dog.*]
Enrique is one of the best players. [The pronoun *one* follows the linking verb *is* and refers to the subject *Enrique.*]

Like subjects and objects, predicate nominatives never appear in prepositional phrases.

EXAMPLES **The prize was a pair of tickets to the movies.** [The word *pair* identifies the subject *prize.* *Tickets* is the object of the preposition *of,* and *movies* is the object of the preposition *to.*]

NOTE: Predicate nominatives may be compound.

EXAMPLE **Hernando de Soto was a soldier and a diplomat.**

▶ EXERCISE 5   **Identifying Predicate Nominatives**

Identify the predicate nominative or nominatives in each of the following sentences.

EXAMPLE   **1. Robert A. Heinlein was one of our country's most important science fiction writers.**
     1. *one*

1. Before he became a writer, Heinlein had been a naval officer and an engineer.
2. Many of Heinlein's "future history" stories have become classics.
3. Heinlein's novels for young people and adults remain top sellers.
4. Published in 1961, *Stranger in a Strange Land* is a novel still enjoyed by many readers.
5. Heinlein was the winner of several Hugo Awards for his writing.

Predicate Adjectives

16e.   A *predicate adjective* is an adjective that follows a linking verb and describes the subject.

EXAMPLES   **An atomic reactor is very powerful.** [The adjective *powerful* follows the linking verb *is* and describes the subject *reactor.*]
     This ground looks swampy. [The adjective *swampy* follows the linking verb *looks* and describes the subject *ground.*]

NOTE: Predicate adjectives may be compound.

     EXAMPLE   **A computer can be fun, helpful, and sometimes frustrating.**

▶ EXERCISE 6   **Identifying Predicate Adjectives**

Identify the predicate adjective or adjectives in each of the following sentences.

EXAMPLE　**1.** San Francisco's Chinatown is large and fascinating.
　　　　　　1. *large, fascinating*

1. The great stone dogs that guard the entrance to Chinatown look a bit frightening.
2. The streets there are crowded, colorful, and full of bustling activity.
3. The special foods at the tearooms and restaurants smell wonderful.
4. To an outsider, the mixture of Chinese and English languages sounds both mysterious and exciting.
5. The art at the Chinese Culture Center is impressive.

　　Some verbs, such as *look, grow,* and *feel,* may be used as either linking verbs or action verbs.

LINKING VERB　The sailor **felt** tired. [*Felt* is a linking verb because it links the adjective *tired* to the subject *sailor.*]

ACTION VERB　The sailor **felt** the cool breeze. [*Felt* is an action verb because it is followed by the direct object *breeze,* which tells what the sailor felt.]

EXERCISE 7　**Identifying Linking Verbs and Subject Complements**

Identify the linking verb and the subject complement in each of the following sentences. Then, identify each complement as a *predicate nominative* or a *predicate adjective.*

EXAMPLE　**1.** The raincoat looked too short for me.
　　　　　　1. *looked; short—predicate adjective*

1. My dog is playful.
2. I am the one who called you yesterday.
3. Many public buildings in the East are proof of I. M. Pei's architectural skill.
4. The downtown mall appeared especially busy today.
5. Sally Ride sounded excited and confident during the television interview.

6. The package felt too light to be a book.
7. These questions seem easier to me than the ones on the last two tests did.
8. The singer's clothing became a symbol that her fans imitated.
9. Some poems, such as "The Bells" and "The Raven," are delightfully rhythmical.
10. While the mountain lion looked around for food, the fawn remained perfectly still.

REVIEW B **Identifying Subject Complements**

Each of the following sentences has at least one subject complement. Identify each complement as a *predicate nominative* or a *predicate adjective*.

EXAMPLE **1.** All the food at the Spanish Club dinner was terrific.
1. *terrific—predicate adjective*

1. These tacos and Juan's fajitas seemed the most popular of the Mexican foods brought to the dinner.
2. The *ensalada campesina,* or peasant salad of Chile, which contained chickpeas, was Rosalinda's contribution.

3. The Ecuadorian tamales not only looked good but also tasted great.
4. The baked fish fillets from Bolivia were spicy and quite appetizing.
5. Peru is famous for its soups, and the shrimp soup was a winner.

6. The noodles with mushroom sauce was a specialty of Paraguay.
7. The Spanish cauliflower with garlic and onions was a treat but seemed too exotic for some students.
8. However, the pan of *hallacas*, the national cornmeal dish of Venezuela, was soon empty.
9. *Arroz con coco*, or coconut rice, from Puerto Rico quickly became the most requested dessert.
10. After dinner, all of us certainly felt full and much more knowledgeable about foods from Spanish-speaking countries.

REVIEW C   **Identifying Verbs and Complements**

Identify the verbs in the following sentences as *action verbs* or *linking verbs*. Then, identify the complements as *direct objects, indirect objects, predicate nominatives,* or *predicate adjectives*.

EXAMPLE   [1] Because they want artistic freedom, many people from other countries become United States citizens.
1. *want—action verb; freedom—direct object; become—linking verb; citizens—predicate nominative*

[1] Gilberto Zaldivar's story is a good example. [2] Zaldivar was an accountant and a community theater producer in Havana, Cuba, in 1961. [3] He became unhappy and frustrated with the Cuban government's control over the arts. [4] So he left his job and his homeland and started a new life in New York City. [5] The change brought Zaldivar many opportunities. [6] It also gave audiences in the United States a new entertainment experience. [7] Zaldivar was a co-founder of the *Repertorio Español* in 1968. [8] This company quickly established a reputation as the country's best Spanish-language theater troupe. [9] Their productions were fresh and unfamiliar to audiences. [10] Throughout the years, the company has performed numerous Spanish classics as well as new plays.

EXERCISE 8 **Using Complements in Speaking**

You're a radio personality, broadcasting live from the grand opening of a record store. Comment on the store, the music it carries, and the customers coming in on the first day of business. Write ten sentences that might be a part of your broadcast. In your sentences, use at least two direct objects, two indirect objects, two predicate nominatives, and two predicate adjectives. Identify the complements you use.

EXAMPLES   **1.** *The weather is beautiful for the grand opening of Music and More.*
beautiful—predicate adjective
2. *Music and More gives you more music for your money.*
you—indirect object; music—direct object

PICTURE THIS

You're among the hundreds of spectators at this spectacular launch of a space shuttle from the Kennedy Space Center in Florida. As the shuttle zooms out of sight, you sit down to write in your diary. You want to record your

GRAMMAR

impressions of the launch. Write a paragraph about the liftoff. Use a combination of action verbs and linking verbs. Underline the complements that you use, and be prepared to identify them as *direct objects, indirect objects, predicate nominatives,* and *predicate adjectives.*

Subject: shuttle launch
Audience: yourself
Purpose: to record an exciting event

Review: Posttest 1

Identifying Complements

Identify each italicized word in the following paragraphs as a *direct object,* an *indirect object,* a *predicate nominative,* or a *predicate adjective.*

EXAMPLES   I enjoy [1] *cooking* but it can be hard [2] *work.*
1. *cooking—direct object*
2. *work—predicate nominative*

My dad has been giving [1] *me* cooking [2] *lessons* since last summer. At first, I was [3] *reluctant* to tell the guys because some of them think that cooking is a girl's [4] *job.* But Dad told me to remind them that we guys eat [5] *meals* just as often as girls do. He also said that cooking is an excellent [6] *way* for us to do our share of the work around the house.

When I began, I could hardly boil [7] *water* without fouling up, but Dad remained [8] *patient* and showed [9] *me* the correct and easiest ways to do things. For example, did you know that water will boil faster if it has a little [10] *salt* in it or that cornstarch can make an excellent thickening [11] *agent* in everything from batter to gravy?

My first attempts tasted [12] *awful,* but gradually I've become a fairly good [13] *cook.* Probably my best complete meal is chicken [14] *stew.* Although stew doesn't require the highest [15] *grade* of chicken, a good baking hen will give [16] *it* a much better taste. I am always very [17] *careful* about picking out the vegetables, too. Our grocer probably thinks that I am too [18] *picky* when I demand the best [19] *ingredients.* I don't care, though, because when I serve my [20] *family* my stew, they say it is their favorite dish.

Review: Posttest 2

Writing Sentences with Complements

Write sentences according to the following guidelines. Underline the direct object, the indirect object, or the subject complement in each sentence.

1. a declarative sentence with a direct object
2. a declarative sentence with a predicate nominative
3. an interrogative sentence with a predicate adjective
4. an imperative sentence with an indirect object
5. an exclamatory sentence with a predicate adjective

17 THE PHRASE

Prepositional, Verbal, and Appositive Phrases

Diagnostic Test

Identifying Phrases

In each of the following sentences, identify the italicized phrase as a *prepositional phrase*, a *participial phrase*, an *infinitive phrase*, a *gerund phrase*, or an *appositive phrase*. Do not separately identify a prepositional phrase that is part of a larger phrase.

EXAMPLE **1.** My brother plans *to marry Maureen in June.*
1. *to marry Maureen in June—infinitive phrase*

1. *Fishing for bass* is my father's favorite pastime.
2. The seagulls *gliding through the air* looked like pieces of paper caught in the wind.
3. The school bus was on time *in spite of the traffic jam.*
4. Ms. Hoban, *my science teacher,* got married last week.
5. There is no time left *to answer your questions.*
6. At the carnival, the band played songs *with a lively samba beat.*

7. He tried *to do his best* in the race.
8. Nobody seems to be very interested in *going to the fireworks display.*
9. Have you seen my cat, *a long-haired Persian with yellow eyes?*
10. Julio said that he prefers the bike *with all-terrain tires and the wider, more comfortable seat.*
11. *Hoping for a new bicycle and a toy robot,* my brother couldn't sleep at all on Christmas Eve.
12. Rachel talked her friends into *watching that Mariah Carey video.*
13. In the United States, citizens have the right *to speak their minds.*
14. My aunt's car, *an old crate with a beat-up interior and a rattly engine,* used to belong to my grandfather.
15. The Mexican artist Diego Rivera enjoyed *painting pictures of children.*
16. Last Sunday, we all piled in the car and went *to the beach, the bowling alley, and the mall.*
17. The shark *chasing the school of fish* looked like a hammerhead.
18. Nobody wanted to read the book, *a thick hardback with a faded cover.*
19. All of the invitations *sent to the club members* had the wrong date on them.
20. Both the Union and the Confederacy recruited Native Americans *to help them during the Civil War.*

17a. A *phrase* is a group of related words that is used as a single part of speech and does not contain a verb and its subject.

VERB PHRASE **should have been told** [no subject]
PREPOSITIONAL **from my sister and me** [no subject or verb]
    PHRASE

NOTE: A group of words that has both a subject and a verb is called a *clause.*

EXAMPLES **Leta is watching television.** [*Leta* is the subject of the verb *is watching.*]
before the train arrived [*Train* is the subject of the verb *arrived.*]

☞ REFERENCE NOTE: For more about clauses, see Chapter 18.

The Prepositional Phrase

17b. A *prepositional phrase* includes a preposition, a noun or a pronoun called the *object of the preposition,* and any modifiers of that object.

EXAMPLES **The Seine River flows through Paris.** [The noun *Paris* is the object of the preposition *through.*]
The car in front of us slid into a snowbank. [The pronoun *us* is the object of the preposition *in front of.* The noun *snowbank* is the object of the preposition *into.*]

☞ REFERENCE NOTE: For a list of commonly used prepositions, see page 474.

Any modifier that comes between the preposition and its object is part of the prepositional phrase.

EXAMPLE **During the stormy night** the horse ran off. [The adjectives *the* and *stormy* modify the object *night.*]

An object of the preposition may be compound.

EXAMPLE **The dish is filled with raw carrots and celery.** [Both *carrots* and *celery* are objects of the preposition *with.*]

Be careful not to confuse an infinitive with a prepositional phrase. A prepositional phrase always has an object that is a noun or a pronoun. An infinitive is a verb form that usually begins with *to.*

PREPOSITIONAL PHRASE   When we went **to Florida,** we saw the old Spanish fort in Saint Augustine.
INFINITIVE   When we were in Florida, we went **to see** the old Spanish fort in Saint Augustine.

☞ REFERENCE NOTE: For more about infinitives, see page 522.

EXERCISE 1   **Identifying Prepositional Phrases**

Identify the prepositional phrase or phrases in each numbered sentence in the following paragraph.

EXAMPLE   [1] Do you recognize the man with a Harlem Globetrotters uniform and a basketball in this picture?
1. *with a Harlem Globetrotters uniform and a basketball; in this picture*

[1] Hubert "Geese" Ausbie was well known for both his sunny smile and his athletic skill during his career. [2] For twenty-five years, Ausbie played on one of the most popular teams in basketball's history. [3] He was a star with the Globetrotters. [4] The all-black team, which was started in 1927, is famous for its humorous performances. [5] But Ausbie discovered that ability must come before showmanship. [6] The combination of skill and humor is what appeals to Globetrotter fans throughout the world. [7] Ausbie, a native of Oklahoma, sharpened his skill on the basketball team at Philander Smith College in Little Rock, Arkansas. [8] While still in college, he tried out for the Globetrotters in 1961. [9] When he retired from the Globetrotters, Ausbie formed a traveling museum of his many souvenirs. [10] His collection includes the autographs of two presidents and boxing gloves from Muhammad Ali.

The Adjective Phrase

17c. An *adjective phrase* is a prepositional phrase that modifies a noun or a pronoun.

An adjective phrase tells *what kind* or *which one.*

EXAMPLES   Wang Wei was a talented painter **of landscapes.** [The phrase modifies the noun *painter,* telling what kind of painter.]
Mrs. O'Meara is the one **on the left.** [The phrase modifies the pronoun *one,* telling which one Mrs. O'Meara is.]

An adjective phrase always follows the word it modifies. That word may be the object of another prepositional phrase.

EXAMPLES   Sicily is an island **off the coast of Italy.** [The phrase *off the coast* modifies the noun *island.* The phrase *of Italy* modifies the object *coast.*]

More than one adjective phrase may modify the same word.

EXAMPLE   The box **of old magazines in the closet** is full. [The phrases *of old magazines* and *in the closet* modify the noun *box.*]

▶ EXERCISE 2   **Identifying Adjective Phrases**

Each of the following sentences contains two adjective phrases. Identify each adjective phrase and the word it modifies.

EXAMPLE   **1.** Megan read a book on the origins of words.
1. *on the origins—book; of words—origins*

1. Mike's sister Tanya, a real terror with a whale of a temper, shouts "Beans!" whenever something goes wrong.
2. Some words and phrases for the expression of anger have their origin in Latin or Greek.

3. Many of us in English class wanted to discuss how people express their annoyance.
4. Imagine what would happen if everybody with a bad temper in the city had a bad day.
5. We agreed that the best thing to do is to avoid people with chips on their shoulders.

The Adverb Phrase

17d. An *adverb phrase* is a prepositional phrase that modifies a verb, an adjective, or an adverb.

An adverb phrase tells *how, when, where, why,* or *to what extent* (such as *how long, how many,* or *how far*).

EXAMPLES   The snow fell **like feathers.** [The phrase modifies the verb *fell,* telling *how* the snow fell.]
The painting looks strange **over the fireplace.** [The phrase modifies the adjective *strange,* telling *where* the painting looks strange.]
Elaine speaks French well **for a beginner.** [The phrase modifies the adverb *well,* telling *to what extent* Elaine speaks French well.]
Mr. Ortiz has taught school **for sixteen years.** [The phrase modifies the verb phrase *has taught,* telling *how long* Mr. Ortiz has taught.]

An adverb phrase may come before or after the word it modifies.

EXAMPLES   The sportswriter interviewed the coach **before the game.**

Before the game the sportswriter interviewed the coach. [In each sentence the phrase modifies the verb *interviewed.*]

More than one adverb phrase may modify the same word.

EXAMPLE   **On April 24, 1990,** the Hubble Space Telescope was launched **into space.** [Both phrases modify the verb phrase *was launched.*]

GRAMMAR

▶ EXERCISE 3   **Identifying Adverb Phrases**

In each of the following sentences, identify the adverb phrase and the word or words it modifies.

EXAMPLE   **1.** The new restaurant was built over a river.
              1. *over a river—was built*

1. The Bali Hai Restaurant has opened across the road.
2. The food is fantastic beyond belief.
3. Almost everyone has gone to the new place.
4. At the Bali Hai you can eat exotic food.
5. None of the items on the menu are too expensive for most people.
6. They enjoy themselves in the friendly atmosphere.
7. People appear happy with the service.
8. For three weeks the Bali Hai has been crowded.
9. When we went there, we were seated on the patio.
10. Off the river blew a cool breeze.

▶ REVIEW A   **Identifying Adjective Phrases and Adverb Phrases**

Identify each prepositional phrase in the sentences in the following paragraph. Then tell whether each phrase is an *adjective phrase* or an *adverb phrase*. Be prepared to tell which word or expression each phrase modifies.

EXAMPLE   **[1]** Through old journals, we have learned much about the pioneers.
              1. *Through old journals—adverb phrase; about the pioneers—adjective phrase*

[1] Few of us appreciate the determination of the pioneers who traveled west. [2] The word *travel* comes from the French word *travailler*, which means "to work," and the pioneers definitely worked hard. [3] A typical day's journey began long before dawn. [4] On the trip westward, people rode in wagons like the ones shown on the next page. [5] During the day the wagon train traveled slowly over the mountains and across plains and deserts. [6] Each evening at dusk, the horses were unhitched from the wagons, and tents were pitched around campfires.

Worthington Whittredge, *Encampment on the Plains.*
Autry Museum of Western Heritage, Los Angeles.

[7] The travelers often established a temporary camp down in a valley for protection from the harsh winter weather. [8] Life in these camps was hard—food was often scarce, and many people never recovered from the hardships. [9] The pioneers who did survive by sheer determination usually continued their journey. [10] When the journey ended, these people worked hard to make homes for their families.

▶ REVIEW B **Using Adjective and Adverb Phrases**

You and your little brother are in a crowd waiting to get on an elevator. Unlike you, your brother is nervous about riding in an elevator with a large group of people. To distract him, you describe how elevators work and tell him about different elevators that you've seen or ridden. Use this drawing and your own thoughts about elevators to write sentences you might say to your brother. In your sentences use at least five adjective phrases and five adverb phrases, and underline them.

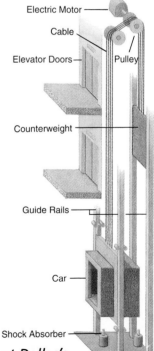

Electric Motor
Cable
Elevator Doors
Pulley
Counterweight
Guide Rails
Car
Shock Absorber

EXAMPLES **1.** *The elevator has an electric motor for the pulley.*
2. *I liked riding the glass elevator at Dallas's Reunion Tower because I could look around the city.*

WRITING APPLICATION

Using Prepositional Phrases in a Story

When you tell a story, you use many details to help your reader picture what happened. Often these details are in prepositional phrases. Adjective phrases tell *what kind* or *which one*. Adverb phrases tell *how, when, where, why,* or *to what extent*.

JUST THE FACTS   The flagship *Revenge* sank.
DETAILS ADDED   The flagship *Revenge* of the Royal Navy sank near the Spanish coast in 1591.

Can you identify the added details as adjective phrases or adverb phrases?

▶ WRITING ACTIVITY

Your class is writing and illustrating a book of original stories. The book will be given to a second-grade class during National Library Week. For the book, write a short story about a search for sunken treasure. In your story, use a variety of adjective and adverb phrases.

Prewriting Begin by thinking about stories you've read or heard about sunken treasures. Then, write down some details from these real or fictional stories. Next, use your imagination to think of a setting and some characters for your own story. Choose a point of view (first-person or third-person) and start writing.

Writing As you write your first draft, try to make your story exciting and interesting for second-grade readers. Since you're telling a story, arrange the events in chronological order. Remember to include details in prepositional phrases whenever possible.

Evaluating and Revising Read the story aloud to a friend or a younger child. Notice what reactions you get from your listener. Does the listener seem interested? Does he or she understand what happens in your story? Have you included enough details to make the story seem real? You may need to cut some details or add some information. New information often can be added easily in prepositional phrases.

GRAMMAR

Proofreading and Publishing Check the verbs in your story. Action verbs appeal to most readers. For more about action verbs, see pages 457–458. Also, check to be sure your verb tenses are correct. Publish your story, along with any illustrations for it, in a class book. Your class may want to read the stories aloud to the younger students.

Verbals and Verbal Phrases

A *verbal* is a form of a verb used as a noun, an adjective, or an adverb. There are three kinds of verbals: the *participle*, the *gerund*, and the *infinitive*.

The Participle

17e. A *participle* is a verb form that can be used as an adjective.

There are two kinds of participles—*present participles* and *past participles.*

Present participles end in *–ing.*

EXAMPLES   The news was **encouraging.** [*Encouraging,* a form of the verb *encourage,* modifies the noun *news.*]
The horses **trotting** past were not frightened by the crowd. [*Trotting,* a form of the verb *trot,* modifies the noun *horses.*]

Most past participles end in *–d* or *–ed*. Others are irregularly formed.

EXAMPLES   The police officers searched the **abandoned** warehouse. [*Abandoned,* a form of the verb *abandon,* modifies the noun *warehouse.*]
Charlie Parker, **known** as Bird, was a talented jazz musician. [*Known,* a form of the verb *know,* modifies the noun *Charlie Parker.*]

Do not confuse a participle used as an adjective with a participle used as part of a verb phrase.

PARTICIPLE   **Planning** their trip, the class learned how to read a road map.
VERB PHRASE   While they **were planning** their trip, the class learned how to read a road map.

PARTICIPLE   Most of the treasure **buried** by the pirates has never been found.
VERB PHRASE   Most of the treasure that **was buried** by the pirates has never been found.

EXERCISE 4   **Identifying Participles**

Identify the participles used as adjectives in the following sentences. Give the noun or pronoun each participle modifies. Be prepared to identify the participle as a *present participle* or a *past participle.*

EXAMPLE   **1.** We heard the train whistling and chugging in the distance.
1. *whistling—train; chugging—train*

1. Records, cracked and warped, were in the old trunk in the attic.
2. Shouting loudly, Carmen warned the pedestrian to look out for the car.
3. The sparkling water splashed in our faces.
4. The papers, aged and yellowed, were found in the bottom of the file cabinet.
5. For centuries the ruins remained there, still undiscovered.

6. Carefully painted and decorated, the piñata glittered in the sunlight.
7. The charging bull thundered across the field.
8. Cheering and clapping, the fans greeted their team.
9. The children, fidgeting noisily, waited eagerly for recess.
10. Recently released, the movie has not yet come to our local theaters.

The Participial Phrase

17f. A *participial phrase* consists of a participle and all of the words related to the participle. The entire phrase is used as an adjective.

A participle may be modified by an adverb and may also have a complement, usually a direct object. A participial phrase includes the participle and all of its modifiers and complements.

EXAMPLES **Seeing itself in the mirror, the duck seemed bewildered.** [The participial phrase modifies the noun *duck*. The pronoun *itself* is the direct object of the present participle *seeing*. The adverb phrase *in the mirror* modifies the present participle *seeing*.]

After a while, we heard the duck **quacking noisily at its own image.** [The participial phrase modifies the noun *duck*. The adverb *noisily* and the adverb phrase *at its own image* modify the present participle *quacking*.]

Then, **disgusted with the other duck,** it pecked the mirror. [The participial phrase modifies the pronoun *it*. The adverb phrase *with the other duck* modifies the past participle *disgusted*.]

A participial phrase should be placed as close as possible to the word it modifies. Otherwise, the sentence may not make sense.

MISPLACED	**Slithering through the grass,** I saw a snake **trimming the hedges this morning.**
CORRECTED	**Trimming the hedges this morning,** I saw a snake **slithering through the grass.**

☞ REFERENCE NOTE: For more information about misplaced participial phrases, see pages 671–672.

▶ EXERCISE 5 **Identifying Participial Phrases**

Identify the participial phrases in the following sentences. Give the word or words that each phrase modifies.

EXAMPLE **1.** Myths are wonderful stories passed on from generation to generation.
1. *passed on from generation to generation—stories*

1. Noted for her beauty, Venus was sought by all the gods as a wife.
2. Bathed in radiant light, Venus brought love and joy wherever she went.
3. Jupiter, knowing her charms, nevertheless married her to Vulcan, the ugliest of the gods.
4. Mars, known to the Greeks as Ares, was the god of war.
5. Terrified by Ares' power, many Greeks did not like to worship him.
6. They saw both land and people destroyed by him.
7. Observing his path, they said that Ares left blood, devastation, and grief behind him.
8. The Romans, having great respect for Mars, made him one of their three chief deities.
9. They imagined him dressed in shining armor.
10. Mars, supposed to be the father of the founders of Rome, has a planet named after him.

▶ EXERCISE 6 **Writing Sentences with Participial Phrases**

Use each of the following participial phrases in a sentence of your own. Place each phrase as close as possible to the noun or pronoun that it modifies.

EXAMPLE **1.** standing in line
1. *Standing in line, we waited twenty minutes for the store to open.*

1. waiting for the bus in the rain
2. passing the store window
3. planning the escape
4. jumping from stone to stone
5. hearing the whistle blow and feeling the train lurch forward

▶ REVIEW C **Using Participles and Participial Phrases to Combine Sentences**

You're the sports editor for the school newspaper. A new writer-photographer just turned in these photographs from a district school track-and-field event. She also wrote these captions to go under the photographs. The information is fine, but you want each caption to be only one sentence long. Use participles and participial phrases to combine each set of sentences.

EXAMPLE **1.** Tamara Jackson nears the finish line in the 100-meter dash. She looks happy because she's run her best.
1. *Looking happy because she's run her best, Tamara Jackson nears the finish line in the 100-meter dash.*

1. In the 100-meter hurdles, Ruth Ann Garcia appears to be leading. She is known for her last-minute bursts of energy.
2. Discus thrower Zack Linquist shifts his weight to his left foot. He twists his body to the right and hurls the discus across the field.

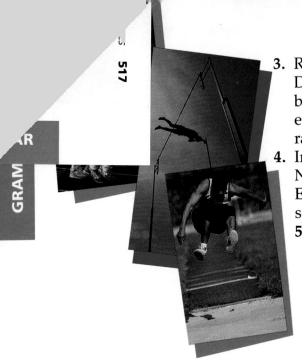

3. Relay team member Krista Davidson reaches for the baton. She has much experience in running relay races.
4. In the pole vault, Dennis Nishimoto clears the crossbar. Every muscle in his body strains as he goes over the bar.
5. Julius McKay shows great promise in the broad jump. Most people favor him to win this year's event.

The Gerund

17g. A *gerund* is a verb form ending in *-ing* that is used as a noun.

SUBJECT	**Jogging** can be good exercise.
PREDICATE NOMINATIVE	My favorite hobby is **fishing**.
OBJECT OF PREPOSITION	Lock the door before **leaving**.
DIRECT OBJECT	Did they enjoy **hiking**?

Do not confuse a gerund with a present participle used as part of a verb phrase or as an adjective.

EXAMPLE **Pausing,** the deer **was sniffing** the wind before **stepping** into the meadow. [*Pausing* is a participle modifying *deer,* and *sniffing* is part of the verb phrase *was sniffing. Stepping* is a gerund, serving as the object of the preposition *before.*]

▶ EXERCISE 7 **Identifying Gerunds**

Find the gerunds in the following sentences. Identify each gerund as a *subject,* a *predicate nominative,* a *direct object,* or an *object of a preposition.* If a sentence does not contain a gerund, write *none.*

EXAMPLE   **1.** Typing is a useful skill.
             1. *Typing—subject*

1. Why won't that dog stop barking?
2. Dr. Martin Luther King, Jr.'s powerful speaking helped draw attention to the civil rights movement.
3. My sister has always enjoyed horseback riding.
4. In the past, working took up most people's time six days a week.
5. I look forward to a rest after this tiring job is done.
6. Uncle Eli's specialty is barbecuing on the grill.
7. Nobody could stand the child's unceasing whine.
8. The most exciting part of the ceremony will be the crowning of the new king.
9. Studying usually pays off in higher scores.
10. Considering the other choices, Melinda decided on walking.

The Gerund Phrase

17h.   A *gerund phrase* consists of a gerund and all the words related to the gerund.

Because a gerund is a verb form, it may be modified by an adverb and may have a complement, usually a direct object. Since a gerund functions as a noun, it may be modified by an adjective. A gerund phrase includes the gerund and all of its modifiers and complements.

EXAMPLES   **Having a part-time job** may interfere with your schoolwork. [The gerund phrase is the subject of the sentence. The noun *job* is the direct object of the gerund *having*. The article *a* and the adjective *part-time* modify *job.*]

The townspeople heard the loud clanging of the fire bell. [The gerund phrase is the direct object of the verb *heard*. The adjectives *the* and *loud* and the adjective phrase *of the fire bell* modify the gerund *clanging.*]

We crossed the stream by **stepping carefully from stone to stone.** [The gerund phrase is the object of the preposition *by.* The adverb *carefully* and the adverb phrases *from stone* and *to stone* modify the gerund *stepping.*]

NOTE: When a noun or a pronoun comes immediately before a gerund, use the possessive form of the noun or pronoun.

EXAMPLES **Michael's** cooking is the best I've ever tasted.
The vultures didn't let anything disturb **their** feeding.

EXERCISE 8 **Identifying Gerund Phrases**

Find the gerund phrases in the following sentences. Identify each phrase as a *subject,* a *predicate nominative,* a *direct object,* or an *object of a preposition.*

EXAMPLE **1.** The rain interrupted their building of the bonfire.
1. *their building of the bonfire—direct object*

1. Angelo's pleading never influenced his mother's decision.
2. The eerie sound they heard was the howling of the wolves.
3. We sat back and enjoyed the slow rocking of the boat.
4. The blue jay's screeching at the cat woke us up at dawn.
5. People supported César Chávez and the United Farm Workers by boycotting grapes.
6. Our greatest victory will be winning the state championship.
7. The frantic darting of the fish indicated that a shark was nearby.
8. She is considering running for class president.
9. Ants try to protect their colonies from storms by piling up sand against the wind.
10. In his later years, Chief Quanah Parker was known for settling disputes fairly.

GRAMMAR

Writing Sentences with Gerund Phrases

Use each of the following gerund phrases in a sentence of your own. Underline the gerund phrase and identify it as a *subject*, a *predicate nominative*, a *direct object*, or an *object of a preposition*.

EXAMPLE   **1.** hiking up the hill
          1. *Hiking up the hill* took us all morning.—
             subject

1. getting up in the morning
2. arguing among themselves
3. refusing any help with the job
4. sharpening my pencil
5. listening to Scott Joplin's ragtime music

Using Gerunds and Gerund Phrases

You and a friend see this experimental car at an auto show, and you're amazed by its design. Many of the car's features are unlike anything on the road now. Do you think this design will really work? Will it sell? Write a short conversation between you and your friend about the car design. Make sure that your conversation contains five gerunds or gerund phrases. Underline each gerund or gerund phrase you use.

EXAMPLE   **1.** *"Wow! Driving a car like that would be*
             great!" I said.

The Infinitive

17i. An *infinitive* is a verb form that can be used as a noun, an adjective, or an adverb. An infinitive usually begins with *to.*

NOUNS **To install** the ceiling fan took two hours. [*To install* is the subject of the sentence.]
Winona's ambition is **to become** a doctor. [*To become* is a predicate nominative referring to the subject *ambition.*]
Shina likes **to skate** but not **to ski.** [*To skate* and *to ski* are direct objects of the verb *likes.*]

ADJECTIVES The best time **to visit** Florida is December through April. [*To visit* modifies *time.*]
If you want information about computers, that is the magazine **to read.** [*To read* modifies *magazine.*]

ADVERBS The gymnasts were eager **to practice** their routines. [*To practice* modifies the adjective *eager.*]
The caravan stopped at the oasis **to rest.** [*To rest* modifies the verb *stopped.*]

NOTE: *To* plus a noun or a pronoun (*to class, to them, to the dance*) is a prepositional phrase, not an infinitive. Be careful not to confuse infinitives with prepositional phrases beginning with *to.*

INFINITIVE I want **to go.**
PREPOSITIONAL PHRASE I want to go **to town.**

▶ EXERCISE 11 **Identifying Infinitives**

Identify the infinitive in each sentence in the following paragraphs.

EXAMPLE [1] June and I decided to be friends the first time we met.
1. *to be*

[1] After school, June and I like to walk home together. [2] Usually, we go to my house or her house to listen to

tapes. [3] Sometimes I get up to dance to the music, but June never does. [4] It's hard for me to sit still when a good song is playing. [5] June finally told me that she had never learned how to dance.

[6] "Do you want me to show you some steps?" I asked.

[7] "I'm ready to try," she answered.

[8] I decided to start with some simple steps. [9] After doing my best to teach her for three weeks, I finally gave up. [10] It's a good thing that June doesn't plan to become a dancer.

The Infinitive Phrase

17j. An *infinitive phrase* consists of an infinitive and its modifiers and complements.

An infinitive may be modified by an adjective or an adverb; it may also have a complement. The entire infinitive phrase may act as an adjective, an adverb, or a noun.

EXAMPLES   The crowd grew quiet **to hear the speaker.** [The infinitive phrase is an adverb modifying the adjective *quiet*. The noun *speaker* is the direct object of the infinitive *to hear.*]

Peanuts and raisins are good snacks **to take on a camping trip.** [The infinitive phrase is an adjective modifying *snacks*. The adverb phrase *on a camping trip* modifies the infinitive *to take.*]

To lift those weights takes a lot of strength. [The infinitive phrase is a noun used as the subject of the sentence. The noun *weights* is the direct object of the infinitive *to lift.*]

▶ EXERCISE 12   **Identifying Infinitive Phrases**

Most of the sentences in the following paragraph contain an infinitive phrase. Identify each infinitive phrase and tell whether it is a *noun,* an *adjective,* or an *adverb.* If there is no infinitive phrase in a sentence, write *none.*

EXAMPLE [1] Taking care of your bicycle is the best way to make it last longer.

    1. *to make it last longer—adjective*

[1] My aunt taught me to take care of my bicycle. [2] We used machine oil to lubricate the chain. [3] She told me to place a drop of oil on each link. [4] Then she showed me the valve to fill the inner tube. [5] Using a hand pump, we added air to the back tire. [6] We were careful not to put in too much air. [7] Next, we got out wrenches to tighten some bolts. [8] My aunt warned me not to pull the wrench too hard. [9] Overtightening can cause as much damage to bolts as not tightening them enough. [10] When we finished, I thanked my aunt for taking the time to give me tips about taking care of my bicycle.

EXERCISE 13   Writing Sentences with Infinitive Phrases

Use each of the following infinitive phrases in a sentence of your own. Underline the infinitive phrase and identify it as a *noun,* an *adjective,* or an *adverb.*

EXAMPLE **1.** to leave school early on Tuesday

    1. *The principal gave me permission <u>to leave school early on Tuesday.</u>—adjective*

1. to give the right answers
2. to go home after school
3. to run after the bus
4. to read the entire book over the weekend
5. to spend the night at my cousin's house

EXERCISE 14   Using Infinitives and Infinitive Phrases

A friend of yours has an opportunity to work at a summer camp as an assistant group leader. The application has been approved, but the camp director wants to know more about your friend. Because you're a good writer, your friend asks you for a letter of recommendation. You decide to make a list of your friend's interests, habits, and good points before beginning to write the letter. Write five sentences that you might include in your letter about your friend. In each sentence, use an infinitive or an infinitive phrase, and underline it.

EXAMPLE **1.** *Pedro likes* <u>*to collect baseball cards*</u>.

GRAMMAR

▶ REVIEW D **Identifying Verbals and Verbal Phrases**

Each of the following sentences contains at least one verbal or verbal phrase. Identify each verbal or verbal phrase as a *gerund*, a *gerund phrase*, an *infinitive*, an *infinitive phrase*, a *participle*, or a *participial phrase*.

EXAMPLE **1.** Visiting Cahokia Mounds State Historic Site in Illinois is a wonderful experience.
1. *Visiting Cahokia Mounds State Historic Site in Illinois—gerund phrase*

1. The Cahokia were a Native American people who built a highly developed civilization in North America more than one thousand years ago.
2. Noting the importance of the Cahokia, the United Nations Educational, Scientific, and Cultural Organization (UNESCO) set aside Cahokia Mounds as a World Heritage Site.
3. After studying the site, archaeologists were able to make a sketch like the one below of the ancient city.
4. The city was destroyed long ago, but the remaining traces of it show how huge it must have been.
5. This thriving community had a population of about 20,000 sometime between A.D. 700 and A.D. 1500.

6. You can see that the people chose or were required to build their houses mostly inside the stockade wall.
7. It's still possible to see many of the earthen mounds.
8. The historic site includes about sixty-eight preserved mounds, which were used mainly for ceremonial activities.
9. Seeing the 100-foot-high Monks Mound is exciting.
10. The mound was built as the place for the city's ruler to live and to govern.

Appositives and Appositive Phrases

17k. An *appositive* is a noun or a pronoun placed beside another noun or pronoun to identify or explain it.

Appositives are often set off from the rest of the sentence by commas. However, when an appositive is necessary to the meaning of the sentence or is closely related to the word it refers to, no commas are necessary.

EXAMPLES   The cosmonaut **Yuri Gagarin** was the first person in space. [The noun *Yuri Gagarin* identifies the noun *cosmonaut.*]

The explorers saw a strange animal, **something** with fur and a bill like a duck's. [The pronoun *something* refers to the noun *animal.*]

John James Audubon, an **artist** and a **naturalist,** is famous for his paintings of American birds in their habitats. [The nouns *artist* and *naturalist* explain the noun *John James Audubon.*]

17l. An *appositive phrase* consists of an appositive and its modifiers.

EXAMPLES   **Officer Webb, one of the security guards,**
apprehended the burglar. [The adjective phrase
of the security guards modifies the appositive
one.]

Black Hawk, a famous chief of the Sauk Indians,
fought hard for the freedom of his people. [The
article *a,* the adjective *famous,* and the adjective
phrase *of the Sauk Indians* modify the
appositive *chief.*]

EXERCISE 15   **Identifying Appositives and Appositive
Phrases**

Identify the appositives or appositive phrases in the following sentences. Give the word or words each appositive or appositive phrase identifies or explains.

EXAMPLE   **1.** My dog, the mutt with floppy ears, can do
tricks.
1. *the mutt with floppy ears—dog*

1. Tacos, tamales, and enchiladas, some of the most
popular Mexican dishes, are served here.
2. This color, midnight blue, is just what I've been
looking for.
3. Two men, a truck driver and a sailor, helped my
father push the car off the road.
4. I'll have a sandwich, tuna salad on rye bread,
please.
5. Miguel has the same class, American history, this
afternoon.
6. Barbara Jordan, one of my heroes, was a strong
champion of both civil and human rights.
7. Shelley asked everyone where her friend Bianca
had gone.
8. Somebody reported the hazard, a pile of trash
containing broken bottles, to the police.
9. Be sure to bring the exact change, fifty cents.
10. They sang the song "I've Been Working on the
Railroad" over and over all the way down the path.

GRAMMAR

> REVIEW E   **Identifying Verbals and Appositives**

Find all the verbals and appositives in the sentences in the following paragraph. Identify each word as an *appositive,* an *infinitive,* a *gerund,* or a *participle.*

EXAMPLE   [1] Skating on the sidewalk, my little brother Shawn tried to do some acrobatics, and that put an end to his playing for a while.

     1. *Skating—participle; Shawn—appositive; to do—infinitive; playing—gerund*

[1] Instead of falling on the soft ground, Shawn managed to hit right on the sidewalk. [2] The concrete, broken and crumbling, cut him in several places on his legs and elbows. [3] We heard his piercing wail all the way up at our house, and my mother and I rushed to see what had happened. [4] By the time we got to him, the cuts had already started bleeding, and he was struggling to get his skates off. [5] Bending down, Mom pulled off the skates and dabbed at the seeping red cuts and scrapes. [6] Shawn, a brave little boy usually, could not keep from crying. [7] Mom carried Shawn to the house, and I followed with his skates, scratched and scraped almost as badly as he was. [8] After cleaning Shawn's cuts, Mom decided to take him to the emergency clinic. [9] The doctor, a young intern, said that she would have to close one of the cuts with stitches. [10] When we got home, Mom said that she hoped Shawn had learned to be more careful, but knowing Shawn, I doubt it.

PICTURE THIS

You are "warming up" with the students in one of the pictures on the next page. Or you're preparing for some other activity that you like to do. A beginner at the activity is watching you and has asked for your help. Write a short paragraph telling the beginner how to prepare for the activity. In your paragraph, use at least one adjective phrase, one adverb phrase, two verbal phrases (participial, gerund, or infinitive), and one appositive phrase.

Subject: "warming up" for an activity
Audience: a beginner
Purpose: to inform

Review: Posttest 1

Identifying Prepositional, Verbal, and Appositive Phrases

Identify each italicized phrase in the following paragraphs as *prepositional*, *participial*, *gerund*, *infinitive*, or *appositive*. Do not separately identify a prepositional phrase that is part of a larger phrase.

EXAMPLES   After [1] *giving me my allowance,* my father
                 warned me [2] *not to spend it all in one place.*
                 1. *giving me my allowance*—gerund
                 2. *not to spend it all in one place*—infinitive

Gina, [1] *my best friend since elementary school,* and I decided [2] *to go to the mall after school yesterday.* Gina suggested [3] *taking the back way* so that we could jog, but I was wearing sandals [4] *instead of my track shoes,* so we just walked. Along the way we saw Cathy [5] *sitting on her front porch* and asked her if she wanted [6] *to join us.* She was earning a little spending money by [7] *baby-sitting her neighbor's children,* though, and couldn't leave.

[8] *Walking up to the wide glass doors at the mall,* Gina and I looked in our purses. We both had a few dollars and our student passes, so we stopped [9] *to get a glass of orange juice* while we checked what movies were playing. None [10] *of the four features* looked interesting to us. However, Deven Bowers, [11] *a friend from school and an usher at the theater,* said that there would be a sneak preview [12] *of a new adventure film* later, and we told him we'd be back then.

Since stores usually do not allow customers to bring food or drinks inside, Gina and I gulped down our orange juice before [13] *going into our favorite dress shop.* We looked [14] *through most of the sale racks,* but none of the dresses, [15] *all of them formal or evening gowns,* appealed to us. A salesclerk asked if we were shopping [16] *for something special.* After [17] *checking with Gina,* I told the clerk we were just looking, and we left.

We walked past a couple of shops—[18] *the health food store and a toy store*—and went into Record World. [19] *Seeing several cassettes by my favorite group,* I picked out one. By the time we walked out of Record World, I'd spent all my money, so we never did get [20] *to go to the movie that day.*

Review: Posttest 2

Writing Sentences with Prepositional, Verbal, and Appositive Phrases

Write ten sentences, using one of the following phrases in each sentence. Follow the directions in parentheses.

EXAMPLE **1.** to write a descriptive paragraph (*use as an infinitive phrase that is the predicate nominative in the sentence*)
1. *Our assignment for tomorrow is to write a descriptive paragraph.*

1. after the game (*use as an adverb phrase*)
2. instead of your good shoes (*use as an adjective phrase*)
3. in one of Shakespeare's plays (*use as an adjective phrase*)
4. going to school every day (*use as a gerund phrase that is the subject in the sentence*)
5. living in a small town (*use as a gerund phrase that is the object of a preposition*)
6. walking through the empty lot (*use as a participial phrase*)
7. dressed in authentic costumes (*use as a participial phrase*)
8. to drive a car for the first time (*use as an infinitive phrase that is the direct object in the sentence*)
9. the best athlete in our school (*use as an appositive phrase*)
10. my favorite pastime (*use as an appositive phrase*)

18 THE CLAUSE

Independent and Subordinate Clauses

Identifying Independent and Subordinate Clauses

Identify each italicized clause in the following sentences as an *independent clause* or a *subordinate clause.* Indicate whether each italicized subordinate clause is used as an *adjective,* an *adverb,* or a *noun.*

EXAMPLES **1.** The customer thumbed through the book, but *it didn't seem to interest her.*
1. *independent clause*

2. Anyone *who gets a high score on this test* will not have to take the final exam.
2. *subordinate clause—adjective*

1. *After it had been snowing for several hours,* we took our sleds out to Sentry Hill.
2. The ring *that I lost at the beach last summer* had belonged to my great-grandmother.

3. If he doesn't get here soon, *I'm leaving.*
4. Do you know *who she is?*
5. I have not seen Shawn *since the football game ended last Saturday night.*
6. *In the morning they gathered their belongings and left* before the sun rose.
7. Nobody knew *that Derrick had worked out the solution.*
8. *The Hopi and the Zuni built their homes out of adobe,* which is sun-dried earth.
9. My dad says never to trust strangers *who seem overly friendly.*
10. *That he had been right* became obvious as the problem grew worse.
11. Julio knew the right answer *because he looked it up in the dictionary.*
12. Today's assignment is to write a three-paragraph composition on *how a bill becomes a law.*
13. On our vacation we visited my dad's old neighbor-hood, *which is now an industrial park.*
14. *Mr. Johnson told us* that in the late 1800s, at least one fourth of all the cowboys in the West were African Americans.
15. Did you get the message *that your mother called?*
16. Tranh raked up the leaves *while his father stuffed them into plastic bags.*
17. The Spanish Club sang several Mexican American *corridos,* which are ballads, and *they were a hit.*
18. We will be over *as soon as Sandy finishes his lunch.*
19. That is the man *whose dog rescued my sister.*
20. Free samples were given to *whoever asked for them.*

18a. A *clause* is a group of words that contains a verb and its subject and is used as a part of a sentence.

Every clause has a subject and a verb. However, not every clause expresses a complete thought.

GRAMMAR

SENTENCE   Writers gathered at the home of Gertrude Stein when she lived in Paris.

                  S   V

CLAUSE   Writers gathered at the home of Gertrude Stein.
[complete thought]

                  S   V

CLAUSE   when she lived in Paris [incomplete thought]

There are two kinds of clauses: the *independent clause* and the *subordinate clause*.

The Independent Clause

18b.   An *independent* (or *main*) *clause* expresses a complete thought and can stand by itself as a sentence.

                       S   V

EXAMPLES   **The sun set an hour ago.** [This entire sentence is an independent clause.]

                    S   V

Jean Merrill wrote *The Pushcart War,* and

                   S   V

Ronni Solbert illustrated the book. [This sentence contains two independent clauses.]

                               S   V

After I finished studying, I went to the movies. [This sentence contains one independent clause and one subordinate clause.]

EXERCISE 1   **Identifying Subjects and Verbs in Independent Clauses**

Identify the subject and verb in each numbered, italicized independent clause in the following paragraph.

EXAMPLE   Before she left for college, [1] *my sister read the comics in the newspaper every day.*
1. *sister—subject; read—verb*

[1] *She told me that Jump Start was one of her* favorites. Since she liked it so much, [2] *I made a point of reading it, too.* [3] *The comic strip was created by this young man, Robb Armstrong,* who lives and works in Philadelphia. [4] *Jump Start features an African American police officer named Joe and his wife, Marcy,* who is a nurse. If you aren't familiar with the strip, [5] *you may not recognize Joe and Marcy standing behind their creator.*

Jump Start reprinted by permission of United Feature Syndicate, Inc.

The Subordinate Clause

18c. A *subordinate* (or *dependent*) *clause* does not express a complete thought and cannot stand alone as a sentence.

A word such as *that, what,* or *since* signals the beginning of a subordinate clause.

EXAMPLES
$$\overset{\text{S} \quad \text{V}}{\textbf{that } \text{I wanted}}$$

$$\overset{\text{S} \quad \text{V}}{\textbf{what } \text{she saw}}$$

$$\overset{\text{S} \qquad \text{V}}{\textbf{since } \text{most plants die without light}}$$

The meaning of a subordinate clause is complete only when the clause is attached to an independent clause.

EXAMPLES   The store did not have the video game **that I wanted.**

The witness told the police officers **what she saw.**

Since most plants die without light, we moved our houseplants closer to the window.

Sometimes the word that begins a subordinate clause is the subject of the clause.

EXAMPLES
$\overset{\text{S}}{}\ \overset{\text{V}}{}$
The animals **that are in the game preserve** are protected from hunters.

$\overset{\text{S}}{}\ \ \overset{\text{V}}{}$
Can you tell me **who wrote "America the Beautiful"**?

▶ EXERCISE 2   **Identifying Independent and Subordinate Clauses**

Identify each of the following groups of words as an *independent clause* or a *subordinate clause*.

EXAMPLE   **1.** as I answered the telephone
1. *subordinate clause*

1. we memorized the lyrics
2. as they sat on the back porch
3. if no one is coming
4. my sister was born on Valentine's Day
5. which everyone enjoyed
6. the flood destroyed many crops
7. the singer wore a silk scarf
8. when the lights were flickering
9. since the first time we talked
10. that the lion's cage was empty

▶ EXERCISE 3   **Identifying Subordinate Clauses and Their Subjects and Verbs**

Identify the subordinate clause in each of the following sentences. Give the subject and the verb of each subordinate clause.

GRAMMAR

EXAMPLE   **1.** My report is about the plague that spread across Europe in the fourteenth century.
   1. *that spread across Europe in the fourteenth century; subject—that; verb—spread*

1. In 1347, trading ships arrived at the Mediterranean island of Sicily from Caffa, which was a port city on the Black Sea.
2. When the sailors went ashore, many of them carried a strange illness.
3. No medicine could save the stricken sailors, who died quickly and painfully.
4. Since it originated in the Black Sea area, the plague was called the Black Death.
5. People who traveled between cities in Europe unknowingly carried the disease with them.
6. Millions of people became sick and died as the plague spread from Sicily across Europe.
7. On this map, you can trace how quickly the plague spread.
8. The terrified survivors thought that the world was coming to an end.
9. No one is sure of the total number of people who died from the dreaded plague.
10. Since medicine offers new ways for controlling plague, the spread of this disease is unlikely today.

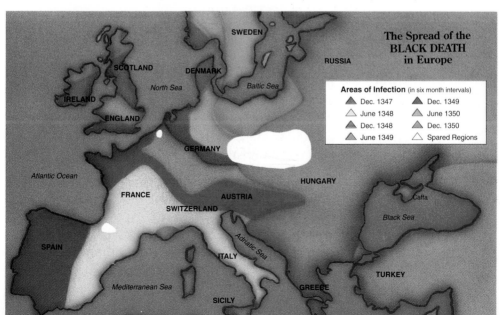

The Spread of the
BLACK DEATH
in Europe

Areas of Infection (in six month intervals)

▲ Dec. 1347   ▲ Dec. 1349
△ June 1348   △ June 1350
▲ Dec. 1348   ▲ Dec. 1350
▲ June 1349   △ Spared Regions

EXERCISE 4   **Writing Sentences with Independent and Subordinate Clauses**

Write a sentence by adding an independent clause to each subordinate clause. Draw one line under the subject and two lines under the verb of each clause.

EXAMPLES   **1.** who came late
         1. *Anica is the volunteer who came late.*
         2. as the horn blared
         2. *As the horn blared, I was running out the door.*

1. when the ice melts
2. if my teacher approves
3. since you insist
4. when they act silly
5. who borrowed my notes
6. as she began to shout
7. when we danced on stage
8. who gave the report
9. since I sleep soundly
10. that I bought yesterday

The Adjective Clause

Like an adjective or an adjective phrase, an adjective clause may modify a noun or a pronoun.

         ADJECTIVE   the **blonde** woman
ADJECTIVE PHRASE   the woman **with blonde hair**
ADJECTIVE CLAUSE   the woman **who has blonde hair**

         ADJECTIVE   a **steel** bridge
ADJECTIVE PHRASE   a bridge **of steel**
ADJECTIVE CLAUSE   a bridge **that is made of steel**

18d.   An *adjective clause* is a subordinate clause that modifies a noun or a pronoun.

An adjective clause usually follows the word it modifies and tells *which one* or *what kind*.

EXAMPLES   Ms. Jackson showed slides **that she had taken in Egypt.** [The adjective clause modifies the noun *slides*, telling *which* slides.]
         Helen Keller was a remarkable woman **who met the challenge of being both blind and deaf.** [The

adjective clause modifies the noun *woman,* telling *what kind* of woman.]
The ones whose flight was delayed spent the night in Detroit. [The adjective clause modifies the pronoun *ones,* telling *which* ones.]

Relative Pronouns

An adjective clause is usually introduced by a *relative pronoun.*

		Relative Pronouns		
that	which	who	whom	whose

A ***relative pronoun*** relates an adjective clause to the word the clause modifies.

EXAMPLES   Leonardo da Vinci was the artist **who painted the *Mona Lisa.*** [The relative pronoun *who* begins the adjective clause and relates to the noun *artist.*]
Everything **that could be done** was done. [The relative pronoun *that* begins the adjective clause and relates to the pronoun *everything.*]

Sometimes a relative pronoun is preceded by a preposition that is part of the adjective clause.

EXAMPLES   Have you read the book **on which the movie is based**?
The young actor **to whom I am referring** is Fred Savage.

In addition to relating a subordinate clause to the rest of the sentence, a relative pronoun also has a function in the subordinate clause.

EXAMPLES   Is this the tape **that is on sale?** [*That* relates the subordinate clause to the word *tape* and also functions as the subject of the subordinate clause.]

> He is a friend **on whom you can always depend.**
> [*Whom* relates the subordinate clause to the word *friend* and functions as the object of the preposition *on.*]

An adjective clause may be introduced by a *relative adverb,* such as *when* or *where.*

EXAMPLES   This is the spot **where we caught most of the fish.**

The time period **when dinosaurs ruled** lasted millions of years.

In some cases, the relative pronoun or adverb can be omitted.

EXAMPLES   We haven't seen the silver jewelry **(that *or* which) she brought back from Mexico.**

Do you remember the time **(when *or* that) the dog caught the skunk?**

EXERCISE 5   **Identifying Adjective Clauses**

Identify the adjective clause in each of the following sentences. Give the relative pronoun and the word that the relative pronoun refers to.

EXAMPLE   **1.** Our friends have a canary that is named Neptune.

    1. *that is named Neptune; that—canary*

1. Proverbs are sayings that usually give advice.
2. Trivia questions have been organized into games that have become quite popular.
3. A black hole, which results after a star has collapsed, can trap energy and matter.
4. A special award was given to the student whose work had improved most.
5. Frances Perkins, who served as secretary of labor, was the first woman to hold a Cabinet position.
6. The problem that worries us now is the pollution of underground sources of water.

GRAMMAR

7. We enjoyed the poems of Gwendolyn Brooks, who for years has been poet laureate of Illinois.
8. In *Walden,* Henry David Thoreau shared ideas that have influenced many.
9. Athena, who ranked as an important Greek deity, protected the city of Athens.
10. A friend is a person whom you can trust.

WRITING APPLICATION

Using Adjective Clauses in Writing a Specific Definition

When you write, you use adjective clauses much as you would use adjectives and adjective phrases. Just as adjective phrases are longer than single-word adjectives, adjective clauses are usually longer than phrases. Because adjective clauses are longer, they can describe more and be more specific.

ADJECTIVE	a **large** building
ADJECTIVE PHRASE	a building **of enormous height**
ADJECTIVE CLAUSE	a building **that towers above all the others**

WRITING ACTIVITY

Sometimes, people misunderstand each other because they aren't thinking of the same meanings for words. For example, what *you* think is a "good" report card may not be the same as what your *parents* think is a "good" report card. Write a paragraph defining one of the people or things listed below or another term that you choose. Use at least four adjective clauses. Underline the clauses you use.

a clean room	a loyal friend	a fun weekend
a good teacher	an ideal pet	a good-looking outfit

Prewriting First, choose a term that interests you. Then, take a few minutes to write down whatever thoughts come to mind about that term. Write specific names and details.

 Writing State your definition(s) of the term—your main idea—in a topic sentence. As you write your supporting sentences, refer to your notes for specific names and details. Make sure that some details are given in adjective clauses.

 Evaluating and Revising Read over your paragraph. Would your reader understand your definition? Would he or she agree with it? Remember that all details in your paragraph should relate to your definition. If they do not, you may need to add, cut, or revise some information. Count the relative pronouns or relative adverbs you've used. That number will tell you how many adjective clauses your paragraph has.

 Proofreading and Publishing As you proofread your paragraph, pay attention to spelling and capitalization. Be sure to capitalize proper nouns and proper adjectives. For more about capitalization, see Chapter 25. You and your classmates may enjoy comparing different definitions of the same term. You could also gather the definitions together to create a class dictionary.

EXERCISE 6   **Identifying Adjective Clauses**

Identify the adjective clause in each of the following sentences. Give the relative pronoun or relative adverb and the word that the pronoun refers to.

EXAMPLE   **1.** Crispus Attucks was an African American patriot who was killed during the Boston Massacre.
    1. *who was killed during the Boston Massacre; who—patriot*

1. Coco Chanel is the woman for whom the perfume is named.
2. Here is the concert hall where we heard the great cello player Pablo Casals.
3. The cello, when played by Pablo Casals, is an instrument to which I could listen for hours.
4. Ella Fitzgerald, who started singing in New York City, is famous throughout the world.
5. The English playwright Christopher Marlowe wrote of Helen of Troy, "Was this the face that launched a thousand ships?"
6. Anita was one of the sopranos who sang in the chorus.
7. In the play *My Fair Lady,* Eliza Doolittle, a poor flower merchant, becomes a woman whom everyone admires.
8. The Kinderhook was the creek in which we found the shells.
9. Janet Flanner, who wrote dispatches from Paris, used the pen name Genêt.
10. The astronauts, to whom travel in the space shuttle is routine, must always keep in shape.

EXERCISE 7   **Using Adjective Clauses**

Go fly a kite! That's what you and the rest of the participants in this year's Smithsonian Kite Festival in Washington, D.C., did. Now that you're back home, your teacher would like you to tell the class about your experiences. Write a brief report about kites or a short story about your experience at the festival. You might want to describe how to make a kite and fly it. Or you might tell about an event that happened at the festival. In your report, include five adjective clauses and underline them. You can use the picture and the diagram on the following page, as well as your own experiences and your imagination, to help you write.

EXAMPLE   **1.** *The kite that I flew looks like the one in the middle of this picture.*

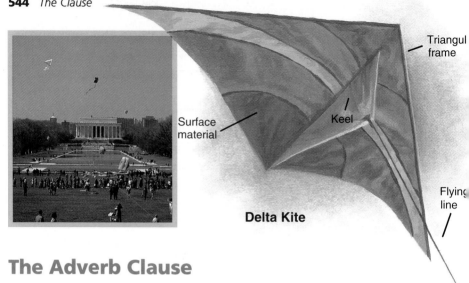

Triangul frame

Surface material

Keel

Flyin line

Delta Kite

The Adverb Clause

Unlike an adverb or an adverb phrase, an adverb clause has a subject and a verb.

ADVERB	You may sit **anywhere.**
ADVERB PHRASE	You may sit **in any chair.**
ADVERB CLAUSE	You may sit **wherever you wish.** [*You* is the subject, and *wish* is the verb.]

18e. An *adverb clause* is a subordinate clause that modifies a verb, an adjective, or an adverb.

An adverb clause tells *where, when, how, why, to what extent,* or *under what condition.*

EXAMPLES   You may sit **wherever you wish.** [The adverb clause modifies the verb *may sit,* telling *where* you may sit.]
　　　　　When winter sets in, many animals hibernate. [The adverb clause modifies the verb *hibernate,* telling *when* many animals hibernate.]
　　　　　My new friend and I talk **as if we've known each other for a long time.** [The adverb clause modifies the verb *talk,* telling *how* my new friend and I talk.]
　　　　　Because the weather was hot, the cool water felt good. [The adverb clause modifies the adjective *good,* telling *why* the water felt good.]

GRAMMAR

Gabrielle can type faster **than I can.** [The adverb clause modifies the adverb *faster*, telling *to what extent* Gabrielle can type faster.]
If it does not rain tomorrow, we will go to Crater Lake. [The adverb clause modifies the verb *will go*, telling *under what condition* we will go to Crater Lake.]

Notice in these examples that an adverb clause does not always follow the word it modifies. When an adverb clause begins a sentence, it is usually followed by a comma.

REFERENCE NOTE: For more information about using commas with adverb clauses, see page 753.

Subordinating Conjunctions

An adverb clause is introduced by a *subordinating con-junction*—a word that shows the relationship between the adverb clause and the word or words that the clause modifies.

Common Subordinating Conjunctions			
after	as though	since	when
although	because	so that	whenever
as	before	than	where
as if	how	though	wherever
as long as	if	unless	whether
as soon as	in order that	until	while

REFERENCE NOTE: The words *after, as, before, since,* and *until* are also commonly used as prepositions. See page 474.

 EXERCISE 8 **Identifying Adverb Clauses**

Identify the adverb clause in each of the following sentences. In each clause, circle the subordinating conjunction, and underline the subject once and the verb twice.

GRAMMAR

EXAMPLE **1.** Although they lived in different regions of North America, Native American children all across the continent enjoyed playing similar kinds of games.
1. (Although) they *lived* in different regions of North America

1. These children used mainly natural objects in games since there were no toy stores.
2. Most Native American children played darts with large feathers as these Arapaho children are doing.
3. If you look closely at the tree, you can see their target, a hole in the trunk.
4. These children are throwing goose feathers attached to bones, but they also used wild turkey feathers whenever they could find them.

5. Although they played many kinds of games, Native Americans in the Southwest especially liked kickball races.
6. The children made balls out of such materials as wood and tree roots before they started playing.
7. After snow had fallen, Seneca children raced small handmade "snow boats."
8. Pine cones were used in many games because they were so easy to find.
9. You can picture some children playing catch with pine cones while others had cone-throwing contests.
10. Games gave the children practice in skills they would need when they became adults.

EXERCISE 9 **Writing Sentences with Adverb Clauses**

Add an adverb clause to each of the following sentences. Write the entire sentence. Circle the subordinating conjunction, and underline the subject of each adverb clause once and the verb twice.

EXAMPLE **1.** The movie finally ended.
1. (After) we spent three hours in the theater, the movie finally ended.

1. Most of the members of the Drama Club auditioned for the play.
2. Erica speaks three languages.
3. We prepared moussaka, a Greek dish with lamb and eggplant, for our Cooking Club's international supper.
4. The Goldmans have visited Acapulco several times on vacation.
5. Jill daydreams in class.

 EXERCISE 10 **Using Adverb Clauses**

Mark Twain's ambition as a boy was to be a steamboat pilot. By the time he was a young man, Twain had served as an apprentice on several steamboats. In *Life on the Mississippi,* Twain tells about his ambition. He begins by writing, "When I was a boy, . . ." Then he goes on to list his childhood ambitions: to be a circus clown, to join a minstrel show, and to be a pirate. Yet even as a child, Twain knew that his "permanent ambition" was to be a steamboat pilot. Write a short paragraph telling about your own ambition or ambitions. In your paragraph, use at least five adverb clauses. Like Twain, you could begin one sentence with the subordinate conjunction *when.* You may want to refer to the list of Common Subordinating Conjunctions on page 545. Be prepared to identify all of the adverb clauses in your paragraph.

EXAMPLE **1.** *When I was a little girl, I wanted to be a doctor.*

GRAMMAR

The Noun Clause

18f. A *noun clause* is a subordinate clause used as a noun.

A noun clause may be used as a subject, a complement (predicate nominative, direct object, indirect object), or an object of a preposition.

SUBJECT	**That Felicia is angry** is obvious.
PREDICATE NOMINATIVE	Three dollars was **what he offered.**
DIRECT OBJECT	The judges determined **who won.**
INDIRECT OBJECT	The sheriff gave **whoever volunteered** a flashlight.
OBJECT OF A PREPOSITION	We agreed with **whatever he said.**

Common Introductory Words for Noun Clauses

who	whoever	which
whom	whomever	whichever
what	whatever	that

The word that introduces a noun clause often has another function within the clause.

EXAMPLES Give a free pass to **whoever asks for one.** [The introductory word *whoever* is the subject of the verb *asks.* The entire noun clause is the object of the preposition *to.*]

Did anyone tell him **what he should do?** [The introductory word *what* is the direct object of the verb *should do—he should do what.* The entire noun clause is the direct object of the verb *did tell.*]

Their complaint was **that the milk smelled sour.** [The word *that* introduces the noun clause but has no other function in the clause. The noun clause is the predicate nominative identifying the subject *complaint.*]

► EXERCISE 11 **Identifying and Classifying
Noun Clauses**

Identify the noun clause in each of the following sentences. Tell whether the noun clause is a *subject*, a *predicate nominative*, a *direct object*, an *indirect object*, or an *object of a preposition*.

EXAMPLE **1.** We couldn't find what was making the noise in the car.
  1. *what was making the noise in the car*—*direct object*

1. Whatever you decide will be fine with us.
2. Whoever takes us to the beach is my friend for life.
3. Do you know what happened to the rest of my tuna sandwich?
4. Stuart is looking for whoever owns that red bicycle.
5. Checking our supplies, we discovered that we had forgotten the flour.
6. The worst flaw in the story is that it doesn't have a carefully developed plot.
7. No, these results are not what we had planned.
8. The painter gave whatever spots had dried another coat of primer.
9. At lunch, my friends and I talked about what we should do as our service project.
10. That Coretta Scott King spoke for peace surprised no one.

► REVIEW A **Identifying Adjective, Adverb, and
Noun Clauses**

Identify each subordinate clause in the following quotations as an *adjective*, an *adverb*, or a *noun*.

1. Look before you leap.
  Old Proverb
2. Do not be afraid of light,
  You who are a child of night.
  Langston Hughes, "Song"

3. You gain strength, courage and confidence by every experience in which you really stop to look fear in the face.

   Eleanor Roosevelt, *You Learn by Living*

4. What I have to say will come from my heart, and I will speak with a straight tongue.

   Chief Joseph, "An Indian's Views of Indian Affairs"

5. For every man who lives without freedom, the rest of us must face the guilt.

   Lillian Hellman, *Watch on the Rhine*

> **REVIEW B**   **Identifying Subordinate Clauses**

Each sentence in the following paragraph contains a subordinate clause. Identify each subordinate clause as an *adjective clause,* an *adverb clause,* or a *noun clause.*

EXAMPLE [1] The Museum of Appalachia, which is in Norris, Tennessee, is a re-created pioneer village.

   1. *which is in Norris, Tennessee—adjective clause*

[1] If you've ever wanted to step into the past, you'll like this museum. [2] You can see many pioneer crafts and

tools that are still used at the museum. [3] For example, the men on the left are splitting shingles with tools that were used in their boyhood. [4] Two other men show how plowing was done before the development of modern equipment. [5] I think that the 250,000 pioneer tools and other items on display will amaze you. [6] What some visitors like to do is to tour the village's log buildings and then take a rest. [7] While they're resting, they can often find some mountain music to listen to. [8] Notice the different instruments that the musicians are playing. [9] The fiddler on the right performs at the museum's Homecoming, which is a yearly fall event. [10] At Homecoming, you might even meet the museum's founder, John Rice Irwin, who grew up in the Appalachian Mountains.

PICTURE THIS

Recently, a multinational group of researchers surprised the world with an announcement. They had developed a device that would allow people to travel back in time.

At the United Nations, world leaders agreed that the device should be used by time travelers for recording information and exploring only. Travelers would neither participate in nor try to change events in the past. Upon returning to the present, travelers would make a full report of their findings to the appropriate UN committee.

You were selected from a large group of volunteers to represent the United States in the first time-travel mission. You've just landed at your destination—San Francisco, California, in 1851. You step out of your time machine into the scene shown on the next page. You're struck by how different everything is, especially the buildings, clothing, and methods of transportation. Before exploring the 1800s any further, you decide to sit down and record your first impressions in your log. Write a paragraph or two describing this place and time. In your

GRAMMAR

log entry, use a variety of clauses. These should include at least three adjective clauses, four adverb clauses, and three noun clauses.

Subject: San Francisco in 1851
Audience: yourself and the members of the United Nations Committee for the Preservation of North American History
Purpose: to record your observations for use in a future report; to inform

The Granger Collection, New York.

Review: Posttest 1

Identifying Independent and Subordinate Clauses

Identify each italicized clause in the following paragraphs as an *independent clause* or a *subordinate clause*. Tell whether each italicized subordinate clause is a *noun*, an *adjective*, or an *adverb*.

GRAMMAR

EXAMPLES   When my mother got a new job, [1] *we had to move to another town.*
1. *independent clause*

[2] *When my mother got a new job,* we had to move to another town.
2. *subordinate clause—adverb*

I didn't want to move [1] *because I didn't want to transfer to another school.* This is the fourth time [2] *that I have had to change schools,* and every time I've wished [3] *that I could just stay at my old school.* [4] *As soon as I make friends in a new place,* I have to move again and leave them behind. Then at the new school [5] *I am a stranger again.*

We lived in our last house for three years, [6] *which is longer than in any other place* [7] *since I was little.* [8] *Living there so long, I had a chance to meet several people* [9] *who became good friends of mine.* My best friends, Chris and Marty, said [10] *that they would write to me,* and I promised to write to them, too. However, the friends [11] *that I've had before* had promised to write, but [12] *after a letter or two we lost touch.* [13] *Why this always happens* is a mystery to me.

I dreaded having to register at my new school two months [14] *after the school year had begun.* By then, everyone else would already have made friends, and [15] *I would be an outsider,* [16] *as I knew from past experience.* There are always some students who bully and tease [17] *whoever is new at school* or anyone else [18] *who is different.* Back in elementary school I would get angry and upset [19] *when people picked on me.* Since then, I've learned how to fit in and make friends in spite of [20] *whatever anyone does to hassle me or make me feel uncomfortable.*

Everywhere [21] *that I've gone to school,* some students always are friendly and offer to show me around. [22] *I used to be shy,* and I wouldn't take them up on their invitations. Since they didn't know [23] *whether I was shy or being unfriendly,* they soon left me alone. Now [24] *whenever someone is friendly to me at a new school or in a new neighborhood,* I fight down my shyness and act friendly myself. It's still hard to get used to new places and new people, but [25] *it's a lot easier with a little help from new friends.*

Review: Posttest 2

Writing Sentences with Independent and Subordinate Clauses

Write your own sentences according to the following instructions. Underline the subordinate clauses.

EXAMPLE **1.** a sentence with an independent clause and an adjective clause
1. *I am going to the game with Guido, who is my best friend.*

1. a sentence with an independent clause and no subordinate clauses
2. a sentence with an independent clause and one subordinate clause
3. a sentence with an adjective clause that begins with a relative pronoun
4. a sentence with an adjective clause in which a preposition precedes the relative pronoun
5. a sentence with an introductory adverb clause
6. a sentence with an adverb clause and an adjective clause
7. a sentence with a noun clause used as a direct object
8. a sentence with a noun clause used as a subject
9. a sentence with a noun clause used as the object of a preposition
10. a sentence with a noun clause and either an adjective clause or an adverb clause

19 SENTENCE STRUCTURE

The Four Basic Sentence Structures

Diagnostic Test

Identifying the Four Kinds of Sentence Structure

Identify each of the following sentences as *simple, compound, complex,* or *compound-complex.*

EXAMPLE **1.** We bought a new computer program that helps with spelling and grammar.
1. *complex*

1. Christina wanted to go to the dance, but she had to baby-sit.
2. When the rabbit saw us, it ran into the bushes.
3. In 1967, Thurgood Marshall became the first African American named to the U.S. Supreme Court.
4. You can either buy a new bicycle tire or fix the old one.
5. Yoko said that this would be the shortest route, but I disagree.

6. There was no way that we could tell what had really happened.
7. Yes, that seems to me like the right answer to the first problem.
8. Mercedes Rodriguez of Miami, Florida, entered and won the Ms. Wheelchair America contest.
9. Do you know who wrote this note and left it on my desk?
10. I'm not sure what you mean, but I think I agree.
11. Nobody is worried about that, for it will never happen.
12. Whatever you decide will be fine with me.
13. Is the movie that we want to see still playing in theaters, or is it available on videocassette?
14. Rammel knew the plan, and he assigned each of us a part.
15. Amphibians and some insects can live both on the land and in the water.
16. The detectives searched for the woman who had been wearing a blue beret, but there weren't any other clues.
17. The tornado cut across the edge of the housing development yesterday morning, and seven homes were destroyed.
18. By July of 1847, the Mormons had reached the Great Salt Lake valley.
19. Before the game started, all the football players ran out onto the field, and everyone cheered.
20. My father stopped to help the family whose car had broken down on the highway.

Sentences may be classified according to *structure*—the kinds and the number of clauses they contain. The four kinds of sentences are *simple, compound, complex,* and *compound-complex.*

☞ REFERENCE NOTE: Sentences may also be classified according to purpose. See pages 422–423.

The Simple Sentence

19a. A *simple sentence* has one independent clause and no subordinate clauses.

              S   V

EXAMPLES The **hairstylist gave** Latrice a new look.

             S   V

            Ernesto has volunteered to organize the recycling campaign.

A simple sentence may have a compound subject, a compound verb, or both.

             S   S   V

EXAMPLES **Beth Heiden** and **Sheila Young won** Olympic medals. [compound subject]

             S   V   V

            Lawrence caught the ball but then **dropped** it. [compound verb]

             S   S   V

            The **astronomer** and her **assistant studied** the

                    V

            meteor and **wrote** reports on their findings. [compound subject and compound verb]

☞ REFERENCE NOTE: For more information about compound subjects and compound verbs, see pages 418–420.

▶ EXERCISE 1   **Identifying Subjects and Verbs in Simple Sentences**

Identify the subjects and the verbs of the following simple sentences. [Note: Some sentences have compound subjects or compound verbs.]

EXAMPLE **1.** Throughout history, people have invented and used a variety of weapons.
         1. *people—subject; have invented, used—verbs*

1. To protect themselves from such weapons, warriors in battle needed special equipment.
2. Some warriors used shields of wood or animal hides.

3. In ancient Assyria, soldiers wore leather armor reinforced with bronze.
4. By 1800 B.C., the Greeks had made the first metal armor out of bronze.
5. Later, the Romans manufactured strong iron armor and designed special equipment, such as shin guards.
6. Before and during the Middle Ages, European knights and foot soldiers often dressed in shirts of chain mail.
7. You can see the tiny steel links of the chains in this close-up drawing.

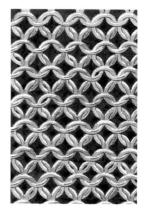

helmet

shoulder piece

8. Compared with chain mail, suits of steel armor gave better protection and therefore became more popular.
9. Helmets and shoulder pieces like these protected a knight's head and neck.
10. To protect his legs and feet, a knight wore greaves and sollerets into battle.

greave (shin guard)

solleret (shoe)

The Compound Sentence

19b. A *compound sentence* has two or more independent clauses but no subordinate clauses.

The independent clauses are usually joined by a coordinating conjunction: *and, but, for, nor, or, so,* or *yet.*

EXAMPLES   **According to legend, Betsy Ross made our first**
                        S   V

                        V   S
flag, but there is little evidence of this. [two independent clauses joined by the conjunction *but*]

              S   V   S   V
The whistle blew, the drums rolled, and the
          S   V
crowd cheered. [three independent clauses, the last two joined by the conjunction *and*]

👉 REFERENCE NOTE: For more information about independent clauses, see page 534.

NOTE: Do not confuse a compound sentence with a simple sentence that contains a compound subject, a compound verb, or both.

                        S   S   V
SIMPLE   **Alberto and Jared increased their speed**
SENTENCE   V
           and passed the other runners. [compound subject and compound verb]

                        S   V   S
COMPOUND   **Alberto led half the way, and then Jared**
SENTENCE   V
           took the lead. [two independent clauses]

The independent clauses in a compound sentence may also be joined by a semicolon.

                               S   V
EXAMPLE   Many mathematical **concepts originated** in North
                         S   V
          Africa; the ancient **Egyptians used** these concepts in building the pyramids.

GRAMMAR

☞ REFERENCE NOTE: For more information on using semicolons in compound sentences, see pages 759–760.

▶ EXERCISE 2   **Identifying Subjects, Verbs, and Conjunctions in Compound Sentences**

Each of the sentences in the following paragraph is a compound sentence. Identify the subject and the verb in the independent clauses in each sentence. Then, give the coordinating conjunction or the mark of punctuation that joins the independent clauses.

EXAMPLE   [1] Many strange things happen backstage during a performance, but the audience usually does not know about them.

    1. *things—subject; happen—verb; audience—subject; does know—verb; but*

[1] The director of a theater-in-the-round visited our class, and we listened to his stories for almost an hour. [2] According to him, the workers in charge of properties are usually alert and careful, yet they still make mistakes sometimes. [3] For example, in one production of *Romeo and Juliet,* the character Juliet prepared to kill herself with a dagger, but there was no dagger on the stage. [4] Audiences at theaters-in-the-round can also be a problem, for they sit very close to the stage. [5] Members of the audience often set things on stage tables, or they hang their coats on the actors' coatracks. [6] Sometimes these actions are overlooked by the stagehands, and the results can be very challenging for the actors. [7] For example, the main clue in one mystery play was a scarf left lying on the stage floor, but the audience had gathered on the stage during intermission. [8] After the intermission, the detective in the play found three scarves instead of one, yet he could not show any surprise. [9] During another mystery drama, a spectator became too involved in the play; he leaped up on the stage and tackled the villain. [10] Directors cannot always predict the reactions of the audience, nor can they always control the audience.

EXERCISE 3

Distinguishing Between Compound Sentences and Compound Subjects and Compound Verbs

Identify the subject(s) and the verb(s) in each sentence in the following paragraph. Then, tell whether the sentence is a *simple sentence* or a *compound sentence*.

EXAMPLE [1] African American actors and actresses performed in many early Hollywood movies.

1. *actors, actresses—subjects; performed—verb; simple sentence*

[2] Hattie McDaniel, for example, made many films, yet she is best known for her role in *Gone with the Wind*.

2. *Hattie McDaniel—subject; made—verb; she—subject; is—verb; compound sentence*

[1] Over the years, African American performers have earned much acclaim and won a number of Academy Awards. [2] Hattie McDaniel in 1939 and Sidney Poitier in 1963 were the first black performers to win Oscars. [3] More recently, Lou Gossett, Jr., and Denzel Washington played supporting roles as military men and won Academy Awards for their performances. [4] Another winner, Whoopi Goldberg, first gained fame as a stand-up comic; then she went on to make several hit movies. [5] Critics praised her performance in *The Color Purple*, and in 1991, she won an Academy Award for playing this funny character in *Ghost*.

The Complex Sentence

19c. A *complex sentence* has one independent clause and at least one subordinate clause.

EXAMPLE When I watch Martha Graham's performances, I feel like studying dance.

> S V
> *Independent Clause* **I feel** like studying dance
>
> S V
> *Subordinate Clause* When **I watch** Martha Graham's performances

EXAMPLE Some of the sailors who took part in the mutiny on the British ship *Bounty* settled Pitcairn Island.

> S V
> *Independent Clause* **Some** of the sailors **settled** Pitcairn Island
>
> S V
> *Subordinate Clause* **who took** part in the mutiny on the British ship *Bounty*

EXAMPLE In *Gone with the Wind,* when Scarlett is faced with near-starvation, she makes a promise that she never will be hungry again.

> *Independent Clause* In *Gone with the Wind,*
>
> S V
> **she makes** a promise
>
> S V
> *Subordinate Clause* when **Scarlett is faced** with near-starvation
>
> S V
> *Subordinate Clause* that **she** never **will be** hungry again

Notice in the examples above that a subordinate clause can appear at the beginning, in the middle, or at the end of a complex sentence.

☞ REFERENCE NOTE: For more information about independent and subordinate clauses, see pages 534–548.

EXERCISE 4

Identifying Independent Clauses and Subordinate Clauses in Complex Sentences

Identify each of the clauses in the following sentences as *independent* or *subordinate*. Be prepared to give the subject and the verb of each clause. [Note: Two sentences have more than one subordinate clause.]

EXAMPLES   **1.** China is a largely agricultural country that has a population of more than one billion people.
   1. *China is a largely agricultural country—independent; that has a population of more than one billion people—subordinate*

   2. Although my brother bought one of those old coins for his collection, it was nearly worthless.
   2. *Although my brother bought one of those old coins for his collection—subordinate; it was nearly worthless—independent*

1. The detective show appeared on television for several weeks before it became popular with viewers.
2. Most of the albums that my parents have from the 1970s are sitting in the corner of the basement behind the broken refrigerator.
3. Richard E. Byrd is but one of the explorers who made expeditions to Antarctica.
4. As studies continued, many important facts about nutrition were discovered.
5. A group of popular singers, who donated their time, recorded a song that made people aware of the problems in Ethiopia.
6. The Hawaiian ruler who wrote the famous song "*Aloha Oe*" ("Farewell to Thee") was Queen Liliuokalani.
7. After we have prepared our report on the history of computers, we may be able to go to the basketball game.

8. Although few students or teachers knew about it, a group of sociologists visited our school to study the relationship between classroom environment and students' grades.
9. While the stage crew was constructing the sets, the performers continued their rehearsal, which went on into the night.
10. Although she had polio as a child, Wilma Rudolph became a top American Olympic athlete.

The Compound-Complex Sentence

19d. A *compound-complex sentence* has two or more independent clauses and at least one subordinate clause.

EXAMPLE Yolanda began painting only two years ago, but already she has been asked to hang one of her paintings at the art exhibit that is scheduled for next month.

	S V
Independent Clause	**Yolanda began** painting only two years ago
	S V
Independent Clause	already **she has been asked** to hang one of her paintings at the art exhibit
	S V
Subordinate Clause	**that is scheduled** for next month

EXAMPLE I have read several novels in which the main characters are animals, but the novel that I like best is *Animal Farm*.

	S V
Independent Clause	**I have read** several novels
	S V
Independent Clause	the **novel is** *Animal Farm*

Subordinate Clause   in which the main

$$\overset{S}{}\ \overset{V}{}$$
characters are animals

$$\overset{S\ \ V}{}$$
Subordinate Clause   that **I like** best

EXAMPLE   When Bill left, he locked the door, but he forgot to turn off the lights.

$$\overset{S\ \ \ V}{}$$
Independent Clause   **he locked** the door

$$\overset{S\ \ \ V}{}$$
Independent Clause   **he forgot** to turn off the lights

$$\overset{S\ \ V}{}$$
Subordinate Clause   When **Bill left**

NOTE: To show how the parts of a compound-complex sentence are related, be sure to use marks of punctuation correctly.

▶ EXERCISE 5   **Identifying Clauses in Compound-Complex Sentences**

Identify each of the clauses in the following sentences as *independent* or *subordinate*.

EXAMPLE   **1.** When they returned from their vacation, they collected their mail at the post office, and they went to the supermarket.
     1. *When they returned from their vacation—subordinate; they collected their mail at the post office—independent; they went to the supermarket—independent*

1. Before we conducted the experiment, we asked for permission to use the science lab, but the principal insisted on teacher supervision of our work.
2. Inside the old trunk up in the attic, which is filled with boxes and toys, we found some dusty photo albums; and one of them contained pictures from the early 1900s.
3. We told them that their plan wouldn't work, but they wouldn't listen to us.

GRAMMAR

4. Every expedition that had attempted to explore that region had vanished without a trace, yet the young adventurer was determined to map the uncharted jungle because he couldn't resist the challenge.
5. The smoke, which grew steadily thicker and darker, billowed through the dry forest; and the animals ran ahead of it as the fire spread quickly.

PICTURE THIS

While on vacation, you borrow the family video camera and head for the seashore. There you find this amazing scene. At first you hide quietly and watch. Then, you decide to capture the scene on film. Back home, you show your tape to a TV reporter, who wants to run your story on the news as soon as possible. But first, you need a short description of how you made the film. Write a paragraph about your experience at the seashore. In your paragraph, use at least one simple sentence, one compound sentence, one complex sentence, and one compound-complex sentence.

Subject: unicorns by the sea
Audience: television viewers
Purpose: to inform viewers about what you saw

Arthur B. Davies, *Unicorns (Legend—Sea Calm)*, (c. 1806). The Metropolitan Museum of Art, Bequest of Lizzie P. Bliss, 1931.

REVIEW

Identifying the Four Kinds of Sentence Structure

Identify each sentence in the following paragraphs as *simple, compound, complex,* or *compound-complex.*

EXAMPLE   **[1]** If he had not practiced, Amleto Monacelli of Venezuela could not have become a champion bowler.
   1. *complex*

[1] People who are learning a new sport begin by mastering basic skills, and they usually are very eager. [2] After people have practiced basic skills for a while, they usually progress to more difficult moves. [3] At this point a beginner is likely to become discouraged, and the temptation to quit grows strong. [4] One of the most common problems that beginners face is coordination; another is muscular aches and pains. [5] If a beginner is not careful, muscles can be injured, yet the strenuous activity usually strengthens the muscle tissues. [6] When enough oxygen reaches the warmed-up muscles, the danger of injury lessens, and the muscles grow in size. [7] At the same time, coordination grows, along with confidence.

[8] The hours of practice that a beginner puts in usually result in rewarding improvements. [9] As a rule, learning something new takes time and work, or it would not seem worthwhile. [10] In sports, as in most other activities, persistence and patience often pay off.

WRITING APPLICATION

Using Compound, Complex, and Compound-Complex Sentences

In writing and in speech, people use all kinds of sentences to express their thoughts and feelings. Simple sentences are

GRAMMAR

best used to express single ideas. To describe more complicated ideas and to show relationships between them, use compound, complex, and compound-complex sentences.

SIMPLE SENTENCES   Yesterday I visited my friend Amy.
                    Then I went to Willa's house.
                    We practiced our dance routine.
COMPOUND-COMPLEX   After I visited my friend Amy
          SENTENCE yesterday, I went to Willa's house,
                    and we practiced our dance routine.

▶ WRITING ACTIVITY

You missed your ride home after school, so you went to a friend's house. No one is at your home now. But you know you should call and leave a message on the answering machine. Write out the message that you will leave. Use a variety of sentence structures.

Prewriting   First, decide what will be in your message. You probably will want to tell where you are and why you are there. Explain why you missed your ride. And you should tell when you'll be home or should make arrangements to be picked up. Make notes about all of these details.

Writing   Use your notes to write your first draft. As you write, remember that your message must be short but clear and informative. Think about how you can combine ideas.

Evaluating and Revising   Read your message aloud and listen to how it sounds. Are your explanations and plans complete? Do they sound logical? Check to be sure that you've used a variety of sentence structures. If you need to combine sentences, review pages 368–377.

Proofreading   Read over your message again, checking for errors in grammar, spelling, and punctuation. For more about punctuating compound sentences, see pages 745–746 and 759–760. For more on using commas with subordinate clauses, see pages 747–748 and 752–753.

Review: Posttest 1

Identifying the Four Kinds of Sentence Structure

Identify each sentence in the following paragraphs as *simple, compound, complex,* or *compound-complex.*

EXAMPLE [1] When my grandmother came to visit, she taught us how to make our own holiday ornaments.

1. *complex*

[1] Last year my grandmother came to stay with us from the middle of December until my brother's birthday in January. [2] While we were getting out the holiday decorations, Mom and Grandma told us all about how people used to make their own decorations. [3] Mom said that she remembered making beautiful decorations and that it used to be a lot of fun, so we decided to try making some of our own.

[4] My dad, my brother, and I drove out to the woods to gather pine cones. [5] We had forgotten to ask what size to get, and since Dad had never made decorations, he didn't know. [6] We decided to play it safe and get all different sizes, which was easy to do because there were pine cones everywhere. [7] My brother picked up all the hard little ones, and my dad and I threw a bunch of medium and big ones into the trunk of the car. [8] When Mom and Grandma saw how many we had, they laughed and said we had enough to decorate ten houses.

[9] First we sorted the cones; the little hard ones went into one pile, and the bigger ones into another. [10] Dad and I painted the little ones silver, and Mom and Grandma painted stripes, dots, and all sorts of other designs on them. [11] Then we tied strings to the tops of the cones; and later, when we put them up, they made great ornaments.

[12] We painted the bigger pine cones all different colors and glued on cranberries and beads, which made each

cone look like a miniature fir tree. [13]We saved some smaller ones for the dining room table, and we put most of the others all around the house. [14]My brother took some to school, too.

[15]Besides the pine-cone decorations, we made some strings to decorate the mantel. [16]My mom got needles and a spool of heavy thread out of her sewing basket, and we strung the rest of the cranberries on six-foot lengths of the thread.

[17]Mom and Grandma cut several more long pieces of thread, and we used them to make strings of popcorn, just like our strings of cranberries. [18]We left some of the popcorn strings white, painted the others different colors, and hung them around the living room and dining room.

[19]Decorating was even more fun than usual, and I think that the whole house looked prettier, too, with all our homemade ornaments. [20]From now on, we're going to make decorations every year.

Review: Posttest 2

Writing a Variety of Sentence Structures

Write your own original sentences according to the following instructions.

EXAMPLE **1.** a compound sentence with two independent clauses joined by *and*
1. *My mother usually gives us tacos for supper once a week, and she makes the best tacos in the world.*

1. a simple sentence with a compound subject
2. a simple sentence with a compound verb
3. a compound sentence with two independent clauses joined by *but*

4. a compound sentence with two independent clauses joined by *or*
5. a complex sentence with a subordinate clause that begins with *that*
6. a complex sentence with a subordinate clause that begins with *who*
7. a complex sentence with a subordinate clause at the beginning of the sentence
8. a complex sentence with a subordinate clause at the end of the sentence
9. a complex sentence with two subordinate clauses
10. a compound-complex sentence

20 AGREEMENT

Subject and Verb, Pronoun and Antecedent

Diagnostic Test

A. Identifying Verbs That Agree with Their Subjects

In each of the following sentences, if the italicized verb agrees with its subject, write C. If the italicized verb does not agree with its subject, write the correct form of the verb.

EXAMPLES **1.** The answers to that question *don't* make sense.
1. C

2. Ms. Suarez, our gym teacher, *don't* know what happened.
2. *doesn't*

1. When *is* Bill's parents coming to pick us up?
2. Mr. Epstein said that it *don't* look like rain today.

3. Neither of the bar mitzvahs *have* been scheduled for next month.
4. Everyone who wears eyeglasses *is* having vision tests today.
5. My baseball bat and my catcher's mitt *was* back in my room.
6. Neither Ésteban nor Tina *have* tried out yet for the play.
7. All of our guests *have* been to Fort Worth's Japanese Garden.
8. *Don't* the team captain plan to put her into the game before it's over?
9. One of the men *have* decided that he will get his car washed.
10. The Bill of Rights *give* American citizens the right to worship where they please.

USAGE

B. Identifying Pronouns That Agree with Their Antecedents

In each of the following sentences, if the italicized pronoun agrees with its antecedent, write C. If the italicized pronoun does not agree with its antecedent, write the correct form of the pronoun.

EXAMPLES **1.** One of the does was accompanied by *her* fawn.
1. C

2. Each of the boys brought *their* permission slip.
2. *his*

11. Have all of the winners taken *their* science fair projects home?
12. Everyone going to the concert should bring *their* own food and lawn chair.
13. Many of the buildings had green ribbons on *its* windows for the Saint Patrick's Day Parade.
14. Neither Stephanie nor Marilyn had worn *their* gym suit to class.

15. Every dog in the show had a numbered tag hanging from *their* collar.
16. Someone in the scout troop camped near poison ivy and has gotten it all over *themselves.*
17. Only a few of the carpenters had brought tools with *them* to the job.
18. My dog was among the contest winners that had *its* pictures taken.
19. According to the teacher, both of those titles should have lines drawn underneath *it.*
20. That Ray Charles song is familiar, but I can't remember *its* title.

Number

Number is the form of a word that indicates whether the word is singular or plural.

20a. When a word refers to one person, place, thing, or idea, it is *singular* in number. When a word refers to more than one, it is *plural* in number.

SINGULAR	book	woman	fox	I	he	each
PLURAL	books	women	foxes	we	they	few

ORAL
PRACTICE 1

Classifying Nouns and Pronouns by Number

Read the following expressions aloud. Tell whether each noun or pronoun is *singular* or *plural.*

1. The lion yawns.
2. The cubs play.
3. No one stays.
4. The refugees arrive.
5. She wins.
6. The play opens.
7. Everyone goes.
8. All applaud.

▷ EXERCISE 1   **Classifying Nouns and Pronouns by Number**

Classify each word as *singular* or *plural*.

EXAMPLE   **1.** cat
           1. *singular*

1. rodeos   6. igloo
2. band   7. geese
3. they   8. we
4. I   9. friends
5. many   10. it

USAGE

Agreement of Subject and Verb

20b. A verb agrees with its subject in number.

(1) Singular subjects take singular verbs.

EXAMPLES   The **car comes** to a sudden stop. [The singular verb *comes* agrees with the singular subject *car.*]
            On that route the **plane flies** at a low altitude. [The singular verb *flies* agrees with the singular subject *plane.*]

(2) Plural subjects take plural verbs.

EXAMPLES   Many **senators oppose** the new tax bill. [The plural verb *oppose* agrees with the plural subject *senators.*]
            Again and again, the **dolphins leap** playfully. [The plural verb *leap* agrees with the plural subject *dolphins.*]

NOTE: Generally, nouns ending in *s* are plural (*candles, ideas, neighbors, horses*), and verbs ending in *s* are singular (*sees, writes, speaks, carries*). For guidelines on forming plurals, see pages 806–810.

The first auxiliary (helping) verb in a verb phrase must agree with its subject.

EXAMPLES **He is building** a bird feeder.
They are building a bird feeder.

Does anyone know the answer?
Do any **students know** the answer?

NOTE: The pronouns *I* and *you* take plural verbs.

EXAMPLES **I walk** to school.
Do you walk to school?
EXCEPTION **I am walking** to school.

▶ EXERCISE 2 Identifying Verbs That Agree in Number with Their Subjects

Choose the form of the verb in parentheses that agrees with the given subject.

EXAMPLE **1.** it (*is, are*)
1. *is*

1. this (*costs, cost*)
2. Chinese lanterns (*glows, glow*)
3. the swimmer (*dives, dive*)
4. we (*considers, consider*)
5. the men (*was, were*)
6. she (*asks, ask*)
7. these (*needs, need*)
8. those tacos (*tastes, taste*)
9. that music (*sounds, sound*)
10. lessons (*takes, take*)

▶ EXERCISE 3 Identifying Verbs That Agree in Number with Their Subjects

For each sentence in the following paragraph, choose the correct form of the verb in parentheses.

EXAMPLE [1] (*Do, Does*) you like rap music?
1. *Do*

[1] The rapper KRS-One (*is, are*) one of my favorite performers. [2] In fact, his picture (*is, are*) hanging in my room. [3] As you can see, KRS's face (*reflects, reflect*) his

positive attitude. [4] KRS (*encourages, encourage*) people to think for themselves. [5] Many performers (*believes, believe*) in using rap music to improve people's lives and to end violence.

hip

hop

USAGE

Prepositional Phrases Between Subjects and Verbs

20c. The number of a subject is not changed by a prepositional phrase following the subject.

NONSTANDARD   The lights on the Christmas tree creates a festive atmosphere.
STANDARD   The **lights** on the Christmas tree **create** a festive atmosphere.

NONSTANDARD   The distance between the two posts for the clothesline are eight feet.
STANDARD   The **distance** between the two posts for the clothesline **is** eight feet.

👉 REFERENCE NOTE: For a discussion of standard and nonstandard English, see pages 394 and 682.

▶ EXERCISE 4   **Identifying Subjects and Verbs That Agree in Number**

Identify the subject in each sentence. Choose the form of the verb in parentheses that agrees with the subject.

EXAMPLE   **1.** The houses on my block (*has, have*) two stories.
   1. *houses—subject; have*

1. The launch of a space shuttle (*attracts, attract*) the interest of people throughout the world.
2. The thermos bottle in the picnic basket (*is, are*) filled with apple juice.
3. My favorite collection of poems (*is, are*) *Where the Sidewalk Ends.*
4. People in some states (*observes, observe*) the fourth Friday in September as Native American Day.
5. The starving children of the world (*needs, need*) food and medicine.
6. The cucumbers in my garden (*grows, grow*) very quickly.
7. Koalas in the wild and in captivity (*eats, eat*) only eucalyptus leaves.
8. The principal of each high school (*awards, award*) certificates to honor students.
9. Stories about Hank Aaron and Willie Mays always (*makes, make*) me want to play baseball.
10. The house beside the city park (*is, are*) where my grandfather was born.

Indefinite Pronouns

Some pronouns do not refer to a definite person, place, thing, or idea and are therefore called *indefinite* pronouns.

> **20d.** The following indefinite pronouns are singular: *anybody, anyone, each, either, everybody, everyone, neither, nobody, no one, one, somebody, someone.*

Pronouns like *each* and *one* are frequently followed by prepositional phrases. Remember that the verb agrees with the subject of the sentence, not with a word in a prepositional phrase.

EXAMPLES   **Everyone was invited** to the celebration.
                 Either of the answers **is** correct.

USAGE

> **One** of the tapes **belongs** to Sabrena.
> **Someone** in the stands **has been waving** at us.

20e. The following indefinite pronouns are plural: *both, few, many, several.*

EXAMPLES **Both** of the apples **are** good.
Few of the guests **know** about the surprise.
Many of the students **walk** to school.
Several of the members **have** not **paid** their dues.

20f. The following indefinite pronouns may be either singular or plural: *all, any, most, none, some.*

The number of the subject *all, any, most, none* or *some* is determined by the number of the object in the prepositional phrase following the subject. If the subject refers to a singular object, the subject is singular. If the subject refers to a plural object, the subject is plural.

EXAMPLES **All** of the fruit **looks** ripe. [*All* refers to the singular object *fruit.*]
All of the pears **look** ripe. [*All* refers to the plural object *pears.*]

Some of the equipment **has been stored** in the garage. [*Some* refers to the singular object *equipment.*]
Some of the supplies **have been stored** in the garage. [*Some* refers to the plural object *supplies.*]

▶ EXERCISE 5 **Identifying Subjects and Verbs That Agree in Number**

Identify the subject in each of the following sentences. Choose the form of the verb in parentheses that agrees with the subject.

EXAMPLE **1.** Each of the marchers (*was, were*) carrying a sign protesting apartheid.
1. *Each—subject; was*

1. All of my friends (*has, have*) had the chicken pox.
2. Everyone at the party (*likes, like*) the hummus dip.
3. Both of Fred's brothers (*celebrates, celebrate*) their birthdays in July.
4. Some of my baseball cards (*is, are*) valuable.
5. None of those rosebushes ever (*blooms, bloom*) in February.
6. Several of those colors (*do, does*) not appeal to me.
7. Many of Mrs. Taniguchi's students (*speaks, speak*) fluent Japanese.
8. Nobody in the beginning painting classes (*has, have*) displayed work in the annual art show.
9. Most of the appetizers on the menu (*tastes, taste*) delicious.
10. One of Georgia O'Keeffe's paintings (*shows, show*) a ram's skull.

▶ REVIEW A **Proofreading a Paragraph for Subject-Verb Agreement**

Many of the sentences in the following paragraph contain errors in agreement of subject and verb. If the verb agrees with its subject, write *C*. If the verb does not agree with its subject, write the correct form of the verb. [Note: Some sentences have more than one verb.]

EXAMPLES [1] One of the best-known prehistoric monuments in the world stand in a field in Britain.
1. *stands*

[2] Everybody today calls the monument Stonehenge, and thousands of people visits it each year.
2. *C; visit*

[1] All of the visitors to Stonehenge wants to know why the structure was built. [2] The huge rocks at Stonehenge almost seems to challenge tourists and scientists alike to uncover their mysteries. [3] Most people easily recognize the monument as it looks in the photograph on the next page. [4] However, nobody are sure how Stonehenge

USAGE

looked long ago. [5] Some of the archaeologists studying the site believes that the drawing below shows how the old Stonehenge looked. [6] Notice that few of the stones remains in their original places. [7] Many visitors to Stonehenge assume that ancient druids built the monument. [8] Most scientists, though, says it was built longer ago—perhaps four thousand years ago. [9] After seeing Stonehenge, few doubt that the stones weighs as much as fifty tons. [10] Of course, nearly everyone seem to have a theory about how these stones were set in place and what they were used for, but no one knows for sure.

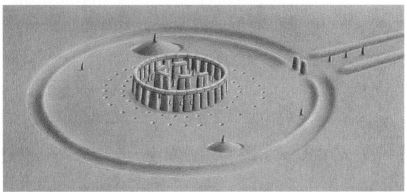

Compound Subjects

20g. Subjects joined by *and* usually take a plural verb.

The following compound subjects joined by *and* name more than one person or thing and take plural verbs.

EXAMPLES **Antonia Brico** and **Sarah Caldwell are** famous conductors. [Two persons are conductors.]
Last year a **library** and a **museum were built** in our town. [Two things were built.]

A compound subject that names only one person or thing takes a singular verb.

EXAMPLES The **captain** and **quarterback** of the team **is** Lyle. [One person is both the captain and the quarterback.]
Chicken and dumplings is a favorite Southern dish. [Chicken and dumplings is one dish.]

 EXERCISE 6 **Choosing Verbs That Agree in Number with Compound Subjects**

Indicate whether the compound subject in each of the following sentences is *singular* or *plural*. Choose the form of the verb that agrees with the compound subject.

EXAMPLE **1.** Cleon and Pam (*is, are*) here.
1. *plural—are*

1. March and April (*is, are*) windy months.
2. My mother and the mechanic (*is, are*) discussing the bill.
3. Monica Seles and Jennifer Capriati (*plays, play*) in the finals today.
4. Red beans and rice (*is, are*) my favorite Cajun dish.
5. (*Does, Do*) Carla and Jean take dancing lessons?
6. (*Is, Are*) the knives and forks in the drawer?
7. English and science (*requires, require*) hours of study.
8. (*Here's, Here are*) our star and winner of the meet.
9. Where (*is, are*) the bread and the honey?
10. (*Does, Do*) an Austrian and a German speak the same language?

20h. Singular subjects joined by *or* or *nor* take a singular verb.

EXAMPLES A **pen** or a **pencil is needed** for this test. [Either one is needed.]
Neither **Miami** nor **Jacksonville is** the capital of Florida. [Neither one is the capital.]

 EXERCISE 7

Choosing Verbs That Agree in Number with Compound Subjects

Choose the form of the verb in parentheses that agrees with the compound subject in each of the following sentences.

EXAMPLE **1.** Neither Theo nor Erin (*has, have*) learned the Jewish folk dance *Mayim, Mayim.*
1. *has*

1. Either Mrs. Gomez or Mr. Ming (*delivers, deliver*) the welcome speech on the first day of school.
2. Our guava tree and our fig tree (*bears, bear*) more fruit than our entire neighborhood can eat.
3. Tuskegee Institute or Harvard University (*offers, offer*) the best courses in Francine's field.
4. Armadillos and anteaters (*has, have*) tubular mouths and long sticky tongues for catching insects.
5. Either the president or the vice-president of the class (*calls, call*) roll every morning.
6. Sarah's report on Booker T. Washington and Sam's report on Quanah Parker (*sounds, sound*) interesting.
7. Red and royal blue (*looks, look*) nice in this bedroom.
8. Bridge or canasta (*is, are*) my favorite card game.
9. Neither my sister nor my brother (*mows, mow*) the lawn without protesting.
10. The tulips and the daffodils (*blooms, bloom*) every April.

20i. When a singular subject and a plural subject are joined by *or* or *nor*, the verb agrees with the subject nearer the verb.

EXAMPLES Neither the **director** nor the **players were** on time for rehearsal. [The verb agrees with the nearer subject, *players.*]
Neither the **players** nor the **director was** on time for rehearsal. [The verb agrees with the nearer subject, *director.*]

USAGE

Whenever possible, avoid this kind of construction by revising the sentence. For instance, the second example above could be revised in the following way.

Both the players and the director were late for rehearsal.

USAGE

▶ EXERCISE 8 **Choosing Verbs That Agree in Number with Compound Subjects**

Choose the form of the verb in parentheses that agrees with the compound subject in each of the following sentences.

EXAMPLE **1.** Both Tyrone and Derrick (*is, are*) going to the Hammer concert.
1. *are*

1. Either Sylvia or her brothers (*washes, wash*) the kitchen floor each Saturday morning.
2. This bread and this cereal (*contains, contain*) no preservatives or dyes.
3. Either the students or the teacher (*reads, read*) aloud during the last ten minutes of each class period.
4. The heavy rain clouds and the powerful winds (*indicates, indicate*) that a hurricane is approaching.
5. Neither the seal nor the clowns (*catches, catch*) the ball that the monkey throws into the circus ring.

▶ REVIEW B **Choosing Verbs That Agree in Number with Their Subjects**

Choose the form of the verb in parentheses that agrees with its subject in each sentence in the following paragraph.

EXAMPLE **[1]** Breads, such as *pan dulce,* and other baked goods (*sells, sell*) well at the Mexican American bakery shown on the next page.
1. *sell*

[1] The wonderful smells at the bakery (*invites, invite*) hungry customers. [2] Children and their parents (*enjoys,*

enjoy) choosing and tasting the baked treats. [3] Display cases and bowls (*holds, hold*) the fresh breads and pastries. [4] Cinnamon rolls with powdered toppings and braided breads (*goes, go*) quickly. [5] Either an *empanada* or some giant biscuits (*are, is*) likely to be someone's breakfast. [6] Pumpkin or sweet potato (*is, are*) often used to fill the *empanadas*. [7] Most children really (*likes, like*) volcano-shaped pastries known as *volcanes*. [8] Raisin bars or a *pañuelo* (*makes, make*) a special after-lunch treat. [9] Bakeries like this one (*prepares, prepare*) mainly traditional Mexican American breads. [10] But holidays and special occasions (*calls, call*) for extra-fancy treats.

Other Problems in Agreement

20j. Collective nouns may be either singular or plural.

A *collective noun* is singular in form but names a group of persons, animals, or things.

Common Collective Nouns			
army	club	fleet	public
assembly	committee	flock	swarm
audience	crowd	group	team
class	family	herd	troop

A collective noun takes a singular verb when the noun refers to the group as a unit. A collective noun takes a plural verb when the noun refers to the individual parts or members of the group.

EXAMPLES   The science **class is taking** a field trip to the planetarium. [The class as a unit is taking a field trip.] Today, the science **class are working** on their astronomy projects. [The members of the class are working on various projects.]

The **family has moved** to Little Rock, Arkansas. [The family as a unit has moved.] The **family have been** unable to agree on where to spend their next vacation. [The members of the family have different opinions.]

EXERCISE 9   **Writing Sentences with Collective Nouns**

Select five collective nouns. Use each noun as the subject of two sentences. In the first sentence, make the subject singular in meaning, so that it takes a singular verb. In the second sentence, make the subject plural in meaning, so that it takes a plural verb.

EXAMPLE   **1.** *The softball team is practicing some new plays.*
The softball team are wearing new uniforms.

20k.   A verb agrees with its subject, not with its predicate nominative.

                      S   V   PN
EXAMPLES   The best **time** to visit **is** weekday mornings.

                      S   V   PN
Weekday **mornings are** the best time to visit.

20l.   When the subject follows the verb, find the subject and make sure the verb agrees with it. The subject usually follows the verb in sentences beginning with *here* or *there* and in questions.

USAGE

EXAMPLES   Here **is** my **seat.**
Here **are** our **seats.**

There **is** an exciting **ride** at the fair.
There **are** exciting **rides** at the fair.

Where **is** the **bread**?
Where **are** the **loaves** of bread?

Does he know them?
Do they know him?

The contractions *here's*, *there's*, and *where's* contain the verb *is* and should be used with only singular subjects.

NONSTANDARD   There's the books.
   STANDARD   There **are** the **books.**
   STANDARD   There**'s** the **book.**

☞ REFERENCE NOTE: For more information about contractions, see pages 783–784.

USAGE

▶ EXERCISE 10   **Choosing Verbs That Agree in Number with Their Subjects**

Choose the form of the verb in parentheses that agrees with the subject in each of the following sentences.

EXAMPLE   **1.** There (*is, are*) many new students this year.
      1. *are*

1. The audience (*loves, love*) the mime performance.
2. (*Here's, Here are*) the Natalie Cole tapes I borrowed.
3. The club (*sponsors, sponsor*) a carwash each March.
4. Andy's gift to Janelle (*was, were*) two roses.
5. Here (*is, are*) the letters I have been expecting.
6. The public (*differs, differ*) in their opinions on the referendum.
7. The map shows that (*there's, there are*) seven countries in Central America.
8. The tennis team usually (*plays, play*) every Saturday morning.
9. His legacy to us (*was, were*) words of wisdom.
10. Where (*is, are*) the limericks you wrote?

20m. The contractions *don't* and *doesn't* must agree with their subjects.

Use *don't* with plural subjects and with the pronouns *I* and *you*.

EXAMPLES   These **gloves don't** fit.
I don't like that song.
You don't have enough money to buy that.

Use *doesn't* with other singular subjects.

EXAMPLES   The **music box doesn't** play.
She doesn't like cold weather.
It doesn't matter.

ORAL PRACTICE 2   **Using *Doesn't* with Singular Subjects**

Read the following sentences aloud. Pay particular attention to the agreement of *doesn't* with the singular subject in each sentence.

1. It doesn't look like a serious wound.
2. She doesn't call meetings often.
3. One doesn't interrupt a speaker.
4. He doesn't play records loudly.
5. Doesn't the television set work?
6. Doesn't Oktoberfest start Saturday?
7. She doesn't play basketball.
8. Fido doesn't like his new dog food.

EXERCISE 11   **Using *Doesn't* and *Don't* Correctly**

Complete each sentence by inserting the correct contraction, *doesn't* or *don't*.

EXAMPLE   **1.** ＿＿ they go to our school?
1. *Don't*

1. ＿＿ anyone in the class know any facts about Susan B. Anthony?

2. Kareem Abdul-Jabbar ___ play professional basketball anymore.
3. They ___ have enough people to form a softball team.
4. Pearl and Marshall ___ need to change their schedules.
5. It ___ hurt to practice the piano an hour a day.
6. ___ the Japanese celebrate spring with a special festival?
7. Those snow peas ___ look crisp.
8. Hector ___ win every track meet; sometimes he places second.
9. ___ anyone know the time?
10. He ___ know the shortest route from Dallas to Peoria.

▶ EXERCISE 12 **Using *Doesn't* and *Don't* Correctly in Sentences**

What do you see when you look at these two images? Do they seem to play tricks on your eyes? These images give your brain false clues. We call such misleading images *optical illusions.* Write five sentences about what you think you see or don't see in each image. Use *doesn't* or *don't* correctly in each sentence.

EXAMPLE   **1.** *I see the goblet, but I don't see the two faces.*

WRITING APPLICATION

Using Verbs That Agree in Number with Collective Nouns

People and animals are often gathered in groups. Therefore, when you write about them, you frequently use collective nouns. Should you use a singular verb or a plural verb with a collective noun? Figuring out which verb form to use can be tricky. Use a singular verb when the noun refers to the group as a unit. Use a plural verb when the noun refers to the individual parts or members of the group.

| GROUP AS A UNIT | The scout troop wants to be in the parade. |
| MEMBERS OF GROUP | The troop haven't asked their parents for permission yet. |

How might you revise the second sentence above to make it clearer?

▶ WRITING ACTIVITY

You are on the committee in charge of organizing your school's participation in the local Thanksgiving Day Parade. Write a brief report about the committee's plans, which you will read at the next student council meeting. Use at least five collective nouns in your report.

Prewriting Write down the names of some clubs or organizations that might be in the parade. What might these groups contribute to the parade? Think about collective nouns to use in your report. You may want to refer to the list on page 585.

Writing Use your notes to help you write your first draft. Begin with a main idea statement that tells other student council members what progress your committee has made. Then, tell about some of the groups that have asked to be in the parade and what those groups are planning to do.

Evaluating and Revising As you read over your report, ask yourself these questions:

- Is it clear what kind of parade is planned?
- Is it clear what groups are involved?
- Have I included important details?
- Do the committee's plans sound logical?

Revise any parts of the report that are unclear. Check to be sure that you've used five collective nouns and the correct verbs with them.

 Proofreading Carefully read your report again. Check for possible sentence fragments and run-on sentences. For more about these kinds of sentence problems, see pages 361–366. Be sure that you've followed the rules in this chapter for subject-verb agreement.

USAGE

 REVIEW C

Proofreading Sentences for Subject-Verb Agreement

Most of the following sentences contain errors in agreement of subject and verb. If a sentence is correct, write C. If a sentence contains an error in agreement, write the correct form of the verb.

EXAMPLE **1.** There is a man and a woman here to see you.
1. *are*

1. Leilani and Yoshi doesn't know how to swim.
2. Carrots are my favorite vegetable.
3. The Seminoles of Florida sews beautifully designed quilts and jackets.
4. Here's the sweaters I knitted for you.
5. Each of these ten-speed bicycles cost more than one hundred dollars.
6. The soccer team always celebrate each victory with a pizza party.

7. The wheelchair division of the six-mile race was won by Randy Nowell.
8. The flock of geese fly over the lake at dawn.
9. Doesn't that Thai dish with chopped peanuts taste good?
10. Where's the bus schedule for downtown routes?

 REVIEW D | **Proofreading a Paragraph for Subject-Verb Agreement**

Some sentences in the following paragraph contain errors in agreement of subject and verb. If a sentence is correct, write *C*. If a sentence contains an error in agreement, write the correct form of the verb.

EXAMPLE [1] **Doesn't these neon signs light up the night sky with color?**
    1. *Don't*

[1] The public have been fascinated with neon lights since they were introduced in the 1920s. [2] There's neon lights in large and small cities all over the world. [3] Times Square in New York City and Tokyo's Ginza district is two places famous for their neon lights. [4] Some of today's neon signs are very large and creative. [5] All of the signs shown below is used in advertising. [6] But nowadays you can also see neon decorations and sculptures. [7] Our science class are learning how neon lights work. [8] Neon lights is made from hollow glass tubes filled with neon gas. [9] An electric current shot through the tube makes the gas glow. [10] The diagrams on the next page clearly show the action of a neon light.

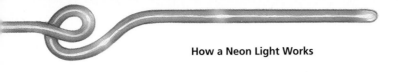

How a Neon Light Works

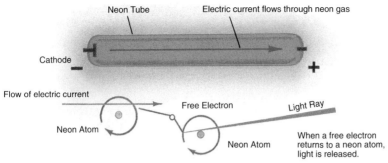

Neon Tube   Electric current flows through neon gas

Cathode

Flow of electric current

Free Electron   Light Ray

Neon Atom

Neon Atom

When a free electron returns to a neon atom, light is released.

▶ EXERCISE 13   Using Correct Subject-Verb Agreement

Your class is making up a trivia game, and you're supposed to contribute five geography questions. You've decided to ask questions about the Great Lakes. Use the information from this map and this chart to write five questions about the Great Lakes. In your questions, use one collective noun, one subject following a verb, and one indefinite pronoun. Be sure to provide answers to your questions.

EXAMPLE   **1.** *What are the names of the five lakes known as the Great Lakes?* [Ontario, Erie, Michigan, Huron, Superior]

2. *Both of these lakes border New York. What are they?* [Ontario, Erie]

USAGE

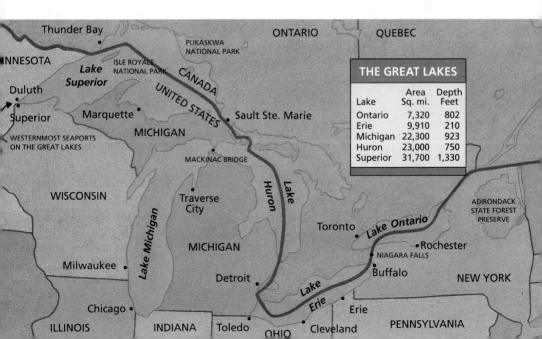

Thunder Bay

ONTARIO   QUEBEC

PUKASKWA NATIONAL PARK

MINNESOTA

Lake **Superior**

ISLE ROYALE NATIONAL PARK   CANADA

UNITED STATES

Duluth

Superior   Marquette

Sault Ste. Marie

WESTERNMOST SEAPORTS ON THE GREAT LAKES

MICHIGAN

MACKINAC BRIDGE

THE GREAT LAKES		
Lake	Area Sq. mi.	Depth Feet
Ontario	7,320	802
Erie	9,910	210
Michigan	22,300	923
Huron	23,000	750
Superior	31,700	1,330

WISCONSIN

Traverse City

Lake Huron

Lake Michigan

MICHIGAN

Toronto

Lake Ontario

ADIRONDACK STATE FOREST PRESERVE

Rochester

NIAGARA FALLS

Milwaukee

Detroit

Buffalo

NEW YORK

Chicago

Lake Erie

Erie

ILLINOIS   INDIANA   Toledo   OHIO   Cleveland   PENNSYLVANIA

Agreement of Pronoun and Antecedent

A pronoun usually refers to a noun or another pronoun, called its ***antecedent.*** Whenever you use a pronoun, make sure that it agrees with its antecedent.

☞ REFERENCE NOTE: For more information about antecedents, see page 436.

20n. A pronoun agrees with its antecedent in number and gender.

Some singular personal pronouns have forms that indicate gender. Masculine pronouns (*he, him, his*) refer to males. Feminine pronouns (*she, her, hers*) refer to females. Neuter pronouns (*it, its*) refer to things (neither male nor female) and sometimes to animals.

EXAMPLES **Bryan** lost **his** book.
Dawn lent **her** book to Bryan.
The **book** had Dawn's name written inside **its** cover.

The antecedent of a personal pronoun can be another kind of pronoun, such as *each, neither,* or *one.* To determine the gender of a personal pronoun that refers to one of these other pronouns, look in the phrase that follows the antecedent.

EXAMPLES **Each** of the men put on **his** hard hat.
Neither of those women got what **she** ordered.

Some antecedents may be either masculine or feminine. When referring to such antecedents, use both the masculine and the feminine forms.

EXAMPLES **No one** on the committee gave **his or her** approval.
Everybody in the class wanted to know **his or her** grade.

Sometimes, using *his or her* to refer to an indefinite pronoun is awkward or confusing. In such cases, use the plural form.

AWKWARD   When the singer walked out onto the stage, everyone clapped his or her hands.
    CLEAR   When the singer walked out onto the stage, everyone clapped their hands.

Even when used correctly, the *his or her* construction sounds awkward to many people. To avoid using *his or her,* try to rephrase the sentence, using a plural pronoun and antecedent.

EXAMPLES   **Everyone** in the club paid **his or her** dues.
All of the club members paid **their** dues.

Each of the mechanics uses **his or her** own tools.
The **mechanics** use **their** own tools.

USAGE

(1) A singular pronoun is used to refer to *anybody, anyone, each, either, everybody, everyone, neither, nobody, no one, one, someone,* or *somebody.*

EXAMPLES   **Everybody** will have an opportunity to express **his or her** opinion.
Each of the birds built **its** own nest.

(2) A singular pronoun is used to refer to two or more singular antecedents joined by *or* or *nor.*

EXAMPLES   **Julio or Van** will bring **his** football.
Neither **the mother nor the daughter** had forgotten **her** umbrella.

NOTE: Although rules (1) and (2) are often disregarded in conversation, they should be followed in writing.

(3) A plural pronoun is used to refer to two or more antecedents joined by *and.*

EXAMPLES   My **mother and father** send **their** regards.
My **dog and cat** never share **their** food.

☞ **REFERENCE NOTE:** For more information on the correct usage and spelling of the pronouns *its, their,* and *your,* see pages 690, 696, and 699.

▶ EXERCISE 14 **Proofreading Sentences for Pronoun-Antecedent Agreement**

Many of the following sentences contain errors in agreement of pronoun and antecedent. If the sentence is correct, write C. If the sentence contains an error in agreement, write the antecedent and the correct form of the pronoun.

EXAMPLE **1.** Everyone in my English class has to give their oral report on Friday.
1. *Everyone—his or her*

1. Either Don or Buddy will be the first to give their report.
2. Several others, including me, volunteered to give mine first.
3. Everybody else in class wanted to put off giving their report as long as possible.
4. Last year my friend Sandy and I figured out that waiting to give our reports was worse than actually giving them.
5. I am surprised that more people didn't volunteer to give his or her reports first.
6. Someone else will be third to give their report; then I will give mine.
7. A few others in my class are going to try to get out of giving his or her reports at all.
8. However, my teacher, Mrs. Goldenburg, said that anyone who does not give an oral report will get an "incomplete" as their course grade.
9. Most of us wish that he or she did not have to give an oral report at all.
10. Since no one can get out of giving their report, though, I'd rather get it over with as soon as possible.

EXERCISE 15   Identifying Antecedents and Writing Pronouns That Agree with Them

Complete each of the following sentences by inserting a pronoun that agrees with its antecedent. Identify the antecedent.

EXAMPLE   **1.** Ann and Margaret wore _____ cheerleader uniforms.
      1. *their—Ann and Margaret*

1. The trees lost several of _____ branches in the storm.
2. Each of the early Spanish missions in North America took pride in _____ church bell.
3. Anthony, do you know whether anyone else has turned in _____ paper yet?
4. Many in the mob raised _____ voices in protest.
5. The creek and the pond lost much of _____ water during the drought.
6. One of my uncles always wears _____ belt buckle off to one side.
7. No person should be made to feel that _____ is worth less than someone else.
8. None of the dogs had eaten all of _____ food.
9. A few of our neighbors have decided to fence _____ backyards.
10. Grant Hill and Scottie Pippen looked forward to _____ chance to play basketball during the 1996 Olympics.

REVIEW E   Proofreading Sentences for Pronoun-Antecedent Agreement

Many of the following sentences contain errors in agreement of pronoun and antecedent. If the sentence is correct, write *C*. If the sentence contains an error in agreement, write the antecedent and the correct form of the pronoun.

EXAMPLE   **1.** Each of the president's Cabinet officers gave their advice about what to do.
      1. *Each—his or her*

1. All of the nation's presidents have had his own Cabinets, or groups of advisers.
2. Shortly after taking office, presidents appoint the members of their Cabinets.
3. Everyone appointed to the Cabinet is an expert in their field.
4. George Washington and John Adams met regularly with his advisers.
5. Neither had more than five people in their Cabinet.
6. The Cabinet received its name from James Madison, the fourth president.
7. Congress and the president have used their power over the years to create new government agencies.
8. In 1979, Shirley M. Hufstedler took their place on the Cabinet as the first Secretary of Education.
9. Neither President Reagan nor President Bush created a new post in their Cabinet.
10. The Cabinet's meeting room now has more than fifteen chairs around their large table.

PICTURE THIS

Lucy never gives Charlie Brown much help. As you can see in the comic strip on the next page, all she has to offer him to inspire their team is a useless personal pronoun. Luckily, you're on the baseball team, too. Help Charlie Brown give the other players a pep talk. Write five sentences that you might say to the team. In at least three of your sentences, use pronouns with Charlie Brown, Lucy, or other team members as antecedents. In your other sentences, use two of the following pronouns: *anybody, each, everybody, nobody, someone.*

Subject: pep talk
Audience: your baseball team
Purpose: to inspire the team to play better

USAGE

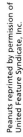

Review: Posttest

A. Identifying Verbs That Agree with Their Subjects

In each of the following sentences, if the italicized verb agrees with its subject, write C. If the italicized verb does not agree with its subject, write the correct form of the verb.

EXAMPLES **1.** The people on the bus *have* all been seated.
1. *C*

2. The fish, bass and perch mostly, *has* started feeding.
2. *have*

1. The swarm of bees *have* deserted its hive.
2. My spelling lessons and science homework sometimes *takes* me hours to finish.
3. Somebody *don't* approve of the new rule.
4. Neither Danny Glover nor Morgan Freeman *stars* in tonight's movie.
5. The mice or the cat *have* eaten the cheese.
6. There *is* probably a few children who don't like strawberries.
7. Most of the guests *likes* the inn's Irish soda bread.
8. Both of those varsity players *exercise* for an hour each day.
9. Evenings *is* the best time to visit her.
10. *Doesn't* those children still take piano lessons?

B. Identifying Pronouns That Agree with Their Antecedents

In each of the following sentences, if the italicized pronoun agrees with its antecedent, write C. If the italicized pronoun does not agree with its antecedent, write the correct form of the pronoun.

EXAMPLES **1.** Either of the men could have offered *their* help.
1. *his*

2. Both of the flowers had spread *their* petals.
2. C

11. Why doesn't somebody raise *their* hand and ask for directions?
12. One of the birds lost most of *their* tail feathers.
13. Sol sold *his* last ticket to Heather.
14. The old tennis court has weeds growing in *their* nets.
15. The Smithsonian's National Museum of the American Indian had closed *their* doors for the day.
16. I don't understand how chameleons sitting on a green leaf or a bush change *their* color.
17. Each of these tests has *their* own answer key.
18. These girls can choose *her* own materials from the supply room.
19. Stan or Ethan will bring *their* guitar.
20. Álvar Núñez Cabeza de Vaca and Fray Junípero Serra suffered great hardships in *his* explorations of the New World.

USAGE

21 USING VERBS CORRECTLY

Principal Parts, Regular and Irregular Verbs

Diagnostic Test

A. Using the Past and Past Participle Forms of Verbs

For each of the following sentences, give the correct form (past or past participle) of the verb in parentheses.

EXAMPLE **1.** We don't know why it (*take*) them so long.
          1. *took*

1. The cat (*lie*) down in front of the warm fire.
2. Since the storm began, the river has (*rise*) four feet.
3. Did you see which way they (*go*)?
4. I have (*write*) for tickets to the Alvin Ailey Dance Theater's next performance.
5. Two runners on our track team have (*break*) the school record for the mile run.

6. When the manager unlocked the door, a mob of shoppers (*burst*) into the store to take advantage of the sale.
7. Larry washed his wool sweater in hot water, and it (*shrink*).
8. The witness said that she (*see*) the blue truck run through the red light.
9. Look in the oven to see if the cake has (*rise*) yet.
10. Everyone should be in class after the bell has (*ring*).
11. Sitting Bull (*name*) his son Crowfoot.
12. Jeanette carefully (*lay*) her coat across the back of the chair.
13. By late December the pond has usually (*freeze*) hard enough to skate on.
14. Several of us (*choose*) to visit the Amish community in Pennsylvania.
15. So far, Dena has (*swim*) fifteen laps around the pool.

USAGE

B. Making Tenses of Verbs Consistent

For each of the following sentences, write the italicized verb in the correct tense.

EXAMPLE   **1.** He looked out the window and *sees* the storm approaching.
       1. *saw*

16. Jan was late, so she *decides* to run the rest of the way.
17. The man at the gate *takes* our tickets and said that we were just in time.
18. My uncle often travels in the Far East and *brought* me fascinating souvenirs.
19. After Sarah told me about the book of Yiddish folk sayings, I *buy* a copy.
20. The waitress brought my order and *asks* me if I wanted anything else.

The Principal Parts of a Verb

The four basic forms of a verb are called the *principal parts* of the verb.

21a. The principal parts of a verb are the **base form,** the **present participle,** the **past,** and the **past participle.**

Notice that the present participle and the past participle require helping verbs (forms of *be* and *have*).

BASE FORM	PRESENT PARTICIPLE	PAST	PAST PARTICIPLE
work	(is) working	worked	(have) worked
sing	(is) singing	sang	(have) sung

EXAMPLES   I **sing** in the school Glee Club.
We **are singing** at the music festival tonight.
Mahalia Jackson **sang** gospels at Carnegie Hall.
We **have sung** all over the state.

NOTE: Some teachers refer to the base form as the infinitive. Follow your teacher's directions in labeling these words.

Regular Verbs

21b. A *regular verb* forms its past and past participle by adding *−d* or *−ed* to the base form.

BASE FORM	PRESENT PARTICIPLE	PAST	PAST PARTICIPLE
use	(is) using	used	(have) used
suppose	(is) supposing	supposed	(have) supposed
attack	(is) attacking	attacked	(have) attacked

Avoid the following common errors when forming the past or past participle of regular verbs:

1. leaving off the *–d* or *–ed* ending

NONSTANDARD	She use to work in the library.
STANDARD	She **used** to work in the library.

NONSTANDARD	Who was suppose to bring the decorations?
STANDARD	Who was **supposed** to bring the decorations?

2. adding unnecessary letters

NONSTANDARD	A swarm of bees attackted us in the orange grove.
STANDARD	A swarm of bees **attacked** us in the orange grove.

NONSTANDARD	Fortunately, no one in the boating accident drownded.
STANDARD	Fortunately, no one in the boating accident **drowned.**

👉 REFERENCE NOTE: For a discussion of standard and nonstandard English, see pages 394 and 682.

ORAL PRACTICE 1   **Using the Past and Past Participle Forms of Regular Verbs**

Read each of the following sentences aloud, stressing the italicized verbs.

1. She has *crossed* this street many times on the way to school.
2. The raccoon *visited* our camp almost every morning last summer.
3. Ryan and Annie *repaired* the engine in less than an hour.
4. Scientists have *discovered* that birds use the sun as a compass.
5. Some people say that Stone Age surgeons in Peru *operated* on the brain.

USAGE

6. Alexandra and Anthony have *baked* Bavarian pretzels for the party.
7. The actors *leaped* across the stage to catch the falling door.
8. Sylvia has *used* her computer every day this week.

> EXERCISE 1 **Using Past and Past Participle Forms of Regular Verbs**

You're an archaeologist in the year 2993. You want to know what life was like in the United States a thousand years ago. While digging for clues, you discover these objects. What are they? What were they used for? Write a brief report about possible uses for these items. (Of course, you really know what these common items are, but imagine yourself as the future scientist.) In your report, use five past forms and five past participle forms of regular verbs. Underline each past and past participle form you use.

EXAMPLE **1.** *I have decided that people used this device to teach their children how to count.*

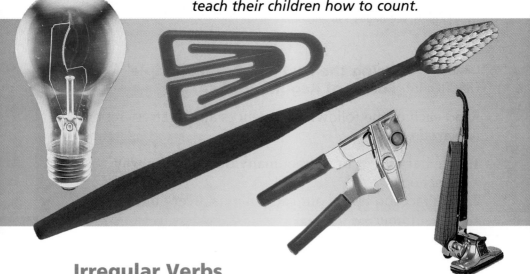

Irregular Verbs

21c. An *irregular verb* forms its past and past participle in some other way than by adding –*d* or –*ed* to the base form.

An irregular verb forms its past and past participle by

- changing vowels *or* consonants
- changing vowels *and* consonants
- making no changes

BASE FORM	PAST	PAST PARTICIPLE
ring	rang	(have) rung
make	made	(have) made
go	went	(have) gone
bring	brought	(have) brought
burst	burst	(have) burst

USAGE

Avoid the following common errors when forming the past or past participle of an irregular verb:

1. using the past form with a helping verb

NONSTANDARD   Carlos has went to the shopping mall.
STANDARD   Carlos **went** to the shopping mall.

or

STANDARD   Carlos **has gone** to the shopping mall.

2. using the past participle form without a helping verb

NONSTANDARD   I seen all of her movies.
STANDARD   I **have seen** all of her movies.

3. adding *–d* or *–ed* to the base form

NONSTANDARD   The right fielder throwed the ball to the shortstop.
STANDARD   The right fielder **threw** the ball to the shortstop.

NOTE: If you are not sure about the principal parts of a verb, look in a dictionary. Entries for irregular verbs give the principal parts of the verb.

The irregular verbs in each of the groups in the charts on the next three pages form their past and past participle in a similar way.

COMMON IRREGULAR VERBS

GROUP I: Each of these irregular verbs has the same form for its past and past participle.

BASE FORM	PRESENT PARTICIPLE	PAST	PAST PARTICIPLE
bring	(is) bringing	brought	(have) brought
build	(is) building	built	(have) built
buy	(is) buying	bought	(have) bought
catch	(is) catching	caught	(have) caught
feel	(is) feeling	felt	(have) felt
find	(is) finding	found	(have) found
get	(is) getting	got	(have) got or gotten
have	(is) having	had	(have) had
hold	(is) holding	held	(have) held
keep	(is) keeping	kept	(have) kept
lay	(is) laying	laid	(have) laid
lead	(is) leading	led	(have) led
leave	(is) leaving	left	(have) left
lend	(is) lending	lent	(have) lent
lose	(is) losing	lost	(have) lost
make	(is) making	made	(have) made
meet	(is) meeting	met	(have) met
pay	(is) paying	paid	(have) paid
say	(is) saying	said	(have) said
sell	(is) selling	sold	(have) sold
send	(is) sending	sent	(have) sent
sit	(is) sitting	sat	(have) sat
spend	(is) spending	spent	(have) spent
spin	(is) spinning	spun	(have) spun
stand	(is) standing	stood	(have) stood
swing	(is) swinging	swung	(have) swung
teach	(is) teaching	taught	(have) taught
tell	(is) telling	told	(have) told
think	(is) thinking	thought	(have) thought
win	(is) winning	won	(have) won

COMMON IRREGULAR VERBS			
GROUP II: Each of these irregular verbs has a different form for its past and past participle.			
BASE FORM	**PRESENT PARTICIPLE**	**PAST**	**PAST PARTICIPLE**
begin	(is) beginning	began	(have) begun
bite	(is) biting	bit	(have) bitten *or* bit
blow	(is) blowing	blew	(have) blown
break	(is) breaking	broke	(have) broken
choose	(is) choosing	chose	(have) chosen
come	(is) coming	came	(have) come
do	(is) doing	did	(have) done
draw	(is) drawing	drew	(have) drawn
drink	(is) drinking	drank	(have) drunk
drive	(is) driving	drove	(have) driven
eat	(is) eating	ate	(have) eaten
fall	(is) falling	fell	(have) fallen
fly	(is) flying	flew	(have) flown
freeze	(is) freezing	froze	(have) frozen
give	(is) giving	gave	(have) given
go	(is) going	went	(have) gone
grow	(is) growing	grew	(have) grown
know	(is) knowing	knew	(have) known
lie	(is) lying	lay	(have) lain
ride	(is) riding	rode	(have) ridden
ring	(is) ringing	rang	(have) rung
rise	(is) rising	rose	(have) risen
run	(is) running	ran	(have) run
see	(is) seeing	saw	(have) seen
shake	(is) shaking	shook	(have) shaken
sing	(is) singing	sang	(have) sung
sink	(is) sinking	sank	(have) sunk
speak	(is) speaking	spoke	(have) spoken
steal	(is) stealing	stole	(have) stolen
swim	(is) swimming	swam	(have) swum

(continued)

USAGE

COMMON IRREGULAR VERBS

GROUP II (*continued*)

take	(is) taking	took	(have) taken
tear	(is) tearing	tore	(have) torn
throw	(is) throwing	threw	(have) thrown
wear	(is) wearing	wore	(have) worn
write	(is) writing	wrote	(have) written

GROUP III: Each of these irregular verbs has the same form for its base form, past, and past participle.

BASE FORM	PRESENT PARTICIPLE	PAST	PAST PARTICIPLE
burst	(is) bursting	burst	(have) burst
cost	(is) costing	cost	(have) cost
cut	(is) cutting	cut	(have) cut
hit	(is) hitting	hit	(have) hit
hurt	(is) hurting	hurt	(have) hurt
let	(is) letting	let	(have) let
put	(is) putting	put	(have) put
read	(is) reading	read	(have) read
set	(is) setting	set	(have) set
spread	(is) spreading	spread	(have) spread

ORAL
PRACTICE 2

Using the Past and Past Participle Forms of Irregular Verbs

Read each of the following sentences aloud, stressing the italicized verb.

1. Ray Charles *has written* many popular songs.
2. Leigh *did* everything the instructions said.
3. She *knew* the best route to take.
4. Maria Tallchief *chose* a career as a dancer.
5. He *ate* chicken salad on whole-wheat bread for lunch.
6. The monkey *had stolen* the food from its brother.
7. Felipe and Tonya *sang* a duet in the talent show.
8. The shy turtle *came* closer to me to reach the lettuce I was holding.

▷ EXERCISE 2   **Using the Past and Past Participle Forms of Verbs**

For each of the following sentences, give the correct form (past or past participle) of the verb in parentheses.

EXAMPLE   **1.** Nobody knew why he (*do*) that.
           1. *did*

1. Did you say that the telephone (*ring*) while I was in the shower?
2. The outfielder (*throw*) the ball to home plate.
3. Diana Nyad (*swim*) sixty miles from the Bahamas to Florida.
4. Uncle Olaf has (*ride*) his new snowmobile up to the remote mountain cabin.
5. The librarian has (*choose*) a book by Jose Aruego.
6. The bean seedlings and the herbs have (*freeze*) in the garden.
7. After she finished the race, she (*drink*) two glasses of water.
8. He (*tell*) me that *waffle, coleslaw,* and *cookie* are words that came from Dutch.
9. We had (*drive*) all night to attend my sister's college graduation exercises.
10. Marianne (*sit*) quietly throughout the discussion.

▷ EXERCISE 3   **Using Correct Verb Forms**

For each of the sentences in the following paragraph, give the correct form (past or past participle) of the verb in parentheses.

EXAMPLE   [1] Have you (*read*) about the Underground Railroad?
           1. *read*

[1] Mr. Tucker, our history teacher, (*write*) the words *Underground Railroad* on the chalkboard. [2] Then he (*draw*) black lines on a map to show us where the Underground Railroad ran. [3] What strange tracks this railroad must have (*have*)! [4] The lines even (*go*) into the Atlantic Ocean.

[5] As you may imagine, this map (*leave*) the class very confused. [6] But then Mr. Tucker explained that no one actually (*ride*) on an underground railroad. [7] The railroad was really a secret network to help slaves who had (*run*) away. [8] Between 1830 and 1860, thousands of slaves (*gain*) their freedom by traveling along the routes marked on this map. [9] The name *Underground Railroad* (*come*) from the use of railroad terms as code words. [10] Mr. Tucker (*say*) that hiding places were called "stations" and that people who helped slaves were called "conductors."

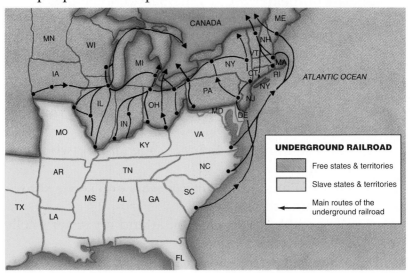

REVIEW A

Proofreading Sentences for Correct Verb Forms

Many of the following sentences contain incorrect verb forms. If the sentence is correct, write *C*. If the sentence has an incorrect verb form, write the correct form.

EXAMPLES **1.** Carmen gave me a menu from the new downtown restaurant.
1. *C*
2. I had spoke to my parents last week about trying this restaurant.
2. *had spoken*

1. My big brother Mark drived us there in Mom's car.
2. We sit down, and the waiter brought our menus.

3. When we arrived at the restaurant, I runned ahead of everyone to tell the hostess we needed five seats.
4. Have you ever drunk water with lemon slices in the glasses?
5. Dad chose the ravioli.
6. My little sister Emilia taked two helpings of salad.
7. The waiter bringed out our dinners on a huge tray.
8. Mark give me a taste of his eggplant parmigiana.
9. Emilia stealed a bite of my lasagna.
10. Dad telled the waiter that the food was delicious.

▶ REVIEW B **Proofreading Sentences for Correct Verb Forms**

Some of the following sentences contain incorrect verb forms. If the sentence is correct, write *C*. If the sentence has an incorrect verb form, write the correct form.

EXAMPLES **1.** Mario has lent me his copy of *Journey to the Center of the Earth.*
1. *C*

2. I thinked I had a copy of this famous novel.
2. *thought*

1. During the 1800s, Jules Verne wrote many scientific adventure tales.
2. Back then, readers founded his stories amazing.
3. Some people believe that he seen into the future.
4. For example, in some novels he telled about space exploration and boats that traveled underwater.
5. These books fascinated readers in the days before space travel and submarines!
6. Verne lead a quiet life but had incredible adventures in his imagination.
7. He gived the world some wonderful stories.
8. Some inventors of modern rockets have said that they read Verne's stories.
9. Some of his books, such as *20,000 Leagues Under the Sea,* have been made into great movies.
10. People have gave Verne the title "Father of Modern Science Fiction."

Verb Tense

21d. The *tense* of a verb indicates the time of the action or state of being expressed by the verb.

Every verb has six tenses.

Present	Past	Future
Present Perfect	Past Perfect	Future Perfect

This time line shows how the six tenses are related to one another.

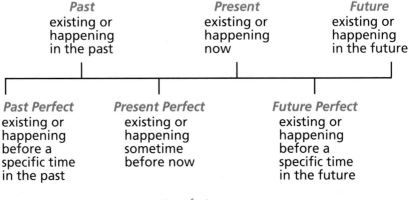

Past	*Present*	*Future*
existing or happening in the past	existing or happening now	existing or happening in the future

Past Perfect	*Present Perfect*	*Future Perfect*
existing or happening before a specific time in the past	existing or happening sometime before now	existing or happening before a specific time in the future

EXAMPLES

present perfect
Melissa **has saved** her money, and now she

present
has enough for a guitar.

past perfect
The scouts **had hiked** five miles before they

past
stopped for lunch.

future perfect
The executive **will have seen** the report by

future
next week and **will make** a decision then.

Listing all the forms of a verb in the six tenses is called *conjugating* a verb.

CONJUGATION OF THE VERB *WRITE*

PRESENT TENSE

SINGULAR	*PLURAL*
I write	we write
you write	you write
he, she, *or* it writes	they write

PAST TENSE

SINGULAR	*PLURAL*
I wrote	we wrote
you wrote	you wrote
he, she, *or* it wrote	they wrote

FUTURE TENSE

SINGULAR	*PLURAL*
I will (shall) write	we will (shall) write
you will write	you will write
he, she, *or* it will write	they will write

PRESENT PERFECT TENSE

SINGULAR	*PLURAL*
I have written	we have written
you have written	you have written
he, she, *or* it has written	they have written

PAST PERFECT TENSE

SINGULAR	*PLURAL*
I had written	we had written
you had written	you had written
he, she, *or* it had written	they had written

FUTURE PERFECT TENSE

SINGULAR	*PLURAL*
I will (shall) have written	we will (shall) have written
you will have written	you will have written
he, she, *or* it will have written	they will have written

USAGE

NOTE: The helping verb *shall* can be used in the second person (*you*) and third person (*he, she, it, they*), as well as in the first person.

Consistency of Tense

21e. Do not change needlessly from one tense to another.

When writing about events that take place in the present, use verbs in the present tense. Similarly, when writing about events that occurred in the past, use verbs in the past tense.

INCONSISTENT When we were comfortable, we begin to do our homework. [*Were* is past tense, and *begin* is present tense.]

CONSISTENT When we **are** comfortable, we **begin** to do our homework. [Both *are* and *begin* are present tense.]

CONSISTENT When we **were** comfortable, we **began** to do our homework. [Both *were* and *began* are past tense.]

INCONSISTENT Suddenly the great door opened, and an uninvited guest comes into the dining hall. [*Opened* is past tense, and *comes* is present tense.]

CONSISTENT Suddenly the great door **opens** and an uninvited guest **comes** into the dining hall. [Both *opens* and *comes* are present tense.]

CONSISTENT Suddenly the great door **opened** and an uninvited guest **came** into the dining hall. [Both *opened* and *came* are past tense.]

EXERCISE 4   **Proofreading a Paragraph to Make the Verb Tense Consistent**

Read the following paragraph and decide whether it should be rewritten in the present or past tense. Then, change the verb forms to make the verb tense consistent.

EXAMPLE [1] At my grandparents' house, I wake up before anyone else and quietly grabbed the fishing pole and head for the pond.

1. *At my grandparents' house, I wake up before anyone else and quietly grab the fishing pole and head for the pond.*

or

At my grandparents' house, I woke up before anyone else and quietly grabbed the fishing pole and headed for the pond.

[1] Across the water, I saw the ripples. [2] "I have to catch some fish," I say to myself. [3] I threw my lure near where I see the ripples and reeled in the line. [4] The fish don't seem interested. [5] I saw more ripples and throw the line in the water again. [6] "I have a strike!" I shout to the trees around me. [7] As I reeled in the line, a beautiful trout jumps out of the water and spit out the hook. [8] Discouraged, I go back to the house. [9] Grandpa was sitting at the kitchen table with a bowl of hot oatmeal for me. [10] I say, "Oh well, maybe tomorrow we'll have fresh trout for breakfast."

PICTURE THIS

You are the scientist who built the huge robot shown on the next page. Now you're testing how well it works. To test its ability to understand speech, you decide to question the robot. You take notes while your assistant asks the robot a series of questions. Write down the conversation between your assistant and the robot. In your notes, use sentences with each of the six verb tenses—present, past, future, present perfect, past perfect, and future perfect. Be sure to use quotation marks around the speakers' exact words. Also, start a new paragraph each time the speaker changes.

Subject: conversation between a robot and a scientist
Audience: yourself and your assistant
Purpose: to record the robot's responses to speech

USAGE

Special Problems with Verbs

Sit and *Set*

(1) The verb *sit* means "to rest in an upright, seated position." *Sit* seldom takes an object.

(2) The verb *set* means "to put (something) in a place." *Set* usually takes an object. Notice that *set* has the same form for the base form, past, and past participle.

BASE FORM	PRESENT PARTICIPLE	PAST	PAST PARTICIPLE
sit (rest)	(is) sitting	sat	(have) sat
set (put)	(is) setting	set	(have) set

EXAMPLES **Let's sit under the tree.** [no object]
Let's set the bookcase here. [Let's set what?
Bookcase is the object.]

The tourists **sat** on benches. [no object]
The children **set** the dishes on the table. [The children set what? *Dishes* is the object.]

We **had sat** down to eat when the telephone rang. [no object]
We **have set** the reading lamp beside the couch. [We have set what? *Lamp* is the object.]

USAGE

ORAL
PRACTICE 3 **Using the Forms of *Sit* and *Set***

Read each of the following sentences aloud, stressing the italicized verb.

1. Let's *sit* down here.
2. Look at the dog *sitting* on the porch.
3. Our teacher *set* a deadline for our term projects.
4. I'd like to *sit* on top of an Aztec pyramid and watch the sun rise.
5. I have always *sat* in the front row.
6. Please *set* the carton down inside the doorway.
7. Where did I *set* my book on judo?
8. After I *set* the mop in the closet, I *sat* down to rest.

EXERCISE 5 **Choosing the Forms of *Sit* and *Set***

For each of the following sentences, choose the correct verb in parentheses. If the verb you choose is a form of *set*, identify its object.

EXAMPLE **1.** Please (*sit, set*) the serving platter on the table.
          1. *set; object—platter*

1. Will you (*sit, set*) down here?
2. Aaron asked to (*sit, set*) the table for our Passover celebration.
3. Jamyce (*sat, set*) down her notebook on the kitchen counter.
4. I have been (*sitting, setting*) here all day.
5. (*Sit, Set*) the fine crystal in the china cabinet.

6. The referee is (*sitting, setting*) the ball on the fifty-yard line.
7. The kitten cautiously (*sat, set*) down beside the Great Dane.
8. Alex had to (*sit, set*) and catch his breath after joining in the Greek chain dance.
9. Let's (*sit, set*) that aside until later.
10. They have been (*sitting, setting*) there for fifteen minutes without saying a word to each other.

Lie and *Lay*

(1) The verb *lie* means "to rest," "to recline," or "to be in a place." *Lie* never takes an object.

(2) The verb *lay* means "to put (something) in a place." *Lay* usually takes an object.

BASE FORM	PRESENT PARTICIPLE	PAST	PAST PARTICIPLE
lie (rest)	(is) lying	lay	(have) lain
lay (put)	(is) laying	laid	(have) laid

EXAMPLES   The cows **are lying** in the shade. [no object]
The servers **are laying** extra napkins beside every plate for the barbecue. [The servers are laying what? *Napkins* is the object.]

The deer **lay** very still while the hunters passed by. [no object]
The soldiers **laid** a trap for the enemy. [The soldiers laid what? *Trap* is the object.]

Rip Van Winkle **had lain** asleep for twenty years. [no object]
The lawyer **had laid** the report next to her briefcase. [The lawyer had laid what? *Report* is the object.]

USAGE

▶ ORAL
PRACTICE 4   **Using the Forms of *Lie* and *Lay***

Read each of the following sentences aloud, stressing the italicized word.

1. Don't *lie* in the sun until you put on some sunscreen.
2. You shouldn't *lay* your papers on the couch.
3. The lion had been *lying* in wait for an hour.
4. The senator *laid* her notes aside after her speech.
5. I have *lain* awake, listening to Spanish flamenco music on the radio.
6. She has *laid* her books on the desk.
7. At bedtime, Toshiro *lies* down on a futon.
8. The exhausted swimmer *lay* helpless on the sand.

▶ EXERCISE 6   **Using the Forms of *Lie* and *Lay***

Complete each of the following sentences by supplying the correct form of *lie* or *lay*. If the verb you use is a form of *lay*, identify its object.

EXAMPLE   **1.** Leo ___ the disk next to the computer.
          1. *laid; object—disk*

1. After the race, Michael Andretti ___ his helmet on the car.
2. My dad was ___ down when I asked him for my allowance.
3. We ___ down some club rules.
4. Have you ever ___ on a water bed?
5. Rammel had ___ his keys beside his wallet.
6. My cat loves to ___ in the tall grass behind our house.
7. My brother left his clothes ___ on the floor until they began to smell.
8. Yesterday that alligator ___ in the sun all day.
9. Lim Sing's great-grandfather ___ railroad track in the United States.
10. The newspaper had ___ in the yard until the sun faded it.

USAGE

▶ REVIEW C

Writing Sentences Using the Forms of *Sit* and *Set* and *Lie* and *Lay*

When your neighbors went on vacation, they asked if you would "pet-sit" their animals. At the time, this sounded like an easy way to earn extra spending money. But you've really earned your money taking care of these three beasts! You've discovered that they can be very wild and stubborn. Write ten sentences about your "pet-sitting" experiences. Use a different verb from the list in each of your sentences.

lies	lay (past form of *lie*)	sat
have laid	set	laid
was sitting	were lying	setting
had set		

EXAMPLE   **1.** *Mr. Whiskers lay in Scruffy's food dish every morning.*

Rise and *Raise*

(1) The verb *rise* means "to go up" or "to get up." *Rise* never takes an object.

(2) The verb *raise* means "to lift up" or "to cause (something) to rise." *Raise* usually takes an object.

BASE FORM	PRESENT PARTICIPLE	PAST	PAST PARTICIPLE
rise (go up)	(is) rising	rose	(have) risen
raise (lift up)	(is) raising	raised	(have) raised

EXAMPLES   My neighbors **rise** very early in the morning. [no object]
Every morning they **raise** their shades to let the sunlight in. [They raise what? *Shades* is the object.]

The full moon **rose** slowly through the clouds last night. [no object]
The cheering crowd **raised** banners and signs over their heads, welcoming the troops home. [The crowd raised what? *Banners* and *signs* are the objects.]

The senators **have risen** from their seats to show respect for the chief justice. [no object]
The wind **has raised** a cloud of dust. [The wind has raised what? *Cloud* is the object.]

ORAL PRACTICE 5   **Using the Forms of *Rise* and *Raise***

Read each of the following sentences aloud, stressing the italicized verb.

1. The reporters *rise* when the president enters the room.
2. Students *raise* their hands to be recognized.
3. They *have raised* the curtain for the first act of the play.
4. Alex Haley *rose* to fame with his book *Roots*.
5. The sun *was rising* over the mountains.
6. The old Asian elephant slowly *rose* to its feet.
7. Who *had risen* first?
8. Two of the Inuit builders *raised* the block of ice and set it in place.

USAGE

EXERCISE 7 **Choosing the Forms of *Rise* and *Raise***

For each of the following sentences, choose the correct verb in parentheses. If the verb you choose is a form of *raise*, identify its object.

EXAMPLE **1.** Please (*raise*, *rise*) your hand when you want to speak.
  1. *raise; object—hand*

1. The steam was (*rising, raising*) from the pot of soup.
2. That discovery (*rises, raises*) an interesting question about the Algonquian people of Canada.
3. The child's fever (*rose, raised*) during the night.
4. The sun (*rises, raises*) later each morning.
5. The teacher will call only on students who (*rise, raise*) their hands.
6. We must (*rise, raise*) the flag before school begins.
7. The student body's interest in this subject has (*risen, raised*) to new heights.
8. The kite has (*risen, raised*) above the power lines.
9. My father promised to (*rise, raise*) my allowance if I pull the weeds.
10. The art dealer (*rose, raised*) the price of the painting by Frida Kahlo.

EXERCISE 8 **Using the Forms of *Rise* and *Raise***

Complete each sentence in the following paragraphs by supplying the correct form of *rise* or *raise*.

EXAMPLE [1] Have you ever ____ before dawn?
  1. *risen*

[1] We girls ____ early to start our hike to Lookout Mountain. [2] From our position at the foot of the mountain, it looked as though it ____ straight up to the skies. [3] But we had not ____ at daybreak just to look at the high peak. [4] We ____ our supply packs to our backs and started the long climb up the mountain. [5] With every step we took, the mountain seemed to ____ that much higher. [6] Finally, after several hours, we reached the

summit and ____ a special flag that we had brought for the occasion. [7] When our friends at the foot of the mountain saw that we had ____ the flag, they knew that all of us had reached the top safely. [8] They ____ their arms and shouted.

[9] Our friends' shouts were like an applause that seemed to ____ from the valley below. [10] Then we felt glad that we had ____ early enough to climb to the top of Lookout Mountain.

▶ REVIEW D **Choosing the Forms of *Sit* and *Set*, *Lie* and *Lay*, and *Rise* and *Raise***

Each of the following sentences has at least one pair of verbs in parentheses. Choose the correct verb from each pair. Be prepared to explain your choices.

EXAMPLE **1.** The audience (*sat, set*) near the stage.
        1. *sat*

1. To study solar energy, our class (*sit, set*) a solar panel outside the window of our classroom.
2. Since I have grown taller, I have (*rose, raised*) the seat on my bicycle.
3. Mr. DeLemos (*lay, laid*) the foundation for the new Vietnamese Community Center.
4. (*Sit, Set*) the groceries on the table while I start dinner.
5. The water level of the stream has not (*risen, raised*) since last summer.
6. Will you (*lie, lay*) the grass mats on the sand so that we can (*lie, lay*) on them?
7. We (*sat, set*) under a beach umbrella so that we wouldn't get sunburned.
8. When the sun (*rises, raises*), I often have trouble (*sitting, setting*) aside my covers and getting up.
9. He left his collection of Isaac Bashevis Singer stories (*lying, laying*) on the table.
10. The crane (*rose, raised*) the steel beam and carefully (*sat, set*) it into place.

REVIEW E

Proofreading a Paragraph for Correct Verb Forms

Some sentences in the following paragraph contain incorrect forms of the verbs *sit* and *set, lie* and *lay,* and *rise* and *raise.* If the sentence is correct, write *C.* If the sentence has an incorrect verb form, write the correct form.

EXAMPLES [1] We rose early for our journey to Havasu Canyon.
1. *C*
[2] I laid awake for hours thinking about the trip.
2. *lay*

[1] I helped Dad sit our bags in the car, and we headed for Havasu Canyon. [2] The canyon, which lies in northern Arizona, is home of the Havasupai Indian Reservation. [3] At the canyon rim, a Havasupai guide helped me up onto a horse and rose the stirrups so that I could reach them. [4] After we rode horses eight miles to the canyon floor, I was tired from setting. [5] Yet I knew I must sit a good example for my younger brother and not complain. [6] As you can see, the trail we took was fairly narrow and lay along the side of a steep, rocky wall. [7] We watched the sun raise high and hot as we rode through this beautiful canyon. [8] I thought about laying down when we reached the village of Supai. [9] Still, I quickly raised my hand to join the next tour to Havasu Falls. [10] When we arrived, I was ready to lay under the spray of the waterfall pictured on the next page.

▶ REVIEW F   **Choosing Correct Verb Forms**

Each of the following sentences has at least one pair of verbs in parentheses. Choose the correct verb from each pair.

EXAMPLE   **1.** Josh (*catched, caught*) seven fish this morning.
              1. *caught*

1. Buffy Sainte-Marie has (*sang, sung*) professionally for more than twenty years.
2. Have you (*began, begun*) your Scottish bagpipe lessons yet?
3. Cindy Nicholas was the first woman who (*swam, swum*) the English Channel both ways.
4. When the baby sitter (*rose, raised*) her voice, the children (*knew, knowed*) it was time to behave.
5. After we had (*saw, seen*) all of the exhibits at the county fair, we (*ate, eat*) a light snack and then (*went, go*) home.
6. The egg (*burst, bursted*) in the microwave oven.
7. He (*lay, laid*) his lunch money on his desk.
8. The loud noise (*breaked, broke*) my concentration.
9. We (*sat, set*) through the movie three times because Cantinflas is so funny.
10. We had (*rode, ridden*) halfway across the desert when I began to wish that I had (*brought, brung*) more water.

USAGE

▶ REVIEW G   **Identifying Correct Verb Forms**

Each sentence in the following paragraph has a pair of verbs in parentheses. Choose the correct verb from each pair.

EXAMPLE   [1] Have you ever (*saw, seen*) an animal using a tool?

    1. *seen*

[1] I had (*thought, thinked*) that only humans use tools. [2] However, scientists have (*spended, spent*) many hours watching wild animals make and use tools. [3] Chimpanzees have been (*saw, seen*) using twigs to catch insects. [4] They (*taken, took*) their sticks and poked them into termite holes. [5] In that way, they (*catched, caught*) termites. [6] I've been (*telled, told*) that some finches use twigs to dig insects out of cracks in tree bark. [7] Sea otters have (*broke, broken*) open shellfish by banging them against rocks. [8] You may have (*knew, known*) that song thrushes also use that trick to get snails out of their shells. [9] Some animals have (*builded, built*) things, using their gluelike body fluids to hold objects together. [10] For example, scientists watched as tailor ants (*spread, spreaded*) their sticky film on leaves to hold them together.

▶ REVIEW H   **Using the Forms of Verbs**

You've always enjoyed riding bicycles. Now you have a chance to help out in your uncle's bicycle repair shop. On your first day there, your uncle gives you a copy of a chart. He tells you to use it to check over every bicycle brought in. Write a letter to a friend, telling about your job at the shop. Use the chart on the next page to describe some of the things that you do when you check a bicycle. In your letter, use the past or past participle forms of ten verbs from the list of Common Irregular Verbs on pages 608–610. Underline these ten verbs.

EXAMPLE   **1.** *One man <u>brought</u> in an old bicycle, and I <u>spent</u> all morning fixing the brakes.*

The Care of the Bicycle

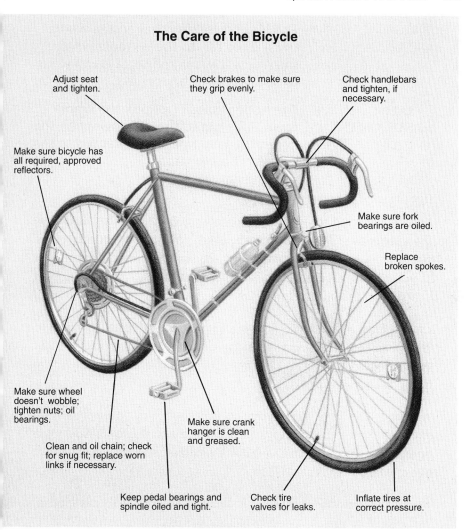

Adjust seat and tighten.

Check brakes to make sure they grip evenly.

Check handlebars and tighten, if necessary.

Make sure bicycle has all required, approved reflectors.

Make sure fork bearings are oiled.

Replace broken spokes.

Make sure wheel doesn't wobble; tighten nuts; oil bearings.

Make sure crank hanger is clean and greased.

Clean and oil chain; check for snug fit; replace worn links if necessary.

Keep pedal bearings and spindle oiled and tight.

Check tire valves for leaks.

Inflate tires at correct pressure.

WRITING APPLICATION

Using Different Verb Forms and Tenses in a Poem

When you write a story, you use verbs to tell what is happening, has happened, or will happen to your characters. To help your readers understand the order of events, you use different verb forms.

INCORRECT FORM
AND INCONSISTENT
TENSE

The huge explosion shaked the whole town. Julie ran to the window when she heard the loud noise. She will want to see what was happening.

CORRECT FORM
AND CONSISTENT
TENSE

The huge explosion **shook** the whole town. Julie **ran** to the window when she **heard** the loud noise. She **wanted** to see what **was** happening.

▶ WRITING ACTIVITY

You've decided to enter a local poetry contest. The theme of the contest is "Modern Adventures." Write a short narrative poem (a poem that tells a story) about a modern adventure. In your poem use at least ten verbs from the list of Common Irregular Verbs on pages 608–610.

Prewriting First, you'll need to pick an adventure story to tell. You could tell a true story or an imaginary one. After you select a story, jot down some specific details that you want to include in your poem.

Writing As you write your rough draft, try to express the excitement of the adventure. You may want to divide your poem into rhymed stanzas. Each stanza could tell a different event of your story.

Evaluating and Revising Ask a friend to read your poem. Is the adventure story easy to follow? Is it interesting? If not, you may want to add, delete, or revise some details. If your poem is a ballad or other traditional type of poem, be sure that the rhythm and rhyme follow that poetic form. Does your poem contain enough sensory details? For more about sensory details, see page 66.

Proofreading Use your textbook to check the spelling of the irregular verbs in your poem. Be sure that you've used ten irregular verbs from the list. And check to see that the forms are correct and the tenses are consistent.

Review: Posttest

A. Using the Past and Past Participle Forms of Verbs

For each of the following sentences, give the correct form (past or past participle) of the verb in parentheses.

EXAMPLES   **1.** The deer (*run*) right in front of our car.
1. *ran*

2. Her dog has (*run*) away from home.
2. *run*

1. She (*buy*) several boxes decorated with colorful Amish designs.
2. Have you (*write*) your history report yet?
3. I don't think I should have (*eat*) that last handful of sunflower seeds.
4. Our teacher (*tell*) us that the ukulele is a musical instrument from Hawaii.
5. She is the nicest person I have ever (*know*).
6. When the medicine finally began to work, his fever (*break*).
7. That phone has (*ring*) every five minutes since I got home.
8. Earl thought and thought, but the answer never (*come*) to him.
9. If that had happened to me, I would have (*freeze*) with fear.
10. Through the murky depths the whales (*sing*) to one another.
11. The coach (*give*) us all a pep talk before the game.
12. We knew that it would start to rain soon because the crickets had (*begin*) chirping.
13. That job shouldn't have (*take*) you all day.
14. The waiter (*bring*) us couscous, a popular North African dish.
15. Though it had (*fall*) from the top of the tree, the baby squirrel was all right.

USAGE

B. Choosing the Forms of *Lie* and *Lay*, *Sit* and *Set*, and *Rise* and *Raise* in Sentences

For each of the following sentences, choose the correct verb in parentheses.

EXAMPLE   **1.** My cat (*lies, lays*) around the house all day.
       1. *lies*

16. We had to wait for the drawbridge to (*rise, raise*) before we could sail out to the bay.
17. (*Sit, Set*) that down in the chair, will you?
18. The treasure had (*lay, lain*) at the bottom of the sea for more than four hundred years.
19. While (*sitting, setting*) on the porch, Nashota read a folk tale about Coyote, the trickster.
20. Look on the other side of any logs (*lying, laying*) in the path to avoid stepping on a snake.

C. Making Tenses of Verbs Consistent

For each of the following sentences, write the italicized verb in the correct tense.

EXAMPLE   **1.** My father looked at his watch and *decides* that it was time to leave.
       1. *decided*

21. Marjorie's sister refused to give us a ride in her car, and then she *asks* us to lend her some money for gas.
22. He says he's sorry, but he *didn't* mean it.
23. The pine trees grow close together and *had* straight trunks.
24. When the show ended, we *get* up to leave, but a crowd had already gathered.
25. Several mechanics worked on my aunt's car before one of them finally *finds* the problem.

22 USING PRONOUNS CORRECTLY

Nominative and Objective Case Forms

Diagnostic Test

Identifying Correct Forms of Pronouns

For each of the following sentences, identify the correct pronoun in parentheses.

EXAMPLE   **1.** When I got home, a package was waiting for
(*I, me*).
  1. *me*

1. Just between you and (*I, me*), I think he's wrong.
2. I don't know (*who, whom*) I'll invite to the dance.
3. We saw (*they, them*) at a Mardi Gras parade in New Orleans.
4. The winners in the contest were Amelia and (*I, me*).
5. The wasp flew in the window and bit (*he, him*) on the arm.

6. Elton and (*she, her*) will give reports this morning.
7. The two scouts who have earned the most merit badges are Angelo and (*he, him*).
8. Several people in my neighborhood helped (*we, us*) boys clear the empty lot and measure out a baseball diamond.
9. Nina usually sits behind Alex and (*I, me*) on the bus every morning.
10. My father and (*he, him*) are planning to go into business together.
11. We thought that we'd be facing (*they, them*) in the finals.
12. May I sit next to Terence and (*he, him*)?
13. The tour guide showed Kimberly and (*she, her*) some Japanese *raku* pottery.
14. My aunt once gave (*me, I*) two dolls made from corn husks.
15. Did you know that it was (*I, me*) who called?
16. Corey's mother and my father said that (*we, us*) boys could go on the field trip.
17. Our friends asked (*we, us*) if we had ever been to San Francisco's Chinatown.
18. Invite (*she, her*) and the new girl in our class to the party.
19. Do you know (*who, whom*) received the award?
20. The best soloists in the band are (*they, them*).

Case

Case is the form of a noun or a pronoun that shows its use in a sentence. There are three cases:

- nominative
- objective
- possessive

The form of a noun is the same for both the nominative and the objective cases. For example, a noun used as a subject (nominative case) will have the same form when used as an indirect object (objective case).

NOMINATIVE CASE   The **singer** received a standing ovation. [subject]

OBJECTIVE CASE   The audience gave the **singer** a standing ovation. [indirect object]

A noun changes its form for the possessive case, usually by adding an apostrophe and an *s*.

POSSESSIVE CASE   Many of the **singer's** fans waited outside the theater.

👉 REFERENCE NOTE: For more about possessive pronouns, see pages 437, 817, 821, and 823.

Unlike nouns, most personal pronouns have different forms for all three cases.

PERSONAL PRONOUNS		
SINGULAR		
NOMINATIVE CASE	OBJECTIVE CASE	POSSESSIVE CASE
I	me	my, mine
you	you	your, yours
he, she, it	him, her, it	his, her, hers, its
PLURAL		
NOMINATIVE CASE	OBJECTIVE CASE	POSSESSIVE CASE
we	us	our, ours
you	you	your, yours
they	them	their, theirs

NOTE: Some teachers prefer to call possessive pronouns (such as *my, your,* and *our*) adjectives. Follow your teacher's directions in labeling possessive forms.

USAGE

USAGE

"So, then . . . Would that be 'us the people' or 'we the people?' "

EXERCISE 1   **Identifying Personal Pronouns and Their Cases**

Each of the sentences in the following paragraph contains at least one personal pronoun. Identify each pronoun and give its case.

EXAMPLE   **[1] Uncle Theo gave us this book about rock stars of the 1950s and 1960s.**
   1. *us—objective*

[1] Why don't you sit down and look through the book with Clarence and me? [2] We want to see what pictures it has of the great African American rock singers. [3] I also look forward to reading more about them! [4] The contributions they made to rock-and-roll affected popular music all over the world. [5] The stars in the pictures on the next page look so different from the performers we have today. [6] That's Chuck Berry doing his famous "duckwalk." [7] These three women were known as the Supremes, and

they had twelve number-one songs. [8] The woman in the middle may look familiar; she is Diana Ross. [9] Fans also liked this male vocal group, the Four Tops, and other groups like them that harmonized. [10] Of course, we can't forget Little Richard, known for his wild piano playing.

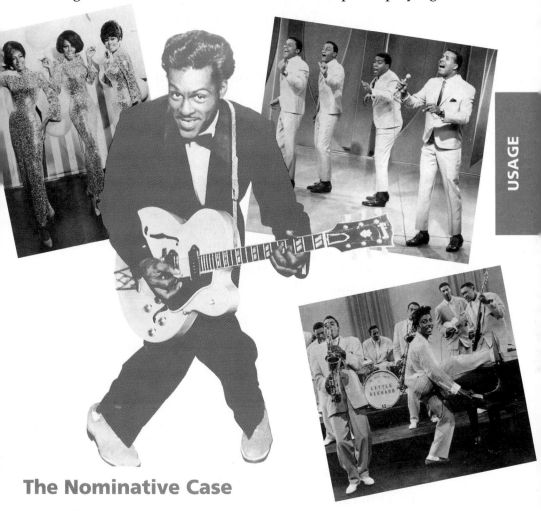

The Nominative Case

22a. A subject of a verb is in the nominative case.

EXAMPLES **I** like classical music. [*I* is the subject of *like.*]
He and **she** sold tickets. [*He* and *she* are the subjects of *sold.*]
They called while **we** were away. [*They* is the subject of *called. We* is the subject of *were.*]

To help you choose the correct pronoun in a compound subject, try each form of the pronoun separately.

EXAMPLE: Candida and (*me, I*) like to dance.
              Me like to dance.
              I like to dance.
ANSWER: Candida and I like to dance.

ORAL PRACTICE 1   Using Pronouns as Subjects

Read the following sentences aloud, stressing the italicized pronouns.

1. *He* and *she* collect seashells.
2. My grandmother and *I* are painting the boat.
3. Both *they* and *we* were frightened.
4. Did Alicia or *she* answer the phone?
5. *We* are giving a fashion show.
6. *You* and *I* will stay behind.
7. Were *he* and *she* on the Old Spanish Trail?
8. My parents and *they* are good friends.

EXERCISE 2   Choosing Personal Pronouns Used as Subjects

Choose appropriate personal pronouns for the blanks in the following sentences. Use a variety of pronouns, but do not use *you* or *it*.

EXAMPLE **1.** ____ and ____ will have a debate.
           1. *We, they*

1. Yesterday she and ____ went shopping.
2. Our cousins and ____ are ready for the race.
3. Neither ____ nor J. B. saw the zydeco band perform.
4. ____ and Lim Sing have copies of the book.
5. When are ____ and ____ coming?
6. Everyone remembers when ____ won the big game.
7. Someone said that ____ and ____ are finalists.
8. Did you or ____ ride in the hot-air balloon?

9. Both ___ and ___ enjoyed the stories about African American cowboys in the Old West.
10. Has ___ or Eduardo seen that movie?

22b. A *predicate nominative* is in the nominative case.

A *predicate nominative* follows a linking verb and explains or identifies the subject of the verb. A personal pronoun used as a predicate nominative follows a form of the verb *be* (*am, is, are, was, were, be,* or *been*).

EXAMPLES   The last one to leave was **he.** [*He* follows the linking verb *was* and identifies the subject *one.*]
              Do you think it may have been **they**? [*They* follows the linking verb *may have been* and identifies the subject *it.*]

USAGE

To help you choose the correct form of a pronoun used as a predicate nominative, remember that the pronoun could just as well be used as the subject in the sentence.

EXAMPLE   The fastest runners are **she** and **I.** [predicate nominatives]
             She and **I** are the fastest runners. [subjects]

☞ REFERENCE NOTE: For more information about predicate nominatives, see page 496.

NOTE: Expressions such as *It's me, That's her,* and *It was them* are accepted in everyday speaking. In writing, however, such expressions are generally considered nonstandard and should be avoided.

▶ EXERCISE 3   **Identifying Personal Pronouns Used as Predicate Nominatives**

For each of the following sentences, identify the correct personal pronoun in parentheses.

EXAMPLE   **1.** It was (*I, me*) at the door.
            1. *I*

1. We hoped it was (*her, she*).
2. That stranger thinks I am (*she, her*).

3. Luckily, it was not (*them, they*) in the accident.
4. It could have been (*she, her*) that he called.
5. Everyone believed it was (*we, us*).
6. It might have been (*him, he*), but I'm not sure.
7. Our opponents could have been (*them, they*).
8. I thought it was (*they, them*) from whom you bought the Cherokee basket.
9. If the singer had been (*her, she*), I would have gone to the concert.
10. Was that Claudia or (*she, her*) who brought the Chinese egg rolls?

▶ REVIEW A **Identifying Personal Pronouns in the Nominative Case**

Each sentence in the following paragraph contains a pair of personal pronouns in parentheses. Choose the correct pronoun from each pair.

EXAMPLE **[1] (*We, Us*) think of Leonardo da Vinci mostly as an artist.**

1. *We*

[1] (*Me, I*) think you probably have seen some paintings by this Italian Renaissance master. [2] (*Him, He*) painted two works that are particularly famous. [3] The *Mona Lisa* and the *Last Supper* are (*they, them*). [4] In science class (*we, us*) were surprised by what our teacher said about Leonardo. [5] (*Her, She*) said that he was also a brilliant inventor. [6] My friend Jill and (*me, I*) were amazed to hear that Leonardo

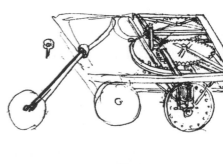

invented a flying machine that looked like a helicopter. [7] Look at the propellers on the flying machine that (*he, him*) drew in 1488. [8] (*Me, I*) was also impressed by his drawing of a spring-driven car. [9] The inventor of the diving bell and the battle tank was (*him, he*), too. [10] Scientists have studied Leonardo's ideas, and (*them, they*) have made models of many of his drawings.

WRITING APPLICATION

Using Pronouns in a Letter to a Magazine

The difference between the rules of spoken English and written English can be confusing. For example, the language you hear spoken at home and in your community determines what sounds "right" to you. But sometimes what *sounds* right is actually a nonstandard usage. To communicate effectively with a wide range of people, you need to learn the rules of standard English.

NONSTANDARD   Ernie and me respect Mr. Ray's decision.
STANDARD   Ernie and I respect Mr. Ray's decision.

▶ WRITING ACTIVITY

A national magazine has asked its readers to send in letters telling about the people they respect the most. A prize will be given to the person who writes the best letter. You decide to enter the contest. Write a letter to the magazine, telling about the person you most respect. You want your writing to appeal to many people, so be sure the pronouns you use follow the rules of standard English.

Prewriting   Begin by thinking about a person you respect. This could be someone you know (such as a family member, a teacher, or a friend). Or it could be someone you have heard or read about (perhaps an author or a scientist). Choose one person to write about. Then, make some notes on why you respect that person.

Writing As you write your first draft, include only the most convincing details from your list. Think about how you want to group these details and how they will fit in your letter. Throughout your letter, use personal pronouns so that you don't keep repeating proper names.

Evaluating and Revising As you read over your letter, imagine that you are a magazine editor. Ask yourself these questions:

- Is it clear why the writer respects the person?
- Has the writer supported all opinions with facts?

Mark any places where more information would be helpful. Delete any unnecessary information. Then, check to be sure that all pronoun antecedents are clear. (For more about antecedents, see pages 436 and 594–596.)

Proofreading and Publishing Recopy your letter following the business letter format on pages 901–906. Check the spellings of all proper names and places. Make sure that all pronouns are used according to the rules of standard English. You and your classmates could display your letters on a Person-of-the-Week bulletin board. You also might want to send a copy of your letter to the person you wrote about.

The Objective Case

22c. A *direct object* is in the objective case.

A *direct object* follows an action verb and tells *who* or *what* receives the action of the verb.

EXAMPLES   **Evan surprised them.** [*Them* tells *whom* Evan surprised.]
Uncle Ramón took me to the rodeo. [*Me* tells *whom* Uncle Ramón took.]
The ranger guided us to the camp. [*Us* tells *whom* the ranger guided.]

To help you choose the correct pronoun in a compound direct object, try each form of the pronoun separately in the sentence.

EXAMPLE: **We met Tara and (*she, her*) at the video arcade.**
We met *she* at the video arcade.
We met *her* at the video arcade.
ANSWER: **We met Tara and her at the video arcade.**

☞ REFERENCE NOTE: For more information about direct objects, see page 491.

▶ EXERCISE 4   **Choosing Pronouns Used as Direct Objects**

Choose appropriate pronouns for the blanks in the following sentences. Use a variety of pronouns, but do not use *you* or *it*.

EXAMPLE   **1.** The teacher helped ____ with the assignment.
1. *us*

1. All five judges have chosen ____ and ____ as the winners.
2. They asked Ms. Shore and ____ for permission.
3. Rita said that she can usually find Alberto and ____ at your house.
4. Did you know Jarvis and ____?
5. The guide directed ____ to New York City's Little Italy neighborhood.
6. Aunt Aggie took ____ and ____ to the zoo.
7. Rochelle told my sister and ____ about the Freddie Jackson concert.
8. Should we call Mark and ____?
9. Do you remember ____ and ____?
10. The dog chased Adam and ____.

22d. An *indirect object* is in the objective case.

An *indirect object* comes between an action verb and a direct object and tells *to whom or what* or *for whom or what.*

EXAMPLES   Coach Mendez gave **them** a pep talk. [*Them* tells *to whom* Coach Mendez gave a pep talk.]
His mother built **him** a footlocker. [*Him* tells *for whom* his mother built a footlocker.]
The science teacher gave **us** posters of the solar system. [*Us* tells *to whom* the teacher gave posters.]

To help you choose the correct pronoun in a compound indirect object, try each form of the pronoun separately in the sentence.

EXAMPLE: Our neighbor gave Kristen and (*I, me*) a job for the summer.
Our neighbor gave *I* a job for the summer.
Our neighbor gave *me* a job for the summer.
ANSWER: Our neighbor gave Kristen and **me** a job for the summer.

☞ REFERENCE NOTE: For more information about indirect objects, see pages 492–493.

▶ ORAL
PRACTICE 2   **Using Pronouns as Direct Objects and Indirect Objects**

Read the following sentences aloud, stressing the italicized pronouns.

1. The hot lentil soup burned Ahmad and *me.*
2. Li showed Raúl and *her* the new kite.
3. The stray dog followed *her* and *him* all the way to school.
4. Did you expect *us* or *them*?
5. The doctor gave *her* and *me* flu shots.
6. Carol helped Sarah and *him* with their chores.
7. Have you seen the Romanos or *them*?
8. After supper Mrs. Karras gave *us* some baklava for dessert.

▶ EXERCISE 5 **Using Personal Pronouns as Indirect Objects**

These photographs show the changing face of Abraham Lincoln, sixteenth President of the United States. He was the first president to have a beard. There's a legend that Lincoln grew his beard after receiving a letter from a young girl. She suggested that Lincoln would look better if he had one. He grew a beard in 1860 and kept it the rest of his life. Do you agree with the girl? Does Lincoln look better with a beard? Write five sentences about what you think of the change. In each sentence, use a personal pronoun as an indirect object. Use at least three different personal pronouns. Underline the indirect object in each of your sentences.

EXAMPLES   **1.** *A beard gives <u>him</u> an important look.*
2. *Lincoln should have written <u>her</u> a letter saying he didn't want a beard.*

USAGE

22e. An *object of a preposition* is in the objective case.

The *object of a preposition* is a noun or a pronoun that follows a preposition. Together, the preposition, its object, and any modifiers of that object make a *prepositional phrase.*

EXAMPLES to **Lee**   in an **hour**   like red **clay**
without **me** near **her**   except **them**
for **him**   by **us**   next to **us**

☞ REFERENCE NOTE: For a list of prepositions, see page 474. For more discussion of prepositional phrases, use pages 506–509.

A pronoun used as the object of a preposition should always be in the objective case.

EXAMPLES When did you mail the package to **them**? [*Them* is the object of the preposition *to.*]
Are you still planning to go to the movies with **us**? [*Us* is the object of the preposition *with.*]
The reward money was divided equally between **him** and **her**. [*Him* and *her* are the objects of the preposition *between.*]

ORAL   **Using Pronouns as Objects of**
PRACTICE 3   **Prepositions**

Read the following sentences aloud, stressing the italicized words.

1. The safari continued *without her* and *me.*
2. Everyone *except us* saw the Navajo rugs.
3. We stood *beside* their families and *them* during the ceremony.
4. Do you have any suggestions *for* Jalene or *me*?
5. The clowns talked *to* Claire and *him.*
6. Give this *to* either your father or *her.*
7. With the help *of* Juan and *her,* we built a fire and set up camp.
8. There was a spelling bee *between us* and *them.*

EXERCISE 6 **Choosing Pronouns Used as Objects of Prepositions**

Choose appropriate pronouns for the blanks in the following sentences. Use a variety of pronouns, but do not use *you* or *it*.

EXAMPLE **1. We could not find all of ____.**
1. *them*

1. The teacher read to André and ____ a saying by Confucius about friendship.
2. I made an appointment for ____ and you.
3. There are some seats behind Lusita and ____.
4. No one except Patrice and ____ was studying.
5. I couldn't have done it without you and ____.
6. Why didn't you speak to Christie and ____?
7. Our team has played basketball against the Jets and ____.
8. I was near you and ____ during the parade.
9. Just between you and ____, I think our chances are good.
10. Did you go with ____ to the Fall Harvest Festival at the Ozark Folk Center?

Special Pronoun Problems

Who and *Whom*

The pronoun *who* has different forms in the nominative and objective cases. *Who* is the nominative form; *whom* is the objective form.

NOTE: In spoken English, the use of *whom* is becoming less common. In fact, when you are speaking, you may correctly begin any question with *who* regardless of the grammar of the sentence. In written English, however, you should distinguish between *who* and *whom*. *Who* is used as a subject or a predicate nominative, and *whom* is used as an object.

USAGE

USAGE

When you are choosing between *who* or *whom* in a subordinate clause, follow these steps:

STEP 1: Find the subordinate clause.
STEP 2: Decide how the pronoun is used in the clause—as subject, predicate nominative, object of the verb, or object of a preposition.
STEP 3: Determine the case of the pronoun according to the rules of standard English.
STEP 4: Select the correct form of the pronoun.

EXAMPLE: Do you know (*who, whom*) they are?
STEP 1: The subordinate clause is (*who, whom*) *they are.*
STEP 2: In this clause, the subject is *they,* the verb is *are,* and the pronoun is the predicate nominative: *they are* (*who, whom*).
STEP 3: A pronoun used as a predicate nominative should be in the nominative case.
STEP 4: The nominative form is *who.*
ANSWER: Do you know **who** they are?

EXAMPLE: Isaac Bashevis Singer, (*who, whom*) I admire, wrote interesting books.
STEP 1: The subordinate clause is (*who, whom*) *I admire.*
STEP 2: In this clause, the subject is *I,* and the verb is *admire.* The pronoun is the direct object of the verb: *I admire* (*who, whom*).
STEP 3: A pronoun used as a direct object should be in the objective case.
STEP 4: The objective form is *whom.*
ANSWER: Isaac Bashevis Singer, **whom** I admire, wrote interesting books.

ORAL
PRACTICE 4   **Using *Who* and *Whom* Correctly**

Read the following sentences aloud, stressing the italicized pronouns.

1. Our team needs a pitcher *who* can throw curve balls.
2. For *whom* do the gauchos in Argentina work?
3. The gauchos work for ranch owners *who* often live in other parts of the world.

4. Dr. Martin Luther King, Jr., was a man *whom* we honor.
5. Is he the new student to *whom* this locker belongs?
6. The Inuit, *who* are sometimes called Eskimos, live along the northern coast of Labrador.
7. *Who* won the speech contest?
8. *Whom* did they suggest for the job?

Pronouns with Appositives

Sometimes a pronoun is followed directly by a noun that identifies the pronoun. Such a noun is called an *appositive.* To help you choose which pronoun to use before an appositive, omit the appositive and try each form of the pronoun separately.

EXAMPLE: **(*We, Us*) cheerleaders practice after school.**
[*Cheerleaders* is the appositive identifying the pronoun.]
We practice after school.
Us practice after school.

ANSWER: **We cheerleaders practice after school.**

EXAMPLE: **The coach threw a party for (*we, us*) players.**
[*Players* is the appositive identifying the pronoun.]
The coach threw a party for *we.*
The coach threw a party for *us.*

ANSWER: **The coach threw a party for us players.**

REFERENCE NOTE: For more information about appositives, see page 526.

EXERCISE 7   **Identifying Correct Forms of Pronouns**

For each of the following sentences, choose the correct pronoun in parentheses.

1. (*Who, Whom*) selected the new team captain?
2. (*We, Us*) students are having a carnival to raise money.
3. The head nurse gave (*we, us*) volunteers a tour of the new hospital wing.

4. Did you know that (*we, us*) girls are going to the concert?

5. From (*who, whom*) did you order the food?

▶ REVIEW B   **Identifying Correct Forms of Pronouns**

For each of the following sentences, identify the correct pronoun in parentheses. Then, tell whether the pronoun is used as the *subject, predicate nominative, direct object, indirect object,* or *object of a preposition.*

EXAMPLE   **1.** Say hello to (*she, her*) and Anna.
            1. *her—object of a preposition*

1. Tulips surround (*we, us*) during May in Holland, Michigan.
2. The audience clapped for Rudy and (*he, him*).
3. The best singer in the choir is (*she, her*).
4. The officer gave (*we, us*) girls a ride home.
5. I wrote a short story about my great-grandpa and (*he, him*) last week.
6. Daniel and (*me, I*) read a book about Pelé, the great soccer player.
7. Last year's winner was (*he, him*).
8. To (*who, whom*) did you send invitations?
9. Please tell me (*who, whom*) the girl in the yellow dress is.
10. (*We, Us*) sisters could help Dad with the dishes.

▶ REVIEW C   **Identifying Personal Pronouns and Their Uses**

Each sentence in the following paragraph contains at least one personal pronoun. Identify each personal pronoun and tell whether it is used as the *subject, predicate nominative, direct object, indirect object,* or *object of a preposition.*

EXAMPLE   [1] I enjoy watching Edward James Olmos in movies and television shows because he always plays such interesting characters.
            1. *I—subject; he—subject*

[1] The cowboy in this picture from the movie *The Ballad of Gregorio Cortez* is he. [2] In the movie, he plays an innocent man hunted by Texas Rangers. [3] The film will give you a good idea of Olmos's acting talents. [4] After I saw him in this movie, I wanted to know more about him. [5] A librarian gave me a book of modern biographies. [6] I read that Olmos's father came from Mexico but that the actor was born in Los Angeles. [7] Growing up, Olmos faced the problems of poverty and gang violence, but he overcame them. [8] Before becoming a successful actor, he played baseball, sang in a band, and moved furniture. [9] In 1978, Olmos's role in the play *Zoot Suit* gave him the big break he needed in show business. [10] Later, the movie *Stand and Deliver*, in which he played math teacher Jaime Escalante, earned him widespread praise.

REVIEW D **Using Correct Forms of Personal Pronouns**

Oh, no! Not *another* test on Friday! You were absent from school all last week, and you're just beginning to catch up. Somehow, you've got to convince your teacher to let you take the test next week. Write ten sentences stating your reasons why the teacher should postpone giving you the test. In your sentences, use at least five personal pronouns in the nominative case and five in the objective case. Underline each personal pronoun you use and be prepared to identify how each is used.

EXAMPLE   **1.** *I was sick last week, and studying for another test would give me eye strain.*

PICTURE THIS

You're a member of this berry-picking party in Massachusetts in 1873. While you're picking berries, everyone talks about all the delicious treats you'll make from the berries. When your bucket is full, you sit down in the shade to relax. You take your journal out of your lunch basket and begin jotting down some notes to help you remember the day. Write a journal entry about berry picking and your plans for this bucket of ripe berries. In your paragraph, use at least five personal pronouns in the nominative case and five in the objective case.

Subject: berry picking
Audience: yourself
Purpose: to record your experience; to plan

Review: Posttest

A. Proofreading for Correct Forms of Pronouns

Most of the following sentences contain at least one pronoun that has been used incorrectly. Identify each of these incorrect pronouns, and then give its correct form. If the sentence is correct, write *C*.

EXAMPLE **1. The teacher told Derek and I a funny story.**
1. *I—me*

1. That announcer always irritates my father and I.
2. The winners of the science fair were Felicia and he.
3. To who did you and Marie send flowers?
4. Us teammates have to stick together, right?
5. Aunt Ida bought we boys some boiled peanuts.
6. Coach Johnson said he was proud of Ling and I.
7. Is he the person who we met at Dan's party?
8. We split the pizza between he and I.
9. My grandmother and me enjoy the English custom of having afternoon tea.
10. The little boy asked Neil and him for help.

B. Identifying Correct Forms of Personal Pronouns

For each sentence in the following paragraph, choose the correct pronoun from the pair in parentheses.

EXAMPLE [1] **Mrs. Lang gave (*we, us*) third-period students a list of good books for summer reading.**
1. *us*

[11] Beth and (*I, me*) plan to read the first five books on Mrs. Lang's list soon. [12] We asked (*she, her*) for some more information about them. [13] (*She, Her*) said that *The Man Who Was Poe* is by Avi. [14] The author of *The True Confessions of Charlotte Doyle* is also (*he, him*). [15] We probably will like Avi's books because (*they, them*) combine fiction and history. [16] Both of (*we, us*) want to read *Where the Lilies Bloom* by Vera and Bill Cleaver, too. [17] Together, the two of (*they, them*) have written sixteen books for young readers. [18] The first book (*I, me*) am going to read is *Jacob Have I Loved* by Katherine Paterson. [19] But Beth said that *A Gathering of Days* by Joan W. Blos will be the first book for (*she, her*). [20] Mrs. Lang told Beth and (*I, me*) that our summer reading project is a good idea.

23 USING MODIFIERS CORRECTLY

Comparison and Placement

Diagnostic Test

A. Using the Correct Forms of Modifiers

The following sentences contain errors in the use of modifiers. Identify the error in each sentence. Then, revise the sentence, using the correct form of the modifier.

EXAMPLE **1.** I never get to have no fun.
      1. *never, no—I never get to have any fun.*

1. Of all the characters in the movie *Robin Hood,* the one played by Morgan Freeman is the most funniest.
2. Alan thinks that this dessert tastes gooder than the others.
3. I couldn't hardly believe she said that.
4. Yoshi is the tallest of the twins.
5. The movie made me curiouser about Spanish settlements in the Philippines.
6. The movie doesn't cost much, but I don't have no money.

7. They offer so many combinations that I don't know which one I like more.
8. The house on Drury Avenue is the one we like the bestest.
9. There's nothing I like to eat for supper more better than barbecued chicken.
10. Why doesn't the teacher give us questions that are more easier?

B. Correcting Misplaced and Dangling Modifiers

Each of the following sentences contains a misplaced or dangling modifier in italics. Revise each sentence so that it is clear and correct.

EXAMPLE   **1.** *Waiting at the curb for the bus,* a car splashed water on me.
     1. *While I was waiting at the curb for the bus, a car splashed water on me.*

11. *Looking in her purse,* two French francs and one Italian lira were all she found.
12. The library has several books about dinosaurs *in our school.*
13. *Sleeping soundly,* Howard woke his father when supper was ready.
14. The book is not in the library *that I wanted to read.*
15. Aunt Lucia sent away a coupon for a free recipe book *in a magazine.*
16. *Alarmed,* a sudden gust of wind swept through the camp and battered our tent.
17. *Left alone for the first time in his life,* a loud sound in the night scared my little brother.
18. *After eating all their food,* we put the cats outside.
19. *Often slaughtered for their tusks,* many African nations prohibit the hunting of elephants.
20. *Sitting in the bleachers,* the outfielder caught the ball right in front of us.

Good and *Well*

23a. Use *good* to modify a noun or a pronoun. Use *well* to modify a verb.

EXAMPLES   Whitney Houston's voice sounded very **good** to me. [*Good* modifies the noun *voice.*]
Whitney Houston sang the national anthem very **well.** [*Well* modifies the verb *sang.*]

Good should never be used to modify a verb.

NONSTANDARD   Paula does good in all her school subjects.
STANDARD   Paula does **well** in all her school subjects.
[*Well* modifies the verb *does.*]

NONSTANDARD   The mariachi band can play good.
STANDARD   The mariachi band can play **well.**
[*Well* modifies the verb *can play.*]

Well can be used as an adjective meaning "in good health" or "healthy."

EXAMPLES   Rammel feels **well** today. [Meaning "in good health," *well* modifies the noun *Rammel.*]

☞ REFERENCE NOTE: For more about *good* and *well,* see page 687.

> ORAL
> PRACTICE
> **Using *Well* Correctly**

Read the following sentences aloud, stressing the modifier *well.*

1. Everyone did *well* on the test.
2. We work *well* together.
3. Do you sing as *well* as your sister does?
4. I can't water-ski very *well.*
5. How *well* can you write?
6. All went *well* for the Korean gymnastics team.
7. Our class pictures turned out *well.*
8. The freshman goalie can block as *well* as the senior.

USAGE

▶ EXERCISE 1 **Using *Good* and *Well* Correctly**

Use *good* or *well* to complete each of the following sentences correctly.

EXAMPLE **1.** We danced ____ at the recital.
 1. *well*

1. Melba did not run as ____ during the second race.
2. The casserole tasted ____ to us.
3. How ____ does she play the part?
4. Everyone could hear the huge Swiss alphorn very ____ when the man played it.
5. He certainly looks ____ in spite of his illness.
6. I gave them directions as ____ as I could.
7. The children behaved very ____.
8. Bagels with cream cheese always taste ____ to him.
9. The debate did not go as ____ as we had hoped.
10. How ____ the pool looks on such a hot day!

Comparison of Modifiers

A *modifier* describes or limits the meaning of another word. The two kinds of modifiers—adjectives and adverbs—may be used to compare things. In making comparisons, adjectives and adverbs take different forms. The specific form that is used depends upon how many syllables the modifier has and how many things are being compared.

ADJECTIVES This building is **tall.** [no comparison]
This building is **taller** than that one. [one compared with another]
This building is the **tallest** one in the world. [one compared with many others]

ADVERBS I ski **frequently.** [no comparison]
I ski **more frequently** than she does. [one compared with another]
Of the three of us, I ski **most frequently.** [one compared with two others]

23b. The three degrees of comparison of modifiers are *positive, comparative*, and *superlative*.

POSITIVE	COMPARATIVE	SUPERLATIVE
weak	weaker	weakest
proudly	more proudly	most proudly
likely	less likely	least likely
bad	worse	worst

Regular Comparison

(1) Most one-syllable modifiers form their comparative and superlative degrees by adding *–er* and *–est*.

POSITIVE	COMPARATIVE	SUPERLATIVE
near	nearer	nearest
bright	brighter	brightest
brave	braver	bravest
dry	drier	driest

👉 REFERENCE NOTE: For guidelines on how to spell words when adding *–er* or *–est*, see pages 803–805.

(2) Some two-syllable modifiers form their comparative and superlative degrees by adding *–er* and *–est*. Other two-syllable modifiers form their comparative and superlative degrees by using *more* and *most*.

POSITIVE	COMPARATIVE	SUPERLATIVE
simple	simpler	simplest
healthy	healthier	healthiest
clearly	more clearly	most clearly
often	more often	most often

When you are not sure about which way a two-syllable modifier forms its degrees of comparison, look up the word in a dictionary.

(3) Modifiers that have three or more syllables form their comparative and superlative degrees by using *more* and *most*.

POSITIVE	COMPARATIVE	SUPERLATIVE
important	more important	most important
creative	more creative	most creative
happily	more happily	most happily
accurately	more accurately	most accurately

USAGE

▶ EXERCISE 2 **Forming the Degrees of Comparison of Modifiers**

Give the forms for the comparative and superlative degrees of the following modifiers.

EXAMPLE **1. long**
       1. *longer; longest*

1. slow   **5.** possible   **9.** seriously
2. cautiously   **6.** short   **10.** loyal
3. early   **7.** easy
4. thankful   **8.** confident

(4) To show decreasing comparisons, all modifiers form their comparative and superlative degrees with *less* and *least*.

POSITIVE	COMPARATIVE	SUPERLATIVE
safe	less safe	least safe
expensive	less expensive	least expensive
often	less often	least often
gracefully	less gracefully	least gracefully

EXERCISE 3 **Using Comparison Forms of Adjectives**

Just look up in any big city and you'll see skyscrapers. They've towered over cities since the 1930s. Skyscrapers have been built all over the world, but the tallest ones are in the United States. The chart below contains information about seven skyscrapers. Use this information to write five sentences comparing these skyscrapers. Use three comparative and two superlative forms of adjectives. Also, make one of your sentences a decreasing comparison, using *less* or *least*. Underline the adjectives you use.

EXAMPLES **1.** *The Empire State Building is* <u>*taller*</u> *than the John Hancock Center.*
2. *Of the seven buildings, the Pittsburgh Plate Glass Building has the* <u>*least*</u> *number of stories.*

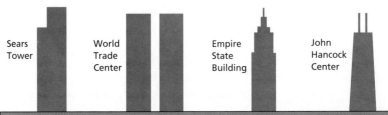

Sears Tower   World Trade Center   Empire State Building   John Hancock Center

SOME INTERESTING SKYSCRAPERS		
Building	Height	Year Completed
Sears Tower, Chicago, IL	110 stories (1,454 feet)	1974
World Trade Center, New York City, NY	110 stories (1,350 feet)	1976
Empire State Building, New York City, NY	102 stories	1931
John Hancock Center, Chicago, IL	100 stories	1969
Chrysler Building, New York City, NY	77 stories	1930
One Liberty Place, Philadelphia, PA	61 stories	1987
Pittsburgh Plate Glass, Pittsburgh, PA	40 stories	1983

USAGE

Irregular Comparison

Some modifiers do not form their comparative and superlative degrees by using the regular methods.

POSITIVE	COMPARATIVE	SUPERLATIVE
far	farther	farthest
good	better	best
well	better	best
many	more	most
much	more	most

 REVIEW A

Forming the Comparative and Superlative Degrees of Modifiers

Give the forms for the comparative and superlative degrees of the following modifiers.

EXAMPLE **1.** wasteful
 1. *more (less) wasteful; most (least) wasteful*

1. sheepish	**6.** quick	**11.** furious	**16.** hot
2. simply	**7.** weary	**12.** enthusiastic	**17.** good
3. much	**8.** easily	**13.** suddenly	**18.** well
4. surely	**9.** many	**14.** frequently	**19.** bad
5. gracious	**10.** tasty	**15.** generous	**20.** old

Use of Comparative and Superlative Forms

23c. Use the comparative degree when comparing two things. Use the superlative degree when comparing more than two.

COMPARATIVE The second problem is **harder** than the first.
 Luisa can perform the gymnastic routine **more gracefully** than I.
 Of the two tape players, this one costs **less**.

USAGE

SUPERLATIVE   Mount Everest is the world's **highest** mountain peak.
This is the **most valuable** coin in my collection.
Of the three dogs, that one barks the **least.**

Avoid the common mistake of using the superlative degree to compare two things.

NONSTANDARD   Of the two plans, this is the best one.
STANDARD   Of the two plans, this is the **better** one.

NONSTANDARD   Felicia is the youngest of the two girls.
STANDARD   Felicia is the **younger** of the two girls.

▶ EXERCISE 4   **Proofreading for Correct Use of Comparative and Superlative Forms**

Some sentences in the following paragraph contain incorrect uses of comparative and superlative forms. For each incorrect form, give the correct form. If a sentence is correct, write *C*.

EXAMPLE   [1] My family spends the most time preparing for Cinco de Mayo than any other family on our block.
   1. *the most—more*

[1] My parents work even more hard than I do to prepare for the holiday. [2] But I get more excited about the parade and festivals. [3] I think Cinco de Mayo is the bestest holiday of the year. [4] At least it's the more lively one in our San Antonio neighborhood. [5] Of all the speakers each year, my father always gives the more stirring speech about the history of the day. [6] Cinco de Mayo celebrates Mexico's most important victory over Napoleon III of France. [7] For me, the better part of the holiday is singing and dancing in the parade. [8] I get to wear the beautifulest dresses you've ever seen. [9] They're even more fancy than the ones worn by the girls in the picture on the next page. [10] Although these white dresses are certainly pretty, they are also less colorful than mine.

23d. Include the word *other* or *else* when comparing a member of a group with the rest of the group.

NONSTANDARD   Jupiter is larger than any planet in the solar system. [Jupiter is one of the planets in the solar system and cannot be larger than itself.]

STANDARD   Jupiter is larger than any **other** planet in the solar system.

NONSTANDARD   Roland can keyboard faster than anyone in his computer class. [Roland is one of the students in his computer class and cannot keyboard faster than himself.]

STANDARD   Roland can keyboard faster than anyone **else** in his computer class.

23e. Avoid using double comparisons.

A *double comparison* is the use of both *–er* and *more* (*less*) or both *–est* and *most* (*least*) to form a degree of comparison. For each degree, comparisons should be formed in only one of these two ways, not both.

NONSTANDARD   The Asian elephant is more smaller than the African elephant.

STANDARD   The Asian elephant is **smaller** than the African elephant.

NONSTANDARD   Ribbon Falls, in Yosemite National Park, is the most beautifulest waterfall I have ever seen.

STANDARD   Ribbon Falls, in Yosemite National Park, is the **most beautiful** waterfall I have ever seen.

EXERCISE 5   **Using the Degrees of Comparison Correctly**

Most of the following sentences contain incorrect forms of comparison. Revise each incorrect sentence, using the correct form. If a sentence is correct, write *C*.

EXAMPLE   **1.** It's the most homeliest dog in the world.
1. *It's the homeliest dog in the world.*

1. Juanita, the pitcher, is worse at bat than any member of the team.
2. The most largest ancient cliff dwellings in Arizona are in Navajo National Monument.
3. That modern sculpture is the most strangest I've ever seen.
4. After watching the two kittens for a few minutes, Rudy chose the most playful one.
5. This morning was more sunnier than this afternoon.
6. Your cough sounds worser today.
7. The music on this album is better for dancing than the music on that one.
8. New York City has a larger population than any city in the United States.
9. Karl likes German sauerkraut more better than Korean kimchi.
10. She was the most talented singer in the show.

EXERCISE 6   **Using Comparisons Correctly in Sentences**

You've been elected president of a new student organization, the We Care Club. Five committees—Environment,

Health, Education, Society, and Family and Friends— were created at the club's first meeting. Now you must appoint committee chairpersons. To help you decide, you're jotting down your thoughts about some possible candidates. Write five sentences comparing the people you consider worthy of each position. In each of your sentences, include the word *other* or *else*. Be sure to avoid double comparisons.

EXAMPLE **1.** *Ray Hampton understands health issues better than anyone else in our school.*

The Double Negative

23f. Avoid using double negatives.

A *double negative* is the use of two negative words to express one negative idea.

Common Negative Words			
barely	never	none	nothing
hardly	no	no one	nowhere
neither	nobody	not (–n't)	scarcely

NONSTANDARD We don't have no extra chairs.
STANDARD We have **no** extra chairs.
STANDARD We **don't** have any extra chairs.

NONSTANDARD He couldn't hardly talk.
STANDARD He **could hardly** talk.

▶ EXERCISE 7 **Correcting Double Negatives**

Revise each of the following sentences, eliminating the double negative.

EXAMPLE **1.** We don't hardly have time to relax.
           1. *We hardly have time to relax.*

1. Josie hasn't never been to Tennessee.
2. Because of the heavy rain, we couldn't scarcely find our way home.
3. He never had no problem with public speaking.
4. The athletes don't hardly have a break between events.
5. The authorities don't allow no passenger cars on Michigan's popular Mackinac Island.
6. By the time I had made sandwiches for everyone else, I didn't have nothing left for me.
7. I never listen to no one who gossips.
8. Your answer doesn't make no difference to me.
9. Don't never say *not* and *scarcely* together.
10. The goalie doesn't have no excuse.

PICTURE THIS

You're the traffic reporter for a local radio station. From the station's helicopter, you give brief, live reports on rush hour traffic. It's almost 5:30 P.M., and this is how the freeway looks. Write a news report about the traffic. In

your report, use at least five of the common negative words listed on page 665. Be sure to avoid using any double negatives.

Subject: traffic report
Audience: radio listeners
Purpose: to inform motorists of traffic conditions

 REVIEW B   **Using Modifiers Correctly**

Most of the following sentences contain errors in the use of modifiers. Revise each incorrect sentence, eliminating the error. If a sentence is correct, write *C*.

EXAMPLE **1.** We don't never stay after school.
           1. *We never stay after school.*

1. Which did you like best—the book or the movie?
2. Gina has more ideas for the festival than anyone.
3. The Suez Canal is more longer than the Panama Canal.
4. I can't hardly reason with her.
5. Jean and Dominic work good as a team.
6. Benita's bruise looks worse today than it did yesterday.
7. They haven't said nothing to us about it.
8. Of the two singers, Natalie Cole has the best voice.
9. Which has better sound, your stereo or mine?
10. The cast performed extremely well.

 REVIEW C   **Proofreading for Correct Use of Modifiers**

Most of the following sentences contain errors in the use of modifiers. If a sentence contains an error, give the correct form of the modifier. If a sentence is correct, write *C*.

EXAMPLE **1.** Of the three programs, the one on Japanese plays was the more interesting.

    1. *more—most*

1. Before the program, I didn't hardly know anything about Japanese theater.
2. I learned that Japanese theater is much more old than theater in many other countries.
3. *No* and *Kabuki* are the two most best-known kinds of Japanese drama.
4. Dating from the Middle Ages, *no* is different from any form of Japanese theater.
5. *No* plays, which are narrated in an ancient language, are performed more slowly than *Kabuki* plays.
6. *No* plays are seen lesser often than the more modern *Kabuki* plays.
7. In the West, we don't have no theater like Japan's *Bugaku* for the Imperial Court.
8. I was more interested in Japan's puppet theater, the *bunraku*, than anyone in my class.
9. Puppet theater performers have a more harder job than other theater performers.
10. I didn't never know that it takes three people to operate one puppet.

Placement of Modifiers

Notice how the meaning of the following sentence changes when the position of the phrase *from Canada* changes.

> The professor **from Canada** gave a televised lecture on famous writers. [The phrase modifies *professor.*]
> The professor gave a televised lecture on famous writers **from Canada**. [The phrase modifies *writers.*]
> The professor gave a televised lecture **from Canada** on famous writers. [The phrase modifies *gave.*]

23g. Place modifying words, phrases, and clauses as close as possible to the words they modify.

A modifier that seems to modify the wrong word in a sentence is called a *misplaced modifier.* A modifier that does not clearly modify another word in a sentence is called a *dangling modifier.*

MISPLACED	My aunt has almost seen all of the documentaries directed by Camille Billops.
CORRECT	My aunt has seen **almost** all of the documentaries directed by Camille Billops.
DANGLING	While vacationing in Mexico, snorkeling was the most fun.
CORRECT	**While vacationing in Mexico,** we had the most fun snorkeling.

USAGE

▶ EXERCISE 8   **Correcting Errors with Modifiers**

Revise each incorrect sentence to eliminate the misplaced or dangling modifier in italics. You may need to add, delete, or rearrange words. If a sentence is correct, write *C.*

EXAMPLE   **1.** *Surprised,* the finish line was only fifty yards away!
          1. *I was surprised that the finish line was only fifty yards away!*

1. Both Dr. Albert Sabin and Dr. Jonas Salk succeeded in *almost* developing polio vaccines at the same time.
2. Kristi Yamaguchi won a gold medal in the 1992 Olympics, *which was for figure skating.*
3. *Looking out the airplane window,* the volcano seemed ready to erupt.
4. *As a new student,* the teacher introduced me to my classmates.
5. *Before eating supper,* your hands must be washed.
6. *Recognized as the first U.S. woman to earn an international pilot's license,* Bessie Coleman dreamed of starting a flying school for African Americans.
7. *Hot and tired,* cold water was what the team needed.

8. Did you look for the black-and-white photographs taken by Grandfather *in that old shoebox*?
9. My uncle got a guide dog from Canine Assistants *that could open cabinets, pull a wheelchair, and go for help.*
10. *Thrilled,* my sister's face lit up when she saw her present.

◢ Prepositional Phrases

A *prepositional phrase* begins with a preposition and ends with a noun or a pronoun.

☞ REFERENCE NOTE: For more information about prepositions, see pages 474–477. For more discussion of prepositional phrases, see pages 475–476 and 506–509.

A prepositional phrase used as an adjective should be placed directly after the word it modifies.

MISPLACED	This book describes Nat Turner's struggle for freedom **by Judith Berry Griffin.**
CORRECT	This book **by Judith Berry Griffin** describes Nat Turner's struggle for freedom.

A prepositional phrase used as an adverb should be placed near the word it modifies.

MISPLACED	Spanish explorers discovered gold along the river that runs near my house **during the 1500s.**
CORRECT	**During the 1500s,** Spanish explorers discovered gold along the river that runs near my house.
CORRECT	Spanish explorers discovered gold **during the 1500s** along the river that runs near my house.

Avoid placing a prepositional phrase where it can modify either of two words. Place the phrase so that it clearly modifies the word you intend it to modify.

MISPLACED	Emily said **in the morning** it might get colder. [Does the phrase modify *said* or *might get?*]
CORRECT	Emily said it might get colder **in the morning.** [The phrase modifies *might get.*]
CORRECT	**In the morning** Emily said it might get colder. [The phrase modifies *said.*]

USAGE

| EXERCISE 9 | **Correcting Misplaced Prepositional Phrases** |

Find the misplaced prepositional phrases in the following sentences. Then, revise each sentence, placing the phrase near the word it modifies.

EXAMPLE **1.** I read that a satellite was launched in the news today.
      1. *I read in the news today that a satellite was launched.*

1. The nature photographer told us about filming a herd of water buffalo in class today.
2. The quick steps of the Texas clog-dancing teams amazed us on the wooden stage.
3. The robotic mannequins drew a huge crowd in the futuristic window display.
4. Many people watched the Fourth of July fireworks in their cars.
5. For my history report, I read three magazine articles on the Statue of Liberty.
6. My aunt has promised me on Saturday that she will take me to the symphony.
7. There is one gymnast who can tumble as well as vault on our gymnastics team.
8. That man bought the rare painting of Pocahontas with the briefcase.
9. The model posed gracefully in front of the statue in the designer gown.
10. We saw the trapeze artist swinging dangerously through our field binoculars.

Participial Phrases

A *participial phrase* consists of a verb form—either a present participle or a past participle—and its related words. A participial phrase modifies a noun or a pronoun.

👉 REFERENCE NOTE: For more information about participial phrases, see pages 515–516. For guidelines on using commas with participial phrases, see pages 747–748 and 753.

USAGE

Like a prepositional phrase, a participial phrase should be placed as close as possible to the word it modifies.

MISPLACED   Bandits chased the stagecoach **yelling wildly.**
  CORRECT   **Yelling wildly,** bandits chased the stagecoach.

MISPLACED   The vase was lying on the floor **broken into many pieces.**
  CORRECT   The vase, **broken into many pieces,** was lying on the floor.

To correct a dangling participial phrase, supply a word that the phrase can modify, or change the phrase to a clause.

DANGLING   **Jogging down the sidewalk,** my ankle was sprained.
  CORRECT   **Jogging down the sidewalk,** I sprained my ankle.
  CORRECT   I sprained my ankle **when I was jogging down the sidewalk.**

DANGLING   **Dressed in warm clothing,** the cold was no problem.
  CORRECT   **Dressed in warm clothing,** we had no problem with the cold.
  CORRECT   **Since we were dressed in warm clothing,** the cold was no problem.

EXERCISE 10   **Correcting Misplaced and Dangling Participial Phrases**

Revise each incorrect sentence to eliminate the misplaced or dangling modifier. You may need to add, delete, or rearrange words. If a sentence is correct, write C.

EXAMPLE   **1.** Dressed in our clown costumes, the police officer waved and smiled.
       1. *Seeing us dressed in our clown costumes, the police officer waved and smiled.*

1. Standing on the dock, the boat didn't look seaworthy to the sailors.
2. Pat found a secret passage exploring the old house.
3. Having brought in plenty of firewood, the cabin soon warmed up, and we fell asleep.

4. Wanting to see more of Mexico City, our vacation grew from one to two weeks.
5. Questioned by reporters, the governor's view on the matter became clear.
6. Suffering from blisters, the runner's chance of winning was slight.
7. Reading a book, my cat crawled into my lap.
8. The old suit hanging in the closet would make the perfect costume for the play.
9. Balancing precariously on the wire, the tricks that the tightrope walker performed were amazing.
10. Exhausted after hiking in the Florida Everglades, a tall, cool glass of water was a welcome sight.

Adjective Clauses

An *adjective clause* is a subordinate clause that modifies a noun or a pronoun. Most adjective clauses begin with a relative pronoun—*that, which, who, whom,* or *whose.*

☞ REFERENCE NOTE: For more information about adjective clauses, see pages 538–540. For more information about punctuating adjective clauses, see pages 747–748.

Like an adjective phrase, an adjective clause should be placed directly after the word it modifies.

MISPLACED His parents traded an old television for a new tape recorder **that they no longer wanted.** [Did his parents no longer want a new tape recorder?]

CORRECT His parents traded an old television **that they no longer wanted** for a new tape recorder.

MISPLACED The book was about insects **that we read.** [Did we read the insects?]

CORRECT The book **that we read** was about insects.

▶ EXERCISE 11 **Correcting Misplaced Adjective Clauses**

Find the misplaced adjective clauses in the following sentences. Then, revise each sentence, placing the clause near the word it modifies.

EXAMPLE **1.** I retyped the first draft on clean paper which I had corrected.
1. *I retyped the first draft, which I had corrected, on clean paper.*

1. The boy is from my school that won the contest.
2. We tiptoed over the ice in our heavy boots, which had begun to crack.
3. The jade sculpture was by a famous Chinese artist that my cousin broke.
4. We sometimes play soccer in one of the parks on nice days that are near the school.
5. Did that telethon achieve its goal that was on for thirty-six hours?
6. Nisei Week is in August, which is celebrated by Japanese Americans in Los Angeles.
7. The friendly man said hello to my mother, whose name I can't remember.
8. The sweater belongs to my best friend that has a V-shaped neck.
9. My married sister has the flu who lives in Ohio.
10. The documentary was filmed in several countries which will be broadcast in the fall.

▶ REVIEW D **Proofreading for Misplaced and Dangling Modifiers**

Most sentences in the following paragraph contain misplaced or dangling modifiers. They may be words, prepositional phrases, participial phrases, or adjective clauses. Revise each sentence that contains a misplaced or dangling modifier. If a sentence is correct, write *C*.

EXAMPLE [1] Living in cold and treeless areas, snow houses are built by some Native Arctic people.
1. *Living in cold and treeless areas, some Native Arctic people build snow houses.*

[1] You've probably seen pictures of houses built of snow on television. [2] Knowing that these houses are igloos, other facts about them may be new to you. [3] At one time, the word *igloo*, which means "shelter,"

applied to all types of houses. [4] However, *igloo* has come to mean houses now built of snow. [5] Used only during the winter, large blocks of snow are stacked together in building igloos. [6] Adapting to their environment long ago, snow houses provided protection against the bitter cold. [7] Look at this drawing, which shows three steps in the building of an igloo. [8] First, blocks are cut by the builders of snow. [9] Arranged in a circle about ten feet across, the builders slant the blocks inward. [10] The finished igloo that you see is dome-shaped and has a hole at the top.

▶ REVIEW E   **Using Modifiers Correctly**

In each of the following sentences, a modifier is used incorrectly. The mistake may result from (1) a confusion of *good* and *well*, (2) an incorrect comparison, (3) the use of a double negative, or (4) a misplaced or dangling modifier. Revise each sentence so that it is clear and correct.

EXAMPLE   **1.** This is the most interesting of the two articles.
           1. *This is the more interesting of the two articles.*

1. During last night's concert, the singing group was protected from being swarmed by guards.

2. The group played before an extremely enthusiastic crowd performing most of their old hits as well as several new tunes.
3. Years ago the singers wore strange costumes and makeup so that fans couldn't hardly tell what their faces looked like.
4. Bored, these gimmicks no longer appealed to the fans after a while.
5. They finally chose the most simply tailored look of the two they had considered.
6. Charmed by the group's new look, a change in their singing style was barely noticed by the fans.
7. Few fans could tell the first time they appeared in public after changing their style how nervous the singers were.
8. "That was the most scariest performance of my career," one singer remarked.
9. Cheering heartily, the singers' fears were relieved.
10. Both the concert and the picnic did exceptionally good at raising funds.

WRITING APPLICATION

Placing Modifying Phrases and Clauses Correctly

Have you ever put together a jigsaw puzzle? Each piece must fit in the right place. If the pieces don't fit properly, the picture appears jumbled. You can think of a sentence as a jigsaw puzzle. The words in the sentence—including any modifying phrases and clauses—are the puzzle pieces. For the sentence to make sense, the words must go in the right places.

MISPLACED   The fans supported the batter cheering and singing.

CORRECT   Cheering and singing, the fans supported the batter.

What kind of picture do you get from the first sentence? from the second sentence? ·

▶ WRITING ACTIVITY

You've just received a letter from a favorite aunt who is a professional athlete. She wants to hear about your sports activities and any sports events you've participated in or seen in person or on television. Write a letter to your aunt, telling her about sports you have been playing and watching. You may also want to make some predictions about upcoming events. Be sure to place modifying phrases and clauses correctly.

Prewriting You'll first need to choose a sports activity or event to write about. You may write about your own experiences in a school or community sport or about a sports event you've seen. Or you may use your imagination. You could look at the sports section of a newspaper for some ideas. Before you begin writing, make notes about the activity or event you find most interesting.

Writing As you write your first draft, try to include specific details that will interest your aunt. Organize your letter so that the details are clear and logical. Be sure to place modifying phrases and clauses as close as possible to the words they modify.

Evaluating and Revising Read over your finished letter. Is it interesting and lively? If not, revise it by adding more adjectives, adverbs, and action verbs to improve your descriptions. Underline all of the prepositional phrases, participial phrases, and adjective clauses. Check to make sure that they are correctly placed near the words they modify.

Proofreading Check your letter for errors in spelling and punctuation, especially in the address, salutation, and closing. For guidelines on correctly capitalizing and punctuating these parts of a personal letter, see pages 726, 739, and 754–755.

Review: Posttest

A. Using the Correct Forms of Modifiers

Most of the sentences in the following paragraphs contain errors in the use of modifiers. Identify each error; then, revise the sentence, using the correct form of the modifier. If a sentence is correct, write C.

EXAMPLE   [1] I didn't want to live nowhere else.
1. *didn't, nowhere—I didn't want to live anywhere else.*

[1] The wonderfullest place in the whole world is my grandmother's house. [2] We used to live there before we got an apartment of our own. [3] Since her house is bigger than any house in the neighborhood, we all had plenty of room. [4] Grandma was glad to have us stay because my dad can fix things so that they're gooder than new. [5] He plastered and painted the walls in one bedroom so that I wouldn't have to share a room no more with my sister. [6] I don't know which was best—having so much space of my own or having privacy from my sister.

[7] My grandmother can sew better than anybody can. [8] She taught my sister and me how to make the beautifullest clothes. [9] She has three sewing machines and my mother has one, but I like Grandma's oldest one better. [10] We started with the more simpler kinds of stitches. [11] After we could do those, Grandma showed us fancier stitches and sewing tricks. [12] For instance, she taught us to wrap thread behind buttons we sew on, so that they will be more easier to button. [13] We learned how to make dresses, skirts, blouses, and all sorts of other things, until now there isn't hardly nothing we can't make.

[14] I was sad when we left Grandma's house, but I like our new apartment more better than I thought I would. [15] Luckily, we moved to a place near my grandmother's, and after school I can go over there or go home— whichever I want to do most.

B. Correcting Misplaced and Dangling Modifiers

Each of the following sentences contains a misplaced or a dangling modifier. Revise each sentence so that it is clear and correct.

EXAMPLE **1.** Tearing away his umbrella, Mr. Pérez became drenched in the storm.
       1. *Tearing away his umbrella, the storm drenched Mr. Pérez.*

16. Our math teacher told us that she had been a nurse yesterday.
17. We read a story written by Jade Snow Wong in class.
18. Destroyed by the fire, the man looked sadly at the charred house.
19. After missing the school bus, my mother gave me a ride in the car.
20. The fox escaped from the hounds pursuing it with a crafty maneuver.
21. Walking through the park, the squirrels chattered at me.
22. The cook will win a new oven that makes the best German potato salad.
23. The squid fascinated the students preserved in formaldehyde.
24. Keeping track of the race with binoculars, the blue car with a yellow roof pulled into the lead.
25. We watched the snow pile up in drifts inside our warm house.

USAGE

24 A GLOSSARY OF USAGE

Common Usage Problems

Diagnostic Test

Identifying and Correcting Errors in Usage

One sentence in each of the following sets contains an error in usage. Choose the letter of the sentence that contains an error. Then revise the sentence, using standard English.

EXAMPLE   **1. a.** I rode a unicycle.
      b. Everyone came except Michael.
      c. What are the side affects of this medicine?
      1. *c. What are the side effects of this medicine?*

  1. a. They bought themselves new pens.
     b. The balloon busted.
     c. Use less flour.
  2. a. She did not feel well.
     b. Leo ought to help us.
     c. Armando hisself bought that.

3. **a.** Jerome could of come.
   b. This book has fewer pages.
   c. He sang well.
4. **a.** We had already been there.
   b. She feels alright now.
   c. We looked everywhere for him.
5. **a.** He behaved badly.
   b. She felt badly about being late.
   c. There is no talking between classes.
6. **a.** We saved ten dollars between the four of us.
   b. Bring a salad when you come.
   c. The chair broke.
7. **a.** She set down.
   b. This news may affect his decision.
   c. They left less milk for me.
8. **a.** I cannot go unless I finish my work first.
   b. Your my friend.
   c. She laid the packages on the table.
9. **a.** My father use to play the piano.
   b. We have a long way to go.
   c. Yesterday I read in the newspaper that Jesse Jackson is in town.
10. **a.** I know how come she left.
    b. It's windy.
    c. He likes this kind of movie.
11. **a.** I am somewhat hungry.
    b. Will you learn me how to ski?
    c. Do as the leader does.
12. **a.** She looks as though she is exhausted.
    b. Meet me outside of the building.
    c. He wrote the letter and mailed it.
13. **a.** The reason that he works is that he wants to save money for a trip.
    b. Your backhand has improved somewhat.
    c. Their are not enough chairs.
14. **a.** I just bought those shoes.
    b. This here ride is broken.
    c. Try to relax.

USAGE

USAGE

15. **a.** I am real happy.
   b. Let's study now and go outside later.
   c. They're new in school.
16. **a.** Take the report when you go.
   b. She might have gone.
   c. Mr. Bennigan he is my English teacher.
17. **a.** We worked for a hour.
   b. She accepted your invitation.
   c. They can hardly see the sign.
18. **a.** Where do you study?
   b. Divide the tasks among the two of us.
   c. If he had been there, I would have seen him.
19. **a.** You should have come.
   b. Less sugar is needed.
   c. It's pedal is stuck.
20. **a.** He likes these kinds of ties.
   b. It looks like a rabbit.
   c. The submarine slowly raised to the surface.

This chapter contains an alphabetical list of common problems in English usage. You will notice throughout the chapter that some examples are labeled *standard* or *nonstandard*. **Standard English** is the most widely accepted form of English. It is used in *formal* situations, such as in speeches and compositions for school, and in *informal* situations, such as in conversation and everyday writing. **Nonstandard English** is language that does not follow the rules and guidelines of standard English.

☞ REFERENCE NOTE: For more discussion of standard and nonstandard English, see page 394.

a, an Use *a* before words beginning with a consonant sound. Use *an* before words beginning with a vowel sound.

EXAMPLES   He did not consider himself **a** hero.
Market Avenue is **a** one-way street.
An oryx is a large antelope.
We waited in line for **an** hour.

accept, except *Accept* is a verb that means "to receive." *Except* may be either a verb or a preposition. As a verb, *except* means "to leave out" or "to exclude"; as a preposition, *except* means "other than" or "excluding."

EXAMPLES I **accept** your apology.
Some students will be **excepted** from this assignment.
Mark has told all his friends **except** Diego.

affect, effect *Affect* is a verb meaning "to influence." *Effect* used as a verb means "to bring about." Used as a noun, *effect* means "the result of some action."

EXAMPLES His score on this test will **affect** his final grade.
Bo and Anica's hard work **effected** a solution to the problem.
The **effects** of the medicine were immediate.

ain't Avoid this word in speaking and writing; it is nonstandard English.

all ready, already *All ready* means "completely prepared." *Already* means "previously."

EXAMPLES The mechanic checked the engine parts to make sure they were **all ready** for assembly.
We have **already** served the refreshments.

all right Used as an adjective, *all right* means "unhurt" or "satisfactory." Used as an adverb, *all right* means "well enough." *All right* should always be written as two words.

EXAMPLES Your work is **all right.** [adjective]
Linda fell off the horse, but she is **all right.** [adjective]
You did **all right** at the track meet. [adverb]

a lot *A lot* should always be written as two words.

EXAMPLE Her family donated **a lot** of money to the Red Cross.

NOTE: Many writers overuse *a lot*. Whenever you run across *a lot* as you revise your own writing, try to replace it with a more exact word or phrase.

EXAMPLE The Spaniards explored a lot of North America and South America.
The Spaniards explored vast areas [or *millions of square miles*] of North America and South America.

among See **between, among.**

anywheres, everywheres, nowheres, somewheres Use these words without the final *s*.

EXAMPLE I didn't go **anywhere** [not *anywheres*] yesterday.

as See **like, as.**

as if See **like, as if, as though.**

at Do not use *at* after *where.*

NONSTANDARD Where is it at?
STANDARD Where is it?

bad, badly *Bad* is an adjective. *Badly* is an adverb.

EXAMPLES The fish tastes **bad.** [*Bad* modifies the noun *fish.*]
The boy's wrist was sprained **badly.** [*Badly* modifies the verb *was sprained.*]

NOTE: In informal usage the expression "feel badly" has become acceptable, though ungrammatical, English.

INFORMAL Marcia felt badly about her low grade.
FORMAL Marcia felt **bad** about her low grade.

▶ EXERCISE 1 **Identifying Correct Usage**

Choose the correct word or expression from the pair in parentheses in each of the following sentences.

EXAMPLE 1. Korea has been in the news (*alot, a lot*) in recent years.
1. *a lot*

1. South Korea occupies the lower half of (*a, an*) peninsula between China and Japan.
2. According to an old Korean saying, you are never out of sight of mountains (*anywheres, anywhere*) in Korea.
3. The 1988 Olympic games in Seoul had a dramatic (*affect, effect*) on Korea's world image.
4. I looked on a map to find out where Korea's Lotte World (*is, is at*).
5. That unique cultural and athletic showcase is (*a, an*) attraction to visitors in Seoul.
6. Many Koreans come to the United States to join family members who (*all ready, already*) live here.
7. In Korea girls practice on their neighborhood swings so that they won't perform (*bad, badly*) in swinging contests during *Tano,* a spring festival.
8. Most boys hope they do (*allright, all right*) in *Tano* wrestling matches.
9. In 1446, King Sejong the Great required the Korean people to use a new alphabet, which scholars and government officials readily (*accepted, excepted*).
10. Even if you (*ain't, aren't*) interested in dancing, you'd probably enjoy watching the lively Korean folk dancers shown here.

USAGE

because See **reason . . . because.**

between, among Use *between* when referring to two things at a time, even though they may be part of a group containing more than two.

EXAMPLES   In homeroom, Carlos sits **between** Bob and me.
Some players practice **between** innings. [Although a game has more than two innings, the practice occurs only between any two of them.]

Use *among* when referring to a group rather than to separate individuals.

EXAMPLES   We saved ten dollars **among** the three of us. [As a group the three saved ten dollars.]
There was disagreement **among** the fans about the coach's decision. [The fans are thought of as a group.]

bring, take *Bring* means "to come carrying something." *Take* means "to go carrying something." Think of *bring* as related to *come* and of *take* as related to *go*.

EXAMPLES   **Bring** your skateboard when you come to my house this weekend.
Please **take** these letters to the post office when you go.

bust, busted Avoid using these words as verbs. Use a form of either *burst* or *break*.

EXAMPLES   The balloon **burst** [not *busted*] when it touched the ceiling.
The vase **broke** [not *busted*] when I dropped it.

could of Do not write *of* with the helping verb *could*. Write *could have*. Also avoid *ought to of, should of, would of, might of,* and *must of*.

EXAMPLE   Reva **could have** [not *could of*] played the piano.

Of is also unnecessary with *had.*

EXAMPLE   If I **had** [not *had of*] seen her, I would have said hello.

doesn't, don't   *Doesn't* is the contraction of *does not. Don't* is the contraction of *do not.* Use *doesn't,* not *don't,* with *he, she, it, this, that,* and singular nouns.

EXAMPLES   He **doesn't** [not *don't*] know how to swim.
The price **doesn't** [not *don't*] include tax.

effect   See **affect, effect.**

everywheres   See **anywheres,** etc.

except   See **accept, except.**

fewer, less   *Fewer* is used with plural words. *Less* is used with singular words. *Fewer* tells "how many"; *less* tells "how much."

EXAMPLES   We have **fewer** tickets to sell than we thought.
These plants require **less** water.

good, well   *Good* is always an adjective. Never use *good* as an adverb. Instead, use *well.*

NONSTANDARD   Nancy sang good at the audition.
STANDARD   Nancy sang **well** at the audition.

Although *well* is usually an adverb, *well* may also be used as an adjective to mean "healthy."

EXAMPLE   He didn't look **well** after eating the entire pizza all by himself.

NOTE: *Feel good* and *feel well* mean different things. *Feel good* means "to feel happy or pleased." *Feel well* means "to feel healthy."

EXAMPLES   I felt **good** [*happy*] when I got an A on my report.
He did not feel **well** [*healthy*] yesterday.

REFERENCE NOTE: For more information about the differences between *good* and *well,* see page 656.

USAGE

had of See **could of.**

had ought, hadn't ought Unlike other verbs, *ought* is not used with *had*.

NONSTANDARD   Eric had ought to help us; he hadn't ought to have missed our meeting yesterday.

STANDARD   Eric **ought to** help us; he **oughtn't to have** missed our meeting yesterday.

or

Eric **should** help us; he **shouldn't have** missed our meeting yesterday.

hardly, scarcely The words *hardly* and *scarcely* convey negative meanings. They should never be used with another negative word.

EXAMPLES   I **can** [not *can't*] **hardly** read your handwriting.
We **had** [not *hadn't*] **scarcely** enough food for everyone.

👉 REFERENCE NOTE: For more examples of double negatives, see page 665.

▶ EXERCISE 2   **Identifying Correct Usage**

Choose the correct word or expression from the pair in parentheses in each sentence.

EXAMPLE   **1.** When you come to my house, (*bring, take*) that interesting book about U.S. presidents.
1. *bring*

1. Theodore Roosevelt must have (*felt good, felt well*) about having the teddy bear named for him.
2. The letter *S* in Harry S Truman's name (*don't, doesn't*) stand for anything.
3. William Henry Harrison served as president (*fewer, less*) days than any other president.
4. Herbert Hoover (*could of, could have*) kept his presidential salary, but he gave it to charity.

5. A president who (*doesn't, don't*) throw the first ball of the baseball season breaks a tradition started in 1910.
6. Both Theodore Roosevelt and Franklin Roosevelt were presidents of the United States; (*between, among*) them, they served a total of twenty years in office.
7. Abraham Lincoln's ability to write (*well, good*) led to his success in politics.
8. Woodrow Wilson believed that countries (*had ought, ought*) to work together in the League of Nations.
9. I (*can hardly, can't hardly*) imagine a president training horses, but Ulysses S. Grant did.
10. When Zachary Taylor went to the White House, he (*brought, took*) his old war horse with him.

▶ REVIEW A **Correcting Errors in Usage**

Each sentence in the following paragraph contains at least one error in usage. Identify each error and write the correct form.

EXAMPLE   **1.** Between the various Native American peoples, there were alot of stories about mythological figures.

            1. *Between—Among; alot—a lot*

1. The Creek people believed that goblins, giants, and dwarfs effected their lives bad.
2. The Micmacs believed that a enormous being named Glooskap created humans and animals everywheres.
3. This picture shows how humans busted into life because of Glooskap's magic.

Wood engraving by Michael McCurdy.

USAGE

USAGE

4. The other animals don't appear to think that Glooskap's new creations are allright.
5. The Tehuelche people of South America tell the story of Elal, a hero who brought fire to where the people were at.
6. When the Mayas heard the thunderous approach of their god Chac, they knew he was taking rain to their fields.
7. The Pawnee people on the plains couldn't hardly help noticing where the stars were.
8. They told stories about Morning Star, who fought good and defeated star monsters.
9. One sad Tewa story is about Deer Hunter, who had ought to have excepted the death of his wife, White Corn Maiden.
10. Her death busted Deer Hunter's heart, causing him to disobey the laws of his people.

he, she, they Do not use an unnecessary pronoun after a noun. This error is called the *double subject.*

NONSTANDARD Nancy Lopez she is a famous professional golfer.

STANDARD Nancy Lopez is a famous professional golfer.

hisself *Hisself* is nonstandard English. Use *himself.*

EXAMPLE Ira bought **himself** [not *hisself*] a lavender polka-dot tie.

how come In informal situations, *how come* is often used instead of *why*. In formal situations, *why* should always be used.

INFORMAL I don't know how come she's not here.

FORMAL I don't know **why** she is not here.

its, it's *Its* is a personal pronoun in the possessive form. *It's* is a contraction of *it is* or *it has.*

EXAMPLES **Its** handle is broken. [possessive pronoun]
It's a hot day. [contraction of *it is*]
It's been a good trip. [contraction of *it has*]

PICTURE THIS

From your bedroom window, you see this amazing sight. The house across the street is lifting off into space! Up until now, the house has appeared to be perfectly normal. However, you have wondered about the house's new owners. You're excited and want to tell your friends all about the liftoff. You decide to jot down your impressions so that you won't forget anything later. Write a page of notes about the house and its strange liftoff. In your notes, use the possessive form *its* five times. Also, use the contraction *it's* (meaning "it is" or "it has") five times.

Subject: a house that lifts off into space
Audience: friends
Purpose: to record details and thoughts; to inform

USAGE

THE MYSTERIES OF HARRIS BURDICK by Chris Van Allsburg. Copyright © 1984 by Chris Van Allsburg. Reprinted by permission of Houghton Mifflin Company. All rights reserved.

kind, sort, type The words *this, that, these,* and *those* should agree in number with the words *kind, sort,* and *type.*

EXAMPLES Whitney likes **this kind** of music.
Those kinds of math problems are easy.

kind of, sort of In informal situations, *kind of* and *sort of* are often used to mean "somewhat" or "rather." In formal English, *somewhat* or *rather* is preferred.

INFORMAL He seemed kind of embarrassed by our compliments.
FORMAL He seemed **somewhat** embarrassed by our compliments.

learn, teach *Learn* means "to acquire knowledge." *Teach* means "to instruct" or "to show how."

EXAMPLES I am **learning** how to use this computer.
My father is **teaching** me how to use this computer.

less See **fewer, less.**

lie, lay See page 620.

like, as In informal situations, the preposition *like* is often used instead of the conjunction *as* to introduce a clause. In formal situations, *as* is preferred.

EXAMPLE I looked up several words in my dictionary, **as** [not *like*] the teacher had suggested.

☞ REFERENCE NOTE: For more information about clauses, see Chapter 18.

like, as if, as though In informal situations, the preposition *like* is often used for the compound conjunction *as if* or *as though.* In formal situations, *as if* or *as though* is preferred.

EXAMPLES They acted **as if** [not *like*] they hadn't heard him.
You looked **as though** [not *like*] you knew the answer.

> **EXERCISE 3** **Identifying Correct Usage**

Choose the correct word or expression from the pair in parentheses in each of the following sentences.

EXAMPLE **1.** I'd like to know (*how come, why*) folk tales about animals that play tricks have always been popular.
  1. *why*

1. People all over the world enjoy stories about a creature that outsmarts (*it's, its*) enemies.
2. (*These kind, These kinds*) of stories are known as trickster tales.
3. In the tales of Native Americans of the Southwest, (*Coyote, Coyote he*) is a trickster who causes disorder and confusion.
4. In one story, Coyote (*kind of, somewhat*) playfully scatters stars across the sky.
5. In South American tales, the trickster Fox talks (*like, as though*) he is clever, but he really isn't.
6. Fox doesn't even understand (*how come, why*) a vulture beats him in a tree-sitting contest.
7. Our teacher (*learned, taught*) us about Brer Rabbit, a famous trickster in African American folklore.
8. Brer Rabbit gets (*himself, hisself*) into a lot of trouble trying to trick Brer Fox.
9. In a funny tale from India, a monkey and a (*crocodile, crocodile they*) play tricks on each other.
10. Just (*as, like*) Aesop's tortoise defeats the hare, Toad wins a race against Donkey in a Jamaican tale.

> **EXERCISE 4** **Using Standard English in a Report**

As a Career Day project, you interviewed a crane operator at a construction site. The operator explained how the different parts of a boom crane work and gave you the drawing shown on the next page. The operator also talked about the hard work involved in moving construction materials. Write a brief report for your classmates, telling how a crane works and what its operator does. Use the

USAGE

drawing below, your memories of cranes you've seen, and your own storytelling abilities to write the report. In your report, use standard English to demonstrate any five of these glossary entries:

he, she, they	kind of, sort of
hisself	learn, teach
how come	lie, lay
its, it's	like, as
kind, sort, type	like, as if

EXAMPLE   *"This type of crane is fun but sometimes scary to operate," Mr. Arlen said.*

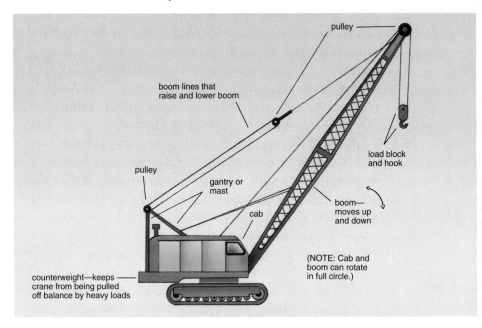

might of, must of See **could of.**

nowheres See **anywheres,** etc.

of Do not use *of* with other prepositions such as *inside*, *off*, and *outside*.

EXAMPLES   He quickly walked **off** [not *off of*] the stage.
She waited **outside** [not *outside of*] the school.
What is **inside** [not *inside of*] this large box?

ought to of See **could of.**

real In informal situations, *real* is often used as an adverb meaning "very" or "extremely." In formal situations, *very* or *extremely* is preferred.

> INFORMAL My mother is expecting a real important telephone call.
> FORMAL My mother is expecting a **very** important telephone call.

reason . . . because In informal situations, *reason . . . because* is often used instead of *reason . . . that.* In formal situations, use *reason . . . that,* or revise your sentence.

> INFORMAL The reason I did well on the test was because I had studied hard.
> FORMAL The **reason** I did well on the test was **that** I had studied hard.
> *or*
> I did well on the test **because** I had studied hard.

rise, raise See pages 622–623.

scarcely, hardly See **hardly, scarcely**

should of See **could of.**

sit, set See pages 618–619.

some, somewhat Do not use *some* for *somewhat* as an adverb.

> NONSTANDARD My math has improved some.
> STANDARD My math has improved **somewhat.**

somewheres See **anywheres,** etc.

sort See **kind, sort, type.**

sort of See **kind of, sort of.**

take See **bring, take.**

teach See **learn, teach.**

than, then *Than* is a conjunction; *then* is an adverb.

EXAMPLES Margo is a faster runner **than** I am.
First we went to the bookstore. **Then** we went to the library.

that See **who, which, that.**

that there See **this here, that there.**

their, there, they're *Their* is the possessive form of *they*. *There* is used to mean "at that place" or to begin a sentence. *They're* is a contraction of *they are*.

EXAMPLES **Their** team won the game.
We are planning to go **there** during spring vacation.
There were twenty people at the party.
They're the best players on the team.

theirself, theirselves *Theirself* and *theirselves* are nonstandard English. Use *themselves*.

EXAMPLE They bought **themselves** [not *theirself* or *theirselves*] a telescope.

them *Them* should not be used as an adjective. Use *those*.

EXAMPLE Karen gave you **those** [not *them*] cassettes yesterday.

this here, that there The words *here* and *there* are unnecessary after **this** and **that.**

EXAMPLE Do you like **this** [not *this here*] shirt or **that** [not *that there*] one?

this kind, sort, type See **kind,** etc.

try and In informal situations, *try and* is often used instead of *try to*. In formal situations, *try to* should be used.

INFORMAL Try and be on time for the party.
FORMAL **Try to** be on time for the party.

EXERCISE 5 **Identifying Correct Usage**

Choose the correct word or expression from the pair in parentheses in each of the following sentences.

EXAMPLE **1.** Athletes find the physical and mental challenges of their sports (*real, very*) exciting.
1. *very*

1. Yosemite Park Ranger Mark Wellman discovered new strengths (*inside of, inside*) himself when he climbed El Capitan.
2. Wellman, paralyzed from the waist down, was anxious to (*try and, try to*) climb the 3,595-foot rock.
3. In this picture, Wellman strains (*somewhat, some*) as he climbs the granite peak in 1989.

4. The reason Wellman was strong enough for the climb is (*because, that*) he had trained for a year.
5. Like Wellman, many people are able to swim, hike, cycle, and canoe in spite of (*there, their*) disabilities.
6. (*Them, Those*) newer, lighter, easier-to-use wheelchairs have helped many people enjoy a wider variety of sports activities.
7. Nowadays, national and state parks offer more services for physically challenged people (*than, then*) they used to offer.
8. (*This here, This*) magazine story lists dozens of sports organizations for athletes who have disabilities.

9. You (*might of, might have*) heard of the National Wheelchair Basketball Association, which sponsors teams and organizes tournaments.
10. Other athletes pride (*themselves, theirselves*) on being able to play wheelchair tennis.

use to, used to Be sure to add the *d* to *use*. *Used to* is the past form.

> EXAMPLE We **used to** [not *use to*] live in Phoenix, Arizona.

way, ways Use *way*, not *ways*, in referring to a distance.

> EXAMPLE They still had a long **way** [not *ways*] to go.

well See **good, well.**

when, where Do not use *when* or *where* incorrectly in writing a definition.

> NONSTANDARD In bowling, a "turkey" is when a person rolls three strikes in a row.
> STANDARD In bowling, a "turkey" is rolling three strikes in a row.

where Do not use *where* for *that*.

> EXAMPLE I read in our newspaper **that** [not *where*] Monica Seles won the tennis tournament.

who, which, that The relative pronoun *who* refers to people only; *which* refers to things only; *that* refers to either people or things.

> EXAMPLES Kim is the only one **who** got the right answer. [person]
> My bike, **which** has ten speeds, is for sale. [thing]
> He is the one person **that** can help you. [person]
> This is the ring **that** I want to buy. [thing]

who's, whose *Who's* is the contraction of *who is* or *who has*. *Whose* is the possessive form of *who*.

EXAMPLE **Who's** keeping score?
Who's been using my typewriter?
Whose baseball glove is this?

without, unless Do not use the preposition *without* in place of the conjunction *unless*.

EXAMPLE My mother said that I can't go to the game **unless** [not *without*] I finish my homework first.

would of See **could of.**

your, you're *Your* is the possessive form of *you. You're* is the contraction of *you are*.

EXAMPLES **Your** dinner is on the table.
You're one of my closest friends.

USAGE

▶ EXERCISE 6 **Identifying Correct Usage**

Choose the correct word or expression from the pair in parentheses in each sentence.

EXAMPLE **1.** I (*use, used*) to know the names of all thirty-three state birds.
1. *used*

1. You may have read (*where, that*) some states have the same state birds.
2. The mockingbird, (*who, which*) mimics other birds, is the state bird of Texas, Mississippi, Arkansas, Tennessee, and Florida.
3. "Mimicking" is (*when a person or an animal imitates another, imitating a person or an animal*).
4. (*Your, You're*) probably familiar with New Mexico's state bird, the roadrunner, from cartoons.
5. My grandfather, (*who's, whose*) a fisherman, often hears the loud calls of Minnesota's state bird, the common loon.
6. The bluebird, state bird of Missouri and New York, (*use, used*) to come around our house.

7. The spunky bird on this baseball player's cap represents both a state and a team quite (*good, well*).
8. (*Without, Unless*) I'm mistaken, you can guess what state claims the Baltimore oriole.
9. It travels a long (*way, ways*) between its summer and winter homes.
10. Would you (*of, have*) guessed that the cardinal is the official bird of the most states?

▶ REVIEW B   **Correcting Errors in Usage**

Most of the following sentences contain an error in usage. If a sentence contains an error, identify the error and write the correct form. If a sentence is correct, write *C*.

EXAMPLE   **1.** It was pirate Jean Laffite which established an early settlement on Texas' Galveston Island.
          1. *which—who (or that)*

1. Since ancient times, pirates they have terrorized the world's seas.
2. Bands of pirates use to build fortified hide-outs from which they attacked ships.
3. I once read where the Roman general Julius Caesar was captured by pirates.
4. My history teacher learned my class about pirates who disrupted shipping along the North African coast.

5. As you may have seen in movies, these pirates preyed upon African, European, and American ships.
6. During the 1600s and 1700s, pirates lived off of the South American coast.
7. One of these pirates, Sir William Kidd, was a real dangerous cutthroat on the Caribbean Sea.
8. You may be surprised to learn that two other fearsome pirates were women.
9. Anne Bonny and Mary Read attacked and robbed alot of ships on the Caribbean.
10. You may think that piracy is a thing of the past, but its still going on in some parts of the world.

WRITING APPLICATION

Using Formal Standard English in a Speech

Listen closely to the speech of a professional radio or TV broadcaster. Then, listen to the conversations of people around you. You'll likely discover quite a difference. On the air, broadcasters use formal standard English to set a serious, businesslike tone. In casual conversation, most people frequently use informal, sometimes even nonstandard, English.

Which of the following sounds like a real newscast?

NEWSCAST 1: At today's press conference, the mayor he was real optimistic about the new recycling program. According to him, if our town had started recycling last year, we could of saved more than $75,000 in landfill and disposal costs. The mayor admitted that recycling ain't a cure-all for our budget problems. But he stressed that these kind of savings takes some of the burden off of the backs of taxpayers.

NEWSCAST 2: At today's press conference, **the mayor** was **extremely** optimistic about the new recycling program. According to him, if our town had started recycling last year, we **could have** saved more than $75,000 in landfill and disposal costs. The mayor admitted that recycling **isn't** a cure-all for our budget problems. But he stressed that **this kind** of savings takes some of the burden **off** the backs of taxpayers.

Written in standard, formal English, Newscast 2 sounds more professional and more believable.

▣▶ WRITING ACTIVITY

A local radio station is sponsoring a speech contest for Earth Day. To enter, contestants must write a speech about an environmental issue. The speech should be no more than three minutes long. The winner gets to read his or her speech on the air. Write a speech for the contest. Use only formal English in your speech.

Prewriting You'll need to choose a specific topic about the environment. Is there an issue that you are especially concerned about? You might brainstorm some ideas with friends or family. You may wish to discuss one of the following subjects: local recycling efforts, pollution, endangered animals, or rain forests. When you've selected a topic, jot down some notes about it. List not only facts and information you've read or heard about the topic but also your feelings about it. Then, make an informal outline of what you want to say.

Writing Use your notes from the prewriting activities as you write the first draft of your speech. You'll want to have an introduction that catches people's attention. Make the main point of your speech very clear in a thesis statement early in your speech. Then, discuss each supporting point in a paragraph or two. Restate your main point in your conclusion. Time your speech to be sure it's no longer than three minutes.

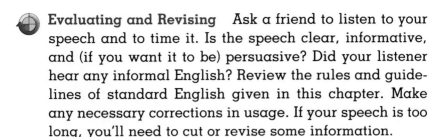

Evaluating and Revising   Ask a friend to listen to your speech and to time it. Is the speech clear, informative, and (if you want it to be) persuasive? Did your listener hear any informal English? Review the rules and guidelines of standard English given in this chapter. Make any necessary corrections in usage. If your speech is too long, you'll need to cut or revise some information.

Proofreading and Publishing   Read the speech to yourself and look for errors in subject-verb agreement. For more about subject-verb agreement, see pages 575–588. Be sure that you don't have any dangling or misplaced modifiers. For more on these, see pages 668–677. Publish your speech by recording it and playing it back for your class. If Earth Day is near, you could ask to read your speech at an Earth Day event.

USAGE

REVIEW C

Revising Sentences by Correcting Errors in Usage

Revise the sentences in the following paragraph to correct each error in usage. [Note: A sentence may contain more than one error.]

EXAMPLE   [1] Our vacation along the Pan American Highway was real interesting.
   1. *real—very* (or *extremely*)

[1] My parents were already to leave as soon as school was out. [2] Mom and Dad planned the trip theirselves so that we'd see alot of country. [3] The Pan American Highway, as the map on the next page shows, runs among North America and South America. [4] Like a bridge, this here highway connects the two continents. [5] Like you can see, Laredo, Texas, is one of the terminals for the highway. [6] That's how come we went to Laredo first.

[7] I enjoyed visiting the towns and seeing the countryside deep inside of Mexico. [8] If you follow along on the map, you'll notice that we than drove through Central America. [9] We crossed the Panama Canal to get to Colombia; their we enjoyed touring the capital, Bogotá. [10] We couldn't of stayed in Venezuela and Chile any longer because both Mom and Dad had to get back to work.

Review: Posttest

Identifying and Correcting Errors in Usage

One sentence in each of the following sets contains an error in usage. Choose the letter of the sentence that contains an error. Then revise the sentence, using standard English.

EXAMPLE   **1. a.** The chicken tastes bad.
  b. Where is the book at?
  c. There was agreement among the five dancers.
  1. *b. Where is the book?*

1. **a.** Bring your notes when you come.
    b. The dish busted.
    c. He could have danced.
2. **a.** I drew an apple.
    b. The cold affects the plant.
    c. We are already to go.

USAGE

3. a. Manuel feels alright today.
   b. She went everywhere.
   c. We have fewer chairs than we need.
4. a. They danced good at the party.
   b. If I had sung, you would have laughed.
   c. You ought to help.
5. a. It's cold.
   b. He made it hisself.
   c. Its knob is broken.
6. a. Teach me the song.
   b. That story is kind of funny.
   c. The dog lay down.
7. a. Mr. Barnes is here.
   b. I know why he left.
   c. This kinds of bikes are expensive.
8. a. These taste like oranges.
   b. Sing as she does.
   c. She might of moved.
9. a. Please come inside the house.
   b. I am real happy.
   c. The reason she laughed was that your dog looked funny.
10. a. I looked for the book, but someone must of misplaced it.
    b. Your forehand has improved somewhat.
    c. He sings better than I do.
11. a. Your coat is beautiful.
    b. You're a fast runner.
    c. I cannot leave without I wash the dishes first.
12. a. She is the student which plays the violin.
    b. We only have a short way to go.
    c. We read in our newspaper that a new store is opening in the mall.
13. a. I use to read mysteries.
    b. Set that crate down here.
    c. This hat is old.
14. a. I gave you them books.
    b. They bought themselves new shirts.
    c. There is the cat.

USAGE

15. **a.** Sit down.
    b. They're smiling.
    c. There team is good.
16. **a.** Gail did not feel well.
    b. Have a orange.
    c. You invited everyone except Cai.
17. **a.** I raised at 8:00 this morning.
    b. Sunscreen lessens the effects of the sun's rays.
    c. We already read the book in class.
18. **a.** You did all right.
    b. They went nowheres.
    c. He looks as if he has lost something.
19. **a.** Nancy's ankle was hurt bad.
    b. The funds were divided among the three cities.
    c. The pipe burst.
20. **a.** I cannot hardly dance.
    b. Warm days make me feel good.
    c. It's pretty.
21. **a.** He must be somewhere.
    b. I can scarcely ride this bike.
    c. The reason I like him is because he is kind.
22. **a.** We have fewer shelves than we need.
    b. Those kinds of shirts are warm.
    c. This morning I laid in bed too long.
23. **a.** Latoya always lays her books on the couch.
    b. Learn how to play this game.
    c. Do like he does.
24. **a.** They are inside of the house.
    b. I will have a sandwich.
    c. He set the chair down.
25. **a.** Their my cats.
    b. Do you need those books?
    c. This house has fourteen rooms.

25 CAPITAL LETTERS

Rules for Capitalization

Diagnostic Test

Proofreading Sentences for Correct Capitalization

Each of the following sentences contains at least one error in capitalization. Correct the errors by changing capitals to lowercase letters or lowercase letters to capitals.

EXAMPLE **1.** The Maxwells enjoyed visiting the southwest, particularly the alamo in San Antonio.
1. *Southwest; Alamo*

1. Is dr. Powell's office at Twenty-First street and Oak drive?
2. On labor day we went to Three Trees State Park.
3. We invited aunt Mae and my cousins to go with us.
4. Our junior high school had a much more successful carnival than Lakeside junior high school did.
5. Did you know that the folk tale "cinderella," which is included in *grimm's fairy tales,* is similar to a tale from ninth-century china?
6. Abe's cousin joined the Peace corps and lived in a small village on the west coast of africa.

7. No fish live in the Great salt lake in Utah.
8. I found out that I could save money by shopping at Al's discount city.
9. We have studied Japanese Culture and the shinto religion.
10. This semester I have English, American History, Spanish, and Industrial Arts I in the afternoon.
11. On saturday and sunday, my mother and i are going to a family reunion in the town where she grew up.
12. The Robinsons live near route 41 not far from Memorial Parkway on the South side of town.
13. At our Wednesday Night meeting, the reverend Terry Witt gave a talk on the beliefs of Lutherans.
14. We salute you, o Caesar!
15. Did you know that thursday was named after the Norse God Thor?
16. The Winter air chilled the scouts to the bone.
17. Dale Evans and Roy Rogers always sang "Happy trails to you" at the end of their television programs.
18. Thurgood Marshall was the first african american appointed to the Supreme court.
19. My Uncle served in the U.S. Army during the Vietnam war.
20. The American revolution took place toward the end of the Age of Enlightenment in the 1700s.

Capital letters are used to

- mark the beginnings of sentences
- distinguish proper nouns from common nouns
- indicate other words that deserve special attention

25a. Capitalize the first word in every sentence.

EXAMPLES **M**ore and more people are discovering the benefits of exercise. **D**aily workouts at the gymnasium or on the running track strengthen the heart.

The first word of a sentence that is a direct quotation is capitalized even if the quotation begins within a sentence.

EXAMPLE   In his *Sacred Meditations,* Francis Bacon states, "**K**nowledge is power."

Traditionally, the first word in a line of poetry is capitalized.

> **H**old fast to dreams
> **F**or if dreams die
> **L**ife is a broken-winged bird
> **T**hat cannot fly.
>
> Langston Hughes, "Dreams"

NOTE: Some modern poets and writers do not follow this style. When you are quoting, follow the capitalization used in the source of the quotation.

👉 REFERENCE NOTE: For more about using capital letters in quotations, see pages 773–774.

25b.   Capitalize the pronoun *I.*

EXAMPLES   They took my lover's tallness off to war,
Left me lamenting. Now **I** cannot guess
What **I** can use an empty heart–cup for.
          Gwendolyn Brooks, "The Sonnet–Ballad"

25c.   Capitalize the interjection *O.*

The interjection *O* is most often used on solemn or formal occasions. It is usually followed by a word in direct address.

EXAMPLES   **O** our Mother the Earth, **O** our Father the Sky,
Your children are we, and with tired backs
We bring you the gifts you love.
          from a traditional song of the Tewa people

Protect us in the battle, **O** great Athena!

MECHANICS

The interjection *oh* requires a capital letter only at the beginning of a sentence.

> Oh, I wish I could tell you how lonely I felt.
>
> Rudolfo A. Anaya, *Tortuga*

Otherwise, *oh* is not capitalized.

EXAMPLE   **We felt tired but, oh, so victorious.**

EXERCISE 1   **Correcting Sentences by Capitalizing Words**

Most of the following sentences contain errors in capitalization. If a sentence is correct, write *C*. If there are errors in the use of capitals, identify the word or words that should be changed.

EXAMPLE   **1. Save us, o Poseidon, on this stormy sea.**
          1. o—O

1. If i need a ride, i will give you a call.
2. Loretta is spending her vacation in Maine, but Oh, how she would like to visit Paris.
3. Ana exclaimed, "oh no, I left my backpack on the bus!"
4. Please accept these gifts, o Lord.
5. Have I told you that my grandmother teaches karate?

25d.   Capitalize proper nouns.

A *common noun* names one of a group of persons, places, or things. A *proper noun* names a particular person, place, or thing.

☞ REFERENCE NOTE: For more about common and proper nouns, see pages 433–435.

A common noun is capitalized only when it begins a sentence or is part of a title. A proper noun is always capitalized.

COMMON NOUNS	PROPER NOUNS
athlete	Florence Griffith Joyner
river	Nile
month	February
team	Los Angeles Dodgers

Some proper nouns consist of more than one word. In these names, short prepositions (those of fewer than five letters) and articles (*a, an, the*) are not capitalized.

EXAMPLES   Statue of Liberty, Alexander the Great

(1) Capitalize the names of persons.

EXAMPLES   Alice Walker, Franklin Chang-Diaz, Ms. Sandoz

(2) Capitalize geographical names.

TYPE OF NAME	EXAMPLES	
Towns, Cities	Jamestown San Diego	Montreal St. Louis
Counties, States	Cook County Georgia	Orange County New Hampshire
Countries	Germany Mexico	Japan New Zealand
Islands	Wake Island Isle of Wight	Attu Molokai
Bodies of Water	Lake Erie Tampa Bay	Kentucky River Indian Ocean
Forests, Parks	Sherwood Forest Palmetto State Park	Yellowstone National Park
Streets, Highways	Madison Avenue Interstate 75	Route 44 West Fourth Street

MECHANICS

NOTE: In a hyphenated street number, the second part of the number is not capitalized.

EXAMPLE   East Seventy-eighth Street

TYPE OF NAME	EXAMPLES	
Mountains	Mount Washington Big Horn Mountains	Sawtooth Range Pikes Peak
Continents	Europe North America	Asia Africa
Regions	Middle East New England	the North the Midwest

NOTE: Words such as *north, east,* and *southwest* are not capitalized when they indicate direction.

EXAMPLES   flying **s**outh for the winter
   northeast of Atlanta

☞ **REFERENCE NOTE:** Some proper nouns, common nouns, titles, and other words are commonly abbreviated. For guidelines on capitalizing abbreviations, see page 739.

▶ EXERCISE 2   ## Writing a Paragraph Using Capitalization Correctly

After visiting this wax museum, you decide to open one of your own. Write a paragraph telling where you'd locate your museum, what you'd name it, and what figures— real, fictional, or imaginary—you'd like to display in it.

EXAMPLE   *I'd open the Waikiki Wax Museum in Waikiki Beach, Hawaii. In it I'd display figures of people from Hawaii's history. One would be Queen Liliuokalani, the last queen of the Hawaiian Islands.*

MECHANICS

(3) Capitalize the names of planets, stars, and other heavenly bodies.

EXAMPLES   **Jupiter, Saturn, Sirius, the Milky Way, the Big Dipper**

NOTE: The word *earth* is not capitalized unless it is used along with the names of other heavenly bodies. The words *sun* and *moon* are not capitalized.

EXAMPLES   Water covers more than 70 percent of the surface of the earth.
Mercury and Venus are closer to the sun than Earth is.

(4) Capitalize the names of teams, organizations, businesses, institutions, and government bodies.

TYPE OF NAME	EXAMPLES	
Teams	Detroit Pistons	Pittsburgh Pirates
	Seattle Seahawks	Southside Raiders
Organizations	African Studies Association	
	Future Farmers of America	
	National Football League	
Businesses	General Cinema Corporation	
	Levi Strauss Associates	
	Kellogg Company	
Institutions	Cary Memorial Hospital	
	Hillcrest Junior High School	
	Antioch College	
Government Bodies	Air National Guard	
	Department of Agriculture	
	Governor's Council on Equal Opportunity	

MECHANICS

NOTE: The word *party* following the name of a political party is usually not capitalized. Some writers, however, do capitalize it in such cases. Either way is correct.

EXAMPLE   Democratic party [*or* Party]

☞ REFERENCE NOTE: Many of the names in this grouping are often abbreviated. For more on abbreviations, see pages 739–740.

(5) Capitalize the names of historical events and periods, special events, and calendar items.

TYPE OF NAME	EXAMPLES	
Historical Events	Revolutionary War Battle of Bunker Hill	Crusades Yalta Conference
Historical Periods	Great Depression Paleozoic Era	Middle Ages Renaissance
Special Events	World Series Olympic Games	Oklahoma State Fair Cannes Film Festival
Calendar Items	Friday October	Memorial Day Fourth of July

NOTE: The name of a season is not capitalized unless it is part of a proper name.

EXAMPLES   the last day of summer
the Oak Ridge Winter Carnival

(6) Capitalize the names of nationalities, races, and peoples.

EXAMPLES   **Greek, Asian, African American, Caucasian, Hispanic, Lakota Sioux**

NOTE: The words *black* and *white* may or may not be capitalized when they refer to races.

EXAMPLE   The first edition of the first black [or Black] newspaper, *Freedom's Journal,* was published on Friday, March 16, 1827.

(7) Capitalize the names of religions and their followers, holy days, sacred writings, and specific deities.

TYPE OF NAME	EXAMPLES	
Religions and Followers	Christianity Zen Buddhism	Muslim Amish

MECHANICS

TYPE OF NAME	EXAMPLES	
Holy Days	Lent Easter	Ramadan Passover
Sacred Writings	Koran Talmud	the Bible New Testament
Specific Deities	God Allah	Holy Spirit Jehovah

NOTE: The word *god* is not capitalized when it refers to a god of ancient mythology. The names of specific gods, however, are capitalized.

EXAMPLE   The trickster **god** in many Native American tales is called **Coyote**.

(8) Capitalize the names of buildings and other structures.

EXAMPLES   **World Trade Center, Golden Gate Bridge, Shubert Theater, Plaza Hotel, Hoover Dam, Eiffel Tower**

MECHANICS

EXERCISE 3   **Correcting Sentences by Capitalizing Words**

Identify the words that should be capitalized in each of the following sentences. If a sentence is correct, write C.

EXAMPLE   **1.** Towering over the surrounding countryside, the san esteban mission is visible for miles.
1. *San Esteban Mission*

1. The mission sits atop a sandstone mesa in valencia county, new mexico.
2. Near San Esteban is the pueblo village of acoma, which is fifty-four miles west-southwest of albuquerque.
3. Almost one thousand years old, acoma is believed to be the oldest continuously inhabited community in the united states.

4. In the seventeenth and eighteenth centuries, the spanish established dozens of catholic missions in new mexico.

5. The main purpose of the missions was to spread christianity among the native peoples, but the outposts also served political and military purposes.

6. This photo of San esteban, which was built between 1629 and 1651, shows the type of mission architecture that developed in that region of the united states.

7. Adobe, a sandy clay commonly used in construction throughout the southwest, covers all the outside surfaces of the building.

8. The building's design is based on the design of churches in central mexico.

9. Those churches, in turn, are regional variations of church buildings in spain.

10. Thus, san esteban, like other new mexican missions, combines various elements of three cultures: native american, mexican, and spanish.

MECHANICS

(9) Capitalize the names of monuments and awards.

TYPE OF NAME	EXAMPLES	
Monuments	**Washington Monument** **Statue of Liberty**	**Vietnam Veterans Memorial**
Awards	**Academy Award** **Pulitzer Prize**	**Newbery Medal** **Purple Heart**

(10) Capitalize the names of trains, ships, airplanes, and spacecraft.

TYPE OF NAME	EXAMPLES	
Trains	*Silver Rocket*	*Orient Express*
Ships	USS *Nimitz*	*Santa Maria*
Airplanes	*Spirit of St. Louis*	*Air Force One*
Spacecraft	*Apollo 11*	*Columbia*

(11) Capitalize the brand names of business products.

EXAMPLES   **N**ike shoes, **B**uick station wagon, **W**rangler jeans
[Notice that the names of the types of products are not capitalized.]

▶ REVIEW A   **Common Nouns and Proper Nouns**

For each proper noun, give a corresponding common noun. For each common noun, give a proper noun.

EXAMPLES   **1.** Independence Hall   **2.** city
1. *building*   **2.** *San Francisco*

1. mountain range
2. Oprah Winfrey
3. historical event
4. river
5. North Dakota
6. Ethiopia
7. Lincoln Memorial
8. spacecraft
9. cereal
10. Environmental Protection Agency

MECHANICS

REVIEW B   **Using Capital Letters Correctly**

Correct each of the following expressions, using capital letters as needed.

EXAMPLE   **1.** a member of the peace corps
           1. *a member of the Peace Corps*

1. decisions of the united states supreme court
2. the apaches of the southwest
3. boulder dam
4. the tomb of the unknown soldier
5. 512 west twenty-fourth street
6. pictures of saturn sent by *voyager* 2
7. the hawaiian island named maui
8. the great lakes
9. monday, april 29
10. the stone age

REVIEW C   **Correcting Sentences by Capitalizing Words**

Identify the words that should be capitalized in each of the following sentences.

EXAMPLE   **1.** Imagine how many flowers it must take to cover just one of these floats for the rose parade!
           1. *Rose Parade*

1. I don't have plans for new year's eve yet, but i know where i'll be on new year's day.
2. Watching the rose parade on TV is a new year's day tradition in my family.
3. The parade takes place each year in pasadena, california, which is northeast of los angeles.
4. The parade is sponsored by the pasadena tournament of roses association.
5. Did you know that the name *pasadena* comes from a ojibwa expression meaning "valley town"?
6. That's a fitting name for a town overlooking a valley at the base of the san gabriel mountains.

7. After the parade, we watch the rose bowl game, which is played in pasadena's brookside park.
8. The oldest postseason college football game in the united states, the rose bowl pits the winner of the big ten conference against the winner of the pacific ten conference.
9. New year's day is nearly always bitterly cold in cleveland, where we live.
10. Yet by the end of the game, we feel as though we've started the new year off with a mini-vacation in california.

▶ REVIEW D Correcting Sentences by Capitalizing Words

Correct the words that should be capitalized in each of the following sentences.

EXAMPLE   **1.** our class visited abraham lincoln's home in springfield, illinois.
   1. *Our; Abraham Lincoln's; Springfield; Illinois*

1. the federal aviation administration regulates airlines only in the united states and not throughout the world.
2. when she was a child, ethel waters lived in chester, pennsylvania.
3. the sacred muslim city of mecca is located in saudi arabia.
4. in chicago, the sears tower and the museum of science and industry attract many tourists.
5. we watched the minnesota twins win the world series in 1991.
6. the valentine's day dance is always the highlight of the winter.
7. several of my friends bought new adidas shoes at the big sporting goods sale in the mall.
8. the citywide food pantry is sponsored and operated by protestants, catholics, and jews.
9. the second-place winners will receive polaroid cameras.
10. jane bryant quinn writes a magazine column on money management.

25e. Capitalize proper adjectives.

A *proper adjective* is formed from a proper noun and is almost always capitalized.

PROPER NOUN	PROPER ADJECTIVE
China	Chinese doctor
Rome	Roman army
Islam	Islamic culture
King Arthur	Arthurian legend

EXERCISE 4 **Correcting Sentences by Capitalizing Proper Nouns and Proper Adjectives**

Capitalize the proper nouns and proper adjectives in each of the following sentences.

EXAMPLE   **1.** A finnish architect, eliel saarinen, designed a
number of buildings in the detroit area.
1. *Finnish; Eliel Saarinen; Detroit*

1. The alaskan wilderness is noted for its majestic
beauty.
2. The syrian and israeli leaders met in geneva.
3. The european cities I plan to visit someday are paris
and vienna.
4. Our american literature book includes hopi poems
and cheyenne legends.
5. The south american rain forests contain many
different kinds of plants and animals.
6. Maria has watched two shakespearean plays on
television.
7. Did you see the exhibit of african art at the library?
8. Our program will feature irish and scottish folk
songs.
9. The language most widely spoken in brazil is
portuguese.
10. Several baptist leaders agreed with the ruling of the
supreme court.

25f.   Do *not* capitalize the names of school subjects,
except languages and course names followed by
a number.

EXAMPLES   I have tests in **English**, **Latin**, and **m**ath.
You must pass **Art I** before taking **Art II**.

▶ EXERCISE 5   **Using Capital Letters Correctly**

Correct each of the following expressions, using capital
letters as needed.

1. a lesson in spanish
2. report for english II
3. a program on chinese customs
4. problems in geometry I
5. studying german, chemistry, and government II

MECHANICS

▶ REVIEW E   **Correcting Sentences by Capitalizing Proper Nouns and Proper Adjectives**

Capitalize the proper nouns and proper adjectives in each of the following sentences.

EXAMPLE   **1.** The natchez trace developed from a series of trails made long before hernando de soto explored the area in 1540.
   1. *Natchez Trace; Hernando de Soto*

1. As the map shows, the natchez trace linked the present-day cities of natchez, mississippi, and nashville, tennessee.
2. From natchez the 450-mile route ran northeast between the big black river and the pearl river.

3. Turning east a few miles north of tupelo, it crossed the tennessee river near muscle shoals, alabama, and then headed into tennessee.
4. Among the peoples living along the trail were the natchez, the chickasaw, the choctaw, and the cherokee.
5. Finding no gold or silver in the area, the spanish explorers turned their attention to what is now the u.s. southwest.
6. At the conclusion of the french and indian war (1754–1763), france was forced to give most of its territory east of the mississippi river to great britain.
7. Near the time of the louisiana purchase of 1803, the natchez trace was improved for use by mail and military wagons traveling to the west.
8. Traffic along the trail increased steadily until the 1830s, when regular steamboat service provided a less dangerous, more comfortable means of travel on the mississippi river.
9. Today a modern highway, named the natchez trace parkway, follows the general route of the ancient path.
10. In an effort to reclaim history, volunteers with the natchez trace trail conference are carving out a hiking trail the entire length of the parkway.

MECHANICS

WRITING APPLICATION

Using Capital Letters Correctly in an Essay

The use of a capital letter or a lowercase letter at the beginning of a word can greatly alter the word's meaning. If a word in a sentence is capitalized or lowercased incorrectly, the sentence may not make sense.

CONFUSING   **We used the heavy-duty Jack at Ben's garage to lift my brother's mustang.** [The meaning of the sentence is *We used the strong person at Ben's garage to lift my brother's horse.*]

CLEAR   **We used the heavy-duty jack at Ben's Garage to lift my brother's Mustang.** [The meaning of the sentence is *We used the equipment at Ben's auto repair shop to lift my brother's car.*]

▶ WRITING ACTIVITY

Your class is putting together a booklet of biographical sketches on the most-admired people in your community. Each student in your class will contribute one biography. Write a short essay about someone you admire. The person can be a friend, a family member, or someone you have never met. In your essay, use capital letters and lowercase letters correctly to help your readers understand precisely what you mean.

Prewriting   Brainstorm to develop a list of people you admire. Then look over your list, and choose the person you admire most. Jot down information about his or her background (such as date and place of birth, upbringing, schooling, and talents), personality traits (such as honesty, courage, creativity, and a good sense of humor), and major achievements. In the case of someone you know, you may wish to interview him or her to gather additional information. Finally, organize your information in an outline.

Writing   Begin your essay with a sentence or two that catches your audience's attention and identifies your subject. Using your notes and outline, write your first draft. In your conclusion, sum up the points you've made, or restate the main idea in your introduction.

Evaluating and Revising   Reread your paper to make sure you've clearly shown why you admire this person. Did you give enough information about him or her, and is the information correct? Add, delete, or rearrange information to make your essay clearer and more interesting.

Proofreading and Publishing Read over your essay again, looking for any errors in grammar, punctuation, or spelling. Pay special attention to your use of capital letters and low-ercase letters. Then, photocopy your paper or input it on a computer. With your classmates, create a booklet of your compositions. You may also wish to include photographs or sketches of the people you've written about. Invite other classes, friends, neighbors, and family members to read your booklet.

25g. Capitalize titles.

(1) Capitalize the title of a person when it comes before a name.

EXAMPLES   There will be a short address by **G**overnor Halsey.
Report to **L**ieutenant Engstrom, please.
Does **M**s. Tam know **D**r. Politi?
This is the church in which the **R**everend Henry Ward Beecher preached.
How many terms did **P**resident Theodore Roosevelt serve?

NOTE: Capitalize a title used alone or following a person's name only when you want to emphasize the position of someone holding a high office.

EXAMPLES   Will the **S**ecretary of **L**abor hold a news conference this afternoon?
The **s**ecretary of our scout troop has the measles.

The crowd grew quiet as the **R**abbi rose to speak at the town meeting.
Is he the **r**abbi at the new synagogue on the corner?

MECHANICS

A title used alone in direct address is usually capitalized.

EXAMPLES   Is the patient resting comfortably, **Nurse**?
What is your name, **Sir** [*or* sir]?

(2) Capitalize a word showing a family relationship when the word is used before or in place of a person's name.

EXAMPLES   I received a letter from **Aunt** Christina and **Uncle** Garth.
When will **Mom** and **Dad** be home?

Do not capitalize a word showing a family relationship when a possessive comes before the word.

EXAMPLE   Angela's **m**other and my **a**unt Daphne coach the softball team.

(3) Capitalize the first and last words and all important words in titles and subtitles of books, magazines, newspapers, poems, short stories, historical documents, movies, television programs, works of art, and musical compositions.

Unimportant words in titles include

- prepositions of fewer than five letters (such as *at, of, for, from, with*)
- coordinating conjunctions (*and, but, for, nor, or, so, yet*)
- articles (*a, an, the*)

☞ REFERENCE NOTE: For a list of prepositions, see page 474.

NOTE: An article (*a, an,* or *the*) before a title is not capitalized unless it is the first word of the title or subtitle.

EXAMPLES   Is that the late edition of the *Chicago Sun-Times*?
I read an interesting story in *The New Yorker*.

TYPE OF NAME	EXAMPLES	
Books	*Dust Tracks on a Road* *River Notes: The Dance of the Herons*	
Magazines	*Sports Illustrated* *Woman's Day*	*Latin American Literary Review*
Newspapers	*The Boston Globe*	*St. Petersburg Times*
Poems	"Refugee Ship" "Mother to Son"	"With Eyes at the Back of Our Heads"
Short Stories	"The Tell-Tale Heart" "Gorilla, My Love"	"My Wonder Horse" "Uncle Tony's Goat"
Historical Documents	Bill of Rights Treaty of Ghent	Emancipation Proclamation
Movies	*Stand and Deliver*	*Back to the Future*
Television Programs	*The Wonder Years* *A Different World*	*FBI: The Untold Stories*
Works of Art	*Mona Lisa*	*Bird in Space*
Musical Compositions	*West Side Story* *Rhapsody in Blue*	"Unforgettable" "On Top of Old Smoky"

MECHANICS

▶ EXERCISE 6   **Correcting Sentences by Capitalizing Words**

Most of the following sentences contain words that should be capitalized. Correct the words requiring capitals. If a sentence is correct, write *C*.

1. During Woodrow Wilson's term as president of the united states, sheep grazed on the front lawn of the White House.
2. When my aunt Inez visited Mexico, she met several of grandmother Villa's brothers and sisters for the first time.
3. All of these pronunciations are correct according to *the american heritage dictionary*.
4. Some of the gods in greek mythology have counterparts in ancient asian and egyptian cultures.

5. Did you hear commissioner of education smathers' speech recommending a longer school day?
6. Was Carrie Fisher in *return of the jedi*?
7. After the secretary read the minutes, the treasurer reported on the club's budget.
8. Elizabeth Speare wrote *the witch of blackbird pond*.
9. My older brother subscribes to *field and stream*.
10. The first politician to make a shuttle flight was senator Jake Garn of Utah.

▶ REVIEW F

Correcting Sentences by Capitalizing Words

Correct the words requiring capitals in each of the following sentences.

1. The andersons hosted an exchange student from argentina.
2. The king ranch in texas is larger than rhode island.
3. At rand community college, ms. epstein is taking three courses: computer programming I, japanese, and english.
4. The sixth day of the week, friday, is named for the norse goddess of love, frigg.
5. The christian holiday of christmas and the jewish holiday of hanukkah are both celebrated in december.
6. My uncle ronald was stationed in the south pacific when he was an ensign.
7. The liberty bell, on display in independence hall in philadelphia, was rung to proclaim the boston tea party and to announce the first public reading of the declaration of independence.
8. Is your mother still teaching an art appreciation class at the swen parson gallery?
9. In the 1920s, zora neale hurston and countee cullen were both active in the movement known as the harlem renaissance.
10. I walk to the eagle supermarket each sunday to buy a copy of the *miami herald* and a quart of tropicana orange juice.

MECHANICS

REVIEW G

Proofreading Sentences for Correct Capitalization

Each of the following sentences contains at least one error in capitalization. Correct the errors by supplying or omitting capitals as necessary.

1. president Roosevelt's saturday talks from the white house were broadcast on the radio.
2. In History class, we learned about these suffragists: elizabeth cady stanton, susan b. anthony, and lucretia c. mott.
3. In April the cherry blossom festival will be celebrated by a Parade through the heart of the City.
4. The 1996 summer olympics were held in atlanta.
5. The rio grande, a major river of north america, forms the Southwestern border of Texas.
6. jane addams, an American Social Reformer who co-founded hull house in chicago, was awarded the 1931 nobel peace prize.
7. Many of the countries of europe are smaller than some states in our country.
8. William Least Heat-Moon began his journey around America, which he tells about in his book *blue highways,* in the southeast.
9. Can we have a surprise Birthday party for uncle Victor, mom?
10. The panama canal connects the atlantic ocean and the pacific ocean.

REVIEW H

Proofreading Sentences for Correct Capitalization

Each of the following sentences contains at least one error in capitalization. Correct the errors by supplying or omitting capitals as necessary.

EXAMPLE **1.** The south african vocal group Ladysmith Black Mambazo sings *a capella*—that is, without instrumental accompaniment.
1. *South African*

1. Ladysmith's music is based on the work songs of black south african miners.
2. In a sense, their music is the south African version of the american blues, which grew out of the work songs of African americans.
3. In 1985, ladysmith was featured on two songs on paul simon's album *graceland*.
4. Those two songs, "homeless" and "diamonds on the soles of her shoes," helped to make the album an enormous hit; it even won a Grammy award.
5. To promote the album, Ladysmith and simon toured the United states, europe, and south America.
6. Most of Ladysmith's songs are in the performers' native language, zulu.
7. Even people who don't understand the Lyrics enjoy the music's power and beauty.
8. Ladysmith has also appeared in eddie murphy's movie *coming to america,* in the famous Music Video *moonwalker,* and on the television shows *Sesame street* and *the Tonight show.*
9. The group's exposure to american music is reflected in two songs on its 1990 album, *two worlds, one heart.*
10. One song is a gospel number, and the other adds elements of Rap music to ladysmith's distinctive sound.

PICTURE THIS

It's 1899. You're aboard this ship, sailing from Seattle, Washington, to Nome, Alaska, where gold was discovered last September. Using the map, write a letter home, telling your family about your trip so far. You may wish to tell about your fellow passengers, the towns and islands you've passed or visited, or the specific things you've seen. You may also wish to tell about your plans. Are you going to Alaska to strike it rich in the goldfields? Do you

aim to start a business? Perhaps you want to be a law officer. Of course, you could be simply looking for adventure. In your letter, use at least five proper nouns and five
proper adjectives.

Subject: sailing to the goldfields in Alaska
Audience: your family
Purpose: to tell about your journey

MECHANICS

Review: Posttest

A. Proofreading Sentences for Correct Capitalization

Each of the following sentences contains at least one error in capitalization. Correct the errors by changing capitals to lowercase letters or lowercase letters to capitals.

EXAMPLE   **1.** The shubert Theater is located at 225 West Forty-Fourth Street in New York.
   1. *Shubert; Forty-fourth*

1. The planet mars was named for the roman God of war.
2. In History class we memorized the Capitals of all the states.
3. Uncle Dave owns one of the first honda Motorcycles that were sold in north America.
4. My cousin gave me a terrific book, *rules of the game,* which illustrates the rules of all sorts of games.
5. Rajiv Gandhi, who was then the prime minister of India, visited Washington, d.c., in June of 1985.
6. The Indus river flows from the Himalaya mountains to the Arabian sea.
7. The writings and television appearances of dr. Carl Sagan have increased public interest in Science.
8. In the afternoons i help Mrs. Parkhurst deliver the *Evening Independent,* a local Newspaper.
9. Many people have left Northern states and moved to the south and west.
10. The Writers Ernest Hemingway, an american, and Robert Service, a canadian, served in the red cross during World war I.
11. Could you please tell me how to get to the chrysler Factory on highway 21 and riverside road?
12. For father's day, let's buy Dad a new power saw.
13. In 1978, the president of egypt and the prime minister of israel shared the nobel peace prize.

14. After we read "fire and ice" by Robert Frost, i wanted to read more of the Poet's work.
15. When i ate Supper at Cam's house, i tried *nuoc mam,* a vietnamese fish sauce.

B. Proofreading Paragraphs for Correct Capitalization

Proofread the following paragraphs, adding or omitting capital letters as necessary.

EXAMPLE   [1] The national park service celebrated its seventy-fifth Anniversary in 1991.
   1. *National Park Service; anniversary*

[16] The national park service was set up as a Bureau of the department of the interior on august 15, 1916. [17] However the beginnings of today's system of National parks go back to 1872, when congress established Yellowstone national park in idaho, montana, and wyoming. [18] In 1906, president Theodore Roosevelt signed the Antiquities act, which authorized the president to declare spanish missions and ancient native american villages as monuments. [19] Of the more than three hundred areas now under the Agency's protection, the one located farthest North is Noatak national preserve in northern Alaska. [20] Farthest east is the Buck Island National Monument on st. Croix, in the u.s. Virgin islands. [21] One park is both the farthest South and the farthest west: the national park of american Samoa, in the South pacific.

[22] Continuing to expand its services to visitors, the national park service in 1991 began compiling a computerized directory of the 3,500,000 civil war Soldiers. [23] The Directory will eventually be installed at all twenty-eight civil war sites maintained by the national park service. [24] It should be popular with the 11,000,000 people who visit those Sites each year. [25] Historians estimate that one half of all americans have Relatives who fought in the civil War, and the question visitors ask most often is, "did my Great-great-grandfather fight here?"

MECHANICS

MECHANICS

SUMMARY STYLE SHEET

Names of Persons

Lupe Serrano	a ballet dancer
Neil A. Armstrong	an astronaut
Martin Luther King, Jr.	a civil rights leader

Geographical Names

Twenty-second Street	a one-way street
Salt Lake City	a city in Utah
in the East, Northwest	traveling east, northwest
Denmark	a country in Europe
Philippine Islands	a group of islands
Pacific Ocean	the largest ocean
Redwood National Park	a park in California
Blue Ridge Mountains	camping in the mountains

Names of Heavenly Bodies

Mars, Pluto, Uranus, Earth	the surface of the earth
North Star	a bright star

Names of Organizations, Businesses, Institutions, Government Bodies

Clarksville Computer Club	the members of the club
Eastman Kodak Company	employed by the company
Pine Bluff High School	a large high school
Department of Transportation	a department of government

Names of Historical Events and Periods, Special Events, Calendar Items

Boston Tea Party	an afternoon tea party
Stone Age	at the age of fourteen
National Chess Tournament	an annual tournament
Memorial Day	a national holiday

Names of Nationalities, Races, Religions

Japanese	a nationality
Caucasian	a race
Christianity	a religion
God	a god of Greek mythology

(continued)

SUMMARY STYLE SHEET *(continued)*

Names of Buildings, Monuments, Awards

the John Hancock Building	an insurance **building**
Aladdin **Motel**	a **motel** in Miami
Mount Rushmore National Memorial	a national **monument**
Pulitzer **Prize**	winning a **prize**

Names of Trains, Ships, Airplanes, Spacecraft

Golden Arrow	a train
Andrea Doria	a ship
Spirit of St. Louis	an airplane
Apollo 11	a spacecraft

Brand Names

Timex watch	a digital watch
Huffy bicycle	a ten-speed bicycle

Names of Languages, School Subjects

English, German, French, Spanish	a native **language**
Algebra I, Science II, Art 101	algebra, science, art

Titles

Governor Martinez	a former **governor**
the President of the United States	the president of the club
Grandfather Bennett	my grandfather
Thank you, Grandfather.	
The War of the Worlds	a book
People Weekly	a magazine
The Dallas Morning News	a newspaper
"Casey at the Bat"	a poem
"The Gift of the Magi"	a short story
Declaration of Independence	a historical **document**
West Side Story	a play, a movie
The Cosby Show	a television program
American Gothic	a painting
"The Star-Spangled Banner"	a national anthem

MECHANICS

26 PUNCTUATION

End Marks, Commas, Semicolons, Colons

Diagnostic Test

Correcting Sentences by Adding End Marks, Commas, Semicolons, and Colons

Write the following sentences, inserting end marks, commas, semicolons, and colons as needed.

EXAMPLE **1.** Have you seen our teacher.Ms. O'Donnell today

1. *Have you seen our teacher, Ms. O'Donnell, today?*

1. Cortez Peters the world's fastest typist can type 250 words per minute and he has won thirteen international typing contests
2. We made a salad with the following vegetables from our garden lettuce cucumbers and cherry tomatoes
3. Running after the bus Dr Sloan tripped and fell in a puddle

4. My first pet which I got when I was six was a beagle I named it Bagel
5. Come in Randy and sit down
6. The soft subtle colors of this beautiful Navajo rug are produced from natural vegetable dyes
7. Well I do know John 3 16 by heart
8. Does anyone know where the crank that we use to open the top windows is
9. The chickens clucked and the ducks squawked however the dogs didn't make a sound
10. Now I recognize her She's in my math class
11. Wow That's the longest home run I've ever hit
12. After the rain stopped the blue jays hopped around the lawn in search of worms
13. Wasn't President John F Kennedy assassinated in Dallas Tex on November 22 1963
14. Soy sauce which is made from soybeans flavors many traditional Chinese and Japanese foods
15. Everybody had told her of course that she couldn't succeed if she didn't try
16. Preparing for takeoff the huge jetliner rolled slowly toward the runway
17. In one of the barns we found an old butter churn
18. Did you see the highlights of the Cinco de Mayo Fiesta on the 6 00 news
19. Her address is 142 Oak Hollow Blvd Mendota CA 93640
20. To get a better view of the fireworks Josh and I rode our bikes to Miller's Hill

MECHANICS

End Marks

An ***end mark*** is a mark of punctuation placed at the end of a sentence. The three kinds of end marks are the *period,* the *question mark,* and the *exclamation point.*

26a. Use a period at the end of a statement.

EXAMPLES One of the figure skaters was Sonja Henie.
"I live in a world of such beautiful stories that I
have to write one every now and then."
from an interview with Pearl Crayton

26b. Use a question mark at the end of a question.

EXAMPLES What is the capital of Canada?
Did Gordon Parks write *The Learning Tree*?

26c. Use an exclamation point at the end of an
exclamation.

EXAMPLES What an exciting time we had!
Wow! What a view!

26d. Use a period or an exclamation point at the end
of a request or a command.

EXAMPLES Please give me the scissors. [a request]
Give me the scissors! [a command]

EXERCISE 1 **Using End Marks**

In the following paragraphs, sentences have been run
together without end marks. Identify the last word of
every sentence, and supply the proper end mark. [Note:
The paragraphs contain a total of ten sentences.]

EXAMPLE **1.** Can you imagine what life was like in
Abraham Lincoln's time
1. *time?*

In New Salem Park, Illinois, you will find a reproduction of the little village of New Salem, just as it was when
Abraham Lincoln lived there A visit to this village reveals
that life in Lincoln's time was harder than it is today

The cabin of the Onstats is not a reproduction but,
instead, is the original cabin where Lincoln spent many

hours In that living room, on that very floor, young Abe studied with Isaac Onstat It was the cabin's only room

Across the way hangs a big kettle once used by Mr. Waddell for boiling wool Mr. Waddell, the hatter of the village, made hats of wool and fur

Do any of you think that you'd like to go back to those days What endurance those people must have had Could we manage to live as they did

26e. Use a period after most abbreviations.

TYPES OF ABBREVIATIONS	EXAMPLES
Personal Names	Pearl S. Buck W.E.B. DuBois
Titles Used with Names	Mr. Mrs. Ms. Jr. Sr. Dr.
States	Ky. Fla. Tenn. Calif.

NOTE: A two-letter state abbreviation without periods is used only when it is followed by a ZIP Code. Both letters of the abbreviation are then capitalized.

EXAMPLE   Austin, **TX 78741**

TYPES OF ABBREVIATIONS	EXAMPLES
Times	A.M. P.M. B.C. A.D.
Addresses	St. Rd. Blvd. P.O. Box
Organizations and Companies	Co. Inc. Corp. Assn.

NOTE: Abbreviations for government agencies and some widely used abbreviations are written without periods. Each letter of the abbreviation is capitalized.

EXAMPLES   UN, FBI, PTA, NAACP, PBS, CNN, YMCA, VHF

If you're not sure whether to use periods with abbreviations, look in a dictionary.

MECHANICS

Abbreviations for units of measure are usually written without periods. However, you should use a period with the abbreviation *in.* (for *inch*) to prevent confusing it with the word *in*.

EXAMPLES   cm, kg, ml, oz, lb, ft, yd, mi

 When an abbreviation with a period ends a sentence, another period is not needed. However, a question mark or an exclamation point is used as needed.

EXAMPLES   This is my friend, J. R.
Have you met Nguyen, J. R.?

REVIEW A   **Correcting Sentences by Adding End Marks**

Write the following sentences, adding end marks where they are needed.

EXAMPLE   1. Look at the beautiful costume this Japanese actor is wearing
1. *Look at the beautiful costume this Japanese actor is wearing!*

1. The picture reminds me of our visit to Little Tokyo last year
2. Have you ever heard of Little Tokyo

3. It's a Japanese neighborhood in Los Angeles, Calif, bordered by First St, Third St, Alameda St, and Los Angeles St
4. Some friends of ours who live in Los Angeles, Mr and Mrs Albert B Cook, Sr, and their son, Al, Jr, introduced us to the area
5. They met our 11:30 AM flight from Atlanta, Ga, and took us to lunch at a restaurant in the Japanese Plaza Village
6. Later we stopped at a bakery for *mochigashi,* which are Japanese pastries, and then we visited the Japanese American Cultural and Community Center on San Pedro St
7. Outside the center is a striking abstract sculpture by Isamu Noguchi, who created the stone sculpture garden at the UNESCO headquarters in Paris, France
8. Next door is the Japan America Theater, which stages a wide variety of works by both Eastern and Western artists
9. Soon, it was time to head for the Cooks's home, at 6311 Oleander Blvd, where we spent the night
10. What a great afternoon we had exploring Japanese culture

MECHANICS

Commas

A *comma* is used to separate words or groups of words so that the meaning of a sentence is clear.

Items in a Series

26f. Use commas to separate items in a series.

Words, phrases, and clauses in a series are separated by commas to show the reader where one item in the series ends and the next item begins.

MECHANICS

WORDS IN A SERIES
Barbecue, hammock, canoe, and *moccasin* are four of the words that the English language owes to American Indians. [nouns]
Always stop, look, and listen before crossing railroad tracks. [verbs]
In the early morning, the lake looked cold, gray, and calm. [adjectives]

PHRASES IN A SERIES
Tightening the spokes, checking the tire pressure, and oiling the gears, Carlos prepared his bike for the race. [participial phrases]
We found seaweed in the water, on the sand, under the rocks, and later in our shoes. [prepositional phrases]
Clearing the table, washing the dishes, and putting everything away took almost an hour. [gerund phrases]

CLAUSES IN A SERIES
We didn't know where we were going, how we would get there, or when we would arrive. [subordinate clauses]
The lights dimmed, the curtain rose, and the orchestra began to play. [short independent clauses]

NOTE: Only *short* independent clauses in a series may be separated by commas. Independent clauses in a series are usually separated by semicolons.

Use a comma before the *and* joining the last two items in a series so that the meaning will be clear.

UNCLEAR   Luanne, Zack and I are going riding. [Is Luanne being addressed, or is she going riding?]

CLEAR   Luanne, Zack, and I are going riding. [Three people are going riding.]

If all items in a series are joined by *and* or *or,* do not use commas to separate them.

EXAMPLES   I voted for Corey **and** Mona **and** Ethan.

For your report you may want to read Jean Toomer's *Cane* **or** Ralph Ellison's *Invisible Man* **or** Richard Wright's *Native Son.*

▶ EXERCISE 2   **Correcting Sentences by Adding Commas**

Insert commas where they are needed in each series in the following sentences.

EXAMPLE   **1.** On their expedition, the explorers took with them 117 pounds of potatoes 116 pounds of beef and 100 pounds of fresh vegetables.
            1. *117 pounds of potatoes, 116 pounds of beef, and 100 pounds of fresh vegetables*

1. Carlos and Anna and I made a piñata filled it with small toys and hung it from a large tree.
2. The four states that have produced the most U.S. presidents are Virginia Ohio Massachusetts and New York.
3. The school band includes clarinets trumpets tubas saxophones trombones flutes piccolos and drums.
4. Most flutes used by professional musicians are made of sterling silver fourteen-carat gold or platinum.
5. We know what we will write about where we will find sources and how we will organize our reports.
6. Squanto became an interpreter for the Pilgrims showed them how to plant corn and stayed with them throughout his life.
7. Sylvia Porter wrote several books about how to earn money and how to spend it borrow it and save it.
8. Last summer I read *The Lucky Stone A Wizard of Earthsea Barrio Boy* and *A Wrinkle in Time.*
9. The San Joaquin kit fox the ocelot the Florida panther and the red wolf are only some of the endangered mammals in North America.
10. I want to visit Thailand Nepal China and Japan.

26g. Use a comma to separate two or more adjectives that come before a noun.

EXAMPLES   An Arabian horse is a fast, beautiful animal.
            Many ranchers depended on the small, tough, sure-footed mustang.

Sometimes the final adjective in a series is closely linked to the noun. When the adjective and the noun are linked in such a way, do not use a comma before the final adjective.

EXAMPLE   Training a frisky colt to become a gentle, dependable riding horse takes great patience.

Notice in this example that no comma is used between *dependable* and *riding* because the words *riding horse* are closely connected.

If you aren't sure whether the final adjective and the noun are linked, use this test. Insert the word *and* between the adjectives. If *and* makes sense, use a comma. In the example, *and* makes sense between *gentle* and *dependable*. *And* doesn't make sense between *dependable* and *riding*.

A comma should never be used between an adjective and the noun immediately following it.

INCORRECT   Mary O'Hara wrote a tender, suspenseful, story about a young boy and his colt.

CORRECT   Mary O'Hara wrote a tender, suspenseful story about a young boy and his colt.

EXERCISE 3   **Correcting Sentences by Adding Commas**

Write the following sentences, adding commas where they are needed.

EXAMPLE   1. A squat dark wood-burning stove stood in one corner.
1. *A squat, dark wood-burning stove stood in one corner.*

1. They made a clubhouse in the empty unused storage shed.
2. This book describes the harsh isolated lives of pioneer women in Kansas.
3. What a lovely haunting melody that tune has!

4. Charlayne Hunter-Gault's skillful probing interviews have made her a respected broadcast journalist.
5. The delicate colorful wings of the hummingbird vibrate up to two hundred times each second.

Compound Sentences

26h. Use a comma before *and, but, or, nor, for, so,* or *yet* when it joins independent clauses.

EXAMPLES   The musical comedy began as an American musical form**, and** its popularity has spread throughout the world.
I enjoyed *The King and I***, but** *Oklahoma!* is still my favorite musical.

When the independent clauses are very short, the comma before *and, but,* or *or* may be omitted.

EXAMPLES   Oscar Hammerstein wrote the words and Richard Rodgers wrote the music.
I'm tired but I can't sleep.
The cat can stay inside or it can go out.

A comma is always used before *nor, for, so,* or *yet* joining independent clauses.

EXAMPLES   We will not give up**, nor** will we fail.
Everyone seemed excited**, for** it was time to begin.
No one else was there**, so** we left.
The water was cold**, yet** it looked inviting.

NOTE: Don't be misled by a simple sentence with a compound verb. A simple sentence has only one independent clause.

SIMPLE SENTENCE WITH COMPOUND VERB   Margo likes golf but doesn't enjoy archery.

COMPOUND SENTENCE   Margo likes golf**,** but she doesn't enjoy archery. [two independent clauses]

☞ REFERENCE NOTE: For more about compound sentences, see pages 559–560. For more about simple sentences with compound verbs, see page 557.

▶ EXERCISE 4   **Correcting Compound Sentences by Adding Commas**

For each of the following sentences, identify the two words that should be separated by a comma. Include the comma. If a sentence is correct, write *C*.

EXAMPLE   **1.** Have you read this article or do you want me to tell you about it?
  1. *article, or*

1. Human beings must study to become architects yet some animals build amazing structures by instinct.
2. The male gardener bower bird builds a complex structure and he decorates it carefully to attract a mate.
3. This bird constructs a dome-shaped garden in a small tree and underneath the tree he lays a carpet of moss covered with brilliant tropical flowers.
4. Then, he gathers twigs and arranges them in a three-foot-wide circle around the display.
5. Tailor ants might be called the ant world's high-rise workers for they gather leaves and sew them around tree twigs to make nests like those shown here.

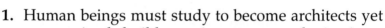

MECHANICS

6. These nests are built in tropical trees and they may be one hundred feet or more above the ground.
7. Adult tailor ants don't secrete the silk used to weave the leaves together but they squeeze it from their larvae.
8. The female European water spider builds a water-proof nest under water and she stocks the nest with air bubbles.
9. This air supply is very important for it allows the spider to hunt underwater.
10. The water spider lays her eggs in the waterproof nest and they hatch there.

Interrupters

| **26i.** | Use commas to set off an expression that interrupts a sentence. |

(1) Use commas to set off a nonessential participial phrase or a nonessential subordinate clause.

A *nonessential* (or *nonrestrictive*) phrase or clause adds information that isn't needed to understand the meaning of the sentence. Such a phrase or clause can be omitted without changing the main idea of the sentence.

NONESSENTIAL PHRASES The spider web, **shining in the morning light,** looked like sparkling lace.
Harvard College, **founded in 1636,** is the oldest college in the United States.

NONESSENTIAL CLAUSES Kareem Abdul-Jabbar, **who retired from professional basketball in 1989,** holds several NBA records.
Joshua eventually overcame his acrophobia, **which is the abnormal fear of being in high places.**

MECHANICS

Do not set off an *essential* (or *restrictive*) phrase or clause. Since such a phrase or clause tells *which one(s)*, it cannot be omitted without changing the meaning of the sentence.

ESSENTIAL PHRASES   All farmers **growing the new hybrid corn** should have a good harvest. [Which farmers?]
The discoveries **made by Einstein** have changed the way people think about the universe. [Which discoveries?]

ESSENTIAL CLAUSES   The book **that you recommended** is not in the library. [Which book?]
Often, someone **who does a good deed** gains more than the person **for whom the deed is done.** [Which someone? Which person?]

NOTE: A clause beginning with *that* is usually essential.

☞ REFERENCE NOTE: For more information about participial phrases, see pages 515–516. For more about subordinate clauses, see pages 535–548.

EXERCISE 5   **Using Commas in Sentences with Nonessential Phrases or Clauses**

Write the following sentences, adding commas to set off the nonessential phrases or clauses. If a sentence is correct, write *C*.

EXAMPLE **1.** My favorite performer is Gloria Estefan who is the lead singer with the Miami Sound Machine.
  1. *My favorite performer is Gloria Estefan, who is the lead singer with the Miami Sound Machine.*

1. Estefan badly injured in a bus accident in 1990 made a remarkable comeback the following year.
2. The accident which occurred on March 20, 1990 shattered one of her vertebrae and almost severed her spinal cord.

MECHANICS

3. The months of physical therapy required after the accident were painful for the singer.

4. Yet less than a year later performing in public for the first time since the accident she sang on the American Music Awards telecast January 28, 1991.

5. On March 1 of that year launching a yearlong tour of Japan, Europe, and the United States she and the band gave a concert in Miami.

6. Estefan who was born in Cuba came to the United States when she was two years old.

7. Her family fleeing the Cuban Revolution settled in Miami where she now lives with her husband, Emilio, and their son, Nayib.

8. The album released to mark her successful comeback is titled *Into the Light*.

9. It contains twelve songs including the first one written by the singer after the accident.

10. Appropriately, that song inspired by a fragment that Emilio wrote as Gloria was being taken to surgery is titled "Coming Out of the Dark."

MECHANICS

(2) Use commas to set off an appositive or an appositive phrase that is nonessential.

EXAMPLES   My best friend**, Nancy,** is studying ballet.
We're out of our most popular flavor**, vanilla.**
Nancy**, my best friend,** has won a dance scholarship.
The Rio Grande**, one of the major rivers of North America,** forms the border between Texas and Mexico.

Do not set off an appositive that tells *which one(s)* about the word it identifies. Such an appositive is essential to the meaning of the sentence.

EXAMPLES   My ancestor **Alberto Pazienza** immigrated to the United States on the ship *Marianna.* [Which ancestor? Which ship?]

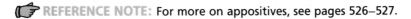 REFERENCE NOTE: For more on appositives, see pages 526–527.

EXERCISE 6   **Using Commas in Sentences to Set Off Appositives and Appositive Phrases**

Write the sentences that require commas. Insert the commas. If a sentence is correct, write C.

EXAMPLE   **1. The dog a boxer is named Brindle.**
            1. *The dog, a boxer, is named Brindle.*

1. The composer Mozart wrote five short piano pieces when he was only six years old.
2. Katy Jurado the actress has appeared in many fine films.
3. Harper Lee author of *To Kill a Mockingbird* is from Alabama.
4. The card game canasta is descended from mah-jongg an ancient Chinese game.
5. Jupiter the fifth planet from the sun is so large that all the other planets in our solar system would fit inside it.
6. The main character in many of Agatha Christie's mystery novels is the detective Hercule Poirot.
7. The writing of Elizabeth Bowen an Irish novelist shows her keen, witty observations of life.
8. Charlemagne the king of the Franks in the eighth and ninth centuries became emperor of the Holy Roman Empire.
9. Chuck Yeager an American pilot broke the sound barrier in 1947.
10. Artist Effie Tybrec a Sioux from South Dakota decorates plain sneakers with elaborate beadwork.

(3) Use commas to set off words used in direct address.

EXAMPLES   **Mrs. Clarkson,** this package is addressed to you.
            Do you know**, Elena,** when the next bus is due?

EXERCISE 7   **Using Commas in Sentences to Set Off Words in Direct Address**

Write the following sentences, adding commas to set off the words in direct address.

EXAMPLE   **1.** Are you hungry Jan or have you had lunch?
   1. *Are you hungry, Jan, or have you had lunch?*

1. Ms. Wu will you schedule me for the computer lab tomorrow?
2. Have you signed up for a baseball team yet Aaron?
3. Your time was good in the hurdles Juanita but I know you can do better.
4. Wear sturdy shoes girls; those hills are hard on the feet!
5. Run Susan; the bus is pulling out!

(4) Use commas to set off a parenthetical expression.

A *parenthetical expression* is a side remark that adds information or relates ideas.

EXAMPLES   The president said, **of course,** that he was deeply disappointed.
   In my opinion, the movie was too violent.
   I will invite Samantha, **I think.**

Commonly Used Parenthetical Expressions		
after all	generally speaking	nevertheless
at any rate	on the other hand	of course
by the way	I believe (hope,	on the contrary
for example	suppose, think)	however
for instance	in my opinion	therefore

Some of these expressions are not always used as interrupters. Use commas only when the expressions are parenthetical.

EXAMPLES   What, **in your opinion,** is the best solution? [parenthetical]
   I have faith **in your opinion.** [not parenthetical]

   Traveling by boat may take longer, **however.** [parenthetical]
   However you go, it will be a delightful trip. [not parenthetical]

MECHANICS

▶ EXERCISE 8   **Using Commas in Sentences to Set Off Parenthetical Expressions**

Write each of the following sentences, using commas to set off the parenthetical expression.

EXAMPLE   **1.** Mathematics I'm afraid is my hardest subject.
           1. Mathematics, I'm afraid, is my hardest subject.

1. The posttest of course covered material from the entire chapter.
2. Your subject should I think be limited further.
3. *Cilantro* by the way is the Spanish name for the herb coriander.
4. Flying however will be more expensive than driving there in the car.
5. After all their hard work paid off.

Introductory Words, Phrases, and Clauses

26j. Use a comma after *yes, no,* or any mild exclamation such as *well* or *why* at the beginning of a sentence.

EXAMPLES   Yes, I understand the problem.
            Well, I think we should ask for help.

26k. Use a comma after an introductory phrase or clause.

Prepositional Phrases

A comma is used after an introductory prepositional phrase if the phrase is long or if two or more phrases appear together.

EXAMPLES   **Underneath the moss-covered rock,** we found a shiny, fat earthworm.
            At night in the desert, the temperature falls rapidly.

If the introductory prepositional phrase is short, a comma may or may not be used.

EXAMPLE   **In the morning,** [or **In the morning**] we'll tour the Caddo burial mounds.

Verbal Phrases

A comma is used after a participial phrase or an infinitive phrase that introduces a sentence.

PARTICIPIAL PHRASE   **Forced onto the sidelines by a sprained ankle,** Carlos was restless and unhappy.

INFINITIVE PHRASE   **To defend the honor of King Arthur's knights,** Sir Gawain accepted the Green Knight's challenge.

Adverb Clauses

An adverb clause may be placed at various places in a sentence. When it begins the sentence, the adverb clause is followed by a comma.

EXAMPLES   **When March came,** the huge ice pack began to melt and break up.

Because I had a sore throat, I could not audition for the school play.

☞ REFERENCE NOTE: For more about prepositional phrases, see pages 506–509. For more about verbal phrases, see pages 515–523. For more about adverb clauses, see pages 544–545.

▶ EXERCISE 9   **Using Commas in Sentences with Introductory Phrases or Clauses**

If a sentence needs a comma, identify the word it should follow, and add the comma. If a sentence is correct, write *C*.

EXAMPLE   **1.** Patented in 1883 Matzeliger's lasting machine, which attached the sole of a shoe to its upper part, revolutionized the shoe industry.
1. *1883,*

MECHANICS

1. Issued in 1991 this stamp honoring inventor Jan Matzeliger is part of the U.S. Postal Service's Black Heritage series.

2. Since the Postal Service began issuing the series in 1978 the stamps have become popular collectors' items.

3. Originally picturing only government officials or national symbols U.S. stamps now feature a wide variety of people, items, and events.

4. As stamps became more varied stamp collecting became even more popular.

5. Because stamps portray our country's culture they fascinate many people.

6. In the United States alone more than twenty million people enjoy stamp collecting.

7. To attract collectors the Postal Service produces limited numbers of special stamps.

8. Collectors can always look forward to adding new stamps because new designs are issued often.

9. To keep their collections from becoming too bulky many collectors concentrate on a single topic.

10. With their treasures safely in albums collectors enjoy examining their first stamps as well as their most recent ones.

Conventional Situations

26l. Use commas in certain conventional situations.

(1) Use commas to separate items in dates and addresses.

EXAMPLES   The delegates to the Constitutional Convention
signed the Constitution on September 17,
1787, in Philadelphia, Pennsylvania.
Each year the Kentucky Derby is held in
Louisville, Kentucky, on the first Saturday
in May.
Passover begins on Wednesday, April 14, this
year.
My grandparents' address is 6448 Higgins Road,
Chicago, IL 60607.

Notice that a comma separates the last item in a date or in an address from the words that follow it. However, a comma does *not* separate a month and a day (*April 14*), a house number and a street name (*6448 Higgins Road*), or a state abbreviation and a ZIP Code (*IL 60607*). A comma also does not separate a month and a year if no day is given (*June 1992*).

NOTE: If a preposition is used between items of an address, a comma is not necessary.

EXAMPLE   He lives at 144 Smith Street **in** Moline,
Illinois.

(2) Use a comma after the salutation of a friendly letter and after the closing of any letter.

EXAMPLES   Dear Aunt Margaret,
Sincerely yours,
Yours truly,

EXERCISE 10   **Correcting Dates, Addresses, and Parts of a Letter by Adding Commas**

Write the following items, inserting commas as needed.

1. 11687 Montana Avenue Los Angeles CA 90049
2. Dresser Road at North First Street in Lynchburg Virginia
3. from December 1 1991 to March 15 1992
4. Dear Joanne
5. Sincerely yours

MECHANICS

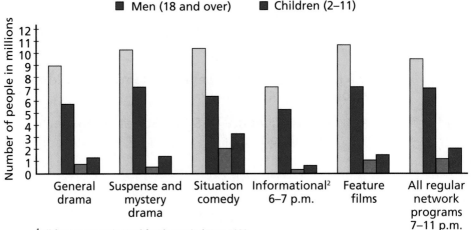

▶ EXERCISE 11   **Writing a Paragraph Using End Marks and Commas Correctly**

Using the graph below, write a paragraph comparing the television viewing patterns of women, men, teenagers, and children. Remember to use commas and end marks where they are needed.

EXAMPLE   *According to the graph, fewer men than women watch regular network programs between 7:00 P.M. and 11:00 P.M.*

Audience Composition by Selected Program Type[1]

Source: Nielsen Media Research, 1990 Nielsen Report on Television.

☐ Women (18 and over)   ■ Teens (12–17)
■ Men (18 and over)   ■ Children (2–11)

Number of people in millions

General drama | Suspense and mystery drama | Situation comedy | Informational[2] 6–7 p.m. | Feature films | All regular network programs 7–11 p.m.

[1]All figures are estimated for the period Nov. 1989.
[2]Multiweekly viewing.

▶ REVIEW B   **Correcting Sentences by Adding End Marks and Commas**

Write the following sentences, adding end marks and commas as needed. If a sentence is correct, write *C*.

EXAMPLE   **1.** I moved from Canton Ohio to Waco Texas in 1985
            1. *I moved from Canton, Ohio, to Waco, Texas, in 1985.*

MECHANICS

1. At the corner of Twelfth St and Park Ave I ran into an old friend
2. Have you ever made the long tiring climb to the head of the Statue of Liberty Alan
3. Oh by the way remind Geraldine to tell you what happened yesterday
4. To prepare for her role in that movie the star observed lawyers at work during a trial
5. Turtles crocodiles alligators frogs and dolphins must breathe air in order to survive
6. His new address is 6731 Wilcox Blvd Hartford CT 06101
7. Junko Tabei one of a team of Japanese women reached the summit of Mount Everest in 1975
8. Students who are late must bring a note from home.
9. Will the twenty-first century begin officially on January 1 2000 or on January 1 2001 Sarah
10. What a great fireworks display that was

REVIEW C   **Correcting a Paragraph by Adding End Marks and Commas**

Write the sentences from the following paragraph, adding end marks and commas where they are needed.

EXAMPLE   [1] Have you ever played chess
         1. *Have you ever played chess?*

[1] To beginners and experts alike chess is a complex demanding game [2] It requires mental self-discipline intense concentration and dedication to long hours of practice [3] Displaying those qualities the Raging Rooks of Harlem tied for first place at the 1991 National Junior High Chess Championship which was held in Dearborn Mich [4] Competing against the Rooks were sixty teams from all across the U S [5] The thirteen- and fourteen-year-old Rooks attended New York City Public School 43 [6] When they returned to New York after the tournament they were greeted by Mayor David Dinkins [7] Becoming media

MECHANICS

celebrities they appeared on television and were interviewed by local newspapers and national news services [8] Imagine how proud of them their friends and families must have been [9] The Rooks' coach Maurice Ashley wasn't surprised that the team did so well in the tournament [10] After all the twenty-five-year-old Ashley is a senior master of the game and his goal is to become the first African American grandmaster

PICTURE THIS

Who's that famous person being honored with a ticker-tape parade? Why, it's none other than you! Write a journal entry about the parade. Tell when and where the parade is taking place, and what you've done to receive such an honor. In addition to these concrete details, record your feelings about the experience. Be sure that you use all three types of end marks. Also, use commas to separate items in a series and to help join independent clauses in a compound sentence.

Subject: being honored with a ticker-tape parade

Audience: yourself at some later date

Purpose: to record information and express your feelings

Semicolons

A *semicolon* is used primarily to join independent clauses that are closely related in meaning.

26m. Use a semicolon instead of a comma between independent clauses when they are not joined by *and, but, or, nor, for, so,* or *yet.*

EXAMPLES　On our first trip to Houston I wanted to see the Astrodome; my little brother wanted to visit the Johnson Space Center.
Our parents settled the argument for us; they took us to both places.

Use a semicolon rather than a period between independent clauses only when the ideas in the clauses are closely related.

EXAMPLE　I called Leon. He will be here in ten minutes.
I called Leon; he will be here in ten minutes.

NOTE:　Very short independent clauses without conjunctions may be separated by commas.

EXAMPLE　The leaves whispered, the brook gurgled, the sun beamed brightly.

26n. Use a semicolon between independent clauses joined by a conjunctive adverb or a transitional expression.

A *conjunctive adverb* or a *transitional expression* shows how the independent clauses that it joins are related.

EXAMPLES　Mary Ishikawa decided not to stay at home; **instead,** she went to the game.
English was Louise's most difficult subject; **accordingly,** she gave it more time than any other subject.
The popular names of certain animals are misleading; **for example,** the koala bear is not a bear.

MECHANICS

Commonly Used Conjunctive Adverbs

accordingly	furthermore	instead	nevertheless
besides	however	meanwhile	otherwise
consequently	indeed	moreover	therefore

Commonly Used Transitional Expressions

as a result	for example	for instance	that is
in addition	in other words	in conclusion	in fact

NOTE: When a conjunctive adverb or a transitional expression *joins* clauses, it is preceded by a semicolon and followed by a comma. When it *interrupts* a clause, however, it is set off by commas.

EXAMPLES You are entitled to your opinion;
  however, you can't ignore the facts.
  You are entitled to your opinion; you
  can't, **however,** ignore the facts.

26o. Use a semicolon rather than a comma before a coordinating conjunction to join independent clauses that contain commas.

EXAMPLES A tall, slender woman entered the large, drafty room; and a short, slight, blonde woman followed her.
  We will practice Act I on Monday, Act II on Wednesday, and Act III on Friday; and on Saturday we will rehearse the entire play.

▶ EXERCISE 12 **Correcting Sentences by Adding Semicolons and Commas**

Write the following sentences, adding semicolons and commas as needed.

EXAMPLE **1.** The gym is on the ground floor the classrooms are above it.
  1. *The gym is on the ground floor; the classrooms are above it.*

1. Scientists have explored almost all areas of the earth they are now exploring the floors of the oceans.
2. Some scientists predict the development of undersea cities however other scientists question this prediction.
3. St. Augustine Florida was the first European settlement in the United States the Spanish founded it in 1565.
4. Mike Powell set a world's record for the long jump in 1991 his leap of 29 feet and 4 1/2 inches beat Bob Beamon's 1968 record by two inches.
5. Some reptiles like a dry climate others prefer a wet climate.
6. Many of today's office buildings look like glass boxes they appear to be made entirely of windows.
7. In April 1912, a new "unsinkable" ocean liner, the *Titanic*, struck an iceberg in the North Atlantic as a result roughly 1,500 persons lost their lives.
8. The *Titanic* carried nearly 2,200 passengers and crew it had enough lifeboats to accommodate less than half of them however.
9. The tragedy brought stricter safety regulations for ships for example the new laws required that ships carry more lifeboats.
10. Today's shipwrecks can produce a different kind of tragedy if a large oil tanker is wrecked for instance the spilled oil damages beaches and kills wildlife.

MECHANICS

Colons

 26p. Use a colon before a list of items, especially after expressions like *as follows* or *the following*.

EXAMPLES Minimum equipment for camping is as follows: bedroll, utensils for cooking and eating, warm clothing, sturdy shoes, jackknife, and rope.

Beyond talent lie all the usual words: discipline, love, luck, but, most of all, endurance.

James Baldwin, from *The Writer's Chapbook*

26q. Use a colon before a statement that explains or clarifies a preceding statement.

When a list of words, phrases, or subordinate clauses follows a colon, the first word of the list is lowercase. When an independent clause follows a colon, the first word of the clause begins with a capital letter.

EXAMPLES   My opinion of beauty was clearly expressed by Margaret Wolfe Hungerford in *Molly Baun***:** "Beauty is in the eye of the beholder."
All books are divisible into two classes**:** the books of the hour, and the books of all time.

John Ruskin, *Of Kings' Treasuries*

26r. Use a colon in certain conventional situations.

(1) Use a colon between the hour and the minute.

EXAMPLES   **11:30** P.M.
4:08 A.M.

(2) Use a colon after the salutation of a business letter.

EXAMPLES   Dear Ms. Gonzalez**:**
Dear Sir or Madam**:**
To Whom It May Concern**:**

(3) Use a colon between chapter and verse in biblical references and between titles and subtitles.

EXAMPLES   Matthew 6**:**9–13
"Easter**:** Wahiawa, 1959"

EXERCISE 13   **Correcting Sentences by Adding Colons**

Write each of the following sentences, inserting a colon as needed.

EXAMPLE   **1.** In Ruth 1 16, Ruth pledges her loyalty to Naomi, her mother-in-law.
1. *In Ruth 1:16, Ruth pledges her loyalty to Naomi, her mother-in-law.*

1. During the field trip our teacher pointed out the following trees sugarberry, papaw, silver bell, and mountain laurel.
2. The first lunch period begins at 11 00 A.M.
3. This is my motto Laugh and the world laughs with you.
4. Using a recipe from *Miami Spice The New Florida Cuisine,* we made barbecue sauce.
5. The artist showed me how to obtain one common flesh tone Mix yellow, white, and a little red.

 REVIEW D

Correcting a Paragraph by Adding End Marks, Commas, Semicolons, and Colons

Write the following paragraph, adding end marks, commas, semicolons, and colons where they are needed.

EXAMPLE   [1] Acadiana La isn't a town it's a region
　　　　1. *Acadiana, La., isn't a town; it's a region.*

[1] Known as Cajun Country the region includes the twenty-two southernmost parishes of Louisiana [2] Did you know that the word *Cajun* is a shortened form of *Acadian* [3] Cajuns are descended from French colonists who settled along the Bay of Fundy in what is now eastern Canada they named their colony Acadie [4] After the British took over the area they deported nearly two thirds of the Acadians in 1755 many families were separated [5] Some Acadians took refuge in southern Louisiana's isolated swamps and bayous [6] They didn't remain isolated however because the Cajun dialect blends elements of the following languages French English Spanish German and a variety of African and Native American languages [7] In 1847 the American poet Henry Wadsworth Longfellow described the uprooting of the Acadians in *Evangeline* a long narrative poem that inspired Joseph Rusling Meeker to paint *The Land of Evangeline* which is shown on the next page. [8] Today most people associate Cajun culture with hot spicy foods and lively fiddle and accordion music

[9] Remembering their tragic history Cajuns sum up their outlook on life in the following saying *Lâche pas la patate* ("Don't let go of the potato") [10] What a great way to tell people not to lose their grip

The Saint Louis Art Museum. Gift of Mrs. W.P. Edgerton, by exchange.

WRITING APPLICATION

Using Punctuation to Make Your Meaning Clear

Punctuation marks haven't always been a part of writing. Ancient Roman texts, like other ancient writings, were hard to read because the words ran together.

EXAMPLE   *SENATUSPOPULUSQUEROMANUS*

Later, Romans began using dots to separate the words.

EXAMPLE   *MAGNO • ET·INVICTO • ACSUPER*

These dots were helpful, but readers still had no way to know where one sentence ended and the next began.

As reading and writing became more widespread, certain practices became standard. Writers left spaces between words and used marks of punctuation to show pauses between ideas. These conventions, which are still followed, made writing easier to read and understand.

▶ WRITING ACTIVITY

A local radio station is sponsoring a contest to select items to put in a time capsule. To enter the contest, write a business letter suggesting one item to include in the time capsule, which will be buried for one hundred years. In your letter, use punctuation marks correctly and follow the rules of business correspondence.

Prewriting   List tangible items (ones you can touch) that show what life in the 1990s is like in the United States. Next, choose the item you think would give people in the 2090s the clearest picture of life today. Finally, make up a name, address, and call letters for the radio station.

Writing   As you draft your letter, keep in mind that a business letter calls for a businesslike tone. Explain *why* the item you're suggesting should be included in the time capsule. Keep your letter brief, and stick to the point.

Evaluating and Revising   To evaluate your letter, ask yourself the following questions:

- Does the item I suggested truly reflect my culture?
- Is the letter easy to follow?
- Is the tone suitable for the form?
- Have I used standard English to present my ideas clearly and reasonably?

Based on your answers to these questions, revise your letter to make it clearer and easier to follow.

Proofreading and Publishing   Proofread your letter carefully, paying special attention to your use of end marks, commas, semicolons, and colons. Make sure that you have followed the proper form for a business letter. (Look on

MECHANICS

pages 901–906 for information about writing business letters.) Then, input your letter on a computer or photocopy it. Compare it with those of your classmates. The class could vote on what ten items they would choose to put in a time capsule.

Review: Posttest

Correcting Sentences by Adding End Marks, Commas, Semicolons, and Colons

Write the following paragraphs, inserting end marks, commas, semicolons, and colons as needed.

EXAMPLE **[1]** Did I ever tell you how our washing machine which usually behaves itself once turned into a foaming monster

 1. *Did I ever tell you how our washing machine, which usually behaves itself, once turned into a foaming monster?*

[1] "Oh no The basement is full of soapsuds" my younger sister Sheila yelled [2] When I heard her I could tell how upset she was [3] Her voice had that tense strained tone that I know so well [4] To see what had alarmed her I ran down to the basement [5] Imagine the following scene The washing machine the floor and much of my sister were completely hidden in a thick foamy flow of bubbles [6] I made my way gingerly across the slippery floor fought through the foam and turned off the machine

[7] This of course merely stopped the flow [8] Sheila and I now had to clean up the mess for we didn't want Mom and Dad to see it when they got home [9] We mopped up soapsuds we sponged water off the floor and

we dried the outside of the washing machine [10] After nearly an hour of steady effort at the task we were satisfied with our work and decided to try the washer

[11] Everything would have been fine if the machine had still worked however it would not even start [12] Can you imagine how upset we both were then [13] Thinking things over we decided to call a repair shop

[14] We frantically telephoned Mr Hodges who runs the appliance-repair business nearest to our town [15] We told him the problem and asked him to come to 21 Crestview Drive Ellenville as soon as possible

[16] When he arrived a few minutes after 4 00 Mr Hodges inspected the machine asked us a few questions and said that we had no real problem [17] The wires had become damp they would dry out if we waited a day before we tried to use the machine again

[18] Surprised and relieved we thanked Mr Hodges and started toward the stairs to show him the way out [19] He stopped us however and asked if we knew what had caused the problem with the suds [20] We didn't want to admit our ignorance but our hesitation gave us away [21] Well Mr Hodges suggested that from then on we measure the soap instead of just pouring it into the machine

[22] Looking at the empty box of laundry powder I realized what had happened [23] It was I believe the first time Sheila had used the washing machine by herself she hadn't followed the instructions on the box

[24] This incident occurred on November 10 1992 and we have never forgotten it [25] Whenever we do the laundry now we remember the lesson we learned the day the washer overflowed

MECHANICS

27 PUNCTUATION

Underlining (Italics), Quotation Marks, Apostrophes, Hyphens, Parentheses, Dashes

Diagnostic Test

A. Proofreading Sentences for the Correct Use of Quotation Marks and Underlining (Italics)

Each of the following sentences contains at least one error in the use of quotation marks or underlining (italics). Write each sentence correctly.

EXAMPLE **1.** Marcella asked, "Did you read Robert Frost's poem Nothing Gold Can Stay in class?"

    1. *Marcella asked, "Did you read Robert Frost's poem 'Nothing Gold Can Stay' in class?"*

1. Uncle Ned reads the Wall Street Journal every day.
2. Fill in all the information on both sides of the form, the secretary said.
3. How many times have you seen the movie of Margaret Mitchell's novel Gone with the Wind?

4. Many of the students enjoyed the humor and irony in O. Henry's short story The Ransom of Red Chief.
5. My little sister asked, Why can't I have a hamster?
6. Please don't sing I've Been Working on the Railroad.
7. Last summer my older sister played in a band on a Caribbean cruise ship named Bright Coastal Star.
8. "Read James Baldwin's essay Autobiographical Notes, and answer both of the study questions," the teacher announced.
9. Dudley Randall's poem Ancestors questions why people always seem to believe that their ancestors were aristocrats.
10. "That artist," Mr. Russell said, was influenced by the Cuban painter Amelia Pelaez del Casal.

B. Proofreading Sentences for the Correct Use of Apostrophes, Hyphens, Parentheses, and Dashes

Each of the following sentences contains at least one error in the use of apostrophes, hyphens, parentheses, or dashes. Write each sentence correctly.

EXAMPLE   **1.** Alices mother said shes read that tomatoes are native to Peru.
1. *Alice's mother said she's read that tomatoes are native to Peru.*

11. Marsha is this years captain of the girls basketball team.
12. Susan B. Anthony 1820–1906 worked to get women the right to vote in the United States.
13. Id never heard of a Greek bagpipe before, but Mr. Karras played one during the folk festival.
14. We couldnt have done the job without you're help.
15. Hes strict about being on time.
16. On my older brothers next birthday, he will turn twenty one.
17. Wed have forgotten to turn off the computer if Maggie hadnt reminded us.

MECHANICS

18. The recipe said to add two eggs, a teaspoon of salt, and one quarter cup of milk.
19. My mothers office is on the twenty second floor.
20. Our dog he's a giant schnauzer is gentle and very well behaved.

Underlining (Italics)

Italics are printed letters that lean to the right, such as *the letters in these words.* In your handwritten or typewritten work, indicate italics by underlining. If your work were to be printed for publication, the underlined words would appear in italics. For example, if you were to write

Born Free is the story of a lioness that became a pet.

the printed version would look like this:

Born Free is the story of a lioness that became a pet.

NOTE: If you use a personal computer, you may be able to set words in italics yourself. Most word-processing software and many printers are capable of producing italic type.

27a. Use underlining (italics) for titles of books, plays, periodicals, works of art, films, television programs, record albums, long musical compositions, trains, ships, aircraft, and spacecraft.

TYPE OF TITLE	EXAMPLES	
Books	*Storyteller* *Barrio Boy*	*A Wrinkle in Time*
Plays	*The Piano Lesson* *Macbeth*	*Visit to a Small Planet*
Periodicals	*Hispanic* *USA Today*	*The New York Times*

MECHANICS

NOTE: The article *the* before the title of a magazine or a newspaper is neither italicized nor capitalized when it is written within a sentence.

EXAMPLE   My parents subscribe to **the** *San Francisco Chronicle.*

TYPE OF TITLE	EXAMPLES	
Works of Art	*The Thinker*	*American Gothic*
	The Last Supper	*Bird in Space*
Films	*Stand and Deliver*	*Do the Right*
	Casablanca	*Thing*
Television Programs	*Life Goes On*	*Wall Street*
	In Living Color	*Week*
Record Albums	*Unforgettable*	*Into the Light*
	No Fences	*Man of Steel*
Long Musical Compositions	*Don Giovanni*	*The Four Seasons*
	A Sea Symphony	*Peer Gynt* suite
Ships	*Calypso*	USS *Nimitz*
	Pequod	*Queen Elizabeth 2*
Trains	*Orient Express*	
	City of New Orleans	
	Garden State Special	
Aircraft	*Enola Gay*	*Spirit of*
	Spruce Goose	*St. Louis*
Spacecraft	*Apollo 12*	USS *Enterprise*
	Voyager I	*Sputnik II*

☞ **REFERENCE NOTE:** For examples of titles that are not italicized but are enclosed in quotation marks, see page 778.

27b. Use underlining (italics) for words, letters, and figures referred to as such.

EXAMPLES   What is the difference between the words *affect* and *effect*?
Don't forget to drop the final *e* before you add *–ing* to that word.
Is the last number a *5* or an *8*?

▶ EXERCISE 1 · **Using Underlining (Italics) in Sentences**

Write and underline the words that should be italicized in each of the following sentences.

EXAMPLE **1.** Have you read The Call of the Wild?
1. *The Call of the Wild*

1. The magazine rack held current issues of National Wildlife, Time, Hispanic, Jewish Monthly, and Sports Illustrated.
2. Sometimes I forget to put the first o in the word thorough, and by mistake I write through.
3. The final number will be a medley of excerpts from George Gershwin's opera Porgy and Bess.
4. Jerry Spinelli won the Newbery Medal for his book Maniac Magee, which is about an unusual athlete.
5. Picasso's painting Guernica is named for a Spanish town that was destroyed by German planes during the Spanish Civil War.
6. My father reads the Chicago Sun-Times because he likes Carl Rowan's column.
7. The first battle between ironclad ships took place between the Monitor and the Merrimac in 1862.
8. The 1989 Irish movie My Left Foot celebrates the accomplishments of a writer and artist who has severe disabilities.
9. The plays Les Misérables and Cats were hits on Broadway and are now on national tours.
10. Janice finally found her mistake; the 4 was in the wrong column.

Quotation Marks

27c. Use quotation marks to enclose a *direct quotation*—a person's exact words.

Be sure to place quotation marks both before and after a person's exact words.

EXAMPLES   "Has anyone in the class swum in the Great Salt
           Lake?" asked Ms. Estrada.
           "I swam there last summer," said Peggy Ann.

Do not use quotation marks for an *indirect quotation*—a rewording of a direct quotation.

DIRECT QUOTATION	Kaya asked, "What is your interpretation of the poem?"
INDIRECT QUOTATION	Kaya asked for my interpretation of the poem.
DIRECT QUOTATION	As Barbara Jordan said in her keynote address to the Democratic National Convention in 1976, "We are willing to suffer the discomfort of change in order to achieve a better future."
INDIRECT QUOTATION	Barbara Jordan said that people will put up with the discomfort of change to have a better future.

27d.   A direct quotation begins with a capital letter.

EXAMPLES   Brandon shouted, "Let's get busy!"
           Abraham Lincoln said, "Those who deny freedom to others deserve it not for themselves."

27e.   When the expression identifying the speaker interrupts a quoted sentence, the second part of the quotation begins with a small letter.

EXAMPLES   "What are some of the things," asked Mrs.
           Perkins, "that the astronauts discovered on the moon?"
           "One thing they found," answered Gwen, "was that the moon is covered by a layer of dust."
           "Gee," Angelo added, "my room at home is a lot like the moon, I guess."

Notice in the examples above that each part of a divided quotation is enclosed in a set of quotation marks. In addition, the interrupting expression is followed by a comma.

MECHANICS

When the second part of a divided quotation is a sentence, it begins with a capital letter.

EXAMPLE   "Any new means of travel is exciting," remarked Mrs. Perkins. "Space travel is no exception."

Notice that a period, not a comma, follows the interrupting expression.

▶ EXERCISE 2   **Correcting Sentences by Adding Capital Letters and Punctuation**

Revise the following sentences by supplying capital letters and marks of punctuation as needed. If a sentence is correct, write *C*.

EXAMPLE   **1.** I think, Phil said, that the Yoruba people of Nigeria are fantastic artists.
   1. *"I think," Phil said, "that the Yoruba people of Nigeria are fantastic artists."*

1. Ella exclaimed, this helmet mask is one of the most amazing things I've ever seen!
2. Mr. Faulkner told the class that the mask weighs eighty pounds and is five feet tall.
3. Don't you think, asked Earl, the figures must have been difficult to carve?
4. Just look at all the detail, Marcia said. it's a beautiful piece of sculpture, but I can't imagine wearing it.
5. Lou explained that the mask was designed to honor the Yoruba people.

27f. A direct quotation is set off from the rest of the sentence by a comma, a question mark, or an exclamation point, but not by a period.

EXAMPLES "I've just finished reading a book about Narcissa Whitman," Alyssa said.
"Was she one of the early settlers in the Northwest?" asked Delia.
"What an adventure!" exclaimed Iola.

27g. A period or a comma is always placed inside the closing quotation marks.

EXAMPLES Ramón said, "Hank Aaron was a better player than Babe Ruth because he hit more home runs in his career."
"But Hank Aaron never hit sixty homers in one year," Paula responded.

27h. A question mark or an exclamation point is placed inside the closing quotation marks when the quotation itself is a question or an exclamation. Otherwise, it is placed outside.

EXAMPLES "Is the time difference between Los Angeles and Chicago two hours?" asked Ken. [The quotation is a question.]
Linda exclaimed, "I thought everyone knew that!" [The quotation is an exclamation.]
What did Jade Snow Wong mean in her story "A Time of Beginnings" when she wrote, "Like the waves of the sea, no two pieces of pottery art can be identical"? [The sentence, not the quotation, is a question.]
I'm angry that Mom said, "You are not allowed to stay out past 10 P.M. on Friday night"! [The sentence, not the quotation, is an exclamation.]

When both the sentence and the quotation at the end of the sentence are questions (or exclamations), only one

MECHANICS

question mark (or exclamation point) is used. It is placed inside the closing quotation marks.

EXAMPLE   Did Elizabeth Barrett Browning write the poem that begins with "How do I love thee?"

EXERCISE 3   **Correcting Sentences by Adding Capital Letters and Punctuation**

Revise the following sentences by supplying capitals and marks of punctuation as needed.

EXAMPLE   **1.** Why she asked can't we leave now
           1. *"Why," she asked, "can't we leave now?"*

1. Mom, will you take us to the soccer field asked Libby
2. Please hold my backpack for a minute, Dave Josh said I need to tie my shoelace
3. Cary asked What is pita bread
4. Did Alison answer It's a round, flat Middle Eastern bread
5. Run Run cried the boys a tornado is headed this way

27i. When you write dialogue (conversation), begin a new paragraph each time you change speakers.

EXAMPLE   "No," I answered, "I do not fish for carp. It is bad luck."
        "Do you know why?" he asked and raised an eyebrow.
        "No," I said and held my breath. I felt I sat on the banks of an undiscovered river whose churning, muddied waters carried many secrets.
        "I will tell you a story," Samuel said after a long silence, "a story that was told to my father . . ."

Rudolfo A. Anaya, *Bless Me, Ultima*

27j. When a quotation consists of several sentences, place quotation marks at the beginning and at the end of the whole quotation.

EXAMPLE   "Memorize all your lines for Monday. Have someone at home give you your cues. Enjoy your weekend!" said Ms. Goodwin.

▶ EXERCISE 4   **Correcting Paragraphs by Adding Punctuation**

Revise the following paragraphs by adding commas, end marks, and quotation marks where necessary.

EXAMPLE   [1] Which would you rather use, a pencil or a pen asked Jody

     1. "Which would you rather use, a pencil or a pen?" asked Jody.

[1] Gordon, do you ever think about pencils Annie asked

[2] I'm always wondering where I lost mine Gordon replied

[3] Well said Annie let me tell you some of the things I learned about pencils

[4] Okay Gordon said I love trivia

[5] People have used some form of pencils for a long time Annie began [6] The ancient Greeks and Romans used lead pencils [7] However, pencils as we know them weren't developed until the 1500s, when people started using graphite

[8] What's graphite asked Gordon

[9] Graphite is a soft form of carbon Annie explained that leaves a mark when it's drawn over most surfaces

[10] Thanks for the information, Annie Gordon said Now, do you have a pencil I can borrow?

27k. Use single quotation marks to enclose a quotation within a quotation.

EXAMPLES   "I said, 'The quiz will cover Unit 2 and your special reports,'" repeated Mr. Allyn.

"What Langston Hughes poem begins with the line 'Well, son, I'll tell you: / Life for me ain't been no crystal stair'?" Carol asked.

271. Use quotation marks to enclose titles of short works such as short stories, poems, articles, songs, episodes of television programs, and chapters and other parts of books.

TYPE OF TITLE	EXAMPLES
Short Stories	"Raymond's Run" "The Rule of Names" "The Tell-Tale Heart"
Poems	"Mother to Son" "The Road Not Taken" "Calling in the Cat"
Articles	"Free Speech and Free Air" "How to Sharpen Your Knife" "Marriage in the '90s"
Songs	"La Bamba" "Amazing Grace" "The Streets of Laredo"
Episodes of Television Programs	"Heart of a Champion" "The Trouble with Tribbles" "An Englishman Abroad"
Chapters and Other Parts of Books	"Learning About Reptiles" "English: Origins and Uses" "Creating a Federal Union"

☞ REFERENCE NOTE: For examples of titles that are italicized, see page 771.

▶ EXERCISE 5 **Correcting Sentences by Adding Quotation Marks**

Revise the following sentences by supplying quotation marks as needed.

EXAMPLE **1.** We sang Greensleeves for the assembly.
1. *We sang "Greensleeves" for the assembly.*

1. Has anyone read the story To Build a Fire? asked the teacher.

MECHANICS

2. I have, said Eileen. It was written by Jack London.
3. Do you know the poem To Make a Prairie?
4. Our chorus will sing When You Wish upon a Star at the recital.
5. In the chapter Workers' Rights, the author discusses César Chávez's efforts to help migrant workers.

> **REVIEW A**   **Correcting Sentences by Adding Punctuation and Capital Letters**

Revise the following sentences by adding marks of punctuation and capital letters as needed. If a sentence is correct, write *C*.

EXAMPLE **1.** Did you read the article about runner Jackie Joyner-Kersee in USA Weekend Lynn asked.
   1. *"Did you read the article about runner Jackie Joyner-Kersee in <u>USA Weekend</u>?" Lynn asked.*

1. Won't you stay pleaded Wynnie there will be music and refreshments later.
2. Hey, Jason, said Chen, you play the drums like an expert!
3. The girls asked whether we needed help finding our campsite.
4. Elise, do you know who said The only thing we have to fear is fear itself asked the teacher.
5. What a wonderful day for a picnic exclaimed Susan.
6. I've read Connie said that Thomas Jefferson loved Italian food and ordered pasta from Italy.
7. When President Lincoln heard of the South's defeat, he requested that the band play Dixie.
8. The latest issue of National Geographic has a long article on rain forests.
9. What can have happened to Francine this time, Tina? Didn't she say I'll be home long before you're ready to leave? Justin asked.
10. Langston Hughes's Dream Deferred is a thought-provoking poem.

MECHANICS

PICTURE THIS

You are a newspaper reporter covering this year's hot-air balloon race. While watching the balloons lift off, you interview some of the people in the crowd around you. You want to use their comments in your news story. For that reason, you quickly write down each speaker's exact words. Write a short article about the balloon liftoff. In your article, quote at least five observers of this event. Use quotation marks and proper punctuation for each quotation.

Subject: hot-air balloon liftoff
Audience: newspaper readers
Purpose: to inform

Apostrophes

An *apostrophe* is used to form the possessive case of nouns and some pronouns, to indicate in a contraction where letters have been omitted, and to form some plurals.

Possessive Case

The *possessive case* of a noun or a pronoun shows owner-ship or relationship.

OWNERSHIP	RELATIONSHIP
Sandra's boat	an **hour's** time
Mother's job	**Julio's** father
your book	**everyone's** choice

27m. To form the possessive case of a singular noun, add an apostrophe and an –*s*.

EXAMPLES   a dog's collar
a moment's notice
one dollar's worth
Charles's typewriter

NOTE: A proper name ending in *s* may take only an apostrophe to form the possessive case if the addition of *'s* would make the name awkward to pronounce.

EXAMPLES   Marjorie Kinnan Rawlings' novels
Hercules' feats
Buenos Aires' population

EXERCISE 6   **Supplying Apostrophes for Possessive Nouns**

Write each noun that should be in the possessive case in the following sentences, and add the apostrophe.

EXAMPLE   **1.** The dogs leash is made of nylon.
1. *dog's*

1. That trucks taillights are broken.
2. The judges were impressed with Veronicas project.
3. Last weeks travel story was about Mindanao, the second largest island of the Philippines.
4. Matthias dream is to have a palomino.
5. Please pack your mothers books.

MECHANICS

27n. To form the possessive case of a plural noun ending in *s*, add only the apostrophe.

EXAMPLES   students' records   doctors' opinions
                  citizens' committee Haines' invitations

To form the possessive case of a plural noun that does not end in *s*, add an apostrophe and an *–s*.

EXAMPLES   women's suits geese's noise
                  mice's tracks children's voices

NOTE: Do not use an apostrophe to form the *plural* of a noun.

INCORRECT	The passenger's showed their tickets to the flight attendant.
CORRECT	The **passengers** showed their tickets to the flight attendant. [plural]
CORRECT	The flight attendant checked the **passengers'** tickets. [plural possessive]

EXERCISE 7   **Forming Plural Possessives**

Give the correct possessive form for each of the following plural expressions.

EXAMPLE   **1.** artists paintings
             1. *artists' paintings*

1. boys boots
2. women careers
3. friends comments
4. three days homework
5. girls parents
6. Joneses cabin
7. men shoes
8. children games
9. cities mayors
10. oxen yokes

27o. Do not use an apostrophe with possessive personal pronouns.

EXAMPLES   These keys are **yours,** not **mine.**
                Are these tapes **ours** or **theirs**?
                His pantomime was good, but **hers** was better.

27p. To form the possessive case of some indefinite pronouns, add an apostrophe and an *–s*.

MECHANICS

EXAMPLES   everyone's opinion
no one's fault
somebody's umbrella

☞ REFERENCE NOTE: For more about possessive personal pronouns, see page 635. For information about indefinite pronouns used as adjectives, see page 442.

▶ EXERCISE 8   **Forming Singular Possessives and Plural Possessives**

Form the singular possessive and the plural possessive of each of the following nouns.

EXAMPLE   **1.** citizen
1. *citizen's; citizens'*

1. book	**4.** mouse	**7.** elephant	**9.** school
2. puppy	**5.** calf	**8.** tooth	**10.** family
3. donkey	**6.** hero		

Contractions

27q. To form a contraction, use an apostrophe to show where letters have been omitted.

A *contraction* is a shortened form of a word, a figure, or a group of words. The apostrophe in a contraction indicates where letters or numerals have been left out.

Common Contractions			
I am	I'm	they had ....they'd	
1993	'93	where is .. where's	
let us	let's	we are.......we're	
of the clock ...	o'clock	he is......... he's	
she would	she'd	you will .... you'll	

The word *not* can be shortened to *n't* and added to a verb, usually without changing the spelling of the verb.

MECHANICS

EXAMPLES
is not . . . . isn't	has not . . . . hasn't
are not . . . . .aren't	have not. . . . . . haven't
does not . . doesn't	had not. . . . . . . hadn't
do not . . . . . . don't	should not. . shouldn't
was not. . . . wasn't	would not . . .wouldn't
were not. . weren't	could not . . . . .couldn't

EXCEPTIONS: will not . . . . . **won't** cannot . . . . . **can't**

Do not confuse contractions with possessive pronouns.

CONTRACTIONS	POSSESSIVE PRONOUNS
It's snowing. [*It is*] **It's** been a long time. [*It has*]	**Its** front tire is flat.
Who's next in line? [*Who is*] **Who's** been helping you? [*Who has*]	**Whose** idea was it?
You're a good friend. [*You are*]	**Your** writing has improved.
They're not here. [*They are*]	**Their** dog is barking.
There's only one answer. [*There is*]	This trophy is **theirs**.

MECHANICS

▶ EXERCISE 9 **Using Apostrophes in a Letter**

You're having a great time, spending your vacation on a relative's ranch in Argentina. The ranch hands, called *gauchos*, are fascinating people, and you're eager to tell your best friend about them. Using pictures that you've taken and notes that you've made, write a letter to your friend, telling about the gauchos on the ranch. (These pictures and notes appear on the next page.) In your letter, use six apostrophes to form the possessive case of nouns and four apostrophes to form contractions. Circle each apostrophe in your letter.

EXAMPLE *Dear Larry,*

Greetings from Argentina! You'd love it here! The gauchos in these pictures work on my uncle's ranch.

MECHANICS

The Gaucho

herds cattle on the Pampas

Pampas—grasslands of central Argentina, ranch country

wears colorful clothes

pants are called <u>bombachas</u>

leather boots, big spurs

sash or leather belt

neckerchief

wears poncho in cold weather

fancy knife called <u>facón</u>

cooks on campfire

works long hours

Plurals

27r. Use an apostrophe and an *–s* to form the plurals of letters, numerals, and symbols, and of words referred to as words.

EXAMPLES   The word has two *d*'s, not one.
Your *2*'s look like *5*'s.
Jazz became quite popular in the 1920's.
Don't use *&*'s in place of *and*'s.

NOTE: In your reading, you may notice that an apostrophe is not always used in forming these four kinds of plurals. Nowadays, many writers omit the apostrophe if the plural meaning is clear without it. However, to make sure that your writing is clear, always use an apostrophe.

▶ EXERCISE 10 **Correcting Sentences by Adding Apostrophes**

Write the correct form of each item that requires an apostrophe in the following sentences.

EXAMPLE **1.** Do you know what youre doing?
  1. *you're*

1. The girls didnt say when theyd be back.
2. Lets find out when the next game is.
3. My cousin Dorothy usually gets all As and Bs on her report card.
4. It isnt correct to use &s in your compositions.
5. Many of the scores on the spelling test were in the 80s and 90s.
6. They cant come with us; theyre studying.
7. Theyll meet us later, if its all right to tell them where were going.
8. Whos signed up for the talent show?
9. Dont those 2s look like zs to you?
10. Your capital Ls and Fs are hard to tell apart.

Hyphens

27s. Use a hyphen to divide a word at the end of a line.

EXAMPLES How long had the new bridge been under con-struction before it was opened?
You can probably find the answer in the alma-nac in the library.

When dividing a word at the end of a line, remember the following rules:

(1) Divide a word only between syllables.

INCORRECT   Lisa wrote her science report on the tyra-
              nnosaurs, the largest meat-eating dinosaurs.
CORRECT   Lisa wrote her science report on the tyran-
              nosaurs, the largest meat-eating dinosaurs.

(2) Do not divide a one-syllable word.

INCORRECT   The fans stood and sang while the band play-
              ed the school song.
CORRECT   The fans stood and sang while the band played
              the school song.

(3) Divide an already hyphenated word at a hyphen.

INCORRECT   I went to the fair with my sister and my broth-
              er-in-law.
CORRECT   I went to the fair with my sister and my brother-
              in-law.

(4) Do not divide a word so that one letter stands alone.

INCORRECT   On their way to Chicago last week, they stayed o-
              vernight in Cincinnati.
CORRECT   On their way to Chicago last week, they stayed
              overnight in Cincinnati.

27t.   Use a hyphen with compound numbers from *twenty-one* to *ninety-nine* and with fractions used as adjectives.

EXAMPLES   thirty-five students
           one-half cup of milk
           forty-eighth state

When a fraction is a noun, do not use a hyphen.

EXAMPLE   **two thirds** of the earth's surface

▶ EXERCISE 11   **Hyphenating Numbers and Fractions**

Write the following expressions, inserting hyphens as needed. If an expression is correct, write C.

EXAMPLE   **1.** thirty one days
            1. *thirty-one*

1. a two thirds majority
2. one half of the coconut
3. one hundred thirty five pages
4. Forty second Street
5. twenty two Amish quilts

▶ REVIEW B   **Forming Contractions**

Form a contraction of each of the following pairs of words.

1. will not	8. should not	15. we are
2. there is	9. let us	16. I am
3. who will	10. I have	17. had not
4. they are	11. you are	18. she is
5. who is	12. does not	19. you will
6. are not	13. he would	20. could not
7. it is	14. has not	

▶ REVIEW C   **Adding Apostrophes, Hyphens, and Underlining**

Write the following sentences, inserting apostrophes, hyphens, and underlining as needed.

EXAMPLE   **1.** Isnt the preface to that edition of Frankenstein twenty four pages long?
            1. *Isn't the preface to that edition of* Frankenstein *twenty-four pages long?*

1. Theres where they live.
2. Wholl go with me to next weeks showing of the French film Small Change?
3. The Lockwood sisters golden retriever is named Storm.

MECHANICS

4. One third of Hollys allowance goes into the bank.
5. From Fifty third Street down to Forty fifth, there are ninety seven businesses.
6. Twenty six student council members (more than a two thirds majority) voted to change the school song.
7. Shelly said that shes always wanted to read Maya Angelou's book I Know Why the Caged Bird Sings.
8. If two thirds of the class has a score below seventy five, well all have to retake the test.
9. Lets find out more about the recovery of Henry VIIIs flagship, the Mary Rose.
10. Ninety seven years ago my great-grandparents left Scotland for the United States.

Parentheses

27u. Use parentheses to enclose material that is added to a sentence but is not considered of major importance.

EXAMPLES   Mohandas K. Gandhi **(1869–1948)** led India's struggle for independence from British rule.
Mrs. Matsuo served us the sushi **(sōō'shē)** that she had prepared.

Material enclosed in parentheses may range from a single word or number to a short sentence. A short sentence in parentheses may stand by itself or be contained within another sentence.

EXAMPLES   Fill in the order form carefully. **(Do not use pencil.)**
My great-uncle Chester **(he's Grandma's brother)** will stay with us during the holidays.

NOTE: Too many parenthetical expressions in a piece of writing can distract readers from the main idea. Keep your meaning clear by limiting the number of parenthetical expressions you use.

MECHANICS

EXERCISE 12   **Writing Sentences with Parentheses**

For each of the following sentences, insert parentheses where they are needed. Be sure not to enclose any words or marks of punctuation that do not belong inside the parentheses.

EXAMPLE   **1.** One of the most popular pets is the house cat *Felis cattus.*

1. *One of the most popular pets is the house cat* (Felis cattus).

1. The old fort it was used during the Civil War has been rebuilt and is open to the public.
2. Most of Yellowstone National Park the oldest national park in the United States is in Wyoming.
3. The writer Langston Hughes 1902–1967 is best known for his poetry.
4. Alligators use their feet and tails to dig water holes also called "gator holes" in marshy fields.
5. On the Sabbath we eat braided bread called challah pronounced khä′lə.

Dashes

Many words and phrases are used *parenthetically;* that is, they break into the main thought of a sentence. Most parenthetical elements are set off by commas or parentheses.

EXAMPLES   The tomato, **however,** is actually a fruit, not a vegetable.

The outcome **(which candidate would be elected governor?)** was in the hands of the voters.

REFERENCE NOTE: For more about using commas with parenthetical expressions, see page 751. For more about using parentheses, see page 789.

Sometimes parenthetical elements demand a stronger emphasis. In such instances, a dash is used.

27v. Use a dash to indicate an abrupt break in thought or speech.

EXAMPLES   Ms. Alonzo—she just left—will be one of the judges of the talent show.
"Right over here—oh, excuse me, Mr. Mills—you'll find the reference books," said the librarian.

 EXERCISE 13   **Writing Sentences with Dashes**

For each of the following sentences, insert dashes where they are needed.

EXAMPLE   **1.** Paul Revere he imported hardware made beautiful jewelry and utensils.
1. *Paul Revere—he imported hardware—made beautiful jewelry and utensils.*

1. A beautiful grand piano it was once played by Chopin was on display in the museum.
2. "I'd like the red no, give me the blue cycling shorts," said Josh.
3. Frederic Remington artist, historian, and lover of the frontier painted the West as it really was.
4. On July 7, 1981, Sandra Day O'Connor she's the first woman associate justice was nominated to the U.S. Supreme Court.
5. Cheryl wondered aloud, "Where in the world oh, my poor Muffy could that hamster be?"

REVIEW D   **Correcting Sentences by Adding Punctuation**

Write the following sentences, supplying punctuation marks where needed. If a sentence is correct, write *C*.

EXAMPLE   **1.** Stans going to the Washingtons Birthday cele bration in Laredo, Texas Teresa said.
1. *"Stan's going to the Washington's Birthday celebration in Laredo, Texas," Teresa said.*

1. Some say that Laredos festivities are the countrys biggest celebration of Washingtons birthday Juan said Isnt that surprising
2. No, not really said Frank The citys large Hispanic population chose to honor George Washington, whom they consider a freedom fighter
3. But Teresa said the citizens also have great respect for Washingtons abilities as a leader
4. Juan said that the annual celebration began back in the 1800s.
5. Do you know theyve extended the birthday party to both sides of the Texas-Mexico border Teresa asked.
6. Thats right Juan said the citizens of Nuevo Laredo in Mexico really enjoy the celebration, too
7. Just look at the colorful costumes in these pictures exclaimed Teresa Can you tell what famous couple these people are portraying

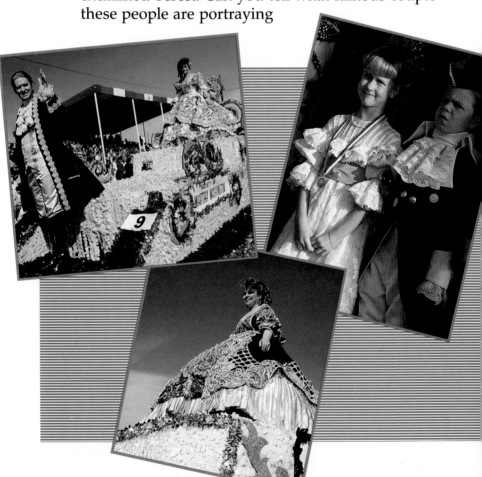

8. Mrs. Serrano she's Juans aunt who lives in Houston has gone to the celebration in Laredo for the past twenty two years.

9. The Laredo Morning Times reported today that a jalapeño-eating contest was part of this years cele bration Angie added.

10. In honor of Washingtons birthday February 22, three fourths of our class read the book Washington by William Jay Jacobs.

Using Quotations in Interviews

When you read an interview in a newspaper or magazine, how do you know exactly what was said? Usually, publishers print the questions and answers of an interview in a very clear format.

EXAMPLE   *Juan Bruce-Novoa:* How do you perceive your role as a writer?
Rolando Hinojosa-Smith: My role is to write and then to try to get the stuff published; in the meantime, I keep writing.

from *Chicano Authors*

Reporters and other interviewers like Juan Bruce-Novoa often use a tape recorder to help them accurately report what was said and to have a permanent record of the interview.

If you were writing a report on Hinojosa-Smith and wanted to use material from the interview above, you would need to quote information from the source material.

EXAMPLE   An interviewer asked Hinojosa-Smith how he saw his role as a writer. The author replied, "My role is to write and then to try to get the stuff published; in the meantime, I keep writing."

MECHANICS

Notice how Hinojosa-Smith's exact words are enclosed in quotation marks. In general, you should follow two rules when using information from source materials.

- When you use someone else's ideas, give him or her credit.
- When you use someone else's words, quote them accurately.

▶ WRITING ACTIVITY

Your class is taking a survey of people's reading habits. Think of five questions you could ask about when and what people read. Then, use these questions to interview at least five people. Based on the information you gather, write a brief report about people and their reading habits. In your report, use quotation marks and correct punctuation to quote people's exact words.

Prewriting First, think of questions to ask. These questions could be about what people read, and how often, when, and why they read. Avoid asking questions that can be answered with a simple *yes* or *no*. Next, select at least five people to interview (perhaps friends, family members, or neighbors). Record the name, age, and occupation of each person. As you conduct your interviews, write down or tape-record what people say. If you want to tape the interview, be sure to ask the interviewee for permission to do so. Think about what reading habits the people you interviewed have in common. For example, you may find that most of them read magazines. Perhaps your survey group's reading habits can be organized by the age or gender of your interviewees. Jot down some notes to help you organize your information.

Writing In the first paragraph of your rough draft, include a statement that summarizes the main idea of your project and findings. Then, use people's answers to your survey questions to support your main idea. Clearly identify each person that you quote.

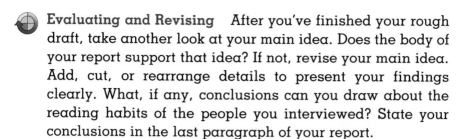

Evaluating and Revising After you've finished your rough draft, take another look at your main idea. Does the body of your report support that idea? If not, revise your main idea. Add, cut, or rearrange details to present your findings clearly. What, if any, conclusions can you draw about the reading habits of the people you interviewed? State your conclusions in the last paragraph of your report.

Proofreading As you proofread your report, check your notes to be sure that you've spelled people's names correctly. Pay special attention to the use of apostrophes to show possessive cases of nouns and pronouns. Finally, be sure that you've put quotation marks around direct quotations and that you've correctly capitalized and punctuated all quotations.

Review: Posttest

A. Proofreading Sentences for the Correct Use of Quotation Marks and Underlining (Italics)

Each of the following sentences requires underlining (italics), quotation marks, or both. Write each sentence correctly.

EXAMPLE **1.** Ted, can you answer the first question? Ms. Simmons asked.
     1. *"Ted, can you answer the first question?" Ms. Simmons asked.*

1. The best chapter in our vocabulary book is the last one, More Word Games.
2. "I answered all the questions, Todd said, but I think that some of my answers were wrong."
3. Star Wars was more exciting on the big movie screen than it was on our small television set.

MECHANICS

4. Mr. Washington asked Connie, "Which flag also included the slogan Don't Tread on Me?"
5. There is a legend that the band on the Titanic played the hymn Nearer My God to Thee as the ship sank into the icy sea.
6. Play the Freddie Jackson tape again, Sam, Rebecca called from her room.
7. Wendy wrote an article called Students, Where Are You? for our local newspaper, the Morning Beacon.
8. In the short story Thank You, M'am by Langston Hughes, a woman helps a troubled boy.
9. "Can I read Treasure Island for my book report? Carmine asked.
10. Every Christmas Eve my uncle recites The Night Before Christmas for the children in the hospital.

B. Proofreading Sentences for the Correct Use of Apostrophes, Hyphens, Parentheses, and Dashes

Each of the following sentences contains at least one error in the use of apostrophes, hyphens, parentheses, or dashes. Write each sentence correctly.

EXAMPLE   1. Ive been thinking about rivers names that come from Native American words.
　　　　　1. *I've been thinking about rivers' names that come from Native American words.*

11. Boater's on the Missouri River may not know that *Missouri* means "people of the big canoes."
12. Have you heard the song about the Souths famous Shenandoah River?
13. The committee voted to help keep the walkway clean along the Connecticut River.
14. I cant remember I wonder how many people have this same problem how many *is* are in the word *Mississippi*.

15. Everybodys favorite tour stop was Mount Vernon, George Washingtons home overlooking the Potomac River.

16. Don't you remember they're story about catching twenty two fish in the Arkansas River?

17. Three fourths of the class couldnt pronounce the name *Monongahela* until we broke it into syllables Mo-non-ga-he-la.

18. His painting of the Mohawk River was good, but her's was better.

19. Ricardos guidebook the one he ordered last month states that the Suwannee is one of Floridas major rivers.

20. Shes lived in Massachusetts for thirty one years but has never before seen the Merrimack River.

MECHANICS

28 SPELLING

Improving Your Spelling

Good Spelling Habits

As your vocabulary grows, you may have difficulty spelling some of the new words. You can improve your spelling by using the following methods.

1. *Pronounce words correctly.* Pronouncing words carefully can often help you to spell them correctly.

   EXAMPLES   athlete: ath • lete [not *ath • e • lete*]
   probably: prob • a • bly [not *pro • bly*]
   library: li • brar • y [not *li • bar • y*]

2. *Spell by syllables.* When you have trouble spelling long words, divide them into syllables. A **syllable** is a word part that can be pronounced by itself. Learning to spell the syllables of a word one at a time will help you master the spelling of the whole word.

   EXAMPLES   gymnasium: gym • na • si • um [four syllables]
   representative: rep • re • sent • a • tive [five syllables]

3. *Use a dictionary.* When you are not sure about the spelling of a word, look in a dictionary. A dictionary will also tell you the correct pronunciations and syllable divisions of words.

4. *Keep a spelling notebook.* The best way to master words that give you difficulty is to list the words and review them frequently. Divide each page of a notebook into four columns.

COLUMN 1   Write correctly the words you frequently misspell.

COLUMN 2   Write the words again, dividing them into syllables and marking the accents. (If you are not sure how to do this, use a dictionary.)

COLUMN 3   Write the words again, circling the parts that give you trouble.

COLUMN 4   Jot down any comments that may help you remember the correct spelling.

EXAMPLE

MECHANICS

Correct Spelling	Syllables and Accents	Trouble Spot	Comments
escape	es•cape'	es(c)ape	Pronounce correctly.
calendar	cal'•en•dar	calend(a)r	Think of <u>days</u> marked on the calendar.
casually	cas'•u•al•ly	casua(lly)	Study rule 28e.

5. *Proofread for careless spelling errors.* Whenever you write, proofread your paper for errors in spelling. By slowly rereading what you have written, you can correct careless errors such as uncrossed *t*'s, undotted *i*'s, and crossed *l*'s.

Spelling Rules

ie and *ei*

28a. Except after *c*, write *ie* when the sound is long *e*.

EXAMPLES achieve believe chief field piece
ceiling conceit deceit deceive receive

EXCEPTIONS either leisure neither
protein seize weird

28b. Write *ei* when the sound is not long *e*.

EXAMPLES foreign forfeit height heir their
freight neighbor reign veil weigh

EXCEPTIONS ancient conscience efficient
friend mischief patience

▶ EXERCISE 1 · **Spelling Words with *ie* and *ei***

The following paragraph contains ten words with missing letters. Add the letters *ie* or *ei* to spell each numbered word correctly.

EXAMPLE Many people know [1] th____r signs in the Chinese zodiac.
1. *their*

My [1] n____ghbor, Mrs. Yee, told me about the Chinese zodiac signs. Not all Chinese people [2] bel____ve in the zodiac. My parents don't, and [3] n____ther do I, but I do think it's interesting. The Chinese zodiac is an [4] anc____nt set of twelve-year cycles named after different animals. According to Mrs. Yee, the [5] ch____f traits in your personality come from your animal sign. At first, I thought this notion was a bit [6] w____rd, but it's not hard to understand. For example, a tiger is supposed to [7] s____ze opportunities [8] f____rcely. That description perfectly fits my brother's [9] fr____nd Mike Chen, who was born in 1974. Mrs. Yee showed me a chart like the one on this page so that I could figure out the signs of all [10] ____ght members of my family.

RAT	OX	TIGER	RABBIT	DRAGON	SNAKE
1972, 1984, 1996	1973, 1985, 1997	1974, 1986, 1998	1975, 1987, 1999	1976, 1988, 2000	1965, 1977, 1989

HORSE	SHEEP	MONKEY	ROOSTER	DOG	BOAR
1966, 1978, 1990	1967, 1979, 1991	1968, 1980, 1992	1969, 1981, 1993	1970, 1982, 1994	1971, 1983, 1995

–cede, –ceed, and –sede

28c.   The only word ending in –*sede* is *supersede*. The only words ending in –*ceed* are *exceed, proceed,* and *succeed*. Most other words with this sound end in –*cede*.

EXAMPLES   **con*cede*   inter*cede*   pre*cede*   re*cede*   se*cede***

 EXERCISE 2   **Proofreading Misspelled Words Ending in –*cede*, –*ceed*, and –*sede***

The following sentences contain five misspelled words ending in –*cede*, –*ceed*, and –*sede*. Identify the errors and spell the words correctly.

EXAMPLE   **1. The guitarist could not procede until the electricity came back on.**
   1. *procede—proceed*

1. Clarence Leo Fender succeded in changing the music business in the 1950s.
2. He improved the design of electric guitars, which quickly superceded acoustic guitars in popular music.

3. The success of Fender's invention probably exceded his wildest dreams.
4. Music critics consede that a new era began with the invention of the electric guitar.
5. Concerts that preceeded Fender's invention were not nearly as loud as modern ones.

Adding Prefixes

A *prefix* is a letter or group of letters added to the begin-ning of a word to change its meaning.

EXAMPLES   dis + honest = **dis**honest
               un + selfish = **un**selfish
               pre + arrange = **pre**arrange

28d. When adding a prefix to a word, do not change the spelling of the word itself.

EXAMPLES   mis + spell = **mis**spell   il + logical = **il**logical
               over + see = **over**see   in + exact = **in**exact

EXERCISE 3   **Spelling Words with Prefixes**

Spell each of the following words, adding the prefix given.

EXAMPLE **1.** un + wrap
           1. *unwrap*

1. im + migrate   3. un + certain   5. semi + circle
2. re + settle   4. il + legal

Adding Suffixes

A *suffix* is a letter or group of letters added to the end of a word to change its meaning.

EXAMPLES   care + less = care**less**
               comfort + able = comfort**able**
               walk + ed = walk**ed**

MECHANICS

28e. When adding the suffix *–ly* or *–ness* to a word, do not change the spelling of the word itself.

EXAMPLES   slow + ly = slow**ly**   dark + ness = dark**ness**
usual + ly = usual**ly** eager + ness = eager**ness**
shy + ly = shy**ly**   shy + ness = shy**ness**

EXCEPTIONS   For words that end in *y* and have more than one syllable, change the *y* to *i* before adding *–ly* or *–ness*.
happy + ly = happ**ily**   lazy + ness = laz**iness**

28f. Drop the final silent *e* before a suffix beginning with a vowel.

EXAMPLES   line + ing = lin**ing**
desire + able = desir**able**
approve + al = approv**al**

EXCEPTIONS   **Keep the final silent *e***
- in a word ending in *ce* or *ge* before a suffix beginning with *a* or *o*:
  *notice + able = notice**able***
  *courage + ous = courage**ous***
- in *dye* before *–ing*: *dye**ing***
- in *mile* before *–age*: *mil**eage***

28g. Keep the final silent *e* before a suffix beginning with a consonant.

EXAMPLES   hope + less = hope**less**
care + ful = care**ful**
awe + some = awe**some**
love + ly = love**ly**
nine + ty = nine**ty**
amuse + ment = amuse**ment**

EXCEPTIONS   nine + th = nin**th**
argue + ment = argu**ment**
true + ly = tru**ly**
judge + ment = judg**ment**
whole + ly = whol**ly**
awe + ful = aw**ful**

MECHANICS

▶ EXERCISE 4   **Spelling Words with Suffixes**

Spell each of the following words, adding the suffix given.

EXAMPLE   **1.** hope + ful
           1. *hopeful*

1. natural + ly   **5.** tease + ing   **9.** confine + ment
2. adore + able   **6.** lucky + ly   **10.** advantage + ous
3. sure + ly   **7.** tune + ful
4. dry + ness   **8.** trace + able

28h.   For words ending in *y* preceded by a consonant, change the *y* to *i* before any suffix that does not begin with *i*.

EXAMPLES   cry + ed = **cried**   duty + ful = **dutiful**
           easy + ly = **easily**   cry + ing = **crying**

28i.   For words ending in *y* preceded by a vowel, keep the *y* when adding a suffix.

EXAMPLES   pray + ing = **praying**   pay + ment = **payment**
           obey + ed = **obeyed**   boy + hood = **boyhood**

EXCEPTIONS   **day—daily   lay—laid   pay—paid   say—said**

28j.   Double the final consonant before a suffix beginning with a vowel if the word

(1) has only one syllable or has the accent on the last syllable

and

(2) ends in a single consonant preceded by a single vowel.

EXAMPLES   sit + ing = **sitting**   occur + ed = **occurred**
           swim + er = **swimmer**   begin + er = **beginner**
           drop + ed = **dropped**   forbid + en = **forbidden**

Otherwise, the final consonant is usually not doubled before a suffix beginning with a vowel.

EXAMPLES   sing + er = singer   final + ist = finalist
           speak + ing = speaking   center + ed = centered

NOTE: In some cases, the final consonant may or may not be
doubled.

EXAMPLES   cancel + ed = canceled   *or*   cancelled
           travel + er = traveler   *or*   traveller

Most dictionaries list both of these spellings as correct.
When you are not sure about the spelling of a word, it is
best to check in a dictionary.

▶ EXERCISE 5   **Spelling Words with Suffixes**

Spell each of the following words, adding the suffix given.

EXAMPLE   **1.** study + ed
          1. *studied*

1. tiny + est   5. display + ed   9. submit + ing
2. trim + ing   6. destroy + ing   10. win + er
3. carry + ed   7. refer + al
4. pity + ful   8. jog + er

▶ REVIEW A   **Proofreading for Misspelled Words**

Most of the following sentences contain a spelling error.
Identify and correct each error. If a sentence is correct,
write C.

EXAMPLE   **1.** The man shown on the next page is not Sam
          Houston or Jim Bowie, but he is a certifyed
          Texas hero.
          1. *certifyed—certified*

1. This industryous blacksmith is William Goyens.
2. In 1820, he moved from North Carolina to Texas,
   where he succeded in several businesses.
3. Goyens acheived his greatest fame as a negotiator
   with the Comanche and the Cherokee peoples.
4. He easily made freinds with the Native Americans
   who traded in the small town of Nacogdoches.

MECHANICS

5. Later, he assisted the Mexican government and then the Texas army in makking peace with their Native American neighbors.
6. General Sam Houston asked Goyens to interceed on behalf of the settlers.
7. Because of Goyens's efforts, the Comanches and the Cherokees agreed to remain on peacful terms with the settlers.
8. In addition to negoti-ating peace treaties, Goyens studied law to protect his own and others' freedoms.
9. People started coming to him with their legal problems, and he unselfishly tried to help them.
10. William Goyens was truely an important force in shaping Texas history.

Forming the Plurals of Nouns

28k. For most nouns, add *—s*.

SINGULAR	desk	idea	shoe	friend	camera	Wilson
PLURAL	desks	ideas	shoes	friends	cameras	Wilsons

28l. For nouns ending in *s, x, z, ch,* or *sh,* add *—es*.

SINGULAR	gas	fox	waltz	inch	dish	Suarez
PLURAL	gases	foxes	waltzes	inches	dishes	Suarezes

▶ EXERCISE 6   **Spelling the Plural Forms of Nouns**

Spell the plural form of each of the following nouns.

EXAMPLE   **1.** right
            1. *rights*

1. dish	5. skyscraper	9. Gómez
2. plumber	6. march	10. tax
3. candle	7. parade	
4. watch	8. republic	

28m. For nouns ending in *y* preceded by a vowel, add *–s.*

SINGULAR	decoy	highway	alley	Riley
PLURAL	decoys	highways	alleys	Rileys

28n. For nouns ending in *y* preceded by a consonant, change the *y* to *i* and add *–es.*

SINGULAR	army	country	city	pony	ally	daisy
PLURAL	armies	countries	cities	ponies	allies	daisies

EXCEPTIONS For proper nouns, add *–s.*
Brady—Bradys   Murphy—Murphys

28o. For some nouns ending in *f* or *fe*, add *–s.* For others, change the *f* or *fe* to *v* and add *–es.*

SINGULAR	belief	thief	sheriff	knife	giraffe
PLURAL	beliefs	thieves	sheriffs	knives	giraffes

NOTE: When you are not sure about how to spell the plural of a noun ending in *f* or *fe*, look in a dictionary.

28p. For nouns ending in *o* preceded by a vowel, add *–s.*

SINGULAR	radio	patio	stereo	igloo	Matteo
PLURAL	radios	patios	stereos	igloos	Matteos

28q. For nouns ending in *o* preceded by a consonant, add *–es.*

SINGULAR	tomato	potato	echo	hero
PLURAL	tomatoes	potatoes	echoes	heroes

EXCEPTIONS For musical terms and proper nouns, add –*s*.

alto—alto**s**	soprano—soprano**s**
Tejano—Tejano**s**	Nakamoto—Nakamoto**s**

NOTE: To form the plural of some nouns ending in *o* preceded by a consonant, you may add either –*s* or –*es*.

SINGULAR	domino	mosquito	banjo	flamingo
PLURAL	domino**s**	mosquito**s**	banjo**s**	flamingo**s**
	or	*or*	*or*	*or*
	domino**es**	mosquito**es**	banjo**es**	flamingo**es**

When you are in doubt about the way to form the plural of a noun ending in *o* preceded by a consonant, check the spelling in a dictionary.

28r. The plural of a few nouns is formed in irregular ways.

SINGULAR	ox	goose	foot	tooth	woman	mouse
PLURAL	ox**en**	g**ee**se	f**ee**t	t**ee**th	w**o**men	m**i**ce

▶ EXERCISE 7   **Spelling the Plurals of Nouns**

Spell the plural form of each of the following nouns. [Note: A word may have more than one correct plural form.]

EXAMPLE   **1.** volcano
                1. *volcanoes or volcanos*

1. monkey	**5.** hoof	**9.** cargo
2. trophy	**6.** proof	**10.** woman
3. Massey	**7.** palomino	
4. diary	**8.** child	

28s. For most compound nouns, form the plural of the last word in the compound.

SINGULAR	bookshelf	push-up	sea gull	ten-year-old
PLURAL	bookshel**ves**	push-up**s**	sea gull**s**	ten-year-old**s**

MECHANICS

28t. For compound nouns in which one of the words is modified by the other word or words, form the plural of the word modified.

SINGULAR	brother-in-law	maid of honor	eighth-grader
PLURAL	brothers-in-law	maids of honor	eighth-graders

28u. For some nouns the singular and the plural forms are the same.

SINGULAR AND PLURAL **trout   sheep   Sioux   deer   moose**

28v. For numbers, letters, symbols, and words used as words, add an apostrophe and –*s*.

EXAMPLES The product of two **4's** is twice the sum of four **2's**.
Notice that the word *committee* has two **m's,** two **t's,** and two **e's.**
Write **$'s** before, not after, amounts of money.
This composition contains too many **so's** and **and's.**

NOTE: In your reading you may notice that some writers do not use apostrophes to form the plurals of numbers, capital letters, symbols, and words used as words.

EXAMPLES Their music is as popular today as it was in the **1970s.**
When dividing, remember to write **R**s before the remainders in the quotients.

However, using an apostrophe is never wrong. Therefore, it is best always to use the apostrophe.

Spelling Numbers

28w. Spell out a number that begins a sentence.

EXAMPLE **Fifteen thousand** people went to see the Milton Nascimento concert.

MECHANICS

28x. Within a sentence, spell out numbers that can be written in one or two words. Use numerals for other numbers.

EXAMPLES   Do you have **two** nickels for **one** dime?
In all, **fifty-two** people attended the family reunion.
More than **160** people were invited.

NOTE: If you use several numbers, some short and some long, write them all the same way. Usually, it is better to write them all as numerals.

INCORRECT   We sold eighty-six tickets to the first dance and 121 tickets to the second dance.
CORRECT   We sold 86 tickets to the first dance and 121 tickets to the second dance.

28y. Spell out numbers used to indicate order.

EXAMPLE   Our team came in **third** [not *3rd*] in the regional track meet.

▶ REVIEW B   **Spelling the Plurals of Nouns**

Spell the plural form of each of the following nouns.

EXAMPLE   **1.** editor in chief
1. *editors in chief*

1. Sioux
2. basketball
3. Japanese
4. son-in-law
5. *i*
6. car pool
7. major general
8. sit-up
9. handful
10. 1900

▶ REVIEW C   **Using Plurals of Nouns**

You and your friends are creating word games for a party on Saturday night. You've decided to write tongue twisters and challenge your friends to read them aloud. Write the plural forms of the following five pairs of words. Then, use words with similar consonant sounds to create hard-to-say sentences. Your tongue-twisting sentences can be silly or serious.

EXAMPLE   **1.** tooth—train
1. *teeth—trains*
*Twyla tickled three tigers' teeth on two trains
to Timbuktu this Thursday.*

1. donkey—dash   **4.** potato—patio
2. O'Reilly—raspberry   **5.** fox—finch
3. moose—mother-in-law

Words Often Confused

People frequently confuse the words in each of the following groups. Some of these words are ***homonyms.*** Their
pronunciations are the same, but their meanings and
spellings are different. Others have the same or similar
spellings.

accept	[verb] *to receive with consent; to give approval to* In 1964, Dr. Martin Luther King, Jr., *accepted* the Nobel Prize for peace.
except	[verb] *leave out from a group;* [prep.] *other than; but* We were *excepted* from the assignment. Everyone will be there *except* Ruben.
advice	[noun] *a recommendation about a course of action* Good *advice* may be easy to give but hard to follow.
advise	[verb] *to recommend a course of action; to give advice* I *advise* you to continue your music lessons if you can.

affect [verb] *to influence; to produce an effect upon*
The explosion of Krakatoa *affected* the
sunsets all over the world.

effect [noun] *the result of an action; consequence*
The phases of the moon have an *effect* on the
tides of the earth's oceans.

---

all ready *all prepared*
The players are *all ready* for the big game.

already *previously*
Our class has *already* taken two field trips.

---

all right [adjective] *satisfactory;* [adverb] *satisfactorily*
[*All right* must be written as
two words. The spelling *alright*
is not acceptable.]
Was my answer *all right?*
Maria did *all right* in the track meet.

MECHANICS

▶ EXERCISE 8   **Using Words Often Confused**

From the choices in parentheses, select the correct word
or words for each of the following sentences.

EXAMPLE   **1.** Anh and her family are (*all ready, already*) to
celebrate Tet, the Vietnamese New Year.
1. *all ready*

1. Do you think my work is (*all right, alright*)?
2. The (*affect, effect*) of the victory was startling.
3. The scientists were (*all ready, already*) to watch the
launching of the rocket.
4. Whose (*advice, advise*) are you going to take?
5. The coach (*advices, advises*) us to stick to the training
rules.
6. Why did you (*accept, except*) Carla from the rule?
7. Her weeks of practice have finally (*affected, effected*)
her game.

8. Juan has (*all ready, already*) learned how to water-ski.
9. Most of the rebels were offered a full pardon and (*accepted, excepted*) it, but the leaders were (*accepted, excepted*) from the offer.
10. Gabriel took my (*advice, advise*) and visited the home of Frederick Douglass in Washington, D.C.

altar	[noun] *a table for a religious ceremony* The *altar* was covered with lilies.
alter	[verb] *to change* The outcome of the election may *alter* the mayor's plan.
all together	*everyone or everything in the same place* The director called us *all together* for one final rehearsal.
altogether	*entirely* He is *altogether* pleased with his victory.
brake	[noun] *a stopping device* Can you fix the *brake* on my bicycle?
break	[verb] *to fracture; to shatter* A high-pitched noise can *break* glass.
capital	*a city; the seat of a government* Olympia is the *capital* of Washington.
capitol	*building; statehouse* Where is the *capitol* in Albany?
choose	[verb; present tense, rhymes with *whose*] *to select* Will you *choose* speech or art as your elective next year?
chose	[verb; past tense, rhymes with *grows*] *selected* Sara *chose* a red pen, not a blue one.

MECHANICS

Frank & Ernest reprinted by permission of Newspaper Enterprise Association, Inc.

EXERCISE 9 **Using Words Often Confused**

From the choices in parentheses, select the correct word or words for each of the following sentences.

EXAMPLE **1.** Mr. Conway said he (*choose, chose*) teaching as a career because he wants to help young people.
1. *chose*

1. The building with the dome is the (*capital, capitol*).
2. By working (*all together, altogether*), we can succeed.
3. Because she loved dramatics, Alice (*choose, chose*) a difficult part in the school play.
4. Be careful not to (*brake, break*) those dishes.
5. That book is (*all together, altogether*) too complicated for you to enjoy.
6. The candles on the (*altar, alter*) of the synagogue glowed beautifully.
7. Why did you (*choose, chose*) that one?
8. A car without a good emergency (*brake, break*) is a menace.
9. Will Carrie's accident (*altar, alter*) her plans to go canoeing on the Buffalo Fork River in Arkansas?
10. Tallahassee is the (*capital, capitol*) of Florida.

clothes	*wearing apparel*
	One can learn a lot about a historical period by studying its styles of *clothes*.
cloths	*pieces of fabric*
	You'll find some cleaning *cloths* in the drawer.

MECHANICS

coarse [adjective] *rough; crude*
The beach is covered with *coarse* brown sand.

course [noun] *path of action; unit of study or route* [also used in the expression *of course*]
If you follow that *course*, you'll succeed.
My mother is taking a *course* in accounting.
The wind blew the ship slightly off its *course*.
You know, of *course*, that I'm right.

consul *a representative of a government in a foreign country*
Who is the American *consul* in Cairo?

council *a group of people who meet together*
The mayor called a meeting of the city *council*.

councilor *member of a council*
The *councilors* discussed several issues.

counsel [noun] *advice;* [verb] *to give advice*
When choosing a career, seek *counsel* from your teachers.
Ms. Jiménez *counseled* me to pursue a career in teaching.

counselor *one who advises*
Who is your guidance *counselor*?

desert [noun] *a dry, sandy region*
The Sahara is the largest *desert* in Africa.

desert [verb] *to abandon; to leave*
Most dogs will not *desert* a friend in trouble.

dessert [noun] *the final course of a meal*
Fruit salad is my favorite *dessert*.

MECHANICS

EXERCISE 10 **Using Words Often Confused**

From the choices in parentheses, select the correct word or words for each of the following sentences.

EXAMPLE **1.** Egypt, of (*course, coarse*), is an ancient country in northeastern Africa.
1. *course*

1. The student (*council, counsel*) voted to have "A Night on the Nile" as its dance theme.
2. In this photograph, many shoppers at an Egyptian market wear Western (*clothes, cloths*).

3. Some, however, wear traditional garments, including (*clothes, cloths*) called *kaffiyehs* wrapped around their heads.
4. In ancient Egypt, pharaohs didn't always follow the advice of their (*councilors, counselors*).
5. The surfaces of some famous Egyptian monuments look (*coarse, course*) from years of exposure to wind and sand.
6. In my geography (*coarse, course*), I learned that Nubians make up the largest minority group in Egypt's population.
7. The American (*consul, council*) in Cairo welcomed the vice-president to Egypt.
8. Camels didn't (*desert, dessert*) their owners when they crossed the Egyptian (*desert, dessert*).

9. Figs, grapes, and dates have long been popular (*deserts, desserts*) in Egypt.
10. In Cairo, the confused tourists looked to their tour director for (*council, counsel*).

formally	*with dignity; according to strict rules or procedures* The mayor delivered the speech *formally*.
formerly	*previously; in the past* Adele Zubalsky was *formerly* the principal of the school.

hear	[verb] *to perceive sounds by ear* Dogs can *hear* sounds that people can't hear.
here	[adverb] *in this place* The treasure is buried *here*.

its	[possessive form of *it*] Mount Fuji is noted for *its* beauty.
it's	[contraction of *it is* or *it has*] *It's* a good idea to open a savings account. *It's* been a long time since I last saw you.

lead	[verb, present tense, rhymes with *feed*] *to go first; to be a leader* A small town in New Hampshire often *leads* the nation in filing its election returns.
led	[verb, past tense of *lead*] *went first* Mr. Tanaka *led* the scout troop back to camp.
lead	[noun, rhymes with *red*] *a heavy metal* Many fishing nets are weighted with *lead* to hold them on the sea bottom.

MECHANICS

> **loose** [adjective, rhymes with *moose*] *not securely attached; not fitting tightly*
> If the knot is too *loose,* the piñata will fall out of the tree.
>
> **lose** [verb, present tense, rhymes with *whose*] *to suffer loss*
> Vegetables *lose* some of their vitamins when they are cooked.

▶ EXERCISE 11　**Using Words Often Confused**

From the choices in parentheses, select the correct word or words for each of the following sentences.

EXAMPLE　**1.** Mary Beth didn't (*loose, lose*) her Southern accent even after she moved to Boston.
　　1. *lose*

1. According to Ethan's map, (*its, it's*) a long way from (*hear, here*) to the park.
2. The ancient Chinese, Greeks, and Romans used (*lead, led*) in their coins.
3. If you don't wait (*hear, here*), we may (*loose, lose*) you in the crowd.
4. Before the club takes up new business, the secretary (*formally, formerly*) reads the minutes of the previous meeting.
5. (*Its, It's*) too bad that the oak tree has lost (*its, it's*) leaves.
6. Didn't you (*hear, here*) me, Charlotte? Come over (*hear, here*) now!
7. The Yankees were ten runs behind, and it seemed certain that they were going to (*loose, lose*).
8. Steffi Graf (*lead, led*) in the first games of the tennis match.
9. My mother told me that our new neighbor, Mr. Brown, was (*formally, formerly*) a colonel in the U.S. Army.
10. That (*loose, lose*) bolt can cause trouble.

passed	[verb, past tense of *pass*] *went by* The people in the car waved as they *passed* us.
past	[noun] *that which has gone by;* [preposition] *beyond* Some people long to live in the *past*. They walked *past* the dozing guard.
peace	*security and quiet order* We are striving for *peace* and prosperity.
piece	*a part of something* Some people can catch fish with a pole, a *piece* of string, and a bent pin.
plain	[adjective] *simple, common, unadorned;* [noun] *a flat area of land* The actors wore *plain* costumes. What is the difference between a prairie and a *plain?*
plane	[noun] *a tool; an airplane; a flat surface* The *plane* is useful in the carpenter's trade. Four single-engine *planes* are in the hangar. In geometry class we learned how to measure the angles of *planes* such as squares and triangles.
principal	[noun] *the head of a school;* [adjective] *main or most important* The *principal* of the school is Mr. Arimoto. What are the *principal* exports of Brazil?
principle	[noun] *a rule of conduct; a main fact or law* Judge Rios is a woman of high *principle*. We discussed some of the basic *principles* of democracy.

MECHANICS

> **quiet** [adjective] *still and peaceful; without noise*
> A *quiet* room is needed for concentrated study.
>
> **quite** [adverb] *wholly or entirely; to a great extent*
> Winters in New England can be *quite* severe.

EXERCISE 12 **Using Words Often Confused**

From the choices in parentheses, select the correct word for each of the following sentences.

EXAMPLE **1.** Summer (*passed, past*) by too quickly!
1. *passed*

1. In some Filipino villages, you can still find (*plain, plane*), practical houses built on bamboo stilts.
2. The summer was not (*quiet, quite*) over before the beginning of school brought a (*quiet, quite*) household once more.
3. This is a main (*principal, principle*) in mathematics.
4. On July 11, 1991, the moon (*passed, past*) between the earth and the sun, causing a total solar eclipse.
5. A (*plain, plane*) is a useful tool.
6. Save me a (*peace, piece*) of that blueberry pie.
7. Have you heard that the new (*principal, principle*) used to be a student here?
8. You can learn much from (*passed, past*) experience.
9. After the long war came a long period of (*peace, piece*).
10. Cattle were grazing over the (*plain, plane*).

> **shone** [verb, past tense of *shine*] *gleamed; glowed*
> The Navajo jeweler polished the silver-and-turquoise ring until it *shone*.
>
> **shown** [verb, past participle of *show*] *revealed*
> A model of the new school will be *shown* to the public next week.

MECHANICS

stationary	[adjective] *in a fixed position* Most of the furnishings of a space capsule must be *stationary*.
stationery	[noun] *writing paper* I need a new box of *stationery*.

than	[conjunction used for comparisons] The Amazon River is longer *than* the Mississippi River.
then	[adverb] *at that time* If the baby is awake by four o'clock, we will leave *then*.

their	[possessive form of *they*] *Their* team seems very skillful.
there	[adverb] *at or in that place;* [also used to begin a sentence] Go *there* in the fall when the leaves are turning. *There* were no objections.
they're	[contraction of *they are*] *They're* rehearsing for a production of *A Soldier's Story*.

threw	[verb, past tense of *throw*] *cast; tossed* Our relief pitcher *threw* nine strikes in succession.
through	[preposition] The ship went *through* the series of locks in the Panama Canal.

MECHANICS

▶ EXERCISE 13 **Using Words Often Confused**

From the choices in parentheses, select the correct word for each of the following sentences.

EXAMPLE **1.** (*There, Their*) are some truly amazing tunnels used for transportation throughout the world.
1. *There*

1. Take a good look at the workers in this photograph because (*their, they're*) part of history.
2. (*Their, They're*) labor helped create a tunnel under the English Channel to link England with France.
3. A documentary about the tunnels through the Alps will be (*shone, shown*) at the library.
4. Huge exhaust fans were constructed to move the (*stationary, stationery*) air in the Holland Tunnel in New York.
5. To run railroad lines all across the United States, workers had to dig many tunnels (*threw, through*) mountains.
6. Used to blast tunnels in mountainsides, explosives (*threw, through*) enormous boulders into the air.
7. The warm sun (*shone, shown*) bright on the snowy top of Mont Blanc, but in the mountain's tunnel it was dark and chilly.
8. We rode the underground, or subway, into London, where I bought some (*stationary, stationery*).
9. Boston's subway is older (*than, then*) New York City's subway.
10. In Paris, we took the subway, called the *métro*, to the Eiffel Tower and (*than, then*) to the Louvre museum.

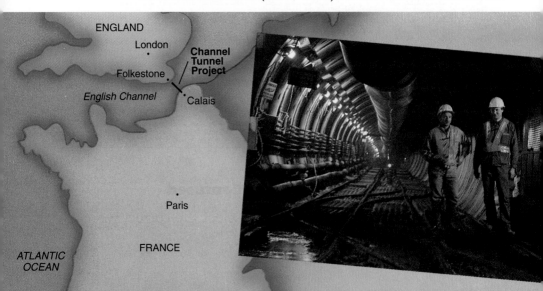

ENGLAND
London
Channel Tunnel Project
Folkestone
English Channel
Calais
Paris
FRANCE
ATLANTIC OCEAN

MECHANICS

to	[preposition; also part of the infinitive form of a verb] Marco Polo began his trip *to* China in 1271. Do you know how *to* make tortillas?
too	[adverb] *also; more than enough* We have lived in Iowa and in Alaska, *too*. It is *too* cold for rain today.
two	*cardinal number between one and three* She borrowed *two* dollars from me.
weak	[adjective] *not strong; feeble* The patient is too *weak* to have visitors.
week	[noun] *seven days* Your pictures of Josh's bar mitzvah will be ready in about a *week*.
weather	[noun] *condition of the air or atmosphere* The *weather* is hot and humid.
whether	[conjunction] *if* Jessica wondered *whether* she should go.
who's	[contraction of *who is* or *who has*] *Who's* representing the yearbook staff? *Who's* read today's newspaper?
whose	[possessive form of *who*] *Whose* report are we hearing today?
your	[possessive form of *you*] *Your* work in math is improving.
you're	[contraction of *you are*] *You're* right on time!

MECHANICS

▶ EXERCISE 14 **Using Words Often Confused**

From the choices in parentheses, select the correct word or words for each of the following sentences.

EXAMPLE   **1.** (*Your, You're*) class gets to visit Minnehaha Park in Minneapolis.
        1. *Your*

1. Jason felt (*weak, week*) after skiing all day in the Sangre de Cristo Mountains of New Mexico.
2. (*Weather, Whether*) we'll go or not depends on the (*weather, whether*).
3. (*Whose, Who's*) books are you carrying?
4. Find out (*whose, who's*) going if you can.
5. Learning (*to, too, two*) roll carved sticks for the Korean game of *yut* wasn't (*to, too, two*) difficult.
6. (*Your, You're*) off your course, captain.
7. We took (*to, too, two*) (*weaks, weeks*) for our trip.
8. The (*weather, whether*) was cloudy in Miami, Florida.
9. Would you enjoy a trip (*to, too, two*) Mars, Flo?
10. Aren't you using (*your, you're*) compass?

▶ REVIEW D   **Proofreading for Misspelled Words**

The following paragraph contains ten spelling errors. Identify and correct each error.

EXAMPLE   [1] Anne Shirley, here portrayed by actress Megan Fallows, found a pieceful life and a loving family on Prince Edward Island.
        1. *pieceful—peaceful*

[1] Does the island's scenery shone in the picture on the next page appeal to you? [2] My family enjoyed the green hillsides and rugged seashore during our two-weak vacation there last summer. [3] Prince Edward Island is quite a beautiful spot, and its Canada's smallest province. [4] Everyone who lives there calls the island PEI, and now I do, to. [5] During our visit, the weather was pleasant, so I lead my parents all over PEI on foot. [6] We walked to several places of interest in Charlottetown, the capitol. [7] I got to chose our first stop, and I selected the farmhouse that's the setting for the novel *Anne of Green Gables*. [8] That novel's main character, Anne Shirley, is someone who's ideas I admire. [9] Walking around "The Garden Province,"

we passed many farms; the principle crop is potatoes.
[10] Take my advise, and visit Prince Edward Island if you
get the chance.

50 Commonly Misspelled Words

ache	cough	guess	once	though
again	could	half	ready	through
always	country	hour	said	tired
answer	doctor	instead	says	tonight
blue	does	knew	shoes	trouble
built	don't	know	since	wear
busy	early	laid	straight	where
buy	easy	meant	sugar	which
can't	every	minute	sure	whole
color	friend	often	tear	women

250 Spelling Words

As you study the following words, pay particular attention to the letters in italics. These letters generally cause
the greatest difficulty in correctly spelling the words.

abandon	actually	appearance
absolutely	advertisement	application
acceptance	against	appreciation
accidentally	aisle	approach
accommodate	amount	argument
accompany	analysis	article
accomplish	anticipate	assistance
achieve	anxiety	authority
acquaintance	apology	awful
acquire	apparent	basis

MECHANICS

beginning
believe
benefit
boundary
bouquet
bulletin
business
cancel
capacity
careless

carrier
ceiling
challenge
choice
choir
chorus
circuit
colonel
column
coming

commercial
committees
competition
completely
conceive
condemn
congratulations
conscience
conscious
control

convenience
courteous
criticism
cylinder
dealt
decision
defense
definite
definition
describe

description
desirable
despair
develop
diamond
difficulties
disappointment
discipline
discussion
distinction

distribution
doctrine
duplicate
economic
eighth
eligible
embarrass
engineering
enthusiasm
eventually

exactly
exaggerate
excellent
existence
experience
experiment
explanation
fascinating
favorite
February

finally
flu
forty
fourth
friendliness
generally
governor
grammar
gratitude
guarantee

guardian
gymnasium
hatred
height
heroine
hesitate
humorous
ignorance
imagination
immediately

incidentally
individual
inferior
initial
inspiration
intelligence
interfere
interrupt
involve
jealous

judgment
knowledge
laboratory
leisure
lengthen
license
lieutenant
loneliness
majority
manufacture

marriage
mechanical
medieval
military
mourn
multiplication
muscular
mystery
naturally
necessary

nickel
nonsense
numerous
obvious
occasionally
occurrence
opinion
opponent
opportunity
orchestra

originally
paid
parallel
parliament
patience
performance
personal
personality
persuade
philosopher

picnicking
planned
pleasant
possess
precede
preferred
prejudice
privilege
probably
procedure

professor
pursuit
qualified
realize
receipt
recognize
recommend
referring
regularly
relieve

repetition
research
response
restaurant
rhythm
satisfied
saucer
schedule
scissors
sense

sentiment
separate
sergeant
shepherd
similar
solemn
source
souvenir
sponsor
straighten

subscription
success
sufficient
suggest
suppress
surprise
surround
suspense
suspicion
tailor

temperament
tendency
theory
therefore
thorough
tobacco
tonsils
tradition
tragedy
transferred

tries
truly
unanimous
unnecessary
unsatisfactory
until
useful
using
utilized
vacuum

variety
various
vein
view
villain
violence
warrant
weird
wholly
writing

MECHANICS

29 CORRECTING COMMON ERRORS

Key Language Skills Review

This chapter reviews key skills and concepts that pose special problems for writers.

- Sentence Fragments and Run-on Sentences
- Subject-Verb and Pronoun-Antecedent Agreement
- Verb Forms
- Pronoun Forms
- Comparison of Modifiers
- Misplaced and Dangling Modifiers
- Capitalization
- Punctuation—Commas, End Marks, Colons, Semicolons, Quotation Marks, and Apostrophes
- Spelling
- Standard Usage

Most of the exercises in this chapter follow the same format as the exercises found throughout the grammar, usage, and mechanics sections. You will notice, however, that two sets of review exercises are presented in standardized test formats. These exercises are designed to provide you with practice not only in solving usage and mechanics problems but also in dealing with these kinds of problems on such tests.

▶ EXERCISE 1   **Correcting Sentence Fragments**

Most of the following groups of words are sentence fragments. If a word group is a sentence fragment, correct it by
adding or deleting words to make a complete sentence or
by attaching it to a complete sentence. You may need to
change the punctuation and capitalization, too. If a word
group is already a complete sentence, write *S*.

EXAMPLE   **1.** The movie about Cleopatra.
   1. *The movie about Cleopatra is playing*
      downtown.

1. Answered the telephone politely.
2. An armadillo's covering of bony plates like armor.
3. Because Alan prefers volleyball to any other team
   sport.
4. After the first winter snow.
5. Someone gave the museum those photographs of
   settlers in the Ozarks.
6. When she returns to the house this afternoon.
7. Delivering the package with postage due.
8. The recycling center now accepting magazines and
   catalogs.
9. Moved here from Germany so that she could study
   at the institute.
10. The kitten walked across the computer keyboard.

▶ EXERCISE 2   **Correcting Run-on Sentences**

Correct each of the following run-on sentences by making
two separate sentences or by combining the two parts of
the run-on sentence to make one complete sentence.

EXAMPLE   **1.** Sign language, or manual speech, is not new,
      in fact, it has a long history.
   1. *Sign language, or manual speech, is not new;*
      in fact, it has a long history.

1. Some people may think that manual speech dates
   from this century the beginnings of manual speech
   go much further back.

2. An Italian physician played an important role in the development of manual speech, I had never heard of him.
3. His name was Girolamo Cardano he lived during the sixteenth century.
4. Cardano proposed the theory that people unable to hear could learn to associate written symbols with objects or actions he thought that people who could not hear or speak could then use such symbols to communicate.
5. In the 1700s, Abbé Charles Michel de L'Epée opened the first free school for people with impaired hearing he devised a manual sign version of spoken French.
6. In 1778, Samuel Heinicke began a school in Germany for people unable to hear, it was the first such school to receive government recognition.
7. The first school in the United States for those unable to hear was founded in 1817 its founder was Thomas Hopkins Gallaudet, a minister from Philadelphia.
8. Laurent Clerc was the first deaf person to teach other deaf people in a school in the United States, in 1816 he came to the United States to help Gallaudet found the Hartford School for the Deaf.
9. Gallaudet University is in Washington, D.C. it is still the world's only liberal arts college for people who are deaf or hard of hearing.
10. Today, American Sign Language is used by at least 500,000 people in the United States and Canada it is the fourth most common language in the United States.

EXERCISE 3 **Correcting Sentence Fragments and Run-on Sentences**

The following groups of words contain fragments, run-ons, and complete sentences. Identify each group of words by writing *F* for a fragment, *R* for a run-on, or *S* for a complete sentence. If a word group is a sentence fragment, correct it by adding or deleting words to make a complete sentence.

Correct each of the run-ons by making it into two separate sentences or by using a comma and a coordinating conjunction. You may also need to change the punctuation and capitalization.

EXAMPLE **1.** The old truck drove very slowly up the hill, a long line of cars followed it.
        1. *R—The old truck drove very slowly up the hill. A long line of cars followed it.*

1. One of the most famous photographs taken during World War II shows soldiers raising the U.S. flag at Iwo Jima.
2. I hope to travel to Asia someday, I want to climb the Himalayas.
3. To uproot the stumps of the trees we cut down in the front yard.
4. Some kinds of spiders, such as the bolas spider, that do not make webs.
5. Played a variety of music from different countries for the dancers.
6. To say no to Robin was hard.
7. Into the forest and across the valley they rode it took until sundown to reach the camp.
8. When a cicada comes out of the ground.
9. My mother's favorite movie is about the composer Mozart, I can't remember its title.
10. Sirius, which is the brightest star that can be seen from Earth at night.

▶ EXERCISE 4 **Correcting Sentence Fragments and Run-on Sentences**

The following paragraph contains sentence fragments, run-on sentences, and complete sentences. First, identify each numbered item by writing *F* for a fragment, *R* for a run-on, or *S* for a complete sentence. Then, revise the paragraph to correct the fragments and run-ons.

EXAMPLE [1] The history of food a delicious subject.
        1. *F—The history of food is a delicious subject.*

[1] There have been many milestones in the history of food production, the development of canned food is one of the most important. [2] Because canned goods fill our stores today. [3] Most people generally take these goods for granted. [4] The story of canned goods begins in the 1700s with Lazzaro Spallanzani his experiments in preserving food were some of the earliest to succeed. [5] Other early experimenters preserved vegetables, fruit, and meat in glass bottles. [6] Using processes in which the bottles of food were heated to very high temperatures. [7] Bottles later replaced with containers made of tin-plated iron. [8] Heating the containers of food kills the bacteria that cause food to spoil. [9] As Louis Pasteur discovered in the mid-1800s. [10] The development of this process, now called pasteurization, made eating canned food safer the eventual invention of the can opener made it easier!

EXERCISE 5

Identifying Verbs That Agree in Number with Their Subjects

For each of the following sentences, choose the form of the verb in parentheses that agrees with the subject.

EXAMPLE   **1.** (*Do, Does*) you know much about cloud formations?
          1. *Do*

1. Learning about clouds (*help, helps*) you predict the weather.
2. Some of the books I used in my report about weather (*give, gives*) detailed information about clouds.
3. Water droplets and ice crystals (*form, forms*) clouds.
4. Many of us (*like, likes*) to look for faces and familiar shapes in clouds overhead.
5. One of the most common types of clouds (*is, are*) the cumulonimbus rain cloud.
6. People often (*call, calls*) these clouds thunderstorm clouds.
7. Clouds of this kind (*produce, produces*) tornadoes and hail at times.

8. My friends Jeffrey and Kate (*don't, doesn't*) remember the name of cloud formations that look like wisps of cotton.
9. Several of these cirrus clouds (*was, were*) in the sky yesterday.
10. Stratus clouds, which often produce drizzle, (*look, looks*) like smooth sheets.

▶ EXERCISE 6   **Proofreading Sentences for Correct Subject-Verb Agreement**

Most of the following sentences contain errors in subject-verb agreement. If a verb does not agree with its subject, give the correct form of the verb. If a sentence is correct, write *C*.

EXAMPLE   **1.** Spanish explorers and missionaries is important in New Mexico's history.
   1. *are*

1. Spanish missions throughout New Mexico attracts many tourists nowadays.
2. Some of these missions has been in continuous use for centuries.
3. Two missions especially interests me.
4. I can't decide whether the Mission of San Agustin de Isleta or the Mission of San Miguel of Santa Fe are my favorite.
5. Both of these missions date from the early seventeenth century.
6. Each of them have survived damage caused by fires and centuries of wear.
7. Antique objects and priceless art lends their beauty to the missions.
8. One of the most noteworthy features of the Santa Fe mission is a bell.
9. The bell, which was brought to Santa Fe in the 1800s, were cast in 1356 in Spain.
10. Churches in Spain and Mexico was home to the bell before it was brought to New Mexico.

▶ EXERCISE 7   **Identifying Pronouns That Agree with Their Antecedents**

For each of the following sentences, choose the pronoun or pair of pronouns in parentheses that agrees with its antecedent or antecedents.

EXAMPLE   **1.** The horse and mule walked toward (*its, their*) owner.
          1. *their*

1. Did your uncle or your father take (*his, their*) fishing license to the pier?
2. Does one of the coats have Kim's initials on (*their, its*) label?
3. Everyone has had (*his or her, their*) turn to play in the game.
4. Ms. Torres and Ms. Lawrence accepted (*her, their*) Community Appreciation Certificates.
5. Anyone may recite (*his or her, their*) poem during the program tonight.
6. Did David or Tim put (*his, their*) jacket on?
7. Neither of my twin stepbrothers has had (*his, their*) first haircut.
8. After careful consideration, each of the women cast (*their, her*) vote.
9. The first grade and the second grade will be taking (*its, their*) field trip tomorrow.
10. Neither Ramona nor Isabel recalled (*her, their*) dream from the night before.

▶ EXERCISE 8   **Proofreading Sentences for Correct Pronoun-Antecedent Agreement**

Most of the following sentences contain errors in agreement of pronoun and antecedent. Identify each incorrect pronoun, and supply the correct form or forms. If the sentence is correct, write *C*.

EXAMPLE   **1.** Tintin, whose adventures spanned the globe, traveled with their dog, Snowy.
          1. *their—his*

1. The Belgian cartoonist Georges Remi created the comic strip character Tintin in the 1920s and set their first adventures in the Soviet Union.
2. Everybody in class who had read Tintin stories had their favorite tales of the adventurous reporter.
3. Both of this character's closest companions, Captain Haddock and Professor Cuthbert Calculus, help his friend Tintin.
4. Each of these men has their own unusual characteristics.
5. Thomson and Thompson, detectives who look alike, add his own silliness to Tintin's travels.
6. Several of the students said that he or she had read the comic strip.
7. Which one of the seven girls remembered to bring their own copy of *Tintin in Tibet*?
8. Julia showed us her drawing of Tintin's dog, Snowy.
9. My grandparents still have some of his or her old Tintin books.
10. Did *Tintin's Travel Diaries* inspire James or Reginald to keep their own travel diary during the summer?

▶ EXERCISE 9 **Writing Correct Verb Forms**

For each of the following sentences, fill in the blank with the correct past or past participle form of the verb given before the sentence.

EXAMPLE **1.** *draw* Kevin has _____ a Japanese pagoda.
　　　　　 1. *drawn*

1. *hike* Most of the club members have _____ on the Appalachian Trail.
2. *know* I have _____ the Katsanos family for years.
3. *steal* Can you believe that Jean Valjean was put in prison because he had _____ a loaf of bread?
4. *try* The baby giraffe _____ to stand immediately after its birth.
5. *spin* The car _____ around twice on the wet road.
6. *build* My dad and my sister _____ a workbench.
7. *make* Who _____ this delicious Irish soda bread?

8. *swim* Our team has _____ in pools this size, but we prefer Olympic-size pools.

9. *suppose* Gary was _____ to rent a funny movie for us to watch tonight.

10. *shake* The wet puppy _____ itself and got water all over Phuong's dress.

EXERCISE 10 **Proofreading for Correct Past and Past Participle Verb Forms**

If a sentence contains an incorrect verb form, write the correct form. If a sentence is correct, write *C*.

EXAMPLE **1.** Have you ever saw a sundial?
1. *seen*

1. I have read Anne Frank's *The Diary of a Young Girl.*
2. The song that Ann and Brian sang use to be popular in the 1950s.
3. Caitlin begun swimming lessons around the age of six.
4. Ben perform that routine for the judges last year.
5. The lizard done its best to catch the fly, but the fly flew away unharmed.
6. Have you wrote a letter recently?
7. The performer told jokes and stories while he danced.
8. Excited about her new idea, Marie gave up on her first plan.
9. Is it true the winner actually run backward in the race?
10. Did you know that Bill "Bojangles" Robinson made up the word *copacetic,* which means "fine" or "excellent"?

EXERCISE 11 **Proofreading for Correct Past and Past Participle Verb Forms**

If a sentence contains an incorrect verb form, write the correct form. If a sentence is correct, write *C*.

EXAMPLE **1.** I have took several lessons in aikido.
1. *taken*

1. Aikido, a Japanese system of self-defense, has interest me for some time.

2. A month ago, I begun lessons at a local martial arts studio.
3. Every time I have went to class, I have been nervous, but I am finally becoming more confident.
4. Our instructor has teached us that the Japanese word *aikido* means "the way of blending energy."
5. He sayed that I can "accept" an attacker's energy and blend my own energy with it to redirect the attack away from myself.
6. Today in class, I saw how redirecting an opponent's energy really works.
7. The aikido holds and movements I choosed played off my opponent's strength.
8. I maked each of these movements without using any unnecessary force.
9. My opponent lunged at me, but he losed his footing when I redirected his energy.
10. My instructor said that attackers are usually throwed off balance by such movements because they expect a person under attack to use force to fight back.

▶ EXERCISE 12 **Identifying Correct Pronoun Forms**

For the following sentences, choose the correct form of each pronoun in parentheses.

EXAMPLE **1.** The new rules do not apply to any of (*us, we*) eighth-graders.
1. *us*

1. Please give (*her, she*) the sequins for the costume.
2. The new paramedics at the stadium are (*they, them*).
3. Sasha and (*he, him*) are good at trivia games.
4. Coach Mendoza adjusted the parallel bars for Paul and (*me, I*).
5. The usher showed (*us, we*) to our seats.
6. My sister and (*me, I*) will help Dad paint our house this summer.
7. A friend of ours sent (*us, we*) a new book of short stories by a popular Venezuelan author.

8. The retirement home where Brad's grandmother lives impressed (*him, he*).

9. Did you give the oranges and apples to (*them, they*) for the picnic?

10. The first ones to arrive in the morning are almost always (*she and I, her and me*).

▶ EXERCISE 13 **Identifying Correct Pronoun Forms**

For each of the following sentences, choose the correct form of the pronoun in parentheses.

EXAMPLE **1. Facts about First Ladies interest (*me, I*).**
1. *me*

1. Hillary Rodham Clinton wrote a book called *It Takes a Village: And Other Lessons Children Teach Us*; last week she autographed copies for (*us, we*).

2. James and (*I, me*) were surprised to learn that Lucy Hayes was the first president's wife to earn a college degree.

3. It was (*her, she*) who was nicknamed Lemonade Lucy.

4. The school librarian gave (*him, he*) an article about Grace Coolidge, who taught children with hearing impairments.

5. Jack showed Eric, Heather, and (*me, I*) a picture of Mrs. Coolidge with Helen Keller.

6. Tell (*them, they*) about Martha Washington's role as hostess of the new nation.

7. The artist who painted the portrait of the elegant Elizabeth Monroe could have been (*him, he*).

8. In his report on Edith Wilson, Nathaniel said that (*she, her*) sewed clothes to send to soldiers during World War I.

9. When she was a delegate to the United Nations, Eleanor Roosevelt championed human rights and worked to secure (*they, them*) for all people.

10. With (*she, her*) as chairperson, the United Nations' Human Rights Commission drafted the Universal Declaration of Human Rights.

▶ EXERCISE 14 **Choosing Correct Regular and Irregular Modifiers**

Choose the correct form of the modifier in parentheses in each of the following sentences.

EXAMPLE **1.** *The Fantasticks* is Jorge's (*favorite, favoritest*) musical.
1. *favorite*

1. *The Fantasticks* has had the (*longer, longest*) run of any musical in New York City.
2. In fact, it is the (*oldest, older*) continuously running musical in the United States.
3. My aunt says that the performance she saw at New York's Sullivan Street Playhouse in 1996 was the (*better, best*) show of any she'd ever seen.
4. She told me that *The Fantasticks* was created by one of the (*most talented, talentedest*) teams of writers for the stage—Tom Jones and Harvey Schmidt.
5. Jones and Schmidt have also written other musicals, but *The Fantasticks* is generally considered to be their (*popularest, most popular*) one.
6. Have you ever seen a musical with a character called something (*more strange, stranger*) than The Man Who Dies?
7. The play has both serious and funny songs; many people like the funny songs (*best, better*).
8. The Handyman, who appears only during the play's intermission, has one of the (*most odd, oddest*) roles in modern theater.
9. The students who put on our school's production of *The Fantasticks* performed (*good, well*).
10. If the play ever comes to your town, you might find it (*more, most*) enjoyable to see than a movie.

▶ EXERCISE 15 **Correcting Double Comparisons and Double Negatives**

For each of the following sentences, identify the incorrect modifier. Then, give the correct form of the modifier.

EXAMPLE **1.** Some of the most prettiest candles are made of beeswax.
1. *most prettiest—prettiest*

1. We wanted to rent a movie but couldn't find none that we all wanted to see.
2. Both Ted and I are learning Spanish, but I am more shyer about speaking it than he is.
3. Kim never wanted to go nowhere near the icy rapids.
4. People in cars are less safer when they do not wear seat belts.
5. We volunteered to help with the preschool art classes because there wasn't nobody else who had the time.
6. Of all the kinds of trees in our neighborhood, which do you think is the least commonest?
7. Moose are the most largest members of the deer family.
8. Don't never use the elevator if a building is on fire.
9. Carrie couldn't scarcely walk after she broke her toe.
10. Kudzu is a Japanese vine that grows more faster than many other plants.

EXERCISE 16 Revising Sentences to Correct Misplaced Modifiers

Each of the following sentences contains a misplaced modifier. Revise each sentence to correct the error.

EXAMPLE **1.** Bathing in the mud, the photographer snapped several photographs of the elephants.
1. *The photographer snapped several photographs of the elephants bathing in the mud.*

1. My dad said today we are going to the beach.
2. The children could see the bacteria using their new microscope.
3. Richard saw the announcement for the book sale on the bulletin board.
4. Changing color to a bright green, we watched the chameleon conceal itself among the leaves.
5. I gave flowers to my friends that I had picked along the roadside.

▶ EXERCISE 17 **Revising Sentences to Correct Misplaced and Dangling Modifiers**

Each of the following sentences contains an error in the use of modifiers. Revise each sentence to correct the error.

EXAMPLE   **1.** Growing in the root cellar, my aunt found a red mushroom.

           1. *My aunt found a red mushroom growing in the root cellar.*

1. I read a book about how the Egyptian pyramids were built yesterday.
2. While making lunch for the visitors, the stove caught on fire.
3. The children played in the puddle with no boots on.
4. Don announced at the meeting he will be asking for volunteers.
5. Running to catch the bus, several books fell out of his backpack.
6. Wobbling, the crowd anxiously watched the tightrope walker.
7. My sister described the giraffe she had seen during our flight back to the United States.
8. Tired of the drought, the rain was greeted with loud cheers.
9. Sparkling in the sunlight, the mockingbird showed no interest in the sapphire ring.
10. While walking along the shoreline, a large, black fossilized shark's tooth caught my eye.

▶ EXERCISE 18 **Identifying Correct Usage**

Choose the correct word or words in parentheses in each of the following sentences.

EXAMPLE   **1.** About (*a, an*) hour before sunrise, the dam almost (*burst, busted*).

           1. *an, burst*

1. (*Doesn't, Don't*) the long-term (*affects, effects*) of global warming concern you?

CORRECTING COMMON ERRORS

2. There (*use to, used to*) be (*fewer, less*) people jogging in my neighborhood.

3. (*Without, Unless*) we have permission, I don't think we ought to (*bring, take*) Dad's new CD player to the beach tomorrow.

4. Marshall (*would of, would have*) gone to the park, but (*then, than*) he changed his mind.

5. We had a difficult time choosing (*between, among*) the two puppies playing together (*inside, inside of*) the large basket.

6. My clarinet playing has improved (*some, somewhat*), but I really (*had ought, ought*) to practice more.

7. Everyone (*accept, except*) John thinks the weather will be (*alright, all right*) for our walk in the park.

8. I (*try and, try to*) go to all of my aunt's softball games because her team plays so (*good, well*).

9. (*Who's, Whose*) going to sleep outside with so many of (*them, those*) mosquitoes around?

10. Randy talks (*like, as if*) he has to ride his bike a long (*way, ways*) on his paper route.

▶ EXERCISE 19 **Correcting Errors in Usage**

Each of the following sentences contains an error in usage. Identify and correct each error.

EXAMPLE **1.** Patrick did so good at the spelling bee that he qualified for the national contest.
1. *good—well*

1. If the tuna-fish salad tastes badly, don't eat any more of it.

2. My stepsister said she would learn me how to play the piano.

3. Please bring these vegetables to your grandmother when you visit her this Friday.

4. I read where a waterspout is the name for a tornado that occurs over a lake or an ocean.

5. The cartoonist which works for our newspaper has a wonderful sense of humor.

6. The *ruble* is an unit of currency used in Russia and Tajikistan.
7. A friendly rivalry arose between all of the members of the soccer team.
8. Late last night, Jack saw a light shining somewheres across the river.
9. Mr. Catalano said that the smallest dinosaurs weren't scarcely larger than chickens.
10. I knew that we should of brought the umbrella with us when we left the house today.

▶ EXERCISE 20 **Correcting Errors in Usage**

Each of the following sentences contains an error in usage. Identify and correct each error.

EXAMPLE **1.** Our class has all ready read about the life of José Luis Muñoz Marín (1898–1980).
1. *all ready—already*

1. Where was Muñoz Marín born at?
2. I read in this here biography that he was born in San Juan, the capital of Puerto Rico.
3. For more then a quarter of a century, Muñoz Marín was Puerto Rico's chief political leader.
4. He worked to help Puerto Ricans build better lives for theirselves.
5. Like Muñoz Marín himself discovered, he had been born at a major turning point in the history of his country.
6. He must of been very popular, for he was elected governor four times.
7. When I read his biography, I learned how come he founded the Popular Democratic Party.
8. John F. Kennedy was the president which awarded Muñoz Marín the Presidential Medal of Freedom.
9. Its fascinating to think of Muñoz Marín's being both a poet and a politician.
10. Did you know that their is a U.S. postage stamp featuring Muñoz Marín?

Grammar and Usage Test: Section 1

DIRECTIONS Read the paragraph below. For each numbered blank, select the word or group of words that best completes the sentence. Indicate your response by shading in the appropriate oval on your answer sheet.

EXAMPLE

The word *organic* _(1)_ "of or related to living things."
1. (A) it means
   (B) meant
   (C) is meaning
   (D) means

SAMPLE ANSWER 1.

Scientists _(1)_ study the prehistoric world _(2)_ carbon dating to determine the age of organic materials such as wood and bone. All living things absorb carbon-14 from the environment into _(3)_ tissues. An organism that has died _(4)_ carbon-14 because _(5)_ no longer takes in air and food. Carbon-14 that was previously absorbed into the organism's tissues _(6)_ at a specific rate. Knowing the rate of breakdown, scientists measure the amount of carbon-14 in an organism's remains to determine how much time _(7)_ since the organism died. Scientists cannot use carbon dating to determine the age of organic material _(8)_ is _(9)_ about 120,000 years, because carbon-14 _(10)_ down and becomes untraceable after that long a time.

---

1. (A) which
   (B) who
   (C) whom
   (D) what

2. (A) they use
   (B) use
   (C) uses
   (D) used

3. (A) its
   (B) his or her
   (C) they're
   (D) their

4. (A) doesn't absorb no more
   (B) don't absorb no more
   (C) doesn't absorb any more
   (D) don't absorb any more

5. (A) he
   (B) she
   (C) it
   (D) they

6. (A) it decays
   (B) decays
   (C) decay
   (D) were decaying

7. (A) passes
   (B) is passing
   (C) have passed
   (D) has passed

8. (A) that
   (B) what
   (C) who
   (D) whom

9. (A) more old then
   (B) older than
   (C) more older than
   (D) older then

10. (A) busts
    (B) busted
    (C) has busted
    (D) breaks

Grammar and Usage Test: Section 2

DIRECTIONS   Either part or all of each of the following sentences is underlined. Using the rules of standard written English, choose the answer that most clearly expresses the meaning of the sentence. If there is no error, choose A. Indicate your response by shading in the appropriate oval on your answer sheet.

EXAMPLE

1. The first Cuban-born woman to become a U.S. Army officer was Mercedes O. Cubria, <u>whom</u> served in the Women's Army Corps.
   (A) whom
   (B) who
   (C) that
   (D) which

SAMPLE ANSWER   1.

1. In basketball, one kind of illegal dribbling <u>is when</u> a player stops dribbling and then begins dribbling again.
   (A) is when
   (B) is that
   (C) is because
   (D) occurs when

2. Karen's sandwich is <u>more tastier than</u> the one I brought.
   (A) more tastier than
   (B) more tastier then
   (C) tastier than
   (D) tastier then

3. <u>Tonya said she had seen a hummingbird at her feeder in the mall today.</u>
   (A) Tonya said she had seen a hummingbird at her feeder in the mall today.
   (B) In the mall today, Tonya said she had seen a hummingbird at her feeder.
   (C) Tonya said in the mall today she had seen a hummingbird at her feeder.
   (D) Tonya said in the mall today at her feeder she had seen a hummingbird.

4. Have the Glee Club and they set down to discuss the program?
    (A) Have the Glee Club and they set
    (B) Have the Glee Club and them sat
    (C) Have the Glee Club and they sat
    (D) Has the Glee Club and they sat

5. For years, Matthew Henson accompanied Robert Peary on expeditions, together, in 1908, they set out to reach the North Pole.
    (A) expeditions, together, in 1908, they set
    (B) expeditions; together, in 1908, they setted
    (C) expeditions, together, in 1908, them setted
    (D) expeditions. Together, in 1908, they set

6. The reason you should wear a helmet is because it can prevent head injuries.
    (A) is because it
    (B) is that it
    (C) is that they
    (D) is when it

7. A dedicated and creative teacher, Anne Sullivan learned Helen Keller how to communicate effectively.
    (A) learned
    (B) taught
    (C) was learning
    (D) teached

8. Between Josh and him lay the exhausted puppy.
    (A) him lay
    (B) he lay
    (C) him laid
    (D) him has laid

9. The treasure that was buried in the abandoned mine.
    (A) The treasure that was buried in the abandoned mine.
    (B) The treasure found buried in the abandoned mine.
    (C) The treasure buried in the abandoned mine.
    (D) The treasure was buried in the abandoned mine.

10. Peering behind the bookcase, a secret passage was discovered by the detective.
    (A) Peering behind the bookcase, a secret passage was discovered by the detective.
    (B) Peering behind the bookcase, the detective discovered a secret passage.
    (C) The detective discovered a secret passage peering behind the bookcase.
    (D) While peering behind the bookcase, a secret passage was discovered by the detective.

▶ EXERCISE 21 **Correcting Errors in Capitalization**

Each of the following groups of words contains at least one capitalization error. Correct the errors either by changing capital letters to lowercase letters or by changing lowercase letters to capital letters.

EXAMPLE   **1.** central avenue in albuquerque, New mexico
            1. *Central Avenue in Albuquerque, New Mexico*

1. venus and jupiter
2. my Aunt Jessica
3. wednesday morning
4. the Jewish holiday hanukkah
5. thirty-fifth street
6. the stone age
7. nobel peace prize
8. Minute maid® orange juice
9. spanish, earth science, and algebra I
10. secretary of state warren christopher

▶ EXERCISE 22 **Correcting Errors in Capitalization**

Each of the following sentences contains errors in capitalization. Correct the errors either by changing capital letters to lowercase letters or by changing lowercase letters to capital letters.

EXAMPLE   **1.** many african americans lived and worked in
            the western United states after the civil war.
            1. *Many African Americans lived and worked in
            the western United States after the Civil War.*

1. one of the most remarkable people from that era is bill pickett, who was born on December 5, 1870.
2. His Father worked on ranches near austin, texas, and pickett grew up watching cowhands work.
3. Pickett began performing rodeo tricks at County fairs, and in 1905, he joined the 101 wild west show in the region then called the oklahoma territory.
4. With this show, Pickett toured the united states, south america, canada, and great britain.

5. i wish i could have seen all the cowboys, cowgirls, horses, buffalo, and longhorn cattle that were part of the show!

6. Pickett portrayed himself in a 1923 silent movie called *the bull-dogger.*

7. Pickett, who died in 1932, was later inducted into the national rodeo cowboy hall of fame.

8. in 1977, the university of oklahoma press published a biography, *bill pickett, bulldogger,* written by colonel bailey c. hanes.

9. a bronze statue of Bill Pickett was dedicated at the fort worth cowtown coliseum in 1987.

10. The Bill Pickett invitational rodeo, which tours all over the united states, draws rodeo talent from around the nation.

▶ EXERCISE 23 **Correcting Sentences by Adding Commas**

Each of the following sentences lacks at least one comma. Write the word that comes before each missing comma, and add the comma.

EXAMPLE **1.** When the Spanish brought the first horses to North America the lives of many American Indians changed.
   1. *America,*

1. Native peoples bred the Spanish horses and developed ponies that could survive on the stubby coarse grass of the Great Plains.

2. These hardy ponies may not have been considered as beautiful as the Spanish horses but they were faster stronger and smarter.

3. Because horses were so highly valued they came to signify status and wealth.

4. These ponies which were useful in the daily activities of American Indians were also ridden into battle.

5. Before riding into a battle Crow warriors painted symbolic designs on themselves and on their ponies.

6. These designs might show that the rider possessed "medicine power" had been on successful horse raids or had lost someone special to him.
7. Colors not just designs had special meanings.
8. The color blue for example represented wounds; red which symbolized courage and bravery represented bloodshed.
9. Often painted on the pony's flanks or under its eyes white clay stripes indicated the number of horses a warrior had captured.
10. Among the Plains Indians warriors who disgraced their enemies by tapping them at close range earned horizontal stripes called "coup" marks.

EXERCISE 24   **Using End Marks and Commas Correctly**

The following sentences need end marks and commas. Write the word or number that comes before each missing end mark or comma, and add the proper punctuation.

EXAMPLE   **1.** Did you sign up for the class trip to Washington Baltimore and Roanoke
1. *Washington, Baltimore, Roanoke?*

1. What for instance would you suggest doing to improve wheelchair access to the theater
2. Well I was standing on the ladder but I still couldn't reach the apples
3. Marta a friend of mine always recycles her aluminum cans and newspapers
4. When I draw with pastels charcoal or chalk I'm careful to wash my hands before touching anything else
5. Watch out for the falling tree branch
6. Is the Spanish Club meeting scheduled for today or tomorrow Lee
7. Adela wrote one letter on May 19 1997 and another on October 5 1997
8. Mr N Q Galvez Ms Alma Lee and Dr Paul M Metz spoke at the nutrition seminar last week

9. What a great idea that is
10. My friends and I like to hike in the mountains water-ski on the lake and jog along the park trails

EXERCISE 25 **Using Semicolons and Colons Correctly**

The following sentences lack necessary colons and semi-colons. Write the word or numeral that comes before and after each missing punctuation mark, and add the proper punctuation.

EXAMPLE **1.** Friday is the day for the band concert all of my family is attending.
    1. *concert; all*

1. I put bread in the oven at 4 15 it should be done soon.
2. We have been keeping the highway clean for three years naturally, no one in the club litters, no matter where he or she is.
3. My brother's favorite movie is *Homeward Bound The Incredible Journey.*
4. We gathered driftwood, shells, and rocks but we also needed sand, glass, and paint for the sculpture.
5. My stepsister Sarah, who is deaf, uses the following electronic devices a doorbell that makes the lights flicker, a telephone that converts speech to written words, and a television with closed captioning.

EXERCISE 26 **Correcting Sentences by Adding Quotation Marks, Other Marks of Punctuation, and Capital Letters**

Revise the following sentences by supplying capital letters and marks of punctuation as needed.

EXAMPLE **1.** Diane asked where is Denali National Park?
    1. *Diane asked, "Where is Denali National Park?"*

1. Natalie Merchant is my favorite singer said Stephen but I haven't heard her newest song yet.
2. Aunt Caroline exclaimed what a beautiful garden you have!

3. To block some of the traffic noise Russell commented the city should plant some trees along this street.
4. The first episode of that new television series is called Once upon a Twice-Baked Potato.
5. Did you see that Francis asked. That player bumped the soccer ball into the goal with his heel
6. Beverly asked why doesn't Janet want to be president of the club?
7. I'll go with you Dee said that sack of birdseed will be too heavy for you to carry back by yourself.
8. I just finished reading the chapter titled Noah Swims Alone, and I really enjoyed it Shawn said.
9. Did Stephanie actually yell I'm out of here before she left the room asked Joel.
10. You've Got a Friend is one of the songs in the movie *Toy Story* Jonathan said.

EXERCISE 27 **Proofreading a Dialogue for Correct Punctuation**

In the following dialogue, correct any errors in the use of quotation marks and other marks of punctuation. Also, correct any errors in the use of capitalization, and begin a new paragraph each time the speaker changes.

EXAMPLES [1] Guess what! Henry exclaimed This Saturday I'm going with my youth group to work on a Habitat for Humanity project
[2] What is Habitat for Humanity Lynn asked

1. "Guess what!" Henry exclaimed. "This Saturday I'm going with my youth group to work on a Habitat for Humanity project."
2. "What is Habitat for Humanity?" Lynn asked.

[1] It's an organization that renovates and builds houses for people who are poor and do not own homes Henry replied. [2] Oh, now I remember Lynn said. Many volunteers help with the work, right [3] Yes that's true Henry answered and the people who will live in the houses also help with the renovating or building of these houses

[4] Are they required to help paint hammer and do whatever else needs to be done? Lynn asked. [5] Yes, and over an extended period of time, they also pay back the building costs Henry explained.

[6] Lynn asked Isn't it expensive to build a house [7] Well Henry responded it does take a lot of money, but volunteer labor, donated construction materials, and skillful management keep the cost of building affordable.

[8] How long has Habitat for Humanity existed, and who started it Lynn asked [9] Our youth group leader told us that Millard and Linda Fuller started Habitat for Humanity in Georgia in 1976 Henry replied

[10] Hey, I think I'll go with you to work on the building project Lynn said.

▶ EXERCISE 28 **Correcting Sentences by Adding Apostrophes**

Write the correct form of each word that requires an apostrophe in the following sentences. If a sentence is already correct, write C.

EXAMPLE   **1.** Didnt the womens team win the tournament last year, too?
1. *Didn't, women's*

1. Theyre looking for Rodneys bucket of seashells that he gathered at the beach.
2. Its anybodys guess who will win!
3. Im glad you enjoyed staying at the Caldwells cabin last weekend.
4. If you help me wash my car this afternoon, I will help you wash yours tomorrow.
5. Isnt ten dollars worth going to be enough?
6. I havent a clue about that.
7. Charles Dickens "A Christmas Carol" is a story youll really enjoy.
8. The mens clothing shop is closed today.
9. Lets go swimming next Wednesday.
10. Tonyas recipes are always a hit at the churchs annual cookoff.

▶ EXERCISE 29 **Correcting Spelling Errors**

If a word in the following list is spelled incorrectly, write the correct spelling. If a word is correctly spelled, write *C.*

EXAMPLE **1.** superceed
 1. *supersede*

1. fryed	**8.** casualy	**15.** ageing
2. receed	**9.** disfigureing	**16.** measurment
3. brief	**10.** mother-in-laws	**17.** denys
4. wifes	**11.** dimmer	**18.** ratioes
5. tempoes	**12.** sliegh	**19.** sheeps
6. Lopezs	**13.** reciept	**20.** tablescloth
7. freewayes	**14.** mishapen	

▶ EXERCISE 30 **Using Words Often Confused**

For each of the following sentences, select the correct word or words from the choices in parentheses.

EXAMPLE **1.** My brother's (*advise, advice*) is usually good.
 1. *advice*

1. When will you hear (*whether, weather*) your poem has been (*accepted, excepted*) for publication?
2. We have (*all ready, already*) planned the field trip.
3. Do you think we will need to (*alter, altar*) our plans?
4. If you could (*choose, chose*) any place in the world to visit, where would you go?
5. Did the town (*counsel, council, consul*) meet today?
6. I'd rather experience the (*piece, peace*) and quiet of the beach (*then, than*) the noise and crowds of the city.
7. (*Its, It's*) good manners to hold the door open for anyone (*whose, who's*) hands are full.
8. The floats (*shown, shone*) brightly in the sunlight as the parade (*passed, past*) by our house.
9. If the (*whether, weather*) is bad, will that (*effect, affect*) our party, or are we having the party indoors?
10. Before turning in plastic bags for recycling, we reuse them (*to, too, two*) or three times.

Mechanics Test: Section 1

DIRECTIONS Each numbered item below contains an underlined group of words. Choose the answer that shows the correct capitalization, punctuation, and spelling of the underlined part. If there is no error, choose answer D (Correct as is). Indicate your response by shading in the appropriate oval on your answer sheet.

EXAMPLE

Thank you very [1] much, Mr. and Mrs. Fernandez for a great visit.

1. (A) much Mr. and Mrs. Fernandez,
   (B) much, Mr. and Mrs. Fernandez,
   (C) much Mr. and Mrs. Fernandez;
   (D) Correct as is

SAMPLE ANSWER 1. Ⓐ ⬤ Ⓒ Ⓓ

1201 Palm Circle
[1] Jacksonville Fla. 32201
[2] April 11 1997

[3] Dear Mr. and Mrs. Fernandez,

    I am so glad that you and Pedro invited me to stay at your home this [4] past weekend, I had a great time. The [5] whether I think was perfect for the activities you planned. The [6] picnic lunches volleyball games, and boat rides were so much fun! I especially enjoyed going fishing in your boat [7] *the ugly duckling*.

    Next weekend my parents are going to have a barbecue party to celebrate [8] my aunt Jessicas birthday. If you would like to join us this coming [9] Saturday at 5:30 P.M. please give us a call sometime this week.

[10] Sincerely yours,

Todd Grinstead

1. (A) Jacksonville, FL 32201
   (B) Jacksonville Fla 32201
   (C) Jacksonville FL 32201
   (D) Correct as is

2. (A) April, 11 1997
   (B) April Eleventh 1997
   (C) April 11, 1997
   (D) Correct as is

3. (A) Dear Mr. and Mrs. Fernandez:
   (B) Dear Mr and Mrs Fernandez:
   (C) Dear Mr. And Mrs. Fernandez,
   (D) Correct as is

4. (A) passed weekend; I had
   (B) past weekend; I had
   (C) passed weekend, I had
   (D) Correct as is

5. (A) whether, I think was
   (B) weather, I think was
   (C) weather, I think, was
   (D) Correct as is

6. (A) picnic lunchs,
   (B) picnic lunchs
   (C) picnic lunches,
   (D) Correct as is

7. (A) *the Ugly Duckling.*
   (B) *The Ugly Duckling.*
   (C) "The Ugly Duckling."
   (D) Correct as is

8. (A) my Aunt Jessica's
   (B) my Aunt Jessicas'
   (C) my aunt Jessica's
   (D) Correct as is

9. (A) Saturday, at 5:30 P.M.
   (B) Saturday at 5:30 P.M.,
   (C) Saturday, at 5:30 PM.,
   (D) Correct as is

10. (A) Sincerely yours',
    (B) Sincerly yours,
    (C) Sincerely yours:
    (D) Correct as is

Mechanics Test: Section 2

DIRECTIONS Each of the following sentences contains an underlined word or group of words. Choose the answer that shows the correct capitalization, punctuation, and spelling of the underlined part. If there is no error, choose answer D (Correct as is). Indicate your response by shading in the appropriate oval on your answer sheet.

EXAMPLE

1. King Louis Philippe of France created the <u>foreign legion</u> in 1831.
   - (A) Foreign Legion
   - (B) Foriegn Legion
   - (C) foriegn legion
   - (D) Correct as is

SAMPLE ANSWER 1. ● Ⓑ Ⓒ Ⓓ

1. My music teacher, <u>Mrs. O'Henry will sing two solos</u> at our school's talent show.
   - (A) Mrs. O'Henry, will sing two soloes
   - (B) Mrs. O'Henry will sing two soloes
   - (C) Mrs. O'Henry, will sing two solos
   - (D) Correct as is

2. "Do we have enough pickets to build the <u>fence,"</u> asked Michelle.
   - (A) fence"
   - (B) fence"?
   - (C) fence?"
   - (D) Correct as is

3. Last Friday <u>my sister-in-laws</u> nephew stopped by.
   - (A) my sister-in-law's
   - (B) my sister's-in-law
   - (C) my sister-in-laws'
   - (D) Correct as is

4. The short story <u>Over the Fence is about three oxen</u> and a frog.
   - (A) 'Over the Fence' is about three oxes
   - (B) 'Over The Fence' is about three oxen
   - (C) "Over the Fence" is about three oxen
   - (D) Correct as is

5. Turn left on <u>Ninety-eighth Street</u>.
   - (A) Ninty-eighth Street
   - (B) Ninety-Eighth Street
   - (C) Ninety-eighth street
   - (D) Correct as is

6. Roberto Clemente twice <u>lead the Pittsburgh Pirates</u> to victory in the World Series.

   (A) lead The Pittsburgh Pirates
   (B) led the Pittsburgh Pirates
   (C) led the Pittsburgh pirates
   (D) Correct as is

7. "How many of you," asked <u>Mr. Reynolds "have</u> seen a painting by the young Chinese artist <u>Wang Yani?"</u>

   (A) Mr. Reynolds, "have
   (B) Mr. Reynolds," have
   (C) Mr. Reynolds, "Have
   (D) Correct as is

8. <u>Those who studied for the test</u> of course, did better than those who did not.

   (A) Those, who studied for the test,
   (B) Those, who studied for the test
   (C) Those who studied for the test,
   (D) Correct as is

9. "Did you <u>say that "it's time to go?"</u> asked Raul.

   (A) say, that 'it's time to go'?"
   (B) say that it's time to go?"
   (C) say that 'It's time to go'?"
   (D) Correct as is

10. My younger sister excels in the following <u>classes Art II, social studies,</u> and English.

    (A) classes art II, social studies,
    (B) classes, Art II, Social Studies,
    (C) classes: Art II, social studies,
    (D) Correct as is

PART THREE

RESOURCES

RESOURCES

30 SPEAKING

Skills and Strategies

Whether you are speaking at school or in the workplace, you can be a more effective communicator if you consider

- your purpose (What are you trying to say?)
- your topic (What are you speaking about?)
- your audience (Who are your listeners?)

The Communication Cycle

Communication takes teamwork. First, a speaker communicates feelings or ideas to listeners. Then the listeners respond to the speaker's message. This response is called *feedback.*

Listeners may respond to a speaker by a *verbal* response, using words (such as "I see what you mean"). Or a listener could make *nonverbal* responses without using any words (such as by applauding).

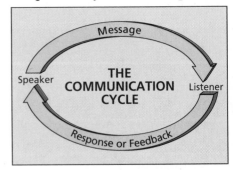

RESOURCES

Nonverbal Communication

Along with words, or verbal signals, you can communicate many meanings with nonverbal signals.

NONVERBAL COMMUNICATION	
NONVERBAL SIGNALS	**EXAMPLES**
Gestures or motions	thumbs up or nodding head (meaning agreement or encouragement), shrugging (uncertainty), shaking head (disagreement)
Facial expressions	smiling, raising an eyebrow, smirking, frowning, grimacing, pouting, or grinning (meanings vary with each situation)
Body language	turning away (rejection), stroking the chin (puzzlement), crossing arms on chest (reluctance, uncertainty)
Sounds	laughing, groaning, giggling (meanings vary with each situation)

Speaking Informally

Impromptu Speaking

Sometimes you need to speak to a group of people without having time to prepare what you want to say. This is called an *impromptu speech.* Remember the following points.

1. *Consider your purpose.* (Are you trying to inform your audience? Do you want to persuade them?)
2. *Consider your topic.* (What are the main ideas you need to say? Do you have time to add details that support or explain your main points?)
3. *Consider your audience.* (Does what you're saying suit the time, place, and audience you're speaking to?)

RESOURCES

Speaking Socially

In most social situations, you can be effective in communicating if you remember to speak clearly and politely.

Speaking on the Telephone

1. Call people at times which are convenient for them.
2. Identify yourself and state your reason for calling.
3. Be polite. Keep your call to a reasonable length.

Giving Instructions or Directions

1. Divide directions into clear, understandable steps.
2. Tell your listener the steps, in order.
3. Check to be sure your listener understands.

Making Social Introductions

1. Be confident. Introduce yourself to others.
2. When introducing others, identify them by name.
3. When you are introducing others, it is customary to speak first to

   - a person of higher job status
   - an older person before a younger person
   - the person you know best

Speaking Formally

Preparing a Speech

A *formal speech* is one given at an arranged time and place. This allows you to prepare carefully beforehand.

Planning Your Speech

When preparing your speech, you will need to consider your purpose, choose a subject, narrow your subject to a limited topic, and gather and arrange your information. See the composition chapters of this textbook for other suggestions.

The following chart shows some common types of speeches, arranged according to their purpose.

IDENTIFYING YOUR PURPOSE		
PURPOSE	**DESCRIPTION OF SPEECH**	**EXAMPLES OF SPEECH TITLES**
To inform	gives facts or explains how to do something	What Makes an Airplane Fly How to Make Your Home a Safer Place
To persuade	attempts to change listeners' opinion or attempts to get listeners to act	Why Getting Suntans May Be a Bad Idea Why Students Should Learn CPR
To entertain	relates an amusing story or incident	My First Experience with Riding a Bicycle

Considering Your Audience

When you plan your speech, you also need to consider your audience's needs and interests.

THINKING ABOUT YOUR AUDIENCE		
QUESTIONS ABOUT AUDIENCE	**EVALUATION**	**YOUR SPEECH WILL NEED**
What does your audience already know about this subject?	very little	to provide background details to inform your listeners about your topic
	a little	to include at least some background detail
	a lot	to focus only on interesting points about the topic
How interested will your audience be in this subject?	very interested	to maintain your listeners' interest
	mildly interested	to stick to parts of the topic your listeners are most interested in
	uninterested	to convince your listeners that this topic is important

RESOURCES

Organizing Your Speech Notes

The most common type of speech is an *extemporaneous speech*. *Extemporaneous* comes from Latin words meaning "from the time." When you give an extemporaneous speech, you prepare an outline of your main points. Then you make note cards for each main point. When you give your speech, you talk directly to the audience just as you would in an impromptu speech. But with an extemporaneous speech, you have prepared your speech and you can refer to your note cards whenever you need to remember your main points.

HOW TO MAKE SPEECH NOTE CARDS

1. Write each main idea on a separate note card.
2. Make a special note card for anything that you plan to read word for word (such as a quotation or a series of dates or statistics that's too hard to memorize).
3. Include a special note card to indicate when to show a chart, diagram, model, or other visual materials.
4. Number your completed cards to keep them in order.

Giving Your Speech

Speaking Expressively

When you speak effectively, you use your voice and your gestures to help convey your meaning to your listeners. Here are some pointers to use when you are speaking.

1. *Stand confidently.* Stand up straight and look alert.
2. *Act naturally.* Use facial expressions and gestures that reflect what you're saying.
3. *Speak clearly.* Speak loudly so that everyone can hear you clearly. Pronounce your words carefully.
4. *Look at your audience.* When you speak, look directly at members of your audience and speak to them directly.

5. *Use variety when you speak.* Use a normal variety of voice patterns as you speak. These are clues that help your audience understand what points you want to emphasize.

- *Volume:* Be loud enough to be heard, but strengthen or soften your tone for emphasis.
- *Pitch:* Use the normal rise and fall of your voice to highlight various ideas.
- *Stress:* Emphasize important words as you speak.
- *Rate:* Speak at a comfortable, relaxed pace.

Speaking Before an Audience

It's normal to feel nervous about speaking in front of an audience. However, you can use the following suggestions to help you stay in control.

1. *Be prepared.* Organize your material carefully and practice using your note cards and any visuals you plan to use during your speech.
2. *Practice your speech.* Each time you rehearse, pretend you're actually giving your speech.
3. *Focus on your purpose.* Think about how you want your speech to affect your audience.

Special Speaking Situations

Making Announcements

When you make an announcement, your main goal is to provide information. Follow these guidelines.

1. When you write your announcement, be brief but include all the most important details.
2. To give your announcement, get your audience's attention and then say your message slowly and clearly.

RESOURCES

Making an Introduction to a Presentation

An introduction is often given before a speaker's presentation or before a short performance. An introduction gets the audience's attention. It also gives an audience background information to explain details about the performance or presentation. This introduction may include information about the speaker or the subject of a speech. Or, it might include background information about a dramatic work, the actors, or the author of the work being presented.

Group Discussions

Setting a Purpose

In many of your classes and in future work situations, you will work with others in groups to accomplish a specific purpose. This purpose may be

- to discuss and share ideas
- to cooperate in group learning
- to solve a problem
- to arrive at a decision or make a recommendation to a larger group or committee

Once your group decides on a purpose, find out how much time will be allowed and identify what you'll need to accomplish within the time limit.

Group Roles in Cooperative Learning

Everyone involved in a group discussion has a specific role. Each role has special responsibilities. For example, your group may choose a chairperson to help keep the discussion moving smoothly. Someone else may be chosen as the secretary or reporter (or recorder), with the responsibility of taking notes during the discussion.

Usually, a group establishes an *agenda,* or outline of the order of topics to follow in a discussion. The agenda may be decided by the chairperson, or it may be decided by the entire group.

A Chairperson's Responsibilities

1. Announce the topic and establish an agenda.
2. Follow the agenda.
3. Encourage each member to participate.
4. Help group members stay on track and avoid disagreements.

A Secretary's or Reporter's Responsibilities

1. Take notes about important information.
2. Prepare a final report.

A Participant's Responsibilities

1. Take an active part in the discussion.
2. Ask questions and listen attentively to others.
3. Cooperate and share information.

Oral Interpretation

Oral interpretation is more like acting in a play than giving a speech. When you perform an oral interpretation, you read a piece of literature expressively to your listeners. You use facial expressions, vocal techniques, and body language to interpret and express the basic meaning of the literary work.

Selecting or Adapting Material

When you are choosing material for an oral interpretation, you usually know the purpose, audience, and occasion for your presentation. You'll also need to think about the length of time allowed for your presentation.

Here are suggestions for finding a literary work for an oral interpretation. You could use a poem, especially one that tells a story (such as an epic poem) or that has a speaker (using the word *I* or featuring a conversation between two characters.) You could use a short story, or a part of a story, that has a beginning, a middle, and an end and that has one or more characters who talk during the story. Or you could use part of a play, such as a scene between two characters.

You may be able to find just the right piece of literature that's already the perfect length. But often, you need to shorten a work. This shortened version is called a *cutting*.

HOW TO MAKE A CUTTING

1. Follow the story line in time order.
2. Cut dialogue tags such as *she whispered sadly.* Instead, use these clues to tell you how to act out the characters' words.
3. Cut parts that don't contribute to the portion of the story you are telling.

You may need to introduce your interpretation to set the scene, tell something about the author of the piece of literature you're presenting, or describe some important events that have already taken place in the story.

Presenting an Oral Interpretation

After you've decided on a piece to present, you'll need to prepare a *reading script.* A reading script is usually typed (double-spaced). It can then be marked to help you with your interpretive reading. For example, you can underline words you want to emphasize.

Rehearse your presentation several different ways until you are satisfied that you have chosen the most effective way to interpret the passage. Use your voice so that it suits your meaning. Vary your body movements and your voice to show that you are portraying different characters and to show important character traits.

 COMPUTER NOTE: Use a word-processing program to prepare your script. You can use bold, italic, or underline formatting to show emphasis or to indicate notes to yourself.

Review

▶ EXERCISE 1   **Practicing Telephone Speaking Situations**

For each of the following situations, explain what you would say to be polite but clear.

1. A salesperson calls while your mother is taking a nap. You don't want to wake her.
2. You're calling the public library to find out if they have issues of *The New York Times* from May of 1991.
3. You're calling your dentist to cancel an appointment.
4. You've dialed the wrong telephone number.

▶ EXERCISE 2   **Giving Directions**

Provide directions for each of the following situations.

1. Give a new neighbor directions to the nearest mall.
2. An out-of-town guest staying at your home needs directions to the nearest restaurant.
3. You're on the yearbook committee. The next meeting is at your house. A member asks you for directions.
4. Direct a new student to the cafeteria.

▶ EXERCISE 3   **Making Social Introductions**

Tell what you might say when making an introduction under each of the following circumstances.

1. You're visiting a friend's house. Your friend's uncle answers the door. Introduce yourself.
2. You're at a school dance. Your date is from another school. [a] Introduce your date to one of your friends. [b] Introduce your date to the chaperon.
3. Your mother comes to pick you up from a new friend's house. Introduce your friend to your mother.

RESOURCES

EXERCISE 4   **Preparing and Giving a Speech**

Choose a topic for a two- to three-minute speech to your English class. Prepare note cards for your speech. Include a visual, such as a chart, diagram, time line, or drawing. Then, give your speech to the class, following the guidelines on pages 864–865 for speaking effectively.

EXERCISE 5   **Making an Announcement**

Write an announcement for a real or imaginary event. Be brief but include all important details.

EXERCISE 6   **Introducing a Speaker**

Prepare an introduction for the speaker of your choice. The speaker can be a sports star, a famous actor or musician, a politician, or your favorite author.

EXERCISE 7   **Conducting a Group Discussion**

Select a group chairperson to lead a discussion on a topic assigned by your teacher or one of your own choosing. Establish an agenda and determine how much time you will have for discussion. The purpose for the discussion is to decide on a list of findings about this topic to be presented to the class.

EXERCISE 8   **Presenting an Oral Interpretation**

Prepare a three-minute oral interpretation to present to your class. Select a portion of a short story, a scene from a play, or a section of a novel that contains a scene for one or two characters. Prepare a reading script. Write a brief introduction.

RESOURCES

31 LISTENING AND VIEWING

Strategies for Listening and Viewing

Hearing is not the same as listening, and seeing is not the same as viewing. When you hear and see, you detect sounds and images. But both listening and viewing are active processes that require you to think about what you hear and see.

Listening with a Purpose

Keeping your purpose in mind as you listen helps you to become a more effective listener. You hear things differently depending on what you are listening for. For example, if you listen to your friends talking, you may only pay enough attention to follow the topic. But if you listen to directions to a new friend's house, you will probably need to pay closer attention in order to find your way. Common purposes for listening are

- for enjoyment or entertainment
- to gain information
- to understand information or an explanation
- to evaluate or form an opinion

Listening for Information

Listening for Details

When you listen for information, you need to listen for details that answer the basic *5W-How?* questions: *Who? What? When? Where? Why?* and *How?* For example, when you are asked to take messages on the telephone, you will need to get important details from the caller, such as

- the caller's name
- whom the call is for
- the caller's message
- the caller's telephone number

Listening to Instructions

Usually, instructions are made up of a series of steps. When you listen to instructions, be sure you understand all the steps you will need to follow.

1. *Listen for the order of steps.* Identify words that tell you when each step ends and the next one begins, such as *first, second, next, then,* and *last.*
2. *Identify the number of steps in the process.* If the instructions are long and complicated, take notes.
3. *Visualize each step.* Imagine yourself actually performing the action. Try to get a mental image of what you should be doing at every step in the process.
4. *Review the steps.* When the speaker is finished, be sure you understand the instructions.

Listening and Responding Politely

To complete the communication cycle, the listener must respond to the speaker. Here's how to respond politely.

1. *Respect the speaker.* Show respect for the speaker's cultural, racial, and religious background. Be tolerant of individual differences.

2. *Don't interrupt.* Pay attention, and save your questions or comments until the speaker has finished.
3. *Keep an open mind.* Be aware of how your own point of view affects the way you judge others' opinions.
4. *Don't judge too soon.* Wait to hear the speaker's whole message before you make judgments.
5. *Ask appropriate questions.* Use a voice loud enough for all to hear. For better understanding, summarize or paraphrase the speaker's point you are questioning.
6. *Use polite, effective gestures.* They should help you emphasize your point and be appropriate to the situation.

Using the LQ2R Method

The LQ2R study method is especially helpful when you are listening to a speaker who is giving information.

L   *Listen* carefully to material as it is being presented.

Q   *Question* yourself as you listen. Make a list, mentally or in your notes, of questions that occur to you.

R   *Recite* mentally the answers to your questions as you discover them, or jot down notes as you listen.

R   *Relisten* as the speaker concludes the presentation. Major points may be summed up or listed again.

Conducting an Interview

An *interview* is a special listening situation. An interview usually takes place between two people, an interviewer and the person being interviewed (called the *interviewee*). The purpose of an interview is to gather information.

Before the Interview
- Decide what information you most want to know.
- Make a list of questions.
- Make an appointment and be on time.

RESOURCES

During the Interview
- Be polite and be patient. Give the interviewee time to answer each question.
- When you ask a question, listen to the answer. If you're not sure you understand, ask questions.
- If you are planning to quote the person directly, it is best to ask permission first.
- Respect the interviewee's opinion. You may ask the other person to explain an opinion, but be polite even if you disagree.
- Conclude by thanking the interviewee.

After the Interview
- Review your notes and write a summary while you still remember the interview clearly.

 COMPUTER NOTE: If you put your interview notes into a computer file, you can keep your notes open on one half of the screen while you write your draft on the other half.

Critical Listening

Critical listening means analyzing and interpreting a speaker's message. You can't remember every word a speaker says. But if you listen critically, you can find the parts of the speaker's message that are most important.

HOW TO LISTEN CRITICALLY	
Find main ideas.	What are the most important points? Listen for clue words a speaker might use, such as *major, main, most important,* or similar words.
Identify significant details.	What dates, names, or facts does the speaker use to support the main points of the speech? What kinds of examples or explanations are used to support the main ideas?

(continued)

RESOURCES

HOW TO LISTEN CRITICALLY *(continued)*	
Distinguish between facts and opinions.	A fact is a statement that can be proved to be true. An opinion is a belief or a judgment about something. It cannot really be proved.
Identify the order of organization.	What order is the speaker using to arrange the ideas—time sequence, spatial order, order of importance?
Note comparisons and contrasts.	Are some details compared or contrasted with others?
Understand cause and effect.	Do some events that the speaker refers to relate to or affect other events?
Predict outcomes and draw conclusions.	What can you reasonably conclude from the facts and evidence you have gathered from the speech?

☞ REFERENCE NOTE: For more information about interpreting and analyzing information, see pages 912–914.

Taking Lecture Notes

When you listen to a speaker, don't just rely on your memory. Taking notes helps you remember information. For example, write key words or phrases the speaker says. You can also use *paraphrasing* and *summarizing.*

Paraphrasing. When you *paraphrase* material, you express it in your own words. As you listen, translate complex terms that the speaker uses into your own words and write your paraphrase in your notes. Use what you already know or your own experience to help you translate the ideas.

Summarizing. When you *summarize,* you write only the speaker's main points. Write these points in your notes.

RESOURCES

Understanding Persuasive Techniques

As a listener, you should be aware of the purpose of the speaker. Many times, speakers (including those on television or radio) have a specific purpose in mind for you, their listener. The speaker's purpose may be:

- to inform you
- to entertain or amuse you
- to persuade you

If the speaker intends to give you information, his or her methods will include techniques for expressing facts or details clearly and accurately. The methods of a speaker who wants to entertain or amuse you will include techniques for performing interesting or comic material. A speaker who wants to persuade you may use one of the following persuasive techniques.

COMMON PERSUASIVE TECHNIQUES USED BY SPEAKERS	
TECHNIQUE	EXPLANATION
Bandwagon	Those who use this technique urge you to "jump on the bandwagon" by suggesting that you should do or believe something because everyone (or everyone admirable or worthwhile) is doing it.
Testimonial	Experts or famous people sometimes give a personal "testimony" about a product or idea. However, the person offering the testimonial may not really know much about that particular product or idea.
"Plain folks"	Ordinary people (or people who pretend to be ordinary) are often used to persuade others. People tend to believe others who seem to be similar to themselves.
Emotional appeals	This technique uses words that appeal to your emotions rather than to your ability to reason.

Becoming a Critical Viewer

You probably know that one part of being a critical reader is evaluating what and how you read. But did you know that you can do the same type of thing when you view television? As a critical viewer, you should ask questions and make judgments about your TV viewing habits.

What Do You Watch, and Why?

When you evaluate your viewing habits, you should question more than the quality of the programs you watch. You should also assess the amount of your television viewing and the kinds of programs you select. These guidelines will help you to evaluate your television habits.

1. *Be selective.* Pay attention to how much of your viewing you actually *choose* to see and how much is "couch-potato" time. Do you watch anything that happens to be on while you are in the room? For every program you actively choose to watch, think about why you chose that program and rejected others.
2. *Evaluate what you see.* Develop **criteria,** or objective standards, for judging various kinds of TV programs. To generate your criteria, consider these questions:
   - Is the program's purpose to entertain, to inform, or to persuade?
   - How well does the program accomplish its purpose?
   - Who is the intended audience, the targeted age group? (Advertisements provide a clue.)
   - How effective is the script, or spoken part, of the program? What makes it excellent or poor?
   - How effective are the visuals? the sound effects or music? What standards can you use to measure them?
   - How effective are the actors? the participants? the moderator?
   - What reasons can you give for making your evaluations?

RESOURCES

3. *Ask yourself questions.* Don't accept what you see and hear uncritically. Ask yourself questions that relate to the type of program you are watching. For example, for a news program, ask: Is this worth my time? What am I learning? Are both sides of a controversial issue presented? How can I tell if this is a fact or someone's opinion? For a talk show, ask: Can I learn something worthwhile from this program? Does the subject affect the lives of many people, or is it just designed to shock or excite the audience? Does the program present any solutions to the situations described?

To sharpen your viewing skills, practice applying the guidelines above on programs you seldom or never watch. When you have done this several times with new programs, you will be ready to critically examine your favorite programs and your viewing habits.

RESOURCES

EXERCISE 1   **Listening to Instructions**

Your teacher will read aloud a set of instructions or directions. When the teacher has finished, write the details of the instructions or directions from memory. Then the teacher will reread the instructions and ask you to check the accuracy of what you remembered.

EXERCISE 2   **Listening Accurately**

Practice listening accurately by making up three information statements and a question about each one, similar to the following numbered examples. The object of the game is to answer all the questions correctly without having to hear the statement read a second time. Pause about five seconds after each question to allow the listeners time to write their answers. Check your listeners' answers to determine how accurately they listened.

1. Here is a series of numbers: *8, 3, 4, 9, 2*. What is the third number?
2. Here is the order of pairs: first, Elvin and Randall; then Carmen and Andrea; last, Vo and Darla. What group is Andrea in?
3. The Mohawk River is in the state of New York, the Brazos River is in Texas, and the Snake River is in Idaho. Where is the Mohawk River?

▶ EXERCISE 3 **Preparing Interview Questions**

Think of a person that you admire and would like to interview. For example, you might imagine an athletic hero, an elected official, a movie star, or someone that you think is admirable or knowledgeable. Prepare ten questions that you would like to ask that person in an interview.

▶ EXERCISE 4 **Listening Critically**

Listen to a short speech presented by your teacher in class. Take brief notes. Then, answer these questions.

1. What do you think is the speaker's purpose? Does the speaker intend to inform, entertain, or persuade you?
2. What are the main ideas expressed in the speech?
3. What details are used to support the main points in the speech? Identify several supporting details.
4. Identify one fact and one opinion from the speech. What reasons are given to support the opinion?
5. Draw a conclusion about the ideas presented in the speech. Did you find the speech convincing? Explain why or why not.

▶ EXERCISE 5 **Recognizing Persuasive Techniques**

Identify the kind of persuasive technique used in each of the following items.

1. "Be a part of the fitness generation. Try the health drink that everyone's talking about."
2. "My opponent for governor is a friend of only the rich."

RESOURCES

3. "As a housewife just like you, I know a good value when I see one. Try Snowy White detergent. It keeps my family looking good for less money."
4. "Superior Motor Oil is a winner. And, as a member of the Super Bowl champion team, I should know something about winning."

▶ EXERCISE 6 **Keeping a Viewing Log**

Keep a log of your television viewing for one week. Include the name, day, and time of the program; the amount of time you watched; the type of program; and the number of commercials.

1. Add up the amount of time you spent viewing. Multiply the total by fifty-two to find out how much time you spend watching TV during a year.
2. Add up the programs of each type that you watched. What types of programs do you prefer?
3. Multiply the number of commercials by fifty-two. How many commercials do you see per year?
4. Compare your viewing time per week and your program preferences with those of your classmates.

▶ EXERCISE 7 **Writing a Television Review**

You are the television reporter for your local newspaper. Your assignment is to review a half-hour comedy or drama. In your review of the program, be sure to include
- the name of program, the time, the date, and the channel
- the type of program, the program's purpose, and the intended audience
- a brief plot summary
- your evaluation (based on the questions in the guidelines on pages 877–878) of the plot, the acting, and the show as a whole

Share your review with your classmates, and compare your evaluation with others who reviewed or watched the same program.

32 THE LIBRARY/ MEDIA CENTER

Finding and Using Information

The best place to look for information is in the library, or media center. To make the most of a library's resources, whether that library is at school, in your community, or in the workplace, you must understand what kinds of information exist and how that information is arranged and classified.

The Arrangement of a Library

Libraries give a number and letter code—a *call number*— to each book. The call number tells you how the book has been classified and where to find it in the library. Most school libraries use the Dewey decimal system to classify and arrange nonfiction books according to their subjects.

Biographies are often placed in a separate section of the library. They are arranged in alphabetical order according to the subjects' last names. If there are several books about the same person, the biographies are then arranged according to the last names of the authors.

In most libraries, books of fiction are located in one specific section. The books are arranged alphabetically by the authors' last names. Books by the same author are arranged alphabetically by the first word of their titles.

Types of Card Catalogs

To find the book you want, look up the call number in the library's card catalog. There are two types of catalogs: the online catalog and the traditional card catalog.

The *online catalog* is stored on a computer. To find the book you want, type in the title, author, or subject of the book. The computer will display the results of the search information on the computer screen.

Search Results from Online Catalog	
Author:	Ashabranner, Brent K., 1921–
Title:	Still a nation of immigrants/Brent Ashabranner; photographs by Jennifer Ashabranner.
Edition:	1st ed.
Published:	New York: Cobblehill Books/Dutton, ©1993.
Description:	ix, 131 p.: ill.; 24 cm.
LC Call No.:	JV6455 .A892 1993
Dewey No.:	325.7320 ASH
ISBN:	0525651306
Notes:	Includes bibliographical references (p. 127–128) and index.
Subjects:	United States—Emigration and immigration—Juvenile literature.
	Immigrants—United States—Juvenile literature.
	United States—Emigration and immigration.
	Immigrants.

The traditional *card catalog* is a cabinet of small drawers containing cards. These cards list books by title, author, and subject. Fiction books have a title card and an author card. Nonfiction books also have a subject card. A *"See"* or *"See also"* card tells you where to find additional information on a subject.

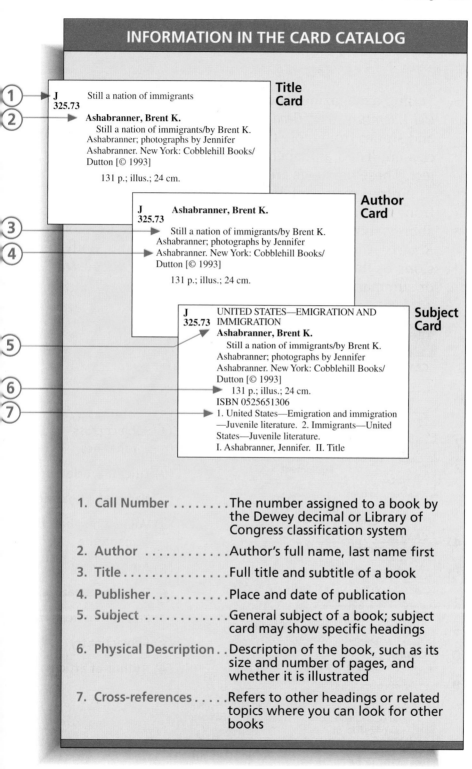

INFORMATION IN THE CARD CATALOG

Title Card

① J 325.73   Still a nation of immigrants

② **Ashabranner, Brent K.**
   Still a nation of immigrants/by Brent K. Ashabranner; photographs by Jennifer Ashabranner. New York: Cobblehill Books/ Dutton [© 1993]

   131 p.; illus.; 24 cm.

Author Card

J 325.73   **Ashabranner, Brent K.**

③   Still a nation of immigrants/by Brent K. Ashabranner; photographs by Jennifer

④   Ashabranner. New York: Cobblehill Books/ Dutton [© 1993]

   131 p.; illus.; 24 cm.

Subject Card

J 325.73   UNITED STATES—EMIGRATION AND IMMIGRATION

⑤   **Ashabranner, Brent K.**
      Still a nation of immigrants/by Brent K. Ashabranner; photographs by Jennifer Ashabranner. New York: Cobblehill Books/ Dutton [© 1993]

⑥   131 p.; illus.; 24 cm.
   ISBN 0525651306

⑦   1. United States—Emigration and immigration —Juvenile literature. 2. Immigrants—United States—Juvenile literature.
   I. Ashabranner, Jennifer. II. Title

1. **Call Number** . . . . The number assigned to a book by the Dewey decimal or Library of Congress classification system

2. **Author** . . . . Author's full name, last name first

3. **Title** . . . . Full title and subtitle of a book

4. **Publisher** . . . . Place and date of publication

5. **Subject** . . . . General subject of a book; subject card may show specific headings

6. **Physical Description** . . Description of the book, such as its size and number of pages, and whether it is illustrated

7. **Cross-references** . . . . . Refers to other headings or related topics where you can look for other books

RESOURCES

Using Reference Materials

The *Readers' Guide*

To find a magazine article, use the *Readers' Guide to Periodical Literature*. The *Readers' Guide* indexes articles, poems, and stories from more than one hundred magazines. Articles are listed alphabetically both by author and by subject. These headings are printed in boldface capital letters.

Entries may contain abbreviations. Use the key at the front of the *Readers' Guide* to find the meaning of these abbreviations. The printed and online versions of the *Readers' Guide* provide the same information. Both versions of the *Readers' Guide* sometimes provide *abstracts,* or summaries, of the articles.

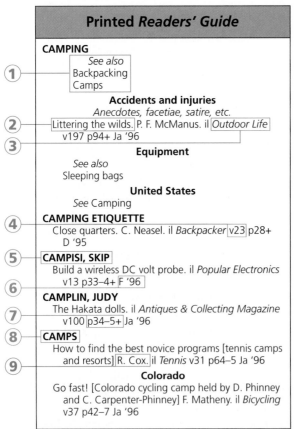

Printed *Readers' Guide*

CAMPING
① — See also
Backpacking
Camps
Accidents and injuries
Anecdotes, facetiae, satire, etc.
② — Littering the wilds. P. F. McManus. il *Outdoor Life*
③ — v197 p94+ Ja '96
Equipment
See also
Sleeping bags
United States
See Camping
④ — **CAMPING ETIQUETTE**
Close quarters. C. Neasel. il *Backpacker* v23 p28+
D '95
⑤ — **CAMPISI, SKIP**
Build a wireless DC volt probe. il *Popular Electronics*
⑥ — v13 p33–4+ F '96
CAMPLIN, JUDY
⑦ — The Hakata dolls. il *Antiques & Collecting Magazine*
v100 p34–5+ Ja '96
⑧ — **CAMPS**
How to find the best novice programs [tennis camps
⑨ — and resorts] R. Cox. il *Tennis* v31 p64–5 Ja '96
Colorado
Go fast! [Colorado cycling camp held by D. Phinney
and C. Carpenter-Phinney] F. Matheny. il *Bicycling*
v37 p42–7 Ja '96

① **Subject cross-reference**

② **Title of article**

③ **Name of magazine**

④ **Volume number of magazine**

⑤ **Author entry**

⑥ **Date of magazine**

⑦ **Page reference**

⑧ **Subject entry**

⑨ **Author of article**

RESOURCES

Result of Online Search of *Readers' Guide*	
AUTHOR:	Neasel, Carla.
TITLE:	Close quarters.
SOURCE:	Backpacker v. 23 (Dec. '95) p. 28+ il.
STANDARD NO:	0277-867X
DATE:	1995
RECORD TYPE:	art
CONTENTS:	feature article
SUBJECT:	Camping etiquette.

 COMPUTER NOTE: If you store the notes from your library research in a computer file, you can rearrange the notes to follow the same order as your outline. Then you won't have to search through piles of paper or to scroll through your file until you find the notes that correspond to the points you're discussing.

Special Information Sources

The *vertical file* is a special file containing up-to-date materials such as pamphlets, newspaper clippings, or government, business, and educational information.

Microforms are reduced-size photographs of pages from various publications. The two most common kinds of microforms are *microfilm* (a roll or reel of film) and *microfiche* (a sheet of film). A special projector enlarges the images to a readable size.

Many libraries use computers to research reference sources. Collections of information are stored on CD-ROMs or diskettes for easy retrieval. Some libraries are linked to *online databases.* These databases store all types of information. Libraries that are linked to the *Internet,* an international network of computers, have access to thousands of information sources. You search for a specific topic by typing a *keyword* or key phrase. Ask your librarian for help in wording your search requests and in using the Internet.

RESOURCES

Reference Works

Most libraries devote a section entirely to reference works. These materials (books, magazines, newspapers, CD-ROMs, and databases) contain information on many subjects.

REFERENCE WORKS	
TYPE	**CONTENT DESCRIPTION**

ENCYCLOPEDIAS
 	
Collier's Encyclopedia
Compton's Encyclopedia
The World Book Multimedia
  Encyclopedia™
	■ multiple volumes
	■ articles arranged alpha-
	  betically by subject
	■ contain general information
	■ may have index or annuals

GENERAL BIOGRAPHICAL
  REFERENCES
 	
Current Biography Yearbook
Dictionary of American
  Biography
Biography Index
  (database)
Webster's New Biographical
  Dictionary
	■ information about birth,
	  nationality, and major
	  accomplishments of
	  outstanding people

SPECIAL BIOGRAPHICAL
  REFERENCES
 	
American Men & Women
  of Science
Contemporary Authors®
  on CD-ROM
Mexican American
  Biographies
	■ information about people
	  noted for accomplishments
	  in various fields or for
	  membership in specific
	  groups

ATLASES
 	
Atlas of World Cultures
National Geographic Atlas
  of the World
	■ maps and geographical
	  information

ALMANACS
 	
The Information Please
  Almanac, Atlas and
  Yearbook
The World Almanac and
  Book of Facts
	■ up-to-date information
	  about current events,
	  facts, statistics, and
	  dates

RESOURCES

(continued)

| REFERENCE WORKS *(continued)* ||
TYPE	CONTENT DESCRIPTION
BOOKS OF QUOTATIONS Bartlett's *Familiar Quotations*	▪ famous quotations indexed or grouped by subject
BOOKS OF SYNONYMS *Roget's International Thesaurus* *Webster's New Dictionary of Synonyms*	▪ lists of more vivid or more exact words to express ideas
LITERARY REFERENCES *Granger's Index to Poetry* *Short Story Index* *Subject Index to Poetry*	▪ information about various works of literature

Newspapers

A daily newspaper has a variety of reading materials in its various sections. Newspaper writers write for different purposes. Readers, like you, read the newspaper for purposes of your own. The following chart shows contents that you may find in a typical newspaper.

| WHAT'S IN A NEWSPAPER? |||
WRITER'S PURPOSE/ TYPE OF WRITING	READER'S PURPOSE	READING TECHNIQUE

to inform
   news stories
   sports
	to gain knowledge or information	Ask yourself the *5W-How?* questions (page 29).

to persuade
   editorials
   comics
   reviews
   ads
	to gain knowledge; to make decisions; or to be entertained	Identify points you agree or disagree with. Find facts or reasons the writer uses.

to be creative or expressive
   comics
   columns
	to be entertained	Identify ways the writer interests you or gives you a new viewpoint or ideas.

EXERCISE 1 **Using the Library**

Answer the following questions to review your under-standing of the library and its resources.

1. Which of the following fiction books would be shelved first: *Barrio Boy*, by Ernesto Galarza, or *Gorilla, My Love*, by Toni Cade Bambara?
2. Using the *Readers' Guide* sample on page 884, find the title of an article by Judy Camplin about Hakata dolls. What magazine printed this article?
3. Using the card catalog or online catalog, find a book about your favorite hobby. Write the title, the author's name, and the call number.
4. Tell which reference work you might use to find infor-mation about the climate and landforms of Antarctica.
5. Tell where to find a pamphlet about air pollution printed by the U.S. Environmental Protection Agency.

EXERCISE 2 **Exploring the Newspaper**

Using a copy of the Sunday newspaper from home or your library, answer the following questions.

1. What part of the newspaper do you read first? Explain whether you read it for information or entertainment.
2. Find one article that gives you information about an event in world news, sports, or entertainment. In this article, find the answers to the *5W-How?* questions (*Who? What? Where? When? Why? How?*).
3. Identify the topic of an editorial or a letter to the editor on the editorial pages. Do you agree or disagree with the writer's opinion? Explain.
4. Find one comic that you think was intended to persuade you. Find another comic that you think was intended just for fun. Explain your choice.
5. Find an ad that makes you want to buy the item shown. What, in the ad, influences you most?

33 THE DICTIONARY

Types and Contents

Types of Dictionaries

There are many types of dictionaries. Each type contains different kinds of information. However, all dictionaries contain certain general features.

TYPES OF DICTIONARIES		
TYPE AND EXAMPLE	NUMBER OF WORDS	NUMBER OF PAGES
Unabridged *Webster's Third New International Dictionary*	460,000	2,662
College/Abridged *Merriam-Webster's Collegiate Dictionary, Tenth Edition*	160,000	1,600
School *The Lincoln Writing Dictionary*	35,000	932
Paperback *The Random House Dictionary*	74,000	1,056

A SAMPLE ENTRY

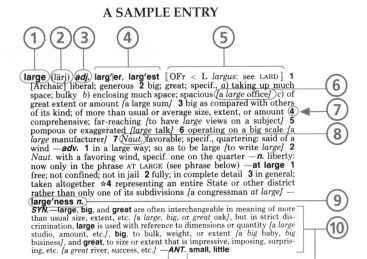

From *Webster's New World College Dictionary*, Third Edition. Copyright © 1996, 1994, 1991, 1988 by Simon & Schuster, Inc. Reprinted by permission of Macmillan USA, a Simon & Schuster Macmillan Company.

1. **Entry word.** The entry word shows the correct spelling of a word and how it is divided into syllables. The entry word may also tell whether the word is capitalized and provide alternate spellings.

2. **Pronunciation.** The pronunciation of a word is shown by the use of accent marks and either phonetic respellings or *diacritical marks* (special symbols placed above the letters). A pronunciation key is provided as a guide to diacritical marks or phonetic symbols.

3. **Part-of-speech labels.** These labels (usually in abbreviated form) indicate how the entry word should be used in a sentence. Some words may be used as more than one part of speech. In this case, a part-of-speech label is provided before each definition.

4. **Other forms.** These may show spellings of plural forms of nouns, tenses of verbs, or the comparative forms of adjectives and adverbs.

5. **Etymology.** The *etymology* is the origin and history of a word. It tells how the word (or its parts) entered the English language.

6. **Examples.** Phrases or sentences may demonstrate how the defined word is to be used.
7. **Definitions.** If there is more than one meaning, definitions are numbered or lettered.
8. **Special usage labels.** These labels identify words that have special meanings or are used in special ways in certain situations.
9. **Related word forms.** These are alternate forms of the entry word, usually created by adding suffixes or prefixes.
10. **Synonyms and antonyms.** Sometimes synonyms and antonyms are listed at the end of a word entry.

COMPUTER NOTE: A spell-checking program highlights unfamiliar letter combinations, often finding proper nouns and special terms. Some programs allow you to add words and thus create your own user dictionary.

Review

 EXERCISE 1 **Finding Alternate Spellings for Words**

Use your dictionary to find an alternate spelling for each of the following words. Tell if one spelling is preferred or more common.

1. anapest
2. abridgment
3. likable

4. savior
5. ameba

EXERCISE 2 **Using the Dictionary to Check for Capitalization**

Look up the following words in a dictionary and explain when they are and are not capitalized. Your dictionary may not give capitalized uses for all the words.

RESOURCES

1. cupid
2. west
3. revolutionary
4. senate
5. democrat

EXERCISE 3 **Dividing Words into Syllables**

Divide the following words into syllables. Use the same method to show syllable division that your dictionary uses.

1. endurance
2. underdog
3. junior
4. socialize
5. flexible

EXERCISE 4 **Finding Part-of-Speech Labels**

Look up each of the following words in a dictionary. Give all the parts of speech listed for each word.

1. fuss
2. incline
3. corner
4. smooth
5. smirk

EXERCISE 5 **Finding Usage Labels**

If your college or unabridged dictionary lists special usage labels for entry words, look up the following words. Write the usage label(s) given for the word or for any of its meanings. If your dictionary has no labels, write *none*.

1. noise
2. glitzy
3. quarter
4. mixture
5. dude

34 VOCABULARY

Learning and Using New Words

You probably encounter many new words every day through conversations, the media, class discussions, and your readings. To acquire a large vocabulary, you should try to recognize clues to the meanings of unfamiliar words. Learning the meanings of frequently used word parts is also helpful in building your vocabulary. By practicing methods shown in this chapter, you can increase your knowledge of words and expand your vocabulary.

Developing a Word Bank

An effective way to increase your vocabulary is by starting a word bank. When you encounter an unfamiliar word, enter the word and its definition in a section of your notebook. Then, write a sentence or phrase to illustrate how each word is used. Check the definition and pronunciation of an unfamiliar word in your dictionary.

COMPUTER NOTE: You can also create a vocabulary file on your computer. Add new words to the end of the file. Then, use your word-processing program's Sort command to arrange the words in alphabetical order.

Learning New Words from Context

Most of the words you encounter are used in combination with other words. The *context* of a word means the words that surround it in a sentence and the whole situation in which the word is used. These surrounding words often provide valuable clues to meaning. Context clues provide meaning in a variety of ways.

USING CONTEXT CLUES	
TYPE OF CLUE	**EXPLANATION**
Definitions and restatements	Look for words that define the term or restate it in other words. ■ Toshio's ambition is to *circumnavigate*—or sail around—the world.
Examples	Look for examples used in context that reveal the meaning of an unfamiliar word. ■ People use all sorts of *conveyances* such as cars, bicycles, rickshaws, airplanes, boats, and space shuttles.
Comparisons	Look for clues that indicate an unfamiliar word is similar to a familiar word or phrase. ■ Those *glaciers* were like huge ice cubes.
Contrast	Look for clues that indicate an unfamiliar word is opposite in meaning to a familiar word or phrase. ■ Don has become quite *apprehensive*, unlike Irene, who has always been easygoing.
Cause and effect	Look for clues that indicate an unfamiliar word is related to the cause or the result of an action, feeling, or idea. ■ Because the clouds looked *foreboding*, we decided to cancel the picnic.

Choosing the Right Word

Since many words have several meanings, you must look at *all* the definitions given for a word. When you meet an unfamiliar word, think about its context. Then, determine the definition that best fits the context.

Some dictionaries include sample contexts to indicate a word's various meanings. Compare the sample contexts given in the dictionary with the context of a new word to make sure you've found the meaning that fits.

Synonyms and Antonyms

A *synonym* is a word that means nearly the same thing as another word. However, words that are synonyms rarely have *exactly* the same meaning. Two words may have the same *denotation,* or dictionary definition, but different *connotations,* or suggested meanings.

The dictionary may list several synonyms for a word. To help you distinguish between synonyms, some dictionaries give *synonym articles*—brief explanations of a word's synonyms and how they differ in meaning. The more often you meet a word in different contexts, the better you will be able to determine its meaning.

The *antonym* of a word is a word with the opposite meaning. Knowing the antonym of a word will often help you understand the first word's meaning. A dictionary sometimes lists antonyms at the end of a word entry.

RESOURCES

Using Word Parts

English words can be classified into two main groups: those that cannot be divided into parts and those that can. Words that cannot be divided into parts are called *base words.* *Plate, grind,* and *large* are examples of base words.

Words that can be divided into parts, like *overhear,* *reception,* and *denial,* are made up of ***word parts.*** The three types of word parts are

- roots
- prefixes
- suffixes

The ***root*** is the foundation a word is built on. It carries the word's core meaning, and prefixes and suffixes are added to it. A ***prefix*** is added before a root; a ***suffix*** is added after a root. For example, in the word *inflexible, in–* is the prefix, *–flex–* is the root, and *–ible* is the suffix.

WORD	PREFIX	ROOT	SUFFIX
predictable	pre–	–dict–	–able
interpersonal	inter–	–person–	–al
disagreement	dis–	–agree–	–ment

Knowing the meanings of word parts can help you figure out the meanings of many unfamiliar words.

COMMONLY USED PREFIXES		
PREFIXES	MEANINGS	EXAMPLES
anti–	against, opposing	antiwar, anticlimax
bi–	two	bimonthly, bilingual
co–	with, together	coexist, codependent
de–	away, from, off, down	debone, debug
extra–	beyond, outside	extralegal, extraordinary
fore–	before, front part of	forehead, foreshadow
hyper–	over, excessive	hypercritical, hypersensitive
inter–	between, among	interpersonal, interact
mis–	badly, not, wrongly	misbehave, misfortune
non–	not	nonprofit, nonsense
over–	above, excessive	overstate, overhead
post–	after, following	postwar, postgraduate
pre–	before	prepayment, preexist

(continued)

RESOURCES

COMMONLY USED PREFIXES (continued)

PREFIXES	MEANINGS	EXAMPLES
re–	back, again	rebuild, reclaim
semi–	half, partly	semiannual, semiprecious
sub–	under, beneath	submarine, substandard
trans–	across, beyond	transplant, transpacific
un–	not, reverse of	unlock, uneven

REFERENCE NOTE: For guidelines on spelling when adding prefixes, see page 802.

COMMONLY USED SUFFIXES

SUFFIXES	MEANINGS	EXAMPLES
NOUNS		
–ance, –ancy	act, quality	admittance, constancy
–ence	act, condition	conference, excellence
–ity	state, condition	reality, sincerity
–ment	result, action	judgment, fulfillment
–tion	action, condition	rotation, selection
–ty	quality, state	safety, certainty
VERBS		
–ate	become, cause	captivate, activate
–en	make, become	deepen, soften
–fy	make, cause	identify, simplify
–ize	make, cause to be	socialize, motorize
ADJECTIVES		
–able	able, likely	readable, lovable
–esque	in the style of, like	picturesque, statuesque
–ible	able, likely	flexible, digestible
–ous	characterized by	dangerous, furious
ADVERB		
–ly	in a (certain) way	urgently, rigidly

 REFERENCE NOTE: For guidelines on spelling when adding suffixes, see pages 802–805.

RESOURCES

Review

▶ EXERCISE 1 **Using Context Clues**

Use context clues to choose the word or phrase that best fits the meaning of each italicized word.

a. drinks
b. lack of concern
c. knowledge
d. drifter

e. kindness
f. transformation
g. myths
h. someone who starts a business

1. Leslie Marmon Silko uses Native American *lore*, or teachings, in her writing.
2. We should encourage *compassion* rather than cruelty.
3. They have a variety of *beverages*, such as milk, juice, iced tea, and water.
4. Jim Bob's *metamorphosis* was so complete that we barely recognized him.
5. Since Pilar disliked working for others, she decided to become an *entrepreneur*.

▶ EXERCISE 2 **Selecting Synonyms to Complete Sentences**

For each sentence below, write the synonym you have selected that best fits the sentence. Use a dictionary to learn the exact meaning of each synonym.

1. My black jacket is made of a new (*fabricated, imitation, synthetic*) material.
2. Some medieval artists had a special (*fashion, technique, system*) for making stained-glass windows.
3. Although the lawyer stayed within the law, she relied on (*guile, trickery, fraud*) to win the case.
4. Under the new government, many of the citizens were (*robbed, deprived, dismantled*) of their rights.
5. You can imagine how (*ridiculous, shaming, humiliating*) it was to drop my tray of food in the cafeteria line.

RESOURCES

EXERCISE 3   **Selecting Antonyms for Specific Words**

For each numbered word below, write the letter of the correct antonym. Use a dictionary if necessary.

1. frustrate	**a.** tiny
2. contemptible	**b.** dawn
3. colossal	**c.** ornamental
4. impertinent	**d.** satisfy
5. upbraid	**e.** wordiness
6. twilight	**f.** biased
7. brevity	**g.** courteous
8. neutral	**h.** admirable
9. functional	**i.** orderly
10. random	**j.** praise

 EXERCISE 4   **Using Prefixes to Define Words**

For each of the following words, give the prefix used and its meaning. Then give the meaning of the whole word. Use a dictionary if necessary.

1. biannual	**6.** transatlantic
2. misfire	**7.** interstate
3. antiviral	**8.** postnatal
4. preheat	**9.** deform
5. nondairy	**10.** subnormal

EXERCISE 5   **Adding Suffixes to Words**

Add the suffix in parentheses to each of the following words. Then give the meaning of the new word and its part of speech. Use a dictionary if necessary. [Hint: The spelling of some words changes when a suffix is added.]

1. appease (*–ment*)	**6.** defense (*–ible*)
2. Roman (*–esque*)	**7.** envy (*–ous*)
3. change (*–able*)	**8.** haste (*–en*)
4. civil (*–ize*)	**9.** defy (*–ance*)
5. beauty (*–fy*)	**10.** employ (*–able*)

RESOURCES

35 LETTERS AND FORMS

Style and Contents

The personal letters you write are an important way of communicating to others your ideas, updates on events in your life, or your feelings. You may also need to write occasional business letters or to fill out printed forms. For each of these, you can improve your effectiveness in communicating if you follow a few simple guidelines.

Addressing an Envelope

Whether you're writing a personal letter or a business letter, you'll need to address an envelope. On your envelope, put your own address in the top left-hand corner. Place the name and address of the person to whom you are writing in the center of the envelope. Make sure all addresses are correct and include ZIP Codes. Use standard two-letter postal abbreviations for states, such as *IA* for Iowa and *NM* for New Mexico.

 COMPUTER NOTE: Most word-processing programs have standard document styles from which to choose. Many programs allow you to create a custom style that you can store and use again.

Writing Informal or Personal Letters

Sometimes an informal letter is the best way to communicate a personal message. Informal or personal letters may include thank-you letters, invitations, or letters of regret.

Thank-you Letters. These are letters that you send to tell someone that you appreciate his or her taking time, trouble, or expense to do something for you. Always respond promptly, and try to say something in your letter in addition to thanking the person. You might mention that you are aware of the person's effort, or tell why the person's gift is special to you.

Invitations. In an informal invitation, include specific information about the occasion, the time and place, and any other special details your guest might need to know (such as that everyone is expected to bring a friend, dress casually, or donate food).

Regrets. A letter of regret is written to inform someone that you will not be able to accept an invitation. You should especially respond in writing to invitations that include the letters *R.S.V.P.* (in French, an abbreviation for "please reply").

Writing Business Letters

The Appearance of a Business Letter

- Use unlined $8\frac{1}{2}'' \times 11''$ paper.
- Type your letter if possible (single-spaced, leaving an extra line between paragraphs). Otherwise, neatly write the letter by hand, using black or blue ink. Check for typing errors and misspellings.
- Center your letter on the paper with equal margins on the sides and at the top and bottom.

RESOURCES

■ Use only one side of the paper. If your letter won't fit on one page, leave a one-inch margin at the bottom of the first page, and carry over at least two lines onto the second page.

These guidelines apply whether you are writing a personal letter to a business or are writing a letter as a workplace employee.

The Parts of a Business Letter

The six parts of a business letter are

(1) the heading
(2) the inside address
(3) the salutation
(4) the body
(5) the closing
(6) the signature

The six parts of a business letter are usually arranged on the page in one of two styles. In the *block form* of a business letter, every part of the letter begins at the left margin, and paragraphs are not indented. In the *modified block form,* the heading, the closing, and your signature are placed to the right of the center of the page. However, the other parts of the letter begin at the left margin, and paragraphs are indented.

Block Style

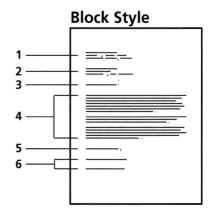

Modified Block Style

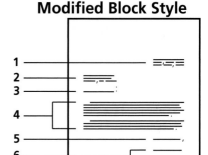

The Heading. The heading usually has three lines:

■ your street address
■ your city, state, and ZIP Code
■ the date the letter was written

The Inside Address. The inside address gives the name and address of the person or company you are writing. If you're directing your letter to someone by name, use a courtesy title (such as *Mr., Ms.,* or *Mrs.*) or a professional title (such as *Dr.* or *Professor*) in front of the person's name. After the person's name, include the person's business title.

The Salutation. The salutation is your greeting. If you are writing to a specific person, begin with *Dear,* followed by a courtesy title or a professional title and the person's name.

The Body. The body is the main part of your letter. This is where you state your message. If your letter contains more than one paragraph, leave a blank line between paragraphs.

The Closing. You should end your letter politely. To close a business letter, use a standard phrase such as *Sincerely, Yours truly,* or *Respectfully yours.*

The Signature. Sign your name in ink below the closing. Type or print your name neatly just below your signature.

HOW TO WRITE EFFECTIVE BUSINESS LETTERS

- *Use a polite, respectful, professional tone.* A courteous letter is much more effective than a rude one.
- *Use standard English.* Avoid slang, contractions, and abbreviations. Informal language that might be acceptable in a telephone conversation or personal letter is not usually acceptable for a business letter.
- *Get to the point.* State the reason for your letter clearly and promptly. Be polite, but don't ramble.
- *Include all necessary information.* Be sure your reader can understand why you wrote and what you are asking.

RESOURCES

Types of Business Letters

The Request or Order Letter

In a request letter, you write to ask for information about a product or service or to request sample materials. In an order letter, you ask for something specific, such as a free brochure advertised in a magazine or an item of merchandise that is listed in a catalog when you don't have a printed order form.

Here is the body of a sample request letter. The writer is asking a state tourism board to send travel information.

My family is planning a two-week vacation in Wyoming in July. We'd like to visit Yellowstone National Park, Jackson Lake, and Grand Teton National Park. Please send me any information— free brochures, pamphlets, or maps—that might help us on the trip. We would be interested in any information about attractions, such as museums or natural rock or cavern formations, that lie on our route.

We'll be driving down from Bozeman in a large camper, so we would also appreciate a list of campsites and fees.

When you are writing a request or order letter, remember the following points.

1. Clearly state your request.
2. If you are requesting information, enclose a self-addressed, stamped envelope.
3. Make your request well in advance of the time you need it.
4. If you want to order something, include all important information. Give the size, color, brand name, or any other specific information. If there are costs involved, add the amount correctly.

The Complaint or Adjustment Letter

If an error has been made or you have a specific complaint, you may write a complaint or adjustment letter.

Here is the body of a sample adjustment letter.

---

387 Mountain Lane
Bozeman, MT 59715
May 25, 1998

Vargas Pool Supply
600 West Main, Suite 100
Cheyenne, WY 82001

Dear Sir or Madam:

On April 30, I ordered a pair of green, heavy-duty swim fins with adjustable straps. In your spring catalog, these fins are item number 820. This morning, however, I received a big, yellow, inflatable sea serpent, which I am returning to you. Please exchange the sea serpent for the swim fins.
Thank you for your help.

Sincerely yours,

Paula Kotran

Paula Kotran

When you are writing a complaint or adjustment letter, remember these points.

1. Register your complaint as soon as possible.
2. Be sure to mention specifics. Necessary details might include the following:
   - why you are unhappy (with the product or service)
   - how you were affected (lost time or money)
   - what solution you believe will correct the problem
3. Keep the tone of your letter calm and courteous.

The Appreciation or Commendation Letter

You write an appreciation or commendation letter to express appreciation, gratitude, or praise for a person, group, or organization. State exactly why you are pleased.

Here is the body of a sample appreciation letter.

> I am writing this letter to thank all of you at the Water Control Board for your help with our team project. The information we gained firsthand on our tour of the facilities was very helpful to our research efforts.
>
> We realize how busy you are with the duties of your work, so the time and patience you gave to our group is sincerely appreciated.
>
> Thanks again for all your help.

Completing Printed Forms

Printed forms differ. However, if you follow a few standard guidelines, you should be able to fill out most forms accurately and completely.

HOW TO FILL OUT FORMS

1. Look over the entire form before you begin.
2. Take note of any special instructions, such as "Please print clearly," or "Use a pencil."
3. Read each item carefully.
4. Supply all the information requested. You may want to indicate that some information requested does not apply to you. In this case, you might use a dash or the symbol N/A, which means "not applicable."
5. When you're finished, proofread your form to make sure you didn't leave any blanks. Also, check for errors and correct them neatly.

Review

EXERCISE 1 **Writing an Informal Letter**

Write an informal letter for one of the following situations, or make up your own situation.

1. You're recovering from the flu. Your friend bought you a book of jokes to read and dropped it off along with your homework assignments.
2. You have been invited to a classmate's going-away party but cannot attend because you will be out of town with your family.
3. You are planning a surprise birthday party for your best friend. Write an invitation letter that includes all the information your guests will need to know.

EXERCISE 2 **Writing a Business Letter**

Write a business letter for one of the situations below and address an envelope for your letter. Make up any details you may need to complete your letter. (Do not mail the letter.)

1. You'd like to order a video game from Computer Games, Inc., 104 Centre Street, Seattle, Washington 98109. The catalog description of the game is too brief, and you want a complete description before you place an order. Make up a name for the video game, or use a brand name you know.
2. Write a letter to the editor of your local newspaper complaining about the lack of news coverage about a recent community event. Explain why you think the newspaper should have covered the event and how this problem can be avoided in the future.
3. Write a letter of appreciation or commendation to a school official or community leader, expressing your thanks for a job well done.

RESOURCES

36 READING, STUDYING, AND TEST TAKING

Using Skills and Strategies

Good grades are usually the result of good reading skills and efficient study habits. In this chapter are strategies for making your reading, studying, and test-taking skills more effective. These strategies will help you earn better grades, finish homework on time, and be prepared for tests—without agony the night before.

Planning a Study Routine

Be realistic when you schedule your study time, and stick to your plan. Here are some suggestions:

1. *Know your assignments.* Write down the assignments you have and their due dates. Be sure you understand the instructions for each assignment.
2. *Make a plan.* Break large assignments into small steps. Keep track of when you should be finished with each step.
3. *Concentrate when you study.* Select an appropriate time and a place where you can focus your attention only on your assignment.

Improving Reading and Study Skills

Reading and Understanding

If you read with a purpose, you will find it much easier to remember what you read. Three of the most common purposes for reading are

- to find specific details
- to find main ideas
- to understand and remember

As you read different materials, adjust your rate of reading to suit your purpose.

READING RATES ACCORDING TO PURPOSE		
READING RATE	PURPOSE	EXAMPLE
Scanning	Reading for specific information or details	Looking for poems written by Hispanic authors in your literature book
Skimming	Reading for main points or important ideas	Reviewing chapters in your science book for key concepts the night before a test
Reading for mastery	Reading closely to understand and remember	Reading a chapter in your history book in order to write a report on the material

Writing to Learn

Writing can help you in the process of learning. You can use your writing to help you organize your thoughts, analyze a problem, record your observations, and plan your work. The following chart shows some of the ways that writing can help you learn.

RESOURCES

TYPE OF WRITING	PURPOSE	EXAMPLE
Freewriting	To help you focus your thoughts	Writing for two minutes to plan an essay for a take-home test
Autobiographies	To help you exa-mine important events in your life	Writing about an event that showed you the value of a good friend
Diaries	To help you recall your impressions and feelings	Writing about your reaction to an idea in your textbook
Journals and Learning Logs	To help you record your observations, ideas, descriptions, solutions, and questions	Jotting down a few questions to raise during a class discussion of an assigned reading
	To help you define or analyze inform-ation, or to propose a solution	Recording your findings as you conduct a science experiment

Using Word-Processing Tools for Writing

A word processor or a computer word-processing program can help you plan, draft, and edit your writing. These tools can make every step of the writing process easier.

Prewriting.   Your rough notes, ideas, or outlines can be revised without having to be copied or retyped.

Writing First Drafts.   You can write, revise, and rear-range as often as you want. At any time, you can use the printer to produce a hard copy, or printout.

Evaluating.   You can make "What if?" revisions. Just save a copy of your document and type in your changes. If you don't like the revisions, you still have the original.

Revising. You can easily make changes and print clean copies without having to repeat steps.

Proofreading. Some word processors have a spell-checking feature, and some even have features that evaluate sentence structure and punctuation.

Publishing. Publishing is easy to do with a word processor. It's simple to print a final copy or even multiple copies with your printer.

Using the SQ3R Reading Method

SQ3R is the name of a reading method developed by an educational psychologist, Francis Robinson. The SQ3R reading method includes five simple steps.

S   *Survey* the entire study assignment. Glance quickly at the headings, subheadings, terms printed in boldface and in italics, and all charts, outlines, illustrations, and summaries.

Q   *Question* yourself. Make a list of questions that you want to be able to answer after you have read the selection.

R   *Read* the material carefully to find answers to your questions. Take notes as you read.

R   *Recite* in your own words answers to each question.

R   *Review* the material by rereading quickly, looking over your questions, and recalling the answers.

You can use the SQ3R method to turn routine assignments into interesting and active reading sessions. When you respond actively to what you are reading, you are more likely to remember what you have read.

RESOURCES

Interpreting and Analyzing What You Read

Every essay, article, or textbook chapter that you read organizes ideas in a pattern that relates them to one another. Interpreting and analyzing these relationships will help you think critically about what you read.

Stated Main Idea. When you look for the main idea of a passage, you are trying to identify the writer's most important point. The main idea may be stated, meaning that the author clearly expresses the major point. A main idea that is stated directly can often be found in one specific sentence.

Implied Main Idea. The main idea may not be stated directly but might be implied, or suggested. You may have to figure out an implied main idea by analyzing the meaning of the details in the passage to decide what overall meaning these details combine to express.

HOW TO FIND THE MAIN IDEA

- Skim the passage to decide what topic the sentences have in common.
- Identify what topic the whole passage is about.
- Identify what the passage says about the topic.
- State the meaning of the passage in your own words.
- Review the passage. If you have correctly identified the main idea, all the details will support it.

 REFERENCE NOTE: For additional information on finding the main idea, whether stated or implied, see pages 62–64.

Reading to Find Relationships Among Details

When you are looking for the meaning of a reading passage, you'll need to understand how the details in the passage are related to the main idea and to each other.

FINDING RELATIONSHIPS AMONG DETAILS

Identify specific details.	Which of the details answer questions such as *Who? What? When? Where? Why?* and *How? (5W-How?* questions)?
Distinguish between fact and opinion.	What can be proved true or false? What expresses a personal belief or attitude?
Identify similarities and differences.	Are there any details that are shown to be similar to or different from one another?
Understand cause and effect.	Do earlier events influence later ones?
Identify an order of organization.	In what kind of order are the details arranged— chronological order, spatial order, order of importance, or some other pattern?

Reading Passage

Garrett Morgan was a famous African American inventor. He was born in 1877 in Kentucky. Raised on a farm, he attended school only through the sixth grade. Later, he moved to Ohio, where he started a sewing-machine repair shop and then a garment business.

His hard work made him prosperous. Reportedly the first black man in Cleveland to own a car, Morgan may have invented the modern traffic signal in response to his experiences in driving. He sold his patent to the General Electric Company for $40,000.

Sample Analysis

DETAIL: When and where was Morgan born?

ANSWER: *He was born in 1877 in Kentucky.*

FACT: Did Morgan receive a formal education?

ANSWER: *No. He only finished the sixth grade.*

TIME ORDER: What did Morgan do after opening a sewing-machine repair shop?

ANSWER: *He started a garment business.*

RESOURCES

Another of Morgan's inventions was the Safety Hood. This device, patented in 1914, originally was made of a helmet and a long breathing tube lined with material to cool and filter incoming air. A separate tube with a valve prevented the return of contaminated air.

Wearing the Safety Hood, a firefighter could breathe clear air for fifteen to twenty minutes. One fire chief from Akron, Ohio, claimed that two of his men wearing Safety Hoods could be more effective in stopping fires than a whole company of firefighters without them.

In 1916, an explosion in Cleveland trapped workers deep in an underground tunnel. The tunnel was filled with deadly gases, and no one could enter. Morgan and his brother arrived, put on Safety Hoods, and— one by one—carried out all of the injured workers. The city of Cleveland rewarded Morgan's heroism with a medal made of solid gold.

During World War I, when American soldiers were exposed to poisonous chlorine gas, Morgan's Safety Hood was updated, becoming the modern gas mask. Over the years, Morgan's inventions have saved countless lives.

CAUSE AND EFFECT: What experience may have led Morgan to invent the traffic signal?
ANSWER: *Driving one of the first cars in Cleveland may have given him experience with traffic problems.*

DIFFERENCE: How did Morgan's Safety Hood provide fresh, breathable air?
ANSWER: *In a tube, incoming air was cooled and filtered, while contaminated air was kept out by a separate tube with a valve.*

OPINION: What did one expert say about Morgan's invention?
ANSWER: *A fire chief said that Morgan's Safety Hood made a few firefighters more effective than a whole company of firefighters without this equipment.*

Applying Reasoning Skills to Your Reading

To think critically about what you read, you evaluate and interpret evidence and facts that you gather from your reading. You may draw *conclusions,* meaning that you make decisions based on clearly expressed facts and evidence.

Or you may make *inferences,* meaning that you make decisions based on evidence that is only hinted at or implied in what you have read.

For example, based on your analysis of the reading passage on pages 913–914, you might draw the following conclusions or inferences about the character of Garrett Morgan.

> Garrett Morgan was financially successful.
> (Evidence: He owned businesses and a car, and he sold his traffic signal patent for $40,000.)
>
> Garrett Morgan's inventions benefited the human race.
> (Evidence: Two of Morgan's major inventions—the traffic signal and the Safety Hood—were safety devices.)

A *valid conclusion* is a conclusion that is based on facts, evidence, or logic. An *invalid conclusion,* however, is not based on logical reasoning and is not grounded on facts or evidence. For example, it is invalid to conclude that Garrett Morgan's prosperity was the result of family wealth. This conclusion is not consistent with facts stated in the reading passage. The reading passage states that Garrett Morgan grew up on a farm and that he only attended school through the sixth grade.

HOW TO DRAW CONCLUSIONS	
Gather all the evidence.	What facts or details have you learned about the subject?
Evaluate the evidence.	What do the facts and details you have gathered tell you about the subject?
Make appropriate connections and draw reasonable conclusions.	What can you reasonably conclude from the evidence that you have gathered and evaluated?

RESOURCES

Reading Graphics and Illustrations

Many of the materials that you read—from textbooks to magazine articles—include visuals such as diagrams, maps, graphs, and illustrations. These visuals make information clearer and easier to understand.

When you read a paragraph filled with detailed information, it is often difficult to understand and remember its meaning. Graphs or diagrams make detailed information much easier to understand. Graphics and illustrations help you understand relationships among sets of facts. For example, the bar graph below shows the final medal standings from the 26th Summer Olympics in 1996.

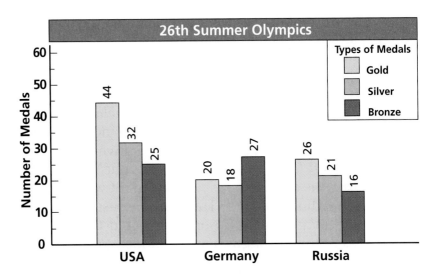

From this graph you can quickly compare the number and the kinds of medals won by three different countries.

Suppose you were a television anchorperson reporting on the Olympics. Information about the medal standings would be very difficult for a viewer to understand quickly. However, if you showed a graph at the same time as you reported the information, it would be easier for the viewer to understand. For example, by looking at the chart, the viewer can immediately see who won the most or the fewest bronze medals.

Graphs such as the one on page 916 help you understand information more easily because you can actually see relationships between the data.

Applying Study and Reading Strategies

As you compare study and reading strategies, you will see that they are simply different ways of organizing and handling information. There are a variety of study and reading strategies. Some of the most common are

- taking notes
- classifying
- organizing information visually
- outlining
- paraphrasing
- summarizing
- memorizing

Taking Notes

If you take careful notes whenever you read or listen to a lecture, your information will already be organized for you when you study, take tests, or write reports.

HOW TO TAKE STUDY NOTES

1. Set off the main subjects as headings in your notes. In a lecture, listen for key words and phrases, such as *first, most important,* or *therefore,* that often introduce main ideas. In a textbook, chapter headings and subheadings usually indicate main topics.
2. Use abbreviations and summarize material in your own words.
3. Note important examples that can help you recall the main ideas.
4. Review your notes soon after you have taken them to be sure you have included all important details.

RESOURCES

Look at the following example. A careful student might take these study notes about the reading passage on pages 913–914. The notes include the main points of the passage. They are grouped with headings that identify the key ideas.

Garrett Morgan

<u>*Biography*</u>

- *Famous African American inventor*
- *Born 1877 in Kentucky*
- *Grew up on farm; only finished 6th grade*
- *Moved to Ohio*
- *Started sewing-machine repair shop, then*
  garment shop

<u>*Achievements*</u>

- *Made money with his work*
- *Possibly first black man in Cleveland with own car*
- *Invented modern traffic signal*
- *Invented the Safety Hood, patented in 1914*
- *Saved men trapped in tunnel; given gold medal*
- *WWI—Safety Hood became gas mask; saved lives*

Classifying

Classification is a way to organize items by arranging them into categories. When you make an outline, you are using classification. You decide which ideas fit together under each heading. In order to decide which group an item belongs in, you identify relationships among the items.

EXAMPLE   What do the following items have in common?
           pancakes, oatmeal, bacon, eggs, cereal
ANSWER   They are common breakfast foods.

You also use classifying when you identify patterns. For example, look at the following sequence of numbers.

What's the next number in the series?

1   3   2   4   3   ___?___

ANSWER   To the first number, 2 is added. This addition produces *3*, the second number. From this number, *1* is subtracted. To the next number, *2* is added. From the fourth number, *1* is subtracted. The pattern is "add 2, subtract 1." Therefore, you should add two to the fifth number, and the next number in the series would be *5*.

Organizing Information Visually

Mapping, diagramming, and charting are techniques that allow you to organize new information so that it is visually presented. This makes the ideas easier to understand.

For example, the passage that follows compares and contrasts the two kinds of elephants.

African and Asian elephants have interesting differences. The African elephant lives on the continent of Africa in areas south of the Sahara. The average African bull elephant is almost eleven and a half feet tall and weighs about six tons. The African elephant has dark gray skin and ears four feet wide, long enough to cover its shoulders. Its forehead forms a smooth curve, and its tusks grow to a length of six to eight feet. The Asian, or Indian, elephant, however, lives in India and in many parts of Southeast Asia. The

RESOURCES

average Asian bull elephant is smaller, standing nine to ten feet tall and weighing about four tons. Its skin is light gray and its ears are only half the width of the African elephant's. The Asian elephant has two humps on its forehead, and its tusks grow to only four or five feet in length. Many have no tusks at all.

AFRICAN ELEPHANT	ASIAN ELEPHANT
lives in Africa, south of the Sahara	lives in India and Southeast Asia
average bull $11\frac{1}{2}$ feet tall	average bull 9 to 10 feet tall
weighs about 6 tons	weighs about 4 tons
dark gray skin	light gray skin
ears 4 feet wide	ears 2 feet wide
tusks 6 to 8 feet long	tusks 4 to 5 feet long

Outlining

An *outline* helps organize important ideas and information. When you make an outline, you group ideas in an organized pattern that makes their order and their relationship to one another clear.

You might make a formal outline, with Roman numerals for headings and capital letters for subheadings. Or, you might use an informal outline form to help you organize information more quickly.

FORMAL OUTLINE FORM

I. Main Point
  A. Supporting Point
    1. Detail
      a. Information or detail

INFORMAL OUTLINE FORM

Main Idea
  Supporting detail
  Supporting detail
  Supporting detail

Paraphrasing

Paraphrasing is a good way to check your understanding of what you read. A *paraphrase* is a restatement of someone else's ideas in your own words. When you paraphrase, you translate complex or poetic ideas into your own words so that they are easier to understand. Your written paraphrase will usually be about the same length as the original. In language arts classes, you may be asked to paraphrase a short passage, such as a poem. Here is an example.

> Desert Noon
> *by Elizabeth Coatsworth*
>
> When the desert lies
> Pulsating with heat
> And even rattlesnakes
> Coil among the roots of the mesquite
> And the coyotes pant at the waterholes—
>
> Far above,
> Against the sky,
> Shines the summit of San Jacinto,
> Blue-white and cool as a hyacinth
> With snow.

Here is a possible paraphrase of the poem.

> The speaker in this poem is observing a desert scene. The heat rising from the ground causes the image of the desert to waver. It's so hot that even the rattlesnakes aren't moving; they're just lying in the shade at the base of desert trees. Coyotes show signs of thirst as they go to places where they usually find water.
>
> By contrast, a mountain, San Jacinto, rises high above the desert, framed by the sky. The top of the mountain is blue and white with snow. It looks cool, like an early spring flower poking through the snow.

RESOURCES

Use the following guidelines when you write a paraphrase.

HOW TO PARAPHRASE

1. Read the selection carefully before you begin.
2. Be sure you understand the main idea of the selection. Look up unfamiliar words in a dictionary.
3. Determine the tone of the selection. (What is the attitude of the writer toward the subject of the selection?)
4. Identify the speaker in fictional material. (Is the poet or a character within the selection speaking?)
5. Write your paraphrase in your own words. Shorten long sentences or stanzas and use your own, familiar vocabulary, but follow the same order of ideas used in the selection.
6. Check to be sure that your paraphrase expresses the same ideas as the original.

You will paraphrase often when you write a research report. In order to avoid *plagiarism,* make sure that you cite the source that you paraphrase. You should always give credit to the person whose ideas you use.

 REFERENCE NOTE: For more about crediting your sources in research reports, see pages 339–342.

Summarizing

A *summary* is a brief restatement of a piece of writing. Like a paraphrase, a summary expresses the ideas of a passage in your own words. However, a summary condenses the original material, presenting only the most important points.

Writing a summary requires critical thinking. You analyze the material that you are condensing. Then you draw conclusions about what should be included in the summary and what can be left out.

HOW TO SUMMARIZE

1. Skim the selection.
2. Reread the passage closely and look for the main ideas and supporting details.
3. Write your summary in your own words. Include only the writer's main ideas and most important supporting points.
4. After you write your draft, evaluate and revise your summary, checking to see that you have covered the most important points. Make sure that the information is clearly expressed. Also be sure that the reader can follow your ideas.

Here's a sample summary of the reading passage found on pages 326–328.

Tropical rain forests are being destroyed. In minutes, a chain saw can cut down a tree that it will take the rain forest 500 years to replace. After the loggers cut the trees, the forest is burned to clear the land for agriculture. When the rain forest is burned, the top coating of ash is rich. The soil underneath, however, is very poor. Soon, crops use it up or rain washes it away, and then desperate farmers try to burn more forest to clear more land.

Losing the rain forests also means trouble for our air. We need trees to absorb carbon dioxide. We also need trees because they recycle oxygen and moisture. When forests are cleared, there are fewer trees to produce oxygen. Also, when the trees are burned, the carbon dioxide that's in them is released into the air. The extra carbon dioxide traps the heat from the sun. The sun's rays enter the atmosphere but can't get out. This process could cause a rise in the global temperature and a change in the world's weather.

RESOURCES

Memorizing

Sometimes, you have to memorize information. If you practice in frequent, short, focused sessions, you are more likely to remember the information. Follow these guidelines to memorize material more efficiently.

HOW TO MEMORIZE	
Memorize only the most important information.	Whenever possible, condense the material you need to remember.
Rehearse the material in different ways.	Copy the material by hand. Recite the material out loud.
Invent memory games.	Form a word from the first letters of important terms, or make up rhymes to help you remember facts and details.

Improving Test-Taking Skills

Preparing for Different Kinds of Tests

It's natural to feel nervous before an important test. However, you can channel your nervous energy in order to do well on the test. Your attitude is the key.

HOW TO PREPARE FOR A TEST
Plan for success. Think of all the things you can do to improve your performance. Know what material will be covered on the test, and make a practical plan to take notes, study, and review the material.
Be confident. If you have studied thoroughly, you know you are prepared. During the test, pay attention only to reading and answering the questions.
Keep trying. Know that you can constantly plan and improve your study effectiveness.

There are two basic types of test questions: *objective* and *essay* questions. Certain strategies can help you prepare for these types of questions.

Objective Tests

Objective test questions appear in many forms. Types of questions include multiple-choice, true/false, matching, reasoning or logic, analogy, and short-answer questions. Objective questions measure your ability to recall and apply specific information, such as dates, names, terms, or definitions. Most objective test questions have only one answer that is scored as correct. For this reason, they are also called *limited-response* or *limited-answer tests.*

You can prepare for objective tests by reviewing the specific information that the test is supposed to cover. The study skills listed earlier in this chapter help you prepare for objective tests.

HOW TO STUDY FOR OBJECTIVE TESTS

1. Answer the study questions in your textbook. Review class notes to identify important terms or facts.
2. Study the information in more than one form. For example, you may be responsible for labeling a map or diagram. Make an unlabeled version and then practice identifying areas on the map.
3. Practice and repeat factual information. Note which items you have difficulty with, and review them.
4. If possible, review all the terms once more, shortly before the actual test.

RESOURCES

For each type of objective test, you may have to adapt your study strategies a little. For example, if your test will include defining key terms, then use flashcards as you study. If problem solving is included, work out practice problems and then check your answers with your textbook.

When you take an objective test, scan the test before you begin. Notice how many items there are on the test and decide how you can budget your time for each item.

Here are some strategies that are effective in handling specific kinds of objective test questions.

Multiple-Choice Questions. Multiple-choice questions require you to select a correct answer from among a number of choices.

EXAMPLE   **1.** Garrett Morgan's design for the Safety Hood was later used to develop
  A the crash helmet.
  B the welding mask.
  Ⓒ the gas mask.
  D the construction worker's safety helmet.

HOW TO ANSWER MULTIPLE-CHOICE QUESTIONS

Read the question or statement carefully.	■ Make sure you understand the key question or statement before examining the choices. ■ Look for words such as *not* or *always* that will limit the correct answers.
Read all the choices before selecting an answer.	■ Eliminate choices that you know are incorrect. ■ Think carefully about the remaining choices and select the one that makes the most sense.

True/False Questions. True/false questions ask you to determine whether a specific, given statement is true or false.

EXAMPLE   **1.** Ⓣ F In the medal tallies in the 26th Summer Olympics, the United States won a greater number of medals than either Germany or Russia.

HOW TO ANSWER TRUE/FALSE QUESTIONS

Read the statement carefully.	■ The whole statement is false if any part of it is false.
Look for word clues.	■ Words such as *always* or *never* limit a statement.

Matching Questions. Matching questions ask you to match the items in one list with the items in another list.

Directions: Match the item in the left-hand column with its description in the right-hand column.

__C__ 1. weight of African bull elephant   **A** about 4 tons

__B__ 2. height of Asian bull elephant   **B** 9 to 10 feet

__D__ 3. height of African bull elephant   **C** about 6 tons

__A__ 4. weight of Asian bull elephant   **D** $11\frac{1}{2}$ feet

HOW TO ANSWER MATCHING QUESTIONS

Read the directions carefully.	Sometimes you won't use all the items listed in one column. Other times items may be matched up to more than one item.
Scan the columns to identify related items.	Match items you know first. Then evaluate items you are less sure about.
Complete the rest of the matching.	Make your best educated guess on remaining items.

RESOURCES

Reasoning or Logic Questions. These questions may test your reasoning abilities more than your knowledge of a specific subject. Reasoning or logic questions often appear on standardized tests. They often ask you to identify the relationship between several items (usually words, pictures, or numbers).

Reasoning questions might ask you to identify a pattern in a number sequence (for example: 14, 35, 49, 84—these are multiples of the number 7). Or you might be asked to predict the next item in a visual sequence. Look at the following example.

What comes next?

1   2   3   4

In this sequence of three drawings, a different square is missing each time from a box of four squares. Therefore, the last drawing in the series should show a square missing in the only position that had not yet been shown with a missing square.

HOW TO ANSWER REASONING OR LOGIC QUESTIONS	
Be sure you understand the instructions.	Reasoning or logic questions are often multiple-choice. On some tests, however, you may need to fill in a blank, complete a number sequence, or even draw a picture.
Analyze the relationship implied in the question.	Look at the question carefully to gather information about the relationship of the various items you are given.
Draw reasonable conclusions.	Evaluate the relationship of the items to decide your final answer.

RESOURCES

Analogy Questions. Analogy questions are special reasoning and logic questions that measure your ability to analyze relationships between words. Analogy questions ask you to recognize the relationship between two words and to identify a pair of words with a similar relationship.

EXAMPLE **1. Directions: Select the appropriate pair of words to complete the analogy.**

DRIVER : CAR :: _____

A engine : truck
B food : stomach
Ⓒ sailor : boat
D family : house

Analogies may also appear as fill-in-the-blank questions.

EXAMPLE **2. Directions: Complete the following analogy.**

STANZA : POEM :: chapter : ___*book*___

HOW TO ANSWER ANALOGY QUESTIONS	
Analyze the first pair of words.	▪ Reason out the relationship between the first two items. (Using Example 1, the relationship between a car and a driver is that a car is controlled by a driver.)
Express the analogy in sentence or question form.	▪ The first example on this page could be read as "A *driver* controls a *car*, just as . . . (what other pair of items among the choices given?)."
Find the best available choice to complete the analogy.	▪ With multiple-choice analogies, select the pair of words that has the same type of relationship between them as the original pair. ▪ For fill-in-the-blank analogies, you are often given one word of the second pair of items, and you are expected to supply the final word. (In Example 2, a *stanza* is a part of a *poem*; a *chapter* is part of a *book*.)

The following chart shows you a few of the most common types of analogy relationships. Many other types of analogies are possible, because there are many ways that any two things can be related.

ANALOGY EXAMPLES	
TYPE OF ANALOGY	**EXAMPLE**
A word to its synonym	FLAT : SMOOTH :: bumpy : rough
A word to its antonym	MOIST : DRY :: sweet : sour
A thing to its cause	COLD : ICE :: heat : fire
A thing to its effect	BLEACH : WHITENESS :: dye : color
A part of something to the whole thing	TWIG : BRANCH :: finger : hand
A whole thing to a part of that thing	BOOK : PAGES :: melody : notes
A thing as part of a category it belongs to	RECLINER : CHAIR :: loveseat : sofa
A thing to a characteristic of that thing	PILLOWS : SOFT :: diamonds : hard
A thing to its use	EARS : HEAR :: nose : smell
An action to the person who performs the action	WRITING : AUTHOR :: cooking : chef
A person who performs an action to the action performed	ARCHITECT : DESIGNING :: farmer : planting
A location to a related location	MONTREAL : CANADA :: Paris : France

Short-Answer Questions.   Short-answer questions require you to show your knowledge in short, precise answers that you write out yourself. Some short-answer questions (such as fill-in-the-blank questions) can be answered with one or a few words. Other types of short-answer questions require you to write a full response, usually one or two sentences.

EXAMPLE   What were Garrett Morgan's two most famous inventions, and how were they useful?

ANSWER   *Garrett Morgan's two most famous inventions were the Safety Hood and the traffic signal. The Safety Hood made it safer for firefighters and rescue workers to do their jobs, and the traffic signal reduced accidents at intersections.*

HOW TO RESPOND TO SHORT-ANSWER QUESTIONS	
Read the question carefully.	Some questions have more than one part, and you will have to include an answer to each part to receive full credit.
Plan your answer.	Briefly decide what you need to include in the answer.
Be as specific as possible in your answers.	Give a complete, precise answer.
Budget your time.	Begin by answering those questions you are certain about. Return later to the questions you are less sure about.

Essay Tests

Essay tests measure your understanding of material you have learned. You are required to write a paragraph or more to answer an essay question.

HOW TO STUDY FOR ESSAY TESTS
1. Read your textbook carefully.
2. Make an outline, identifying the main points and important details.
3. Try making up your own essay questions and practice writing out the answers.
4. Evaluate and revise your practice answers. Check your notes and textbook for accuracy and the composition section of this textbook for help in writing.

RESOURCES

There are several steps you should take before you begin an essay test. You should quickly scan the questions. How many essay questions are you expected to answer? Are you allowed to choose from several items? Which of them do you think you can answer best? After you have determined these issues, plan how much time to spend on each answer, and stay on this schedule.

Read the question carefully. You may be asked for an answer that contains several parts.

Pay attention to important terms in the question. Essay questions on tests usually require specific responses. Each task is expressed with a verb. Become famiiiar with the key verbs and what type of response each one calls for.

ESSAY TEST QUESTIONS		
KEY VERB	**TASK**	**SAMPLE QUESTION**
argue	Take a viewpoint on an issue and give reasons to support this opinion.	Argue whether or not students who receive good grades should be excused from routine home-work assignments.
analyze	Take something apart to see how each part works.	Analyze the major effects of the destruction of the rain forests.
compare	Point out likenesses.	Compare Carmen Maymi and Herman Badillo as famous Puerto Ricans.
contrast	Point out differences.	Contrast Travis's life in *Old Yeller* with a typical routine of a modern teenager.
define	Give specific details that make something unique.	Define the term *symbiosis* as it is used in biology.

(continued)

ESSAY TEST QUESTIONS *(continued)*		
KEY VERB	TASK	SAMPLE QUESTION
demonstrate (also illustrate, present, show)	Provide examples to support a point.	Demonstrate the importance of the ozone layer to the world's weather.
describe	Give a picture in words.	Describe incidents from "A Walk to the Jetty" that Jamaica Kincaid recalls as she prepares to leave her home.
discuss	Examine in detail.	Discuss the term *passive resistance.*
explain	Give reasons.	Explain the popularity of Winston Churchill during World War II.
identify	Point out specific characteristics.	Identify the types of poetic meter.
interpret	Give the meaning or significance of something.	Interpret the impact of the discovery of penicillin.
list (also outline or trace)	Give all steps in order or all details about a subject.	List the events that led to the landing of an American on the moon.
summarize	Give a brief overview of the main points.	Summarize the myth of Prometheus the fire-bringer.

RESOURCES

Take a moment to use prewriting strategies. After considering the key verbs in the question, write notes or a rough outline on scratch paper to help you decide what you want to say and how you want to say it.

Allow time to evaluate and revise after you write your essay. While you are writing your essay, you won't have time to edit very much. However, as soon as you finish, look over what you have written. You can check for simple errors as well as for omission of important points. Make sure you have answered every part of each question.

QUALITIES OF A GOOD ESSAY ANSWER

- The essay is well organized.
- The main ideas and supporting points are clearly expressed.
- The sentences are complete and well written.
- There are no distracting errors in spelling, punctuation, or grammar.

Review

 EXERCISE 1 **Choosing an Appropriate Reading Rate**

Identify the reading rate that best fits each of the following situations.

1. You are reading the instructions to a new game so you will understand how to teach several of your friends to play the game.
2. You are looking through current issues of *National Geographic* to find articles about ancient temples in Southeast Asia.
3. You need to write an outline of the main points in a history chapter about the Industrial Revolution.
4. You are reading a short story by Gabriel García Márquez, knowing you are expected to discuss the meaning of it in tomorrow's English class.
5. You are trying to find in your history book the date of John F. Kennedy's assassination.

► EXERCISE 2   **Applying the SQ3R Reading Method**

Use the SQ3R method while reading a magazine article or a textbook chapter that you need to read for a class. List at least five questions while you are reading. Then write a brief answer to each one.

► EXERCISE 3   **Reading: Analyzing Details in a Passage**

Answer the following questions about the reading passage on pages 913–914.

1. What are two facts or details about Garrett Morgan (other than those facts and details already noted in the sample analysis)?
2. What was Morgan's contribution to traffic safety?
3. What two types of businesses did Morgan start while he lived in Ohio?
4. What happened in Cleveland in 1916 that helped Morgan's invention become recognized as a life-saving device?
5. Why was Morgan's Safety Hood important during World War I?

► EXERCISE 4   **Reading: Drawing Conclusions and Making Inferences**

Using the reading passage on pages 913–914, identify the evidence or the reasoning that you might need to use in making the following inferences or in drawing the following conclusions.

1. Garrett Morgan knew a great deal about practical engineering.
2. Garrett Morgan gained knowledge on his own that he used in his inventions.
3. Garrett Morgan and his brother were men of considerable strength and stamina.
4. Garrett Morgan was considered a hero by the city of Cleveland.

RESOURCES

EXERCISE 5 **Reading: Interpreting Graphic Information**

Using the graph on page 916, answer the following questions.

1. How many gold medals did the United States win in the 26th Summer Olympics?
2. What is the difference between the number of medals won by the United States and by Germany?
3. Which nation won the most bronze medals?
4. Which nation won the most silver medals?
5. What is the difference between the number of medals won by Germany and by Russia?

EXERCISE 6 **Analyzing Your Note-Taking Method**

For one day, take notes in all of your classes by using the techniques suggested on page 917. Write a paragraph, comparing and contrasting your usual method and this new method. Be sure to address these points: How are the two methods similar? How are they different? Which works better? Why?

EXERCISE 7 **Identifying Classifications**

For each of the following groups, identify the category.

1. peso, franc, dollar, rupee, yen
2. barley, wheat, oats, rice, millet
3. Benjamin Franklin, Thomas Paine, Paul Revere, George Washington, Benedict Arnold
4. Lake Superior, Lake Michigan, Lake Huron, Lake Erie, Lake Ontario
5. gila monster, alligator, grass snake, tortoise

EXERCISE 8 **Reading: Applying Visual Organization**

After reading the following paragraph, make a chart or other visual representation of its contents. Use your graphic to answer the numbered questions.

The Nile River and the Congo River are two of the great rivers of the world. Both are vital waterways to their home continent, Africa. For example, electricity is generated from power plants built on each river.

The Nile flows mostly through desert country. The Nile has a total length of over 4,000 miles and is located in east and northeast Africa. The Nile's main branches are the White Nile, originating at Lake Victoria, and the Blue Nile, beginning at Lake Tana. The Nile gains about 21 percent of its total volume from the Atbara River, another of its important tributaries. The mouth of the Nile is the Mediterranean Sea. The Congo, with a total length of 2,900 miles, is located in central Africa. It originates between the nations of Zaire and Zambia, and flows through warm, wet lands. Its mouth is at the Atlantic Ocean.

1. Where are the Nile and Congo Rivers located?
2. What is the total length of the Nile River? of the Congo River?
3. Where is the mouth of the Congo River?
4. What is the difference between the lands through which the Nile and the Congo flow?

▶ EXERCISE 9   **Reading: Paraphrasing a Poem**

Read the following short poem by Robert Frost. Then write a paraphrase of the poem.

A Time to Talk
by Robert Frost

When a friend calls to me from the road
And slows his horse to a meaning walk,
I don't stand still and look around
On all the hills I haven't hoed,
And shout from where I am, "What is it?"

> No, not as there is a time to talk.
> I thrust my hoe in the mellow ground,
> Blade-end up and five feet tall,
> And plod: I go up to the stone wall
> For a friendly visit.

▶ EXERCISE 10   **Analyzing Essay Questions**

Identify the key verb(s) in each of the following essay questions. Do not write an essay answer. Just state briefly what task you would need to do to answer the question.

1. Compare the populations and physical sizes of Tokyo, Mexico City, and New York City.
2. Analyze the effect of the narrator on the message of Isaac Bashevis Singer's story "Zlateh the Goat."
3. While many people consider television a waste of time, others consider it important for the modern world. They point out its potential for educating and informing citizens. Argue your opinion about the value of television. Be sure to use specific examples.
4. Describe how to print a document on one of your school's computers.
5. Compare and contrast a violin and a viola.
6. Summarize how courts settle disputes in the United States.
7. Demonstrate the historical importance of the March on Washington on August 28, 1963.
8. Trace the path of blood circulation through the human heart.
9. Define the type of humor represented in the writings of Mark Twain and O. Henry.
10. Stonehenge—located on the Salisbury Plain in Wiltshire, England—has fascinated scientists, archaeologists, and historians for centuries. Identify some of the characteristics of Stonehenge that make it so fascinating.

DIAGRAMING SENTENCES

A *sentence diagram* is a picture of how the parts of a sentence fit together. It shows how the words in the sentence are related.

Subjects and Verbs (pages 409–423)

To diagram a sentence, first find the simple subject and the verb (simple predicate), and write them on a horizontal line. Then separate them with a vertical line.

EXAMPLES   The reporter dashed to the fire.

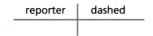

Have you been studying?

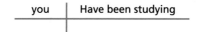

Notice that a diagram shows the capitalization but not the punctuation of a sentence.

Understood Subjects (page 423)

To diagram an imperative sentence, place the understood subject *you* in parentheses on the horizontal line.

EXAMPLE   Listen to the beautiful music.

▶ EXERCISE 1 **Diagraming Simple Subjects and Verbs**

Diagram only the simple subjects and the verbs in the following sentences.

EXAMPLE **1.** Midas is a character in Greek mythology.

Midas	is

1. Midas ruled the kingdom of Phrygia.
2. One of the gods gave Midas the power to turn anything into gold.
3. Soon this gift became a curse.
4. Do you know why?
5. Read the story of King Midas in a mythology book.

Compound Subjects (page 418)

EXAMPLE **Vines** and **weeds** grew over the old well.

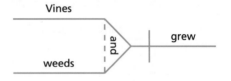

Compound Verbs (pages 419–420)

EXAMPLE We ran to the corner and barely caught the bus.

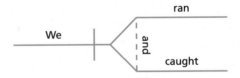

Compound Subjects and Compound Verbs (page 372)

EXAMPLE **Ken** and **LaDonna dived** into the water and **swam** across the pool.

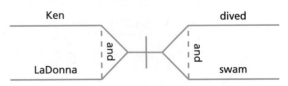

▶ EXERCISE 2   **Diagraming Simple Subjects and Verbs**

Diagram the simple subjects and the verbs in the following sentences.

EXAMPLE   **1.** Nikki and Chris chopped the cilantro and added it to the salsa.

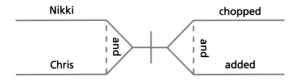

1. Mr. Carrington collects aluminum cans and returns them for recycling.
2. The students and the faculty combined their efforts and defeated the proposal.
3. The plane circled above the landing field but did not descend.
4. Pencil and paper are needed for tomorrow's math assignment.
5. Rita Moreno and her costar prepared for the scene.

Adjectives and Adverbs (pages 445–448 and 469–472)

Both adjectives and adverbs are written on slanted lines below the words they modify. Notice that possessive pronouns are diagramed in the same way adjectives are.

Adjectives (pages 445–448)

EXAMPLE   **bright** star   **a special** person   **her favorite** class

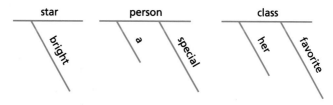

Two or more adjectives joined by a connecting word are diagramed this way:

EXAMPLE   **a lovely** and **quiet** place

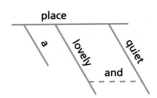

▶ EXERCISE 3   **Diagraming Adjectives**

Diagram the following groups of words.

1. mighty warrior
2. long, exciting movie
3. short and funny story
4. my final offer
5. the slow but persistent turtle

Adverbs (pages 469–472)

EXAMPLES   studies **hard**   does **not** exercise **daily**

When an adverb modifies an adjective or another adverb, it is placed on a line connected to the word it modifies.

EXAMPLES   **extremely** strong wind   tried **rather** hard

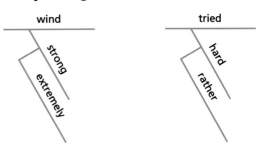

► EXERCISE 4   **Diagraming Adverbs**

Diagram the following groups of words.

1. answered quickly
2. listened quite intently
3. dangerously sharp curve
4. never plans very carefully
5. may possibly happen

► REVIEW A   **Diagraming Sentences That Contain Adjectives and Adverbs**

Diagram the following sentences.

1. The shutters rattled quite noisily.
2. We are definitely leaving tomorrow.
3. The anxious motorist drove much too far.
4. Our turn finally came.
5. The new car had not been damaged badly.

Objects (pages 491–493)

Direct Objects (page 491)

A direct object is diagramed on the horizontal line with the subject and verb. A vertical line separates the direct object from the verb. Notice that this vertical line does not cross the horizontal line.

EXAMPLE   The rain cleaned the **street.**

Compound Direct Objects (page 491)

EXAMPLE   We sold **lemonade** and **oranges.**

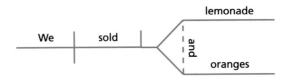

Indirect Objects (pages 492–493)

To diagram an indirect object, write it on a short horizontal line below the verb. Connect the indirect object to the verb by a slanted line.

EXAMPLE   The artist showed **me** his painting.

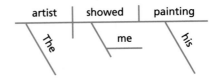

Compound Indirect Objects (page 493)

EXAMPLE   The company gave **Jean** and **Corey** summer jobs.

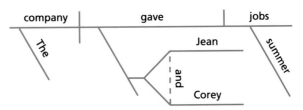

EXERCISE 5   **Diagraming Sentences That Contain Direct Objects and Indirect Objects**

Diagram the following sentences.

1. Placido Domingo signed photographs and programs.
2. Cara's sister taught her the rules.
3. The cashier handed the children balloons.
4. The judges awarded Jelisa and Rae the prizes.
5. Snow gives motorists and pedestrians trouble.

Subject Complements (pages 496–497)

A subject complement is placed on the horizontal line with the simple subject and the verb. The subject complement comes after the verb and is separated from it by a line slanting toward the subject. This slanted line shows that the complement refers to the subject.

Predicate Nominatives (page 496)

EXAMPLE   William Least Heat-Moon is an **author.**

Compound Predicate Nominatives (page 496)

EXAMPLE   The contestants are **Joan** and **Dean.**

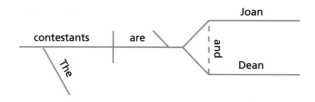

Predicate Adjectives (page 497)

EXAMPLE   The river looked **deep.**

Compound Predicate Adjectives (page 497)

EXAMPLE   This Chinese soup tastes **hot** and **spicy**.

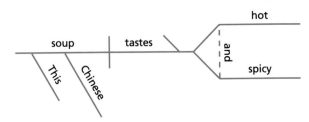

► EXERCISE 6 **Diagraming Sentences That Contain Subject Complements**

Diagram the following sentences.

1. Is Freddie Jackson your favorite singer?
2. The air grew cold and damp.
3. Sir Francis Drake was a brave explorer.
4. The chimpanzees seemed tired but happy.
5. My shoes looked worn and dusty.

► REVIEW B **Diagraming Sentences That Contain Complements**

Diagram the following sentences.

1. Her mother was a motorcycle mechanic.
2. Don and Maria rehearsed their parts.
3. The Gypsies' origin remains mysterious and strange.
4. The girls made themselves bracelets and necklaces.
5. My favorite Mexican foods are tamales and tacos.

Phrases (pages 505–527)

Prepositional Phrases (pages 506–509)

Prepositional phrases are diagramed below the word they modify. Write the preposition that introduces the phrase on a line slanting down from the modified word. Then, write the object of the preposition on a horizontal line extending from the slanting line.

Adjective Phrases (page 508)

EXAMPLES   paintings **by famous artists**

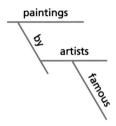

cloth **from Costa Rica and Guatemala**

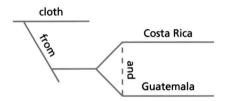

Adverb Phrases (page 509)

EXAMPLES   walked **along the road**

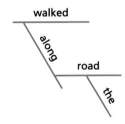

went **with Hollis and Dave**

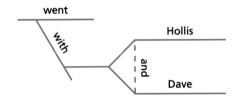

When a prepositional phrase modifies the object of another prepositional phrase, the diagram looks like this:

EXAMPLE camped on the side **of a mountain**

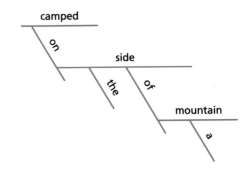

▶ EXERCISE 7 **Diagraming Prepositional Phrases**

Diagram the following word groups.

1. invited to the celebrations
2. a glimpse of the famous ruler
3. one of the people in the room
4. read about the Vietnamese and their history
5. drove to a village near Paris

▶ REVIEW C **Diagraming Sentences That Contain Prepositional Phrases**

Diagram the following sentences.

1. The number of whales is decreasing.
2. Hundreds of animal species are being protected by concerned citizens.
3. Citrus fruits are grown in California and Florida.
4. Many historic events have been decided by sudden changes in the weather.
5. The defeat of the debate team resulted from a lack of preparation.

Verbals and Verbal Phrases (pages 513–523)

Participles and Participial Phrases (pages 513–516)

Participles are diagramed in the same way that other adjectives are.

EXAMPLE   José comforted the **crying** baby.

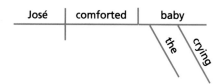

Participial phrases are diagramed as follows:

EXAMPLE   **Shaking the manager's hand,** Teresa accepted her new job.

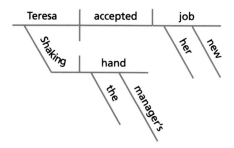

Notice that the participle has a direct object (*the manager's hand*), which is diagramed in the same way that the direct object of a main verb is.

Gerunds and Gerund Phrases (pages 518–520)

EXAMPLES   I enjoy **swimming.** [gerund used as direct object]

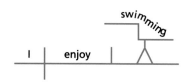

Being slightly ill is no excuse for **missing two days of baseball practice.** [Gerund phrases used as subject and as object of preposition. The first gerund has a subject complement (*ill*); the second gerund has a direct object (*days*).]

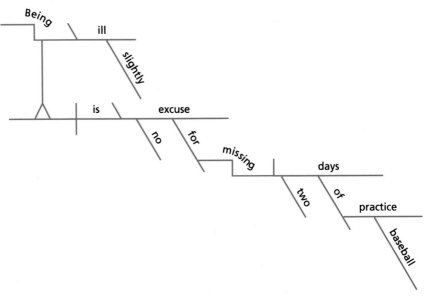

Infinitives and Infinitive Phrases (pages 522–523)

EXAMPLES **To write** is her ambition. [infinitive used as subject]

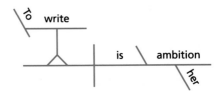

He was the first one **to solve that tricky problem.** [infinitive phrase used as adjective]

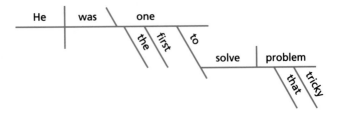

Marge was hoping **to go with us.** [infinitive phrase used as direct object]

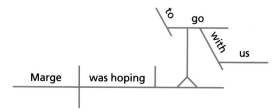

She called **to invite us over.** [infinitive phrase used as adverb]

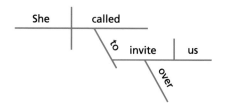

 EXERCISE 8 **Diagraming Sentences That Contain Verbal Phrases**

Diagram the following sentences.

1. Taking that shortcut will cut several minutes off the trip.
2. I want to watch *Nova* tonight.
3. That is my cat licking its paws.
4. Did they stop to ask directions?
5. Checking the time, Wynetta rushed to the gym.

Appositives and Appositive Phrases (pages 526–527)

To diagram an appositive or an appositive phrase, write the appositive in parentheses after the word it explains.

EXAMPLES   Our cousin **Iola** is a chemical engineer.

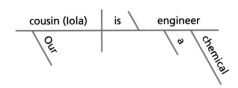

Bill Cosby, **the popular TV star,** is also the author of a best-selling book.

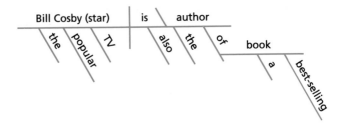

Subordinate Clauses (pages 535–548)

Adjective Clauses (pages 538–540)

Diagram an adjective clause by connecting it with a broken line to the word it modifies. Draw the broken line between the relative pronoun and the word that it relates to. [Note: The words *who, whom, whose, which,* and *that* are relative pronouns.]

EXAMPLES   The grades **that I got last term** pleased my parents.

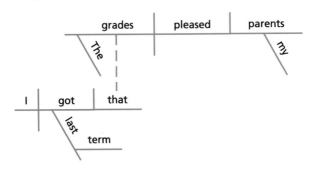

Adverb Clauses (pages 544–545)

Diagram an adverb clause by using a broken line to connect the adverb clause to the word it modifies. Place the subordinating conjunction that introduces the adverb clause on the broken line.

EXAMPLE **When I got home from school,** I ate an apple.

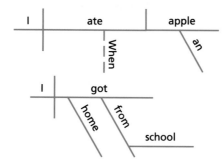

Noun Clauses (page 548)

Diagram a noun clause by connecting it to the independent clause with a solid line.

EXAMPLES Olivia knew **what she wanted.** [The noun clause is the direct object of the independent clause. The word *what* is the direct object in the noun clause.]

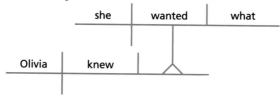

When the introductory word of the noun clause does not have a specific function in the noun clause, the sentence is diagramed in this way:

EXAMPLE The problem is **that they lost the map.** [The noun clause is the predicate nominative of the independent clause. The word *that* has no function in the noun clause except as an introductory word.]

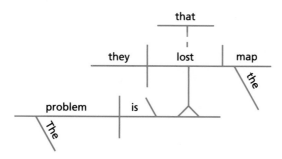

▶ EXERCISE 9 **Diagraming Sentences That Contain Subordinate Clauses**

Diagram the following sentences.

1. The test that we took on Friday was hard.
2. If I had not studied Thursday night, I could not have answered half the questions.
3. Our teacher announced what would be on the test.
4. Several friends of mine were not paying attention when the teacher gave the assignment.
5. My friends who did not know what to study are worried now about their grades.

Sentences Classified According to Structure (pages 556–565)

Simple Sentences (page 557)

EXAMPLE **Tracy is building a birdhouse in industrial arts class.** [one independent clause]

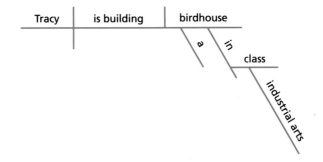

Compound Sentences (pages 559–560)

The second independent clause in a compound sentence is diagramed below the first and is joined to it by a coordinating conjunction.

EXAMPLE Darnell threw a good pass, but Clay did not catch it. [two independent clauses]

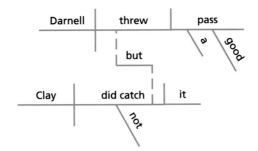

▶ EXERCISE 10   **Diagraming Compound Sentences**

Diagram the following compound sentences.

1. I want a motorboat, but Jan prefers a sailboat.
2. The bus stopped at the restaurant, and all of the passengers went inside.
3. Our club is very small, but it is growing.
4. Shall we meet you at the station, or will you take a taxi?
5. In Arizona the temperature is often high, but the humidity always remains low.

Complex Sentences (page 562)

EXAMPLE Before they left the museum, Lester and Jessica visited the exhibit of masks from Nigeria and the Ivory Coast. [one subordinate clause and one independent clause]

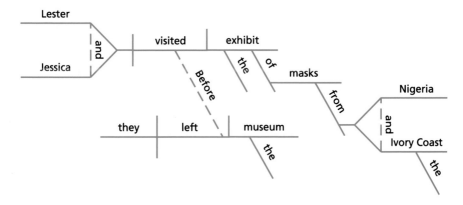

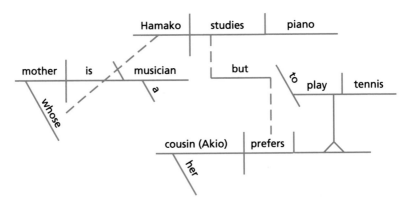

☞ REFERENCE NOTE: See pages 952–953 for more information on diagraming the three different kinds of subordinate clauses— adjective clauses, adverb clauses, and noun clauses.

▶ EXERCISE 11   **Diagraming Complex Sentences**

Diagram the following complex sentences.

1. One book that has won a Pulitzer Prize is *Pilgrim at Tinker Creek.*
2. Invite whomever you wish.
3. The satellite will be launched if the weather remains good.
4. The knight in black armor fought whoever would challenge him.
5. Alexander the Great, who conquered most of the known world, died at the age of thirty-three.

Compound-Complex Sentences (pages 564–565)

EXAMPLE   Hamako, whose mother is a musician, studies piano, but her cousin Akio prefers to play tennis. [two independent clauses and one subordinate clause]

▶ REVIEW D   **Diagraming Sentences**

Diagram the following sentences.

1. Diego Rivera and Rufino Tamayo were two important Mexican artists of this century.

2. Mom wanted to fly to Utah, but Dad and I wanted to drive there.
3. Our new neighbors, the Chens, come from Taiwan, which is an island off the coast of China.
4. When I returned to the store, the purple shirt had been sold, so I bought the blue one.
5. For my report, I wrote about Katherine Anne Porter and Eudora Welty, two Southern authors.

Glossary of Terms

Abstract noun An abstract noun names an idea, a feeling, a quality, or a characteristic. (See page 435.)

Action verb An action verb is a verb that expresses physical or mental action. (See page 457.)

Adjective An adjective is a word used to modify a noun or a pronoun. (See page 445.)

Adjective clause An adjective clause is a subordinate clause that modifies a noun or a pronoun. (See page 538.)

Adjective phrase An adjective phrase is a prepositional phrase that modifies a noun or a pronoun. (See page 508.)

Adverb An adverb is a word used to modify a verb, an adjective, or another adverb. (See page 469.)

Adverb clause An adverb clause is a subordinate clause that modifies a verb, an adjective, or an adverb. (See page 544.)

Adverb phrase An adverb phrase is a prepositional phrase that modifies a verb, an adjective, or an adverb. (See page 509.)

Agreement Agreement refers to the correspondence, or match, between grammatical forms. For example, the number and person of a subject and verb, and the number and gender of a pronoun and its antecedent, should always agree, or match. (See Chapter 20.)

Aim An aim is one of the four basic purposes, or reasons, for writing. (See pages 7 and 22.)

Antecedent An antecedent is a noun to which a pronoun refers. (See page 436.)

Antonym The antonym of a word is a word with the opposite meaning of that word. (See page 895.)

Appositive An appositive is a noun or a pronoun placed beside another noun or pronoun to identify or explain it. (See page 526.)

Appositive phrase An appositive phrase is made up of the appositive and its modifiers. (See page 526.)

Article *A, an,* and *the* are the most frequently used adjectives and are called articles. *A* and *an* are **indefinite articles.** Each indicates that a noun refers to one of a general group. *The* is a **definite article.** It indicates that a noun refers to someone or something in particular. (See page 446.)

Audience An audience is the person(s) who reads or listens to what the writer or speaker says. (See page 33.)

Base form One of the four principal parts of a verb. (See page 604.)

Body The body of a composition is one or more paragraphs that state and develop the composition's main points. (See page 108.)

Brainstorming Brainstorming is a technique for finding ideas by saying what comes to mind in response to a word without stopping to judge what's said. (See page 27.)

Business letter A business letter is a formal letter written to request something, complain or seek the correction of a problem, or express appreciation. (See page 901.)

Call number A call number is a number and letter code a library assigns to a book to tell how the book has been classified and where it has been placed on the shelves. (See page 881.)

Card catalog The library's card catalog is a cabinet or electronic database that contains listings of books by title, author, and subject. (See page 882.)

Case Case is the form of a noun or pronoun that shows its use in a sentence. (See page 634.)

Chronological order Chronological order is a way of arranging details in a paragraph or composition according to when events or actions take, or have taken, place. (See page 75.)

Classification Classification is a strategy of development in which a writer looks at a subject as it relates to other subjects in a group. (See page 79.)

Clause A clause is a group of words that contains a verb and its subject and is used as part of a sentence. (See page 533.)

Cliché A cliché is a vague and overused expression. (See page 399.)

Clustering Clustering, or **webbing,** is a technique for finding writing ideas and gathering information by breaking a large subject into its smaller parts, creating a visual map of the writer's thoughts. (See page 28.)

Coherence Coherence, in a paragraph or composition, is a quality achieved when all the ideas are clearly arranged and connected. (See page 71.)

Collective noun A collective noun is a word that names a group. (See page 433.)

Colloquialism A colloquialism is a colorful, widely used expression of conversational language. (See page 396.)

Common noun A common noun names any one of a group of persons, places, or things and is not capitalized unless it begins a sentence. (See page 433.)

Comparative degree Comparative degree is the form a modifier takes when comparing two things. (See page 661.)

Complement A complement is a word or group of words that completes the meaning of a verb. (See page 488.)

Complex sentence A complex sentence has one independent clause and at least one subordinate clause. (See page 562.)

Compound noun A compound noun is two or more words used together as a single noun. (See page 432.)

Compound sentence A compound sentence has two or more independent clauses but no subordinate clauses. (See page 559.)

Compound subject A compound subject consists of two or more subjects that are joined by a conjunction and have the same verb. (See page 418.)

Compound verb A compound verb consists of two or more verbs or verb phrases that are joined by a conjunction and have the same subject. (See page 419.)

Compound-complex sentence A compound-complex sentence contains two or more independent clauses and at least one subordinate clause. (See page 564.)

Conclusion A conclusion reinforces the main idea and brings the composition to a definite close. (See page 110.)

Conclusion A conclusion is a decision reached by reasoning from clearly expressed facts and evidence found in a reading passage or other materials. It may be **valid** or **invalid.** (See page 915.)

Concrete noun A concrete noun names an object that can be perceived by one or more of the senses. (See page 435.)

Conjunction A conjunction is a word used to join words or groups of words. **Coordinating conjunctions** connect words or groups of words used in the same way. **Correlative conjunctions** also connect words used in the same way and are always used in pairs. (See page 478.)

Connotation The connotation of a word is the meaning, association, or emotion suggested by a word. (See page 895.)

Context The context of a word includes the surrounding words and the way the word is used. (See page 894.)

Contraction A contraction is a shortened form of a word, a figure, or a group of words. (See page 783.)

Creative writing Creative writing is writing that aims at creating literature: stories, poems, songs, and plays. (See page 7.)

D

Declarative sentence A declarative sentence makes a statement and is followed by a period. (See page 422.)

Demonstrative pronoun A demonstrative pronoun points out a person, a place, a thing, or an idea. (See page 440.)

Denotation The denotation of a word is its direct, plainly expressed meaning—the meaning a dictionary lists. (See page 895.)

Description Description is a strategy of development in which a writer uses sensory details to describe something. (See page 74.)

Dialect A dialect is a distinct version or variety of a language used by a particular group of people. Dialects of a language may differ from one another in vocabulary, grammar, and pronunciation. A dialect may be **regional** or **ethnic**. (See page 392.)

Dialogue Dialogue consists of the words that characters say in a story. (See page 202.)

Direct object A direct object is a noun or a pronoun that receives the action of the verb or shows the result of the action. It tells *what* or *whom* after an action verb. (See page 491.)

Direct quotation A direct quotation is a person's exact words and is enclosed in quotation marks. (See page 772.)

Double negative A double negative is the use of two negative words to express one negative idea. (See page 665.)

E

Early plan An early plan, sometimes called an **informal outline,** is a writer's rough plan for a composition in which he or she groups and orders information. (See page 97.)

End marks An end mark is a punctuation mark that is placed at the end of a sentence to indicate the purpose of the sentence. (See page 737.)

Essay test An essay test is a test that requires a student to think carefully about material learned and to express his or her understanding of that material, in writing, in an organized way. (See page 931.)

Essential clause/Essential phrase An essential (or **restrictive**) clause or phrase is necessary to the meaning of a sentence. (See page 748.)

Evaluating Evaluating is the stage in the writing process in which a writer goes over a draft, making judgments about its strengths and weaknesses in content, organization, and style. (See pages 6 and 43.)

Evaluation Evaluation is a strategy of development in which a writer makes judgments about a subject in an attempt to determine its value. (See page 82.)

Example An example is a specific instance, or illustration, of a general idea. (See page 68.)

Exclamatory sentence An exclamatory sentence shows excitement or expresses strong feeling and is followed by an exclamation point. (See page 423.)

Expository writing. *See* Informative writing.

Expressive writing Expressive writing is writing that aims at expressing a writer's feelings and thoughts. (See page 7.)

F

Fact A fact is something that can be checked and proved to be true by concrete information. (See page 67.)

Feedback Feedback is the listener's response to a speaker's message. (See page 860.)

Figure of speech A figure of speech is a word or a group of words that has a meaning other than its literal one. (See page 165.)

5W-How? **questions** The *5W-How?* questions—*Who? What? Where? When? Why? How?*—are questions a writer uses to collect information about a subject. (See page 29.)

Formal outline A formal outline is a highly structured, clearly labeled writing plan. It has a set pattern, using letters and numbers to label main headings and subheadings. (See page 99.)

Formal speech A formal speech is carefully prepared and given at an arranged time and place. (See page 862.)

Freewriting Freewriting is a technique for finding ideas in which the writer writes whatever pops into his or her head without regard to form. **Focused freewriting,** or **looping,** is a technique in which a writer focuses on one word or phrase from his or her original freewriting and uses it to start freewriting again. (See page 25.)

G

Gerund A gerund is a verb form ending in *–ing* that is used as a noun. (See page 518.)

Gerund phrase A gerund phrase contains a gerund and all the words related to the gerund. (See page 519.)

H

Homonyms Homonyms are words that are spelled differently and that mean different things, but are pronounced alike. (See page 811.)

I

Imperative sentence An imperative sentence gives a command or makes a request and is followed by either a period or an exclamation point. (See page 423.)

Impromptu speech An impromptu speech is a short speech made on the spur of the moment, with little or no time for development or preparation of ideas. (See page 861.)

Indefinite pronoun An indefinite pronoun refers to a person, a place, or a thing that is not specifically named. (See page 442.)

Independent clause An independent (or **main**) clause expresses a complete thought and can stand by itself as a sentence. (See page 534.)

Indirect object An indirect object is a noun or pronoun that comes between a transitive verb and its direct object and tells *to whom* or *for whom* the action of the verb is done. (See page 492.)

Indirect quotation An indirect quotation is a rewording or paraphrasing of something a person has said. (See page 773.)

Infinitive An infinitive is a verb form, usually preceded by *to,* that can be used as a noun, an adjective, or an adverb. (See page 522.)

Infinitive phrase An infinitive phrase consists of an infinitive and its modifiers and complements. (See page 523.)

Informative writing Informative writing is writing that aims at conveying information or explaining something. (See page 7.)

Instructions Instructions are a form of writing in which a writer explains how to use or do something. (See page 228.)

Intensive pronoun An intensive pronoun emphasizes a noun or another pronoun. (See page 438.)

Interjection An interjection is a word used to express emotion. It has no grammatical relation to other words in the sentence. (See page 480.)

Interrogative pronoun An interrogative pronoun introduces a question. (See page 440.)

Interrogative sentence An interrogative sentence asks a question and is followed by a question mark. (See page 423.)

Interview An interview is a special listening situation with the specific purpose of gathering information that usually takes place between two people, an interviewer and the person being interviewed (called the *interviewee*). (See page 873.)

Intransitive verb An intransitive verb expresses action (or tells something about the subject) without passing the action from a doer to a receiver. (See page 459.)

Introduction An introduction begins a composition and should catch the reader's interest and present the main idea. (See page 104.)

Irregular verb An irregular verb is a verb that forms its past and past participle in some other way than by adding *-d* or *-ed* to the infinitive form. (See page 606.)

Jargon Jargon consists of words and phrases that have special meanings for particular groups of people. (See page 400.)

Linking verb A linking verb links, or connects, the subject with a noun, a pronoun, or an adjective in the predicate. (See page 461.)

Main idea A main idea is the idea around which a paragraph or composition is organized. (See pages 62 and 97.)

Metaphor A metaphor is a figure of speech that directly compares two things without using the word *like* or *as*. A metaphor says that something *is* something else. (See page 165.)

Modifier A modifier describes or limits the meaning of another word. (See page 657.)

Narration Narration is a strategy of development in which a writer relates events or actions over a period of time. (See page 75.)

Nonessential clause/Nonessential phrase A nonessential (or **nonrestrictive**) clause or phrase adds information that is not needed to understand the meaning of the sentence. It is set off by commas. (See page 747.)

Noun A noun is a word used to name a person, a place, a thing, or an idea. (See page 430.)

Noun clause A noun clause is a subordinate clause used as a noun. (See page 548.)

Number Number is the form of a word that indicates whether the word is singular or plural. (See page 574.)

O

Object An object receives the action of a transitive verb. (See page 459.)

Object of the preposition The noun or pronoun that ends a prepositional phrase is the object of the preposition that begins the phrase. (See page 506.)

Objective test An objective test is a test that may contain multiple-choice, true/false, matching, reasoning or logic, analogy, or short-answer questions. (See page 925.)

Opinion An opinion is a belief or attitude. (See page 261.)

Oral interpretation Oral interpretation is an expressive presentation of a literary work to an audience. (See page 867.)

Order of importance Order of importance is a way of arranging details in a paragraph or composition according to the details' levels of importance. (See page 82.)

P

Paraphrase A paraphrase is a restatement of someone's ideas in different words. (See pages 875 and 921.)

Parenthetical expression A parenthetical expression is a side remark that adds information or relates ideas. (See page 751.)

Participial phrase A participial phrase contains a participle and all of the words related to the participle. (See page 515.)

Participle A participle is a verb form that can be used as an adjective. (See page 513.)

Personal letter A personal letter is an informal letter in which a writer might thank someone for something, invite someone to a particular event or occasion, or reply to an invitation he or she has received. (See page 901.)

Personal narrative A personal narrative is a form of writing in which an author explores and shares the meaning of an experience that was especially important to him or her. (See Chapter 4.)

Personal pronoun A personal pronoun refers to the one speaking (*first person*), the one spoken to (*second person*), or the one spoken about (*third person*). (See page 437.)

Personification Personification is a figure of speech in which human characteristics are given to nonhuman things. (See page 166.)

Persuasive essay A persuasive essay is a form of writing in which a writer supports an opinion and tries to persuade an audience. (See Chapter 8.)

Persuasive writing Persuasive writing is writing that aims at persuading people to change their minds about something or to act in a certain way. (See page 7.)

Phrase A phrase is a group of related words that is used as a single part of speech and does not contain a verb and its subject. (See page 505.)

Plot The plot is the series of events in a story that follow each other and cause each other to happen. The plot centers on a **conflict,** or problem, that the main character faces. (See page 198.)

Point of view Point of view is the vantage point, or position, from which a writer tells a story. (See page 200.)

Positive degree Positive degree is the form of a modifier when only one thing is being described. (See page 658.)

Predicate The predicate is the part of a sentence that says something about the subject. The **simple predicate,** or **verb,** is the main word or group of words within the **complete predicate.** The complete predicate is composed of the main verb and its modifiers. (See page 413.)

Predicate adjective A predicate adjective is an adjective that follows a linking verb and describes the subject. (See page 497.)

Predicate nominative A predicate nominative is a noun that follows a linking verb and identifies the subject or refers to it. (See page 496.)

Prefix A prefix is a letter or group of letters added to the beginning of a word to change its meaning. (See page 802.)

Preposition A preposition is a word used to show the relationship of a noun or a pronoun to some other word in the sentence. (See page 474.)

Prepositional phrase A prepositional phrase is a group of words beginning with a preposition and ending with a noun or a pronoun. (See page 506.)

Prewriting Prewriting is the first stage in the writing process. In this stage, a writer thinks and plans, figures out what to write about, collects ideas and details, and makes a plan for presenting ideas. (See pages 6 and 24.)

Principal parts of a verb The principal parts of a verb are the verb's forms: the *base form,* the *present participle,* the *past,* and the *past participle.* (See page 604.)

Pronoun A pronoun is a word used in place of a noun or more than one noun. (See page 436.)

Proofreading Proofreading is the stage of the writing process in which a writer carefully reads a revised draft to correct mistakes in grammar, usage, and mechanics. (See pages 6 and 50.)

Proper adjective A proper adjective is formed from a proper noun and begins with a capital letter. (See page 448.)

Proper noun A proper noun names a particular person, place, thing, or idea and is always capitalized. (See page 433.)

Publishing Publishing is the last stage of the writing process. In this stage, a writer makes a final, clean copy of a paper and shares it with an audience. (See pages 6 and 51.)

Purpose Purpose is the reason for writing or speaking: to express yourself; to be creative; to entertain; to explain, inform, or explore; or to persuade. (See page 33.)

R

Reflexive pronoun A reflexive pronoun refers to the subject and directs the action of the verb back to the subject. (See page 438.)

Regular verb A regular verb is a verb that forms its past and past participle by adding *–d* or *–ed* to the base form. (See page 604.)

Relative pronoun A relative pronoun introduces a subordinate clause and relates an adjective clause to the word that the clause modifies. (See pages 440 and 539.)

Research report A research report is a form of writing in which a writer presents factual information that he or she has discovered through exploration and research. (See Chapter 10.)

Revising Revising is the stage of the writing process in which a writer goes over a draft, making changes in its content, organization, and style in order to improve it. (See pages 6 and 43.)

Run-on sentence A run-on sentence is two or more complete sentences run together as one. (See page 364.)

Sentence A sentence is a group of words that contains a subject and a verb and expresses a complete thought. (See page 406.)

Sentence base The sentence base consists of the subject and the verb of a sentence. (See page 417.)

Sentence fragment A sentence fragment is a part of a sentence that does not express a complete thought. (See pages 361 and 406.)

Setting The setting is where and when a story takes place. (See page 197.)

Simile A simile is a figure of speech that compares two basically unlike things, using the word *like* or *as.* (See page 165.)

Simple sentence A simple sentence has one independent clause and no subordinate clauses. (See page 557.)

Slang Slang consists of made-up words and old words used in new ways. (See page 396.)

Spatial order Spatial order is a way of arranging details in a paragraph or composition by ordering them according to how they are spaced—nearest to farthest, left to right, and so on. (See page 74.)

Statement of opinion A statement of opinion is a sentence in which a writer clearly states a topic and his or her opinion about it. (See page 262.)

Stringy sentence A stringy sentence is a sentence that has too many independent clauses, often strung together with words like *and* or *but.* (See page 378.)

Subject The subject is the part of a sentence that tells whom or what the sentence is about. The **simple subject** is the main word or group of words within the **complete subject.** The complete subject consists of the simple subject and its modifiers. (See page 409.)

Subject complement A subject complement completes the meaning of a linking verb and identifies or describes the subject. (See page 496.)

Subordinate clause A subordinate (or **dependent**) clause does not express a complete thought and cannot stand alone as a sentence. (See page 535.)

Subordinating conjunction A subordinating conjunction is a word that shows the relationship between an adverb clause and the word or words that the clause modifies. (See page 545.)

Suffix A suffix is a letter or group of letters added to the end of a word to change its meaning. (See page 802.)

Summary A summary is a restatement, in shortened form, of the main points of a passage, a speech, etc. (See pages 875 and 922.)

Superlative degree Superlative degree is the form a modifier takes when comparing more than two things. (See page 661.)

Supporting sentences Supporting sentences are sentences in a paragraph or composition that give specific details or information to support the main idea. (See page 66.)

Syllable A syllable is a word part that can be pronounced by itself. (See page 798.)

Synonym A synonym is a word that has a meaning similar to but not exactly the same as another word's. (See page 895.)

T

Tense The tense of a verb indicates the time of the action or state of being expressed by the verb. (See page 614.)

Topic sentence A topic sentence is the sentence that expresses the main idea of a paragraph. (See page 63.)

Transitional words and phrases Transitional words and phrases connect ideas in a paragraph or composition by showing how ideas and details are related. (See page 71.)

Transitive verb A transitive verb is an action verb that expresses an action directed toward a person or thing. (See page 459.)

U

Unity Unity, in a paragraph or composition, is a quality achieved when all the sentences or paragraphs work together as a unit to express or support one main idea. (See page 69.)

V

Verb A verb is a word used to express an action or a state of being. (See page 457.)

Verb phrase A verb phrase consists of a main verb preceded by at least one **helping verb,** or **auxiliary verb.** (See page 464.)

Verbal A verbal is a form of a verb used as a noun, an adjective, or an adverb. (See page 513.)

W

"What if?" questions Asking "What if?" questions is a creative thinking technique that can help a writer draw upon imagination to explore ideas for writing. (See page 31.)

Word bank A word bank is a writer's storehouse of words that he or she can use in writing. (See pages 164 and 893.)

Writer's journal A writer's journal is a written record of a person's experiences, feelings, questions, and thoughts. (See page 25.)

Writing Writing is the stage in the writing process in which a writer puts his or her ideas into sentences and paragraphs, following a plan for presenting the ideas. (See pages 6 and 41.)

Writing process The writing process is the series of stages or steps that a writer goes through to develop ideas and to communicate them clearly in a piece of writing. (See pages 6 and 22.)

Glossary

This glossary is a short dictionary of words found in the professional writing models in this textbook. The words are defined according to their meanings in the context of the writing models.

Pronunciation Key

Symbol	Key Words	Symbol	Key Words
a	asp, fat, parrot	b	bed, fable, dub, ebb
ā	ape, date, play, break, fail	d	dip, beadle, had, dodder
ä	ah, car, father, cot	f	fall, after, off, phone
e	elf, ten, berry	g	get, haggle, dog
ē	even, meet, money, flea, grieve	h	he, ahead, hotel
i	is, hit, mirror	j	joy, agile, badge
ī	ice, bite, high, sky	k	kill, tackle, bake, coat, quick
ō	open, tone, go, boat	l	let, yellow, ball
ô	all, horn, law, oar	m	met, camel, trim, summer
σο	look, pull, moor, wolf	n	not, flannel, ton
o͞o	ooze, tool, crew, rule	p	put, apple, tap
yo͞o	use, cute, few	r	red, port, dear, purr
yσο	cure, globule	s	sell, castle, pass, nice
oi	oil, point, toy	t	top, cattle, hat
ou	out, crowd, plow	v	vat, hovel, have
u	up, cut, color, flood	w	will, always, swear, quick
ur	urn, fur, deter, irk	y	yet, onion, yard
ə	a in ago	z	zebra, dazzle, haze, rise
	e in agent	ch	chin, catcher, arch, nature
	i in sanity	sh	she, cushion, dash, machine
	o in comply	th	thin, nothing, truth
	u in focus	*th*	then, father, lathe
ər	perhaps, murder	zh	azure, leisure, beige
		ŋ	ring, anger, drink

Abbreviation Key

adj.	adjective	*prep.*	preposition
adv.	adverb	*vi.*	intransitive verb
n.	noun	*vt.*	transitive verb
pl.	plural		

a·fi·cio·na·do [ə fish'ə nä'dō] *n.*
A person who likes, knows about,
and devotedly pursues some interest or activity.

ail·ment [āl'mənt] *n.* An illness.

a·larm·ist [ə lärm'ist] *adj.* Of or like
a person who spreads exaggerated
reports of danger.

am·bi·tion [am bish'ən] *n.* A strong
desire to succeed.

au·to·bi·o·graph·i·cal [ôt'ō bī'ə
graf'i kəl] *adj.* About one's own
life story.

a·verse [ə vʉrs'] *adj.* Unwilling or
not inclined; opposed (to).

bade [bad] *vt.* Commanded.

bar·ren [bar'ən] *adj.* Empty.

be·moan [bē mōn'] *vt.* To feel sorry
about something.

bi·zarre [bi zär'] *adj.* Very odd or out
of the ordinary; unexpected and
unbelievable.

Brown·ing [broun'iŋ], **Elizabeth Barrett** *n.* (1806–1861) An English poet.

Brown·ing [broun'iŋ], **Robert** *n.*
(1812–1889) An English poet.

Car·roll [kar'əl], **Lewis** *n.* (1832–1898)
An English writer.

clab·ber [klab'ər] *n.* Thick, sour milk.

clad [klad] *adj.* Dressed or clothed.

con·scious·ly [kän'shəs lē] *adv.* Done
with a knowledge or awareness of.

con·ser·va·tion·ist [kän'sər vā'shən
ist] *n.* A person who promotes the
preservation of natural resources.

con·vey [kən vā'] *vt.* To communicate.

co-op [kō'äp'] *n.* Short for **cooperative**;
an apartment house, store, society,
or other organization owned and
operated by those who use its
facilities or buy its goods.

cov·ey [kuv'ē] *n.* A small flock of
birds.

de·but [dā byōō'] *n.* An introduction
to the public, as of an actor; a
career's beginning.

de·fi·ance [dē fī'əns] *n.* The act of
openly challenging an opposition.

dell [del] *n.* A small valley.

de·pict [dē pikt'] *vt.* To describe.

Dick·ens [dik'ənz], **Charles** *n.* (1812–
1870) The English writer who wrote
Oliver Twist and *A Christmas Carol.*

doff [däf] *vt.* To take off one's hat in
greeting.

drove [drōv] *n.* A great number of
something, such as people or
animals.

eaves·drop·per [ēvz'dräp ər] *n.* One
who listens secretly to others'
conversations.

El·ling·ton [el'iŋ tən], **Duke** *n.*
(1899–1974) A U.S. jazz musician,
bandleader, and composer.

en·hance [en hans'] *vt.* To improve
the quality of.

ep·i·dem·ic [ep'ə dem'ik] *n.* The
quick spreading of a disease.

flat [flat] *n.* An area of level land.

flush [flush] *vt.* To drive out game
birds from their cover.

G

gas plate [gas plāt] *n.* A small, portable stove.

gran·deur [grän′jər] *n.* Magnificence.

gru·el·ing [groo′əl iŋ] *adj.* Extremely harsh and exhausting.

H

half nel·son [haf nel′sən] *n.* A type of wrestling hold.

haugh·ty [hôt′ē] *adj.* Showing too much pride in oneself.

hum·ding·er [hum′diŋ′ər] *n.* A slang word for a person or thing of excellence.

I

ice·box [īs′bäks′] *n.* An insulated box that holds ice for keeping foods cold.

in·flu·en·za [in′floo en′zə] *n.* A contagious viral disease.

in·or·di·nate·ly [in ôr′də nit lē] *adv.* Excessively.

in·tact [in takt′] *adj.* Untouched; kept whole and uninjured.

L

Le·o·pold [lē′ə pōld′], **Aldo** *n.* (1887–1948) A U.S. naturalist, one of only one hundred trained foresters working for the U.S. Forest Service in 1909; he later became a private forestry and wildlife consultant.

M

mag·ma [mag′mə] *n.* Molten rock within the earth.

Mag·na Car·ta [mag′nə kär′tə] *n.* The document that King John of England was forced to sign in 1215, giving civil and political rights to the people.

Mar·shal [mär′shəl], **Bob** *n.* (1942–) The first recreation chief of the U.S. Forest Service. He has worked to preserve lands.

mel·an·chol·y [mel′ən käl′ē] *n.* Sadness and gloom.

met·a·phor·i·cal [met′ə fôr′i kəl] *adj.* Not meant to be taken literally.

Milne [miln], **A(lan) A(lexander)** *n.* (1882–1956) An English playwright and novelist.

Mil·ton [mil′tən], **John** *n.* (1608–1674) The English poet who wrote *Paradise Lost.*

mi·nor·i·ty [mī nôr′ə tē] *n.* Less than half of a group.

Muir [myoor], **John** *n.* (1838–1914) The naturalist who worked to make Yosemite a national park and gained support from Theodore Roosevelt for 148,000,000 acres for forest reserves.

mul·ti·tude [mul′tə tood] *n.* A large number of people or things.

mu·tant [myoo′tənt] *adj.* Of or produced by a sudden change in some inheritable characteristic in a plant or animal.

my·col·o·gist [mī käl′ə jist] *n.* A person who studies fungi.

P

per·ti·nent [pur′tə nənt] *adj.* Having to do with the matter at hand.

phi·los·o·phy [fə läs′ə fē] *n.* The love of or search for wisdom or knowledge.

pig·eon·hole [pij′ən hōl′] *v.* To categorize or classify.

poised [poizd] *vi.* Balanced.

pro·to·zo·an [prōt′ō zō′ən] *n.* A member of the animal subkingdom Protozoa. Protozoans are usually single-celled and microscopic and are either water-dwelling or parasitic organisms.

pul·sate [pul′sāt′] *v.* To throb or move rhythmically; quiver.

pur·ga·tive [pur′gə tiv] *n.* A substance that causes a bowel movement.

quell [kwel] *vt.* To quiet or put an end to.

roil [roil] *vt.* To stir up; to agitate; to move turbulently.

room·er [rōōm'ər] *n.* A person who lives in a rented room.

schoon·er [skōōn'ər] *n.* A ship with two or more masts.

scle·ro·ti·um [skli rō'shē əm] *n.* In various fungi, a hardened mass of threads that stores food material and can remain dormant for long periods.

sem·i·pro·fes·sion·al [sem'i prə fesh'ə nəl] *adj.* Engaged in for pay but not as a full-time occupation.

shale [shāl] *n.* Fine-grained, layered rock, formed by the hardening of clay, mud, or silt.

slack [slak] *adj.* Loose.

sock·dol·a·ger [säk däl'ə jər] *n.* Something outstanding.

sphere [sfir] *n.* Something round; a ball.

sphe·roid [sfir'oid] *n.* An object that is almost but not completely round.

spore [spōr] *n.* A small reproductive organ associated with many non-flowering plants (such as fungi, mosses, or ferns), with bacteria, and with some protozoans.

stoop [stōōp] *n.* A small porch with steps.

strick·en [strik'ən] *adj.* Affected by something upsetting.

sub·tle·ty [sut"l tē] *n.* The condition of not being obvious.

syc·a·more [sik'ə môr'] *n.* A kind of maple tree with yellow flowers.

tas·sel [tas'əl] *n.* A group of strings hanging from the knot where they are tied together.

Ten·ny·son [ten'i sən] **Alfred** *n.* (1808–1892) An English poet.

ter·res·tri·al [tə res'trē əl] *adj.* Of or relating to the earth.

tin·ker [tink'ər] *n.* A person who makes minor repairs.

tongue [tuŋ] *n.* A language.

top·ple [täp'əl] *vt.* To cause to fall over.

tou·can [tōō'kan'] *n.* A fruit-eating bird of tropical America, characterized by its large beak and bright colors.

tour·ni·quet [tʉr'ni kit] *n.* A device, such as a bandage twisted about a limb, to control bleeding.

trend [trend] *n.* A current style.

tu·mult [tōō'mult'] *n.* Noisy uproar of a crowd.

Twain [twān], **Mark** *n.* (1835–1910) American humorist and writer.

un·con·scious·ly [un kän'shəs lē] *adv.* Done without a knowledge or awareness of.

un·heed·ed [un hēd'id] *adv.* Not having attention being paid.

un·sur·passed [un sər past'] *adj.* Not outdone; best.

ver·min [vʉr'mən] *n. pl.* Various harmful bugs or small animals that are difficult to control.

vis·age [viz'ij] *n.* The face and its expressions.

viv·id·ly [viv'id lē] *adv.* Done in a clear or realistic way.

writh·ing [rī*th*'iŋ] *vi.* Squirming or twisting of the body.

Index

D

INDEX

P

Q

INDEX

W

Y

Z

Acknowledgments

For permission to reprint copyrighted material, grateful acknowledgment is made to the following sources:

Andrews and McMeel: From "Chapter 9: Use It Again . . . and Again . . . and Again . . ." from *50 Simple Things Kids Can Do to Save the Earth* by The Earth Works Group. Copyright © 1990 by John Javna.

Atheneum Books for Young Readers, an imprint of Simon & Schuster: From *Rockhound Trails* by Jean Bartenbach. Copyright © 1977 by Jean Bartenbach.

Ballantine Books, a division of Random House, Inc.: From "WHAT TO DO IN A WILDERNESS MEDICAL EMERGENCY" from *Dave Barry's Only Travel Guide You'll Ever Need* by Dave Barry. Copyright © 1991 by Dave Barry.

Susan Bergholz Literary Services, New York: From *Bless Me Ultima* by Rudolfo A. Anaya. Copyright © 1972 by Rudolfo A. Anaya. Published by Warner Books in hardcover and mass market editions; originally published by TQS Publications, Berkeley, CA. All rights reserved. From "Salomon's Story" from *Tortuga* by Rudolfo A. Anaya. Copyright © 1979 by Rudolfo A. Anaya. Published by University of New Mexico Press, Albuquerque, NM. All rights reserved.

Boy Scouts of America: From "Are There Martians on Mars?" from "A Home on the Martian Range" by Scott Stuckey from *Boy's Life*, July 1990. Copyright © 1990 by Boy Scouts of America.

Gwendolyn Brooks: From "The Sonnet-Ballad" from *Blacks* by Gwendolyn Brooks. Copyright © 1987 by Gwendolyn Brooks. Published by The David Company. Reissued by Third World Press, 1991. "Robert, Who Is Often a Stranger to Himself" from *Bronzeville Boys and Girls* by Gwendolyn Brooks. Copyright © 1956 by Gwendolyn Brooks Blakely.

Curtis Brown Ltd.: From "Strange and Terrible Monsters of the Deep" by William Wise from *Boy's Life*, February 1978. Copyright © 1978 by The Boy Scouts of America.

Juan Bruce-Novoa and University of Texas Press, Inc.: From *Chicano Authors: Inquiry by Interview* by Juan Bruce-Novoa. Copyright © 1980 by Juan Bruce-Novoa.

Children's Television Workshop: From "Paradise Lost" by Elizabeth Vitton from *3–2–1 Contact*, December 1990, pp. 7–9. Copyright © 1990 by Children's Television Workshop, New York, NY. All rights reserved.

Cobblestone Publishing, Inc., 7 School Street, Peterborough, NH 03458: From "Energy: Powering a Nation" by Laurel Sherman from *Cobblestone*, vol. 11, no. 10, October 1990. Copyright © 1990 by Cobblestone Publishing, Inc.

Coffee House Press: From "Part I: Emile" from *Brazil Maru* by Karen Tei Yamashita. Copyright © 1992 by Karen Tei Yamashita.

Ruth Cohen, Inc., on behalf of Lensey Namioka: From "The All-American Slurp" by Lensey Namioka from *Visions*, edited by Donald R. Gallo. Copyright © 1987 by Lensey Namioka. Published by Delacorte Press.

Coward-McCann, Inc.: "Desert Noon" from *Compass Rose* by Elizabeth Coatsworth. Copyright 1929 by Coward-McCann, Inc.; copyright renewed © 1957 by Elizabeth Coatsworth.

Stanley Crouch: From "The Duke's Blues" by Stanley Crouch from *The New Yorker*, April 19 & May 6, 1996, p. 158. Copyright © 1996 by Stanley Crouch.

Crown Publishers Inc.: "Travel Tip: How to Use Chopsticks" from *Dave Barry Does Japan* by Dave Barry. Copyright © 1992 by Dave Barry.

Kent Dannen: From "Ban Dogs from Trails?" by Kent Dannen from *Dog Fancy,* June 1988. Copyright © 1988 by Kent Dannen.

DC Comics: Superman Trademark slogan. ™ DC Comics. All rights reserved.

E. L. Doctorow: Unpublished quotation by E. L. Doctorow. Copyright © 1993 by E. L. Doctorow.

Doubleday, a division of Bantam Doubleday Dell Publishing Group, Inc.: "Tuesday, 4 April, 1944" (Retitled: "Becoming a Journalist") and from "March 7, 1944" from *Anne Frank: The Diary of a Young Girl* by Anne Frank. Copyright 1952 by Otto H. Frank.

Dutton Signet, a division of Penguin Books USA Inc.: From "The Letter" from *Max Perkins, Editor of Genius* by A. Scott Berg. Copyright © 1978 by A. Scott Berg.

Paul S. Eriksson, Publisher: From a journal entry by Mary Garfield from *Small Voices* by Josef and Dorothy Berger.

Farrar, Straus & Giroux, Inc.: From *A Wind in the Door* by Madeleine L'Engle. Copyright © 1974 by Crosswicks, Ltd.

HarperCollins Publishers, Inc.: "Jimmy Jet and His TV Set" from *Where the Sidewalk Ends* by Shel Silverstein. Copyright © 1974 by Evil Eye Music, Inc.

HarperCollins Publishers Limited: From *Survive the Savage Sea* by Dougal Robertson. Copyright © 1973 by Dougal Robertson.

Highlights for Children, Inc., Columbus, OH: From "Billy Mills" by Della A. Yannuzzi from *Highlights for Children,* January 1990. Copyright © 1990 by Highlights for Children, Inc. From "Pictures of the Poor" by Elsa Marston from *Highlights for Children,* September 1990. Copyright © 1990 by Highlights for Children, Inc.

Hill & Wang, a division of Farrar, Straus & Giroux, Inc.: "Thank You, M'am" from *Short Stories* by Langston Hughes. Copyright © 1996 by Ramona Bass and Arnold Rampersad.

International Creative Management, Inc.: From "On the Ball" from *Five Seasons* by Roger Angell. Copyright © 1972 by Roger Angell.

Stephen King: From "Everything You Need to Know About Writing Successfully in Ten Minutes" by Stephen King from *The Writer's Handbook,* edited by Sylvia K. Burack. Copyright © 1990 by Stephen King.

Alfred A. Knopf, Inc.: From "Along the Colorado" from *The Secret Worlds of Colin Fletcher* by Colin Fletcher. Copyright © 1989 by Colin Fletcher. From "Dream Deferred" ("Harlem"), from "Dreams," and from "Song" from *Collected Poems* by Langston Hughes. Copyright © 1994 by the Estate of Langston Hughes. From "Mother to Son" from *Selected Poems* by Langston Hughes. Copyright 1926 by Alfred A. Knopf, Inc.; copyright renewed 1954 by Langston Hughes. "Alta Weiss" from *Baseball: An Illustrated History,* narrative by Geoffrey C. Ward, based on a documentary filmscript by Geoffrey C. Ward and Ken Burns. Copyright © 1994 by Baseball Film Project, Inc.

Nedra Newkirk Lamar: "Does a Finger Fing?" by Nedra Newkirk Lamar.

Larry Leonard: Quotation by Jean Auel from "Jean Auel" by Larry Leonard from *On Being a Writer,* edited by Bill Strickland. Copyright © 1984 by Larry Leonard.

Ray Lincoln Literary Agency, Elkins Park House, 107–B, Elkins Park, PA: From "The Big Bang" from *Mount St. Helens: A Sleeping Volcano Awakens* by Marian T. Place. Copyright © 1981 by Marian T. Place.

Liveright Publishing Corporation: From "An Interview with Ann Petry" from *Interviews with Black Writers,* edited by John O'Brien. Copyright © 1973 by Liveright Publishing Corporation.

Sterling Lord Literistic, Inc.: From "The Log Jam" from *River Notes: The Dance of Herons* by Barry Holstun Lopez. Copyright © 1979 by Barry Holstun Lopez.

Los Angeles Times Syndicate: From "Get Eco-logical" from "Earth SOS" from *Seventeen Magazine*, April 1991. Copyright © 1991 by Seventeen Magazine. Distributed by the Los Angeles Times Syndicate. From "Disaster Hits Home" by Jennifer Cohen from *Seventeen Magazine,* March 1990. Copyright © 1990 by Seventeen Magazine. Distributed by the Los Angeles Times Syndicate.

David Low: From "Winterblossom Garden" by David Low from *Ploughshares*, vol. 8, no. 4, 1982. Copyright © 1982 by David Low.

Macmillan USA, a Simon & Schuster Macmillan Company: Entry "large" and "Pronunciation Key" from *Webster's New World College Dictionary*, Third Edition. Copyright © 1996, 1994, 1991, 1988 by Simon & Schuster Inc. From "Zion National Park/Utah" from *National Park Guide* by Michael Frome. Copyright © 1991 by Simon & Schuster Inc.

Anne McCaffrey and agent, Virginia Kidd: From "The Smallest Dragonboy" by Anne McCaffrey. Copyright © 1973 by Anne McCaffrey. First appeared in *Science Fiction Tales.*

National Council of Teachers of English: "A Letter to Gabriela, A Young Writer" by Pat Mora from *English Journal,* vol. 79, no. 5, September 1990. Copyright © 1990 by the National Council of Teachers of English. From "Joyce Carol Thomas" from *Speaking for Ourselves,* compiled and edited by Donald R. Gallo. Copyright © 1990 by the National Council of Teachers of English.

National Geographic World, the official magazine for Junior Members of the National Geographic Society: From "Animal Body Talk" from *National Geographic World*, no. 175, March 1990. Copyright © 1990 by National Geographic Society.

Nielsen Media Research: Chart, "Audience Composition by Selected Program Type (Average Minute Audience)" from *1990 Nielsen Report on Television* by Nielsen Media Research. Copyright © 1990 by Nielsen Media Research.

Omni: From "Road Warrior" by Bob Berger from *Omni*, March 1990. Copyright © 1990 by Omni Publications International, Ltd. From "Making Fun" by A.J.S. Rayl from *Omni,* November 1990. Copyright © 1990 by Omni Publications International, Ltd.

Pantheon Books, a division of Random House, Inc.: From "The Sound of Flutes" by Henry Crow Dog from *The Sound of Flutes and Other Indian Legends,* edited by Richard Erdoes. Text copyright © 1976 by Richard Erdoes.

Popular Science Magazine: From "Water World" by Tony Reichhardt from *Popular Science*, February 1996, p. 70. Copyright © 1996 by Times Mirror Magazines Inc. Distributed by Los Angeles Times Syndicate.

Byron Preiss Visual Publications, Inc.: From "A Cautionary Tale" from *A Kid's Guide to How to Save the Planet* by Billy Goodman, illustrated by Paul Meisel. Copyright © 1990 by Byron Preiss Visual Publications, Inc.

Gail Provost: Quote by Ellen Goodman from "Ellen Goodman" by Gary Provost from *On Being a Writer,* edited by Bill Strickland. Copyright © 1981 by Gary Provost.

Random House, Inc.: From *I Know Why the Caged Bird Sings* by Maya Angelou. Copyright © 1969 by Maya Angelou. From *Gorilla, My Love* by Toni Cade Bambara. Copyright © 1966 by Toni Cade Bambara.

School Library Journal: From a book review by Kathleen Odean on the book *Lyddie* by Katherine Paterson from *School Library Journal*, vol. 37, no. 2, February 1991. Copyright © 1991 by School Library Journal.

PHOTO CREDITS

COVER: Ralph J. Brunke Photography

TABLE OF CONTENTS: Page vii(t), Lois Ellen Frank/Westlight; vii(c), Craig Aurness/Westlight; vii(b), Mark Wagoner/Picturesque; viii, The Kobal Collection; ix(t), Culver Pictures; ix(b), Brown Brothers; xii, Walter Chandoha; xv(t), François Gohier/Photo Researchers; xv(b), Sturgis McKeever/National Audubon Society/Photo Researchers; xvii, Bettmann Archives; xxi, Jerry Wachter/Focus on Sports; xxiii, Obremski/The Image Bank; xxiv(l), Pictorial Press Limited/Star File; xxiv(r), Michael Ochs Archives; xxviii, Wide World Photos; xxxi, James Newberry; xxxii, HRW Photo by John Langford; xxxiv, Courtesy of Pat Mora.

INTRODUCTION: Page 4, Comstock; 5, HRW photo by Russell Dian; 6, Will McIntyre/Tony Stone Images; 7, M. Durrance/Photo Researchers.

CHAPTER 1: Page 19, AP/Wide World Photos; 26, The Bettmann Archive; 29, Gerry Ellis/Ellis Nature Photography; 30, Nawrocki Stock Photography; 35, Laurence Parent; 39, Culver Pictures; 40(bl), Don & Pat Valenti/Tony Stone Images ; 40(cl), Skjold/Nawrocki Stock Photo; 40(cr), T. Rosenthal/Superstock; 40(br), Myrleen Ferguson Cate/PhotoEdit; 42, S. Vidler/Superstock; 45(l), (r), Benjamin Mendlowitz; 47, George Holton/Photo Researchers; 49, Frank Lane Agency/Bruce Coleman Inc.; 51(l), Jeff Schultz/AlaskaStock Images; 51(r), Greg Martin/AlaskaStock Images.

CHAPTER 2: Page 56(t), Lois Ellen Frank & Craig Aurness/Westlight; 56(b), Mark Wagoner/Picturesque; 57, Lois Ellen Frank & Craig Aurness/Westlight; 58, Victor Duran © Sylvia Duran Sharnoff; 60, © Sylvia & Stephen Sharnoff; 63, D. Sprague/WeatherStock; 64, T. Murphy/SuperStock; 65, Bill Bachman/Photo Researchers; 67, David Weintraub/Photo Researchers; 70, HRW Collection; 71(l), Anne Marie Weber/Adventure Photo; 71(r), David Hiser/Photographers Aspen; 73, UPI/Bettmann Newsphotos; 76, AP/Wide World Photos; 80, Mary Gow; 81(l), Gerad Lacz/Peter Arnold; 81(r), Mike & Moppet Reed/Animals Animals; 82, AKG London.

CHAPTER 3: Page 90, Luis Castaneda/The Image Bank; 102(l), Gamma Liaison; 102(r), The Kobal Collection; 103, Walt Disney Pictures/The Kobal Collection; 105, Courtesy of HarperCollins; 107(t), NASA; 107(b), Archive Photos; 111(bl), (br), Roy Britt/WeatherStock; 112(l), Brunskill/Bob Thomas Sports Photography;

112(r), The Bettmann Archive; 114, Dennis O'Conner II/Paul Bardagjy Photography.

CHAPTER 4: Page 119, Culver Pictures; 121, UPI/Bettmann; 124(l), Fukuhara, Inc./Westlight; 124(r), James Newberry; 124(inset), U.S. Forest Service; 126(l), AP/Wide World Photos; 126(r), AP/Wide World Photos; 127, Adrienne T. Gibson/Animals Animals; 132, Rick Stewart/Allsport; 134, James Newberry; 148(cr), Brown Brothers; 149(t), NASA; 149(bl), Globe Photos; 149(br), Ken Regan/Camera 5.

CHAPTER 5: Page 155, James Newberry; 158(tl), Smith/Gamma Liaison; 158(tr), Rivera Collection/Superstock; 158(bl) HRW photo by Peter Van Steen; 158(br), P. R. Productions/SuperStock; 159, Walter Chandoha; 160, Al Grillo/AlaskaStock; 162, P. R. Dunn; 165, HRW photo by Eric Beggs; 169, HRW photo by Lance Schriner; 171, Library of Congress; 175, Park Street; 178, Courtesy of Ray Young Bear; 179, John Running/Black Star; 181, James Newberry; 182(l), Walter Chandoha; 182(r), HRW photo by Eric Beggs; 183, A. Cosmos Blank/Photo Researchers.

CHAPTER 6: Page 195, Tom Bean/Tony Stone Images; 197, both images Nawrocki Stock Photo; 212, Courtesy of Pat Mora; 220, James Newberry.

CHAPTER 7: Page 233, HRW photo by Pat Dunn; 240, courtesy of Sterling Publishing Co.; 242, 243, Walter Chandoha; 249, HRW photo by Peter Van Steen; 253, James Newberry.

CHAPTER 8: Page 263, Tim Davis/Duomo; 265, James Newberry; 270, Archives Division, Texas State Library; 272, Kent & Donna Dannen; 275, James Newberry; 283(l), Rick Reinhard/Impact Visuals; 283(r), John Harrington/Black Star; 284, James Newberry; 287(b), James Newberry.

CHAPTER 9: Page 300(tl), HRW photo by Eric Beggs; 303, Paul J. Sutton/Duomo Photography; 309, Mark Antman/The Image Works; 310, Toris Von Wolfe/Everett Collection; 316, Kathleen Carr/Index Stock; 321, Archive Photos; 323(cl), Peter Fetters/Matrix; 323(c), Nawrocki Stock Photo; 323(c), Lawrence Barns/Black Star; 323(cr), Nawrocki Stock Photo; 323(bc), Theo Westenberger/Sygma; 323(br), Ken Regan/Camera 5.

CHAPTER 10: Page 326, Gary Braasch/Tony Stone Images; 327, Randall Hyman; 331, Park Street; 334, François Gohier/Photo Researchers; 336(l), HRW Photo by John Langford; 336(r), John Griffin/The Image Works; 338(t), Sturgis McKeever/National Audubon Society/Photo Researchers; 338(b), James Newberry; 346(l),

Archive Photos; 346(c), Sipa Press; 346(r), Sygma; 347(l)(c), HRW photo by Peter Van Steen; 347(r), HRW Photo by Sam Dudgeon; 348, Everett Collection, Inc.; 349, AP/Wide World Photos; 355, ©1965 by Elizabeth Borton de Trevino. Courtesy of Farrar, Straus & Giroux.

CHAPTER 11: Page 361, Carol Boone; 362(l), Culver; 363, UPI/Bettmann; 366, Jim Corwin/ Tony Stone Images; 367, Francis Le Guen/Sygma; 368(l), Paramount Studios/SuperStock; 368(r), Sygma; 370, Frederic Lewis/American Stock; 372, John Cancalosi/Natural Selection; 376(l), D. Done/SuperStock; 376(r), M. Thonig/ H. Armstrong Roberts; 377(tl), Luis Castaneda/ The Image Bank; 377(c), Nick Nicholson/ The Image Bank; 380, Bettmann Archive.

CHAPTER 12: Page 400, Paramount Studios/ SuperStock.

CHAPTER 13: Page 413, Ronald C. Modra/ Sports Illustrated ©Time, Inc.; 416, Bridgeman Art Library/Art Resource; 421, Courtesy of the Austin American-Statesman.

CHAPTER 14: Page 431, National Anthropological Archives/National Museum of Natural History/ Smithsonian Institution; 435, G. Ahrens/ H. Armstrong Roberts; 441, Henry J. Kokojan/ The Stockhouse; 445, Courtesy of Concord Jazz; 452(l), Ken Dequaine/Third Coast Stock Source; 452(r), David A. Jentz/Third Coast Stock Source.

CHAPTER 15: Page 458, Nin Berman/Sipa Press; 463(all), Scott Newton; 466, Cotton Coulson/ Woodfin Camp & Associates; 473(l), P. B. Kaplan/ Photo Researchers; 473(r), Frank Schreider/Photo Researchers; 477, *Cows Watching Plane,* John Held, Jr., Courtesy of Illustration House, Inc.; 480, Gwendolen Cates/Sygma; 483, Bonnie Timmons/ The Image Bank.

CHAPTER 16: Page 494, Professional Rodeo Cowboys Association; 499, Phillip Kretchmar/The Image Bank; 501, NASA.

CHAPTER 17: Page 507, Jerry Wachter/Focus on Sport; 517(l), (r), © David Madison 1996; 518(t), Pat Caruso/Sportschrome East/West; 518(c), © David Madison 1996; 518(b), Mitchell R. Reibel/Sportschrome East/West; 529 (all) James Newberry.

CHAPTER 18: Page 544, John Neubauer/ Uniphoto Picture Agency; 550(all), Museum of Appalachia; 552(r), Nawrocki Stock Photo.

CHAPTER 19: Page 558, Musee de l'Armée, Paris/Art Resource; 561, Paramount/Shooting Star.

CHAPTER 20: Page 577, © Mark Seliger; 581, Robert Harding Picture Library; 585, HRW photo by Eric Beggs; 592(l), Craig Aurness/Westlight; 592(c), Rob Atkins/The Image Bank; 592(r), Obremski/The Image Bank.

CHAPTER 21: Page 606(all), HRW photos by Eric Beggs; 618, Steven Guarnaccia/The Image Bank; 622(l), Alexandra Buxbaum/Nawrocki Stock Photo; 622(c), Nawrocki Stock Photo; 622(r), Zephyr Pictures/Nawrocki Stock Photo; 626, Steve Allen/Peter Arnold, Inc.; 627, Jerry Jacka/Jerry Jacka Photography.

CHAPTER 22: Page 636, Nawrocki Stock Photo; 637(tl), Michael Ochs Archives; 637(tr), Michael Ochs Archives; 637(c), Pictorial Press Limited/ Star File; 637(br), Michael Ochs Archives; 640(t), Biblioteca Ambrosiana, Milan; 640(b), Bibliothèque Nationale, Paris; 645(l), Library of Congress; 645(cl), The Lincoln Museum, Fort Wayne, Indiana, a part of Lincoln National Corporation; 645(cr),(r), Library of Congress; 651, Collector's Showcase; 652, Nawrocki Stock Photo.

CHAPTER 23: Page 663, Craig Aurness/ Westlight; 666, Uniphoto, Inc.

CHAPTER 24: Page 685, Cameramann International, Inc.; 697, Chris Falkenstein; 700, Al Tielemans/Duomo.

CHAPTER 25: Page 712, Andrew A. Wagner; 716, Sandak, Inc.; 719(tl), Andy Caulfield/The Image Bank; 719(tr), Paul Nehrenz/The Image Bank; 719(b), Andy Caulfield/The Image Bank; 722, Courtesy of McGraw-Hill; 731, Ross Alistair/SuperStock.

CHAPTER 26: Page 740, Mike Powers; 746, Kjell B. Sandved/Photo Researchers, Inc.; 754, U.S. Postal Service; 758, Wide World Photos.

CHAPTER 27: Page 774(br), Collection of the Newark Museum, Purchase 1985, The Members' Fund; 780, Dr. E. R. Degginger/Color-Pic, Inc.; 785(tl), Robert Frerck/Woodfin Camp & Associates; 785(tc),(tr),(bl),(br), Loren McIntyre/Woodfin Camp & Associates; 792(all), Michael Sullivan/TexaStock.

CHAPTER 28: Page 806, Courtesy of Hendrick-Long Publishing Co.; 816, H. Gruyaert/Magnum Photos; 822, R. Gaillardi/Gamma Liaison; 825(l), Richard Sullivan/Shooting Star; 825(r), G. Hunter/SuperStock.

ILLUSTRATION CREDITS

Brian Battles—112, 113, 114, 165, 252, 416, 494, 511, 525, 558, 581, 593, 629, 731, 746, 754, 889

Kate Beetle—259

Kim Behm—15, 123

Linda Blackwell—171, 209

Keith Bowden—ix, xxix, 98, 148, 332, 384, 386, 537, 599, 612, 694, 704, 822

Paul Casale—14

Rondi Collette—64, 220, 232, 233, 239, 240, 326, 327, 328, 370, 421, 589

Chris Ellison—204, 207, 208, 544

Richard Erickson—62, 242, 243, 265

Janice Fried—x, 152, 153, 490, 719

Tom Gianni—366, 494

John Hanley—211, 372

Mary Jones—268

Linda Kelen—xiii, 68, 256, 257, 258, 383, 389, 398, 399

Susan Kemnitz—xiv, 290, 291, 318

Tatjana Krizmanic—224–225

Rich Lo—xxiii, 355, 592–593

Judy Love—xi, 8, 12, 13, 186–187, 188, 189, 190, 191, 192, 295, 296, 298, 546, 675

Richard Murdock—69, 156, 157, 801

Jack Scott—401

Steve Shock—vi, xxvi–xxvii, 20, 93, 94–95

Chuck Solway—521

Troy Thomas—xvi, xvii, 380

Nancy Tucker—80